BBC PRONOUNCING
DICTIONARY
OF BRITISH NAMES

BERTELSMANN INFO SERV		
NN1		
NB1		
NC1		
NE1		
NH1		10.92
NL1		
NM1		
NP1		
NT1		
NV1		
NN2		

BBC PRONOUNCING DICTIONARY
OF BRITISH NAMES

WITH AN APPENDIX OF
CHANNEL ISLANDS NAMES

Edited and Transcribed by

G. M. MILLER

M.B.E., M.A.

LONDON
OXFORD UNIVERSITY PRESS
1971

Oxford University Press, Ely House, London W. 1

GLASGOW NEW YORK TORONTO MELBOURNE WELLINGTON
CAPE TOWN SALISBURY IBADAN NAIROBI DAR ES SALAAM LUSAKA ADDIS ABABA
BOMBAY CALCUTTA MADRAS KARACHI LAHORE DACCA
KUALA LUMPUR SINGAPORE HONG KONG TOKYO

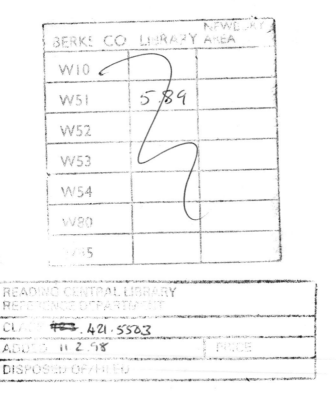
PRINTED IN GREAT BRITAIN

PREFACE

In this book the BBC has gathered together the fruits of more than forty years of research into the pronunciation of proper names in the United Kingdom. The book was compiled primarily for the use of members of staff, but the BBC hopes that it will prove useful to many other readers. Here they will find the pronunciation which as nearly as possible represents the usage of the inhabitants of the place or of the family bearing the name listed. Although the BBC does not, and never did, impose pronunciations of its own on English words, the myth of 'BBC English' dies hard. It owed its birth no doubt to the era before the Second World War, when all announcers and perhaps a majority of other broadcasters spoke the variety of Southern English known as Received Pronunciation, which is the type of English spoken by those educated at public schools; but there was nothing esoteric about this way of speaking, nothing exclusive to the BBC, and in its pre-war setting it came to be accepted as the natural mode of communication over the air. Even today, when a much wider variety of voices is heard, the old style is still regarded as having an important place in broadcasting. The good announcer remains, as far as the BBC is concerned, the pleasant, unobtrusive speaker who does not distract attention from his subject matter by causing embarrassment, unwitting amusement, or resentment among intelligent listeners. He is the mouthpiece for the BBC's official pronouncements, the man who links programmes, announces concerts, narrates opera scripts, reads bulletins prepared in the newsroom, and generally undertakes the exacting task of interpreting other people's work, only occasionally displaying his own versatility by taking part in particular programmes.

In the early 1960s, the BBC felt that it would be more realistic to throw the stage open to the men behind the scenes, so that news men participated personally in news broadcasts, meteorologists gave us our weather forecasts, policemen enlisted our aid direct from Scotland Yard, and the BBC

Motoring Unit kept us hourly aware of traffic problems. This created a greater sense of immediacy between the listener and those at the heart of the event. Naturally, there was no longer insistence on purely southern usage, as these experts are likely to be drawn from all parts of the country. Their prime advantage is that they are informed and articulate on their own subject, and consequently easy to follow. They hold the interest and sympathy of the listener because of their expertise. At the same time, a more colloquial element has been introduced, which has disposed even further of a sense of formality. Individual departments are of course responsible for avoiding the pitfall of employing the man who is patently neither adequate speaker nor expert. In both radio and television, News Division has experimented widely. London television presentation announcers, on the other hand, continue to be drawn from the ranks of RP speakers, while domestic radio presentation has extended its range to take in several Commonwealth announcers. In the BBC's European and World Service English language broadcasts, understandably, Southern English RP remains the accepted norm for all announcers, both in news bulletins and in programmes. As well as the need to overcome the occasional vagaries of short-wave reception, there is the consideration that to a very large number of listeners English is a foreign tongue, and a stable style of pronunciation greatly helps intelligibility. It is also appreciated by the world-wide followers of BBC English by Radio programmes.

There is one sphere, however, in which the BBC expects conformity from all its official broadcasters, and that is in the treatment of British proper names. It is felt that, as a matter of courtesy, the bearer of a name or title should be referred to by the pronunciation which he himself prefers ; and that place names should be pronounced as they are locally, with perhaps rare exceptions where there is a recognized 'national' pronunciation. A name is usually a matter of vital moment to those closely and often emotively concerned with it, and unfavourable reaction to a mispronunciation, with all the lack of interest and care that the latter implies, is immediate. On the BBC's part, the size of the Pronunciation Unit's telephone bills must be considered one small testimony to its endeavour to keep in close touch with personal and local usage. It is this Unit, which emerged as the direct heir to the BBC's Advisory

Committee on Spoken English in 1939, that continues to carry out the Committee's far-sighted recommendations in regard to both English and foreign language problems. It is worth pausing for a moment to study the calibre of the Committee itself, which was set up in 1926 by the Director-General, Mr. J. C. W. Reith, later Lord Reith. Foremost among its members were four linguistic specialists—Arthur Lloyd James, Professor of Phonetics at the School of Oriental and African Studies in the University of London, who acted as honorary secretary to the Committee and linguistic adviser to the announcers; Daniel Jones, Professor of Phonetics at University College London, a phonetician of world repute, whose close association with the BBC continued until his death in 1967; H. C. Wyld, Merton Professor of English Language and Literature in the University of Oxford; and Harold Orton, later to become Professor of English Language and Medieval Literature in the University of Leeds. Among the members of the main Committee over the years were the Poet Laureate Robert Bridges, Sir Johnston Forbes-Robertson, George Bernard Shaw, Sir Julian Huxley, Lord David Cecil, Sir Kenneth Clark, Lady Cynthia Asquith, Rose Macaulay, and many others of distinction. After some early lively battles on matters of principle, the members settled down to collecting information for inclusion in a successive range of booklets covering the pronunciation of English, Scottish, Welsh, and Northern Irish place names, and of British family names and titles. All their findings, published before 1939, have been incorporated in this present book, together with much evidence acquired since that time.

I wish to acknowledge my indebtedness to Professor A. Lloyd James and Professor Daniel Jones, who were responsible for the inception of this collection and for the principles on which it is based, and with whom I had the constant pleasure of working during their years as the Corporation's Linguistic Advisers; to my colleague, Elspeth D. Anderson, who has not only collaborated closely throughout the preparation of the dictionary, but who did much of the research over a long period of years; to R. L. W. Collison, formerly BBC Librarian and now Professor of Library Service in the University of California, Los Angeles, who advised on the more intricate aspects of indexing; to Dr. Aled Rhys Wiliam, formerly of the BBC in Wales and now Director of Audio-Visual Media at the

INTRODUCTION

A CURIOUS witness to the remarkable diversity of provenance of the inhabitants of the British Isles is the fact that the first entry in this dictionary should be *Aagaard* and the last *Zabiela* —names more immediately suggesting an affinity with Scandinavia and the Iberian Peninsula. Here, however, the recording of pronunciations rather than research into historical origins has been the aim. The book includes titles, family names (i.e. surnames), certain Christian names (or personal first names), place names, those of institutions and societies, and adjectival forms of proper names, drawn from England, Wales, Scotland, Northern Ireland, the Isle of Man, and the Channel Islands— the last appearing in a separate appendix. Some names, like that of *Mr. Yehudi Menuhin*, appear because their owners, although not technically of British nationality, have made their homes here and are very much a part of the British scene. It is not an exhaustive collection, and not every pronunciation of every name is represented; only those for which satisfactory evidence was available have been included. Local clergy, town clerks and their staff, postal and police officials, and many private citizens have contributed—sometimes very extensively —to the information on place names. Advice on personal names has been most carefully sought from the individuals concerned, or from members of their families or other sources close to them. Although it is naturally outside the scope of the book to record the many popular versions of pronunciations used by those professing no local or personal knowledge of the names, there are cases, like those of *Carlisle* and *Newcastle*, in which an accepted 'national' pronunciation has been recorded, even although it is not necessarily the most general one among the educated local population. Many historians, artists, musicians, scientists, and others have been consulted about present-day spoken forms of historic names. Descendants of historical personages, too, have sometimes provided interesting information about past and present usage. For entries like *Wriothesley*, where evidence was elusive, various written sources were also consulted.

Spellings

For place-name spellings, the authorities accepted have been the handbook entitled *Post Offices in the United Kingdom*, issued by H.M. Postmaster General in October 1964, and the 1961 *Census, England and Wales, Index of Place Names*, issued by H.M. Stationery Office; but guidance was also sought from Bartholomew's *Survey Gazetteer of the British Isles* and from the *Gazetteer of Welsh Place-Names* of the Board of Celtic Studies of the University of Wales. Spellings of titles were verified in *Debrett*.

Titles

The pronunciation of a title has been linked, according to its origin, sometimes with a family name and sometimes with a place name. In the case of an historic hereditary title where the line of succession has come to an end, or the title is in abeyance, and the last holder's pronunciation is known to us, this has been recorded, as appropriate, as an *earldom, viscountcy*, or *barony*. Likewise, the term *barony* appears in association with certain family names to record the specific pronunciation of one who has been a life peer. A place name has sometimes been retained in a title, not because it is an integral part of the title, but because of its pronunciation interest. This situation arises when the place name, in this particular form, appears only in the title and is not to be found elsewhere, e.g. *Viscount Green-wood of Holbourne, Baron Tedder of Glenguin*. The opportunity to record the pronunciation might otherwise be lost. There are titles, on the other hand, where the territorial designation is included as a matter of course because it is an essential distinguishing feature of the title, e.g. *Baron Douglas of Barloch, Baron Douglas of Kirtleside*.

County names

Names of counties after place names have been omitted, except in those cases where doubt could arise. There are frequent occurrences of two or more places of the same name in separate counties, or even in the same county, where local usage calls for differing treatment. There are also several places of the same name, with the same pronunciation, located in a variety of counties. In all these cases the counties have been named. Also, when a river flows through more than one county, those counties have been identified.

Indexing

Names of the same spelling and consisting of a single word appear in the sequence of Christian name (i.e. personal first name), family name (i.e. surname), and place name. A title, if isolated, precedes all of these, but titles are generally associated with particular family or place names. For greater visual clarity, titles, family names (followed by *f.n.*), Christian names (followed by *C.n.*), and distinguishing county names have been italicized, in contrast to place names, which are shown in roman type. In names of two or more component parts the system of alphabetization does not always follow the pattern to which we are accustomed in telephone directories and gazetteers, but conforms to a word-by-word order which is intended to make the name leap more readily to the eye. This is achieved by placing these forms in one group, separate from and preceding their compound counterparts, e.g.

> Bishop Auckland
> Bishop's Frome
> Bishop's Lydeard
> Bishop's Nympton
> Bishop's Stortford
> Bishop's Waltham
> Bishopston
> Bishopwearmouth.

Family names introduced by the separate prefixes *D' De, Del, De la, Des, Du, La, Le, Les* are similarly treated. Thus, in Channel Islands names, *De Veulle* will be found in the group above *Decaux, Derouet*, and *Du Feu* above *Dubras*, although in strict letter-by-letter alphabetical order their precedence would be reversed. The advantage of this arrangement is that the eye is not confused by the juxtaposition of whole and broken names. Some deviations from the principle have been made inevitable by a page division, or where an isolated name eludes rigid classification.

It will be observed that the *Mac* group of family names has been segregated from the *M*'s in general and precedes them. The result is that sometimes an arbitrary decision has been made in placing certain names like *Machray, Mahaddie, Makgill*, because of their orthography, in the main group, although etymologically they may belong to the *Mac*'s. Optional ways of writing this initial syllable, according to family preference, are exemplified in the name *Macgregor*, *MacGregor*, *McGregor*, *M'Gregor*.

St., the standard abbreviation of *Saint* in family names and place names, is treated for alphabetical purposes as if it were written in full. In general, the name of saints associated with these islands occur, as do other Christian names, in their due alphabetical places throughout the book. Certain of them, however, having come to the notice of the BBC in the form of names of individual churches or hospitals, have found their place in this edition alphabetically under *St.*, intermingled with place names and family names. They are distinguished by being written in bold italics on the same principle as that of ordinary personal names.

Key to pronunciation

Two systems have been employed to indicate pronunciation, one for the benefit of those acquainted with the International Phonetic Association's method of writing sounds and the other for the general user. In the IPA system, a 'multiliteral' transcription has been used, with the addition of italicized [ə], [h], [r], [p], [d], to indicate variant pronunciations. For the second method an English modified spelling system has been used which, after its explanations have been studied, should be immediately obvious to most English speakers. The systems have been adapted to Received Pronunciation, which is familiar alike to BBC announcers and to listeners and viewers in this country and overseas, whether it happens to be their own type of speech or not.

Vowels

IPA symbol	English modified spelling	Words containing sound
i	ee	see
ɪ	i	pity
e	e	get
æ	a	hat
ɑ	aa	father
ɒ	o	not
ɔ	aw	law

ʊ	ŏŏ	book
u	oo	food
ʌ	u	but
ə	ă, ĕ, ŏ, ŭ	*a*bout, butter
ɜ	er, ur, ir	fern, fur, fir
	ö	*is used to indicate this same centralized vowel sound in cases where there is no 'r' in the original spelling*, e.g. Beinn Laoigh [ben ˈlɜɪ] (ben lö́-i) De Veulle [də ˈvɜl] (dĕ vö́ll) Des Voex [deɪ ˈvɜ] (day vö́)

Exotic vowels

More or less as in French

æ̃	a*ng*	vin
ɑ̃	aa*ng*	banc
õ	õ*ng*	bon
ɛː	e	fèvre

Diphthongs

ɛə	air	there
ɪə	eer	here
ʊə	ŏŏr	poor
eɪ	ay	day
aɪ	ī	high
aʊ	ow	now
oʊ	ō	no
ɔɪ	oy	boy

Consonants

p, b, t, d, k, m, n, l, r, f, v, s, z, h, w are used in both transcriptions with their customary English values.

Otherwise the symbols are:

g	g	get
x	ch	Scottish *loch*
tʃ	ch, tch	church
dʒ	j	jet

ṇ	n	see note on syllabic n
ŋ	ng	sing
ḷ	l	see note on syllabic l
ɬ	<u>hl</u>	Welsh *llan*
θ	<u>th</u>	thin
ð	<u>th</u>	there
ʃ	<u>sh</u>	shut
ʒ	<u>zh</u>	*s* in *measure*
r̩	r̩	*is used in French-type pronunciations to denote devoiced, non-syllabic* r *following* p, t. e.g. *Earl of Ypres* [ipr̩] (eepr)
ʜw	wh	where
j	y	yes

Stress symbols

In the IPA transcription main stress is indicated by the symbol ˈ preceding the stressed syllable, and secondary stress by the symbol ˌ. In modified spelling, secondary stress is not shown, but main stress is indicated by an acute accent ′ above the syllable. Thus *Altarnun* appears as [ˌæltərˈnʌn] (altărnún).

Use of hyphens

The use of hyphens in the IPA script has been kept to a minimum, except for printer's divisions at the end of lines; but hyphens have been introduced to avoid the ambiguity which might arise when [ɪə] and [ɔɪ] are employed not as diphthongs but in each case as two distinct vowels. *Flawith* makes the point particularly well, as its pronunciation allows two such variants, [ˈflɔ-ɪθ] (fláw-ith) and [flɔɪθ] (floyth). In modified spelling hyphens are used more frequently, and generally for obvious reasons. A less obvious treatment becomes necessary in a name like the Welsh *Dewi*, where the use of open [e] (e) before [w] (w) constitutes a sound sequence unfamiliar to most users of the Received Pronunciation of English, and where the pronunciation [ˈdewɪ] has been written (dé-wi). Similarly, the Irish name *Mulcahy*, pronounced [mʌlˈkæhɪ], with *a* as in *cat*, has been written (mulká-hi).

The two systems

In the actual text IPA symbols are enclosed, for clarity, in square brackets, [ ], and modified spelling pronunciations in rounded brackets, ( ). The two methods are systematically related, although the precision of the IPA system cannot be quite matched by the other, and certain concessions have had to be made in the modified spelling system in order to avoid misinterpretation. For example, the sound corresponding to [ju] appears as (yoo) at the beginning of a pronunciation, as in *Udall* ['ˈjudəl] (yoódawl), but in all other cases as (ew); that corresponding to [ɔr] is generally written (or), but before another vowel, or following (w), it becomes (awr), so that *Dorey* ['ˈdɔrɪ] (dáwri) may not be mistaken for ['ˈdɒrɪ] (dórri), and that the initial syllables *Ward-*, *Wark-*, *Warm-*, pronounced [wɔrd-] (wawrd-) [wɔrk-], (wawrk-), [wɔrm-] (wawrm-), should not be confused with the English words *word*, *work*, and *worm*. A convention of the modified spelling is that it is in general related to the original spelling of the name, so that *Burghersh* is written (búrgersh), although the two vowel sounds are the same. Wherever they occur, the modified spellings (ăr), (ĕr), (ŭr) are merely different representations of the same sound. A double consonant, or in appropriate cases (ck), is used to make the open nature of the preceding vowel more obvious, as in *Debenham* ['ˈdebənəm] (débběnăm), *Pakenham* ['ˈpækənəm] (páckěnăm).

Exotic vowels

As the key to pronunciation shows, the nasalization of a vowel in IPA script is indicated by the use of a tilde ~ over it; in modified spelling, it is shown by writing an italicized *ng* after the vowel. Of the nasal vowels the first, [æ̃] (a*ng*), is related to the [æ] (a) of English *hat*; the second, [ɑ̃] (aa*ng*), to the [ɑ] (aa) sound of English *father*; and the third, [õ] (õ*ng*), to the close *o* used by many Scots, Irish, and Welsh speakers in the word *no*. The vowel [ɛ:]—the only instance in which the IPA length mark [:] has been used, incidentally—is a lengthened version of the first vowel in English *ever*. In Southern English usage [eɪ] (ay) is generally substituted for this sound, but there are names in which a closer approximation to the foreign sound is usual.

Syllabic l

In the numerous cases in which final syllables spelt *-al, -all, -el -ell, -il, -ill, -ull* are pronounced as a syllabic *l*, no indeterminate vowel has been introduced into either system of pronunciation and they are written simply as *l*, e.g. *Dougall* [ˈdugl] (doogl), *Mitchell* [ˈmɪtʃl] (mitchl), *Sempill* [ˈsempl] (sempl), *Minshull* [ˈmɪnʃl] (minshl). When a syllabic *l* occurs in the middle of a word, however, it becomes necessary to introduce a syllabic mark, [ˌl], in the IPA script, and to use a hyphen in an appropriate place in the modified spelling. Thus, *Chittlehamholt* is written [ˈtʃɪtl̩əmhoʊlt] (chíttl-ăm-hōlt), to suggest that, in the more careful pronunciation at least, the *l* would constitute a syllable in itself.

Syllabic n

There is a good deal of variety in the treatment of final unstressed syllables in which the following consonants are preceded by a vowel, and followed by another vowel plus *n*: [t] (t), [d] (d), [s] (s), [z] (z), [ʃ] (sh), [ʒ] (zh). Although the majority usually in relaxed speech make the *n* syllabic, some endeavour, even in informal speech, always to retain the indeterminate vowel, and this has been indicated by writing [ən] with an italicized, alternative [ə] in IPA script, and (ăn), (ĕn), (ŏn), (ŭn), not merely (n), in modified spelling, e.g. *Beaton* [ˈbitən] (béetŏn), *Marsden* [ˈmɑrzdən] (maárzdĕn). Occasionally, on the other hand, it becomes necessary to accommodate a syllabic *n* in the middle of a name, and this is done by writing [n̩], with a syllabic mark, in IPA script and using a hyphen to show the suitable break in modified spelling, e.g. *Adeney* [ˈeɪdn̩ɪ] (áydn-i).

Italicised [ə] *in IPA transcription*

Although the use of italicized [ə] in the IPA transcription has been restricted largely to endings where syllabic *n* may occur, it could feasibly be extended to cover such further possible variants as [-bərə], [-bərɪ], [-dʒəm], [-ʃəm], [-rəm], [-rən] [-wəl]. This would not in most cases affect the present modified spelling renderings.

Orthographic r

Where *r* occurs in the spelling, its presence is acknowledged in both pronunciation systems. In those cases, however, in which it is in general omitted by Southern English speakers, it is written as italicized [*r*] in the IPA version.

It is thus italicized

(1) before consonants e.g. *Parnell* [pɑr'nel] (paarnéll)

(2) in final positions e.g. *Grosvenor* ['grouvnər] (gróv-nŏr) except when this is a linking *r*, as mentioned below.

It is not italicized

(1) in initial positions e.g. *Renwick* ['renɪk] (rénnick)

(2) after consonants e.g. *Tregoning* [trɪ'gɒnɪŋ] (trĕgónning)

(3) as linking *r* between two words, where the second word begins with a vowel e.g. *Over Alderley* ['ouvər 'ɔldərlɪ] (óver áwldĕrli)

The devoiced [r̥] (r), used in the *Earl of Ypres* and similar names, occurs only after the unvoiced plosives *p, t*. It is employed to guard against the possible interpretation of the single-syllable [ipr̥] (eepr) as two syllables, ['ipər] (eéper).

Initial orthographic rh

Rh occurs particularly at the beginning of Welsh names and is generally an indication that the *r* is a strong voiceless sound in the Welsh language; but, as this is a pronunciation not usually employed by non-Welsh speakers, it has not been shown in the modified spelling pronunciation. Its presence in Welsh, however, is acknowledged by writing [*hr*] in IPA script, so that *Rhos*, for example, appears as [*h*rous] (rōss).

Orthographic rhiw

This root may occur initially, medially, or finally in Welsh place names. To pronounce it as one syllable, [*h*rju] (rew), is normal in Welsh, but not in RP usage, and it has in general been treated as [*h*rɪ'u] (ri-oó).

Initial orthographic wh

While most southern speakers, at least, habitually make no distinction in pronunciation between such pairs of words as *Wales* and *whales*, others regularly do. It is a matter of usage in particular regions or speech groups. Allowance has been made for both schools here by writing (ʍw] in IPA script, and by showing (wh) in modified spelling, e.g. *Whitefield* [ˈʍwaɪt-fild] (whítefeeld). In those cases in which there has been no evidence of the existence of a pronunciation with [hw], no [h] has been shown. A further possible treatment of the spelling occurs in the name *Whewell*, pronounced [ˈhjuəl] (héw-ĕl).

Final orthographic -ian, -ien, -ion, -ear, -ier -iour, -iel, -iol

In all cases where the pronunciation of these syllables has been indicated in IPA script as [-ɪən], [-ɪər], [-ɪəl], it can be taken for granted that the alternatives [-jən], [-jər], [-jəl] are acceptable variations, e.g. *Fabian* [ˈfeɪbɪən] (fáybi-ăn), *Ollier* [ˈɒlɪər] (ólli-er), *Baliol* [ˈbeɪlɪəl] (báyli-ŏl) can also be [ˈfeɪbjən] (fáyb-yăn), [ˈɒljər] (ól-yer), [ˈbeɪljəl] (báyl-yŏl).

Attributive stress

An aspect of stress to be remembered is that, although a two- or three-syllable name may be stressed on the final syllable when used in isolation, more often than not the stress moves to the first syllable when it is used attributively. For example, *Thorness* by itself is pronounced [θɔrˈnes] (thornéss); but *Thorness Bay*, in the natural rhythm of the English language, becomes [ˈθɔrnes ˈbeɪ] (thórness báy). This point has not been elaborated in individual cases, but taken for granted, and the stress shown is that which would apply if the name were used in isolation.

Initial Dun- and Strath- in Celtic names

The unstressed initial syllables *Dun-* and *Strath-* in Scottish and Northern Irish names have been shown in this book only as [dʌn-] (dun-) and [stræθ-] (strath-), which is the way in which they are pronounced in careful speech; but in colloquial use they are just as often pronounced [dən-] (dŭn-) and [strəθ-] (străth-), and a footnote to this effect appears on the relevant pages.

Welsh names

Those who are already aware of the complex linguistic situation arising from the differing pronunciations of North and South Wales on the one hand, and from the existence of a demotic and classical language on the other, will appreciate that

the BBC's need to adapt individual pronunciations still further
to the speech of English announcers must inevitably produce
different solutions from those which might appear in a work of
exclusively Welsh interest. It can be taken for granted, however,
that a BBC announcer is expected at least to distinguish between *l* and *ll* in those Welsh names in which these consonants
would be differentiated by local educated speakers of English.
Professor A. Lloyd James, whose comprehensive collection of
Welsh names and their pronunciations was published by the
BBC in 1934 in *Broadcast English IV*, found it necessary to
recommend considerably anglicized versions for the use of
announcers in London and the rest of the country. In the present
work extensive advice on the adaptation of these names and
many others has been given by Dr. Aled Rhys Wiliam and
Mr. Jack Windsor Lewis, and, if there has been any failure
to adopt their recommendations, the fault is certainly not
theirs. Orthography was checked largely against *A Gazetteer of
Welsh Place-Names* prepared by the Language and Literature
Committee of the Board of Celtic Studies of the University of
Wales, but in cases where this was at variance with *Post Offices
in the United Kingdom* the final decision was allowed to rest
with the latter, as it is the forms used there which are most
likely to appear in national newspapers and in BBC news
bulletins. For the same reason it was considered inappropriate
to include such exclusively Welsh-language forms as *Meirion-
nydd* for *Merioneth* or *Morgannwg* for *Glamorgan*. Nevertheless,
the Committee's admirable principle of making stress patterns
clear by the use of hyphens has been followed wherever possible.
In Welsh names stressed at the regular penultimate syllable no
hyphens are necessary. The appearance of a hyphen before the
final syllable, however, reveals that stress falls on that syllable,
e.g. *Troedrhiw-fuwch*. The practical benefit of the system is
perhaps most evident in two-syllable names which, in North
Wales, tend usually to be stressed on the first (or penultimate)
syllable, whereas in the South their counterparts are often
stressed on the second (or final) syllable, thus, *Penrhos* in
Caernarvonshire, but *Pen-rhos* in Breconshire, Monmouthshire,
and Montgomeryshire. Hyphens are in general also used before
and after the definite article in three-syllable names where the
stress falls on the last syllable, as in *Pen-y-bank*, *Pen-y-fan*,
Pont-y-clun.

Abbreviations of county names

Beds.	Bedfordshire
Berks.	Berkshire
Bucks.	Buckinghamshire
Cambs.	Cambridgeshire
Glos.	Gloucestershire
Hants.	Hampshire
Herts.	Hertfordshire
Hunts.	Huntingdonshire
Lancs.	Lancashire
Leics.	Leicestershire
Lincs.	Lincolnshire
Middx.	Middlesex
Northants.	Northamptonshire
Notts.	Nottinghamshire
Oxon.	Oxfordshire
Ross.	Ross and Cromarty
Salop	Shropshire
Staffs.	Staffordshire
Wilts.	Wiltshire
Worcs.	Worcestershire
Yorks.	Yorkshire

County names which have no such accepted abbreviations, and which consist of the name of the county town with the suffix *-shire*, are written in this book with a full stop, e.g. *Aberdeen.*, *Derby*. Northern Irish counties and the county of *Durham* are preceded by the abbreviation *Co.*, thus, *Co. Antrim*. Otherwise, county names appear written in full, without a full stop, as *Anglesey, Cumberland*.

Other abbreviations

A.-S.	Anglo-Saxon
c.	century
cf.	compare
C.n.	Christian name
Co.	County
e.g.	for example
F.M.	Field-Marshal
f.n.	family name
H.M.	Her Majesty's

H.R.H.	His *or* Her Royal Highness
i.e.	that is
I.o.M.	Isle of Man
IPA	International Phonetic Association
M.P.	Member of Parliament
nr.	near
q.v.	which see
R.A.F.	Royal Air Force
RP	Received Pronunciation
Rt. Hon.	Right Honourable
Rt. Rev.	Right Reverend
St.	Saint

Works of reference

Bartholomew's *Survey Gazetteer of the British Isles.* Ninth Edition Reprint. Edinburgh

Geographia *Commercial Gazetteer of Great Britain.* 1958. London

Ordnance Survey one inch to the mile maps

English Place-name Society county publications. Up to 1967. London

Post Offices in the United Kingdom, issued by H.M. Postmaster General. October 1964. London

Census 1961, *England and Wales, Index of Place Names,* issued by H.M. Stationery Office. London

A Gazetteer of Welsh Place-Names (Second Edition) prepared by The Language and Literature Committee of the Board of Celtic Studies of the University of Wales. February 1958. Cardiff

Debrett's *Peerage, Baronetage, Knightage, and Companionage.* 1968. London

Burke's *Peerage, Baronetage and Knightage.* 1967. London

Who's Who. Up to and including 1968. London

Crockford's *Clerical Directory.* Up to and including 1968. O.U.P.

Everyman's English Pronouncing Dictionary by Daniel Jones (Thirteenth Edition). January 1967. London

Webster's *Pronouncing Biographical Dictionary* (Second Edition). 1961. London

A Dictionary of British Surnames by P. H. Reaney (Second Impression). 1961. London

A Dictionary of English and Welsh Surnames by C. W. Bardsley. 1901. London

The Oxford Dictionary of English Christian Names (Second Edition). 1949. O.U.P.

Chambers's *Biographical Dictionary*. 1963. Edinburgh

The Concise Dictionary of National Biography Part I. (1953 Impression). O.U.P.

Aagaard, f.n. ['eɪgɑrd] (áygaard)
Abady, Temple, composer ['templ 'æbədɪ] (témpl ábbǎdi)
Abbey Cwmhir ['æbɪ kʊm'hɪər] (ábbi kŏŏm-heér)
Abbey St. Bathans ['æbɪ snt 'bæθənz] (ábbi sĭnt báthǎnz)
Abbiss, f.n. ['æbɪs] (ábbiss)
Abbots Bromley ['æbəts 'brɒmlɪ] (ábbŏts brómli)
Abbotsham ['æbətsəm] (ábbŏtsǎm)
Abbotsinch ['æbətsɪnʃ] (ábbŏtsinsh)
Abbotskerswell ['æbəts'kɜrzwəl] (ábbŏtskérzwĕl)
Abbs, f.n. [æbz] (abz)
Abdela, f.n. [æb'delə] (abdéllǎ)
Abel, f.n. ['eɪbl] (aybl)
Abelard, f.n. ['æbəlɑrd] (ábbĕlaard) Appropriate also for the ~ Music Ensemble.
Abelard-Schuman, publishers and printers ['æbəlɑrd 'ʃumən] (ábbĕlaard shŏŏmǎn)
Abelé, f.n. ['eɪbəlɪ] (áybĕli)
Aberaeron, also spelt **Aberayron** [ˌæbər'aɪrən] (abbərírŏn)
Aberaman [ˌæbər'æmən] (abbĕrámmǎn)
Aberangell [ˌæbər'æŋel̸] (abbĕráng-ehl)
Aberarth [ˌæbər'ɑrθ] (abbĕraárth)
Aberavon [ˌæbər'ævən] (abbĕrávvŏn)
Aberayron see Aberaeron.
Aberbargoed [ˌæbər'bɑrgoɪd] (abbĕrbaárgoyd); [ˌæbər'bɑrgɒd] (abbĕrbaárgod); [ˌæbər'bɑrgəd] (abbĕrbaárgawd)
Aberbeeg [ˌæbər'big] (abbĕrbeég)
Aberbran [ˌæbər'bran] (abbĕrbraán)
Abercairney [ˌæbər'kɜrnɪ] (abbĕrkaírni)
Abercanaid [ˌæbər'kænaɪd] (abbĕrkánnĭd)
Abercarn [ˌæbər'kɑrn] (abbĕrkaárn)
Aberchalder [ˌæbər'kɒldər] (abbĕrkáwlder)
Aberchirder [ˌæbər'kɜrdər] (abbĕrkírder)
Abercrave [ˌæbər'kreɪv] (abbĕrkráyv)
Abercrombie, f.n. ['æbərkrʌmbɪ] (ábbĕrkrumbi); ['æbərkrɒmbɪ] (ábbĕrkrombi) The first is appropriate for Sir Patrick ~, architect, and Sir Lascelles ~, poet.
Abercwmboi [ˌæbərkʊm'boɪ] (abbĕrkŏŏm-bóy)
Abercynon [ˌæbər'kʌnən] (abbĕrkúnnŏn)
Aberdare [ˌæbər'dɛər] (abbĕrdaír) Appropriate also for Baron ~.
Aberdaron [ˌæbər'dærən] (abbĕrdárrŏn)
Aberdeen [ˌæbər'din] (abbĕrdeén)

Aberdeen and Temair, Marquess of [ˌæbər'din ənd tɪ'mɛər] (abbĕrdeén ǎnd tĕmaír)
Aberdonian, native of Aberdeen [ˌæbər'dounɪən] (abbĕrdóniǎn)
Aberdour, Aberdeen., Fife [ˌæbər'dauər] (abbĕrdówr)
Aberdovey [ˌæbər'dʌvɪ] (abbĕrdúvvi)
Aberdulais [ˌæbər'dɪləs] (abbĕrdíllǎss)
Aberedw [ˌæbər'eɪdu] (abbĕráydoo)
Abererch [ˌæbər'ɛərx] (abbĕraírch)
Aberfan [ˌæbər'væn] (abbĕrván)
Aberfeldy [ˌæbər'feldɪ] (abbĕrféldi)
Aberffraw [ə'bɛərfrau] (ǎbaírfrow)
Aberffrwd [ˌæbər'frud] (abbĕrfroód)
Abergavenny, Marquess of [ˌæbər'genɪ] (abbĕrgénni)
Abergavenny [ˌæbərgə'venɪ] (abbĕrgǎvénni)
Abergele [ˌæbər'geleɪ] (abbĕrgéllay)
Abergorlech [ˌæbər'gɔrləx] (abbĕrgórlĕch)
Abergwessin [ˌæbər'gwesɪn] (abbĕrgwéssin)
Abergwili [ˌæbər'gwɪlɪ] (abbĕrgwílli)
Abergwynfi [ˌæbər'gwɪnvɪ] (abbĕrgwínvi)
Abergynolwyn [ˌæbərgʌn'ʊlwɪn] (abbĕrgunólwin)
Aberhafesp [ˌæbər'hævesp] (abbĕrhávvesp)
Aberkenfig [ˌæbər'kenfɪg] (abbĕrkénfig)
Aberlady [ˌæbər'leɪdɪ] (abbĕrláydi)
Aberllefenni [ˌæbərlə'venɪ] (abbĕrhlĕvénni)
Aberlour [ˌæbər'lauər] (abbĕrlówr)
Abermorddu [ˌæbər'mɔrðɪ] (abbĕrmórthi)
Abermule [ˌæbər'mjul] (abbĕrméwl)
Abernant [ˌæbər'nænt] (abbĕrnánt)
Abernethy, Lord [ˌæbər'neθɪ] (abbĕrnéthi)
Abernethy, Inverness., Perth. [ˌæbər'neθɪ] (abbĕrnéthi)
Aberpedwar [ˌæbər'pedwɑr] (abbĕrpédwaar)
Aberpergwm [ˌæbər'pɛərgʊm] (abbĕrpaírgŏŏm)
Aberporth [ˌæbər'pɔrθ] (abbĕrpórth)
Abersoch [ˌæbər'soux] (abbĕr-sŏch)
Abersychan [ˌæbər'saxən] (abbĕr-súchǎn)
Aberthaw [ˌæbər'θɔ] (abbĕr-tháw)
Abertillery [ˌæbərtɪ'lɛərɪ] (abbĕrtiláiri)
Abertridwr [ˌæbər'trɪduər] (abbĕrtrídŏŏr)
Abertysswg [ˌæbər'tʌsʊg] (abbĕrtússŏŏg)
Aberuchill [ˌæbər'ʊxɪl] (abbĕrŏŏchill)

Aberuthven [ˌæbərˈɪvən] (abbĕrívvĕn)
Aberystwyth [ˌæbərˈɪstwɪθ] (abbĕríst-with); [ˌæbərˈʌstwɪθ] (abbĕrústwith)
Abinger [ˈæbɪndʒər] (ábbinjer) *Appropriate also for Baron ~.*
Abinger Hammer [ˈæbɪndʒər ˈhæmər] (ábbinjer hámmer)
Abington [ˈæbɪŋtən] (ábbingtŏn)
Aboyne [əˈbɔɪn] (ăbóyn) *Appropriate also for the Earl of ~.*
Abram [ˈæbrəm] (ábrăm)
Abridge [ˈeɪbrɪdʒ] (áybrij)
Abse, *f.n.* [ˈæbzɪ] (ábzi)
Aby [ˈeɪbɪ] (áybi)
Achanalt [ˌæxəˈnælt] (achănált)
Acharacle [əˈxærəkl] (ăchárrăkl)
Acharn [əˈxɑrn] (ăchaárn)
Achdalieu [ˌæxdəˈluː] (achdăloŏ)
Acheson, *f.n.* [ˈætʃɪsən] (átchĕssŏn)
Achmore, *also spelt* Auchmore [ˈæxˈmɔr] (ách-mór)
Achnacarry [ˌæxnəˈkærɪ] (achnăkárri)
Achnasheen [ˌæxnəˈʃiːn] (achnăsheén)
Achonry, *f.n.* [ˈækənrɪ] (áckŏnri); [əˈkɒnrɪ] (ăkónri)
Achray, Loch [əˈxreɪ] (ăchráy)
Ackroyd, *f.n.* [ˈækrɔɪd] (áckroyd)
Acland, *f.n.* [ˈæklənd] (áckländ)
Acle [ˈeɪkl] (aykl)
Acol [ˈeɪkɒl] (áykol)
Acomb, *f.n.* [ˈeɪkəm] (áykŏm)
Acomb [ˈeɪkəm] (áykŏm)
Acontius, Jacobus, *Elizabethan philosopher and engineer* [dʒəˈkoʊbəs əˈkɒntɪəs] (jăkóbŭss ăkóntiŭss); [əˈkɒnʃɪəs] (ăkónshi-ŭss) *He hailed from the Tirol and was originally Jacopo Aconzio,* [ˈjækəpoʊ əˈkɒntsɪoʊ] (yáckŏpō ăkóntsiō)
Acott, *f.n.* [ˈeɪkɒt] (áykot)
A'court, *f.n.* [ˈeɪkɔrt] (áykort)
Acraman, *f.n.* [ˈækrəmən] (áckrămăn)
Acrefair [ˌækrəˈvaɪər] (ackrévír)
Acrise [ˈeɪkrɪs] (áykreess); [ˈeɪkrɪs] (áykriss)
Acton Burnell [ˈæktən bərˈnel] (ácktŏn burnéll)
Adair, *f.n.* [əˈdɛər] (ădaír)
Adam, *f.n.* [ˈædəm] (áddăm)
Adare, *f.n.* [əˈdɛər] (ădaír) *Appropriate also for Viscount ~.*
Adbaston [ˈædbəstən] (ádbăstŏn)
Adburgham, *f.n.* [ˌædˈbɜrgəm] (ad-búrgăm)
Adcock, *f.n.* [ˈædkɒk] (ádkock)
Addlestone [ˈædlstoʊn] (áddlstŏn)
Adeane, Sir Michael, *soldier and courtier* [əˈdiːn] (ădeén)
Adel [ˈædl] (addl)
Adel cum Eccup [ˈædl kəm ˈekəp] (áddl kŭm éckŭp)
Adeyfield [ˈeɪdɪfiːld] (áydi-feeld)
Adgie, *f.n.* [ˈædʒɪ] (ájji)
Adie, *f.n.* [ˈeɪdɪ] (áydi)
Adisham [ˈædɪʃəm] (áddishăm)

Adlard, *f.n.* [ˈædlɑrd] (ádlaard)
Adlestrop [ˈædlstrɒp] (áddl-strop)
Adney, Richard, *flautist* [ˈeɪdnɪ] (áydn-i)
Adshead, *f.n.* [ˈædzhed] (ádz-hed)
Adur, River [ˈeɪdər] (áydŭr)
Adversane [ˈædvərseɪn] (ádvĕrssayn)
Advie [ˈædvɪ] (ádvi)
Adwick-le-Street [ˈædɪk lə ˈstrit] (áddick lĕ street)
Ady, *f.n.* [ˈeɪdɪ] (áydi)
Adye, *f.n.* [ˈeɪdɪ] (áydi)
Ae [eɪ] (ay)
Aelred, C.n. [ˈeɪlred] (áylred)
Afford, *f.n.* [ˈæfərd] (áffŏrd)
Affric, Loch *and* River [ˈæfrɪk] (áffrick)
Aflalo, *f.n.* [əˈflɑloʊ] (áflaălō)
Afon, River [ˈævən] (ávvŏn)
Afon Wen [ˈævən ˈwen] (ávvŏn wén)
Afton, *f.n.* [ˈæftən] (áfftŏn)
Agar, *f.n.* [ˈeɪgər] (áygăr); [ˈeɪgɑr] (áygaar)
Agate, *f.n.* [ˈeɪgət] (áygăt); [ˈægət] (ággăt)
Agen Allwedd [ˈægen ˈælwəð] (ággen áhl-wĕth)
Ager, *f.n.* [ˈeɪgər] (áyger); [ˈædʒər] (ájjer); [ˈeɪdʒər] (áyjer)
Aghaeully [ˌæxəˈkʌlɪ] (achăkúlli)
Aghaderg [ˌæxəˈdɜrg] (achădérg) *Another form is* Aghaderrick, *q.v.*
Aghaderrick [ˌæxəˈderɪk] (achădérrick) *see also* Aghaderg.
Aghadowey [ˌæxəˈduɪ] (achădoŏ-i)
Aghagallon [ˌæxəˈgælən] (achăgálŏn)
Aghalee [ˌæxəˈliː] (achăleé)
Aghanloo [ˈɑnluː] (aánloo)
Aghavea [ˌæxəˈveɪ] (achăváy)
Agivey [əˈgɪvɪ] (ăgívvi)
Aglionby, *f.n.* [ˈæglɪənbɪ] (ággli-ŏnbi)
Agnellus, C.n. [æɡˈneləs] (ag-néllŭss)
Agnew, *f.n.* [ˈægnju] (ág-new)
Ago, *f.n.* [ˈɑgoʊ] (aágō)
Aguilar, *f.n.* [əˈgwɪlər] (ăgwíllăr)
Agutter, *f.n.* [əˈgʌtər] (ăgútter)
Aherne, *f.n.* [əˈhɜrn] (ăhérn)
Ahoghill [əˈhɒxɪl] (ăhóchill)
Aichroth, *f.n.* [ˈeɪkrɒθ] (áykroth)
Aikman, *f.n.* [ˈeɪkmən] (áykmăn)
Ailesbury, Marquess of [ˈeɪlzbərɪ] (áylz-bŭri)
Ailort, Loch *and* River [ˈaɪlərt] (flŏrt)
Ailsa, Marquess of [ˈeɪlsə] (áylssă)
Ailsa Craig [ˈeɪlzə ˈkreɪg] (áylză kráyg)
Ainley, *f.n.* [ˈeɪnlɪ] (áynli)
Ainscough, *f.n.* [ˈeɪnzkoʊ] (áynzkō)
Ainscow, *f.n.* [ˈeɪnzkoʊ] (áynzkō)
Aird, *f.n.* [ˈɛərd] (aird)
Airdrie [ˈɛərdrɪ] (aírdri)
Airlie, Earl of [ˈɛərlɪ] (aírli)
Airor [ˈɛərər] (aírŏr)
Aish [æʃ] (ash)
Aisher, *f.n.* [ˈeɪʃər] (áysher)
Aislaby, Co. Durham, Yorks. [ˈeɪzlbɪ] (áyzlbi)
Aisthorpe [ˈeɪsθɔrp] (áyss-thorp)
Aistrop, *f.n.* [ˈeɪstrɒp] (áysstrop)
Aitchison, *f.n.* [ˈeɪtʃɪsən] (áytchissŏn)

Aithsting ['eɪθstɪŋ] (áyth-sting)
Aitken, *f.n.* ['eɪtkɪn] (áytkĕn); ['eɪkən] (áykĕn)
Aitkenhead, *f.n.* ['eɪkənhed] (áykĕn-hed)
Aitkin, *f.n.* ['eɪtkɪn] (áytkin); ['eɪkɪn] (áykin)
Aked, *f.n.* ['eɪkɪd] (áykĕd)
Akeld ['eɪkeld] (áykeld)
Akeman ['eɪkmən] (áykmăn)
Akerman, *f.n.* ['eɪkərmən] (áykĕrmăn); ['ækərmən] (áckĕrmăn)
Akers, *f.n.* ['eɪkərz] (áykĕrz); ['ækərz] (áckĕrz)
Akery, *f.n.* ['eɪkəri] (áykĕri)
Akhurst, *f.n.* ['ækhɜrst] (áck-hurst)
Akister, *f.n.* ['eɪkɪstər] (áykister)
Akroyd, *f.n.* ['ækrɔɪd] (áckroyd)
Akst, *f.n.* [ækst] (ackst)
Alan, *f.n. and C.n.* ['ælən] (álăn)
Alanbrooke, *Viscount* ['ælənbrʊk] (álănbrŏŏk)
Alasdair, *C.n.*, *also spelt* **Alastair**, **Alistair** ['elɪstər] (álister)
Alastair, *C.n. see Alasdair.*
Albany, *f.n.* ['ɔlbənɪ] (áwlbăni)
Albemarle, *Earl of* ['ælbəmɑrl] (álbĕmaarl)
Alberbury ['ɔlbərbərɪ] (áwlbĕrbŭri)
Albery, *f.n.* ['ɔlbəri] (áwlbĕri)
Albon, *f.n.* ['ælbən] (álbŏn)
Albourne ['ɔlbɔrn] (áwlborn)
Albrighton [ɔl'braɪtən] (awlbrítŏn) *Appropriate for both places of the name in Shropshire.*
Albu, *f.n.* ['ælbju] (álbew)
Albury ['ɔlbərɪ] (áwlbŭri)
Alce, *f.n.* [æls] (alss)
Alcester, *f.n.* ['ɔlstər] (áwlsster)
Alcester ['ɔlstər] (áwlsster)
Alciston ['ɔlsɪstən] (áwlssistŏn)
Alcock, *f.n.* ['ælkɒk] (álkock); ['ɔlkɒk] (áwlkock) *The first was the pronunciation of Sir John ~, airman, and of Sir Walter ~, organist and composer.*
Alconbury ['ɔlkənbərɪ] (áwlkŏnbŭri); ['ɔkənbərɪ] (áwkŏnbŭri)
Aldborough ['ɔldbərə] (áwldbŭră)
Aldbourne ['ɔlbɔrn] (áwlborn)
Aldbrough ['ɔldbrə] (áwldbră)
Aldbury ['ɔldbərɪ] (áwldbŭri); ['ɔlbərɪ] (áwlbŭri)
Alde, *River* [ɔld] (awld)
Aldeburgh ['ɔlbərə] (áwlbŭră) *Home of the ~ Festival.*
Aldeby ['ɔldəbɪ] (áwldĕbi)
Aldeguer, *f.n.* ['ɔldɪgər] (áwldĕger)
Aldenham, *Baron* ['ɔldnəm] (áwldn-ăm)
Aldenham ['ɔldənəm] (áwldĕnăm)
Alder, *f.n.* ['ɔldər] (áwldĕr)
Alderbury ['ɔldərbərɪ] (áwldĕrbŭri)
Aldergrove ['ɔldərgrovv] (áwldĕrgrŏv)
Alderley, *Nether and Over* ['ɔldərlɪ] (áwldĕrli)
Aldermaston ['ɔldərmɑstən] (áwldĕrmaastŏn)

Alderney, *Viscount* ['ɔldərnɪ] (áwldĕrni)
Aldershot, *Hants., Northants.* ['ɔldərʃɒt] (áwldĕr-shot)
Alderson, *f.n.* ['ɔldərsən] (áwldĕrssŏn)
Alderton, *f.n.* ['ɔldərtən] (áwldĕrtŏn)
Alderwasley [ˌældərwəz'li] (aldĕrwázleě); [ˌældərz'li] (alĕrzleě)
Aldham, *f.n.* ['ɔldəm] (áwldăm)
Aldhelm, *C.n.* ['ɔldhelm] (áwld-helm)
Aldington, *Baron* ['ɔldɪŋtən] (áwldingtŏn)
Aldous, *f.n.* ['ɔldəs] (áwldŭss)
Aldred, *f.n.* ['ɔldrɪd] (áwldrĕd); ['ɒldrɪd] (ól-drĕd)
Aldridge, *f.n.* ['ɔldrɪdʒ] (áwldrij)
Aldwark ['ɔldwərk] (áwldwŭrk)
Aldwick ['ɔldwɪk] (áwldwick)
Aldwych ['ɔldwɪtʃ] (áwldwitch)
Aled, *Welsh C.n.* ['æled] (áled)
Alethorpe ['eɪlθɔrp] (áyl-thorp)
Alexander of Tunis and Errigal, *Viscount* [ˌælɪg'zɑndər əv 'tjunɪs ənd 'erɪgɒl] (alĕgzaánder ŏv téwniss ănd érrigawl)
Alfold ['ɒlfovld] (áwlfŏld); ['ælfovld] (álfŏld); ['ɑfovld] (aáfŏld)
Alford, *Kenneth*, *composer* ['ɔlfərd] (áwlfŏrd)
Alford, *Aberdeen.* ['ɑfərd] (aáfŏrd)
Alford, *Lincs.* ['ɔlfərd] (áwlfŏrd)
Alfreton ['ɔlfrɪtən] (áwlfrĕtŏn); ['ɒlfrɪtən] (ólfrĕtŏn)
Alfriston [ɒl'frɪstən] (awlfrístŏn)
Algar, *f.n.* ['ælgər] (álgăr)
Algarkirk ['ɔlgərkɜrk] (áwlgárkirk); ['ɒldʒərkɜrk] (áwljárkirk)
Alger, *f.n.* ['ælgər] (álger)
Aline, *Loch and River* ['ælɪn] (álin)
Alington, *f.n.* ['ælɪŋtən] (álingtŏn) *Also the pronunciation of the Barony.*
Alistair, *C.n. see Alasdair.*
Alkborough ['ɔlkbərə] (áwlkbŭră)
Alkham ['ɔlkəm] (áwlkăm); ['ɔkəm] (áwkăm)
Alkin, *f.n.* ['ælkɪn] (álkin)
Alkington, *Glos.* ['ɔlkɪŋtən] (áwlkingtŏn)
Alkington, *Salop* ['ɔkɪŋtən] (áwkingtŏn); ['ɔlkɪŋtən] (áwlkingtŏn)
Alkrington ['ɔlkrɪŋtən] (áwlkringtŏn)
Allaker, *f.n.* ['æləkər] (áláker)
Allam, *Edward*, *composer* ['æləm] (álăm)
Allard, *f.n.* ['ælard] (álaard)
Allason, *f.n.* ['æləsən] (álássŏn)
Allaun, *f.n.* [ə'lɒn] (áláwn)
Allenby, *Viscount* ['ælənbɪ] (álĕnbi)
Aller ['ɒlər] (óller); ['ɔlər] (áwler)
Allerton ['ɒlərtən] (óllĕrtŏn); ['ælərtən] (álĕrtŏn)
Allerton Mauleverer ['ælərtən mɔ'levərər] (álĕrtŏn mawlévvĕrer)
Allesley ['ɒlzlɪ] (áwlzli)
Allestree ['ɑlɪstri] (álĕsstree)
Allet ['ælɪt] (álĕt)
Alleyn Old Boys, *past members of Alleyn's School*, *Dulwich* ['ælɪn] (álĕn)
Alleyn Park, *Dulwich* ['ælɪn] (áleen)

Alleyn's School, *Dulwich* ['ælɪnz] (álĕnz)

Alleyne, *f.n.* [æ'leɪn] (aláyn); [æ'liːn] (aleén); ['ælɪn] (álĕn)

Alleyne's Grammar School, *Stevenage* ['ælɛɪnz] (álaynz)

Alleynian, *one educated at Dulwich College* [ə'leɪnɪən] (áláynián)

Allfrey, *f.n.* ['ɔlfrɪ] (áwlfri)

Ailhusen, *f.n.* [ɔl'hjuːzən] (awl-héwzĕn)

Allibone, *f.n.* ['ælɪboʊn] (álibōn)

Allighan, *f.n.* ['ælɪɡən] (áligán)

Allingham, *f.n.* ['ælɪŋəm] (áling-ăm)

Allington ['ælɪŋtən] (álingtŏn)

Alliss, *f.n.* ['ælɪs] (áliss)

Allitt, *f.n.* ['ælɪt] (álit)

Allner, *f.n.* ['ɔlnər] (áwlner)

Alloa ['æloʊə] (álō-á)

Allsebrook, *f.n.* ['ɔlsbrʊk] (áwlssbrŏŏk)

Allsopp, *f.n.* ['ɔlsɒp] (áwlssop)

Allt, *f.n.* [ɒlt] (awlt)

Allt-Rhyd-y-Groes ['æɬt,riːdə'grɔɪs] (áḥlt-reed-ă-gróyss)

Alma-Tadema, *f.n.* ['ælmə 'tædɪmə] (álmă táddĕmă) *This is also the pronunciation generally associated with the Anglo-Dutch painter.*

Almeley ['æmlɪ] (ámli); ['aməlɪ] (a'amĕli)

Almer ['ælmər] (álmer)

Almey, *f.n.* ['ælmɪ] (álmi)

Almond, *f.n.* ['amənd] (a'amŏnd)

Almondbank ['amənd'bæŋk] (a'amŏndbánk)

Almondbury ['eɪmbərɪ] (áymbŭri); ['ɒmbərɪ] (áwmbŭri); ['ælməndbərɪ] (ál-mŏndbŭri)

Almondsbury ['amzbərɪ] (a'amzbŭri)

Aln, *River* [æln] (aln)

Alne, *Yorks.* [ɒn] (awn)

Alne, Great *and* **Little,** *Warwick.* [ɒn] (awn); [ɒln] (awln)

Alness, *Barony of* ['ɒlnes] (áwlness)

Alness ['ɒlnɪs] (áwlnĕss); ['ælnɪs] (álnĕss)

Alnham ['ælnəm] (álnăm)

Alnmouth ['ælnmaʊθ] (áln-mowth); ['eɪlmaʊθ] (áylmowth)

Alnwick, *f.n.* ['ænɪk] (ánnick)

Alnwick ['ænɪk] (ánnick)

Aloysius, *C.n.* [æloʊ'ɪʃəs] (alō-íshŭss)

Alpass, *f.n.* ['ɔlpəs] (áwlpáss)

Alperton ['ælpərtən] (álpĕrtŏn)

Alpheton [æl'fiːtən] (alfeétŏn)

Alpington ['ælpɪŋtən] (álpingtŏn)

Alport, *f.n.* ['ɔlpɔrt] (áwlport) *Appropriate also for Baron ~.*

Alresford, *f.n.* ['ɒlzfərd] (áwlzfŏrd)

Alresford, *Essex* ['ɑlsfərd] (a'alssfŏrd); ['eɪlsfərd] (áylssfŏrd)

Alresford, *Hants.* ['ɒlsfərd] (áwlssfŏrd); ['ɑlzfərd] (a'alzfŏrd)

Alrewas ['ɒlrəs] (áwlrăss); ['ɒlrəwəs] (áwlrĕwáss)

Alsager [ɔl'seɪdʒər] (awlssáyjer); ['ɒlsədʒər] (áwlssájer)

Alsatia, *old name for* **Whitefriars,** *London* [æl'seɪʃə] (alsáyshá)

Alscott ['ɒlskət] (áwlsskŏt) *But see pronunciation of Alverdiscott, which is the more usual form.*

Alsh, *Loch* [ælʃ] (alsh)

Alsop, *f.n.* ['ɒlsɒp] (áwlssop)

Alston, *f.n.* ['ɒlstən] (áwlstŏn)

Alston ['ɒlstən] (áwlstŏn)

Alstone ['ælstən] (álstŏn)

Alswyck Hall, *Buntingford* ['æsɪk] (ássick)

Alt, *River* [ɒlt] (awlt)

Altarnun [,ælter'nʌn] (altärnún)

Altcar ['ɒltkər] (áwltkaar)

Altham, *f.n.* ['ɒlθəm] (áwl-thăm)

Altham ['ɒlθəm] (áwl-thăm); ['æltəm] (áltăm); ['ɒltəm] (áwltăm)

Althorne ['ɒlθɔrn] (áwl-thorn)

Althorp ['ɒltrəp] (áwltrŏp) *Appropriate also for Viscount ~.*

Althorpe ['ɒlθɔrp] (áwl-thorp)

Altimeg Hill ['ɒltɪmeg] (áwltimeg)

Altnabreac [,æltnə'brek] (altnábréck)

Altnaveigh [,æltnə'veɪ] (altnáváy)

Altofts ['ɒltɒfts] (áwltŏfts); ['ɒltəs] (óltŭss)

Alton ['ɒltən] (áwltŏn)

Altries ['æltrɪz] (áltriz)

Altrincham ['ɒltrɪŋəm] (áwltring-ăm)

Altsigh ['ælt'ʃiː] (ált-shée)

Alty, *f.n.* ['ɒltɪ] (áwlti)

Alun, *Welsh C.n.* ['ælɪn] (álin)

Alva ['ælvə] (álvá)

Alvarez, *f.n.* [æl'vɑrɪz] (alvaárĕz)

Alvaston ['ælvəstən] (álvástŏn)

Alvechurch ['ɒlvtʃɜrtʃ] (áwlv-church)

Alveley ['ævlɪ] (ávvli)

Alverdiscott [,ælvər'dɪskət] (alvĕr-dísskŏt) *A less usual form of this name is* Alscott, *q.v.*

Alverstoke ['ælvərstoʊk] (álvĕrstōk)

Alverthorpe ['ɒlvərθɔrp] (áwlvĕr-thorp)

Alves ['avɪs] (a'avĕss)

Alvescot ['ɒlskət] (áwlsskŏt); ['ælskət] (álsskŏt); ['ælvɪskɒt] (álvĕsskot)

Alveston ['ælvɪstən] (álvĕstŏn)

Alvie ['ælvɪ] (álvi)

Alvingham ['ɒlvɪŋəm] (áwlving-ăm) *Appropriate also for Baron ~.*

Alvington, *Glos.* ['ælvɪŋtən] (álvingtŏn)

Alvington, West, *Devon* ['ɒlvɪŋtən] (áwlvingtŏn)

Alwalton ['ɒlwɒltən] (áwl-wawltŏn)

Alwin Gallery, *London* ['ɒlwɪn] (áwlwin)

Alwinton ['ælwɪntən] (álwintŏn)

Alwoodley ['ɒlwʊdlɪ] (áwl-wŏŏdli)

Alwyn, Kenneth, *conductor* ['ɒlwɪn] (áwlwin)

Alwyn, William, *composer* ['ælwɪn] (álwin)

Alyth ['eɪlɪθ] (áylith)

Amadeus String Quartet [,æmə'deɪəs] (ammădáy-ŭss)

Amaury, f.n. ['eɪmərɪ] (áymări)
Ambersham ['æmbərʃəm] (ámbĕr-shăm)
Am Bodach [æm 'bɒtəx] (am bóttách)
Ambrosden ['æmbroʊzdən] (ámbrŏzdĕn)
Amen Corner, *City of London* ['eɪmen] (áymen)
Amen House, *City of London* ['eɪmen] (áymen)
Amer, f.n. ['eɪmər] (áymer)
Amersham ['æmərʃəm] (ámmĕr-shăm)
Amey, f.n. ['eɪmɪ] (áymi)
Amherst, f.n. ['æmərst] (ámmĕrst); ['æmhɜrst] (ám-herst) *The first is the pronunciation of Earl ~ and of Baron ~ of Hackney.*
Amici String Quartet [ə'miːtʃɪ] (ămeétchi)
Amies, f.n. ['eɪmɪz] (áymiz)
Amis, Kingsley, author ['kɪŋzlɪ 'eɪmɪs] (kíngzli áymiss)
Amiss, f.n. ['eɪmɪs] (áymiss)
Amlwch ['æmlʊx] (ámlŏŏch)
Amman, *River* ['æmən] (ámmăn)
Ammanford ['æmənfərd] (ámmănfŏrd)
Ammon, Barony of ['æmən] (ámmŏn)
Ammonds, f.n. ['æməndz] (ámmŏndz)
Amoore, f.n. ['eɪmʊər] (áymŏŏr); ['eɪmɔr] (áymor)
Amor, f.n. ['eɪmɔr] (áymor)
Amore, f.n. ['eɪmɔr] (áymor)
Amory, f.n. ['eɪmərɪ] (áymŏri) *Appropriate also for Viscount ~.*
Amos, f.n. ['eɪmɒs] (áymoss)
Amphlett, f.n. ['æmflɪt] (ámflĕt)
Ampleforth ['æmplfərθ] (ámpl-forth)
Ampney Crucis ['æmpnɪ 'krusɪs] (ámpni kroóssiss)
Ampney St. Peter ['æmpnɪ snt 'piːtər] (ámpni sint peéter)
Ampthill ['æmthɪl] (ámt-hil) *Appropriate also for Baron ~.*
Amroth ['æmrəθ] (ámroth)
Amulree [ˌæml'riː] (amml-reé) *Appropriate also for Baron ~.*
Amwell, Baron ['æmwəl] (ámwĕl)
Anahoe [ˌænə'huː] (annă-hoó)
An Athain, *Loch* ['lɒx ən 'ɑn] (lóch ăn aán)
Ancaster, *Earl of* ['æŋkəstər] (ánkăster)
Ancoats ['æŋkoʊts] (ánkŏts)
An Comunn Gaidhealach, *Highland Association* [ən 'kɒmən 'gaɪləx] (ăn kómmŭn gílăch)
Anderson, f.n. ['ændərsən] (ándĕrssŏn)
Andover ['ændoʊvər] (ándŏver) *Appropriate also for Viscount ~.*
Andoversford ['ændoʊvərzfɔrd] (ándŏvĕrzford)
Andrade, f.n. ['ændreɪd] (ándrayd)
Andreas ['ændrəs] (ándráss)
Andreetti, f.n. [ˌændrɪ'etɪ] (andri-étti)
Andreoli, f.n. [ˌændrɪ'oʊlɪ] (andri-óli)
Aneurin, Welsh C.n. [ə'naɪrɪn] (ănírin)
Angarrick [əŋ'gærɪk] (ăng-gárrick)
Angas, f.n. ['æŋgəs] (áng-gáss)

Angell, f.n. ['eɪndʒl] (aynjl)
Angersleigh ['eɪndʒərzlɪ] (áynjĕrzlee)
Angerstein, John Julius, 18-19th-c. merchant and art collector ['æŋgərstaɪn] (áng-gĕrstīn)
Angharad, Welsh C.n. [æŋ'hærəd] (ang-hárrăd)
Angier, f.n. ['ændʒɪər] (ánjeer)
Angle ['æŋgl] (áng-gl)
Anglesey ['æŋglsɪ] (áng-gl-si) *Appropriate also for the Marquess of ~.*
Angmering ['æŋmərɪŋ] (áng-mĕring)
Angus ['æŋgəs] (áng-gŭss) *Appropriate also for the Earl of ~.*
Anick ['enɪk] (áynick)
Anido, f.n. ['ænɪdoʊ] (ánnidō)
Anketell, f.n. ['æŋkətl] (ánkĕtl)
Anlaby ['ænləbɪ] (ánlăbi)
Annacloy [ˌænə'klɔɪ] (annăklóy)
Annaghmore [ˌænəx'mɔr] (annáchmór)
Annahilt [ˌænə'hɪlt] (annăhílt)
Annalong [ˌænə'lɒŋ] (annălóng)
Annaly, f.n. ['ænəlɪ] (ánnáli) *Appropriate also for Baron ~.*
Annear, f.n. [ə'nɪər] (ăneér)
Annells, f.n. ['ænlz] (annlz)
Annereau, f.n. ['ænərou] (ánnĕrō)
Annesley, f.n. ['enzlɪ] (ánzli) *Appropriate also for Earl ~.*
Annesley ['ænɪzlɪ] (ánnĕzli); ['ænzlɪ] (ánzli)
Annet ['ænɪt] (ánnĕt)
Annett, f.n. ['ænɪt] (ánnĕt)
Anscombe, f.n. ['ænskəm] (ánsskŏm)
Ansorge, f.n. ['ænsɔrdʒ] (ánssorj)
Anstice, f.n. ['ænstɪs] (ánstiss)
Anstruther, f.n. ['ænstrʌðər] (ánstruther)
Anstruther ['ænstrʌðər] (ánstruther)
Anstye [æn'staɪ] (anstí)
An Teallach [æn 'tʃæləx] (an chálách)
Anthony, f.n. ['æntənɪ] (ántŏni) ['ænθənɪ] (ánthŏni)
Antiquis, f.n. [æn'tɪkwɪs] (antíckwiss)
Antony ['æntənɪ] (ántŏni)
Antrim ['æntrɪm] (ántrim) *Appropriate also for the Earl of ~.*
Antrobus, f.n. ['æntrəbəs] (ántrŏbŭss)
Anwick, f.n. ['ænɪk] (ánnick)
Anwoth ['ænwɒθ] (ánwoth)
Apethorpe ['æpθɔrp] (áp-thorp); ['eɪpθɔrp] (áyp-thorp)
Aplvor, Denis, Welsh composer ['denɪs æp'aɪvər] (dénnis ap-ívŏr)
Appel, f.n. [ə'pel] (ăpéll)
Appelbe, f.n. [ə'pelbɪ] (ăpélbi)
Appleby, f.n. ['æplbɪ] (ápplbi)
Appletreewick ['æpltriːwɪk] (áppltreewíck)
Aprahamian, Felix, music critic ['fiːlɪks ˌæprə'heɪmɪən] (feéliks appră-háymiăn)
Apuldram ['æpldrəm] (áppldrăm)
Arabin, f.n. [ə'ræbɪn] (árábbin)
Arbikie [ɑr'bɪkɪ] (aarbeéki)
Arbirlot [ɑr'bərlət] (aarbírlŏt)
Arblaster, f.n. ['ɑrblastər] (aárblaastər)

Arboe [ɑr'boʊ] (aarbṓ)
Arborfield ['ɑrbərfīld] (aárbŏrfeeld)
Arbroath [ɑr'broʊθ] (aarbrṓth)
Arbuthnot, f.n. [ɑr'bʌθnət] (aarbúthnŏt)
Arbuthnott, Viscount of [ɑr'bʌθnət] (aarbúthnŏt)
Arcedeckne, f.n. [ɑrtʃ'dikən] (aartchdeèkĕn)
Ardagh, f.n. ['ɑrdə] (aárdǎ)
Ardcharnich [ɑrd'tʃɑrnɪx] (aard-chaárnich)
Ardee, Baron of [ɑr'di] (aardeè)
Ardeer [ɑr'dɪər] (aardeèr)
Ardeonaig [ɑr'dʒoʊneɪg] (aarjŏ́nayg); [ɑr'dʒoʊnɪg] (aarjŏ́nig)
Ardersier [ˌɑrdər'sɪər] (aardĕrsseèr)
Ardgay [ɑrd'gaɪ] (aard-gí)
Ardglass [ɑrd'glæs] (aardgláss)
Ardgour [ɑrd'gaʊər] (aardgówr)
Ardilaun, Barony of [ˌɑrdɪ'lɒn] (aardiláwn)
Ardingly [ˌɑrdɪŋ'laɪ] (aarding-lí)
Ardivachar Point [ˌɑrdɪ'væxər] (aardivácẖǎr)
Ardizzone, Edward, painter and illustrator [ˌɑrdɪ'zoʊnɪ] (aardizṓni)
Ardkeen [ɑrd'kin] (aardkeèn)
Ardkenneth [ɑrd'kenɪθ] (aardkénnĕth)
Ardlamont Point [ɑrd'læmənt] (aardlámmŏnt)
Ardmore [ɑrd'mɔr] (aardmór)
Ardnadam [ɑrd'nædəm] (aard-náddǎm)
Ardnamurchan [ˌɑrdnə'mɜrxən] (aardnǎmúrcẖǎn)
Ardoch ['ɑrdɒx] (aárdoch)
Ardovie [ɑr'dʌvɪ] (aardúvvi)
Ardoyne [ɑr'dɔɪn] (aardóyn)
Ardrishaig [ɑr'drɪʃɪg] (aardríshig); [ɑr'drɪʃeɪg] (aardríshayg)
Ardrossan [ɑr'drɒsən] (aardróssǎn)
Ardtalnaig [ɑrd'tælneɪg] (aardtálnayg)
Ardvasar [ɑrd'vɑzər] (aardvaázǎr)
Ardwick ['ɑrdwɪk] (aárdwick)
Arenig [ə'renɪg] (ărénnig)
Arfon ['ɑrvon] (aárvon)
Argall, f.n. ['ɑrgɒl] (aárgawl)
Argoed ['ɑrgɔɪd] (aárgoyd)
Argyll [ɑr'gaɪl] (aargíl) *Appropriate also for the Duke of ~.*
Arieli, Celia, pianist ['sɪlɪə ˌærɪ'elɪ] (seèliǎ arri-élli)
Aris, f.n. ['ɛərɪs] (aíriss); ['ɑrɪs] (aáriss)
Arisaig ['ærɪseɪg] (árrissayg)
Ariss, f.n. ['ɛərɪs] (aíriss)
Arkaig, Loch ['ɑrkeɪg] (aárkayg)
Arkell, f.n. ['ɑrkl] (aárkl); [ɑr'kel] (aarkéll)
Arkesden ['ɑrksdən] (aárksdĕn)
Arkholme with Cawood ['ɑrkhoʊm wɪð 'keɪwʊd] (aárk-hōm with káy-wŏ̄od)
Arlecdon ['ɑrlɛkdən] (aárlĕkdŏn)
Arlen, f.n. ['ɑrlən] (aárlĕn)
Arlesey ['ɑrlzɪ] (aárlzi)
Arleston ['ɑrlstən] (aárlstŏn)
Arlingham ['ɑrlɪŋəm] (aárling-ǎm)

Armadale, *Inverness., Sutherland, West Lothian* ['ɑrmədeɪl] (aármǎdayl)
Armagh, f.n. [ɑr'mɑ] (aarmaá)
Armagh [ɑr'mɑ] (aarmaá)
Armoy [ɑr'mɔɪ] (aarmóy)
Arnell, Richard, composer [ɑr'nel] (aarnéll)
Arnott, f.n. ['ɑrnət] (aárnŏt)
Aronowitz, f.n. [ə'rɒnəwɪts] (ărónnŏwits) *Appropriate for Cecil ~, viola player, and for John ~, pianist.*
Aros ['ɑrɒs] (aáross)
Arpinge ['ɑrpɪndʒ] (aárpinj)
Arram, f.n. ['ærəm] (árrǎm)
Arran ['ærən] (árrǎn) *Appropriate also for the Earl of ~.*
Arrantash, f.n. ['ærəntæʃ] (árrǎntash)
Arreton ['ærɪtən] (árrĕtŏn)
Arrochar ['ærəxər] (árrŏcẖǎr)
Arthington, f.n. ['ɑrθɪŋtən] (aárthingtŏn)
Arthog ['ɑrθɒg] (aár-thog)
Arthurlie ['ɑrθərlɪ] (aárthŭrli)
Arthy, f.n. ['ɑrθɪ] (aárthi)
Articlave [ɑrtɪ'kleɪv] (aartikláyv)
Arun, River ['ærən] (árrŭn)
Arundel ['ærəndl] (árrŭndl) *Appropriate also for the Earl of ~.*
Arundell of Wardour, Barony of ['ærəndl əv 'wɔrdər] (árrŭndl ŏv wáwrdŭr)
Arvel, Welsh C.n. ['ɑrwel] (aárwel)
Ascham, Roger, 16th-c. scholar ['æskəm] (ásskǎm)
Ascog ['æskɒg] (ásskog)
Ascoli, f.n. ['æskəlɪ] (ásskŏli)
Asgarby ['æzgərbɪ] (ázgǎrbi)
Ashampstead ['æʃəmstɛd] (áshǎmsted)
Ashbee, f.n. ['æʃbɪ] (áshbi)
Ashburnham ['æʃbɜrnəm] (áshburnǎm)
Ashburton, Baron ['æʃbərtən] (áshbŭrtŏn)
Ashburton [æʃ'bɜrtən] (ashbúrtŏn)
Ashby ['æʃbɪ] (áshbi)
Ashby St. Ledgers ['æʃbɪ snt 'ledʒərz] (áshbi sĭnt léjjĕrz)
Ashby Woulds ['æʃbɪ 'woʊldz] (áshbi wṓldz)
Ashby-de-la-Launde ['æʃbɪ də lə 'lɒnd] (áshbi dĕ lǎ láwnd)
Ashby-de-la-Zouch ['æʃbɪ də lə 'zuʃ] (áshbi dĕ lǎ zoósh)
Ashcombe, Baron ['æʃkəm] (áshkŏm)
Ashill, *Norfolk, Somerset* ['æʃhɪl] (áshhil)
Ashkenazi, f.n. [ˌæʃkɪ'nɑzɪ] (ashkĕnaázi)
Ashmanaugh ['æʃ'mænə] (ásh-mánnǎ)
Ashmolean Museum, *Oxford* [æʃ'moʊlɪən] (ashmṓliǎn)
Ashop Clough ['æʃəp 'klʌf] (áshŏp klúff)
Ashorne ['æʃhɔrn] (ásh-horn)
Ashort, f.n. ['æʃərt] (áshŏrt)
Ashow ['æʃoʊ] (áshō)
Ashreigney [æʃ'reɪnɪ] (ash-ráyni)
Ashton Keynes ['æʃtən 'keɪnz] (áshtŏn káynz)

Ashton - in - Makerfield [ˈæʃtən ɪn ˈmeɪkərfɪld] (áshtŏn in máykĕrfeeld)

Ashurst [ˈæʃhɜːst] (ásh-hurst)

Ashwellthorpe [ˈæʃwəlθɔːp] (áshwĕl-thorp)

Aske, *f.n.* [æsk] (assk)

Askern [ˈæskɜːn] (ásskern)

Askerswell [ˈæskərzwel] (ásskĕrzwel)

Askew, *f.n.* [ˈæskjuː] (ásskew)

Askham [ˈæskəm] (ásskăm)

Aslackby [ˈeɪzlbɪ] (áyzlbi)

Aslockton [ˈæzlɒktən] (ázlocktŏn)

Aspatria [æsˈpeɪtrɪə] (asspáytriă)

Aspel, *f.n.* [ˈæspel] (ásspel) ; [ˈæspl] (asspl)

Aspland, *f.n.* [ˈæsplænd] (ásspland)

Aspley Guise [ˈæsplɪ ˈɡaɪz] (ásspli gíz)

Asquith, *f.n.* [ˈæskwɪθ] (ásskwith) *Family name of the Earl of Oxford and ~.*

Assersohn, *f.n.* [ˈæsərsən] (ássĕrssŏn)

Assheton, *f.n.* [ˈæʃtən] (áshtŏn)

Assinder, *f.n.* [ˈæsɪndər] (ássinder)

Assynt [ˈæsɪnt] (ássint)

Astell, *f.n.* [æsˈtel] (asstéll)

Asterby [ˈeɪstərbɪ] (áysstĕrbi)

Asthall Leigh [ˈæstɒl ˈliː] (ásstawl leé) ; [ˈæstɒl ˈleɪ] (ásstawl láy)

Astins, *f.n.* [ˈæstɪnz] (ásstinz)

Aston Ingham [ˈæstən ˈɪŋəm] (ásstŏn íng-ăm)

Aston Rowant [ˈæstən ˈrouənt] (ásstŏn rŏ-ănt)

Astor, *Viscount* [ˈæstər] (ásstŏr)

Atchison, *f.n.* [ˈætʃɪsən] (átchissŏn)

Atha, *f.n.* [ˈeɪθə] (áthă)

Athawes, *f.n.* [ˈæθɔːz] (áthawz) ; [ˈæθɒz] (át-hawz)

Athelney [ˈæθəlnɪ] (áthĕlni)

Atherstone [ˈæθərstoun] (áthĕrstŏn)

Atherton, *f.n.* [ˈæθərtən] (áthĕrtŏn) ; [ˈæðərtən] (áthĕrtŏn)

Atherton [ˈæðərtən] (áthĕrtŏn) ; [ˈæθərtən] (áthĕrtŏn)

Athill, *f.n.* [ˈæðɪl] (áthil) ; [ˈæθɪl] (át-hil) ; [ˈæθɪl] (áthil)

Athlone, *Earldom of* [æθˈloun] (athlŏ́n)

Athlumney, *Barony of* [əθˈlʌmnɪ] (áthlúmni)

Atholl, *Duke of* [ˈæθl] (athl)

Atienza, *f.n.* [ˌætɪˈenzə] (atti-énză)

Attewell, *f.n.* [ˈætwel] (átwel)

Attleborough [ˈætlbrə] (áttl-bră) ; [ˈætlbərə] (áttl-bŭră)

Attlee, *Earl* [ˈætlɪ] (áttli)

Aubertin, *f.n.* [ˈoubərtɪn] (ŏ́bĕrtin)

Aubery, *f.n.* [ˈobərɪ] (áwbĕri)

Auchaber [ɒˈxabər] (ochaáber)

Auchendennan [ˌɒxənˈdenən] (ochĕn-dénnăn)

Auchengeich Colliery [ˌɒxənˈɡɪx] (ochĕn-geéch)

Auchenlochan [ˌɒxənˈlɒxən] (ochĕn-lóchăn)

Auchernach Lodge [ɒˈxɛərnəx] (ochaïr-năch)

Auchinachie, *f.n.* [ɒˈxɪnəxɪ] (ochínnăchi)

Auchincruive [ˌɒxɪnˈkruːv] (ochin-kroóv)

Auchindachie, *also spelt* **Auchindachy** [ɒˈxɪnəxɪ] (ochínnăchi)

Auchindoir [ˌɒxɪnˈdɔɪər] (ochindóyr)

Auchinleck, *Field Marshal Sir Claude* [ˌɒxɪnˈlek] (ochinléck)

Auchinleck [ˌɒxɪnˈlek] (ochinléck)

Auchinleck, Boswell of [ˈbɒzwəl əv ˈæflek] (bózwĕl ŏv áffleck)

Auchmore *see* Achmore.

Auchnagatt [ˌɒxnəˈɡæt] (ochnăgát)

Auchterarder [ˌɒxtərˈardər] (ochtĕraár-der)

Auchterderran [ˌɒxtərˈderən] (ochtĕr-dérrăn)

Auchterhouse [ˈɒxtərhaus] (óchtĕr-howss)

Auchterless [ˌɒxtərˈles] (ochtĕr-léss)

Auchterlonie, *f.n.* [ˌɒxtərˈlounɪ] (ochtĕr-lŏ́ni)

Auchtermuchty [ˌɒxtərˈmʌxtɪ] (ochtĕr-múchti)

Auckingill [ˈɒkɪŋɡɪl] (óckin-gil) ; [ˈaukɪŋɡɪl] (ówkin-gil)

Auden, W. H., *poet* [ˈɒdən] (áwdĕn)

Audigier, *f.n.* [ˈɒdɪʒeɪ] (áwdizhay)

Audlem [ˈɒdləm] (áwdlĕm)

Audus, *f.n.* [ˈɒdəs] (áwdŭss)

Auerbach, *f.n.* [ˈɔrbæk] (órback)

Augener, *f.n.* [ˈɒɡɪnər] (áwgĕner)

Augher [ˈɒxər] (óchr)

Aughertree [ˈɒfərtri] (óffĕrtree) ; [ˈæfərtri] (áffĕrtree)

Aughnacloy [ˌɒxnəˈklɔɪ] (ochnăklóy)

Aughrim [ˈɒxrɪm] (óchrim)

Aughton, *nr. Lancaster, Lancs.* [ˈæftən] (áfftŏn)

Aughton, *nr. Ormskirk, Lancs.* [ˈɒtən] (áwtŏn)

Aughton, *Yorks.* [ˈɒtən] (áwtŏn)

Augill Castle [ˈɒɡɪl] (áwgil)

Augustine, *f.n.* [ɒˈɡʌstɪn] (awgústin)

Aukin, *f.n.* [ˈɒkɪn] (áwkin)

Auld, *f.n.* [ɒld] (awld)

Auldearn [ɒldˈɜːn] (awldérn)

Auldgirth [ˈɒldɡɜːθ] (áwld-girth)

Auliff, *f.n.* [ˈɒlɪf] (áwlif)

Aultbea [ɒltˈbeɪ] (awltbáy)

Ault Hucknall [ˈɒlt ˈhʌknəl] (áwlt húcknăl)

Aumonier, Stacy, *author* [ˈsteɪsɪ ouˈmounɪeɪ] (stáyssi ōmŏ́ni-ay)

Aunger, *f.n.* [ˈɒndʒər] (áwnjer)

Aust [ɒst] (awsst)

Austen, *f.n.* [ˈɒstən] (ósstĕn) ; [ˈɒstɪn] (áwsstĕn)

Austin, *f.n.* [ˈɒstɪn] (ósstin) ; [ˈɒstɪn] (áwsstin)

Austwick, *f.n.* [ˈɒstwɪk] (ósstwick)

Austwick [ˈɒstwɪk] (áwsstwick) ; [ˈɒstɪk] (ósstick)

Auton, *f.n.* [ˈɒtən] (áwtŏn)

Auty, *f.n.* [ˈɒtɪ] (áwti)

Ava, *Earl of* [ˈavə] (aávă)

Avann, *f.n.* [əˈvæn] (ăván)

Avaulds ['jævlz] (yavvlz)

Avebury ['eɪvbərɪ] (áyvbŭri); ['eɪbərɪ] (áyburi)

Aveley ['eɪvlɪ] (áyvli)

Aveling, *f.n.* ['eɪvəlɪŋ] (áyvĕling); ['eɪvlɪŋ] (áyvling)

Ave Maria Lane, *City of London* ['ɑvɪ məˈriə] (aávi máree-ă)

Avening ['eɪvnɪŋ] (áyv-ning)

Averham ['ɛərəm] (áǐrăm)

Averill, *f.n.* ['æverɪl] (ávvĕril)

Avern, *f.n.* ['ævərn] (ávvĕrn); [əˈvɜrn] (ăvérn)

Aves, *f.n.* [eɪvz] (ayvz)

Aveton Gifford ['ɒtən ˈdʒɪfərd] (áwtŏn jíffŏrd); ['eɪvtən ˈdʒɪfərd] (áyvtŏn jíffŏrd)

Aviemore [ˌævɪˈmɔr] (avvimór)

Avill ['ævɪl] (ávvil)

Avington ['ævɪŋtən] (ávvingtŏn)

Avishays, *also spelt* **Avishayes** ['ævɪsheɪz] (ávvis-hayz); ['ævɪʃeɪz] (ávvishayz) *The spelling* Avishays *and the first pronunciation apply to the historic house and the agricultural and sporting estate.* Avishayes, *pronounced either way, is appropriate for the modern housing site.*

Avison, *f.n.* ['eɪvɪsən] (áyvissŏn); ['ævɪsən] (ávvissŏn) *The former is the North country pronunciation, and was quite probably that of the 18th-c. composer, who hailed from Newcastle. However, there is no positive evidence about it, and in English musical circles he is generally given the second pronunciation.*

Avoch, *f.n.* ['ævɒx] (ávvŏ<u>ch</u>)

Avoch [ɒx] (aw<u>ch</u>)

Avon, *Earl of* ['eɪvən] (áyvŏn)

Avon, *Loch and River, Banff.* [ɑn] (aan)

Avon, *River, Central Scotland* ['eɪvən] (áyvŏn)

Avon, *River, Devon* ['ævən] (ávvŏn)

Avon, *River, tributary of the Severn* ['eɪvən] (áyvŏn) *This river flows through Stratford-upon-Avon, and the counties of Northampton, Leicester, Warwick, and Gloucester.*

Avon Carrow ['eɪvən ˈkærou] (áyvŏn kárrŏ)

Avon Tyrell ['eɪvən ˈtɪrəl] (áyvŏn tírrĕl)

Avonmouth ['eɪvənmauθ] (áyvŏnmowth)

Avonwick ['ævənwɪk] (ávvŏn-wick)

Avory, *f.n.* ['eɪvərɪ] (áyvŏri)

Awbery, *f.n.* ['ɔbərɪ] (áwbĕri)

Awbridge ['eɪbrɪdʒ] (áybrij); ['ɑbrɪdʒ] (aábrij)

Awliscombe ['ɒlɪskəm] (áwlisskŏm)

Awre [ɔr] (or)

Awsworth ['nzwərθ] (ózwŭrth)

Axholme ['ækshoum] (ácks-hōm)

Axmouth ['æksmauθ] (ácksmowth)

Axon, *f.n.* ['æksən] (ácksŏn)

Ayckbourn, *f.n.* ['eɪkbərn] (áykborn)

Aycliffe ['eɪklɪf] (áyklif)

Ayer, *f.n.* [ɛər] (air)

Ayers, *f.n.* [ɛərz] (airz); ['eɪərz] (áy-ĕrz)

Ayerst, *f.n.* ['eɪərst] (áy-ĕrst); ['aɪərst] (í-ĕrst)

Aykroyd, *f.n.* ['eɪkrɔɪd] (áykroyd)

Aylburton ['eɪlbərtən] (áylburtŏn)

Aylen, *f.n.* ['eɪlən] (áylĕn)

Ayles, *f.n.* [eɪlz] (aylz)

Aylesbeare ['eɪlzbɪər] (áylzbeer)

Aylesford, *Earl of* ['eɪlzfərd] (áylzfŏrd)

Aylesham ['eɪlʃəm] (áyl-shăm)

Ayling, *f.n.* ['eɪlɪŋ] (áyling)

Aylsham ['eɪlʃəm] (áyl-shăm); ['eɪlsəm] (áylssăm)

Aylward, *f.n.* ['eɪlwərd] (áylwărd); ['eɪlwərd] (áylwawrd)

Aylwen, *f.n.* ['eɪlwɪn] (áylwĕn)

Aynho ['eɪnhou] (áyn-hō)

Ayot St. Lawrence ['eɪət snt ˈlɒrəns] (áy-ŏt sĭnt lórrĕnss)

Ayr [ɛər] (air)

Ayris, *f.n.* ['ɛərɪs] (áiriss)

Ayrst, *f.n.* [ɛərst] (airst)

Ayscough, *f.n.* ['eɪzkou] (áyzkō); ['eɪskou] (ásskō); ['æskou] (ásskō)

Aysgarth ['eɪzgɑrθ] (áyzgaarth)

Aytoun, William Edmonstoune, *Scottish poet* ['edmənstən ˈeɪtən] (édmŏnstŏn áytŏn)

Aza, *f.n.* ['eɪzə] (áyză)

B

Babell, William, *composer* ['beɪbl] (baybl)

Babell ['bæbel] (bábbehl)

Babraham ['beɪbrəm] (báybrăm)

Bach, *f.n.* [bɑk] (baak)

Bacharach, *f.n.* ['bækəræk] (báckărack)

Bache, *f.n.* [beɪtʃ] (baytch); [beɪʃ] (baysh)

Bachymbyd Bach [bəˈxʌmbɪd ˈbɑx] (bă<u>ch</u>úmbid baá<u>ch</u>)

Backhouse, *f.n.* ['bækəs] (báckŭss); ['bækhaus] (báck-howss)

Bacon, *f.n.* ['beɪkən] (báykŏn)

Baconian, *pertaining to Francis Bacon* [beɪˈkounɪən] (baykóniăn)

Bacup ['beɪkəp] (báykŭp)

Bacuzzi, *f.n.* [bəˈkʌzɪ] (băkúzzi)

Badcock, *f.n.* ['bædkou] (bádkō)

Baddeley, *f.n.* ['bædəlɪ] (báddĕli); ['bædlɪ] (bádli)

Baddesley, North ['bædzlɪ] (bádzli)

Baddesley, South ['bædɪzlɪ] (báddĕzli); ['bædzlɪ] (bádzli)

Baddesley Clinton ['bædɪzlɪ ˈklɪntən] (báddĕzli klíntŏn); ['bædzlɪ ˈklɪntən] (bádzli klíntŏn)

Baddesley Ensor ['bædızlı 'enzɔr] (báddĕzli énzor); ['bædzlı 'enzɔr] (bádzli énzor)

Badel, Alan, actor [bə'del] (bådéll)

Badeley, Barony of ['bædlı] (bádli)

Badenoch, f.n. ['beɪdnɒk] (báyd-nock)

Badenoch ['bædənɒx] (báddĕno<u>ch</u>)

Baden-Powell, Baron ['beɪdən 'pouəl] (báydĕn pô-ĕl)

Bader, Group-Captain Douglas ['badər] (baáder)

Badgworthy Water, also spelt **Bagworthy** ['bædʒərı 'wotər] (bájjĕri wáwter)

Badham, f.n. ['bædəm] (báddăm)

Badoney [bə'dounı] (bådóni)

Baelz, f.n. [belts] (belts)

Bage, f.n. [beɪdʒ] (bayj)

Bagehot, f.n. ['bædʒət] (bájjŏt); ['bæɡət] (bággŏt) The first was the pronunciation of Walter ~, economist and journalist.

Bagenal, f.n. ['bæɡnəl] (bágnăl); ['bæɡənəl] (bággĕnăl)

Baggallay, f.n. ['bæɡəlı] (bággăli)

Bagier, f.n. ['beɪdʒər] (báyjer)

Bagillt ['bæɡıhlt] (bággih<u>l</u>t)

Baginton ['bæɡıntən] (bággintŏn)

Baglan ['bæɡlən] (bág/lăn)

Bagnari, f.n. [bæɡ'narı] (bag-naárí)

Bagnell, f.n. ['bæɡnəl] (bágnĕl)

Bagot, Baron ['bæɡət] (bággŏt)

Bagrie, f.n. ['bæɡrı] (bágri)

Bagrit, f.n. ['bæɡrıt] (bágrit)

Baguley, f.n. ['bæɡəlı] (bággŭli)

Baguley ['bæɡəlı] (bággŭli); ['bæɡlı] (bágli)

Bagworthy Water see Badgworthy Water.

Baigent, f.n. ['beɪdʒənt] (báyjĕnt)

Bailey, f.n. ['beɪlı] (báyli)

Bailhache, f.n. ['beɪlhætʃ] (báyl-hatch)

Baillieston ['beɪlıstən] (báylistŏn)

Baillieu, f.n. ['beɪljuː] (báylew) Appropriate also for Baron ~.

Baillon, f.n. ['beɪlən] (báylŏn)

Baird, f.n. [bɛərd] (baird)

Bairstow, f.n. ['bɛərstou] (baírsstō)

Bakewell ['beɪkwel] (báykwel)

Bala ['bælə] (bálă)

Balby ['bolbı] (báwlbi)

Balch, f.n. [bolʃ] (bawlsh)

Balchen, f.n. ['bæltʃın] (báltchĕn) This is the pronunciation associated with the 18th-c. Admiral of the name.

Balchin, Nigel, author ['boltʃın] (báwl-chin)

Balcomb, f.n. ['bolkəm] (báwlkŏm)

Balcombe ['bolkəm] (báwlkŏm)

Balcon, Sir Michael, film producer ['bolkən] (báwlkŏn)

Balden, f.n. ['boldən] (báwldĕn)

Baldernock [bæl'dərnək] (baldérnŏk)

Balderston, f.n. ['boldərstən] (báwldĕrstŏn)

Baldhu [bæl'dju] (baldéw); [bol'dju] (bawldéw); [bol'du] (bawldoó)

Baldick, f.n. ['boldık] (báwldick)

Baldock, f.n. ['boldɒk] (báwldock)

Baldock ['boldɒk] (báwldock)

Baldovan [bæl'dɒvən] (baldóvvăn)

Baldovie [bæl'dʌvı] (baldúvvi)

Baldragon [bæl'dræɡən] (bal-drággŏn)

Baldry, f.n. ['boldrı] (báwldri)

Baldwin of Bewdley, Earl ['boldwın əv 'bjudlı] (báwldwin ŏv béwdli)

Balerno [bə'lɜrnou] (bălérnō) Appropriate also for Baron ~.

Balfour, f.n. ['bælfər] (bálfŭr); ['bælfɔr] (bálfor)

Balfour, Earl of ['bælfɔr] (bálfor)

Balfour of Burleigh, Baron ['bælfər əv 'bɜrlı] (bálfŭr ŏv búrli)

Balfour of Inchrye, Baron ['bælfər əv ın'raı] (bálfor ŏv insh-rí)

Balfron [bæl'frɒn] (balfrón)

Balgavies [bæl'ɡævız] (balgávviz)

Balgay [bæl'ɡeı] (balgáy)

Balgedie [bæl'ɡedı] (balgéddi)

Balgonie, f.n. [bæl'ɡounı] (balgóni)

Balguy, f.n. ['bolɡı] (báwlgi)

Baliol, f.n. ['beɪlıəl] (báyli-ŏl)

Balivanich [ˌbælɪ'vænıx] (balivánni<u>ch</u>)

Ball, f.n. [bol] (bawl)

Ballabrooie, I.o.M. [ˌbælə'bruı] (balăbroó-i)

Ballachulish [ˌbælə'hulıʃ] (balăhoólish)

Ballacraine, I.o.M. [ˌbælə'kreın] (balăkráyn)

Ballagh ['bælə] (bálă)

Ballagher, f.n. ['bæləɡər] (báláger)

Ballam ['bæləm] (bálăm)

Ballantine, f.n. ['bæləntaın] (bálăntĭn)

Ballantrae [ˌbælən'treı] (balăn-tráy)

Ballantyne, f.n. ['bæləntaın] (bálăntĭn)

Ballard, f.n. ['bælard] (bálaard); ['bælərd] (bálărd)

Ballardie, f.n. [bə'lardı] (bălaárdi)

Ballasalla, I.o.M. [ˌbælə'sælə] (balăssálă)

Ballater ['bælətər] (bálăter)

Ballaugh [bə'laf] (bălaáf)

Ballechin [bə'lexın] (bălé<u>ch</u>in)

Balleine, f.n. [bæ'len] (balén)

Ballham, f.n. ['bɒləm] (báwlăm)

Ballig [bə'lıɡ] (bálíg)

Ballinahatty [ˌbælınə'hætı] (balinăhátti)

Ballinamallard [ˌbælınə'mælərd] (balinămálărd)

Ballinaskeagh [ˌbælınə'skeı] (balinăskáy)

Ballindalloch [ˌbælın'dæləx] (balindáló<u>ch</u>)

Ballinderry [ˌbælın'derı] (balindérri)

Ballinger ['bælındʒər] (bálinjer)

Ballingry [bə'lıŋɡrı] (balíng-gri)

Ballinluig [ˌbælın'luıɡ] (balinloó-ig)

Ballintogher [ˌbælın'tɒxər] (balintó<u>ch</u>er)

Ballintoy [ˌbælın'toı] (balintóy)

Balliol College, Oxford University ['beɪlıəl] (báyli-ŏl); ['beɪljəl] (báyl-yŏl)

Balloch, *Dunbarton., Inverness., Perth.*
['bælǝx] (bálŏ<u>ch</u>)
Balloch Buie ['bælǝx 'buɪ] (bálŏ<u>ch</u> boó-i)
Ballochmyle [ˌbælǝx'maɪl] (balŏ<u>ch</u>míl)
Balloo [bæ'lu] (baloó)
Ballyards [ˌbælɪ'ɑːdz] (bali-aárdz)
Ballyaughlis [ˌbælɪ'ɒxlɪs] (bali-ó<u>ch</u>liss)
Ballybannon [ˌbælɪ'bænǝn] (balibánnŏn)
Ballycairn [ˌbælɪ'kɛǝrn] (balikaírn)
Ballycarry [ˌbælɪ'kærɪ] (balikárri)
Ballycastle [ˌbælɪ'kɑsl] (balikaássl)
Ballyclare [ˌbælɪ'klɛǝr] (baliklaír)
Ballycoan [ˌbælɪ'kouǝn] (balikŏ-án)
Ballycopeland [ˌbælɪ'kouplǝnd] (bali-kŏplánd)
Ballycultra [ˌbælɪkǝl'trɔ] (balikŭltráw)
Ballydavey [ˌbælɪ'deɪvɪ] (balidáyvi)
Ballydivity [ˌbælɪ'dɪvɪtɪ] (balidívviti)
Ballydougan [ˌbælɪ'dugǝn] (balidoógǎn)
Ballydrain [ˌbælɪ'dreɪn] (balidráyn)
Ballyeglish [ˌbælɪ'eglɪʃ] (bali-églish)
Ballyfinaghy [ˌbælɪ'fɪnǝxɪ] (balifínnǎ<u>ch</u>i)
Ballygally [ˌbælɪ'gælɪ] (baligáli)
Ballygawley [ˌbælɪ'gɔlɪ] (baligáwli)
Ballygilbert [ˌbælɪ'gɪlbǝrt] (baligílbĕrt)
Ballygomartin [ˌbælɪgou'mɑrtɪn] (bali-gōmaártin)
Ballygowan [ˌbælɪ'gauǝn] (baligówăn)
Ballygrainey [ˌbælɪ'greɪnɪ] (baligráyni)
Ballyhackamore [ˌbælɪ'hækǝmɔr] (bali-háckǎmor)
Ballyhalbert [ˌbælɪ'hælbǝrt] (bali-hálbĕrt)
Ballyhanwood [ˌbælɪ'hænwʊd] (bali-hánwŏ̄od)
Ballyholme [ˌbælɪ'houm] (bali-hŏ́m) ¶
Ballyhornan [ˌbælɪ'hornǝn] (bali-hórnǎn)
Ballykelly [ˌbælɪ'kelɪ] (balikélli)
Ballykilbeg [ˌbælɪkɪl'beg] (balikilbég)
Ballykinlar [ˌbælɪ'kɪnlǝr] (balikínlár)
Ballylesson [ˌbælɪ'lesǝn] (baliléssŏn)
Ballylumford [ˌbælɪ'lʌmfǝrd] (balilúmfŏrd)
Ballymacarrett [ˌbælɪmǝ'kærɪt] (bali-mǎkárrĕt)
Ballymachan [ˌbælɪ'mæxǝn] (bali-má<u>ch</u>ǎn)
Ballymaconaghy [ˌbælɪmǝ'kɒnǝxɪ] (bali-mǎkónnǎ<u>ch</u>i)
Ballymaconnell [ˌbælɪmǝ'kɒnl] (bali-mǎkónnl)
Ballymacormick [ˌbælɪmǝ'kɔrmɪk] (bali-mǎkórmick)
Ballymaguigan [ˌbælɪmǝ'gwɪgǝn] (bali-mǎgwíggǎn)
Ballymena [ˌbælɪ'minǝ] (balimeénǎ)
Ballymenoch [ˌbælɪ'minǝx] (balimeé-nŏ<u>ch</u>)
Ballymoney [ˌbælɪ'mʌnɪ] (balimúnni)
Ballynafeigh [ˌbælɪnǝ'faɪ] (balináff)
Ballynahinch [ˌbælɪnǝ'hɪnʃ] (balináhínsh)
Ballynure [ˌbælɪ'njuǝr] (balinyŏ̄or)
Ballyquintin [ˌbælɪ'kwɪntɪn] (balikwíntin)
Ballyrashane [ˌbælɪrǝ'ʃeɪn] (balirásháyn)

Ballyrobert [ˌbælɪ'rɔbǝrt] (balirŏbbĕrt)
Ballyronan [ˌbælɪ'rounǝn] (balirŏnǎn)
Ballyroney [ˌbælɪ'rounɪ] (balirŏ́ni)
Ballysallagh [ˌbælɪ'sælɪ] (bali-sáli)
Ballysillan [ˌbælɪ'sɪlǝn] (bali-síllǎn)
Ballystockart [ˌbælɪ'stɒkǝrt] (bali-stóckǎrt)
Ballywalter [ˌbælɪ'wɒltǝr] (bali-wáwlter)
Ballywillan [ˌbælɪ'wɪlǝn] (bali-wíllǎn)
Balmacara [ˌbælmǝ'kɑrǝ] (balmákaárǎ)
Balmaghie [ˌbælmǝ'gi] (balmágeé)
Balmaha [ˌbælmǝ'hɑ] (balmáhaá)
Balmedie [bæl'medɪ] (balméddi)
Balmer, f.n. ['bɑmǝr] (baámer)
Balmerino, f.n. [bæl'mɛǝrnɪ] (balmaírni)
Balmoral, *Aberdeen., Co. Antrim* [bæl-'mɒrǝl] (balmórrǎl)
Balnain [bæl'neɪn] (balnáyn)
Balnave, f.n. [bæl'neɪv] (balnáyv)
Balne [bɒn] (bawn)
Balniel, Lord [bæl'nɪl] (balneél)
Balogh, Baron ['bælɒg] (bálog)
Balornock House [bǝ'lɔrnǝk] (bǎlórnŏk)
Balquharn [bæl'hwɑrn] (bal-whaárn)
Balquhidder [bæl'hwɪdǝr] (bal-whídder); [bæl'kwɪdǝr] (bal-kwídder)
Balsall Heath ['bɒlsl 'hiθ] (báwlssl heéth)
Balshagray [bæl'ʃægreɪ] (bal-shágray)
Balsham ['bɒlʃǝm] (báwl-shám)
Balston, f.n. ['bɒlstǝn] (báwlstŏn)
Baltasound ['bɒltǝsaʊnd] (báwltǎssownd)
Bambrough, f.n. ['bæmbrǝ] (bámbrǎ)
Bamburgh ['bæmbǝrǝ] (bámbŭrǎ)
Bamfyld, f.n. ['bæmfɪld] (bámfeeld)
Bamont, f.n. ['beɪmǝnt] (báymŏnt)
Banagher ['bænǝxǝr] (bánnǎ<u>ch</u>er)
Banavie ['bænǝvɪ] (bánnǎvi)
Banbridge [bæn'brɪdʒ] (banbríj)
Bance, f.n. [bæns] (banss)
Banchory ['bæŋkǝrɪ] (bánkŏri); ['bænxǝrɪ] (bán<u>ch</u>ŏri)
Banff [bæmf] (bamf); [bænf] (banf)
Bangor, Viscount ['bæŋgǝr] (báng-gŏr)
Bangor, *Caernarvon., Co. Down, Flint.* ['bæŋgǝr] (báng-gŏr)
Banham, f.n. ['bænǝm] (bánnǎm)
Bank-Ffos-Felen [ˌbæŋk foʊs 'velɪn] (bank fōss véllĕn)
Bankyfelin [ˌbæŋkǝ'velɪn] (bankǎvéllin)
Bannard, f.n. ['bænǝrd] (bánaard)
Bannatyne, f.n. ['bænǝtaɪn] (bánnătǐn)
Bannatyne, Port [pɔrt 'bænǝtɪn] (port bánnátin)
Bantham ['bæntǝm] (bántăm)
Banyard, f.n. ['bænjɑrd] (bán-yaard)
Bapchild ['bæptʃaɪld] (báp-chǐld)
Barachnie [bǝ'ræxnɪ] (bǎrá<u>ch</u>ni)
Barassie [bǝ'ræsɪ] (bǎrássi)
Barbirolli, Sir John, conductor [ˌbɑrbɪ-'rɒlɪ] (baarbirólli)
Barbour, f.n. ['bɑrbǝr] (baárbŭr)
Barcaldine [bɑr'kældɪn] (baarkáldin)
Barcloy [bǝr'klɔɪ] (bǎrklóy)
Barcombe [bǝr'kǝm] (baárkŏm)

Bardgett, Herbert, *conductor* ['bɑrdʒet] (baárjet)

Bardill, *f.n.* ['bɑrdl] (baárdl); ['bɑrdɪl] (baárdil)

Bareau, Paul, *economist* ['pɒl 'bærɒʊ] (páwl bárrō)

Bargany [bɑr'genɪ] (baargénni)

Bargeddie [bɑr'gedɪ] (baargéddi)

Barger, *f.n.* ['bɑrdʒər] (baárjer)

Bargery, *f.n.* ['bɑrdʒərɪ] (baárjĕri)

Bargh, *f.n.* [bɑrdʒ] (baarj); [bɑrf] (baarf)

Bargoed ['bɑrgɔɪd] (baárgoyd)

Barham, *f.n.* ['bærəm] (bárrăm); ['bɑrəm] (baárăm) *The second is appropriate for Baron* ~.

Barham ['bærəm] (bárrăm)

Barharrow [bɑr'hærɒʊ] (baar-hárrō)

Barholm ['bærəm] (bárrŏm)

Baring, *f.n.* ['beərɪŋ] (baíring)

Baring-Gould, The Revd. Sabine, *author and hymn-writer* ['seɪbɪn 'beərɪŋ 'gʊld] (sáybin baíring goóld)

Baripper [bə'rɪpər] (bărípper)

Barkisland ['bɑrkɪslənd] (baárkisslánd); ['bɑslənd] (baássländ)

Barklye [bɑrk'laɪ] (baarklí)

Barlaston ['bɑrləstən] (baárlăstŏn)

Barlborough ['bɑrlbərə] (baárl-bŭră); ['bɑrbərə] (baárbŭră)

Barlestone ['bɑrlstɒʊn] (baárlsstōn)

Barmouth ['bɑrməθ] (baármūth)

Barnabe, *f.n.* ['bɑrnəbɪ] (baárnăbi)

Barnadier, *f.n.* [ˌbɑrnə'dɪər] (baarnădeér)

Barnard, *f.n.* ['bɑrnɑrd] (baárnaard); ['bɑrnərd] (baárnărd)

Barnard Castle ['bɑrnərd 'kɑsl] (baárnărd kaássl)

Barnard Gate ['bɑrnərd 'geɪt] (baárnărd gáyt)

Barnardiston, *f.n.* [ˌbɑrnər'dɪstən] (baarnărdístŏn)

Barnbow [bɑrn'bɒʊ] (baarnbó)

Barnett, *f.n.* ['bɑrnɪt] (baárnĕt)

Barnoldswick [bɑr'nɒʊldzwɪk] (baarnŏ́ldzwick); ['bɑrlɪk] (baárlick)

Barou, *f.n.* [bə'ruː] (băroó)

Barraclough, *f.n.* ['bærəklʌf] (bárrăkluff)

Barrass, *f.n.* ['bærəs] (bárráss)

Barraud, *f.n.* ['bærɒʊ] (bárrō)

Barrogil Castle ['bærɒʊgɪl] (bárrōgil) *Former name of the Castle of Mey, q.v.*

Barrow-in-Furness ['bærɒʊ ɪn 'fɜrnɪs] (bárrō in fúrnĕss)

Barry ['bærɪ] (bárri)

Barsham ['bɑrʃəm] (baár-shăm) *Appropriate for* ~ *in Norfolk; East, West and North* ~ *in Suffolk; and the historic East* ~ *Manor.*

Barstow, *f.n.* ['bɑrstɒʊ] (baársstō)

Bartestree ['bɑrtɪstrɪ] (baártĕstree)

Barthomley ['bɑrθəmlɪ] (baárthŏmli)

Bartleet, *f.n.* ['bɑrtlɪt] (baártleet)

Bartlett, *f.n.* ['bɑrtlɪt] (baártlĕt)

Barton-in-Fabis ['bɑrtən ɪn 'feɪbɪs] (baártŏn in fáybiss)

Barttelot, *f.n.* ['bɑrtɪlɒt] (baártĕlot)

Baruck, *f.n.* [bə'rʊk] (băroŏk)

Barugh, *f.n.* [bɑrf] (baarf)

Barugh [bɑrk] (baark)

Barwick, *f.n.* ['bærɪk] (bárrick)

Barwick, *Herts., Norfolk, Somerset* ['bærɪk] (bárrick)

Barwick-in-Elmet ['bærɪk ɪn 'elmɪt] (bárrick in élmĕt)

Baschurch ['bæstʃɜrtʃ] (báss-church)

Baseden, *f.n.* ['beɪzdən] (báyzdĕn)

Baseley *f.n.* ['beɪzlɪ] (báyzli)

Basevi, George, *19th-c. architect* [bə'seɪvɪ] (bássáyvi)

Basford, *suburb of Nottingham* ['beɪsfərd] (báyssfŏrd)

Basford, *Staffs.* ['bæsfərd] (bássfŏrd)

Basildon ['bæzldən] (bázldŏn)

Baslow ['bæzlɒʊ] (bázlō)

Bason, *f.n.* ['bæsən] (bássŏn)

Bassaleg ['beɪzlɪg] (báyzlig); [bæ'sæleg] (bassáleg)

Bassenthwaite ['bæsənθweɪt] (bássĕnthwayt)

Bassetlaw ['bæsɪt'lɒ] (bássĕtláw)

Bassingbourn ['bæsɪŋbɔrn] (bássingborn)

Bassingthwaite, *f.n.* ['bæsɪŋθweɪt] (bássingthwayt)

Basterfield, *f.n.* ['bæstərfɪld] (básstĕrfeeld)

Bastie, *f.n.* ['bæstɪ] (bássti)

Bastonford ['bæstənford] (básstŏnford)

Baswich ['bæsɪdʒ] (bássij); ['bæsɪtʃ] (bássitch)

Bateson, *f.n.* ['beɪtsən] (báytsŏn)

Batham, *f.n.* ['beɪθəm] (báythăm)

Bathavon ['bɑθeɪvən] (baáth-ayvŏn)

Bathealton ['bætltən] (báttltŏn)

Batheaston [bɑθ'istən] (baatheéstŏn); ['bætɪstən] (báttistŏn)

Bather, *f.n.* ['bæðər] (báther); ['bæθər] (báther)

Bathford [bɑθ'fɔrd] (baathfórd)

Batho, *f.n.* ['bæθɒʊ] (báthō); ['beɪθɒʊ] (báythō)

Bathurst, *f.n.* ['bæθɜrst] (báthurst); ['bæθhɜrst] (báth-hurst) *The first is appropriate for Earl* ~ *and for Viscount Bledisloe's family name.*

Batley ['bætlɪ] (bátli)

Battagel, *f.n.* ['bætədʒl] (báttăjl)

Battersea ['bætərsɪ] (báttĕrssi)

Battershill, *f.n.* ['bætərʃɪl] (báttĕr-shil)

Battes, *f.n.* ['bætɪs] (báttĕss)

Battine, *f.n.* ['bætin] (bátteen)

Battisford ['bætɪsfərd] (báttisfŏrd)

Battishill, *f.n.* ['bætɪʃɪl] (bátti-shil)

Battlesbridge ['bætlzbrɪdʒ] (báttlz-brij)

Battye, *f.n.* ['bætɪ] (bátti)

Baty, *f.n.* ['beɪtɪ] (báyti)

Baudains, *f.n.* ['bɒʊdeɪnz] (bṓdaynz)

Baufield, *f.n.* ['bɑʊfɪld] (bówfeeld)

Baugh, *f.n.* [bɔ] (baw)
Baughan, *f.n.* [bɔn] (bawn); ['bɔən]
(báw-ăn); ['bɒfən] (bóffăn)
Baughen, *f.n.* [bɔn] (bawn); ['bɔən]
(báw-ên); ['bɒfən] (bóffĕn)
Baulch, *f.n.* [bɔltʃ] (bawltch)
Baumber, *f.n.* ['bɒmbər] (báwmber)
Baumber ['bɒmbər] (báwmber)
Baverstock, *f.n.* ['bævərstɒk] (bávvĕr-stock)
Bavin, *f.n.* ['bævɪn] (bávvin)
Bawburgh ['beɪbər] (báyber); ['bɔbərə]
(báwbŭră)
Bawdeswell ['bɔdzwəl] (báwdzwĕl)
Bawdsey ['bɔdzɪ] (báwdzi)
Bawor, *f.n.* ['bauər] (bówer)
Baxandall, *f.n.* ['bæksəndɔl] (báck-săndawl)
Bayard, *f.n.* ['beɪɑrd] (báy-aard)
Baylham ['beɪləm] (báylăm)
Baynard's Green ['beɪnɑrdz 'grin]
(báynaardz greén)
Bazalgette, *f.n.* ['bæzldʒet] (bázzl-jet)
Bazeley, *f.n.* ['beɪzlɪ] (báyzli)
Bazell, *f.n.* [bə'zel] (băzéll)
Bazett, *f.n.* ['bæzɪt] (bázzĕt)
Bazin, *f.n.* ['beɪzɪn] (báyzin)
Beachy Head ['bitʃɪ 'hed] (beétchi héd)
Beaconsfield, *Earldom of* ['bikənzfild]
(beékŏnzfeeld)
Beaconsfield ['bekənzfild] (béckŏnz-feeld); ['bikənzfild] (beékŏnzfeeld)
Beaford ['bifərd] (beéfŏrd)
Beaglehole, *f.n.* ['biglhoʊl] (beégl-hōl)
Beahan, *f.n.* ['biən] (beé-ăn)
Beament, *f.n.* ['bimənt] (beémĕnt)
Beaminster ['bemɪnstər] (bémminster)
Beamish, *f.n.* ['bimɪʃ] (beémish)
Beamont, *f.n.* ['bimɒnt] (beémont)
Bean, *f.n.* [bin] (been)
Beanacharan, *Loch* [ˌbjænə'xærən]
(byannáchárrăn)
Beanes, *f.n.* [beɪnz] (baynz)
Beaney, *f.n.* ['binɪ] (beéni)
Beardsall, *f.n.* ['bɪərdsl] (beerdssl)
Beardsell, *f.n.* ['bɪərdsl] (beerdssl)
Beardsley, *f.n.* ['bɪərdzlɪ] (beérdzli)
Appropriate for Aubrey ~, 19th-c. artist.
Beare [bɪər] (beer)
Beare Green ['bɛər 'grin] (baír greén)
Bearley ['bɪərlɪ] (beérli)
Bearpark ['bɪər'pɑrk] (beér-paárk)
Bearsden [bɛərz'den] (bairzdén)
Bearsted ['bɜrsted] (bérsted); ['bɛərsted]
(baírsted); *The first is appropriate for*
Viscount ~.
Bearstone ['bɪərstən] (beérstŏn)
Bearwardcote ['bærəkət] (bárrăkŏt)
Beastall, *f.n.* ['bistl] (beestl)
Beattie, *f.n.* ['bitɪ] (beéti)
Beattock ['bitək] (beétŏk)
Beatty, *Earl* ['bitɪ] (beéti)
Beauchamp ['bitʃəm] (beétchăm) *Ap-propriate also for Earl ~.*
Beauchief ['bitʃɪf] (beétchif)

Beauclerk, *f.n.* ['boʊklɛər] (bóklair)
Appropriate also for the Duke of St.
Albans' family name.
Beaudesert [boʊ'dezərt] (bōdézzĕrt);
[ˌboʊdɪ'zɛər] (bōdĕzaír); ['belzər] (bélzer)
Beaudesert Park ['boʊdɪzɛər 'pɑrk]
(bōdĕzair paárk)
Beaufort, *Duke of* ['boʊfərt] (bófŏrt)
Beaufoy, *f.n.* ['boʊfɔɪ] (bófoy)
Beaulieu ['bjulɪ] (béwli)
Beauly ['bjulɪ] (béwli)
Beaumanor [boʊ'mænər] (bōmánnŏr)
Beaumaris [boʊ'mærɪs] (bōmárriss)
Beaumont, *f.n.* ['boʊmənt] (bómŏnt)
Appropriate also for Baroness ~.
Beaumont ['bimənt] (beémŏnt)
Beausale ['bjusl] (bewssl)
Beauvoir, *f.n.* ['boʊvwɑr] (bóvwaar)
Beavan, *f.n.* ['bevən] (bévvăn)
Beavis, *f.n.* ['bivɪs] (beéviss)
Beavon, *f.n.* ['bevən] (bévvŏn)
Beaworthy ['biwɜrðɪ] (beè-wurthi);
['bauərɪ] (bówĕri)
Beba, *f.n.* ['bibə] (beébă)
Bebe, *f.n.* ['bibɪ] (beébi)
Becher's Brook ['bitʃərz 'brʊk] (beè-chĕrz brŏok)
Bechervaise, *f.n.* ['betʃərveɪz] (bétchĕr-vayz); ['beʃərveɪz] (béshĕrvayz)
Bechhofer, *f.n.* ['bekhoʊfər] (béck-hōfer)
Becke, *f.n.* [bek] (beck)
Beckermet [be'kɜrmɪt] (beckérmĕt)
Beckles, *f.n.* ['beklz] (becklz)
Bective, *Earl of* ['bektɪv] (bécktiv)
Bedale, *Yorks.* ['bidl] (beedl) *The local*
~ Hunt, however, is pronounced
['bideɪl] (beédayl).
Bedales School, *Hants.* ['bideɪlz] (beè-daylz)
Beddall, *f.n.* ['bedɔl] (béddawl)
Beddau ['beðaɪ] (béthī)
Beddgelert [beɪð'gelərt] (bayth-géllĕrt)
Beddingham [ˌbedɪŋ'hæm] (bedding-hám)
Beddoes, *Thomas Lovell*, *19th-c. poet*
and dramatist ['lʌvl 'bedoʊz] (lúvvl
béddōz)
Bedel, *f.n.* ['bidl] (beedl)
Bedells, *f.n.* [bɪ'delz] (bĕdéllz)
Bedenham ['bedənəm] (béddĕnăm)
Bedford ['bedfərd] (bédfŏrd) *Appropriate*
also for the Duke of ~.
Bedham [bed'hæm] (bed-hám)
Bedlinog [bed'linɒg] (bedleénog)
Bedruthan [bɪ'drʌðən] (bĕdrúthăn)
Bedwas ['bedwæs] (bédwass)
Bedwellty [bed'weltɪ] (bed-wéhlti)
Beebee, *f.n.* ['bibɪ] (beébee)
Beeleigh ['bilɪ] (beélee); ['bilɪ] (beéli)
Beesands ['bisændz] (beé-sandz)
Beese, *f.n.* [biz] (beez)
Beeswing ['bizwɪŋ] (beézwing)
Beetham, *f.n.* ['biθəm] (beéthăm)
Beetham ['biðəm] (beéthăm)
Begbroke ['begbrʊk] (bégbrŏok)

Begelly [bɪ'gelɪ] (bĕgélli)
Begent, f.n. ['bidʒənt] (beéjĕnt)
Beggearn Huish ['begərn 'hjuːʃ] (béggern héw-ish)
Beguildy [bɪ'gaɪldɪ] (bĕgíldi)
Behague, f.n. [bɪ'heɪg] (bĕ-háyg)
Beharrell, f.n. [bɪ'hærəl] (bĕ-hárrĕl)
Behnes, William, 19th-c. sculptor ['beɪnɪz] (báynĕz); [beɪnz] (baynz) *These pronunciations are based merely on usage, not on historical evidence. The sculptor was of German origin.*
Behrens, f.n. ['bɛərənz] (baírĕnz)
Beighton, f.n. ['beɪtən] (báytŏn)
Beighton, *Derby.* ['beɪtən] (báytŏn); ['baɪtən] (bítŏn)
Beighton, *Norfolk* ['baɪtən] (bítŏn); ['beɪtən] (báytŏn)
Beinn a'Chaolais [ˌben ə 'xœɪlɪʃ] (ben ă chŏ-ílish)
Beinn-an-Oir [ˌben ən 'ɔr] (ben ăn ór)
Beinn Eighe *see* Ben Eay.
Beinn Laoigh [ben 'lœɪ] (ben lŏ-i)
Beinn Siantaidh [ben 'ʃɪəntɪ] (ben sheé-ănti)
Beint, f.n. [baɪnt] (bīnt)
Beit, f.n. [baɪt] (bīt) *Appropriate for Alfred and Sir Otto ~, the financiers and philanthropists associated with the Rhodes foundation.*
Beith, f.n. [biθ] (beeth)
Beith [biθ] (beeth)
Bekesbourne ['biksbɔrn] (beéksborn)
Bekonscot, *model village in Beaconsfield* ['bekənzkɒt] (béckŏnzkot)
Belah, River ['bilə] (beélă)
Belaugh ['bɪlə] (beélaa); ['bɪlɔ] (beélaw); ['bɪloʊ] (beélō); ['bɪlu] (beéloo)
Belbroughton [bel'brɒtən] (belbráwtŏn)
Belchamp Otten ['belʃəm 'ɒtən] (bélshăm óttĕn)
Belchamp St. Paul ['belʃəmp snt 'pɔl] (bélshămp sĭnt páwl)
Belchem, f.n. ['beltʃəm] (béltchĕm)
Belcher, f.n. ['beltʃər] (béltcher)
Belchier, f.n. ['belʃɪeɪ] (béishi-ay)
Belcoo [bel'ku] (belkoó)
Belfast [bel'fast] (belfaást); ['belfast] (bélfaast)
Belim, f.n. ['belɪm] (béllim)
Belisha, f.n. [bɪ'lɪʃə] (bĕleéshă)
Bellaghy [be'læxɪ] (belláchi)
Bellairs, f.n. [be'lɛərz] (belláirz)
Bellak, f.n. ['belæk] (béllack)
Bellamy, f.n. ['beləmɪ] (béllămi)
Bellars, f.n. ['belɑrz] (béllaarz)
Bellasis, f.n. ['beləsɪs] (béllássiss); [be-'leɪsɪs] (belláyssiss)
Bellasis, *Co. Durham* ['beləsɪs] (béllássiss)
Bellasis, *Northumberland* [bɪ'læsɪs] (bĕlássiss)
Bellchambers, f.n. ['beltʃeɪmbərz] (béllchaymbĕrz)
Belleau ['beloʊ] (béllō); ['belju] (béllew)
Belleek [bɪ'lik] (bĕleék)

Bellenger, f.n. ['belɪndʒər] (béllĕnjer)
Belle Tout, *site of the old Beachy Head lighthouse* ['bel 'tut] (béll toót)
Bellew, f.n. ['belju] (béllew)
Bellinger, f.n. ['belɪndʒər] (béllinjer)
Bellingham, f.n. ['belɪŋhəm] (bélling-hăm); ['belɪŋəm] (bélling-ăm); ['belɪndʒəm] (béllinjăm)
Bellingham ['belɪndʒəm] (béllinjăm)
Bellm, f.n. ['beləm] (béllĕm)
Belloc, Hilaire, author and poet ['hɪlɛər 'belɒk] (híllair béllock)
Bellshill, *Lanark., Midlothian* ['belz'hɪl] (bélz-híll)
Bellyse, f.n. ['belɪs] (bélliss)
Belmore, f.n. ['belmɔr] (bélmor)
Beloe, f.n. ['bɪloʊ] (beélō)
Beloff, f.n. ['belɒf] (bélloff)
Belsay ['belsɪ] (bélssi)
Belthorn ['belθɔrn] (bél-thorn)
Beltinge ['beltɪndʒ] (béltinj)
Beltingham ['beltɪndʒəm] (béltinjăm)
Belvedere [ˌbelvɪ'dɪər] (belvĕdeér)
Belvoir, f.n. ['bivər] (beéver)
Belvoir ['bivər] (beéver)
Belvoir Park, *Belfast* ['bivər] (beéver)
Bembaron, f.n. [bem'bærən] (bembárrŏn)
Bemersyde ['bimərsaɪd] (beémĕr-sīd)
Ben Cruachan [ben 'kruəxən] (ben kroó-ăchăn)
Ben Eay, *also spelt* Beinn Eighe [ben 'eɪ] (ben áy)
Ben Ime [ben 'imə] (ben eémĕ)
Ben Ledi [ben 'ledɪ] (ben léddi)
Ben Macdhui [ˌben mək'duɪ] (ben măkdoó-i)
Ben Nevis [ben 'nevɪs] (ben névviss)
Ben Rhydding [ben 'rɪdɪŋ] (ben rídding)
Ben Venue [ˌben və'nju] (ben vĕnéw)
Ben Vrackie [ben 'vrækɪ] (ben vrácki)
Benacre ['benerkər] (bénayker)
Benbecula [ben'bekjʊlə] (benbéck-yŏŏlă)
Bendelow, f.n. ['bendɪloʊ] (béndĕlō)
Benderloch ['bendərlɒx] (béndĕrloch)
Benefield ['benɪfɪld] (bénnĕfeeld)
Benenden ['benəndən] (bénnĕndĕn); [ˌbenən'den] (bennĕn-dén) *The latter is rarely heard now.*
Benenson, f.n. ['benənsən] (bénnĕnssŏn)
Benest, f.n. ['benest] (bénnest) [bɪ'nest] (bĕnést)
Benet, f.n. ['benɪt] (bénnĕt) *From the history of the name it seems probable that this was the pronunciation of the 16th-c. madrigal composer, J. Benet.*
Beneveian, Loch, *also spelt* Benevean [ˌbenɪ'viən] (bennĕveé-ăn)
Beney, f.n. ['binɪ] (beéni)
Bengeo ['bendʒoʊ] (bénjō)
Bengough, f.n. ['bengɒf] (bén-goff)
Benhall ['benl] (bennl)
Benhar [ben'hɑr] (ben-haár)
Benians, f.n. ['benɪənz] (bénniănz)
Benke, f.n. ['beŋkɪ] (bénki)
Bennachie [ˌbenə'xɪ] (bennăcheé)

Bennane Head ['benən 'hed] (bénnăn héd)

Bennellick, f.n. [bɪ'nelɪk] (bĕnéllick)

Bennett f.n. ['benɪt] (bénnĕt)

Benoliel, f.n. [‚benoʊ'lɪəl] (bennōlee-ĕl)

Bensham ['benʃəm] (bén-shăm)

Benson, f.n. ['bensən] (bénssŏn)

Benson ['bensən] (bénssŏn)

Benstead, f.n. ['bensted] (bénsted)

Bentall, f.n. ['bentəl] (béntawl)

Benthall, f.n. ['bentəl] (béntawl); ['ben-θəl] (bén-thawl)

Benthall ['bentəl] (béntawl)

Bentham, f.n. ['benθəm] (bén-thăm); ['bentəm] (béntăm) *The first is appropriate for Jeremy ~, 18-19th-c. author and founder of University College London.*

Bentinck, f.n. ['bentɪŋk] (béntink) *A member of the family asserts that* ['bentɪk], (béntick), *is simply a popular misconception.*

Bentine, f.n. [ben'tin] (benteen)

Bentwich, f.n. ['bentwɪtʃ] (béntwitch)

Benzie, f.n. ['benzɪ] (bénzi)

Beoley ['bilɪ] (beéli)

Beowulf, A.-S. epic hero ['beɪoʊwʊlf] (báy-ō-wŏŏlf); ['beɪowʊlf] (báy-ŏ-wŏŏlf)

Beragh ['bɛərə] (baíră)

Bere Alston ['bɪər 'ɔlstən] (beér áwlstŏn)

Bere Regis ['bɪər 'ridʒɪs] (beér reéjiss)

Beregi, f.n. ['berəgɪ] (bérrĕgi)

Berenson, f.n. ['berənsən] (bérrĕnssŏn)

Beresford, f.n. ['berɪsfərd] (bérrĕsfŏrd)

Berger, f.n. ['bɜrdʒər] (bérjer)

Bergh Apton [bɜr 'æptən] (ber áptŏn)

Bergonzi, f.n. [bər'ɡʊnzɪ] (bĕrgónzi)

Beringer, f.n. ['berɪndʒər] (bérrinjer)

Beriosova, Svetlana, ballerina [svet-'lanə bɛər'jɒsəvə] (svetlaáná bairyóssŏvá)

Berkeley, f.n. ['bɑrklɪ] (baárkli) *Appropriate also for Baroness ~.*

Berkeley ['bɑrklɪ] (baárkli)

Berkhamsted ['bɜrkəmsted] (bérkămsted); ['bɑrkəmsted] (baárkămsted)

Berkley ['bɑrklɪ] (baárkli)

Berkshire ['bɑrkʃər] (baárk-sher)

Berkswell ['bɑrkswel] (baárkswel); ['bɜrkswel] (bérkswel)

Berkswich ['bɑrkswɪtʃ] (baárkswitch)

Berkyngechirche, *A.-S. name for Barking-by-the-Tower* ['bɑrkɪŋtʃərtʃ] (baárking church)

Bermange, f.n. [bər'mɑʒ] (bĕrmaángzh)

Bermel, f.n. [bər'mel] (bĕrméll)

Bernal, f.n. [bər'næl] (bĕrnál); ['bɜrnəl] (bérnál)

Bernard, Anthony, composer and conductor ['æntənɪ bər'nɑrd] (ántŏni bĕrnaárd)

Bernays, f.n. [bər'neɪz] (bĕrnáyz)

Bernelle, f.n. [bər'nel] (bĕrnéll)

Bernera ['bɜrnərə] (bérnĕră)

Berners, Baroness ['bɜrnərz] (bérnĕrz)

Bernhard, C.n. ['bɜrnərd] (bérnárd)

Bernhard, f.n. ['bɜrnhɑrd] (bérn-haard); [bɜrn'hɑrd] (bern-haárd)

Bernhardt, f.n. ['bɜrnhɑrt] (bérn-haart)

Bernicia, *part of ancient Northumbria* [bər'nɪʃɪə] (bĕrníshă)

Bernstein, f.n. ['bɜrnstaɪn] (bérnstīn); ['bɜrnstin] (bérnsteen)

Berrick Salome ['berɪk 'sæləm] (bérrick sálōm)

Berriew ['berɪu] (bérri-oo)

Berrynarbor [‚berɪ'nɑrbər] (berrinaárbŏr)

Bertera, f.n. [bɛər'tɛərə] (bairtaíră)

Berthengam [bər'θeŋgəm] (bĕrthéngăm)

Berthon, f.n. ['bɜrθən] (bérthŏn)

Berthoud, f.n. ['bɜrtu] (bértoo)

Bertie, f.n. ['bɑrtɪ] (baárti) *Family name of the Earl of Lindsey and Abingdon.*

Bertie of Thame, *Viscountcy of* ['bɑrtɪ əv 'teɪm] (baárti ŏv táym)

Bertin, f.n. ['bɜrtɪn] (bértin)

Berwick ['berɪk] (bérrick) *Appropriate also for the Barony of ~.*

Berwick St. John ['berɪk snt 'dʒɒn] (bérrick sint jón)

Berwick-upon-Tweed ['berɪk əpɒn 'twid] (bérrick ŭpon tweéd)

Berwin ['bɛərwɪn] (baírwin)

Besant, f.n. [bɪ'zænt] (bĕzánt); ['besənt] (béssănt); ['bezənt] (bézzănt) *The second was the pronunciation of Annie ~, social reformer.*

Bescoby, f.n. ['beskoʊbɪ] (béskōbi)

Besier, f.n. ['besjeɪ] (béss-yay); ['bezjeɪ] (béz-yay)

Besley, f.n. ['bezlɪ] (bézli)

Bessant, f.n. ['besənt] (béssănt)

Bessborough, Earl of ['bezbərə] (bézbŭră)

Bessell, f.n. ['besl] (bessl); [bɪ'sel] (bĕsséll)

Besselsleigh ['beslz'li] (bésslz-leé)

Bessone, f.n. [be'soʊn] (bessón)

Besthorpe ['besθɔrp] (béss-thorp)

Beswick, f.n. ['bezɪk] (bézzick)

Beswick ['bezɪk] (bézzick)

Betham, f.n. ['betəm] (béttăm)

Bethell, f.n. ['beθl] (bethl)

Bethersden ['beθərzdən] (béthĕrzdĕn)

Bethesda [be'θezdə] (bethézdă)

Bethune, f.n. ['bitn] (beetn); [bɪ'θjun] (bĕthéwn)

Betjeman, John, *poet and author* ['betʃɪmən] (bétchĕmăn)

Betsham ['betsəm] (bétsăm)

Betteshanger ['betshæŋər] (béts-hanger)

Bettws Bledrws ['betʊs 'bledrʊs] (béttŏŏss blédrŏŏss)

Bettws-y-Coed ['betʊs ə 'kɔɪd] (béttŏŏss ă kóyd)

Bettws-yn-Rhos ['betʊs ən 'hroʊs] (béttŏŏss ăn rṓss)

Beuden, f.n. ['bjudən] (béwdĕn)

Beuttler, f.n. ['bɔɪtlər] (bóytler)

Bevan, Aneurin, politician [ə'naɪrɪn
ˈbevən] (ănírin bévvăn)
Bevercotes ['bevərkoʊts] (bévvĕrkōts)
Bevere ['bevərɪ] (bévvĕri)
Beveree ['bevərɪ] (bévvēree)
Beveridge of -Tuggal, Barony of
['bevərɪdʒ əv 'tʌgl] (bévvĕrij ŏv túggl)
Beves, f.n. ['bivɪs] (beévĕss)
Bevin, f.n. ['bevɪn] (bévvin)
Bevins, f.n. ['bevɪnz] (bévvinz)
Bevir, f.n. ['bivər] (beévir)
Bevis, f.n. ['bivɪs] (beéviss)
Bevis Marks, *district of London* ['bivɪs
ˈmɑːks] (beéviss maárks)
Bewaldeth [bjuˈældəθ] (bew-áldĕth)
Bewdley ['bjuːdlɪ] (béwdli)
Bewes, f.n. [bjuz] (bewz)
Bewick, f.n. ['bjuɪk] (béw-ick) *Appro-
priate for Thomas ~, 18-19th-c. wood
engraver, and therefore also for ~'s swan.*
Bews, f.n. [bjuz] (bewz)
Bewsher, f.n. ['bjuʃər] (béwsher)
Beyer, f.n. [beər] (bair) ; ['baɪər] (bí-er)
Beyfus, f.n. ['beɪfəs] (báyfŭss)
Beynon, f.n. ['baɪnən] (bínŏn) ; ['beɪnən]
(báynŏn)
Beyton ['beɪtən] (báytŏn)
Bezant, f.n. [bɪ'zænt] (bĕzánt) ; ['bezənt]
(bézzănt)
Bezer, f.n. ['bizər] (beézer)
Bezzant, f.n. [bɪ'zænt] (bĕzánt)
Bias, f.n. ['baɪəs] (bí-ăss)
Bibury ['baɪbərɪ] (bíbŭri)
Bicester ['bɪstər] (bísster) *Appropriate
also for Baron ~.*
Bichard, f.n. ['biʃɑːd] (beé-shaard)
Bickerdike, f.n. ['bɪkərdaɪk] (bíckĕrdík)
Bickleigh ['bɪklɪ] (bícklee)
Biddenden ['bɪdəndən] (bíddĕndĕn)
Biddestone ['bɪdɪstən] (bíddĕstŏn)
Biddlesden ['bɪlzdən] (bílzdĕn)
Biddulph, f.n. ['bɪdʌlf] (bíddulf)
Biddulph ['bɪdʌlf] (bíddulf)
Bideford ['bɪdɪfərd] (bíddĕfŏrd)
Biden, f.n. ['baɪdən] (bídĕn)
Bidwell, f.n. ['bɪdwel] (bídwel)
Biek, f.n. [bik] (beek)
Bierer, f.n. ['bɪərər] (beérer)
Bierley ['baɪərlɪ] (bírli)
Bierton ['bɪərtən] (beértŏn)
Bigelow, f.n. ['bɪgɪloʊ] (bíggĕlō)
Bigham, f.n. ['bɪgəm] (bígăm)
Bignian ['bɪnjən] (bín-yăn)
Bilainkin, George, author [bɪ'leɪŋkɪn]
(biláynkin)
Bilbster ['bɪlpstər] (bílpster)
Bildeston ['bɪldɪstən] (bíldĕstŏn)
Bilgora, f.n. [bɪl'gɔːrə] (bilgórră)
Billenness, f.n. ['bɪlnɪs] (bíllĕnĕss)
Billericay [ˌbɪlə'rɪkɪ] (bíllĕrícki)
Billesdon ['bɪlzdən] (bílzdŏn)
Billinge ['bɪlɪndʒ] (bíllinj)
Billingham ['bɪlɪŋhəm] (bílling-hăm)
Billmeir, f.n. ['bɪlmaɪər] (bílmír)
Bilsington ['bɪlzɪŋtən] (bílzingtŏn)

Bilyard, f.n. ['bɪljɑːd] (bíl-yaard)
Binderton ['bɪndərtən] (bíndĕrtŏn)
Binge, Ronald, composer [bɪndʒ] (binj)
Binsey ['bɪnzɪ] (bínzi)
Bion, f.n. ['biən] (beé-ŏn)
Birchenough, f.n. ['bɜrtʃɪnʌf] (bír-
chĕnuff)
Birkbeck, f.n. ['bɜrbek] (bírbeck) ; ['bɜrk-
bek] (bírkbeck)
Birkbeck College, *University of London*
['bɜrkbek] (bírkbeck)
Birkenhead [ˌbɜrkən'hed] (birkĕn-héd) ;
['bɜrkənhed] (bírkĕn-hed) *The second is
appropriate for the Earl of ~.*
Birmingham ['bɜrmɪŋəm] (bírming-ăm)
Birnam ['bɜrnəm] (bírnăm)
Birnbryer, f.n. ['bɜrnbraɪər] (bírnbrī-er)
Birnie, f.n. ['bɜrnɪ] (bírni)
Birsay ['bɜrzeɪ] (bírzay)
Birstall ['bɜrstɔl] (bírstawl)
Biscombe, f.n. ['bɪskəm] (bískŏm)
Biscovey ['bɪskəveɪ] (bískŏvay)
Bisham ['bɪsəm] (bíssăm)
Bishop Auckland ['bɪʃəp 'ɔklənd]
(bíshŏp áwklănd)
Bishop's Frome ['bɪʃəps 'frum] (bíshŏps
froóm)
Bishop's Lydeard ['bɪʃəps 'lɪdɪərd]
(bíshŏps líddi-árd)
Bishop's Nympton ['bɪʃəps 'nɪmtən]
(bíshŏps nímtŏn)
Bishop's Stortford ['bɪʃəps 'stɔrfərd]
(bíshŏps stórfŏrd)
Bishop's Waltham ['bɪʃəps 'wɔlθəm]
(bíshŏps wáwl-thăm) ; ['bɪʃəps 'wɔltəm]
(bíshŏps wáwltăm)
Bishopston ['bɪʃəpstən] (bíshŏpstŏn)
Bishopwearmouth ['bɪʃəp'wɪərmaʊθ]
(bíshŏp-weérmowth)
Bispham, f.n. ['bɪspəm] (bíspăm) ; ['bɪs-
fəm] (bísfăm)
Bispham ['bɪspəm] (bíspăm)
Bissell, f.n. ['bɪsl] (bissl)
Bissoe ['bɪsoʊ] (bíssō)
Bistre ['bɪstər] (bísster)
Bithell, f.n. ['bɪθl] (bithl)
Bittesby ['bɪtsbɪ] (bítsbi)
Bitteswell ['bɪtɪzwel] (bíttĕzwel)
Bizeray, f.n. ['bɪzəreɪ] (bízzĕray)
Bizony, f.n. [bɪ'zoʊnɪ] (bizóni)
Blabhein *see* Blaven.
Blaby ['bleɪbɪ] (bláybi)
Blackadder, River ['blækədər] (bláck-
ăder)
Blackawton [blæk'ɔtən] (black-áwtŏn)
Black Bourton ['blæk 'bɔrtən] (bláck
bórtŏn)
Blackley ['bleɪklɪ] (bláykli)
Blackness [blæk'nes] (blacknéss)
Blackwater [blæk'wɔtər] (black-wáwter)
Blackwater Burn ['blækwɔtər] (bláck-
wawter)
Blackwood ['blæk'wʊd] (bláck-woŏd)
Blacon ['bleɪkən] (bláykŏn)
Bladon [bleɪdən] (bláydŏn)

Blaen-Cwm [blaɪnˈkʊm] (blīn-kŏŏm)
Blaen Llynfi [blaɪn ˈɬʌnvɪ] (blīn hlŭnvi)
Blaen-Plwyf [ˈblaɪn ˈpluːɪv] (blīn plooʹ-iv); [ˈblaɪn ˈpluːɪ] (blīn plooʹ-i)
Blaen-y-Cwm, *Glamorgan, Monmouth.* [ˌblaɪnəˈkʊm] (blīnăkŏŏm)
Blaenau Festiniog [ˈblaɪnaɪ fesˈtɪnjɒg] (blīnī festín-yog)
Blaenavon [blaɪnˈævən] (blīnávvŏn)
Blaenclydach [blaɪnˈklɪdəx] (blīn-klíddăch)
Blaengarw [blaɪnˈgæru] (blīn-gárroo)
Blaengwawr [blaɪnˈgwauər] (blīn-gwówr)
Blaengwrach [blaɪnˈgwrɑx] (blīn-gwraăch); [blaɪnˈgrɑx] (blīn-graăch) *Welsh speakers pronounce 'gwrach' as one syllable by treating the 'w' as a rounding of the lips to accompany the 'r'.*
Blaenhirwaun Colliery [blaɪnˈhərwaɪn] (blīn-hírwīn)
Blaenhonddan [blaɪnˈhɒnðən] (blīn-hónthăn)
Blaenllecha [blaɪnˈɬexə] (blīn-hléchă)
Blaenpenal [blaɪnˈpenl] (blīn-pénnl)
Blaenporth [blaɪnˈpɔrθ] (blīn-pórth)
Blagrave, f.n. [ˈblægreɪv] (blágrayv)
Blagrove, f.n. [ˈbleɪgroʊv] (bláygrŏv)
Blaikie, f.n. [ˈbleɪkɪ] (bláyki)
Blaina [ˈblaɪnə] (blīnă)
Blair Atholl [blɛər ˈæθl] (blair áthl)
Blairgowrie [blɛərˈgaurɪ] (blairgówri)
Blaisdon [ˈbleɪzdən] (bláyzdŏn)
Blakehope [ˈbleɪkəp] (bláykŏp)
Blakeney, f.n. [ˈbleɪknɪ] (bláyk-ni)
Blakeney [ˈbleɪknɪ] (bláyk-ni)
Blakenham [ˈbleɪkənəm] (bláykĕnăm) *Appropriate also for Viscount ∼.*
Blakesley [ˈbleɪkslɪ] (bláyksli)
Blakiston, f.n. [ˈbleɪkɪstən] (bláykistŏn); [ˈblækɪstən] (bláckistŏn)
Blakstad, f.n. [ˈblækstæd] (bláckstad)
Blamire, f.n. [bləˈmaɪər] (blămír)
Blamires, f.n. [bləˈmaɪərz] (blămírz)
Blanchard, f.n. [ˈblæntʃɑrd] (blánchaard); [ˈblæntʃərd] (blántchărd)
Blanchett, f.n. [ˈblæntʃɪt] (blántchĕt)
Blanchland [ˈblænʃlənd] (blánshlănd)
Blandford, Marquess of [ˈblændfərd] (blándfŏrd)
Blanshard, f.n. [ˈblænʃɑrd] (blán-shaard)
Blantyre [ˈblæntaɪər] (blántīr)
Blarmacfoldach [ˌblɑrməkˈfoʊltjəx] (blaarmăk-fŏlt-yắch)
Blaston [ˈbleɪstən] (bláysstŏn)
Blaven, *also spelt* **Blabhein** [ˈblɑvən] (bláavěn)
Blaydon Haughs [ˈbleɪdən ˈhɒfs] (bláydŏn hóffs)
Bleackley, f.n. [ˈblɪklɪ] (bleékli)
Bleadon [ˈblɪdən] (bleédŏn)
Bleaklow [ˈblɪkloʊ] (bleéklŏ)
Blea Moor [ˈblɪ ˈmʊər] (bleé mŏŏr)
Blean, *Yorks.* [blem] (blayn)
Blean Forest, *Kent* [blɪn] (bleen)

Bleaney, f.n. [ˈblɪnɪ] (bleéni)
Blease, f.n. [bliz] (bleez)
Bleazard, f.n. [ˈblɪzɑrd] (bleézaard)
Blech, f.n. [blek] (bleck)
Blech String Quartet [blek] (bleck)
Bleddfa [ˈbleðvə] (bléthvă)
Bledisloe, Viscount [ˈbledɪsloʊ] (blédisslŏ)
Blemundsbury House, *Holborn, London* [ˈblemzbərɪ] (blémzbŭri)
Blencathara [blenˈkæθrə] (blen-káthră)
Blenheim Palace [ˈblenəm] (blénněm)
Blennerhassett, f.n. [ˈblenərhæsɪt] (blénněr-hassĕt); [ˌblenərˈhæsɪt] (blenər-hássĕt)
Bles, f.n. [bles] (bless) *Appropriate also for Geoffrey ∼, publishers.*
Bletsoe [ˈbletsoʊ] (blétsŏ)
Blezard, f.n. [ˈblezɑrd] (blézzaard)
Blidworth [ˈblɪdwɜrθ] (blídwurth)
Bligh, f.n. [blaɪ] (blī)
Blindell, f.n. [ˈblɪndl] (blindl)
Blindley Heath [ˈblaɪndlɪ ˈhiθ] (blíndli heéth)
Blin-Stoyle, f.n. [ˈblɪn ˈstɔɪl] (blín stóyl)
Blishen, Edward, author [ˈblɪʃən] (blísh-ĕn)
Blisland [ˈblɪzlənd] (blízlănd)
Blisworth [ˈblɪzwɜrθ] (blízwurth)
Blithfield [ˈblɪfɪld] (bliffeeld)
Blizard, f.n. [ˈblɪzɑrd] (blízzaard)
Blofield [ˈbloʊfɪld] (blŏfeeld)
Blogue, f.n. [bloʊg] (blŏg)
Blois, f.n. [blɔɪs] (bloyss)
Blom, Eric, music critic [blɒm] (blom)
Blomefield, f.n. [ˈblumfɪld] (bloomfeeld)
Blomfield, f.n. [ˈblɒmfɪld] (blómfeeld); [ˈblʌmfɪld] (blúmfeeld); [ˈblʌmfɪld] (blúmfild); [ˈbloʊmfɪld] (blŏŏmfeeld); [ˈblʌmfɪld] (blúmfild) (bloomfeeld)
Blo Norton [ˈbloʊ ˈnɔrtən] (blŏ nórtŏn)
Blonstein, f.n. [ˈblɒnstɪn] (blónsteen)
Bloundelle, f.n. [ˈblʌndl] (blundl)
Blount, f.n. [blʌnt] (blunt)
Blower, f.n. [ˈbloʊər] (blŏ-er); [ˈblauər] (blówer)
Bloxwich [ˈblɒkswɪtʃ] (blóckswitch)
Blundell, f.n. [ˈblʌndl] (blundl)
Blundellian, one educated at Blundell's School [blʌnˈdelɪən] (blundélliăn)
Blundeston [ˈblʌndɪstən] (blúndĕstŏn)
Bluntisham [ˈblʌntɪʃəm] (blúnti-shăm); [ˈblʌntɪsəm] (blúntissăm)
Blyth, f.n. [blaɪ] (blī); [blaɪð] (blīth); [blaɪθ] (blīth) *The first is appropriate for Baron ∼.*
Blyth [blaɪð] (blīth)
Blyth, *River* [blaɪð] (blīth)
Blythborough, f.n. [ˈblaɪbərə] (blíbŭră)
Blythburgh [ˈblaɪbrə] (blíbră)
Blytheman, William, Tudor composer [ˈblaɪθmən] (blíthmăn)
Blythswood [ˈblaɪðzwʊd] (blíthz-wŏŏd)
Blyton, f.n. [ˈblaɪtən] (blítŏn)
Boadicea, queen of the Iceni [ˌboʊədɪˈsiə] (bŏădisseeă) *Another form is Boudicca, q.v.*

Boady, f.n. ['boʊdɪ] (bŏ́di)
Boaks, f.n. [boʊks] (bōks)
Boarhunt ['bɔrhʌnt] (bór-hunt); ['bʊrənt] (bóŕrŭnt)
Boase, f.n. [boʊz] (bōz)
Boath, f.n. [boʊθ] (bōth)
Boat of Garten ['boʊt əv 'gɑrtən] (bŏ́t ŏv gaártĕn)
Boatte, f.n. [boʊt] (bōt)
Bobbingworth ['bɒbɪŋwɜrθ] (bóbbing-wurth) *The post office is* Bovinger, *q.v.*
Bochaton, f.n. ['bɒkətən] (bóckătŏn)
Boconnoc [bə'kɒnək] (bŏkónnŏk)
Bocquet, f.n. ['boʊkeɪ] (bŏ́kay)
Boddam - Whetham, f.n. ['bɒdəm 'wetəm] (bóddăm wéttăm)
Boddey, f.n. ['bɒdɪ] (bóddi)
Bodedern [bɒd'eɪdɛərn] (boddáydairn); [bɒd'edɛərn] (boddéddairn)
Bodelwyddan [ˌbɒdl'wiðən] (boddl-weéthăn)
Bodenham ['bɒdənəm] (bóddĕnăm)
Bodfari [bɒd'færɪ] (bodfárri)
Bodffordd ['bɒtfɔrð] (bótforth)
Bodiam ['boʊdɪəm] (bŏ́diăm); ['bɒdɪəm] (bóddiăm)
Bodilly [bə'dɪlɪ] (bŏdílli)
Bodinnar, f.n. ['bɒdmɑr] (bóddinaar)
Bodleian Library, *Oxford* [bɒd'liən] (bodleé-ăn); ['bɒdlɪən] (bódli-ăn)
Bodnant ['bɒdnænt] (bód-nant)
Bodorgan [bɒd'ɔrgən] (bodórgăn)
Bodriggy [bə'drɪgɪ] (bŏdríggi)
Bodrugan's Leap [bə'drʌgən] (bŏdrúggăn)
Bodryngallt [bɒd'rɪŋælt] (bodríng-ahlt)
Boduan [bə'diən] (bŏdeé-ăn)
Body, f.n. ['bɒdɪ] (bóddi)
Boehm, f.n. [boʊm] (bōm); ['boʊəm] (bŏ́-ĕm)
Boevey, f.n. ['buvɪ] (boóvi)
Boffey, f.n. ['bɒfɪ] (bóffi)
Bogany Point ['bɒgənɪ] (bóggăni)
Boger, f.n. ['boʊdʒər] (bŏ́jer)
Boggart Hole Clough ['bɒgərt 'hoʊl 'klʌʃ] (bóggărt hŏl klúff)
Boggis, f.n. ['bɒgɪs] (bóggiss)
Boghall Bridge ['bɒghɒl] (bóg-hawl)
Boharm [boʊ'hɑrm] (bō-haárm)
Bohn, f.n. [boʊn] (bōn)
Bohunt Manor, *Liphook, Hants.* ['boʊhʌnt] (bŏ́-hunt)
Boileau, f.n. ['bɔɪloʊ] (bóylō)
Bois, f.n. [bɔɪz] (boyz)
Boisdale ['bɔɪzdeɪl] (bóyzdayl)
Boisragon, f.n. ['bɒrəgən] (bórrăgŏn)
Boissevain, f.n. ['bwazɪveɪn] (bwaázĕvayn)
Boissier, f.n. ['bɔɪsjər] (bóyss-yer)
Boivie, f.n. ['beɪvɪ] (báyvi)
Bolam, f.n. ['boʊləm] (bŏ́lăm)
Bolam ['boʊləm] (bŏ́lăm)
Boland, f.n. ['boʊlənd] (bŏ́lănd)
Boldon ['boʊldən] (bŏ́ldŏn)

Boldre, f.n. ['boʊldər] (bŏ́lder)
Boldre ['boʊldər] (bŏ́lder)
Bolenow [bə'lenoʊ] (bŏlénnō)
Boleskine [bɒ'leskɪn] (boléskin)
Boleyn, f.n. [bə'lɪn] (bŏlín); ['bʊlɪn] (bŏ́olin); [bʊ'lɪn] (bŏoleén) *The first two are most popularly associated with Anne ~.*
Bolger, f.n. ['bɒldʒər] (bóljer)
Bolingbroke and St. John, *Viscount* ['bʊlɪŋbrʊk ənd 'sɪndʒən] (bŏ́oling-brŏok ănd sínjŏn)
Bolingey [bə'lɪndʒeɪ] (bŏlínjay)
Bolitho, f.n. [bə'laɪθoʊ] (bŏlíthō)
Bolitho [bə'laɪθoʊ] (bŏlíthō)
Bollin, *River* ['bɒlɪn] (bóllin)
Bollinger, f.n. ['bɒlɪndʒər] (bóllinjer)
Bollingham ['bɒlɪndʒəm] (bóllinjăm); ['bɒlɪŋəm] (bólling-ăm)
Bolloten, f.n. ['bɒlətən] (bóllŏtĕn)
Bolney ['boʊlnɪ] (bŏ́lni); ['boʊnɪ] (bŏ́ni)
Boinhurst ['boʊnhɜrst] (bŏ́n-hurst)
Bols, f.n. [boʊlz] (bōlz)
Bolsover, f.n. ['bɒlsoʊvər] (bólssōver)
Bolsover ['boʊlzoʊvər] (bŏ́lzōver)
Bolston ['boʊlsən] (bŏ́lssŏn)
Bolton by Bowland ['boʊltən baɪ 'bɒlənd] (bŏ́ltŏn bī bóllănd); ['boʊltən baɪ 'boʊlənd] (bŏ́ltŏn bī bŏ́lănd)
Boltz, f.n. [boʊlts] (bōlts)
Bolventor [bɒl'ventər] (bolvéntŏr)
Bomere Heath ['boʊmɪər 'hiθ] (bŏ́meer heéth)
Bompas, f.n. ['bʌmpəs] (búmpăss)
Bonallack, f.n. [bə'nælək] (bŏnálăk)
Bonaly [bɒ'nælɪ] (bonáli)
Bonar, f.n. ['bɒnər] (bónnăr)
Bonar Bridge ['boʊnər 'brɪdʒ] (bŏ́năr bríj); ['bɒnər 'brɪdʒ] (bónnăr bríj)
Bonavia, f.n. [ˌbɒnə'viə] (bonnăveé-ă)
Bonawe [bɒn'ɔ] (bonnáw)
Boncath ['bɒŋkæθ] (bóng-kath)
Bondi, f.n. ['bɒndɪ] (bóndi)
Bo'ness [boʊ'nes] (bōnéss)
Bonett, f.n. ['bɒnɪt] (bónnĕt)
Boney, f.n. ['bʌnɪ] (búnni)
Bonifazi, f.n. [ˌbɒnɪ'fætsɪ] (bonnifátsi)
Boningale ['bɒnɪŋgeɪl] (bónning-gayl)
Bonkyl ['bɒŋkl] (bonkl)
Bonnetard, f.n. ['bɒnɪtard] (bónnĕtaard)
Bonnett, f.n. ['bɒnɪt] (bónnĕt)
Bonome, f.n. ['bɒnəm] (bónnŏm)
Bonong, f.n. [bə'nɒŋ] (bŏnóng)
Bonskeid [bɒn'skid] (bonsskeéd)
Bonsor, f.n. ['bɒnsər] (bónssŏr)
Bontddu [bɒnt'ðɪ] (bont-theé)
Bontine, f.n. [bɒn'tin] (bonteén); ['bɒntɪn] (bóntin)
Bontnewydd [bɒnt'newɪð] (bontné-with)
Bonvilston ['bɒnvɪlstən] (bónvilstŏn); ['boʊlstən] (bŏ́lstŏn)
Bonvit, f.n. ['bɒnwɪt] (bónwit)
Bonymaen [ˌbɒnə'maɪn] (bŏnămín)
Bonynge, Richard, harpsichordist ['bɒnɪŋ] (bónning)

Bonython, *f.n.* [bɒˈnaɪðən] (bonnÿthŏn)
Boobbyer, *f.n.* [buˈbaɪər] (boobí-er)
Boobyer, *f.n.* [ˈbubjər] (boób-yer)
Boord, *f.n.* [bɔrd] (bord)
Boosbeck [ˈbuzbek] (boózbeck)
Boost, *f.n.* [bust] (boost)
Booth, *f.n.* [buð] (booth)
Boothby, *Baron* [ˈbuðbɪ] (boóthbi)
Boothman, *f.n.* [ˈbuðmən] (boóthmăn)
Boothroyd, *f.n.* [ˈbuθrɔɪd] (boóthroyd)
Booy, *f.n.* [bɔɪ] (boy)
Boquhanran [bouˈhwænrən] (bŏ-whán-răn); [bouˈhwɒnrən] (bŏ-whónrăn)
Boreel, *f.n.* [bɒˈreɪl] (borráyl)
Borenius, *f.n.* [bəˈrinɪəs] (bŏreéniŭss)
Borestone [ˈbɔrˈstoun] (bór-stŏn)
Borgue, *Caithness, Kirkcudbright.* [bɔrg] (borg)
Borlase, *f.n.* [ˈbɔrleɪs] (bórlayss)
Borodale,*Viscount* [ˈbɒrədeɪl](bórrŏdayl)
Borrett, *f.n.* [ˈbɒrɪt] (bórrĕt)
Borrowash [ˈbʌrouwɒʃ] (búrrŏ-wosh); [ˈbɒrouæʃ] (bórrŏ-ash); [ˈbɒrouwɒʃ] (bórrŏ-wosh)
Borrowes, *f.n.* [ˈbʌrouz] (búrrŏz)
Borth [bɔrθ] (borth)
Borthwick, *f.n.* [ˈbɔrθwɪk] (bórthwick)
Borwick, *f.n.* [ˈbɒrɪk] (bórrick)
Borwick [ˈbɒrɪk] (bórrick)
Bosahan [bəˈseɪn] (bŏssáyn)
Bosanquet, *f.n.* [ˈbouzənket] (bŏzănket)
Boscastle [ˈbɒskɑsl] (bósskaassl) [ˈbɒskæsl] (bósskassl)
Boscaswell [bɒsˈkæzwəl] (bŏsskázwĕl)
Boscawen, *f.n.* [bɒsˈkouən] (boskŏ-ĕn); [bəsˈkouən] (bŏskŏ-ĕn); [bɒsˈkɔən] (bos-káw-ĕn) *The first is the pronunciation of Viscount Falmouth's family name.*
Boscawen [bɒsˈkauən] (bŏskówĕn)
Boscobel [ˈbɒskəbel] (bósskŏbel) *Appropriate also for ~ House, where Charles II hid after the Battle of Worcester.*
Bosfranken [bəsˈfræŋkən] (bŏsfránkĕn)
Bosham [ˈbɒzəm] (bózzăm)
Boshell, *f.n.* [ˈbouʃl] (bŏshl)
Bosher, *f.n.* [ˈboʊʃər] (bŏsher)
Boshier, *f.n.* [ˈboʊʃər] (bŏsher)
Bosinney [bəˈsɪnɪ] (bŏssínni)
Bosisto, *f.n.* [bəˈsɪstou] (bŏssísstŏ)
Bosistow [bəˈsɪstou] (bŏssísstŏ)
Boskenwin [bəsˈkenwɪn] (bŏsskénwin)
Bosleake [bəsˈlik] (bŏssleék)
Bosley, *f.n.* [ˈbɒslɪ] (bóssli)
Bossom, *f.n.* [ˈbɒsəm] (bóssŏm)
Bosullow [bəˈsʌlou] (bŏssúllŏ)
Boswall, *f.n.* [ˈbɒzwəl] (bózwăl)
Boswell *of Auchinleck* [ˈbɒzwəl əv ˈæflek] (bózwĕl ŏv áffleck)
Bosworth [ˈbɒzwərθ] (bózwŭrth)
Boteler, *f.n.* [ˈboutlər] (bŏtler)
Bothamsall [ˈbɒðəmsɔl] (bóthăm-sawl)
Bothel and Threapland [ˈbɒθl ənd ˈθriplənd] (bóthl ănd threépländ)
Bothenhampton [ˌbɒθənˈhæmptən] (bothĕn-hámptŏn)

Bothnagowan [ˌbɒθnəˈgauən] (bothnăgów-ăn)
Bothwell, *f.n.* [ˈbɒðwəl] (bóthwĕl); [ˈbɒθwəl] (bóthwĕl)
Bothwellhaugh [ˈbɒðwəlˈhɒx] (bóthwĕlhóch)
Botriphnie [bouˈtrɪfnɪ] (bŏtrífni)
Bottesford [ˈbɒtɪsfərd] (bóttĕsfŏrd); [ˈbɒtsfərd] (bótsfŏrd)
Bottisham [ˈbɒtɪʃəm] (bótti-shăm)
Bottome, Phyllis, *author* [bəˈtoum] (bŏtốm)
Bottrall, *f.n.* [ˈbɒtrəl] (bótrăl)
Bottwnog [bɒˈtunɒg] (bottoŏnog)
Boty, *f.n.* [ˈboutɪ] (bŏti)
Bouch, Sir Thomas, *19th-c. civil engineer* [bautʃ] (bowtch)
Boucher, *f.n.* [ˈbautʃər] (bówtcher)
Bouchier, *f.n.* [ˈbautʃər] (bówtcher)
Boucicault, Dion, *actor-manager* [ˈdaɪən ˈbusɪkou] (df-ŏn boóssikŏ)
Boud, *f.n.* [baud] (bowd)
Boudicca, *queen of the Iceni* [ˈbudɪkə] (boódickă); [bouˈdɪkə] (bŏdíckă) *Another form is Boadicea, q.v.*
Bough, *f.n.* [bɒf] (boff)
Boughey, *f.n.* [ˈbouɪ] (bŏ-i)
Boughrood [ˈbɒxrud] (bóchrood)
Boughton, *f.n.* [ˈbautən] (bówtŏn); [ˈbɒtən] (báwtŏn) *The first is appropriate for Rutland ~, the composer.*
Boughton, *Cheshire, Kent* [ˈbɒtən] (báwtŏn)
Boughton, *Hunts., Northants.* [ˈbautən] (bówtŏn)
Boughton, *Notts.* [ˈbutən] (boótŏn); [ˈbautən] (bówtŏn)
Boughton Aluph [ˈbɒtən ˈæləf] (báwtŏn álŭf)
Boughton Malherbe [ˈbɒtən ˈmælərbɪ] (báwtŏn málĕrbi)
Boughton Monchelsea [ˈbɒtən ˈmʌntʃlsɪ] (báwtŏn múntchlssi)
Bould, *f.n.* [bould] (bŏld)
Boulge [buldʒ] (boolj); [bouldʒ] (bŏlj)
Boulmer [ˈbumər] (boómer)
Boult, Sir Adrian, *conductor* [ˈeɪdrɪən ˈboult] (áydriăn bŏlt)
Boultham [ˈbutəm] (boótăm); [ˈbuðəm] (boóthăm)
Boulton, *f.n.* [ˈboultən] (bŏltŏn)
Boulton [ˈboultən] (bŏltŏn)
Boumphrey, *f.n.* [ˈbʌmfrɪ] (búmfri)
Boundstone [ˈbaundstoun] (bówndstŏn)
Bouquet, *f.n.* [ˈbukeɪ] (boókay)
Bourchier, *f.n.* [ˈbautʃər] (bówtcher)
Bourdillon, *f.n.* [bɔrˈdɪlən] (bordíllŏn); [bərˈdɪljən] (bordíl-yŏn); [bərˈdɪljən] (bŭrdíl-yŏn) *The first is appropriate for Tom ~, mountaineer.*
Bourke, *f.n.* [bɜrk] (burk) *Appropriate also for the family name of the Earl of Mayo.*

Bourlet, *f.n.* ['bʊərleɪ](bŏŏrlay);['bʊərlet] (bŏŏrlet)
Bourne, *f.n.* [bɔrn] (born); [bʊərn] (bŏŏrn); [bɜrn] (burn)
Bourtie ['bʊərtɪ] (bŏŏrti)
Bourton, *f.n.* ['bɔrtən] (bórtŏn)
Bourton ['bɔrtən] (bórtŏn)
Bourton-on-the-Water ['bɔrtən ɒn ðə 'wɔtər] (bórtŏn on thĕ wáwter)
Bourtree Bush ['bʊərtrɪ 'bʊʃ] (bŏŏrtri bŏŏsh)
Bousfield, *f.n.* ['baʊsfɪld] (bówssfeeld)
Bouskell, *f.n.* ['baʊskl] (bowsskl)
Boustead, *f.n.* ['baʊstɪd] (bówsstĕd)
Boutal, *f.n.* ['baʊtl] (bowtl)
Boutall, *f.n.* ['baʊtl] (bowtl); [bu'tæl] (bootál)
Boutell, *f.n.* [bu'tel] (bŏŏtéll)
Boutflower, *f.n.* ['baʊflaʊər] (bŏflower); ['buflaʊər] (bŏŏflower)
Bouttell, *f.n.* [bu'tel] (bŏŏtéll)
Boutwood, *f.n.* ['baʊtwʊd] (bówt-wŏŏd)
Bouverie, *f.n.* [bu'vɛərɪ] (boŏvĕri)
Boveney ['bʌvnɪ] (búvni)
Bovenschen, *f.n.* ['bʊʊvənʃən] (bŏvĕn-shĕn) [bʊʊ'vɒnʃən] (bŏvón-shĕn)
Boverton ['bɒvərtən] (bóvvĕrtŏn)
Bovey Tracy ['bʌvɪ 'treɪsɪ] (búvvi tráyssi)
Bovingdon ['bɒvɪŋdən] (bóvvingdon); ['bʌvɪŋdən] (búvvingdŏn)
Bovinger ['bɒvɪndʒər] (bóvvinjer) *This is the post office for the parish of Bobbingworth, q.v.*
Bovington ['bɒvɪŋtən] (bóvvingtŏn)
Bow [bʊʊ] (bŏ)
Bow Fell ['bʊʊ 'fel] (bŏ féll)
Bow of Fife ['baʊ əv 'faɪf] (bów ŏv fíf)
Bow Street, *Cardigan* ['bʊʊ strit] (bŏ street)
Bowater, *f.n.* ['bʊʊwɔtər] (bŏ-wawter)
Bowden, *f.n.* ['bʊʊdən] (bŏdĕn); ['baʊdən] (bówdĕn) *The first is appropriate for Baron ~, the second for the family name of Baron Aylestone.*
Bowden ['baʊdən] (bówdĕn)
Bowder Stone ['baʊdər stʊʊn] (bówder stŏn)
Bowdon, *f.n.* ['bʊʊdən] (bŏdŏn)
Bowdon ['bʊʊdən] (bŏdŏn)
Bowe, *f.n.* [bʊʊ] (bŏ)
Bowen, *f.n.* ['bʊʊɪn] (bŏ-ĕn)
Bower, *f.n.* ['baʊər] (bówer)
Bowerman, *f.n.* ['baʊərmən] (bówĕrmăn)
Bowers Gifford ['baʊərz 'gɪfərd](bówĕrz gíffŏrd)
Bowes, *f.n.* [bʊʊz] (bŏz)
Bowes, [bʊʊz] (bŏz)
Bowes-Lyon, *f.n.* ['bʊʊz 'laɪən] (bŏz lí-ŏn) *Family name of the Earl of Strathmore.*
Bowes Park ['bʊʊz 'pɑrk] (bŏz·páark)
Bowett, *f.n.* ['baʊɪt] (bówĕt)
Bowhill, *f.n.* ['bʊʊhɪl] (bŏ-hil)
Bowie, *f.n.* ['baʊɪ] (bów-i); ['bʊʊɪ] (bŏ-i)

Bowker, *f.n.* ['baʊkər] (bówker)
Bowland ['bɒlənd] (bóllănd)
Bowlby, *f.n.* ['bʊʊlbɪ] (bŏlbi)
Bowles, *f.n.* [bʊʊlz] (bŏlz)
Bowley, *f.n.* ['bʊʊlɪ] (bŏli)
Bowling ['bʊʊlɪŋ] (bŏling)
Bowman, *f.n.* ['bʊʊmən] (bŏmăn)
Bowmore ['bʊʊ'mɔr] (bŏ-mór)
Bown, *f.n.* [baʊn] (bown)
Bownas, *f.n.* ['bʊʊnəs] (bŏnăss)
Bowness, *f.n.* [bʊʊ'nes] (bŏnéss)
Bowness, *Cumberland,* *Westmorland* ['bʊʊnes] (bŏness)
Bowra, Sir Maurice, *scholar and author* ['baʊrə] (bówră)
Bowser, *f.n.* ['baʊzər] (bówzer)
Bowtell, *f.n.* [bʊʊ'tel] (bŏtéll)
Bowyer, *f.n.* ['bʊʊjər] (bŏ-yer)
Bowyer Tower, *Tower of London* ['bʊʊjər] (bŏ-yer)
Boyagis, *f.n.* ['bɔɪədʒɪs] (bóy-ăjiss)
Boydell, *f.n.* [bɔɪ'del] (boydéll)
Boyd-Orr, *Baron* ['bɔɪd 'ɔr] (bóyd ór)
Boyndlie ['bɔɪndlɪ] (bóyndli)
Boys, *f.n.* [bɔɪz] (boyz)
Boz, *pen-name of Charles Dickens* [bɒz] (bozz) *Professor Daniel Jones notes that* [bʊʊz] (bŏz), *which was the original pronunciation, is not often heard now.*
Bozeat ['bʊʊzɪæt] (bŏzi-at)
Braaid [breɪd] (brayd)
Braal [brɔl] (brawl)
Brabant, *f.n.* ['bræbənt] (brábbănt); [brə'bænt] (brăbánt)
Brabazon of Tara, *Baron* ['bræbəzən əv 'tɑrə] (brábbăzŏn ŏv taáră)
Brabin, *f.n.* ['breɪbɪn] (bráybin)
Brabourne['breɪbɔrn](bráyborn);['breɪbərn] (bráybŭrn) *The second is appropriate for Baron ~.*
Brabrooke, *f.n.* ['breɪbrʊk] (bráybrŏŏk)
Brabyn, *f.n.* ['breɪbɪn] (bráybin)
Brabyn's Brow Canal ['bræbɪnz 'braʊ] (brábbinz brów)
Bracadale ['brækədeɪl] (bráckădayl)
Bracher, *f.n.* ['breɪtʃər] (bráytcher)
Braco ['breɪkʊʊ] (bráykŏ)
Bracon Ash ['brækən æʃ] (bráckŏn ash)
Braddell, *f.n.* ['brædl] (braddl)
Braddock, *f.n.* ['brædək] (bráddŏk)
Braddock ['brædək] (bráddŏk)
Bradenham ['brædənəm] (bráddĕnăm)
Bradford, *f.n.* ['brædfərd] (brádfŏrd)
Bradish, *f.n.* ['breɪdɪʃ] (bráydish)
Bradlaugh, *f.n.* ['brædlɔ] (brádlaw)
Braemar [breɪ'mɑr] (braymaár)
Braeriach [breɪ'rɪəx] (bray-rée-ăch)
Braham, *f.n.* ['breɪəm] (bráy-ăm)
Brahams, *f.n.* ['breɪəmz] (bráy-ămz)
Brahan, *f.n.* [brɒn] (brawn)
Brahan Castle [brɒn] (braan) *Appropriate also for the ~ seer, Scottish soothsayer.*
Braich-y-Pwll [ˌbraɪx ə 'puɬ] (brích ă poŏhl)

Braid, *f.n.* [breɪd] (brayd)
Brainin, *f.n.* ['braɪnɪn] (bri'nin)
Brainshaugh ['breɪnzhɑf] (bráynz-haaf)
Braithwaite, *f.n.* ['breɪθweɪt] (bráyth-wayt)
Braithwell ['breɪθwel] (bráythwel)
Bramall, *f.n.* ['bræmɔl] (brámawl)
Brambletye ['bræmbltaɪ] (brámbltī)
Bramcote ['bræmkɒt] (brámkott)
Bramerton ['bræmərtən] (brámmĕrtŏn)
Bramhall ['bræmhɔl] (brám-hawl)
Bramhope ['bræmhoʊp] (brám-hōp)
Brancaster Staithe ['bræŋkəstər 'steɪð] (bránkáster stáyth)
Brancepeth ['branspəθ] (braánsspĕth)
Brandane, *f.n.* [bræn'deɪn] (brandáyn)
Brandeston ['brændɪstən] (brándĕstŏn)
Brandis Corner ['brændɪs 'kɔrnər] (brándiss kórner)
Brandiston ['brændɪstən] (brándistŏn)
Brandlesholme ['brændlzhoʊm] (brándlzhōm)
Brangwyn, *f.n.* ['bræŋgwɪn] (bránggwin)
Brant-Broughton ['brænt 'brutən] (bránt broótŏn)
Brantham ['brænθəm] (brán-thăm)
Brashaw, *f.n.* ['breɪʃɔ] (bráy-shaw)
Brasher, *f.n.* ['breɪʃər] (bráysher)
Brass, *f.n.* [bras] (braass)
Brassey, *f.n.* ['bræsɪ] (brássi)
Brassington, *f.n.* ['bræsɪŋtən] (brássing-tŏn)
Brasted ['breɪstɪd] (bráyssted)
Bratoft ['breɪtɒft] (bráytoft)
Braughing ['bræfɪŋ] (bráffing)
Braun, *f.n.* [braʊn] (brown)
Braund, *f.n.* [brɒnd] (brawnd)
Braunholtz, *f.n.* ['braʊnhoʊlts] (brównhōlts)
Braunstone ['brɒnstən] (bráwnstŏn)
Braunton ['brɒntən] (bráwntŏn)
Bravington, *f.n.* ['brævɪŋtən] (brávving-tŏn)
Brawdy ['brɔdɪ] (bráwdi)
Brazell, *f.n.* [brə'zel] (brăzéll)
Brazil, *f.n.* ['bræzl] (brazzl); ['bræzɪl] (brázzil)
Brea [breɪ] (bray)
Breadalbane [brɪ'dælbən] (brĕdálbăn); [brɪ'dɔlbən] (brĕdáwlbăn) *The second is appropriate for the Earl of ~.*
Breadsell, *f.n.* [bred'sel] (bredsséll)
Breage [breɪg] (brayg); [brig] (breeg)
Breakey, *f.n.* ['breɪkɪ] (bráyki)
Brealey, *f.n.* ['brɪəlɪ] (breé-áli)
Breamore ['bremər] (brémmŏr)
Brean [brin] (breen)
Breaston ['bristən] (breésstŏn)
Breay, *f.n.* [breɪ] (bray)
Brech, *f.n.* [brek] (breck)
Brechfa ['brexvə] (bréchvă)
Brechin, *f.n.* ['brɪxɪn] (breéchin)
Brechin ['brɪxɪn] (breéchin)
Brecon ['brekən] (bréckŏn)

Bredin, *f.n.* ['brɪdɪn] (breédin)
Bredon ['brɪdən] (breédŏn)
Bredwardine [ˌbredwɔr'daɪn] (bred-wárdīn)
Brehony, *f.n.* [brɪ'hoʊnɪ] (brĕ-hóni)
Breich [brix] (breech)
Breidden ['braɪðən] (brīthĕn)
Breightmet ['braɪtmɪt] (brītmĕt); ['breɪtmɪt] (bráytmĕt)
Breinton ['breɪntən] (bráyntŏn)
Brenack, *f.n.* ['brenək] (brénnăk)
Brenard, *f.n.* ['brenɑrd] (brénnaard)
Brenchley ['brentʃlɪ] (bréntchli)
Brenel, *f.n.* [brɪ'nel] (brĕnéll)
Brent Eleigh ['brent 'ɪlɪ] (brént eéli)
Brenzett ['brenzɪt] (brénzĕt)
Brereton, *f.n.* ['brɛərtən] (bráirtŏn); ['brɪərtən] (breértŏn)
Brereton ['brɪərtən] (breértŏn)
Bresler, *f.n.* ['brezlər] (brézler)
Bressay ['breseɪ] (bréssay)
Bretforton ['brefərtən] (bréffĕrtŏn); ['bretfərtən] (brétfŏrtŏn)
Brettargh Holt ['bretər 'hoʊlt] (bréttăr hŏlt)
Brettell, *f.n.* [brɪ'tel] (brĕtéll)
Brewis, *f.n.* ['bruɪs] (broó-iss)
Brewood [brud] (brood)
Breydon Water ['breɪdən 'wɒtər] (bráydŏn wáwter)
Brian, Havergal, *composer* ['hævərgəl 'braɪən] (hávvĕrgăl brí-ăn)
Bricett ['braɪsɪt] (bríssĕt)
Brickell, *f.n.* [brɪ'kel] (brickéll)
Bricusse, *f.n.* ['brɪkəs] (bríckŭss)
Bridburg, *f.n.* ['brɪdbɜrg] (brídburg)
Bridell ['brɪdeɫ] (bríddehl)
Bridestowe ['brɪdɪstoʊ] (bríddĕstō); ['brɪdstoʊ] (brídstō)
Bridge Blean ['brɪdʒ 'blin] (brij bleén)
Bridge of Gaur ['brɪdʒ əv 'gɔr] (bríj ŏv gór)
Bridge of Orchy ['brɪdʒ əv 'ɔrxɪ] (bríj ŏv órchi)
Bridgend [brɪdʒ'end] (brij-énd)
Bridgette, *f.n.* [brɪ'dʒet] (brijét)
Bridgnorth ['brɪdʒnɔrθ] (bríj-north)
Bridie, James, *author* ['braɪdɪ] (brídi) *Pen name of Dr. O. H. Mavor.*
Bridlington ['brɪdlɪŋtən] (brídlingtŏn)
Bridson, *f.n.* ['braɪdsən] (brídssŏn)
Bridstow ['brɪdstoʊ] (brídstō)
Brierley, *f.n.* ['braɪərlɪ] (brí-ĕrli); ['brɪərlɪ] (breérli)
Brierley Hill ['braɪərlɪ 'hɪl] (brí-ĕrli híll)
Brierly, *f.n.* ['braɪərlɪ] (brí-ĕrli)
Briers, *f.n.* ['braɪərz] (brí-ĕrz)
Brighouse ['brɪghaʊs] (bríg-howss)
Brighstone ['braɪstən] (brísstŏn)
Brightholmlee ['braɪtəmlɪ] (brítŏmli)
Brightling ['braɪtlɪŋ] (brítling)
Brightlingsea ['braɪtlɪŋsɪ] (brítling-see)
Brighton ['braɪtən] (brítŏn)
Briginshaw, *f.n.* ['brɪgɪnʃɔ] (bríggin-shaw)

Briley, f.n. ['braɪlɪ] (brílī)
Brilles, f.n. ['brɪlɪs] (brílĕss)
Brimacombe, f.n. ['brɪməkum] (brímmăkoom)
Brimblecombe, f.n. ['brɪmblkoum] (brímblkōm)
Brimilow, f.n. ['brɪmɪloʊ] (brímmilō)
Brind, f.n. [brɪnd] (brínd)
Brinkheugh ['brɪŋkhjuf] (brínk-hewf)
Brinscall ['brɪnskl] (brínsskl)
Brinsea ['brɪnzɪ] (brínzi)
Briody, f.n. ['braɪədɪ] (brí-ŏdi)
Brisco, f.n. ['brɪskoʊ] (brískō)
Brithdir, *Glamorgan, Merioneth* ['brɪθdɪər] (bríthdeer)
Briton Ferry ['brɪtən 'ferɪ] (bríttŏn férri)
Britwell Salome ['brɪtwəl 'sæləm] (brítwĕl sálŏm)
Brize Norton ['braɪz 'nɔrtən] (bríz nórtŏn)
Broadclyst ['brɒdklɪst] (bráwdklĭst)
Broad Halfpenny Down ['brɒd 'hɑfpenɪ 'daʊn] (bráwd haáf-penni dówn)
Broadhembury [brɒd'hembərɪ] (brawd-hémbŭri)
Broadis, f.n. ['brɒdɪs] (bráwdiss)
Broadwas ['brɒdwəs] (bráwd-wǎss)
Broadwoodwidger ['brɒdwʊd'wɪdʒər] (bráwdwŏod-wíjjer)
Broady, f.n. ['broʊdɪ] (bróđi)
Brocas, Viscount ['brɒkəs] (bróckǎss)
Broderick, f.n. ['brɒdərɪk] (bróddĕrick)
Brodick ['brɒdɪk] (bróddick)
Brodie, f.n. ['broʊdɪ] (bróđi)
Brodrick, f.n. ['brɒdrɪk] (bródrick)
Broe, f.n. [broʊ] (brō)
Brogan, f.n. ['broʊgən] (brógǎn)
Brogyntyn [brɒ'gʌntɪn] (broggúntin)
Broke, f.n. [brʊk] (brŏok)
Bromborough ['brɒmbərə] (brómbŭrǎ)
Brome [broʊm] (brōm)
Brome [brum] (broom)
Bromet, f.n. ['brɒmɪt] (brómmĕt)
Bromford ['brɒmfərd] (brómfŏrd)
Bromham ['brʌməm] (brúmmǎm)
Bromhead, f.n. ['brʌmhed] (brúm-hed)
Bromholm ['brʊmhoʊm] (brŏom-hōm)
Bromley, f.n. ['brʌmlɪ] (brúmli); ['brɒmlɪ] (brómli)
Bromley, *Kent* ['brɒmlɪ] (brómli) *The old pronunciation,* ['brʌmlɪ] (brúmli), *seems to have succumbed completely to the spelling pronunciation.*
Brompton ['brɒmptən] (brómptŏn)
Brompton Ralph ['brɒmptən 'rælf] (brómptŏn rálf)
Bromsgrove ['brɒmzgroʊv] (brómzgrōv)
Bromwich *see* West Bromwich.
Bronant ['brɒnənt] (brónnǎnt)
Brongwendraeth [brɒn'gwendraɪθ] (bron-gwéndrīth)
Brongwyn ['brɒŋgwɪn] (brón-gwin)
Bronllys ['brɒnɬɪs] (brón-ḥleess)

Brontë, f.n. ['brɒntɪ] (brónti) *Appropriate for authors Charlotte, Anne, and Emily Jane ~.*
Bronydd ['brɒnɪð] (brónnĭth)
Bron-y-Foel [ˌbrɒnə'vɔɪl] (bronnǎvóyl)
Brookes, f.n. [brʊks] (brŏoks)
Broomieknowe [ˌbrumɪ'naʊ] (broomi-nów)
Brora ['brɔrə] (bráwrǎ)
Broseley ['broʊzlɪ] (brózli)
Brough, f.n. [brʌf] (bruff)
Brough, *Caithness* [brʊx] (broḥ)
Brough, *Westmorland, Yorks.* [brʌf] (bruff)
Brough-under-Stainmore ['brʌf ʌndər 'steɪnmɔr] (brúff-undĕr-stáynmor) *More simply* Brough.
Broughall, f.n. ['brɒvəl] (brów-ăl)
Broughall ['brɒfl] (bróffl)
Brougham, f.n. [brum] (brŏom); ['broʊəm] (brô-ăm); ['bruəm] (broó-ăm); [broʊm] (brōm)
Brougham [brum] (broom)
Brougham and Vaux, Baron ['brum ənd 'vɒks] (brŏom ǎnd váwks)
Broughshane, Baron [brə'ʃeɪn] (brŏ-sháyn)
Broughshane [broʊ'ʃeɪn] (brō-sháyn)
Broughton, f.n. ['brɒtən] (bráwtŏn); ['braʊtən] (brówtŏn) *The first is appropriate for Baron Fairhaven's family name.*
Broughton, *Cumberland, Denbigh., Flint., Hants., Lancs., Lincs., Oxon., Peebles., Salop, Staffs., Yorks.* ['brɒtən] (bráwtŏn)
Broughton, *Northants.* ['braʊtən] (brówtŏn)
Broughton, Drake's ['dreɪks 'brɒtən] (dráyks bráwtŏn)
Broughton, Nether ['neðər 'brɒtən] (néther bráwtŏn)
Broughton, Upper ['ʌpər 'brɒtən] (úpper bráwtŏn)
Broughton Astley ['brɒtən 'æstlɪ] (bráwtŏn ástli)
Broughton-in-Furness ['brɒtən ɪn 'fɜrnɪs] (bráwtŏn in fúrnĕss)
Broughty Ferry ['brɒtɪ 'ferɪ] (brótti férri)
Browell, f.n. ['brɒvəl] (brówĕl)
Browett, f.n. ['broʊɪt] (brô-ĕt)
Brownjohn, f.n. ['braʊndʒɒn] (brówn-jon)
Broxis, f.n. ['brɒksɪs] (brócksiss)
Bruar ['bruər] (broó-ăr)
Bruce Lockhart, f.n. ['brus 'lɒkərt] (broóss lóckărt)
Bruce of Melbourne, Viscountcy of ['brus əv 'melbərn] (broóss ǒv mélbŭrn)
Bruche [bruʃ] (broosh)
Bruck, f.n. [brʊk] (brŏok)
Brudenell, Baron ['brudənəl] (broódĕnĕl)
Bruen, f.n. ['bruɪn] (broó-ĕn)
Brundall ['brʌndl] (brúndl)

Brundrett, *f.n.* ['brʌndrɪt] (brúndrĕt)
Brunel, Sir Isambard, *19th-c. engineer*
['ɪzəmbɑrd bruˈnel] (ízzămbaard brŏŏnéll)
Bruning, *f.n.* ['brunɪŋ] (broóning)
Brunner, *f.n.* ['brʌnər] (brúnner)
Bruntisfield, *Baron* ['brʌntsfɪld] (brúntsfeeld)
Bruxner, *f.n.* ['brʊksnər] (brŏŏksner)
Brydon, *f.n.* ['braɪdən] (brídŏn)
Brydone, *f.n.* ['braɪdən] (brídŏn)
Bryher ['braɪər] (brí-er)
Brymbo ['brɪmboʊ] (brímbō)
Brymer, *f.n.* ['braɪmər] (brímer)
Brynamman [brɪnˈæmən] (brinámmăn)
Bryncethin [brɪnˈkeθɪn] (brin-kéthin)
Bryncoch [brɪnˈkoʊx] (brin-kôch)
Bryncroes [brɪnˈkrɔɪs] (brin-króyss)
Bryneglwys [brɪnˈeɡlʊɪs] (brinéglŏŏ-iss)
Bryn Euryn [brɪn ˈaɪrɪn] (brin frín)
Brynglas [brɪnˈɡlɑs] (brin-gláass)
Bryngwyn ['brɪŋɡwɪn] (bríng-gwin)
Brynhyfryd [brɪnˈhʌvrɪd] (brin-húvvrid)
Bryniau [ˈbrʌnjaɪ] (brún-yī)
Bryning, *f.n.* ['braɪnɪŋ] (bríning)
Brynkir ['brɪŋkɪər] (brínkeer)
Brynmawr [brɪnˈmaʊər] (brin-mówr)
Brynmenyn [brɪnˈmenɪn] (brin-ménnin)
Brynrefail [brɪnˈrevaɪl] (brin-révvīl)
Brynsiencyn [brɪnˈʃeŋkɪn] (brin-shénkin)
Buachaille Etive Mór ['buəxeɪl ˈetɪv ˈmɔr] (boó-áchayl éttiv mór)
Buccleuch [bəˈklu] (bŭklóo) *Appropriate also for the Duke of* ~.
Buchan, *f.n.* ['bʌxən] (búchăn); ['bʌkən] (búckăn) *The first is appropriate for John* ~, *first Baron Tweedsmuir, author and statesman.*
Buchan ['bʌxən] (búchan) *Appropriate also for the Earl of* ~.
Buchanan, *f.n.* [bəˈkænən] (bŭkánnăn); [bjuˈkænən] (bewkánnăn) *The first is appropriate for Professor Colin* ~, *author of the* ~ *Report* (Traffic in Towns). *It is also normal Scottish usage.*
Buchell, *f.n.* [buˈʃel] (boo-shéll)
Bucher, *f.n.* ['bʊʃər] (bŏŏsher)
Buchinch ['bak'ɪnʃ] (búck-ínsh)
Buchlyvie [bʌkˈlaɪvɪ] (bucklívi)
Bucke, *f.n.* [bjuk] (bewk)
Buckeridge, *f.n.* ['bʌkərɪdʒ] (búckĕrij)
Buckfastleigh ['bʌkfɑst'li] (búckfaastleè)
Buckie ['bʌkɪ] (búcki)
Buckingham ['bʌkɪŋəm] (búcking-ăm)
Buckinghamshire, *Earl of* ['bʌkɪŋəm-ʃər] (búcking-ăm-sher)
Buckland Filleigh ['bʌklənd 'fɪlɪ] (búckländ fílli)
Buckland Tout Saints ['bʌklənd 'tu 'seɪnts] (búckländ toó sáynts)
Buddig, *Welsh C.n.* ['bɪðɪɡ] (bíthig)
Bude [bjud] (bewd)
Budle ['bjudl] (bewdl)

Budleigh Salterton ['bʌdlɪ 'sɔltərtən] (búdli sáwltĕrtŏn)
Budock ['bjudək] (béwdŏk)
Bueb, *f.n.* ['bjueb] (béw-eb)
Buerton ['bjuərtən] (béwĕrtŏn)
Buesst, *f.n.* [bjust] (bewsst)
Buggé, *f.n.* ['bugeɪ] (boógay)
Buggs, *f.n.* [bjuɡz] (bewgz); [bʌɡz] (buggz)
Bught Park, *Inverness* [bʌxt] (bucht)
Bugle ['bjuɡl] (bewgl)
Buick, *f.n.* ['bjuɪk] (béw-ick)
Builth Wells ['bɪlθ 'welz] (bílth wéllz)
Buist, *f.n.* ['bjuɪst] (béw-ist); [bjust] (bewsst)
Buittle ['bɪtl] (bittl); ['bjutl] (bewtl)
Bukatzsch, *f.n.* ['bjukætʃ] (béwkatch)
Bukht, *f.n.* [bʌkt] (buckt)
Bulbrook, *f.n.* ['bʊlbrʊk] (bŏŏlbrŏŏk)
Bulcote ['bʊlkət] (bŏŏlkŏt)
Buley, *f.n.* ['bjulɪ] (béwli)
Bulkeley ['bʊklɪ] (bŏŏkli)
Bulkley, *f.n.* ['bʌlklɪ] (búlkli)
Bullard, *f.n.* ['bʊlərd] (bŏŏlárd); ['bʊlard] (bŏŏlaard)
Bulleid, *f.n.* ['bʊlɪd] (bŏŏleed); [bʊˈlɪd] (bŏŏleéd)
Bullimore, *f.n.* ['bʊlɪmɔr] (bŏŏlimor)
Bullough, *f.n.* ['bʊlə] (bŏŏlă); ['bʊloʊ] (bŏŏlō)
Bullus, *f.n.* ['bʊləs] (bŏŏlŭss)
Bulphan ['bʊlvən] (bŏŏlvăn)
Bulteel, *f.n.* ['bʊltɪl] (bŏŏlteel)
Bultitude, *f.n.* ['bʌltɪtjud] (búltitewd)
Bulverhythe [ˌbʊlvər'haɪð] (bŏŏlvĕr-híth)
Bulwer, *f.n.* ['bʊlwər] (bŏŏlwer)
Bulwick ['bʊlɪk] (bŏŏlick)
Bumpus, *f.n.* ['bʌmpəs] (búmpŭss)
Bunchrew [bʌn'kru] (bunkroó); [bən'kru] (bŭnkroó)
Bunessan [bən'esən] (bŭnéssăn)
Bungay ['bʌŋɡɪ] (búng-gi)
Bunwell ['bʌnwəl] (búnwĕl)
Burbury, *f.n.* ['bɜrbərɪ] (búrbŭri)
Burcher, *f.n.* ['bɜrtʃər] (búrtcher)
Bure, *River* [bjʊər] (byŏŏr)
Bures [bjʊərz] (byŏŏrz)
Burgate ['bɜrɡeɪt] (búrgayt)
Burges, *f.n.* ['bɜrdʒɪz] (búrjĕz)
Burgess, *f.n.* ['bɜrdʒɪs] (búrjĕss)
Burgh, *f.n.* ['bʌrə] (búrră); [bɜrɡ] (burg); [bɜr] (bur) *The first is appropriate for Baron* ~.
Burgh [bɜrɡ] (burg)
Burgh Castle ['bʌrə 'kɑsl] (búrră kaássl)
Burgh Heath ['bʌrə 'hiθ] (búrră heéth); ['bɜr 'hiθ] (búr heéth)
Burgh House, *Hampstead* [bɜrɡ] (burg)
Burgh St. Peter ['bʌrə snt-'pitər] (búrră sĭnt peéter)
Burgh-by-Sands ['brʌf baɪ 'sændz] (brúff bī sándz)
Burgh-le-Marsh ['bʌrə lə 'mɑrʃ] (búrră lĕ maársh)

Burghclere ['bɜrkleər] (búrklair) *Appropriate also for the Barony of* ~.

Burghead [bɜrg'hed] (burg-héd)

Burghersh, Baron ['bɜrgɜrʃ] (búrgersh)

Burghfield ['bɜrfild] (búrfeeld)

Burghley, Baron ['bɜrlɪ] (búrli)

Burgin, f.n. ['bɜrgɪn] (búrgin); ['bɜrdʒɪn] (búrjin)

Burgoyne, f.n. ['bɜrgɔɪn] (búrgoyn)

Burham ['bʌrəm] (búrrăm)

Burhop, f.n. ['bʌrəp] (búrrŏp)

Buriton ['berɪtən] (bérritŏn)

Burke, f.n. [bɜrk] (burk)

Burke-Collis, f.n. ['bɜrklɪs] (baárkliss)

Burleigh Castle ['bɜrlɪ] (búrli)

Burlingjobb [ˌbɜrlɪŋ'dʒɒb] (burling-jób)

Burlton, f.n. ['bɜrltən] (búrltŏn)

Burnaston ['bɜrnəstən] (búrnăstŏn)

Burnell, f.n. [bɜr'nel] (burnéll)

Burneside ['bɜrnɪsaɪd] (búrnĕssĭd); ['bɜrnsaɪd] (búrnssĭd)

Burness, f.n. [bɜr'nes] (burnéss)

Burnet, f.n. ['bɜrnɪt] (búrnĕt)

Burnett, f.n. ['bɜrnɪt] (búrnĕt); [bɜr'net] (burnét)

Burngullow [bɜrn'gʌloʊ] (burn-gúllō)

Burnhope ['bɜrnhoʊp] (búrn-hōp)

Burntisland [bɜrnt'aɪlənd] (burnt-fländ)

Burpham, *Surrey, Sussex* ['bɜrfəm] (búrfăm)

Burrator ['bʌrə'tɔr] (búrră-tór)

Burravoe ['bʌrəvoʊ] (búrrăvō)

Burray ['bʌreɪ] (búrray)

Burringham ['bʌrɪŋəm] (búrring-ăm)

Burrough, f.n. ['bʌroʊ] (búrrō); ['bʌrə] (búrră)

Burroughes, f.n. ['bʌroʊz] (búrrōz)

Burroughs, f.n. ['bʌroʊz] (búrrōz)

Burry Estuary ['bʌrɪ] (búrri)

Burry Holmes ['bʌrɪ 'hoʊmz] (búrri hŏmz)

Burry Port ['bʌrɪ 'pɔrt] (búrri pórt)

Burscough ['bɜrskoʊ] (búrsskō)

Bursledon ['bɜrzldən] (búrzldŏn)

Burslem ['bɜrzləm] (búrzlĕm)

Burstall, f.n. ['bɜrstɔl] (búrsstawl)

Burt, f.n. [bɜrt] (burt)

Burtchaell, f.n. ['bɜrtʃl] (burtchl)

Burton Lazars ['bɜrtən 'læzərz] (búrtŏn lázzărz)

Burton Pedwardine ['bɜrtən 'pedwərdaɪn] (búrtŏn pédwărdĭn)

Burton Pynsent ['bɜrtən 'pɪnsənt] (búrtŏn pínssĕnt)

Burtonwood ['bɜrtən'wʊd] (búrtŏn-wŏŏd)

Burwardsley ['bɜrwərdzlɪ] (búrwărdzli)

Burwarton ['bɜrwərtən] (búrwártŏn)

Burwash ['bɜrwɒʃ] (búrwosh)

Burwasher, native of Burwash ['bʌrəʃər] (búrrăsher)

Burwell, f.n. ['bɜrwel] (búrwel); ['bɜrwəl] (búrwĕl)

Burwell ['bɜrwel] (búrwel)

Bury, f.n. ['berɪ] (bérri); ['bjʊərɪ] (byŏŏri) *The first is appropriate for Viscount* ~.

Bury ['berɪ] (bérri)

Bury Fen ['berɪ 'fen] (bérri fén)

Bury St. Edmunds ['berɪ snt 'edməndz] (bérri sĭnt édmŭndz)

Busby, f.n. ['bʌzbɪ] (búzzbi)

Bushby, f.n. ['bʊʃbɪ] (bŏŏshbi)

Bushelle, f.n. [bʊ'ʃel] (bŏŏ-shéll)

Buskell, f.n. ['bʌskl] (busskl)

Busler, f.n. ['bʌzlər] (búzzler)

Bussell, f.n. ['bʌsl] (bussl)

Busutilli, f.n. [ˌbʊsʊ'tɪlɪ] (bŏŏssŏŏtílli)

Busvine, f.n. ['bʌzvaɪn] (búzzvīn)

Buszard, f.n. ['bʌzərd] (búzzărd)

Butchart, f.n. ['bʊtʃart] (bŏŏtchaart); ['bʊtʃərt] (bŏŏtchărt)

Bute [bjut] (bewt) *Appropriate also for the Marquess of* ~.

Buthlay, f.n. ['bʌθleɪ] (búthlay)

Butler-Bowdon, f.n. ['bʌtlər 'boʊdən] (bútler bóōdŏn) *Family name relating to the Barony of Grey de Ruthyn.*

Butley, *Cheshire, Suffolk* ['bʌtlɪ] (bútli)

Butlin, f.n. ['bʌtlɪn] (bútlin)

Buttar, f.n. ['bʌtar] (búttaar)

Butterwick ['bʌtərwɪk] (búttĕrwick); ['bʌtərɪk] (búttĕrick)

Buxhall ['bʌksɔl] (búcksawl)

Buxeman, f.n. ['bjuzmən] (béwzmăn)

Bwlch Gwyn [bʊlx 'gwɪn] (bŏŏlch gwín)

Bwlch Moch [bʊlx 'moʊx] (bŏŏlch mŏch)

Bwlch Newydd [bʊlx 'newɪð] (bŏŏlch né-with)

Bwlch-y-Cibau [ˌbʊlxə'kibaɪ] (bŏŏlchăkeébĭ)

Bwlchllan [bʊlx'hæn] (bŏŏlch-hlán)

Bwlchysarnau [ˌbʊlxə'sɑrnaɪ] (bŏŏlchăsaárnĭ)

Bwllfa ['bʊɬvə] (bŏŏhlvă)

Byam, f.n. ['baɪəm] (bí-ăm)

Byatt, f.n. ['baɪət] (bí-ăt)

Byham, f.n. ['baɪəm] (bí-ăm)

Byker ['baɪkər] (bíker)

Bylaugh ['bilɑ] (beélaa); ['biloʊ] (beélō); ['baɪlɑ] (bíflaa); ['baɪloʊ] (bíflō)

Bylchau ['bʌlxaɪ] (búlchĭ)

Byllam, f.n. ['bɪləm] (bíllăm)

Bynea ['bɪnjə] (bín-yă)

Byrne [bɜrn] (birn)

Byron, f.n. ['baɪərən] (bírŏn)

Byshottles ['baɪʃɒtlz] (bí-shottlz)

Bysouth, f.n. ['baɪsaʊθ] (bíssowth)

Bysshe, f.n. [bɪʃ] (bish) *Appropriate also for Percy* ~ *Shelley.*

Bythesea, f.n. ['bɪθsi] (bíth-see)

Bytheway, f.n. ['baɪðəweɪ] (bíthĕway); ['baɪθweɪ] (bíth-way)

Byward Tower, *Tower of London* ['baɪwərd] (bí-wărd)

C

Caban Coch ['kæbən 'koʊx] (kábbăn kṓch)

Cabell, f.n. ['kæbl] (kabbl)

Cabot, f.n. ['kæbət] (kábbŏt) *This is the pronunciation generally used for John and Sebastian ~, explorers.*

Cabourn ['keɪbɔrn] (káyborn)

Cabrach ['kæbrəx] (kábrǎch); ['kɑbrəx] (káabrǎch)

Caccia, f.n. ['kætʃə] (kátchǎ) *Appropriate for Baron ~.*

Cachemaille, f.n. ['kæʃmaɪl] (káshmīl); ['kæʃmeɪl] (káshmayl)

Cadbury, f.n. ['kædbəri] (kádbŭri)

Cadby, f.n. ['kædbɪ] (kádbi)

Caddonfoot [ˌkædən'fʊt] (kaddŏnfṓŏt)

Cadeby, *Lincs., Yorks.* ['keɪdbɪ] (káydbi)

Cadell, f.n. ['kædl] (kaddl) *Appropriate also for Jean ~, actress.*

Cader Idris ['kædər 'ɪdrɪs] (kádder ídriss)

Cadgwith ['kædʒwɪθ] (káj-with); ['kædʒwɪθ] (káj-with)

Cadishead ['kædɪzhed] (káddiz-hed)

Cadle, f.n. ['keɪdl] (kaydl)

Cadle ['kædleɪ] (kádlay)

Cadogan, Earl [kə'dʌgən] (kădúggăn)

Cadoux, f.n. ['kædu] (káddoo)

Cadoxton ['kædəkstən] (káddŏkstŏn)

Cadwaladr, Dilys, Welsh poet ['dɪlɪs kæd'wælədər] (díllis kadwálăder)

Cadwaladyr, f.n. [kæd'wælədər] (kadwálăder)

Cadwallader, f.n. [kæd'wɒlədər] (kadwóllăder)

Cadwgan, f.n. [kə'dʊgən] (kădṓŏgăn)

Cadzow, f.n. ['kædzoʊ] (kádzō)

Cadzow ['kædzoʊ] (kádzō)

Caegarw [kaɪ'gæru] (kīgárroo)

Caenby ['keɪnbɪ] (káynbi); ['keɪənbɪ] (káy-ĕnbi)

Caerau ['kaɪraɪ] (kírī)

Caerbwdi Bay [kaɪər'budɪ] (kírboódi)

Caer Caradoc ['kaɪər kə'rædɒk] (kír kărádŏck)

Caerdeon [kɑr'deɪən] (kaardáy-ŏn)

Caergeiliog [kaɪər'gaɪljɒg] (kírgíl-yog) .

Caergwrle [kaɪər'gʊərleɪ] (kírgŏŏrlay)

Caergybi [kaɪər'gʌbɪ] (kīrgúbbi)

Caerhayes, *also spelt* **Carhays** [kɑr'heɪz] (kaar-háyz); [kə'reɪz] (kăráyz) *Historians prefer the spelling* Carhays.

Caerhayes Castle [kɑr'heɪz] (kaar-háyz)

Caerhun [kaɪər'hin] (kīr-heén)

Caerlaverock [kɛər'lævərɒk] (kairlávvĕrock)

Caerleon [kɑr'liən] (kaarleé-ŏn)

Caernarvon [kər'nɑrvən] (kărnaárvŏn)

Caerphilly [kər'fɪlɪ] (kărfílli)

Caersalem [kaɪər'sæləm] (kīr-sá1ĕm)

Caersws [kaɪər'sus] (kīr-soóss)

Caerwent [kaɪər'went] (kīrwént)

Caerwys ['kaɪərwɪs] (kírwiss)

Caffarey, f.n. ['kæfərɪ] (káffări)

Caffery, f.n. ['kæfərɪ] (káffĕri)

Caffyn, f.n. ['kæfɪn] (káffin)

Cahan, f.n. [kɑn] (kaan)

Cahir, Irish C.n. ['kæhər] (ká-hir)

Cahusac, f.n. [kə'hjusæk] (kăhéwssack)

Caiger, f.n. ['keɪdʒər] (káyjer)

Caillard, f.n. ['kaɪɑr] (kí-aar)

Caird, f.n. [kɛərd] (kaird)

Cairnbulg ['kɛərn'bʌlg] (kaírn-búlg)

Cairngorms ['kɛərn'gɔrmz] (kaírn-górmz)

Cairntoul [kɛərn'tul] (kairntoól); [kɛərn-'taʊl] (kairntówl)

Caister ['keɪstər] (káyster)

Caistor ['keɪstər] (káystŏr)

Caithness, Earl of ['keɪθnes] (káythness)

Caithness ['keɪθnɪs] (káythnĕss)

Caius, f.n. [kɪz] (keez)

Caius College *see* Gonville and Caius College.

Calcot, f.n. ['kɒlkət] (káwlkŏt); ['kælkət] (kálkŏt)

Calcot ['kælkət] (kálkŏt)

Calcott, f.n. ['kɒlkət] (káwlkŏt); ['kælkət] (kálkŏt)

Caldarvan [kəl'dɑrvən] (kăldaárvăn)

Caldbeck ['kɒldbek] (káwldbeck); ['kɒdbek] (káwdbeck); ['kʊdbek] (kódbeck)

Caldcleugh, f.n. ['kɒldklʌf] (káwldkluff); ['kɑldklʌf] (kaáldkluff)

Caldecote, Viscount ['kɒldɪkət] (káwldĕkŏt)

Caldecott ['kɒldɪkət] (káwldĕkŏt)

Caldercruix [ˌkɒldər'kruks] (kawldĕrkroóks)

Calderon, f.n. ['kældərən] (káldĕrŏn); ['kɒldərən] (káwldĕrŏn)

Caldmore ['kɑmər] (kaámŏr)

Caldow, f.n. ['kældoʊ] (káldō)

Caldwell, f.n. ['kɒldwel] (káwldwel)

Caldy ['kɒldɪ] (káwldi)

Caldy Island ['kɒldɪ aɪlənd] (káwldi íländ)

Caledon ['kælɪdən] (kálĕdŏn) *Appropriate also for the Earl of ~.*

Calenick [kə'lenɪk] (kălénnick)

Calfe, f.n. [kɑf] (kaaf)

Calgary, f.n. ['kælgərɪ] (kálgări)

Calke [kɔk] (kawk)

Calkwell, f.n. ['kokwel] (káwkwel)

Calladine, f.n. ['kælədɪn] (kálădeen)

Callaghan, f.n. ['kæləhən] (kálăhán)

Callaly ['kælølɪ] (káláli)

Callander ['kæləndər] (kálánder)

Callernish ['kælərnɪʃ] (kálĕrnish)

Callestick [kə'lestɪk] (kálĕstick); ['klestɪk] (kléstick)

Callieu, f.n. ['kæl'ju] (kal-yoó)

Callington ['kælɪŋtən] (kálingtŏn)

Callis Mill, *Hebden Bridge, Yorks.* ['kælɪs] (káliss)

Calne [kɑn] (kaan)

Calow ['keɪloʊ] (káylō) ; ['kɒloʊ] (káwlō)
Calshot ['kælʃɒt] (kál-shot)
Calstock ['kælstɒk] (kálstock)
Calthorpe, *f.n.* ['kɔlθɔrp] (káwl-thorp);
['kælθɔrp] (kál-thorp) *The first is appropriate for Baron* ~.
Calthorpe ['kælθɔrp] (kál-thorp)
Calton, *Glasgow* ['kɑltən] (kaáltŏn)
Calton Hill, *Edinburgh* ['kɒltən 'hɪl]
(káwltŏn hĭll)
Calveley ['kɑvlɪ] (kaávlĭ) ; ['kɒvlɪ] (kávvlĭ)
Calver, *f.n.* ['kælvər] (kálver) ; ['kɑvər]
(kaáver)
Calverhall ['kælvərhɒl] (kálvĕr-hawl)
Calverley ['kɑvərlɪ] (kaávĕrli) ; ['kɒvlɪ]
(kávvlĭ) *The first is appropriate for Baron* ~.
Calver Sough ['kɑvər 'sʌf] (kaáver súff)
Calvert, *f.n.* ['kælvərt] (kálvĕrt) ; ['kɒl-vərt] (káwlvĕrt)
Calverton ['kælvərtən] (kálvĕrtŏn);
['kɑvərtən] (kaávĕrtŏn)
Calvine [kæl'viːn] (kalveén)
Calvocoressi, *f.n.* [ˌkælvəkə'resɪ] (kalvŏ-kŏréssi)
Calwell, *f.n.* ['kɒlwəl] (káwl-wĕl)
Cam, River [kæm] (kam)
Camascross [ˌkæməs'krɒs] (kammăs-króss)
Camasunary [ˌkæmə'sjuːnərɪ] (kammă-séwnări)
Cambois ['kæməs] (kámmŭss) ; ['kæmɪs]
(kámmiss)
Camborne ['kæmbɔrn] (kámborn)
Cambrian, *pertaining to Wales* ['kæm-brɪən] (kámbriăn)
Cambridge ['keɪmbrɪdʒ] (káymbrij)
Cambusavie [ˌkæmbəs'ævɪ] (kambŭss-ávvi)
Cambusbarron [ˌkæmbəs'bærən] (kam-bŭssbárrŏn)
Cambuslang [ˌkæmbəs'læŋ] (kambŭss-láng)
Cambusnethan [ˌkæmbəs'neθən] (kam-bŭssnéthăn)
Cameley ['keɪmlɪ] (káymli)
Camelford ['kæmlfərd] (kámmlfŏrd)
Camelon ['kæmələn] (kámmĕlŏn)
Camerer-Cuss, *f.n.* ['kæmərər 'kʌs]
(kámmĕrer kúss)
Cameron of Lochiel, *f.n.* ['kæmərən əv
lɒ'xiːl] (kámmĕrŏn ŏv lochẽel)
Camerton ['kæmərtən] (kámmĕrtŏn)
Camlachie [kæm'læxɪ] (kamláchi)
Cammaerts, *f.n.* ['kæmərts] (kámmĕrts)
Camoys, *Baron* ['kæmɔɪz] (kámmoyz)
Campagnac, *f.n.* [kæm'pænjæk] (kam-pán-yack) ; [kəm'pænjæk] (kămpán-yack)
Campbell, *f.n.* ['kæmbl] (kambl)
Campbell of Monzie, *f.n.* ['kæmbl əv
mə'niː] (kámbl ŏv mŏneé)
Campbeltown ['kæmbltaʊn] (kámbl-town) ; ['kæmbltən] (kámbltŏn)
Campden, *f.n.* ['kæmdən] (kámdĕn)
Appropriate also for Viscount ~.

Campey, *f.n.* ['kæmpɪ] (kámpi)
Campoli, Alfredo, *violinist* [æl'freɪdoʊ
'kæmpəlɪ] (alfráydō kámpŏli)
Campsall ['kæmpsl] (kampssl)
Campsie ['kæmpsɪ] (kámpsi)
Camrose ['kæmroʊz] (kámrōz)
Camulodunum, *Roman name for Colchester* ['kæmjʊloʊd'junəm] (kám-yōō lōōd-yoōnŭm) ; ['kæmʊloʊd'unəm] (kámoō-lōōd-oónŭm)
Camus, *f.n.* ['kæməs] (kámmŭss)
Candler, *f.n.* ['kændlər] (kándler)
Candlin, *f.n.* ['kændlɪn] (kándlin)
Canelle, *f.n.* [kə'nel] (kănéll)
Canewdon [kə'njudən] (kănéwdŏn)
Canna ['kænə] (kánnă)
Cannel, *f.n.* [kə'nel] (kănéll)
Cannell, *f.n.* ['kænl] (kannl)
Canon Frome ['kænən 'frum] (kánnŏn froōm)
Canon Pyon ['kænən 'paɪən] (kánnŏn pí-ŏn)
Canonbury ['kænənbərɪ] (kánnŏnbŭri)
Cantabrigian, *pertaining to Cambridge or its University* [ˌkæntə'brɪdʒɪən] (kantá-brijjián)
Cantamir, *f.n.* ['kæntəmɪər] (kántămeer)
Cantelo, *f.n.* ['kæntɪloʊ] (kántĕlō)
Cantelowes Gardens, *London park*
['kæntɪloʊz] (kántĕlōz)
Canter, *f.n.* ['kæntər] (kánter)
Canterbury ['kæntərbərɪ] (kántĕrbŭri)
Cantuar, *Archbishop of Canterbury's signature* ['kæntjʊar] (kánt-yōō-aar)
Canwick ['kænɪk] (kánnick) ; ['kænwɪk]
(kánwick)
Caol [kɜl] (kŏll)
Capaldi, *f.n.* [kə'pældɪ] (kăpáldi)
Cap Coch [kæp 'koʊx] (kap kŏch)
Cape Cornwall [keɪp 'kɔrnwəl] (kayp kórnwăl)
Capel, *f.n.* ['keɪpl] (kaypl)
Capel, *Kent, Suffolk, Surrey* ['keɪpl]
(kaypl)
Capel Curig ['kæpl 'kɪrɪg] (káppl kírrig)
Capel Mair ['kæpl 'maɪər] (káppl mír)
Capel Mawr ['kæpl 'maʊər] (káppl mówr)
Capel-le-Ferne ['keɪpl lə 'fɜrn] (káypl lĕ férn)
Capell, *f.n.* ['keɪpl] (kaypl)
Capener, *f.n.* ['keɪpənər] (káypĕner)
Capenhurst ['keɪpənhɜrst] (káypĕnhurst)
Capern, *f.n.* ['keɪpərn] (káypĕrn)
Cape Wrath [keɪp 'rɑθ] (kayp raáth) ;
[keɪp 'rɒθ] (kayp ráwth)
Capheaton [kæp'hitən] (kap-heétŏn)
Caplan, *f.n.* ['kæplən] (káplăn)
Capon, *f.n.* ['keɪpən] (káypŏn)
Caporn, *f.n.* ['keɪpɔrn] (káyporn)
Cappercleuch ['kæpərklux] (káppĕr-klooch)
Capron, *f.n.* ['keɪprən] (káyprŏn)
Caputh ['keɪpəθ] (káypŭth)

Caradoc, Welsh C.n., also spelt Caradog [kə'rædɒk] (kărádock)
Caradon ['kærədən] (kárrádŏn) *Appropriate also for Baron ~.*
Caravias, f.n. [ˌkærə'viəs] (karrăveé-ăss)
Carbery, f.n. ['karbəri] (káarbĕri)
Carbis Bay ['karbɪs 'beɪ] (káarbiss báy)
Carbost ['karbɒst] (káarbosst)
Carburton ['karbərtən] (káarbŭrtŏn)
Cardenden [ˌkardən'den] (kaardĕndén)
Cardiff ['kardɪf] (káardif)
Cardigan ['kardɪgən] (kaárdigăn) *Appropriate also for the Earl of ~.*
Cardinall, f.n. ['kardɪnl] (káardinnl)
Cardinham [kar'dɪnəm] (kaardínnăm)
Cardnell, f.n. ['kardnel] (káard-nel)
Cardowan [kar'dauən] (kaardówăn)
Cardross ['kardrəs] (káardrŏss)
Cardus, Neville, author ['nevl 'kardəs] (névvl káardŭss)
Careglefn [ˌkærɪg'levn] (karrĕg-lévvn)
Careston ['karɪstən] (kaáréstŏn)
Carew, f.n. [kə'ru] (kăroó) ; ['kɛərɪ] (káíri) *The first is appropriate for Baron ~, and for Thomas ~, 17th-c. poet.*
Carew ['kɛərɪ] (káíri) ; ['kɛəru] (káíroo)
Carewe, f.n. [kə'ru] (kăroó)
Carfin ['kar'fɪn] (káar-fín)
Carfraemill ['karfreɪ'mɪl] (káarfraymíll)
Cargen ['kargən] (káargĕn)
Cargill, f.n. [kar'gɪl] (kaargíll) ; ['kargɪl] (káargil)
Carham ['kærəm] (kárrăm)
Carharrack [kar'hærək] (kaar-hárrăk) ; [kər'hærək] (kăr-hárrăk)
Carhays, *see* Caerhayes.
Carholme Racecourse, *Lincoln* ['karhoʊm] (káar-hōm)
Caridia, f.n. [kə'rɪdɪə] (kăríddiă)
Carinish ['karɪnɪʃ] (káarinish)
Carkeet-James, f.n. ['karkɪt 'dʒeɪmz] (káarkeet jáymz)
Carland ['karlænd] (káarland)
Carleton, f.n. ['karltən] (káarltŏn)
Carleton Road, *London* [kar'lɪtən] (kaarleétŏn)
Carleton Forhoe ['karltən 'fɔrhoʊ] (kaárltŏn fór-hō)
Carlill, f.n. ['kar'lɪl] (káar-líll)
Carline, f.n. ['karlaɪn] (káarlïn)
Carlinghow [ˌkarlɪŋ'hau] (kaarling-hów)
Carlisle, f.n. [kar'laɪl] (kaarlíl)
Carlisle [kar'laɪl] (kaarlíl) ; ['karlaɪl] (káarlïl) *The first is recognised national usage; the second is preferred locally. The first is also appropriate for the Earl of ~.*
Carlops ['karlɒps] (káarlops)
Carlton Colville ['karltən 'kɒlvɪl] (káarltŏn kólvil)
Carluke [kar'luk] (kaar-loók)
Carlyon, f.n. [kar'laɪən] (kaarlĩ-ŏn)
Carlyon Bay [kar'laɪən] (kaarlĩ-ŏn)
Carmarthen [kər'marðən] (kărmaár-thĕn)
Carmedy, f.n. ['karmədɪ] (káarmĕdi)

Carmel ['karmel] (káarmel)
Carmichael, f.n. [kar'maɪkl] (kaarmíkl) ; [kar'mɪxl] (kaarmíchl)
Carmyllie [kar'maɪlɪ] (kaarmíli)
Carnalea [ˌkarnə'li] (kaarnáleé)
Carnane [kar'nem] (kaarnáyn)
Carnarvon, Earl of [kər'narvən] (kărnaárvŏn)
Carn Brea ['karn 'breɪ] (káarn bráy)
Carnearney [kar'nɛərnɪ] (kaarnaárni)
Carnegie, f.n. [kar'negɪ] (kaarnéggi) ; [kar'neɪgɪ] (kaarnáygi) *The first is that of the Earl of Northesk's family name. Both pronunciations are current in Scotland, and usage for the ~ Trust consequently varies with individual speakers.*
Carnegy, f.n. [kar'negɪ] (kaarnéggi) ; [kar'neɪgɪ] (kaarnáygi)
Carnell, f.n. [kar'nel] (kaarnéll)
Carnkie [karn'kaɪ] (kaarnkí)
Carnlough ['karnlɒx] (káarnloch)
Carnmenellis [ˌkarnmɪ'nelɪs] (kaarnmĕnéllis)
Carnmoney [karn'mʌnɪ] (kaarn-múnni)
Carno ['karnoʊ] (káarnō)
Carnoustie [kar'nustɪ] (kaarnoósti)
Carntyne [karn'taɪn] (kaarn-tín)
Carnwadric [karn'wɔrdrɪk] (kaarn-wáwrdrick)
Carnwath [karn'wɒθ] (kaarnwóth)
Carnyorth [karn'jɔrθ] (kaarn-yórth)
Caro, f.n. ['karoʊ] (káarō)
Caroe, f.n. ['kɛəroʊ] (káírō) ; ['kæroʊ] (kárrō)
Caroe, Sir Olaf, diplomatist and writer ['oʊlæf 'kɛəroʊ] (ólaf kaírō)
Carolan, f.n. ['kærələn] (kárrŏlăn)
Caron, f.n. ['kærɒn] (kárron)
Carothers, f.n. [kə'rʌðərz] (kărúthĕrz)
Carpmael, f.n. ['karpmeɪl] (káarpmayl)
Carr, f.n. [kar] (kaar)
Carrad, f.n. ['kærəd] (kárrăd)
Carrawburgh Fort ['kærəbrʌf] (kárrăbruff)
Carrbridge ['kar'brɪdʒ] (káar-bríj)
Carreghofa [ˌkærɪg'hoʊvə] (karrĕg-hóvă)
Carrell, f.n. [kə'rel] (kăréll)
Carreras, f.n. [kə'rɪərəz] (kăreérăz)
Carrick-a-Rede [ˌkærɪkə'rid] (karrick-ă-reéd)
Carrickfergus [ˌkærɪk'fɜrgəs] (karrick-férgŭss)
Carrick - Mannan [ˌkærɪk'mænən] (karrick-mánnăn)
Carrigans, f.n. ['kærɪgənz] (kárrigănz)
Carrodus, f.n. ['kærədəs] (kárrŏdŭss)
Carrothers, f.n. [kə'rʌðərz] (kărúthĕrz)
Carrowdore ['kærədɔr] (kárrădor)
Carrowreagh, *Co. Antrim* [ˌkæroʊ'riə] (karrō-reé-ă)
Carrowreagh, *Co. Down* [ˌkæroʊ'reɪ] (karrō-ráy)
Carruth, f.n. [kə'ruθ] (kărooth)
Carruthers, f.n. [kə'rʌðərz] (kărúthĕrz)
Carryduff [ˌkærɪ'dʌf] (karridúff)

Carse, f.n. [kɑrs] (kaárss)
Carse of Gowrie ['kɑrs əv 'gaʊrɪ] (kaárss ŏv gówri)
Carsfad [kɑrs'fæd] (kaarss-fád)
Carshalton [kɑr'ʃɔltən] (kaar-sháwltŏn)
Although apparently no longer heard, there was, within living memory, a pronunciation [keɪs'hɔtən] (kayss-háwtŏn).
Carsluith [kɑr'sluθ] (kaar-slóoth)
Carsphairn [kɑrs'fɛərn] (kaarss-faírn)
Carstairs, f.n. [kɑr'stɛərz] (kaar-staírz); ['kɑrstɛərz] (kaárstairz)
Carstairs [kɑr'stɛərz] (kaar-staírz)
Carthusian, one educated at Charterhouse School [kɑr'θjuːzɪən] (kaar-théwziăn)
Cartmel ['kɑrtməl] (kaártmĕl)
Cartmel Fell ['kɑrtməl 'fel] (kaártmĕl féll)
Carton de Wiart, f.n. ['kɑrtən də 'waɪərt] (kaártŏn dĕ wí-ărt)
Cartwright, f.n. ['kɑrtraɪt] (kaártrīt)
Carus, f.n. ['kɛərəs] (kaírŭss)
Caruth, f.n. [kə'ruθ] (kăróoth)
Caruthers, f.n. [kə'rʌðərz] (kărúthĕrz)
Carvell, f.n. [kɑr'vel] (kaarvéll)
Carwadine, f.n. ['kɑrwədɪn] (kaárwădeen)
Carwardine, f.n. ['kɑrwərdɪn] (kaárwărdeen); [ˌkɑrwər'dɪn] (kaarwărdeén)
Carway ['kɑrweɪ] (kaárway)
Carwinnen [kɑr'wɪnən] (kaarwínnĕn)
Carwithen, f.n. [kɑr'wɪðən] (kaar-wíthĕn)
Cary, f.n. ['kɛərɪ] (kaíri)
Carysfort, f.n. ['kɛərɪsfɔrt] (kárrisfort)
Casasola, f.n. [ˌkæsə'soʊlə] (kassăssốlă)
Cascob ['kæskɒb] (kásskob)
Casdagli, f.n. [kæz'dæglɪ] (kazdágli)
Casley, f.n. ['keɪzlɪ] (káyzli)
Caslon, f.n. ['kæzlɒn] (kázzlon)
Casselden, f.n. ['kæsldən] (kássldĕn)
Cassillis, Earl of ['kæslz] (kasslz)
Cassillis ['kæslz] (kasslz)
Cassini, f.n. [kə'siːnɪ] (kăsseéni)
Cassiobury Park, *Herts.* ['kæsɪoʊbərɪ 'pɑrk] (kássiŏbŭri paárk)
Casson, f.n. ['kæsən] (kássŏn)
Castagnola, f.n. [ˌkæstə'noʊlə] (kasstă-nốlă)
Castaldini, f.n. [ˌkæstəl'dɪnɪ] (kasstäl-deéni)
Castell, f.n. [kæs'tel] (kasstéll)
Castellain, f.n. ['kæstɪleɪn] (kásstĕlayn)
Castellan, f.n. ['kæstelən] (kásstellăn)
Castell Coch ['kæsteɬ 'koʊx] (kásstehl kŏch)
Castelnau, *London thoroughfare* ['kɑslnɔ] (kaásslnaw); ['kɑslnoʊ] (kaásslnō)
Castle Baynard ['kɑsl 'beɪnɑrd] (kaássl báynaard)
Castle Bromwich ['kɑsl 'brɒmɪtʃ] (kaássl brómmitch); ['kɑsl 'brʌmɪdʒ] (kaássl brúmmij)
Castle Cary ['kɑsl 'kɛərɪ] (kaássl kaíri)
Castle Combe ['kɑsl 'kuːm] (kaássl koóm)

Castle Donington ['kɑsl 'dʌnɪŋtən] (kaássl dúnningtŏn)
Castle Douglas ['kɑsl 'dʌgləs] (kaássl dúgláss)
Castle Malwood ['kɑsl 'mɒlwʊd] (kaássl máwlwŏŏd)
Castle-an-Dinas ['kɑsl ən 'daɪnəs] (kaássl ăn dínăss)
Castle of Mey ['kɑsl əv 'meɪ] (kaássl ŏv máy)
Castlebay ['kɑslbeɪ] (kaásslbay)
Castlecaulfield [ˌkɑsl'kɔfɪld] (kaassl-káwfeeld)
Castledawson [ˌkɑsl'dɔsən] (kaassl-dáwssŏn)
Castlederg [ˌkɑsl'dɜrg] (kaassl-dérg)
Castledoor [ˌkɑsl'dɔr] (kaassl-dór)
Castlereagh [ˌkɑsl'reɪ] (kaassl-ráy)
Castlerock [ˌkɑsl'rɒk] (kaassl-róck)
Castlerosse, Viscountcy of ['kɑslrɒs] (kaásslross)
Castletown, *Caithness* ['kɑsltaʊn] (kaássltown)
Castletown, *I.o.M.* ['kɑsl'taʊn] (kaássl-tówn)
Castleward [ˌkɑsl'wɔrd] (kaassl-wáwrd)
Castlewellan [ˌkɑsl'welən] (kaassl-wéllăn)
Castley, f.n. ['kæstlɪ] (kásstli)
Caston ['kæstən] (kaástŏn); ['kæsən] (kássŏn)
Catchpole, f.n. ['kætʃpoʊl] (kátchpōl)
Catcleugh ['kætklʌf] (kátkluff); ['kætklɪf] (kátkleef)
Catelinet, f.n. ['kætlɪneɪ] (kátlinay)
Cater, f.n. ['keɪtər] (káyter)
Catesby, f.n. ['keɪtsbɪ] (káytsbi)
Cathays [kə'teɪz] (kătáyz)
Cathcart [kæθ'kɑrt] (kath-kaárt)
Cathedine [kə'θedɪn] (kăthéddin)
Catherwood, f.n. ['kæθərwʊd] (káthĕr-wŏŏd); ['kæðərwʊd] (káthĕr-wŏŏd)
Cathie, f.n. ['keɪθɪ] (káythi)
Cathles, f.n. ['kæθlz] (kathlz)
Cathro, f.n. ['kæθroʊ] (káthrō)
Catinthewell [ˌkætɪt'wel] (kattit-wéll)
Cation, f.n. ['keɪʃən] (káy-shŏn)
Catmur, f.n. ['kætmər] (kátmŭr)
Cato, f.n. ['keɪtoʊ] (káytō)
Caton, f.n. ['keɪtən] (káytŏn)
Caton ['keɪtən] (káytŏn)
Cator, f.n. ['keɪtər] (káytŏr)
Catrine ['kætrɪn] (kátrin)
Catriona, C.n. [kə'triənə] (kătreé-ŏnă)
Cattanach, f.n. ['kætənəx] (káttănăch)
Cattell, f.n. [kə'tel] (kătéll)
Catterline, f.n. ['kætərlaɪn] (káttĕrlīn)
Cattewater, *see* Catwater.
Cattistock ['kætɪstɒk] (káttistock)
Catto, Baron ['kætoʊ] (káttō)
Catwater, The ['kætwɒtər] (kátwawter)
The spelling Cattewater *appears to be an older variation.*
Caughey, f.n. ['kæxɪ] (káchi)
Caulcutt, f.n. ['kɒlkət] (káwlkŭt)

Caulfeild, f.n. ['kɔfild] (káwfeeld)
Caulfield, f.n. ['kɔfild] (káwfeeld)
Caunce, f.n. [kɒns] (kawnss); [kʊns] (konss)
Causer, f.n. ['kɔzər] (káwzer)
Causley, f.n. ['kɔzlɪ] (káwzli); ['keɪzlɪ] (káyzli)
Causton, Thomas, 16th-c. composer ['kɔstən] (káwsstŏn) *Also sometimes spelt Caustun or Cawston.*
Caute, f.n. [kɒʊt] (kŏt)
Cautley, f.n. ['kɔtlɪ] (káwtli)
Cava Island ['kavə] (kaávă)
Cavan, Earl of ['kævən] (kávvăn)
Cavanagh, f.n. ['kævənə] (kávvănă); [kə'vænə] (kăvánnă)
Cavander, f.n. ['kævəndər] (kávvănder)
Cavell, f.n. ['kævl] (kavvl); [kə'vel] (kăvéll) *The first is appropriate for Nurse Edith ~.*
Cavenagh, f.n. ['kævənə] (kávvĕnă)
Cavers ['keɪvərz] (káyvĕrz)
Cavers Hill ['keɪvərz 'hɪl] (káyvĕrz hĭll)
Caversham ['kævərʃəm] (kávvĕr-shăm)
Caverswall ['kævərzwɔl] (kávvĕrz-wawl)
Cavey, f.n. ['keɪvɪ] (káyvi)
Cawardine, f.n. [kɒ'wardɪn] (kaw-waárdin)
Cawdine, f.n. ['kerɪg 'gwɪnnɪən] (kérrig gwĭnni-ŏn)
Cawood, f.n. ['keɪwʊd] (káy-wŏŏd)
Cawood, *Lancs. see* Arkholme *with* Cawood.
Cawood, *Yorks.* ['keɪwʊd] (káy-wŏŏd)
Cawsand ['kɒsənd] (káwssănd)
Cawston, f.n. ['kɒstən] (káwstŏn) *see also Thomas Causton.*
Cawston ['kɒstən] (káwstŏn)
Cayzer, f.n. ['keɪzər] (káyzer)
Cazabon, f.n. ['kæzəbɒn] (kázzăbon)
Cazalet, f.n. ['kæzəlɪt] (kázzălĕt)
Cazalet-Keir, f.n. ['kæzəlɪt 'kɪər] (kázzălĕt keér)
Cazenove, f.n. ['kæzɪnoʊv] (kázzĕnōv)
Cearns, *f.n.* [kɛərnz] (kairnz)
Cecil, f.n. ['sesl] (sessl); ['sɪsl] (sissl) *The first is the pronunciation of the Marquess of Exeter's family name. The second, being that of the Marquess of Salisbury's family, is appropriate for Lord David ~ and for the late Viscount ~ of Chelwood.*
Cedric, C.n. ['sedrɪk] (sédrick); ['sɪdrɪk] (seédrick)
Cefn ['kevn] (kevvn)
Cefn Caeau [ˌkevn 'kaɪaɪ] (kevvn kí-I)
Cefn Coed [ˌkevn 'kɔɪd] (kevvn kóyd)
Cefn Golau [ˌkevn 'gɒlaɪ] (kevvn góllī)
Cefn Hirgoed [ˌkevn 'hərɡɔɪd] (kevvn hírgoyd)
Cefn Mably [ˌkevn 'mæblɪ] (kevvn mábbli)
Cefn Mawr [ˌkevn 'maʊər] (kevvn mówr)
Cefn-y-Bedd, *Denbigh., Flint.* [ˌkevn ə 'beɪð] (kevvn ă báyth)
Cefneithyn [ˌkevn'aɪθɪn] (kevvn-íthin)
Cefnpennar [ˌkevn'penər] (kevvnpénnăr)
Ceinwen, Welsh C.n. ['kaɪnwen] (kínwen)

Ceirchiog ['kaɪərxjɒɡ] (kírch-yog)
Ceiriog ['kaɪrɪɒɡ] (kírí-og)
Cellan, f.n. ['keɪən] (kéhlăn)
Celner, f.n. ['selnər] (sélner)
Celoria, f.n. [sɪ'lɔrɪə] (sĕláwriă)
Celt, *member of Celtic race* [kelt] (kelt); [selt] (selt) *In Scotland and Northern Ireland the second is the more popular, and the only pronunciation ever heard for the Glasgow Celtic and Belfast Celtic football teams is* ['seltɪk] (séltick).
Cemmaes ['kemaɪs] (kémmíss)
Cemmes Road ['kemɪs 'roʊd] (kémmiss rŏd)
Cenarth ['kenɑrθ] (kénnaarth)
Cennydd, Welsh C.n. ['kenɪð] (kénnith)
Centlivre, Susannah, 17-18th-c. playwright and actress [sɪnt'lɪvər] (sintleéver); [sɪnt'lɪvər] (sintlívver) *There appears to be no positive evidence about her own pronunciation, and today she is known by both.*
Cerely, f.n. ['sɪərlɪ] (seérli)
Ceri, Welsh C.n. ['kerɪ] (kérri)
Ceridwen, Welsh C.n. [kə'rɪdwen] (kĕrídwen)
Cerig Gwynion ['kerɪg 'gwɪnɪən] (kérrig gwínni-ŏn)
Cerne Abbas ['sɜrn 'æbəs] (sérn ábbăss)
Cernioge [kɛərn'jɒɡeɪ] (kairn-yóggay)
Cerrig-y-Drudion ['kerɪg ə 'drɪdjɒn] (kérrig-ă-dríd-yon)
Cesarewitch, horse race [sɪ'zærəwɪtʃ] (sĕzárrĕwitch)
Ceserani, f.n. [ˌsɪzə'ranɪ] (seezĕraáni)
Cestrian, native of Chester ['sestrɪən] (séstriăn)
Chabot, f.n. ['ʃæboʊ] (shábbō)
Chaceley ['tʃeɪslɪ] (cháyssli)
Chacewater ['tʃeɪswɒtər] (cháyss-wawter)
Chacombe ['tʃeɪkəm] (cháykŏm) *An older spelling is* Chalcombe.
Chaddesden ['tʃædzdən] (chádzdĕn) ['tʃædzən] (chádzĕn)
Chaddlehanger ['tʃædlhænər] (cháddlhang-er); ['tʃælmər] (cháling-er)
Chadshunt ['tʃædzhʌnt] (chádz-hunt); ['tʃædzʌnt] (chádzunt)
Chafer, f.n. ['tʃeɪfər] (cháyfer)
Chaffe, f.n. [tʃeɪf] (chayf)
Chaffey, f.n. ['tʃeɪfɪ] (cháyfi)
Chagrin, Francis, composer ['fransɪs 'ʃægrã] (fraánsiss shágrang)
Chain, *f.n.* [tʃeɪn] (chayn)
Chalcombe *see* Chacombe.
Chaldon ['tʃɔldən] (cháwldŏn)
Chalfont, Baron ['tʃælfɒnt] (chálfont)
Chalfont St. Giles ['tʃælfənt snt 'dʒaɪlz] (chálfŏnt sĭnt jílz); ['tʃafənt snt 'dʒaɪlz] (chaáfŏnt sĭnt jílz)
Chalfont St. Peters ['tʃælfənt snt 'piːtərz] (chálfŏnt sĭnt peétĕrz); ['tʃafənt snt 'piːtərz] (chaáfŏnt sĭnt peétĕrz)
Chalford ['tʃælfərd] (chálfŏrd)

Chalgrove ['tʃælgrouv] (chálgrōv)
Chalker, *f.n.* ['tʃɔkər] (cháwker)
Chalkley, *f.n.* ['tʃɔklɪ] (cháwkli)
Challacombe ['tʃæləkəm] (chálákŏm)
Challands, *f.n.* ['tʃæləndz] (chálăndz)
Challis, *f.n.* ['tʃælɪs] (cháliss)
Challock ['tʃɒlək] (chóllŏk)
Challoner, *f.n.* ['tʃælənər] (chálŏner)
Challow, East *and* **West** ['tʃælou] (chálō)
Chalmers, *f.n.* ['tʃamərz] (chaámĕrz);
['tʃælmərz] (chálmĕrz) *The first is appro-*
priate for the Barony of ∼.
Chaloner, *f.n.* ['tʃælənər] (chálŏner)
Chalvey ['tʃavɪ] (chaávi); ['tʃalvɪ]
(chaálvi)
Chalvington ['tʃælvɪŋtən] (chálvingtŏn);
['tʃalvɪŋtən] (chaálvingtŏn)
Chamberlain, *f.n.* ['tʃeɪmbərlɪn] (cháym-
bĕrlin); ['tʃeɪmbərleɪn] (cháymbĕrlayn)
Chamier, *f.n.* ['ʃæmɪər] (shámmi-er)
Champany ['tʃæmpənɪ] (chámpăni)
Champelovier, *f.n.* [ˌtʃæmpə'louvɪər]
(champĕlóvi-er)
Champernowne, *f.n.* ['tʃæmpərnaun]
(chámpĕrnown)
Champneys, *f.n.* ['tʃæmpnɪz] (chámpniz)
Chandler, *f.n.* ['tʃandlər] (chaándler)
Chandos, *f.n.* ['ʃændɒs] (shándoss);
['tʃændɒs] (chándoss) *The first is appro-*
priate for Viscount ∼.
Chandos-Pole, *f.n.* ['ʃændɒs 'pul] (shán-
doss pool)
Changue [tʃæŋ] (chang)
Channon, *f.n.* ['tʃænən] (chánnŏn)
Chaorunn, Loch ['xɜrən] (chúr-ŭn)
Chapel of Garioch ['tʃæpl ə 'gɪərɪ]
(cháppl ŏ géeri)
Chapel-en-le-Frith ['tʃæpl en lə 'frɪθ]
(cháppl en lĕ fríth)
Chapin, *f.n.* ['tʃeɪpɪn] (cháypin)
Chappell, *f.n.* ['tʃæpl] (chappl)
Chappory, *f.n.* ['tʃæpərɪ] (cháppŏri)
Chaproniere, *f.n.* [ˌʃæprə'nɪər] (shaprŏ-
neér)
Chardet, *f.n.* ['ʃardeɪ] (shaárday)
Charig, *f.n.* ['tʃærɪg] (chárrig)
Charing ['tʃɛərɪŋ] (cháiring); ['tʃærɪŋ]
(chárring)
Charlecote Park ['tʃarlkout 'park]
(chaárlkŏt paárk)
Charlemont, *Viscount* ['tʃarlɪmənt]
(chaárlĕmŏnt)
Charlestown ['tʃarlztaun] (chaárlztown)
Charleton, *f.n.* ['tʃarltən] (chaárltŏn)
Charleton ['tʃarltən] (chaárltŏn)
Charmouth ['tʃarmauθ] (chaármowth)
Charoux, Siegfried, *sculptor* ['sɪgfrid
ʃə'ru] (seégfreed shăroó)
Charques, *f.n.* ['tʃarkwɪz] (chaárkwĕz);
['ʃarkwɪz] (shaárkwĕz)
Charrosin, Frederick, *composer* ['tʃær-
ousɪn] (chárrōssin)

Charteris, *f.n.* ['tʃartərɪs] (chaártĕriss);
['tʃartərz] (chaártĕrz) *The first is appro-*
priate for the family name of the Earl of
Wemyss.
Chartershaugh ['tʃartərzhaf] (chaár-
tĕrz-haaf)
Chartres, *f.n.* ['tʃartərz] (chaártĕrz)
Chaston, *f.n.* ['tʃæstən] (chásstŏn)
Chater, *f.n.* ['tʃeɪtər] (cháyter)
Chathill ['tʃæt'hɪl] (chát-híll)
Chaudoir, *f.n.* ['ʃoudwar] (shŏdwaar)
Chaul End ['tʃɒl 'end] (cháwl énd)
Chavasse, *f.n.* [ʃə'væs] (shăváss)
Chawleigh ['tʃɒlɪ] (cháwli)
Chaworth, Baron ['tʃawərθ] (chaá-
wŭrth)
Cheadle Hulme ['tʃidl 'hjum] (cheédl
héwm); ['tʃidl 'hum] (cheédl hoóm)
Chearsley ['tʃɪərzlɪ] (cheérzli)
Chediston ['tʃedɪstən] (chéddistŏn)
Chedzoy ['tʃedzɔɪ] (chédzoy)
Cheesman, *f.n.* ['tʃizmən] (cheézmăn)
Cheetham, *f.n.* ['tʃitəm] (cheétăm)
Cheetham Hill ['tʃitəm 'hɪl] (cheétăm
híll)
Cheke, *f.n.* [tʃik] (cheek)
Cheldon ['tʃeldən] (chéldŏn)
Chelfham ['tʃelfəm] (chélfăm)
Chelioti, *f.n.* [ˌkelɪ'outɪ] (kelli-óti)
Chellaston ['tʃeləstən] (chéllăstŏn)
Chelmer, Baron ['tʃelmər] (chélmĕr)
Chelmondiston ['tʃelmstən] (chélmstŏn)
Chelmsford ['tʃelmsfərd] (chélmssfŏrd);
['tʃemsfərd] (chémssfŏrd)
Chelsea ['tʃelsɪ] (chélssi) *Appropriate also*
for Viscount ∼.
Chelsham ['tʃelʃəm] (chél-shăm)
Chelveston [tʃel'vestən] (chelvéstŏn)
Chenappa, *f.n.* ['tʃenəpə] (chénnăpă)
Chenevix, *f.n.* ['tʃenɪvɪks] (chénnĕvicks);
['ʃenɪvɪks] (shénnĕvicks)
Chenevix-Trench, *f.n.* ['ʃenɪvɪks 'trentʃ]
(shénnĕvicks trénch)
Cheney, *f.n.* ['tʃeɪnɪ] (cháyni)
Chenies, *f.n.* ['tʃeɪnɪz] (cháyniz)
Chenies ['tʃeɪnɪz] (cháyniz); ['tʃinɪz]
(cheéniz)
Chenil Galleries, *London* ['tʃenɪl]
(chénnil)
Chepstow ['tʃepstou] (chépstō)
Chequerbent ['tʃekərbent] (chéckĕrbent)
Cherhill ['tʃerɪl] (chérril)
Cherkley Court ['tʃɜrklɪ 'kort] (chérklï
kórt)
Cherrill, *f.n.* ['tʃerɪl] (chérril)
Cherwell, *Barony of* ['tʃarwel] (chaárwell)
Cherwell, River ['tʃarwəl] (chaárwĕl)
Chesham, Baron ['tʃeʃəm] (chéshăm)
Chesham ['tʃeʃəm] (chéshăm); ['tʃesəm]
(chéssăm)
Chesham Bois ['tʃesəm 'bɔɪz] (chéssăm
bóyz)
Cheshire ['tʃeʃər] (chésher)
Cheshunt ['tʃesənt] (chéssŭnt)
Chesil Beach ['tʃezl 'bitʃ] (chézzl beétch)

Chesneau, *f.n.* ['tʃesnoʊ] (chéssnō)
Chesney, *f.n.* ['tʃeznɪ] (chézni)
Chester-le-Street ['tʃestər lɪ strit] (chéstĕrli-street)
Chestle, *f.n.* ['tʃesl] (chessl)
Cheswardine ['tʃezwərdaɪn] (chézwărdīn)
Chesworth, *f.n.* ['tʃezwɜrθ] (chézwurth)
Chetham's Hospital, *Manchester* ['tʃetəmz] (chéttămz)
Chetham-Strode, Warren, *author* ['wɒrən 'tʃetəm 'stroʊd] (wórrĕn chéttăm strōd)
Chettiscombe ['tʃetɪskəm] (chéttiskŏm); ['tʃeskəm] (chéskŏm)
Chetwode, *f.n.* ['tʃetwʊd] (chétwŏŏd) *Appropriate also for Baron* ~.
Chetwynd, *f.n.* ['tʃetwɪnd] (chétwind) *Appropriate also for Viscount* ~.
Chevalier, *f.n.* [ʃɪ'vælɪeɪ] (shĕváli-ay); *Appropriate also for Albert* ~, *music-hall artist*.
Chevallier, *f.n.* [ˌʃevə'lɪər] (shevvăleér)
Cheveley Park ['tʃivlɪ 'park] (cheévli paárk)
Chevening ['tʃivnɪŋ] (cheév-ning)
Chevenix, *f.n.* ['ʃevɪnɪks] (shévvĕnicks)
Chevet ['tʃevɪt] (chévvĕt)
Chevington ['tʃevɪŋtən] (chévvingtŏn)
Chevins, *f.n.* ['tʃevɪnz] (chévvinz)
Cheviot Hills ['tʃivɪət] (cheéviŏt); ['tʃevɪət] (chévviŏt) *A theory that the first of these two pronunciations is used north of the Border, and the other on the English side, has been discredited by observation over a long period. The truth appears to be that the former is almost invariably used in the Border country, in both England and Scotland, and that it is speakers from further south who favour the second. A third pronunciation,* ['tʃɪvɪət] (chívviŏt), *has been heard in Edinburgh for the cloth of the name*.
Chewton, *Viscount* ['tʃutən] (choótŏn)
Cheylesmore ['tʃaɪlzmɔr] (chílzmor) *Appropriate also for Baron* ~.
Cheyne, *f.n.* ['tʃeɪnɪ] (cháyni); [tʃeɪn] (chayn); [tʃɪn] (cheen)
Chichele, Henry, *15th-c. benefactor and founder of All Souls College, Oxford* ['tʃɪtʃɪlɪ] (chítchĕli)
Chiddention, *f.n.* ['tʃɪdənʃən] (chíddĕnshŏn)
Chiddingly [ˌtʃɪdɪŋ'laɪ] (chidding-lí)
Chidel, *f.n.* [tʃɪ'del] (chidéll)
Chideock ['tʃɪdək] (chíddŏck)
Chidgey, *f.n.* ['tʃɪdʒɪ] (chíjji)
Chidlow ['tʃɪdloʊ] (chídlō)
Chiene, *f.n.* [ʃin] (sheen)
Chigwell ['tʃɪgwəl] (chígwĕl)
Chilbolton [tʃɪl'boʊltən] (chilbóltŏn)
Childerditch ['tʃɪldərdɪtʃ] (chíldĕrditch)
Childerhouse, *f.n.* ['tʃɪldərhaʊs] (chíldĕrhowss)

Childers, Erskine, *author* ['ɜrskɪn 'tʃɪldərz] (érsskin chíldĕrz)
Childerstone, *f.n.* ['tʃɪldərstoʊn] (chíldĕrstōn)
Childer Thornton ['tʃɪldər 'θɔrntən] (chílder thórntŏn)
Child's Ercall ['tʃaɪldz 'arkl] (chíldz aárkl)
Childwall ['tʃɪlwɒl] (chíl-wawl)
Childwick Bury ['tʃɪlɪkbərɪ] (chíllickbŭri)
Childwick Green ['tʃɪlɪk 'grin] (chíllick greén)
Chilham ['tʃɪləm] (chíllăm)
Chillesford ['tʃɪlzfərd] (chílzfŏrd)
Chillingham ['tʃɪlɪŋəm] (chílling-ăm)
Chiltern Hills ['tʃɪltərn] (chíltĕrn)
Chilton Foliat ['tʃɪltən 'foʊlɪət] (chíltŏn fóliăt)
Chilver, *f.n.* ['tʃɪlvər] (chílver)
Chilvers Coton ['tʃɪlvərz 'koʊtən] (chílverz kótŏn)
Chinnery, *f.n.* ['tʃɪnərɪ] (chínnĕri)̣
Chipping Campden ['tʃɪpɪŋ 'kæmdən] (chípping kámdĕn)
Chipping Norton ['tʃɪpɪŋ 'nɔrtən] (chípping nórtŏn)
Chipping Sodbury ['tʃɪpɪŋ 'sɒdbərɪ] (chípping sódbŭri)
Chirbury ['tʃɜrbərɪ] (chírbŭri)
Chirk [tʃɜrk] (chirk)
Chisholm, *f.n.* ['tʃɪzəm] (chízzŏm)
Chisledon ['tʃɪzldən] (chízzldŏn)
Chissell, *f.n.* [tʃɪ'zel] (chizéll); ['tʃɪzl] (chizzl)
Chiswell, *f.n.* ['tʃɪzwel] (chízwel); ['tʃɪzwəl] (chízwĕl)
Chiswick ['tʃɪzɪk] (chízzick)
Chiswick Eyot ['tʃɪzɪk 'eɪt] (chízzick áyt)
Chittlehamholt ['tʃɪtləmhoʊlt] (chíttlăm-hōlt)
Chivas, *f.n.* ['ʃɪvæs] (shívvass)
Chivenor ['tʃɪvnər] (chívnŏr)
Chivers, *f.n.* ['tʃɪvərz] (chívvĕrz)
Choat, *f.n.* [tʃoʊt] (chōt)
Choate, *f.n.* [tʃoʊt] (chōt)
Chobham ['tʃɒbəm] (chóbbăm)
Cholmeley, *f.n.* ['tʃʌmlɪ] (chúmli)
Cholmondeley, *f.n.* ['tʃʌmlɪ] (chúmli) *Family name of Baron Delamere*.
Cholmondeley ['tʃʌmlɪ] (chúmli) *Appropriate also for the Marquess of* ~.
Cholmondeston ['tʃɒmsən] (chómssŏn)
Cholsey ['tʃoʊlzɪ] (chólzi)
Chomley, *f.n.* ['tʃʌmlɪ] (chúmli)
Chorlton, *f.n.* ['tʃɔrltən] (chórltŏn)
Chote, *f.n.* [tʃoʊt] (chōt)
Choveaux, *f.n.* [ʃə'voʊ] (shŏvṓ); ['tʃoʊvoʊ] (chóvō)
Chovil, *f.n.* ['tʃoʊvɪl] (chóvil)
Chown, *f.n.* [tʃaʊn] (chown)
Chowns, *f.n.* [tʃaʊnz] (chownz)
Chrimes, *f.n.* [kraɪmz] (krīmz)
Chrishall ['krɪʃəl] (kríss-hawl)

Christian Malford ['krɪstjən 'mɒlfərd] (kríst-yăn máwlfŏrd)

Christie, f.n. ['krɪstɪ] (kríssti)

Christison, f.n. ['krɪstɪsən] (krístissŏn)

Christleton ['krɪsltən] (kríssltŏn)

Christopherson, f.n. [krɪs'tɒfərsən] (kristóffěrsŏn)

Christow ['krɪstoʊ] (krísstŏ)

Chroisg, Loch [xrɔɪsk] (chroysk)

Chronnell, f.n. ['krɒnl] (kronnl)

Chruikhorn, f.n. ['krʊkhɔrn] (króokhorn)

Chryston ['kraɪstən] (krísstŏn)

Chulmleigh ['tʃʌmlɪ] (chúmli)

Chumleigh ['tʃʌmlɪ] (chúmli)

Churchill, f.n. ['tʃɜrtʃɪl] (chúrchil)

Churchman, f.n. ['tʃɜrtʃmən] (chúrchmăn)

Churchstowe ['tʃɜrtʃstoʊ] (chúrch-stŏ)

Chute, f.n. [tʃut] (choot)

Chuter, f.n. ['tʃutər] (chóoter)

Chuter-Ede, f.n. ['tʃutər 'id] (chóoter eéd) *Pronunciation of the late Baron* ∼.

Chwilog ['xwilɒg] (chweélog)

Chyandour ['ʃaɪəndaʊər] (shf-ăndowr); ['tʃaɪəndaʊər] (chf-ăndowr)

Chynoweth, f.n. [ʃɪ'noʊəθ] (shinnŏ-ĕth)

Chysoyster [tʃaɪ'sɒstər] (chíssáwster)

Chyvelah [ʃɪ'vilə] (shiveélă)

Cilan ['kɪlən] (killăn)

Cilcain ['kɪlkaɪn] (kílkĭn)

Cilcarw [kɪl'kæru] (kilkárroo)

Cilcen ['kɪlken] (kílken)

Cilcennin [kɪl'kenɪn] (kilkénnin) *Appropriate also for the Viscountcy of* ∼.

Cilcewydd [kɪl'kewɪð] (kilké-wíth)

Cilfrew [,kɪlvrɪ'u] (kilvri-oó)

Cilfynydd [kɪl'vʌnɪð] (kilvúnnith)

Cilgerran [kɪl'gerən] (kilgérrăn)

Cilie Aeron ['kɪljeɪ 'aɪrɒn] (kíl-yay fron)

Ciliene [kɪl'jeneɪ] (kil-yénnay)

Cilmery [kɪl'merɪ] (kilmérri)

Cilrhedyn [kɪl'ʰredɪn] (kilréddin)

Cilybebyll [,kɪlə'bebɪl] (killăbébbihl)

Cil-y-Cwm [,kɪlə'kum] (killákŏŏm)

Cil-y-Maenllwyd [,kɪlə'mænhlʊɪd] (killămán-hlŏ̄oid)

Cimla ['kɪmlə] (kímlă)

Cinque Ports ['sɪŋk pɒrts] (sínk ports)

Cippenham ['sɪpənəm] (síppěnăm)

Cipriani, 18th-c. Florentine-English painter [,sɪprɪ'ɑnɪ] (sipri-aáni)

Cirencester ['saɪərənsestər] (sírěnsester); ['sɪsɪtər] (síssiter)ₐ *The latter, although no longer commonly heard, has not entirely disappeared from use. For some, it is particularly associated with one of the older spellings, Ciceter.*

Citrine, f.n. [sɪ'trin] (sitreén) *Appropriate also for Baron* ∼.

Clachan ['klæxən] (kláchán)

Clackmannan [klæk'mænən] (klackmánnăn); [klək'mænən] (klăkmánnăn)

Clady, Co. *Tyrone* ['klædɪ] (kláddi)

Clady Circuit, *Belfast* ['klædɪ] (kláddi)

Cladymore [,klædɪ'mɔr] (kladdimór)

Claerwen, River ['klaɪərwen] (klír-wen)

Clagh Ouyre ['klæk 'aʊər] (kláck ówr)

Clague, f.n. [kleɪg] (klayg); [kleg] (kleg)

Clandeboye ['klændɪbɔɪ] (klándĕboy)

Clannaborough ['klænəbərə] (klánnăbŭră)

Clanricarde, f.n. [klæn'rɪkərd] (klanríckărd) *Appropriate also for the Earl of* ∼.

Clapworthy ['klæpərɪ] (kláppěri)

Clarabut, f.n. ['klærəbʌt] (klárrăbut)

Clarach ['klærəx] (klárrǎch)

Clarbeston ['klɑrbəstən] (klaárbĕstŏn)

Clare, f.n. [klɛər] (klair)

Clarendon, Earl of ['klærəndən] (klárrĕndŏn)

Clarina, Barony of [klə'raɪnə] (klărínă)

Claringbull, f.n. ['klærɪŋbʊl] (klárringbŏŏl)

Clarke, f.n. [klɑrk] (klaark)

Claro, f.n. ['klɛəroʊ] (kláirŏ)

Clatteringshaws Loch ['klætərɪŋʃɒz] (kláttěring-shawz)

Claudy ['klɒdɪ] (kláwdi)

Claughton, f.n. ['klɒtən] (kláwtŏn)

Claughton, *Cheshire* ['klɒtən] (kláwtŏn)

Claughton, *Lancs.* ['klæftən] (kláfftŏn)

Claughton-on-Brock, *Lancs.* ['klaɪtən ɒn 'brɒk] (klítŏn on bróck)

Clausen, f.n. ['klɒsən] (kláwssĕn)

Clauson, f.n. ['klɒsən] (kláwssŏn)

Claverdon ['klævərdən] (klávvěrdŏn); ['klɑrdən] (klaárdŏn)

Claverham ['klævərəm] (klávvěrăm)

Claverhouse,f.n. ['kleɪvərhaʊs] (kláyvěrhowss)

Claverhouse ['kleɪvərhaʊs] (kláyvěrhowss) *Appropriate also for John Graham of* ∼, *Scottish soldier.*

Clavering, f.n. ['kleɪvərɪŋ] (klávvěring)

Clavering ['kleɪvərɪŋ] (kláyvěring)

Claverley ['klævərlɪ] (klávvěrli)

Claverton ['klævərtən] (klávvěrtŏn) *Appropriate also for* ∼ *Down.*

Clayhidon ['kleɪhaɪdən] (kláy-hĭdŏn)

Cleal, f.n. [klil] (kleel)

Cleanthous, f.n. [klɪ'ænθəs] (kli-ánthŭss)

Clearwell ['klɪər'wel] (kleérwéll); [klɪər'wel] (kleerwéll); ['klɪərwel] (kleérwell)

Cleary, f.n. ['klɪərɪ] (kleéri)

Cleasby, f.n. ['klizbɪ] (kleézbi)

Clease, f.n. [klis] (kleess)

Cleather, f.n. ['kleðər] (kléther)

Cleator ['klitər] (kleétŏr)

Cleckheaton [klek'hitən] (kleck-heétŏn)

Cledwyn, Welsh C.n. ['kledwɪn] (klédwin)

Clegyr ['klegər] (kléggir)

Clehonger ['klɒŋgər] (klóng-ger)

Cleland, f.n. ['klelənd] (klélländ); ['klilənd] (kleéländ)

Cleland ['klelənd] (klélländ)

Clemak, f.n. ['klimæk] (kleémack)

Clemenger, f.n. ['klemɪndʒər] (klémměnjer)

Clemo, f.n. ['klemoʊ] (klémmō)
Clenchwarton ['klenʃwɔrtən] (klénshwawrtŏn)
Clennell, f.n. [klɪ'nel] (klĕnéll)
Cleobury, f.n. ['kloʊbərɪ] (klóbŭri); ['klɪbərɪ] (kleébŭri)
Cleobury Mortimer ['klɪbərɪ 'mɔrtɪmər] (klíbbŭri mórtimer)
Cleobury North ['klɪbərɪ 'nɔrθ] (klíbbŭri nórth)
Clerici, f.n. ['klerɪsɪ] (klérrissi)
Clerk, f.n. [klɑrk] (klaark)
Clerke, f.n. [klɑrk] (klaark)
Clervaux ['klɛərvoʊ] (kláirvō); ['klɛərvoks] (kláirvawks)
Clery, f.n. ['klɪərɪ] (kleéri)
Clevedon ['klivdən] (kleévdŏn)
Cleveleys ['klivlɪz] (kleévliz)
Cleverdon, f.n. ['klevərdən] (klévvĕrdŏn)
Cleverley, f.n. ['klevərlɪ] (klévvĕrli)
Cleverly, f.n. ['klevərlɪ] (klévvĕrli)
Cleworth, f.n. ['kluərθ] (kloó-ŭrth)
Cley [klaɪ] (klī); [kleɪ] (klay)
Clibborn, f.n. ['klɪbərn] (klíbborn)
Cliburn ['klɪbərn] (klíbburn)
Clickhimin, Loch ['klɪkɪmɪn] (klíckimin)
Cliddesden ['klɪdɪzdən] (klíddĕzdĕn)
Cliffords Mesne ['klɪfərdz 'min] (klíffŏrdz meén)
Clifton Reynes ['klɪftən 'reɪnz] (klíftŏn ráynz)
Climie, f.n. ['klaɪmɪ] (klími)
Clipsham ['klɪpʃəm] (klíp-shăm); ['klɪpshəm] (klíps-hăm)
Clipstone, *Notts.* ['klɪpstoʊn] (klípstŏn)
Clitheroe ['klɪðəroʊ] (klíthĕrō) *Appropriate also for Baron* ~.
Clitherow, f.n. ['klɪðəroʊ] (klíthĕrō)
Cliveden ['klɪvdən] (klívdĕn)
Cloan [kloʊn] (klōn)
Clocaenog [kloʊ'kaɪnɒg] (klōkínog)
Cloete, f.n. [kloʊ'itɪ] (klō-eéti); ['klutɪ] (kloóti)
Clogher, f.n. ['klɒxər] (klócher)
Clogher ['klɒxər] (klócher)
Cloghmore [klɒx'mɔr] (klochmór)
Clogwyn Du'r Arddu [kloʊ'gʊɪn dɪər 'arðɪ] (klōgoó-in deer aárthee)
Clogwyn-y-Person [kloʊ'gʊɪn ə 'pɛərsɒn] (klōgoó-in ă paírsson)
Clompus, f.n. ['klɒmpəs] (klómpŭss)
Clonaneese [ˌklɒnə'nis] (klonnáneéss)
Clonard ['klɒnərd] (klónnărd)
Clonbrock, f.n. [klɒn'brɒk] (klonbróck)
Cloncurry, f.n. [klɒn'kʌrɪ] (klon-kúrri)
Clonmacate [ˌklɒnmə'keɪt] (klonmăkáyt)
Clonmell, f.n. [klɒn'mel] (klon-méll)
Clonmore, f.n. [klɒn'mɔr] (klon-mór)
Clontivrim [klɒn'tɪvrɪm] (klontívvrim)
Clontoe [klʌn'toʊ] (kluntó)
Clopet, f.n. ['kloʊpeɪ] (klópay)
Clophill ['klɒphɪl] (klóp-hill)
Close, f.n. [kloʊs] (klōss)
Clother, f.n. ['kloʊðər] (klóther)

Clough, f.n. [klʌf] (kluff)
Clough, *Co. Down* [klɒx] (kloch)
Clough, River, *Yorks.* [klʌf] (kluff)
Clougha Pike ['klɒfə 'paɪk] (klóffă pīk)
Cloughenery [ˌklɒxə'nɛərɪ] (klochĕnaíri)
Cloughey ['klɒxɪ] (klóchi)
Cloughfold ['klʌf'foʊld] (klúff-fōld)
Cloughmills [klɒx'mɪlz] (klochmíllz)
Cloughogue [klɒx'oʊg] (klochóg)
Cloughton ['klaʊtən] (klówtŏn); ['kloʊtən] (klótŏn)
Clousta ['klustə] (kloóstá)
Clouston, f.n. ['klustən] (kloósstŏn); ['klaʊstən] (klówsstŏn)
Clouston, J. Storer, author ['storər 'klustən] (stáwrer kloósstŏn)
Clovelly [kloʊ'velɪ] (klōvélli)
Clovenfords [ˌkloʊvən'fɔrdz] (klōvĕnfórdz)
Cloverley ['klɒvərlɪ] (klóvvĕrli)
Clow, f.n. [kloʊ] (klō)
Clowes, f.n. [klaʊz] (klowz); [kluz] (klooz)
Clowne [klaʊn] (klown)
Cluanie, Loch ['kluːnɪ] (kloóni); ['kluənɪ] (kloó-ăni)
Clucas, f.n. ['klukəs] (kloókáss)
Clulow, f.n. ['kluloʊ] (kloólō)
Clumber Park ['klʌmbər 'park] (klúmber paárk) *This gives its name to the Clumber spaniel.*
Clun [klʌn] (klun) *Appropriate also for Baron* ~.
Clunbury ['klʌnbərɪ] (klúnbŭri)
Clunes, *Inverness., Perth.* [klunz] (kloonz)
Clungunford [klʌn'gʌnfərd] (klun-gúnfŏrd)
Clunie, *Banff., Perth.* ['klunɪ] (kloóni)
Clunies, f.n. ['klunɪz] (kloóniz)
Cluntoe [klʌn'toʊ] (kluntó)
Clunton ['klʌntən] (klúntŏn)
Cluse, f.n. [kluz] (klooz)
Clutsam, f.n. ['klʌtsəm] (klútsăm)
Clutton ['klʌtən] (klúttŏn)
Clwyd, Baron ['kluːɪd] (kloó-id)
Clwyd, River ['kluːɪd] (kloó-id)
Clydach, *Glamorgan* ['klɪdəx] (klíddăch)
Clyde, River [klaɪd] (klīd)
Clydesmuir, Baron ['klaɪdzmjʊər] (klízmyŏŏr)
Clyffe Pypard ['klɪf 'paɪpərd] (klíff pípaard)
Clynder ['klɪndər] (klínder)
Clynderwen [klɪn'dɛərwən] (klindaírwĕn)
Clynnog ['klʌnɒg] (klúnnog)
Clynnogfawr ['klʌnɒg'vaʊər] (klúnnogvówr)
Clypse Circuit, *I.o.M.* [klɪps] (klips)
Clyro ['klaɪroʊ] (klírō)
Clyst, River [klɪst] (klisst)
Clywedog Valley [klɪ'wedɒg] (kliwéddog)
Cnwch Coch ['knux 'koux] (knoóch kóch) *Initial -k is pronounced.*
Coad, f.n. [koʊd] (kōd)

Coade, f.n. [koʊd] (kōd) *Appropriate also for the terra-cotta known as ~ stone, developed in the 18th c. by Mrs. Eleanor ~.*

Coagh [koʊx] (kŏ͞oh)

Coalbrookdale ['koʊlbrʊk'deɪl] (kṓl-brŏŏk-dáyl)

Coalisland [koʊl'aɪlənd] (kōlíland)

Coalsnaughton [koʊlz'nɔtən] (kōlznáw-tŏn)

Coase, f.n. [koʊz] (kōz)

Cobairdy [koʊ'bɛərdɪ] (kōbáírdi)

Cobban, f.n. ['kɒbən] (kóbbăn)

Cobbold, f.n. ['kɒboʊld] kóbbōld) *Appropriate also for Baron ~.*

Coberley ['kʌbərlɪ] (kúbbĕrli)

Coberman, f.n. ['koʊbərmən] (kṓbĕrman)

Cobley, f.n. ['kɒblɪ] (kóbbli)

Cochran, f.n. ['kɒxrən] (kóchrăn); ['kɒkrən] (kóckrăn)

Cochrane, f.n. ['kɒxrən] (kóchrăn); ['kɒkrən] (kóckrăn)

Cockayne, f.n. [kɒ'keɪn] (kockáyn)

Cockbridge ['kɒkbrɪdʒ] (kóck-brij)

Cockburn, f.n. ['koʊbərn] (kṓbŭrn)

Cockburnspath ['koʊbərnzpaθ] (kṓbŭrnzpaath)

Cockcroft, f.n. ['kɒkkrɒft] (kóck-kroft); ['koʊkrɒft] (kṓkroft) *The first is appropriate for Sir John ~, physicist.*

Cockell, f.n. ['kɒkl] (kockl)

Cockenzie [kə'kenzɪ] (kŏkénzi)

Cockerell, f.n. ['kɒkərəl] (kóckĕrĕl)

Cockerington ['kɒkərɪŋtən] (kóckĕring-tŏn)

Cockerline, f.n. ['kɒkərlaɪn] (kóckĕrlĭn)

Cockernhoe ['kɒkərnhoʊ] (kóckĕrn-hō)

Cockett ['kɒkɪt] (kóckĕt)

Cockley Cley ['kɒklɪ 'klaɪ] (kóckli klĭ)

Cockroft, f.n. ['kɒkrɒft] (kóckroft); ['koʊkrɒft] (kṓkroft)

Cocks, f.n. [kɒks] (kocks)

Cockshott, f.n. ['kɒkʃɒt] (kŏ-shot)

Cockshut, f.n. ['kɒkʃʌt] (kóck-shut)

Cockshutt ['kɒkʃʌt] (kóck-shut)

Codicote ['kɒdɪkət] (kóddikŏt)

Codsall ['kɒdsl] (kodssl)

Coe, f.n. [koʊ] (kō)

Coed Camlyn Nature Reserve [kɔɪd 'kæmlɪn] (koyd kámlin)

Coed Dolgarrog [ˌkɔɪd dɒl'gærɒg] (koyd dolgárrog)

Coed-ffranc [kɔɪd'fræŋk] (koydfránk)

Coed Gorswen [ˌkɔɪd gɔrs'wen] (koyd gorss-wén)

Coed Poeth [kɔɪd 'pɔɪθ] (koyd póyth)

Coed Rheidol Nature Reserve [kɔɪd 'hraɪdɒl] (koyd rídol)

Coed Tremadoc Nature Reserve [ˌkɔɪd trɪ'mædɒk] (koyd trĕmádock)

Coed-y-Brenin [ˌkɔɪdə'brenɪn] (koyd-ă-brénnin)

Coedpenmaen [ˌkɔɪdpen'maɪn] (koyd-pen-mín)

Coegnant Colliery ['kɔɪgnænt] (kóyg-nant)

C 4609   C

Coetmore, f.n. ['kɔɪtmɔr] (kóytmor)

Cogan Pill ['koʊgən 'pɪl] (kōgán pĭll)

Cogenhoe, f.n. ['kʊknoʊ] (kŏ͞oknō)

Cogenhoe ['kʊknoʊ] (kŏ͞oknō); ['koʊgən-hoʊ] (kṓgĕn-hō)

Cogers, The, *London inn* ['kɒdʒərz] (kójjĕrz)

Coggeshall, f.n. ['kɒgzɒl] (kógzawl)

Coggeshall ['kɒgɪʃl] (kóggĕshl); ['kɒksl] (kocksl)

Coghill, f.n. ['kɒghɪl] (kóg-hil)

Coghlan, f.n. ['koʊlən] (kṓlăn)

Cogill, f.n. ['koʊgɪl] (kṓgil)

Cogry ['kɒgrɪ] (kógri)

Cohen, f.n. ['koʊɪn] (kṓ-ĕn)

Coinneach Odhar, *the Brahan Seer* ['kɒnjəx 'oʊər] (kón-yăch ṓ-ĕr)

Coity ['kɔɪtɪ] (kóyti)

Coke, f.n. [kʊk] (kŏ͞ok); [koʊk] (kōk) *The first is appropriate for the Earl of Leicester's family name.*

Colan ['kɒlən] (kóllăn)

Colaton Raleigh ['kɒlətən 'rɒlɪ] (kóllătŏn ráwli)

Colborn, f.n. ['koʊbərn] (kṓbŭrn)

Colborne, f.n. ['koʊlbərn] (kṓlbŭrn); ['kɒlbərn] (kólborn)

Colbren ['kɒlbren] (kólbren)

Colbrook ['koʊlbrʊk] (kṓlbrŏŏk)

Colbury ['koʊlbərɪ] (kṓlbŭri)

Colby, f.n. ['kɒlbɪ] (kólbi)

Colbyiathes ['koʊlbɪ'leɪθs] (kṓlbi-láyths)

Colchester ['koʊltʃɪstər] (kṓltchĕster)

Colclough, f.n. ['koʊklɪ] (kṓkli); ['koʊlklʌf] (kṓlkluff)

Cold Hesledon ['koʊld 'hesldən] (kṓld héssldŏn)

Coldred ['koʊldred] (kṓldred)

Coldrick, f.n. ['koʊldrɪk] (kṓldrick)

Coldwaltham ['koʊld'wɒləm] (kṓld-wáwl-thăm)

Coleclough, f.n. ['koʊlklaʊ] (kṓlklow)

Coleford ['koʊlfərd] (kṓlfŏrd)

Colehan, f.n. ['koʊləhən] (kṓlĕhăn)

Colehill ['kɒlhɪl] (kól-hil); ['koʊlhɪl] (kṓl-hil)

Coleman, f.n. ['koʊlmən] (kṓlmăn)

Coleorton [kɒl'ɔrtən] (kolórtŏn)

Coleraine [koʊl'reɪn] (kōlráyn) *Appropriate also for Baron ~.*

Coleridge, f.n. ['koʊlrɪdʒ] (kṓlrij)

Coleridge Taylor, Avril, *composer* ['eɪvrɪl 'koʊlrɪdʒ 'teɪlər] (áyvril kṓlrij táylŏr)

Colerne ['kʌlərn] (kúllĕrn)

Coleshill ['koʊlzhɪl] (kṓlz-hil)

Colintraive ['kɒlɪn'traɪv] (kollintrív)

Collard ['kɒlard] (kóllaard)

Collaro, f.n. [kə'laroʊ] (kŏlaárō)

Colles, f.n. ['kɒlɪs] (kólliss)

Collet, f.n. ['kɒlɪt] (kóllĕt)

Colley, f.n. ['kɒlɪ] (kólli)

Collier, f.n. ['kɒlɪər] (kólli-er)

Collingbourne Ducis ['kɒlɪŋbɔrn 'djuːsɪs] (kólling-born déwsiss)

Collinge, f.n. ['kɒlɪndʒ] (kóllinj)
Collinson, f.n. ['kɒlɪnsən] (kóllinsŏn)
Collison, f.n. ['kɒlɪsən] (kóllissŏn)
Collopy, f.n. ['kɒləpɪ] (kóllŏpi)
Collow, f.n. ['kɒloʊ] (kóllō)
Colman, f.n. ['kɒlmən] (kólmăn); ['koʊlmən] (kṓlmăn)
Colmer, f.n. ['kɒlmər] (kól-mer)
Colmonell [ˌkɒlmɒ'nel] (kolmonnéll)
Colnaghi, London fine art dealers ['koʊlnagɪ] (kṓlnaagi)
Colnbrook ['koʊnbrʊk] (kṓnbrŏŏk); ['koʊlnbrʊk] (kṓlnbrŏŏk)
Colne, f.n. [koʊn] (kōn)
Colne, *Essex, Lancs.* [koʊn] (kōn)
Colne, *River, Yorks.* [koʊn] (kōn) *Appropriate also for the ~ Valley Parliamentary Division.*
Colne Engaine [ˌkoʊn ən'geɪn] (kōn ĕn-gáyn)
Colney ['koʊnɪ] (kṓni)
Colney Heath ['koʊnɪ 'hiθ] (kṓni heéth)
Coln St. Aldwyn ['koʊn snt 'ɒldwɪn] (kṓn sĭnt áwldwin)
Colomb, f.n. ['kɒləm] (kóllŏm)
Colonsay ['kɒlənzeɪ] (kóllŏnzay)
Colquhoun, f.n. [kə'hun] (kŏ-hoṓn)
Colsell, f.n. ['koʊlsl] (kṓlssl)
Colston Basset ['koʊlstən 'bæsɪt] (kṓlstŏn bássĕt)
Coltart, f.n. ['koʊltart] (kṓltaart)
Coltishall ['koʊltɪsəl] (kṓltissál); ['koʊltɪʃl] (kṓltishl); ['koʊltɪsəl] (kṓltissawl); ['koʊlsl] (kṓlssl)
Colum, f.n. ['kɒləm] (kóllŭm)
Colvend [kɒlv'end] (kolvénd)
Colville, f.n. ['kɒlvɪl] (kólvil)
Colville of Culross, Viscount ['kɒlvɪl əv 'kurɒs] (kólvil ŏv koṓ-ross)
Colvin, f.n. ['kɒlvɪn] (kólvin)
Colwall ['kɒlwəl] (kólwăl)
Colwich ['kɒlwɪtʃ] (kólwitch)
Colwick ['kɒlɪk] (kóllick); ['kɒlwɪk] (kólwick)
Colworth ['kɒlwɜrθ] (kólwurth)
Colwyn Bay ['kɒlwɪn 'beɪ] (kólwin báy)
Colyford ['kɒlɪfərd] (kóllifŏrd)
Colyton ['kɒlɪtən] (kóllitŏn) *Appropriate also for Baron ~.*
Coman, f.n. ['koʊmən] (kṓmăn)
Combe, f.n. [kum] (koom); [koʊm] (kōm)
Combe Cross ['kum 'krɒs] (koṓm króss)
Combe in Teignhead ['kum ɪn tɪn'hed] (koṓm in tin-héd)
Comben, f.n. ['kɒmbən] (kómbĕn)
Combepyne *see* Combpyne.
Comber, f.n. ['kɒmbər] (kómber)
Comber ['kʌmbər] (kúmber)
Comberbach ['kʌmberbætʃ] (kúmbĕrbatch)
Combermere, Viscount ['kʌmbərmɪər] (kúmbĕrmeer)
Combermere Barracks ['kʌmbərmɪər] (kúmbĕrmeer); ['kɒmbərmɪər] (kómbĕrmeer)

Comberow ['kumroʊ] (koṓmrō)
Combpyne, *also spelt* Combepyne ['kum'paɪn] (koṓm-pín)
Combrook ['kɒmbrʊk] (kómbrŏŏk)
Combsies ['kumzɪz] (koṓmziz); ['kʌmzɪz] (kúmziz)
Combwich ['kʌmɪdʒ] (kúmmij); ['kʌmɪtʃ] (kúmmitch); ['kumɪdʒ] (koṓmij); ['kumɪtʃ] (koṓmitch)
Comer, f.n. ['koʊmər] (kṓmer)
Comerford, f.n. ['kɒmərfərd] (kómmĕrfŏrd)
Comiston ['kɒmɪstən] (kómmistŏn)
Compton, f.n. ['kʌmptən] (kúmptŏn); ['kɒmptən] (kómptŏn) *The first is correct for the Marquess of Northampton's family name. It is also appropriate for Sir ~ Mackenzie, author; Fay ~, actress; and Denis ~, cricketer.*
Compton-Burnett, Ivy, author ['kʌmptən 'bɜrnɪt] (kúmptŏn búrnĕt)
Compton, *Berks.* ['kɒmptən] (kómptŏn)
Compton, *Hants.* ['kʌmptən] (kúmptŏn)
Compton Castle ['kɒmptən 'kasl] (kómptŏn káassl)
Compton Chamberlayne ['kɒmptən 'tʃeɪmbərlɪn] (kómptŏn cháymbĕrlin)
Compton Down ['kɒmptən 'daʊn] (kómptŏn dówn)
Compton Pauncefoot ['kɒmptən 'pɒnsfʊt] (kómptŏn páwnssfŏŏt)
Compton Valence ['kɒmptən 'væləns] (kómptŏn válénss)
Compton Wynyates, *also spelt* Wyniates, Winyates ['kɒmptən 'wɪnjeɪts]; ['kʌmptən 'wɪnjeɪts] *The first is the local village pronunciation. The second is used appropriately by the Marquess of Northampton for his family seat.*
Comrie, f.n. ['kɒmrɪ] (kómri)
Comrie ['kɒmrɪ] (kómri)
Comyn, f.n. ['kʌmɪn] (kúmmin)
Comyns, f.n. ['kʌmɪnz] (kúmminz)
Conan, f.n. and C.n. ['kɒnən] (kónnăn); ['koʊnan] (kṓnăn)
Conan Doyle, Sir Arthur, author ['koʊnən 'dɔɪl] (kṓnăn dóyl) *This is the family pronunciation, although he is also popularly known as* ['kɒnən] (kónnăn).
Conant, f.n. ['kɒnənt] (kónnănt); ['koʊnənt] (kṓnănt)
Conbeer, f.n. ['kɒnbɪər] (kónbeer)
Concannon, f.n. [kɒn'kænən] (konkánnŏn)
Condicote ['kɒndɪkət] (kóndikŭt)
Condorrat [kən'dɒrət] (kŏndórrăt)
Condover ['kʌndoʊvər] (kúndŏver)
Conesford, Baron ['kɒnɪsfərd] (kónnĕsfŏrd)
Conger Hill ['kɒŋgər] (kóng-ger)
Congresbury ['kɒŋzbrɪ] (kóngzbri); ['kumzbərɪ] (koṓmzbŭri) *The first is the local pronunciation; the other is said to originate in Bristol.*

Conibear, f.n. ['koʊnɪbeər] (kŏnibair)
Coningham,f.n. ['kʌnɪŋəm](kúnning-ăm)
Coningsby ['kɒnɪŋzbɪ] (kónningzbi);
['kʌnɪŋzbɪ] (kúnningzbi)
Conington ['kɒnɪŋtən] (kónning-tŏn)
Conisbee, f.n. ['kɒnɪzbɪ] (kónnizbi)
Conisbrough, *also spelt* **Conisborough**
['kɒnɪsbərə] (kónnissbŭrå)
Coniscliffe, High *and* **Low** ['kɒnɪsklɪf]
(kónniss-kliff)
Conisholme ['kɒnɪshoʊm] (kónnis-
hōm); ['kɒnɪzhoʊm] (kónniz-hōm);
['kɒnɪʃoʊm] (kónni-shōm)
Coniston Water ['kɒnɪstən 'wɔtər]
(kónnistŏn wáwter)
Conlig [kən'lɪg] (kŏnlíg)
Connah's Quay ['kɒnəz 'kiː] (kónnăz keé)
Connaught, *Dukedom of* ['kɒnɔt]
(kónnawt)
Connell, f.n. ['kɒnl] (konnl)
Connelly, f.n. ['kɒnəlɪ] (kónnĕli); [kə-
'nelɪ] (kŏnélli)
Connolly, f.n. ['kɒnəlɪ] (kónnŏli)
Connor ['kɒnər] (kónnŏr)
Connor Downs ['kɒnər 'daʊnz] (kónnŏr
dównz)
Connswater ['kɒnzwɔtər] (kónz-wawter)
Conolly, f.n. ['kɒnəlɪ] (kónnŏli)
Conon ['kɒnən] (kónnŏn)
Consett ['kɒnsɪt] (kónssĕt); ['kɒnset]
(kónsset)
Constable, f.n. ['kʌnstəbl] (kúnstăbl);
['kɒnstəbl] (kónstăbl) *In the absence of
positive evidence about his own usage, the
painter, John ~, is today given either
pronunciation; but it seems possible that
the first was the more likely.*
Constable Burton ['kʌnstəbl 'bɜrtən]
(kúnstăbl búrtŏn)
Constantine, f.n. ['kɒnstəntaɪn] (kón-
stăntīn)
Constantine ['kɒnstəntaɪn] (kónstăntīn)
Contin ['kɒntɪn] (kóntin)
Conway, River ['kɒnweɪ] (kónway)
Conwil Cayo ['kɒnwɪl 'kaɪoʊ] (kónwil
kí-ō)
Conybeare, f.n. ['kɒnɪbɪər] (kónnibeer);
['kʌnɪbɪər] (kúnnibeer)
Conyer ['kʌnjər] (kún-yer); ['kɒnjər]
(kón-yer)
Conyers, f.n. ['kɒnjərz] (kón-yĕrz)
Conyngham, *Marquess* ['kʌnɪŋəm]
(kúnning-ăm)
Cooden ['kudən] (koódĕn); [ku'den]
(koodén)
Cookstown ['kʊkstaʊn] (kŏokstown)
Coolin Hills *see* Cuillin.
Coombs, f.n. [kumz] (koomz)
Coope, f.n. [kup] (koop)
Coopersale ['kupərseɪl] (koópĕrssayl)
Copelin, f.n. ['kɒuplɪn] (kŏplin)
Copestake, f.n. ['kɒpsteɪk] (kópstayk)
Copleston, f.n. ['kɒplstən] (kópplstŏn)
Copley, f.n. ['kɒplɪ] (kópli)
Copped Hall ['kɒpt 'hɔl] (kópt háwl)

Coppela, f.n. ['kɒpɪlə] (kóppĕlå)
Copperashouse ['kɒpərzhaʊs] (kóppĕrz-
howss)
Coppinger, f.n. ['kɒpɪndʒər] (kóppinjer)
Copplestone ['kɒplstən] (kópplstŏn)
Coppull ['kɒpl] (koppl)
Copthall ['kɒptəl] (kóptawl); ['kɒpthɒl]
(kópt-hawl)
Coquet, *River* ['koʊkɪt] (kŏkĕt)
Coquet Island ['koʊkɪt] (kŏkĕt)
Corbally, f.n. ['kɔrbəlɪ] (kórbăli)
Corbally [kɔr'bælɪ] (korbáli)
Corbet, f.n. ['kɔrbɪt] (kórbĕt)
Corbett, f.n. ['kɔrbɪt] (kórbĕt)
Corbishley, f.n. ['kɔrbɪʃlɪ] (kórbishli)
Corbould, f.n. ['kɔrboʊld] (kórbōld)
Corbridge ['kɔrbrɪdʒ] (kórbrij)
Corcoran, f.n. ['kɔrkərən] (kórkŏrăn);
['kɔrkrən] (kórkrăn)
Cordeaux, f.n. ['kɔrdoʊ] (kórdō)
Cordell, f.n. [kɔr'del] (kordéll)
Coren, f.n. ['kɒrən] (kórrĕn)
Corina, f.n. [kə'rinə] (kŏreénă)
Cork and Orrery, *Earl of* ['kɔrk ənd
'ɒrərɪ] (kórk ănd órrĕri)
Corken, f.n. ['kɔrkən] (kórkĕn)
Corkin, f.n. ['kɔrkɪn] (kórkin)
Corlett, f.n. ['kɔrlɪt] (kórlĕt)
Cornhill [kɔrn'hɪl] (korn-híll)
Cornillie, f.n. [kɔr'nɪlɪ] (korneéli)
Cornwall ['kɔrnwəl] (kórnwăl)
Cornwallis, f.n. [kɔrn'wɒlɪs] (korn-
wólliss) *Appropriate also for Baron ~.*
Corpach ['kɔrpəx] (kórpách)
Corpusty ['kɔrpəstɪ] (kórpústi)
Corregan Rocks [kə'regən] (kŏréggăn)
Corrie ['kɒrɪ] (kórri)
Corriehalloch [ˌkɒrɪ'hæləx] (korri-
hálŏch)
Corriemulzie [ˌkɒrɪ'mʌlzɪ] (korri-múlzi)
Corrievreckan [ˌkɒrɪ'vrekən] (korri-
vréckăn)
Corringham ['kɒrɪŋəm] (kórring-ăm)
Corris ['kɒrɪs] (kórriss)
Corrour [kɒ'rʊər] (korroŏr)
Corsellis, f.n. [kɔr'selɪs] (korsséllis)
Corsham ['kɔrʃəm] (kór-shăm)
Corslwyn, f.n. ['kɔrslʊɪn] (kórsslŏŏ-in)
Corstorphine [kɔr'stɔrfɪn] (körsstórfin)
Cors Tregaron Nature Reserve ['kɔrs
trɪ'gærən] (kórss trĕgárrŏn)
Cortachy ['kɔrtaxɪ] (kórtáchi)
Corteen, f.n. [kɔr'tin] (korteén)
Coruisk, Loch [kə'rʊʃk] (kŏroŏshk)
Corvedale, Viscount ['kɔrvdeɪl] (kórv-
dayl)
Corwen ['kɔrwən] (kórwĕn)
Cory, f.n. ['kɔrɪ] (káwri)
Coryton, f.n. ['kɒrɪtən] (kórritŏn)
Coryton ['kɒrɪtən] (kórritŏn)
Coseley ['koʊzlɪ] (kŏzli)
Cosen, Benjamin, *17th-c.* *composer,*
also spelt Cosin, Cosyn ['kʌzən] (kúzzĕn)
Cosens, f.n. ['kʌzənz] (kúzzĕnz)
Cosford ['kɒsfərd] (kóssfŏrd)

Cosham ['kɒsəm] (kóssăm)

Cosin, Benjamin see Cosen.

Cossall ['kɒsl] (kossl)

Cossington ['kæsɪŋtən] (kússingtŏn); ['kæzɪŋtən] (kúzzingtŏn)

Costain, f.n. [kɒs'teɪn] (kostáyn)

Costello, f.n. [kə'steloʊ] (kŏstéllō); ['kɒstəloʊ] (kóstĕlō)

Costelloe, f.n. ['kɒstəloʊ] (kóstĕlō)

Costessey ['kɒsi] (kóssi)

Costin, f.n. ['kɒstɪn] (kóstin)

Coston ['koʊsn] (kóssŏn)

Coswinsawson [ˌkɒzwɪn'sɒsən] (kozwin-sáwssŏn); [kə'zɒsən] (kŏzáwssŏn)

Cosyn, Benjamin see Cosen.

Cotehele [kə'til] (kŏteél); [kət'hil] (kŏtheél)

Cotesbach ['koʊtsbætʃ] (kótsbatch)

Cotgrave ['kɒtɡreɪv] (kótgrayv)

Cotham ['kɒtəm] (kóttăm)

Cothay, f.n. ['koʊθeɪ] (kó-thay)

Cothelstone ['kʌɒlstən] (kúthlstŏn); ['kɒtlstən] (kóttlstŏn)

Cotheridge ['kɒðərɪdʒ] (kóthĕrij)

Cotherstone ['kʌðərstən] (kúthĕrstŏn)

Cothi, River ['kɒθi] (kóthi)

Cothill ['kɒt'hɪl] (kót-híll)

Cotmanhay ['kɒtmənheɪ] (kótmăn-hay)

Coton, f.n. ['koʊtən] (kótŏn)

Coton ['koʊtən] (kótŏn)

Cotswolds, The ['kɒtswoʊldz] (kóttswōldz)

Cottell, f.n. [kə'til] (kŏteél)

Cottenham, *Earl of* ['kɒtnəm] (kót-năm)

Cottesbrooke ['kɒtɪsbrʊk] (kóttĕsbrŏŏk)

Cottesloe, Baron ['kɒtsloʊ] (kótslō)

Cottesmore ['kɒtsmɔr] (kóttsmor)

Cottrell, f.n. ['kɒtrəl] (kóttrĕl); [kə'trel] (kŏtréll)

Couch, f.n. [kutʃ] (kootch)

Coucher, f.n. ['kaʊtʃər] (kówtcher)

Couchman, f.n. ['kuʃmən] (koóshmăn)

Coughlan, f.n. ['kɒxlən] (kóchlăn); ['kɒɡlən] (kóglán)

Coughlin, f.n. ['kɒxlɪn] (kóchlin); ['kɒɡlɪn] (kóglin)

Coughton, *Hereford.* ['koʊtən] (kótŏn)

Coughton, *Warwick.* ['koʊtən] (kótŏn); ['kaʊtən] (kówtŏn) *The first is usual for the National Trust property of ~ Court.*

Coughtrey, f.n. ['kaʊtrɪ] (kówtri); ['kɒtrɪ] (káwtri); ['kutrɪ] (koótri); ['koʊtrɪ] (kótri); ['kɒftrɪ] (kófftri)

Coughtrie, f.n. ['kɒftrɪ] (kófftri)

Coul [kul] (kool)

Coulcher, f.n. ['kultʃər] (koóltcher)

Couldrey, f.n. ['kuldrɪ] (koóldri); ['kuldreɪ] (koóldray); ['koʊldrɪ] (kóldri)

Couldry, f.n. ['kuldrɪ] (koóldri)

Couldwell, f.n. ['kuldwel] (kóldwel)

Coull, *Aberdeen., Fife* [kul] (kool)

Coulling, f.n. ['kulɪŋ] (koóling)

Coulman, f.n. ['koʊlmən] (kólmăn)

Coulport ['kulpɔrt] (koólport)

Coulsdon ['koʊlzdən] (kólzdŏn); ['kulzdən] (koólzdŏn)

Coulshaw, f.n. ['kulʃə] (koól-shaw)

Coulson, f.n. ['koʊlsən] (kólssŏn); ['kulsən] (koólssŏn)

Coulston, f.n. ['kulstən] (koólstŏn)

Coult, f.n. [koʊlt] (kōlt); [kult] (koolt)

Coulter, f.n. ['kultər] (koólter); ['koʊltər] (kólter)

Coulthard ['kultɑrd] (koóltaard); ['koʊlθɑrd] (kól-thaard)

Coulton, f.n. ['koʊltən] (kóltŏn)

Councell, f.n. ['kaʊnsl] (kownssl)

Coundon ['kaʊndən] (kówndŏn)

Counihan, f.n. ['kunɪhən] (koónihăn)

Countess Wear ['kaʊntɪs 'wɪər] (kówntĕss weér)

Countisbury ['kaʊntɪsbərɪ] (kówntissbŭri)

Coupar Angus [ˌkupər 'æŋɡəs] (koopăr áng-gŭss)

Coupe, f.n. [kup] (koop)

Couper, f.n. ['kupər] (koóper)

Coupland, f.n. ['kuplənd] (koóplănd); ['koʊplənd] (kóplănd)

Coupland ['kuplənd] (koóplănd); ['koʊplənd] (kóplănd)

Coupland Beck ['koʊplənd 'bek] (kóplănd béck)

Courtauld, f.n. ['kɔrtoʊ] (kórtō); ['kɔrtoʊld] (kórtōld) *Although the first is the pronunciation of the late Samuel ~'s family, the latter is now invariably used for the ~ Institutes and for the firm of ~s Ltd.*

Courtenay, f.n. ['kɔrtnɪ] (kórtni)

Courthope, f.n. ['kɔrθoʊp] (kórt-hōp); ['kɔrtoʊp] (kórtōp) *The first is appropriate for the Barony of ~.*

Courtney, f.n. ['kɔrtnɪ] (kórtni)

Courtown, Earl of ['kɔrtaʊn] (kórtown)

Cousens, f.n. ['kʌzənz] (kúzzĕnz)

Couser, f.n. ['kaʊzər] (kówzer)

Cousland, f.n. ['kaʊzlænd] (kówzland)

Cousland ['kaʊzlənd] (kówzlănd)

Coutts, f.n. [kuts] (koots)

Couzens, f.n. ['kʌzənz] (kúzzĕnz)

Cove, f.n. [koʊv] (kŏv)

Covehithe ['koʊv'haɪð] (kŏv-hfth)

Coveley, f.n. ['koʊvəlɪ] (kóvĕli)

Covell, f.n. [koʊ'vel] (kōvéll); [kə'vel] (kŏvéll)

Coven, f.n. ['koʊvən] (kóvĕn)

Coven ['koʊvən] (kóvĕn)

Coveney, f.n. ['koʊvənɪ] (kóvĕni)

Coveney ['koʊvnɪ] (kóv-ni)

Covenham ['koʊvənəm] (kóvĕnăm)

Covenhope ['kɒnəp] (kónnŏp); ['koʊvənhoʊp] (kóvĕn-hōp)

Covent Garden ['kɒvənt 'ɡɑrdən] (kóvvĕnt gaárdĕn); ['kʌvənt] (kúvvĕnt)

Coventry, f.n. ['kʌvəntrɪ] kúvvĕntri); ['kɒvəntrɪ] (kóvvĕntri)

Coventry

Coventry ['kɒvəntrɪ] (kóvvĕntri); ['kʌvəntrɪ] (kúvvĕntri) *The first is appropriate for the Earl of ~. The second, however, is commonly used in the expression, 'to send someone to ~'.*

Coverack ['kʌvəræk] (kúvvĕrack); ['kɒvəræk] (kóvvĕrack)

Covington, f.n. ['kɒvɪŋtən] (kóvvĭngtŏn)

Cowal ['kauəl] (kówăl); [kaul] (kowl)

Coward, f.n. ['kauəd] (kówărd)

Cowbit ['kʌbɪt] (kúbbit)

Cowbridge ['kaubrɪdʒ] (kówbrij)

Cowcher, f.n. ['kautʃər] (kówtcher)

Cowden ['kauden] (kowdén)

Cowdenbeath [ˌkaudən'biθ] (kowdĕn-beéth)

Cowderoy, f.n. ['kaudərɔɪ] (kówdĕroy)

Cowdray, Viscount ['kaudrɪ] (kówdri)

Cowell, f.n. ['kauəl] (kówĕl); ['kouəl] (kṓ-ĕl)

Cowen, f.n. ['kauɪn] (kówĕn); ['kouɪn] (kṓ-ĕn)

Cowie, f.n. ['kauɪ] (kówi)

Cowin, f.n. ['kauɪn] (kówin)

Cowlairs ['kau'leərz] (ków-laírz)

Cowles, f.n. [kaulz] (kowlz); [koulz] (kōlz)

Cowley, *Oxon.* ['kaulɪ] (kówli)

Cowley, *Yorks.* ['kaulɪ] (kówli); ['koulɪ] (kṓli)

Cowling, *Lancs.* ['kaulɪŋ] (kówling); ['koulɪŋ] (kṓling)

Cowling, *Yorks.* ['koulɪŋ] (kṓling)

Cowlinge ['kulɪndʒ] (koólinj)

Cowpe [kaup] (kowp)

Cowpen ['kupən] (koópĕn)

Cowpen Bewley ['kupən 'bjulɪ] (koópĕn béwli)

Cowper, f.n. ['kupər] (koóper); ['kaupər] (kówper) *The first is appropriate for the 18th-c. poet, William ~.*

Cowper Powys, John, author ['kupər 'pouɪs] (koóper pṓ-iss)

Cowplain ['kaupleɪn] (kówplayn)

Cowsill, f.n. ['kauzɪl] (kówzil)

Cowtan, f.n. ['kautən] (kówtăn)

Coxe, f.n. [kɒks] (kocks)

Coyne, f.n. [kɔɪn] (koyn)

Coytrahen [ˌkɔɪtrə'heɪən] (koytră-háy-ĕn)

Cozens, f.n. ['kʌzənz] (kúzzĕnz)

Cozens-Hardy, Baron ['kʌzənz 'hardɪ] (kúzzĕnz haárdi)

Craddock, f.n. ['krædək] (krádŏck)

Cradley, *Hereford.* ['krædlɪ] (krádli)

Cradley, *Worcs.* ['kreɪdlɪ] (kráydli)

Cradley Heath ['kreɪdlɪ 'hiθ] (kráydli heéth)

Cradock, f.n. ['krædək] (krádŏck); ['kreɪdɒk] (kráydock)

Craen, f.n. [kreɪn] (krayn)

Crafthole ['krafθoul] (kraáft-hōl)

Crag Lough ['kræg 'lɒf] (krág lóff)

Craigani Point [kreɪ'ɡanɪ] (kraygaáni)

Craigantlet [kreɪg'æntlət] (kraygántlĕt)

Craigavad [ˌkreɪɡə'væd] (kraygávád)

Craigavon [kreɪɡ'ævən] (kraygávvŏn) *Appropriate also for Viscount ~.*

Craig Cerrig Gleisiad Nature Reserve ['kraɪɡ 'kerɪɡ 'ɡlaɪsɪæd] (kríg kérrig glíssi-ad)

Craigellachie [kreɪ'ɡeləxɪ] (kraygéllǎchi)

Craigendoran [ˌkreɪɡən'dɒrən] (kraygĕndórrán)

Craigie, f.n. ['kreɪɡɪ] (kráygi)

Craigie ['kreɪɡɪ] (kráygi)

Craiglockhart [kreɪg'lɒkərt] (krayglóckárt)

Craiglour - Achin [kreɪg'laurəxɪn] (krayglówrǎchin) *also written* Craig Lowrigan, *and pronounced* [kreɪg 'laurɪɡən] (krayg lówrigán)

Craignure [kreɪg'njuər] (krayg-nyoór)

Craig-ny-Baa, *I.o.M., also spelt* **Cregny-Baa** ['kreɪg nɪ 'ba] (kráyg-ni-baá)

Craig Willies Hill [kreɪg 'wɪlɪz] (krayg wílliz)

Craig-y-Deryn [ˌkraɪɡ ə 'derɪn] (kríg-ă-dérrin)

Craig-y-Llyn [ˌkraɪɡ'ə 'ɬɪn] (kríg-ă-ḥlín)

Craig-y-Nos [ˌkraɪɡə'nous] (kríɡǎnṓss)

Crail [kreɪl] (krayl)

Cramond ['kræmənd] (krámmŏnd)

Cranagh ['krænə] (kránnǎ)

Crank ny Mona, *I.o.M.* ['kræŋk nɪ 'mounə] (kránk ni mṓnǎ)

Cranleighan, one educated at Cranleigh School ['kræn'liən] (kranleé-ăn)

Crarae ['krærɪ] (krárri)

Crashaw, Richard, 17th-c. poet ['kræʃɔ] (kráshaw)

Crask of Aigas ['kræʃk əv 'eɪɡəʃ] (kráshk ŏv áygǎsh)

Craske, f.n. [krask] (kraask)

Craster, f.n. ['krastər] (kraáster)

Crathes ['kræθɪz] (kráthĕz)

Crathie ['kræθɪ] (kráthi)

Crathorn, f.n. ['kreɪθɔrn] (kráy-thorn)

Crathorne, Baron ['kreɪθɔrn] (kráy-thorn)

Crauford, f.n. ['krɔfərd] (kráwfŏrd)

Craven Arms ['kreɪvən 'armz] (kráyvĕn aármz)

Crawford and Balcarres, Earl of ['krɔfərd ənd bæl'kærɪs] (kráwfŏrd ánd balkárrĕss)

Crawght, f.n. [krɔt] (krawt)

Crawhall, f.n. [krə'hɒl] (krǎ-háwl)

Crawley, f.n. ['krɔlɪ] (kráwli)

Crawshaw, f.n. ['krɔʃo] (kráw-shaw)

Crawshay, f.n. ['krɔʃeɪ] (kráw-shay)

Crawt, f.n. [krɔt] (krawt)

Crayford ['kreɪfərd] (kráyfŏrd)

Creacombe ['krikəm] (kreékŏm)

Creagan ['kriɡən] (kreégăn)

Creagh, f.n. [kreɪ] (kráy)

Creaghan, f.n. ['kriɡən] (kreégăn)

Creak, f.n. [krik] (kreek)

Crean, f.n. [krin] (kreen)

Creaney, f.n. ['krinɪ] (kreéni)

Creasy, f.n. ['krisɪ] (kreéssi)
Creaton, Great *and* Little ['kritən] (kreétŏn)
Creber, f.n. ['kribər] (kreéber)
Crebilly [krə'bɪlɪ] (krĕbílli)
Credenhill ['kredənhɪl] (kréddĕnhil); ['kridənhɪl] (kreédĕnhil)
Crediton ['kredɪtən] (krédditŏn)
Cree, f.n. [kri] (kree)
Crees, f.n. [kriz] (kreez)
Creese, f.n. [kris] (kreess)
Creetown ['kritaʊn] (kreétown)
Cregagh ['kreɪɡə] (kráygă)
Cregeen, f.n. [krɪ'dʒin] (krĕjeén)
Cregneish [kreg'niʃ] (kreg-neésh)
Creg-ny-Baa *see* Craig-ny-Baa.
Crehan, f.n. ['kriən] (kreé-ăn)
Creich [krix] (kreech)
Creighton, f.n. ['kraɪtən] (krítŏn); ['kreɪtən] (kráytŏn)
Creigiau ['kraɪɡjaɪ] (kríg-yī)
Cremer, f.n. ['krimər] (kreémer)
Cremyll ['kremɪl] (krémmil)
Creran, Loch ['krɪərən] (kreérăn)
Crerar, f.n. ['krɛərər] (kraírăr); ['krɪərər] (kreérăr)
Creswell, f.n. ['krezwəl] (krézwĕl)
Creswell, *Derby.* ['kreswel] (krésswel); ['kreswəl] (krésswĕl)
Creswick, f.n. ['krezɪk] (krézzick)
Creunant, *also spelt* Crynant ['kraɪnənt] (krínănt)
Crevenagh ['krevənə] (krévvĕnă)
Crewkerne ['krukɜrn] (króokern)
Crianlarich [ˌkriən'lærɪx] (kreeănlárrich)
Cribbett, f.n. ['krɪbɪt] (kríbbĕt)
Crib-Goch ['krib 'gɒx] (kreéb góch)
Crib-y-Ddysgl [ˌkrib ə 'ðɪskl] (kreeb ă thískl)
Cribyn ['krɪbɪn] (kreébin)
Criccieth ['krɪkɪəθ] (krícki-ĕth)
Crich [kraɪtʃ] (krītch)
Crichel Down ['krɪtʃl 'daʊn] (krítchl dówn)
Crichton, f.n. ['kraɪtən] (krítŏn)
Crickadarn [krɪk'kædərn] (krickáddărn)
Cricket Malherbie ['krɪkɪt 'mælərbɪ] (kríckĕt málĕrbi)
Crickhowell [krɪk'haʊəl] (krick-hówĕl)
Crieff [krif] (kreef)
Crier, f.n. ['kraɪər] (krí-er)
Criggion ['krɪɡjɒn] (kríg-yon)
Crighton, f.n. ['kraɪtən] (krítŏn)
Crimond ['krɪmənd] (krímmŏnd)
Crimplesham ['krɪmplʃəm] (krímplshăm)
Crinan ['krɪnən] (krínnăn)
Cringleford ['krɪŋɡlfərd] (kríng-gifŏrd)
Cringletie [krɪŋ'letɪ] (kring-létti)
Crisell, f.n. [krɪ'sel] (krisséll)
Crisp, f.n. [krɪsp] (krisp)
Critchley, f.n. ['krɪtʃlɪ] (krítchli)
Crittall, f.n. ['krɪtəl] (kríttawl)
Croal, River [kroʊl] (krōl)

Croall, f.n. [kroʊl] (krōl)
Croan, f.n. [kroʊn] (krōn)
Croasdell, f.n. ['kroʊzdel] (krōzdel)
Crockernwell ['krɒkərnwel] (króckĕrnwel)
Crocketford ['krɒkɪtfərd] (króckĕtfŏrd)
Croesfaen [krɔɪs'vaɪn] (kroyss-vín)
Croesor ['krɔɪsər] (króyssor)
Croesyceiliog [ˌkrɔɪsə'kaɪljɒɡ] (kroyssăkíl-yog)
Croghan, f.n. ['kroʊən] (krō-ăn)
Croham Hurst ['kroʊəm 'hɜrst] (krō-ăm húrst)
Croke, f.n. [kroʊk] (krōōk)
Crom [krɒm] (kromm)
Cromac ['krʌmək] (krúmmăk)
Cromartie, Earl of ['krɒmərtɪ] (krómmărti)
Cromarty ['krɒmərtɪ] (krómmărti)
Crombie, f.n. ['krɒmbɪ] (krómbi); ['krʌmbɪ] (krúmbi)
Crome, f.n. [kroʊm] (krōm)
Cromer ['kroʊmər] (krōmer) *Appropriate also for the Earl of* ∼.
Cromey, f.n. ['krʌmɪ] (krúmmi)
Cromford ['krɒmfərd] (krómfŏrd)
Cromie, f.n. ['kroʊmɪ] (krōmi)
Cromlech ['krʌmlex] (krúmlĕch)
Crommelin, f.n. ['krʌmlɪn] (krúmlin)
Crompton, Samuel, inventor of weaving-shuttle ['krɒmptən] (krómptŏn)
Crondall ['krʌndl] (krundl); ['krɒndl] (krondl)
Cronin, f.n. ['kroʊnɪn] (krōnin)
Crookating ['krʊkətɪŋ] (króŏkáting)
Crook of Devon ['krʊk əv 'devən] (króŏk ŏv dévvŏn)
Croome d'Abitot ['krum 'dæbɪtoʊ] (kroóm dábbitō)
Cropredy ['krɒprədɪ] (króprĕdi)
Crosby ['krɒzbɪ] (krózbi)
Crosier, f.n. ['kroʊʒər] (krōzher); ['kroʊzɪər] (krōzi-er)
Crosland, f.n. ['krɒslənd] (krósslănd)
Crossbychan [krɒs'bʌxən] (krossbúchăn)
Crossgar [krɒs'ɡɑr] (krossgaár)
Crosshill ['krɒs'hɪl] (króss-híll)
Crossmaglen [ˌkrɒsmə'ɡlen] (krossmăglén)
Crossmyloof [ˌkrɒsmɪ'luf] (krossmiloóf)
Crosthwaite-Eyre, f.n. ['krɒsθweɪt 'ɛər] (króss-thwayt aír)
Crostwick ['krɒstwɪk] (króst-wick); ['krɒstɪk] (króstick); ['krɒsɪk] (króssick)
Crothers, f.n. ['krʌðərz] (krúthĕrz)
Crouch, f.n. [kraʊtʃ] (krowtch)
Crouch [krutʃ] (krootch)
Croucher, f.n. ['kraʊtʃər] (krówtcher)
Croughton ['kroʊtən] (krótŏn)
Crow, f.n. [kroʊ] (krō)
Crowan ['kraʊən] (krówăn)
Crowcombe ['kroʊkəm] (krókŏm)
Crowcroft, f.n. ['kroʊkrɒft] (krókroft)
Crowden, f.n. ['kraʊdən] (krówdĕn)

Crowden ['kroʊdən] (krṓděn)
Crowder, f.n. ['kraʊdər] (krówder)
Crowdy, f.n. ['kraʊdɪ] (krówdi)
Crowe, f.n. [kroʊ] (krṓ)
Crowest, f.n. ['kroʊɪst] (krṓ-ĕst)
Crowlas ['kraʊləs] (krówlăss)
Crowle, Lincs. [kroʊl] (krōl); [krul] (krool)
Crowle, Worcs. [kroʊl] (krōl); [kraʊl] (krowl)
Crowley, f.n. ['kroʊlɪ] (krṓli)
Crows-an-Wra ['kraʊzənreɪ] (krówzăn-ray)
Crowson, Lamar, pianist [lə'mɑr 'kraʊsən] (lămaár krówssŏn)
Crowther, f.n. ['kraʊðər] (krówther)
Croxdale ['krɒksdəl] (krócksdăl)
Croxton, Lincs. ['krɒkstən] (króckstŏn); ['kroʊsən] (krṓssŏn)
Croxton, Norfolk ['krɒkstən] (króckstŏn)
Croxton, South, Leics. ['kroʊsən] (krṓssŏn); ['kroʊstən] (krṓsstŏn); ['kroʊzən] (krṓzŏn)
Croxton Kerrial ['kroʊsən 'kerɪəl] (krṓssŏn kérriăl)
Croyland ['kroʊlənd] (krṓlănd)
Crozier, f.n. ['kroʊzɪər] (krózi-er); ['kroʊʒər] (krṓzher)
Cruachan, Falls of ['kruəxən] (kroó-ăchăn)
Cruchley, f.n. ['krʌtʃlɪ] (krútchli)
Cruddas, f.n. ['krʌdəs] (krúddáss)
Cruden Bay ['krudən 'beɪ] (kroóděn báy)
Crudwell ['krʌdwel] (krúdwĕl)
Crug-y-Bar [ˌkrig ə 'bɑr] (kreeg ă baár)
Crug-y-Byddar [ˌkrig ə 'bʌðər] (kreeg ă búthǎr)
Cruickshank, f.n. ['krʊkʃæŋk] (kroŏk-shank)
Cruikshank, f.n. ['krʊkʃæŋk] (kroŏk-shank)
Crum, f.n. [krʌm] (krum)
Crumlin, Co. Antrim, Monmouth. ['krʌmlɪn] (krúmlin)
Crunwere ['krʌnwɛər] (krúnwair)
Crutwell, f.n. ['krʌtwəl] (krútwĕl)
Cruwys Morchard ['kruz 'mɔrtʃərd] (kroóz mórtchárd)
Crwys, Welsh C.n. ['kruɪs] (kroó-iss)
Crwys ['kruɪs] (kroó-iss)
Cryer, f.n. ['kraɪər] (krí-er)
Crymmych ['krʌmɪx] (krúmmich)
Crynant see Creunant.
Crysell, f.n. ['kraɪsl] (kríssl)
Cubert ['kjubərt] (kéwbĕrt)
Cubitt, f.n. ['kjubɪt] (kéwbit)
Cuchullin Hills see Cuillin.
Cuckfield ['kʊkfild] (koŏkfeeld)
Cuckmere ['kʊkmɪər] (koŏkmeer)
Cuckney ['kʌknɪ] (kúckni)
Cucksey, f.n. ['kʊksɪ] (koŏksi)
Cuckston, f.n. ['kʊkstən] (koŏkstŏn)
Cuddeford, f.n. ['kʌdɪfərd] (kúddĕford)
Cuddesdon ['kʌdzdən] (kúdzdŏn)
Cuffe, f.n. [kʌf] (kuff)

Cuillin Hills, also spelt Coolin, Cuchullin ['kulɪn] (koólin)
Culbone ['kʌlboʊn] (kúlbōn)
Culcavey [kəl'keɪvɪ] (kŭlkáyvi)
Culcheth ['kʌltʃəθ] (kúltchĕth)
Culdrose [kʌl'droʊz] (kuldrōz)
Culduthel [kʌl'dʌθl] (kuldúthl)
Culf, f.n. [kʌlf] (kulf)
Culgaith [kʌl'geɪθ] (kulgáyth); [kʊl'geɪθ] (koŏlgáyth)
Culham ['kʌləm] (kúllăm)
Culhane, f.n. [kʌl'heɪn] (kul-háyn)
Culkein ['kʊlkeɪn] (koŏlkayn)
Cullamore [ˌkʌlə'mɔr] (kullámór)
Cullavoe see Cullivoe.
Cullen, f.n. ['kʌlən] (kúllĕn)
Cullen ['kʌlən] (kúllĕn)
Cullercoats ['kʌlərkoʊts] (kúllĕrkōts)
Cullinan, f.n. ['kʌlɪnən] (kúllinán)
Cullivoe, also spelt Cullavoe ['kʌlɪvoʊ] (kúllivō)
Culloden [kə'lɒdən] (kŭlóddĕn); [kə'loʊdən] (kŭlṓdĕn)
Cullompton ['kʌləmptən] (kúllŏmptŏn); [kə'lʌmptən] (kŭlámptŏn)
Cullybackey [ˌkʌlɪ'bækɪ] (kullibácki)
Culm [kʌlm] (kulm)
Culme-Seymour, f.n. ['kʌlm 'siɱɔr] (kúlm seémor)
Culmstock ['kʌlmstɒk] (kúlm-stock)
Culnady [kəl'nædɪ] (kŭlnáddi)
Culpeper, f.n. ['kʌlpepər] (kúll-pepper)
Culross, f.n. ['kʌlrɒs] (kúlross)
Culross ['kurəs] (koó-rŏss)
Culsalmond [kʌl'sæmənd] (kul-sámmŏnd)
Culter, Aberdeen., Lanark. ['kutər] (koóter)
Cultra [kəl'trɒ] (kŭltráw)
Cults, Aberdeen., Fife [kʌlts] (kults)
Culzean Castle [kə'leɪn] (kŭláyn)
Cumberbeach, f.n. ['kʌmbərbɪtʃ] (kúmbĕrbeetch)
Cumberland ['kʌmbərlənd] (kúmbĕrlănd)
Cumbernauld [ˌkʌmbər'nɒld] (kumbĕrnáwld)
Cumbrae, Great and Little ['kʌmbreɪ] (kúmbray)
Cumdivock [kʌm'dɪvək] (kumdívvŏk)
Cumine, f.n. ['kʌmɪn] (kúmmin)
Cuminestown ['kʌmɪnztaʊn] (kúmminz-town)
Cuming Museum, London ['kʌmɪŋ] (kúmming)
Cummertrees ['kʌmər'triz] (kúmmĕr-treéz)
Cumnock ['kʌmnək] (kúmnŏk)
Cumnor ['kʌmnər] (kúmnŏr)
Cumrew [kʌm'ru] (kumroó); [ˌkʌmrɪ'u] (kumri-oó)
Cumwhinton [kʌm'hwɪntən] (kum-whín-tŏn)
Cunard, f.n. [kju'nɑrd] (kewnaárd)
Cundell, f.n. ['kʌndl] (kundl)

Cuneo, Terence, *painter* ['kjuniou] (kéwniŏ)

Cuningham, *f.n.* ['kʌnɪŋəm] (kúnningăm)

Cuninghame, *f.n.* ['kʌniŋəm] (kúnningăm)

Cunliffe, *f.n.* ['kʌnlɪf] (kúnlif)

Cunningham of Hyndhope, *Viscountcy of* ['kʌnɪŋəm əv 'haɪndhoup] (kúnningăm ŏv hínd-hōp)

Cunobelin, *ancient king, also spelt* **Cunobeline** [ku'nɒbəlɪn] (koŏnóbbĕlin)

Cunynghame, *f.n.* ['kʌnɪŋəm] (kúnningăm)

Cupar ['kupər] (koŏpăr)

Cupit, *f.n.* ['kjupɪt] (kéwpit)

Curgenven, *f.n.* [kər'genvən] (kŭrgénvĕn); [kər'gɪnvən] (kŭrgínvĕn)

Curigwen, *Welsh C.n.* [kə'rɪgwen] (kŭrígwen)

Curle, *f.n.* [kɜrl] (kurl)

Curraghmore [ˌkʌrə'mɔr] (kurrămór)

Curran, *f.n.* ['kʌrən] (kúrrăn)

Currell, *f.n.* ['kʌrəl] (kúrrĕl)

Currie ['kʌri] (kúrri)

Curry Rivel ['kʌri 'raɪvl] (kúrri rívl)

Cursiter, *f.n.* ['kɜrsɪtər] (kúrssiter)

Cursley, *f.n.* ['kɜrzli] (kúrzli)

Cursue, *f.n.* [kɜr'sju] (kursséw)

Curteis, *f.n.* ['kɜrtɪs] (kúrtiss)

Curthoys, *f.n.* [kɜr'tɔɪz] (kurtóyz); [kɜr'θɔɪz] (kur-thóyz); ['kɜrθɔɪz] (kúrthoyz)

Curtois, *f.n.* ['kɜrtɔɪz] (kúrtoyz); ['kɜrtɪs] (kúrtiss)

Cury ['kjʊəri] (kyoŏri)

Cury Cross ['kjʊəri 'krɒs] (kyoŏri króss)

Cury Hunt ['kjʊəri] (kyoŏri)

Curzon, *Viscount* ['kɜrzən] (kúrzŏn)

Cusack, *f.n.* ['kjusæk] (kéwssack)

Cusgarne [kəz'garn] (kŭzgaárn)

Cush, *f.n.* [kʊʃ] (koŏsh)

Cushendall [ˌkʊʃən'dɔl] (koŏshĕndáwl)

Cushendun, *Barony of* [ˌkʌʃən'dʌn] (kushĕndún)

Cushendun [ˌkʊʃən'dʌn] (koŏshĕndún)

Cushine, *f.n.* ['kʊʃaɪn] (koŏshín)

Cushing, *f.n.* ['kʊʃɪŋ] (koŏshing)

Cutforth, *f.n.* ['kʌtfɔrθ] (kútforth)

Cuthbe, *f.n.* ['kʌθbɪ] (kúthbi)

Cuthill, *f.n.* ['kʌθɪl] (kúth-il)

Cutner, *f.n.* ['kʌtnər] (kútner)

Cuttell, *f.n.* [kə'tel] (kŭtéll)

Cuttress, *f.n.* ['kʌtrɪs] (kúttrĕss)

Cuxham ['kʊksəm] (koŏksăm); ['kʌksəm] (kúcksăm)

Cuxwold ['kʌkswoʊld] (kúckswōld)

Cuyler, *f.n.* ['kaɪlər] (kíler)

Cwm [kʊm] (koŏm)

Cwm Avon [kʊm 'ævən] (koŏm ávvŏn)

Cwm Ffrwd [kum 'frud] (koŏm froŏd)

Cwm Idwal Nature Reserve [kʊm 'ɪdwəl] (koŏm ídwăl)

Cwm Prysor [kʊm 'prʌsor] (koŏm prússor)

Cwm Silyn [kʊm 'sɪlɪn] (koŏm síllin)

Cwm Tryweryn [ˌkʊm trɪ'werɪn] (koŏm tri-wérrin)

Cwm-yr-Eglwys [ˌkʊm ər 'eglʊɪs] (koŏm-ŭr-églŏiss)

Cwmaman [kʊm'æmən] (koŏmámmăn)

Cwmamman [kʊm'æmən] (koŏmámmăn)

Cwmann [kʊm'æn] (koŏmán)

Cwmannogisaf [kʊm'ænɒg'ɪsæv] (koŏmánnog-íssav)

Cwmbach [kʊm'bax] (koŏmbaách)

Cwmbran [kʊm'brɑn] (koŏmbraán)

Cwmbwrla [kʊm'bʊərlə] (koŏmboŏrlă)

Cwmcarn [kʊm'karn] (koŏmkaárn)

Cwmcelyn [kʊm'kelɪn] (koŏmkéllin)

Cwmclydach [kʊm'klɪdəx] (koŏmklíddăch)

Cwmcothi [kʊm'kɒθɪ] (koŏmkóthi)

Cwmdare [kʊm'dɛər] (koŏmdaír)

Cwmdu [kʊm'di] (koŏm-deé)

Cwmfelin [kʊm'velɪn] (koŏmvéllin)

Cwmfelinfach [kʊmˌvelɪn'vax] (koŏmvellinvaách)

Cwmffrwdoer [ˌkʊmfrud'ɔɪər] (koŏmfroodóyr)

Cwmgiedd [kʊm'gɪəð] (koŏmgee-ĕth)

Cwmgors [kʊm'gɔrs] (koŏmgórss)

Cwmgwrach [kʊm'gwrax] (koŏmgwraách); [kʊm'grax] (koŏmgraách). *Welsh speakers pronounce 'gwrach' as one syllable by treating the 'w' as a rounding of the lips to accompany the 'r'.*

Cwmllynfell [kʊm'ɬʌnveɬ] (koŏm-hlúnvehl)

Cwmmawr [kʊm'maʊər] (koŏm-mówr)

Cwmparc [kʊm'park] (koŏmpaárk)

Cwmpennar [kʊm'penər] (koŏmpénnăr)

Cwmrheidol [kʊm'ʰraɪdɒl] (koŏmrhídol)

Cwmstradllyn [kʊm'stræd⁴ɪn] (koŏmstrádhlin)

Cwmsyflog [kʊm'sɪvjɒg] (koŏmssív-yog)

Cwmtillery [ˌkʊmtɪ'lɛəri] (koŏmtiláiri)

Cwmtwrch [kʊm'tʊərx] (koŏmtoŏrch)

Cwmyglo [ˌkʊmə'glou] (koŏmágló)

Cwmyoy [kʊm'jɔɪ] (koŏm-yóy)

Cwmystwyth [kʊm'ʌstwɪθ] (koŏmústwith)

Cyfarthfa [kə'varθə] (kŭvaárth-vă)

Cyfeiliog [kə'vaɪljɒg] (kŭvíl-yog)

Cyfoeth-y-Brenin ['kʌvɔɪθ ə 'brenɪn] (kúvvoyth ă brénnin)

Cyfronydd [kə'vrɒnɪð] (kŭvrónnith)

Cymau ['kʌmaɪ] (kúmmī)

Cymmer ['kʌmər] (kúmmer)

Cymmrodorion Society, *London Welsh society* [ˌkʌmrə'dɒrɪən] (kumrŏdórri-ŏn)

Cynan, *Welsh C.n.* ['kʌnən] (kúnnăn)

Cyncoed [kɪn'kɔɪd] (kin-kóyd)

Cynddylan, *Welsh C.n.* [kʌn'ðʌlən] (kun-thúllăn)

Cynghordy [kʌŋ'hərdɪ] (kung-hórdi)

Cynlais ['kʌnlaɪs] (kúnlíss)

Cynog ['kʌnɒg] (kúnnog)

Cynon, *River* ['kʌnən] (kúnnŏn)

Cynric, *Welsh C.n.* ['kʌnrɪk] (kúnrick)
Cyntwell ['sɪntwel] (síntwel)
Cynull Mawr ['kʌnɨɬ 'mauǝr] (kúnnihl mówr)
Cynwyd ['kʌnuɪd] (kúnnŏŏ-id)
Cyriax, *f.n.* ['sɪrɪæks] (sírri-acks)
Cyster, *f.n.* ['sɪstǝr] (sísster)
Cysyllte [kǝ'sʌɬteɪ] (kŭssúhltay)

D

D'Abbes, *f.n.* [dæbz] (dabz)
D'Abernon, *Viscountcy of* ['dæbǝrnǝn] (dábbĕrnŏn)
D'Abreu, *f.n.* ['dæbru] (dábroo)
D'Aeth, *f.n.* [deθ] (deth); [deɪθ] (dayth)
D'Aguilar, *f.n.* ['dægwɪlǝr] (dágwillăr)
D'Albiac, *f.n.* ['dɒlbɪæk] (dáwlbi-ack)
D'Alton, *f.n.* ['dɒltǝn] (dáwltŏn)
D'Ambrumenil, *f.n.* [dæm'brʌmǝnǝl] (dambrúmmĕnĕl)
D'Antal, *f.n.* ['dæntl] (dantl)
d'Avigdor-Goldsmid, *f.n.* ['dævɪgdǝr 'gouldsmɪd] (dávvigdor góldsmid)
D'Egville, *f.n.* ['degvɪl] (dégvil)
d'Erlanger, *f.n.* ['dɛǝrlãʒeɪ] (daírlaangzhay)
D'Eyncourt, *f.n.* ['deɪnkɔrt] (dáynkort); ['deɪnkǝrt] (dáynkŭrt)
D'Olier, *f.n.* [dɒ'lɪǝr] (dolleér); ['douljeɪ] (dól-yay)
d'Urfey, Thomas, *17th-c. poet and songwriter* ['duǝrfeɪ] (doórfay)
Daborn, *f.n.* ['deɪbɔrn] (dáyborn)
Dacombe, *f.n.* ['deɪkǝm] (dáykŏm)
Dacre, *Barony of* ['deɪkǝr] (dáyker)
Dacre of Gillesland, *Baron* ['deɪkǝr ǝv 'gɪlzlǝnd] (dáyker ŏv gílzlănd)
Dacres, *f.n.* ['deɪkǝrz] (dáykĕrz)
Daer Water ['dar 'wɒtǝr] (daár wáwter)
Dafen ['dævǝn] (dávvĕn)
Dafydd, *Welsh C.n.* ['dævɪð] (dávvith)
Daggar, *f.n.* ['dægǝr] (dággăr)
Dagul, *f.n.* ['deɪgl] (daygl)
Daiches, *f.n.* ['deɪʃɪs] (dáyshĕss); ['daɪxɪs] (díchĕss)
Dailly ['deɪlɪ] (dáyli)
Daimpré, *f.n.* ['dæmpreɪ] (dámpray)
Dakeyne, *f.n.* [dǝ'keɪn] (dăkáyn)
Dakin, *f.n.* ['deɪkɪn] (dáykin)
Dalbeattie [dǝl'bɪtɪ] (dálbeéti)
Dalberg, *f.n.* ['dælbɜrg] (dálberg)
Dalbury Lees ['dɒlbǝrɪ 'liz] (dáwlbŭri leéz)
Dalby, *f.n.* ['dɒlbɪ] (dáwlbi); ['dælbɪ] (dálbi)
Dalby, *Leics.* ['dɒlbɪ] (dáwlbi); ['dɒlbɪ] (dólbi)
Dalby, *Lincs.* ['dɒlbɪ] (dáwlbi)
Daldy, *f.n.* ['dældɪ] (dáldi)

Dalgety [dǝl'getɪ] (dálgétti)
Dalgleish, *f.n.* [dæl'gliʃ] (dalgleésh)
Dalguise [dæl'gaɪz] (dalgíz)
Dalhousie, Earl of [dæl'hauzɪ] (dalhówzi) *Appropriate also for ~ Castle.*
Daliburgh ['dælɪbǝrǝ] (dálibŭră)
Daligan, *f.n.* ['dælɪgǝn] (dáligăn)
Dalkeith [dæl'kiθ] (dalkeéth) *Appropriate also for the Earl of ~.*
Dall, *f.n.* [dæl] (dal); [dɒl] (dawl)
Dalley, *f.n.* ['dælɪ] (dáli)
Dalling, *f.n.* ['dælɪŋ] (dáling)
Dallington, *Sussex* ['dælɪŋtǝn] (dálingtŏn); ['dɒlɪŋtǝn] (dóllingtŏn)
Dally, *f.n.* ['dælɪ] (dáli)
Dalmeny [dæl'menɪ] (dalménni); [dǝl'menɪ] (dălménni) *The first is appropriate for Baron ~.*
Dalmunzie [dæl'mʌŋɪ] (dalmúng-i)
Dalnacardoch [ˌdælnǝ'kardǝx] (dalnăkaárdŏch)
Dalnaspidal [ˌdælnǝ'spɪdl] (dalnă-spíddl)
Dalquhandy [dǝl'hwɒnɪ] (dál-whónni)
Dalriada [ˌdælrɪ'ædǝ] (dalri-áddă)
Dalry, Ayr., Edinburgh, Kirkcudbright. [dǝl'raɪ] (dálrí)
Dalrymple, *f.n.* [dǝl'rɪmpl] (dălrímpl); [dæl'rɪmpl] (dalrímpl); ['dælrɪmpl] (dálrimpl) *The first is appropriate for the family name of the Earl of Stair and thus also for Viscount ~.*
Dalrymple [dǝl'rɪmpl] (dălrímpl)
Dalserf [dǝl'sɜrf] (dál-sérf)
Dalton, *f.n.* ['dɒltǝn] (dáwltŏn)
Dalway, *f.n.* ['dɒlweɪ] (dáwlway)
Dalwhinnie [dǝl'hwɪnɪ] (dál-whínni)
Daly, *f.n.* ['deɪlɪ] (dáyli)
Dalyell of the Binns, *f.n.* [di'el ǝv ðǝ 'bɪnz] (dee-éll ŏv thĕ bínz)
Dalzell, *f.n.* [di'el] (dee-éll); ['dælzel] (dálzel) *The first is appropriate for Baron Hamilton of ~.*
Dalziel, *f.n.* [di'el] (dee-éll); ['dælzil] (dálzeel)
Dalziel [di'el] (dee-éll)
Dalziel of Kirkcaldy, *Barony of* [di'el ǝv kǝr'kɒdɪ] (dee-éll ŏv kirkóddi)
Dalziel of Wooler, *Barony of* ['dælzil ǝv 'wulǝr] (dálzeel ŏv woóler)
Damant, *f.n.* [dǝ'mænt] (dămánt)
Damems ['dæmǝmz] (dámmĕmz)
Damerell, *f.n.* ['dæmǝrǝl] (dámmĕrĕl)
Damerham ['dæmǝrǝm] (dámmĕrăm)
Damiano, *f.n.* [ˌdæmi'anou] (dammi-aánŏ)
Dammarell, *f.n.* ['dæmǝrǝl] (dámmărĕl)
Dampier, *f.n.* ['dæmpɪǝr] (dámpi-er)
Danckwerts, *f.n.* ['dæŋkwǝrts] (dánkwĕrts)
Dancy, *f.n.* ['dænsɪ] (dánssi)
Dancyger, *f.n.* ['dænsɪgǝr] (dánssiger)
Dangan, *Viscount* ['dæŋgǝn] (dáng-găn)
Daniell, *f.n.* ['dænjǝl] (dán-yĕl)
Dannreuther, *f.n.* ['dænrɔɪtǝr] (dánroyter)

Danvers, f.n. ['dænvərz] (dánvĕrz)
Danygraig [ˌdænə'graɪg] (dannăgríg)
Darcy de Knayth, Baroness ['dɑrsi də 'neɪθ] (daárssi dĕ náyth)
Darent, River ['dærənt] (dárrĕnt)
Darenth ['dærənθ] (dárrĕnth)
Daresbury ['dɑrzbəri] (daárzbŭri) *Appropriate also for Baron ~.*
Darewski, f.n. [də'ruskɪ] (dărooóski)
Dargavel, f.n. ['dɑrgəvel] (daárgăvel)
Darite [də'raɪt] (dărít)
Darlaston ['dɑrləstən] (daárlástŏn)
Darlington ['dɑrlɪŋtən] (daárlingtŏn)
Darlow, f.n. ['dɑrloʊ] (daárlō)
Darnac, f.n. ['dɑrnæk] (daárnack)
Darowen [də'roʊən] (dărō-ĕn)
Darragh, f.n. ['dærəx] (dárrăch)
Darranlas [ˌdærən'lɑs] (darránlaáss)
Darsham ['dɑrʃəm] (daár-shăm)
Dartmouth ['dɑrtməθ] (daártmŭth)
Darvall, f.n. ['dɑrvəl] (daárvăl)
Darvel ['dɑrvəl] (daárvĕl)
Darvell, f.n. ['dɑrvəl] (daárvĕl)
Darwen ['dɑrwɪn] (daárwĕn); ['dærən] (dárrĕn)
Daryll, f.n. ['dærɪl] (dárril)
Dasent, f.n. ['deɪsənt] (dáyssĕnt)
Dashper, f.n. ['dæʃpər] (dáshper)
Dassells ['dæslz] (dasslz)
Datyner, f.n. ['dætɪnər] (dáttiner)
Daubeney, f.n. ['dɔbnɪ] (dáwb-ni)
Daugleddyf [daɪ'gleðɪv] (díglétthiv) *Another form,* **Daugleddau,** *may be pronounced* [daɪ'gleðaɪ] (díglétthi)
Dauncey, f.n. ['dɔnsɪ] (dáwnsси)
Dauntsey, f.n. ['dɔntsɪ] (dáwntssi)
Dauthieu, f.n. ['doʊtjø] (dót-yö)
Davaar [də'vɑr] (dăvaár)
Davenham ['deɪvənəm] (dáyvĕnăm); ['deɪməm] (dáynăm)
Davenport, f.n. ['dævənport] (dávvĕnport)
Daventry ['dævəntrɪ] (dávvĕntri); ['deɪntrɪ] (dáyntri) *The first is appropriate for Viscount ~.*
Davidge, f.n. ['dævɪdʒ] (dávvij)
Davidson, f.n. ['deɪvɪdsən] (dáyvidssŏn)
Davidstow ['deɪvɪdstoʊ] (dáyvidstō)
Davie, f.n. ['deɪvɪ] (dáyvi) see also *Thorpe Davie.*
Davies, f.n. ['deɪvɪs] (dáyviss)
Davin, f.n. ['dævɪn] (dávvin)
Davinson, f.n. ['dævɪnsən] (dávvinsŏn)
Davion, f.n. ['dævɪən] (dávvi-ŏn)
Daviot, Gordon, author ['dævɪət] (dávviŏt) *Although Elizabeth McIntosh derived this pen-name from the Inverness-shire village of Daviot, she chose to pronounce it differently.*
Daviot, Aberdeen., Inverness. ['deɪvɪət] (dáyvi-ŏt)
Davis, f.n. ['deɪvɪs] (dáyviss)
Davison, f.n. ['deɪvɪsən] (dáyvissŏn)
Davson, f.n. ['dævsən] (dávssŏn)
Dawbarn, f.n. ['dɔbərn] (dáwbărn)

Dawick, Viscount ['dɔ-ɪk] (dáw-ick)
Dawnay, f.n. ['dɔnɪ] (dáwni)
Daymond, f.n. ['deɪmənd] (dáymŏnd)
Ddôl [ðoʊl] (thōl)
Dduallt ['ðiæɬt] (thée-ahlt)
De'ath, f.n. [di'æθ] (dee-áth)
De Bathe, f.n. [də 'bɑθ] (dĕ baáth)
De Beer, f.n. [də 'bɪər] (dĕ beér)
De Blank, The Rt. Revd. Joost ['joʊst də 'blæŋk] (yŏst dĕ blánk)
De Blaquiere, Barony of [də 'blækjər] (dĕ bláck-yer)
De Bounevialle, f.n. [də 'bunvɪæl] (dĕ boónvi-al)
De Broke, f.n. [də 'brʊk] (dĕ brŏŏk)
De Bruyne, f.n. [də 'bruneɪ] (dĕ broónay)
De Buf, f.n. [də 'bʌf] (dĕ búff)
De Bunsen, f.n. [də 'bʌnsən] (dĕ búnssĕn)
De Burgh, f.n. [də 'bɜrg] (dĕ búrg)
De Buriatte, f.n. [də 'bjʊərɪæt] (dĕ byoóri-at)
De Candole, f.n. [də 'kændoʊl] (dĕ kándōl)
De Carteret, f.n. [də 'kɑrtrɪt] (dĕ kaártrĕt)
De Casembroot, f.n. [də 'kæsəmbrut] (dĕ kássĕmbroot)
De Chair, f.n. [də 'tʃɛər] (dĕ chaír); [də 'ʃɛər] (dĕ shaír)
De Comarmond, f.n. [də kə'mɑrmənd] (dĕ kŏmaármŏnd)
De Coucey, f.n. [də 'kusɪ] (dĕ koóssi)
De Courcey, f.n. [də 'kɔrsɪ] (dĕ kórssi)
De Courcy, f.n. [də 'kɔrsɪ] (dĕ kórssi); [də 'kʊərsɪ] (dĕ koórssi); [də 'kɜrsɪ] (dĕ kúrssi) *The first is appropriate for Baron Kingsale's family name.*
De Crespigny, f.n. [də 'krepɪnɪ] (dĕ kréppini)
De Cusance, f.n. [də 'kuzɑns] (dĕ koózaanss)
De Eresby, f.n. ['dɪərzbɪ] (deérzbi)
De Felice, f.n. [ˌdi fɪ'lis] (dee fĕleéss)
De Ferranti, f.n. [ˌdə fə'ræntɪ] (dĕ fĕránti)
De Francia, f.n. [də 'frɑnsɪə] (dĕ fraánsiă)
De Francquen, f.n. [də 'fræŋkwɪn] (dĕ fránkwĕn)
De Frece, f.n. [də 'fris] (dĕ freéss)
De Freitas, f.n. [də 'freɪtəs] (dĕ fráytăss)
De Garis, f.n. [də 'gærɪs] (dĕ gárriss)
De Gaury, f.n. [də 'gɔrɪ] (dĕ gáwri)
De Gernier, f.n. [də 'dʒɜrnɪər] (dĕ jérni-er)
De Glehn, f.n. [də 'glen] (dĕ glén)
de Grunwald, Anatole, film producer ['ænətɒl də 'grunvæld] (ánnătol dĕ groónvald)
De Guingand, f.n. [də 'gæ̃gã] (dĕ gáng-gaang)
De Hoghton, f.n. [də 'hɒtən] (dĕ háwtŏn)
De Jonge, f.n. [də 'jʌŋ] (dĕ yúng)
De Krassel, f.n. [də 'kræsl] (dĕ krássl)
De Labilliere, f.n. [ˌdə lə'bɪljər] (dĕ laabíl-yer)

De Larrinaga, *f.n.* [də ˌlærɪˈnagə] (dĕ larrinaágǎ)
De Laubenque, *f.n.* [də ˈloʊbeŋk] (dĕ lṓbenk)
De Lestang, *f.n.* [də ˈleɪtã] (dĕ láytaang)
De Lingen, *f.n.* [də ˈlɪŋən] (dĕ líng-ĕn)
De Lisle, *f.n.* [də ˈlaɪl] (dĕ líl)
De L'Isle, *Viscount* [də ˈlaɪl] (dĕ líl)
De Lotbinière, *f.n.* [də ˈloʊbɪnjɛər] (dĕ lṓbin-yair)
De Manio, *f.n.* [də ˈmænɪoʊ] (dĕ mánniṓ)
De Mauley, *Baron* [də ˈmɔlɪ] (dĕ máwli)
De Minvielle, *f.n.* [də ˈmenvəl] (dĕ ménvĕl)
De Moleyns, *f.n.* [də ˈmʌlɪnz] (dĕ múllĕnz); [ˈdeməlɪnz] (démmṓleenz) *The first is appropriate in the title of Baroness Strange of Knokin, Hungerford and ~. see Eveleigh-de-Moleyns.*
De Montalt, *Baron* [ˌdemənt'ælt] (demmŏntált)
De Montmorency, *f.n.* [də ˌmɒntməˈrensɪ] (dĕ montmŏrénssi); [də ˌmõməˈrãsɪ] (dĕ mõngmŏraángssi) *The second was the pronunciation of the late Viscount of Mountmorres.*
De Muralt, *f.n.* [də ˈmjʊərælt] (dĕ myṓŏralt)
De Nevers, *f.n.* [də ˈnevərz] (dĕ névvĕrz)
De Nys, *f.n.* [də ˈnis] (dĕ neéss)
De Peyer, *f.n.* [də ˈpaɪər] (dĕ pí-er)
De Polnay, *f.n.* [də ˈpɒlneɪ] (dĕ pólnay)
De Reyghère, *f.n.* [də ˈreɪgər] (dĕ ráyger)
De Rohan, *f.n.* [də ˈroʊən] (dĕ rṓ-ǎn)
De Sales, *f.n.* [də ˈsalz] (dĕ saálz)
De Salis, *f.n.* [də ˈsælɪs] (dĕ sáliss); [də ˈsalz] (dĕ saálz)
De Saram, *f.n.* [də ˈsɛərəm] (dĕ saírǎm)
De Satgé, *f.n.* [də ˈsætdʒeɪ] (dĕ sátjay)
De Saubergue, *f.n.* [də ˈsoʊbɜrg] (dĕ sṓberg)
De Saumarez, *f.n.* [də ˈsɒmərɪz] (dĕ sómmǎrĕz); [də ˈsɒmərez] (dĕ sómmǎrezz) *The first is appropriate for Baron ~.*
De Saxe, *f.n.* [ˌdə ˈsæks] (dĕ sácks)
De Selincourt, *f.n.* [də ˈselɪnkɔrt] (dĕ séllin-kort)
De Sevin, *f.n.* [ˌdə sɪˈvɪn] (dĕ sĕveén)
De Soissons, *f.n.* [də ˈswasõ] (dĕ swaássõng)
De Stein, *f.n.* [də ˈstaɪn] (dĕ stín)
De Thuillier, *f.n.* [də ˈtwɪlɪər] (dĕ twillier)
De Valera, *f.n.* [ˌdə vəˈlɛərə] (dĕ vǎláĭrǎ)
De Vesci, *Viscount* [də ˈvesɪ] (dĕ véssi)
De Veulle, *f.n.* [də ˈvɜl] (dĕ vŏll)
De Villiers, *f.n.* [də ˈvɪlərz] (dĕ víllĕrz); [də ˈvɪljərz] (dĕ víl-yĕrz) *The first is appropriate for Baron ~.*
De Vitré, *f.n.* [də ˈvɪtrɪ] (dĕ veétri)
De Warfaz, *f.n.* [də ˈwɔrfæz] (dĕ wáwrfaz)
De Yevele, *f.n.* [də ˈjivəlɪ] (dĕ yeévĕli) *Appropriate for Henry ~, 14th-c. master-mason and architect.*

De Zoete, *f.n.* [də ˈzut] (dĕ zoót)
De Zouche, *f.n.* [də ˈzuʃ] (dĕ zoósh)
De Zulueta, *f.n.* [də ˌzuluˈetə] (dĕ zooloo-éttǎ)
De la Bedoyère, *f.n.* [də la ˌbedwəˈjɛər] (dĕ laa bedwá-yaír)
De la Bere, *f.n.* [ˌdeləˈbɪər] (dellábeér)
de la Ferté, *f.n.* [ˌdə la ˈfɛərteɪ] (dĕ laa faírtay)
De la Fuente, *f.n.* [ˌdə lə fuˈentɪ] (dĕ lǎ fŏo-énti)
De la Haye, *f.n.* [ˌdə la ˈheɪ] (dĕ laa háy)
De la Mahotiere, *f.n.* [də la ˌmaoʊˈtjɛər] (dĕ laa maa-ō-tyaír)
de la Mare, *f.n.* [ˌdeləˈmɛər] (dellámaír); [ˈdeləmɛər] (déllǎmair) *The first is appropriate for the poet, Walter ~.*
De la Motte, *f.n.* [ˌdə la ˈmɒt] (dĕ laa mótt)
De-la-Noy, *f.n.* [ˈdelənɔɪ] (déllǎnoy)
De la Pasture, *f.n.* [də ˈlæpətʃər] (dĕ láppǎtcher)
de la Pole, *f.n.* [ˌdə la ˈpul] (dĕ laa poól)
De la Rue, *f.n.* [ˌdeləˈru] (dellároó)
De la Salle, *f.n.* [ˌdə la ˈsal] (dĕ laa saál)
De la Torre, *f.n.* [ˌdə la ˈtɔr] (dĕ laa tór)
De La Warr, *Earl* [ˈdeləwɛər] (déllǎwair)
Del Mar, *Norman*, *conductor* [del ˈmar] (del maár)
Del Renzio, *f.n.* [del ˈrenzɪoʊ] (del rénziō)
Del Riego, *Teresa*, *composer* [təˈreɪzə del rɪˈeɪgoʊ] (tĕráyzǎ del rɪ-áygō)
Del Strother, *f.n.* [del ˈstrʌðər] (del strúther)
del Tufo, *f.n.* [del ˈtufoʊ] (del toófō)
Des Champs, *f.n.* [ˈdeʃən] (déshǎn); [ˈdeɪʃã] (dáy-shaang)
Des Graz, *f.n.* [deɪ ˈgra] (day graá)
Des Voeux, *f.n.* [deɪ ˈvɜ] (day vŏ)
Deakin, *f.n.* [ˈdikɪn] (deékin)
Dealtry, *f.n.* [ˈdɔltrɪ] (dáwltri)
Deamer, *f.n.* [ˈdimər] (deémer)
Dearden, *f.n.* [ˈdɪərdən] (deérdĕn)
Dearmer, *f.n.* [ˈdɪərmər] (deérmer)
Dearne, *River* [dɜrn] (dern)
Dearnley, *f.n.* [ˈdɜrnlɪ] (dérnli)
Dearsley, *f.n.* [ˈdɪərzlɪ] (deérzli)
Dearth, *f.n.* [dɜrθ] (derth)
Deas, *f.n.* [diz] (deez)
Dease, *f.n.* [dis] (deess)
Deason, *f.n.* [ˈdisən] (deéssŏn)
Debach [ˈdebɪdʒ] (débbij)
Debbane, *f.n.* [dɪˈbæn] (dĕbánn)
Deben, *River* [ˈdibən] (deébĕn)
Debeney, *f.n.* [ˈdebənɪ] (débbĕni)
Debenham, *f.n.* [ˈdebənəm] (débbĕnǎm)
Debenham [ˈdebənəm] (débbĕnǎm)
Debes, *f.n.* [dɪˈbez] (dĕbézz)
Deby, *f.n.* [ˈdibɪ] (deébi)
Dechmont, *Lanark.*, *West Lothian* [ˈdexmənt] (déchmŏnt)
Decies, *Baron* [ˈdiʃɪz] (deésheez)
Decimus, *f.n.* [ˈdesɪməs] (déssimŭss)
Dederich, *f.n.* [ˈdedərɪtʃ] (déddĕritch)
Dedow, *f.n.* [ˈdidoʊ] (deédō)

Deffee, f.n. [dɪ'fi] (dĕfeé)
Defferary, f.n. [ˌdefə'reərɪ] (defférairi)
Defoe, Daniel, 18th-c. author [də'fou] (dĕfó)
Defrates, f.n. [dɪ'freɪts] (dĕfráyts)
Defries, f.n. [də'fris] (dĕfreéss)
Deganwy [dɪ'gænʊɪ] (dĕgánoo-i)
Dehaney, f.n. [də'heɪnɪ] (dĕ-háyni)
Dehn, f.n. [deɪn] (dayn)
Deighton, f.n. ['daɪtən] (dítŏn); ['deɪtən] (dáytŏn)
Deighton ['ditən] (deétŏn)
Deildre Isaf ['daɪldrɪ 'ɪsæv] (díldri íssav)
Deiniolen [daɪn'jɒlən] (dīn-yóllĕn)
Dekker, f.n. ['dekər] (décker)
Delabole ['deləbovl] (déllábōl); [ˌdelə-'boʊl] (dellábóĺ)
Delacombe, f.n. ['deləkum] (déllákoom)
Delacour, f.n. ['deləkʊər] (déllákoŏr)
Delafons, f.n. ['deləfɒnz] (délláfonz)
Delahaye, f.n. ['deləheɪ] (délláhay)
Delamain, f.n. ['deləmeɪn] (déllámayn)
Delamere, Baron [ˌdelə'mɪər] (dellá-meér)
Delamere, f.n. ['deləmɪər] (déllámeer)
Delaney, f.n. [dɪ'leɪnɪ] (dĕláyni)
Delap, f.n. [də'læp] (dĕláp)
Delapré Abbey ['deləpreɪ] (déllápray)
Delargy, f.n. [də'lɑrgɪ] (dĕlaárgi)
Delbanco, f.n. [del'bænkoʊ] (delbánkō)
Delephine, f.n. ['deləpin] (déllépeen)
Delevingne, f.n. ['delɪvɪn] (déllĕveen)
Delfont, f.n. ['delfɒnt] (délfont)
Delgaty Castle, *also spelt* Delgatie ['delgətɪ] (délgáti)
Delius, Frederick, composer ['dilɪəs] (deéliŭss)
Deloitte, f.n. [də'lɔɪt] (dĕlóyt)
Delomosne, f.n. ['deləmoʊn] (déllŏmōn)
Delph [delf] (delf)
Delury, f.n. [də'lʊərɪ] (dĕlóŏri)
Delval, f.n. [del'væl] (delvál)
Demant, f.n. [dɪ'mænt] (dĕmánt)
Demel, f.n. ['deml] (demml)
Demuth, f.n. [dɪ'mjuθ] (dĕméwth); ['demət] (démmŭt); [dɪ'muθ] (dĕmóŏth)
Denbigh ['denbɪ] (dénbi) *Appropriate also for the Earl of ~.*
Deneke, f.n. ['denɪkɪ] (dénnĕki) *Appropriate for the Clara Sophie ~ scholarship at Oxford University.*
Dengie ['dendʒɪ] (dénji)
Denholm ['denəm] (dénnŏm)
Denholme ['denhɒlm] (dénhollm)
Dening, f.n. ['denɪŋ] (dénning)
Denne, f.n. [den] (den)
Dennehy, f.n. ['denɪhɪ] (dénnĕhi)
Denney, f.n. ['denɪ] (dénni)
Dennistoun ['denɪstən] (dénnistŏn)
Dent, f.n. [dent] (dent)
Dent-de-Lion ['dændɪlaɪən] (dándilī-ŏn)
Denton ['dentən] (déntŏn)
Denwick ['denɪk] (dénnick)
Deopham ['dipəm] (deépam); ['difəm] (deéfám)

Deptford ['detfərd] (déttfŏrd)
Derby ['dɑrbɪ] (daárbi) *Appropriate also for the Earl of ~.*
Derbyshire, f.n. ['dɑrbɪʃər] (daárbisher)
Dereham ['dɪərəm] (deérăm)
Deri, f.n. ['dɛərɪ] (daíri)
Deri ['derɪ] (dérri)
Dering, f.n. ['dɪərɪŋ] (deéring)
Deritend [ˌderɪt'end] (derrit-énd)
Dernawilt [ˌdɜrnə'wɪlt] (dernăwílt)
Derriaghy [ˌderɪ'æxɪ] (derri-áchi)
Derry ['derɪ] (dérri)
Derrygonnelly [ˌderɪ'gɒnəlɪ] (derri-gónnĕli)
Derrylin [ˌderɪ'lɪn] (derrilín)
Dersingham ['dɜrzɪŋəm] (dérzing-ăm)
Derville, f.n. ['dɜrvɪl] (dérvil)
Dervock ['dɜrvək] (dérvŏk)
Derwen ['dɛərwɪn] (daírwĕn)
Derwendeg [ˌdɛərwɪn'deɪg] (dairwĕn-dáyg)
Derwenlas [ˌdɛərwɪn'lɑs] (dairwĕnlaáss)
Derwent, Baron ['dɑrwənt] (daárwĕnt)
Derwenthaugh ['dɛərwənthɑf] (daír-wĕnt-haaf)
Derwentwater ['dɜrwəntwɔtər] (dér-wĕnt-wawter)
Desart, Earldom of ['dezərt] (dézzärt)
Desbois, f.n. [deɪ'bwɑ] (daybwaá)
Desborough, f.n. ['dezbərə] (dézbŭră) *Appropriate also for the Barony of ~.*
Desch, f.n. [deʃ] (desh)
Deschamps, f.n. ['deʃən] (déshăn); ['deɪʃã] (dáy-shaaŋg)
Desertmartin [ˌdezərt'mɑrtɪn] (dezzért-maártin)
Desford ['desfərd] (déssfŏrd)
Desforges, f.n. [deɪ'fɔrdʒ] (dayfórj)
Desoutter, f.n. [dɪ'sutər] (dĕssoóter)
Desvaux, f.n. [dɪ'voʊ] (dĕvó); [deɪ'voʊ] (dayvó)
Deuchar, f.n. ['djuxər] (déwchăr)
Deuchrie Dod ['djuxrɪ 'dɒd] (déwchri dód)
Deugh, Water of [djux] (dewch)
Devall, f.n. [dɪ'væl] (dĕvál)
Devaney, f.n. [dɪ'veɪnɪ] (dĕváyni)
Devas, f.n. [dɪ'væs] (dĕváss)
Develin, f.n. [dɪ'velɪn] (dĕvéllin)
Deveney, f.n. ['dɪvnɪ] (deévni)
Devenish, f.n. ['devənɪʃ] (dévvĕnish); ['dɪvənɪʃ] (deévĕnish)
Deverell, f.n. ['devərəl] (dévvĕrĕl)
Devereux, f.n. ['devəruks] (dévvĕrooks); ['devəreks] (dévvĕrecks); ['devərə] (dévvĕră); ['devəru] (dévvĕroo) *The first is that of the family name of Viscount Hereford, although the second is said to be usual in the counties of Hereford and Montgomery. A descendant of the Elizabethan Robert ~, Earl of Essex, also favours the first pronunciation.*
Deveron, River ['devərən] (dévvĕrŏn)

Devers, f.n. ['dɪvərz] (déevĕrz) ; ['devərz] (dévvĕrz)

Deveson, f.n. ['dɪvɪsən] (deevĕssŏn)

Devey, f.n. ['dɪvɪ] (deévi)

Devine, f.n. [dɪ'vɪn] (dĕvèen) ; [dɪ'vaɪn] (dĕvín)

Devlin, f.n. ['devlɪn] (dévlin)

Devoke Water ['devək 'wɔtər] (dévvŏk wáwter)

Devol, f.n. [dɪ'voʊl] (dĕvŏl)

Devon ['devən] (dévvŏn)

Devon, River, *Perth.-Kinross-Clackmannan.-Stirling.* ['devən] (dévvŏn)

Devon, River, *Notts.* ['dɪvən] (deèvŏn)

Devonald, f.n. ['devənəld] (dévvŏnáld)

Devons, f.n. ['devənz] (dévvŏnz)

Devoran ['devərən] (dévvŏrăn) ; ['devrən] dévrŏn)

Dewar, f.n. ['djʊər] (dyŏŏ-ăr)

Dewes, f.n. [djuz] (dewz)

Dewi, Welsh C.n. ['dewɪ] (dé-wi)

Dewrance, f.n. ['djʊərəns] (dyŏŏrănss)

Dey, f.n. [deɪ] (day)

Dhooge, f.n. [doʊg] (dōg)

Dhu Varren ['du 'værən] (doó várrĕn)

Diack, f.n. ['daɪək] (dí-ăk)

Diane, C.n. [daɪ'æn] (dī-ánn) ; [dɪ'æn] (di-ánn)

Dibden Purlieu ['dɪbdən 'pɜrlju] (díbdĕn púrlew)

Dichmont, f.n. ['dɪtʃmɒnt] (dítchmont)

Dicksee, f.n. ['dɪksɪ] (dícksi)

Dielhenn, f.n. ['dɪlən] (deélĕn)

Dienes, f.n. [dɪnz] (deenz)

Digbeth Institute, *Birmingham* ['dɪgbeθ] (dígbeth)

Digges, f.n. [dɪgz] (digz)

Dighty Water ['dɪxtɪ 'wɔtər] (díɣti wáwter)

Diglis ['dɪglɪs] (dígliss)

Dihewid [di'hewɪd] (deehé-wid)

Dilger, f.n. ['dɪldʒər] (díljer)

Dilhorne, Viscount ['dɪlən] (díllŏn)

Dilhorne ['dɪlərn] (díllŏrn) ; ['dɪlərn] (díllorn)

Dilke, f.n. [dɪlk] (dilk)

Dilworth, f.n. ['dɪlwɜrθ] (dílwurth)

Dilwyn, Welsh C.n., also spelt Dillwyn ['dɪlwɪn] (dílwin)

Dilwyn, f.n. ['dɪlwɪn] (dílwin)

Dimbleby, f.n. ['dɪmblbɪ] (dímblbi)

Diment, f.n. ['daɪmənt] (dímĕnt)

Dimmock, f.n. ['dɪmək] (dímmŏk)

Dimoline, f.n. ['dɪməlɪn] (dímmŏleen)

Dimont, f.n. ['daɪmənt] (dímŏnt)

Dinuantes, f.n. [ˌdɪmju'æntiz] (dimmewánteez)

Dinas, *Glamorgan, Pembroke.* ['dɪnæs] (deènass)

Dinas Mawddwy ['dɪnæs 'maʊðuɪ] (deènass mówthoo-i)

Dinas Oleu ['dɪnæs 'oʊlaɪ] (deènass ŏlī)

Dinas Powis ['dɪnəs 'paʊɪs] (dínnăss pówiss)

Dinchope ['dɪntʃəp] (díntchŏp)

Dinedor ['daɪn'dor] (dín-dór)

Dinefwr Castle [dɪ'nevʊər] (dinévvŏŏr) *Welsh form of Dynevor, q.v.*

Dines, f.n. [daɪnz] (dīnz)

Dingestow ['dɪndʒɪstoʊ] (dínjĕstō)

Dinglay, f.n. ['dɪŋgleɪ] (díng-glay)

Dingley, f.n. ['dɪŋlɪ] (díng-li) ; ['dɪŋglɪ] (díng-gli)

Dingwall ['dɪŋwɒl] (díng-wawl) ; ['dɪŋwəl] (díng-wăl)

Dinorwic [dɪ'nɔrwɪk] (dinórwick)

Diosy, f.n. [di'oʊzɪ] (dee-ózi)

Diptford ['dɪpfərd] (dípfŏrd)

Dirac, f.n. [dɪ'ræk] (diráck)

Diseworth ['daɪzwɜrθ] (dízwurth)

Disgwylfa [dɪs'gwɪlvə] (dissgwílvá)

Disley, f.n. ['dɪzlɪ] (dízzli)

Dispain, f.n. ['dɪspeɪn] (dísspayn)

Disraeli, f.n. [dɪz'reɪlɪ] (dizráyli)

Diss [dɪs] (diss)

Disserth ['dɪsərθ] (díssĕrth)

Dittisham ['dɪtɪsəm] (díttissăm) ; ['dɪtɪʃəm] (ditti-shăm) ; ['dɪtsəm] (dítsăm)

Divell, f.n. ['daɪvl] (dívl)

Divine, f.n. [dɪ'vaɪn] (divín)

Divis ['dɪvɪs] (dívviss)

Dixey, f.n. ['dɪksɪ] (dícksi)

Doagh [doʊx] (dō<u>ch</u>)

Dobrée, Bonamy, scholar and writer ['bɒnəmɪ 'doʊbreɪ] (bónnămi dóbray)

Dochart, River ['dɒxərt] (dó<u>ch</u>árt)

Docherty, f.n. ['dɒxərtɪ] (dó<u>ch</u>ĕrti)

Dochfour, Loch [dɒx'fʊər] (do<u>ch</u>fŏŏr)

Docwra, f.n. ['dɒkrə] (dóckrá)

Dodgson, Charles, mathematician and author of 'Alice in Wonderland' ['dɒdsən] (dódssŏn) *Not* [dɒdʒ-] (doj-), *as one might expect.*

Dodman ['dɒdmən] (dódmăn)

Dodwell, f.n. ['dɒdwəl] (dódwĕl) ; ['dɒdwel] (dódwel)

Doepel, f.n. [doʊ'pel] (dōpéll)

Doggett, f.n. ['dɒgɪt] (dóggĕt)

Doherty, f.n. ['dɒxərtɪ] (dó<u>ch</u>ĕrti) ; ['dɒhərtɪ] (dó-hĕrti) ; ['doʊhərtɪ] (dó-hĕrti) ; ['doʊərtɪ] (dó-ĕrti)

Doig, f.n. [dɔɪg] (doyg) ; ['doʊɪg] (dŏ-ig)

Dolan, f.n. ['doʊlən] (dŏlăn)

Dolau ['doʊlaɪ] (dóli)

Dolaucothi [ˌdoʊlaɪ'kɒθɪ] (dollī-kóthi)

Dolbadarn [dɒl'bædərn] (dolbáddărn)

Dolbenmaen [ˌdɒlben'maɪn] (dolbenmín)

Dolcoath [dəl'koʊθ] (dŏlkóth)

Doldowlod [dɒl'daʊlɒd] (doldówlod)

Dolemore, f.n. ['dɒlɪmɔr] (dóllĕmor)

Dolforwyn [dɒl'vɔrwɪn] (dolvórwin)

Dolgarrog [dɒl'gærɒg] (dolgárrog)

Dolgellau [dɒl'geɪaɪ] (dolgé<u>hl</u>ī) ; [dɒl'geɪr] (dolgé<u>hl</u>) Dolgellau *has superseded* Dolgelley *as the official spelling.*

Dolgelley *see* Dolgellau.

Dolgoch [dɒl'goʊx] (dolgó<u>ch</u>)

Dolhendre [dɒl'hendrɪ] (dol-héndri)

Dollan, f.n. ['doʊlən] (dŏlăn)

Dolmetsch, f.n. ['dɒlmetʃ] (dólmetch)
Dolton ['dɒultən] (dólton)
Dolwyddelan [ˌdɒlwɪ'ðelən] (dolwi-théllăn)
Dol-y-Gaer [ˌdɒlə'ɡɛər] (dollăgaïr)
Domleo, f.n. ['dɒmlɪoʊ] (dómliō)
Donaghadee [ˌdɒnəxə'diː] (donnăchădee)
Donaghcloney [ˌdɒnə'kloʊnɪ] (donnáklōni)
Donaghey, f.n. ['dɒnəxɪ] (dónnăchi)
Donaghmore [ˌdɒnəx'mɔːr] (donnăchmór)
Donaghy, f.n. ['dɒnəxɪ] (dónnăchi)
Donat, Robert, actor ['dɒunæt] (dŏnat)
Doncaster ['dɒŋkəstər] (dónkăster)
Done, f.n. (dɒun) (dōn)
Donegall, Marquess of ['dɒnɪɡɒl] (dónněgawl)
Donelly, f.n. ['dɒnəlɪ] (dónněli)
Doneraile, Viscount ['dʌnəreɪl] (dúnněrayl)
Dongray, f.n. ['dɒŋɡreɪ] (dóng-gray)
Doniach, f.n. ['dɒnjæk] (dón-yack)
Donibristle [ˌdɒnɪ'brɪsl] (donnibríssl)
Donington, Barony of ['dʌnɪŋtən] (dúnningtŏn)
Donington, Lincs., Salop ['dɒnɪŋtən] (dónningtŏn)
Donington-on-Bain ['dɒnɪŋtən ɒn 'beɪn] (dónningtŏn on báyn); ['dʌnɪŋtən ɒn 'beɪn] (dúnningtŏn on báyn)
Donkleywood ['dɑŋklɪwʊd] (dúnkliwŏod)
Donlevy, f.n. [dɒn'liːvɪ] (donleévi)
Donmall, f.n. ['dɒnməl] (dónmăl)
Donne, f.n. (dɒn) (donn); (dʌn) (dun) *Usage varies for the 17th-c. poet and divine, John* ~.
Donnellan, f.n. ['dɒnələn] (dónnělăn)
Donnelly, f.n. ['dɒnəlɪ] (dónněli)
Donohoe, f.n. ['dʌnəhu] (dúnnŏhoo); ['dɒnəhu] (dónnŏhoo)
Donoughmore, Earl of ['dʌnəmɔr] (dúnnŏmor)
Donovan, f.n. ['dʌnəvən] (dúnnŏvăn); ['dɒnəvən] (dónnŏvăn)
Doran, f.n. ['dɔrən] (dáwrăn)
Dore, f.n. [dɔr] (dor)
Dornoch ['dɔrnəx] (dórnŏch)
Dorset ['dɔrsɪt] (dórssĕt)
Dorté, f.n. ['dɔrtɪ] (dórti)
Dotrice, f.n. [də'trɪs] (dŏtreéss)
Douai College, also spelt **Douay** ['daʊeɪ] (dów-ay) *The* ~ *Bible is pronounced both* ['dʊeɪ] (doŏ-ay) *and* ['daʊeɪ] (dów-ay).
Doublebois ['dʌblbɔɪz] (dúbbl-boyz)
Douch, f.n. [dutʃ] (dootch)
Doudney, f.n. ['daʊdnɪ] (dówdni); ['dudnɪ] (doŏdni)
Dougall, f.n. ['dugl] (doogl)
Dougan, f.n. ['dugən] (doŏgăn)
Dougherty, f.n. ['dɒxərtɪ] (dóchĕrti); ['doʊərtɪ] (dŏ-ĕrti)
Doughton ['dʌftən] (dúfftŏn)
Doughty, f.n. ['daʊtɪ] (dówti)
Douglas, f.n. and C.n. ['dʌɡləs] (dúgláss)

Douglas-Home, f.n. ['dʌɡləs 'hjum] (dúgláss héwm) *This is the family name of the Earls of Home. The pronunciation is thus appropriate for Sir Alec* ~, *politician, Henry* ~, *ornithologist, and William* ~, *playwright.*
Douglas of Barloch, Baron ['dʌɡləs əv bar'lɒx] (dúgláss ŏv baarlóch)
Douglas and Clydesdale, Marquess of ['dʌɡləs ənd 'klaɪdzdeɪl] (dúgláss ănd klídzdayl)
Douglas of Kirtleside, Barony of ['dʌɡləs əv 'kɜrtlsaɪd] (dúgláss ŏv kírtl-sīd)
Douie, f.n. ['djuɪ] (déw-i); ['duɪ] (doŏ-i); ['daʊɪ] (dów-i)
Doulting ['dɒultɪŋ] (dólting); ['daʊltɪŋ] (dówlting)
Doulton, f.n. ['doʊltən] (dōltŏn)
Doune, Lord [dun] (doon)
Doune, Dunbarton., Perth. [dun] (doon)
Dounreay ['dunreɪ] (doŏnray) *There is an older form,* Downreay, *pronounced* ['daʊnreɪ] (dównray).
Douro, Marquess ['dʊəroʊ] (doŏrō)
Dousland ['daʊzlənd] (dówzlănd)
Douthwaite, f.n. ['daʊθweɪt] (dówth-wayt)
Dovaston, f.n. ['dʌvəstən] (dúvvăstŏn)
Dove, River [dʌv] (duvv); [doʊv] (dōv)
Dovedale ['dʌvdeɪl] (dúvdayl)
Dovenby ['dʌvənbɪ] (dúvvĕnbi)
Dovendale ['dʌvəndeɪl] (dúvvĕndayl)
Dover ['doʊvər] (dŏver)
Doverdale, Barony of ['dʌvərdeɪl] (dúvvĕrdayl)
Doveridge ['dʌvərɪdʒ] (dúvvĕrij)
Dovey, f.n. ['doʊvɪ] (dŏvi); ['dʌvɪ] (dúvvi)
Dovey, River ['dʌvɪ] (dúvvi) *The Welsh spelling is* Dyfi.
Dow, f.n. [daʊ] (dow)
Dowanhill ['daʊənhɪl] (dówăn-hil)
Dowd, f.n. [daʊd] (dowd)
Dowdall, f.n. ['daʊdl] (dowdl)
Dowden, f.n. ['daʊdən] (dówdĕn)
Dowdeswell ['daʊdzwəl] (dówdzwĕl)
Dower, f.n. ['daʊər] (dówer)
Dowie, f.n. ['daʊɪ] (dów-i)
Dowlais ['daʊləs] (dówláss)
Dowland, John 16–17th-c. lutenist and composer ['daʊlənd] (dówlănd)
Dowland ['daʊlənd] (dówlănd)
Dowle, f.n. [daʊl] (dowl)
Down [daʊn] (down)
Downend [daʊn'end] (down-énd)
Downes, f.n. [daʊnz] (downz)
Downpatrick [daʊn'pætrɪk] (down-pátrick)
Downreay see Dounreay.
Dowsby ['daʊzbɪ] (dówzbi)
Dowse, f.n. [daʊs] (dowss)
Dowsing, Inner and Outer ['daʊzɪŋ] (dówzing)
Doyle, f.n. [dɔɪl] (doyl)
Dozmary Pool ['dɒzmrɪ 'pul] (dóz-mri poŏl)

Draffen, *f.n.* ['dræfən] (dráffĕn)
Draffin, *f.n.* ['dræfɪn] (dráffĭn)
Drage, *f.n.* [dreɪdʒ] (drayj)
Drakelow ['dreɪkloʊ] (dráyklō)
Drake's Broughton ['dreɪks 'brɒtən] (dráyks bráwtŏn)
Draughton, *Northants.* ['drɒtən] (dráwtŏn)
Draughton, *Yorks.* ['dræftən] (dráfftŏn)
Dravers, *f.n.* ['dreɪvərz] (dráyvĕrz)
Dreaper, *f.n.* ['dreɪpər] (dráyper)
Drefach [dre'vɑx] (drevaách)
Drellingore ['drelɪŋɡɔr] (drélling-gor)
Drever, *f.n.* ['drɪvər] (dreéver)
Drewe, *f.n.* [dru] (droo)
Drewsteignton ['druz'teɪntən] (droóztáyntŏn)
Dreyer, *f.n.* ['draɪər] (drí-er)
Drian Gallery, *London art gallery* ['driən] (dreé-ăn)
Dribbell, *f.n.* [drɪ'bel] (dribéll)
Driberg, *f.n.* ['draɪbɜrɡ] (dríberg)
Driby ['draɪbɪ] (dríbi)
Drighlington ['drɪɡlɪŋtən] (dríglingtŏn); ['drɪlɪŋtən] (dríllingtŏn)
Drimnin ['drɪmnɪn] (drímnin)
Droeshout, Martin, *17th-c. Anglo-Flemish engraver, also spelt Maerten* ['mɑrtɪn 'drushaʊt] (maártin droósshowt)
Drogheda, *Earl of* ['drɒɪɪdə] (dróy-ĕ-dă)
Drogo Castle ['droʊɡoʊ] (drṓgō)
Dromantine *see* Drumantine.
Dromara [drə'mærə] (drŏmárrǎ)
Dromgoole, *f.n.* [drɒm'ɡul] (dromgoól)
Dromore, *Co. Down, Co. Tyrone* [drə'mɔr] (drŏmór)
Dronfield ['drɒnfɪld] (drónfeeld)
Drower, *f.n.* ['draʊər] (drówer)
Droylsden ['drɔɪlzdən] (dróylzdĕn)
Drucker, *f.n.* ['drʊkər] (droóker)
Drughorn, *f.n.* ['drʌɡhɔrn] (drúg-horn)
Druiff, *f.n.* ['druɪf] (droó-iff)
Druimuachdar *see* Drumochter.
Drumalbyn, *Baron* [drʌm'ælbɪn] (drumálbin)
Drumaness [ˌdrʌmə'nes] (drummănéss)
Drumantine, *also spelt* **Dromantine** ['drʌməntaɪn] (drúmmántĭn)
Drumaroad [ˌdrʌmə'roʊd] (drummărṓd)
Drumbeg [drəm'beɡ] (drŭmbég)
Drumbo [drəm'boʊ] (drŭmbṓ)
Drumelzier [drʌ'mɪljər] (drummeél-yer)
Drumhain ['drʊmɪn] (droómin)
Drumlithie [drʌm'lɪθɪ] (drumlíthi)
Drummond, *f.n.* ['drʌmənd] (drúmmŏnd)
Drummore [drə'mɔr] (drŭmór)
Drumnadrochit [ˌdrʌmnə'drɒxɪt] (drumnădróchit)
Drumoak [drʌm'oʊk] (drummṓk)
Drumochter [drə'mʊxtər] (drŭmóchter) *The Gaelic spelling is* Druimuachdar.
Drumquhassle [drʌm'hwæsl] (drumwhássl)

Drumry [drʌm'raɪ] (drum-rí)
Drumsheugh [drʌm'ʃux] (drum-shoóch)
Drury, *f.n.* ['drʊərɪ] (droóri)
Drws-y-Nant [ˌdrusə'nænt] (droossánánt)
Dryburgh, *f.n.* ['draɪbərə] (dríbŭră)
Dryburgh Abbey ['draɪbərə] (dríbŭră)
Drymen ['drɪmən] (drímmĕn)
Dryrange ['draɪ'reɪndʒ] (drí-ráynj)
Drysllwyn ['drɪslʊɪn] (dríssloṓ-in)
Du Boulay, *f.n.* [dʊ 'buleɪ] (dōṓ boólay)
Du Buisson, *f.n.* ['djubɪsən] (déwbissŏn)
Du Cane, *f.n.* [dju 'keɪn] (dew káyn)
Du Cann, *f.n.* [dju 'kæn] (dew kánn)
Du Cros, *f.n.* [dju 'kroʊ] (dew krṓ)
Du Croz, *f.n.* [dju 'kroʊ] (dew krṓ)
Du Deney, *f.n.* [dju 'denɪ] (dew dénni)
du Maurier, *f.n.* [du 'mɒrɪeɪ] (doo mórri-ay) *This is the family pronunciation of Sir Gerald ~, actor-manager, and of Daphne ~, author.*
Du Parcq, *Barony of* [du 'pɑrk] (doo paárk)
Du Plat, *f.n.* [dju 'plɑ] (dew plaá)
Du Sautoy, *f.n.* [dʊ 'soʊtɔɪ] (dōṓ sótoy)
Du Seautois, *f.n.* ['djusøtɔɪ] (déwssĕtoy)
Du Toit, *f.n.* [dju 'twɑ] (dew twaá); [du 'twɑ] (doo twaá)
Dubens, *f.n.* ['djubənz] (déwbĕnz)
Dubh Artach Rocks ['du 'ɑrtəx] (doó aartách)
Ducharme, *f.n.* [du'ʃɑrm] (doo-shaárm)
Duchemin, *f.n.* ['duʃəmɪn] (doóshĕmin)
Duchesne, *f.n.* [du'ʃeɪn] (doo-sháyn); [dju'ʃeɪn] (dew-sháyn)
Duchin, *f.n.* ['dutʃɪn] (doótchin)
Ducie, *Earl of* ['djusɪ] (déwssi)
Ducrow, *f.n.* [dju'kroʊ] (dewkrṓ)
Duddeston ['dʌdɪstən] (dúddĕstŏn)
Duddleswell ['dʌdlzwel] (dúddlzwel)
Dudeney, *f.n.* ['djudnɪ] (déwd-ni); ['djudnɪ] (déwdn-i); ''djudŋeɪ] (déwdn-ay); ['dudnɪ] (doód-ni)
Dudhope, *Viscount* ['dʌdəp] (dúddŏp)
Duerden, *f.n.* ['djuərdən] (dyoórdĕn)
Duff, *f.n.* [dʌf] (duff)
Duffell, *f.n.* ['dʌfl] (duffl)
Dufferin and Ava, *Marquess of* ['dʌfərɪn ənd 'ɑvə] (dúffĕrin ánd aávǎ)
Duffes, *f.n.* ['dʌfɪs] (dúffĕss)
Dufftown ['dʌftaʊn] (dúfftown); ['dʌftən] (dúfftŏn)
Duffus, *f.n.* ['dʌfəs] (dúffüss)
Dufour, *f.n.* [du'fʊər] (doófoŏr)
Dugan, *f.n.* ['dugən] (doógăn) *Appropriate also for the Barony of ~ of Victoria.*
Duggan, *f.n.* ['dʌɡən] (dúggăn)
Duggin, *f.n.* ['dʌɡɪn] (dúggin)
Duggleby, *f.n.* ['dʌɡlbɪ] (dúgglbi)
Duguid, *f.n.* ['djuɡɪd] (déwgid)
Duirinish, *Argyll, Ross., Skye* ['djuərɪnɪʃ] (dyoórinish)
Dukesfield ['dʌksfɪld] (dúcksfeeld)
Dukinfield ['dʌkɪnfɪld] (dúckinfeeld)
Dulais ['dɪlaɪs] (dílliss); ['dɪləs] (dílláss)

Duley, f.n. ['djulɪ] (déwli)
Dull [dʌl] (dull)
Dullatur ['dʌlətər] (dúllătŭr)
Dullea, f.n. [dju'leɪ] (dewláy); [dʌ'leɪ] (dulláy)
Dullingham ['dʌlɪŋəm] (dúlling-ăm)
Dulnain, River ['dʌlnən] (dúlnăn)
Dulnain Bridge ['dʌlnən 'brɪdʒ] (dúlnăn bríj)
Duloe ['djulov] (déwlō)
Dulson, f.n. ['dʌlsən] (dúlssŏn)
Dulwich ['dʌlɪdʒ] (dúllij); ['dʌlɪtʃ] (dúllitch)
Dumaresq, f.n. [dʊ'merɪk] (dŏŏmérrik); [dju'merɪk] (dewmérrik)
Dumas, f.n. [dju'mɑ] (dewmaá)
Dumbarton [dəm'bɑrtən] (dŭmbaártŏn)
Dumfries [dəm'fris] (dŭmfreéss) *Appropriate also for the Earl of ~.*
Dumont, f.n. [dju'mɒnt] (dewmónt); [dy'mõ] (dümŏ́ng)
Dunadry [dʌn'ædrɪ] (dunádri)
Dunalastair [dʌn'ælɪstər] (dunálistăr)
Dunalley, Baron [dʌn'ælɪ] (dunáli)
Dunball ['dʌnbɔl] (dúnbawl)
Dunbar, f.n. [dʌn'bɑr] (dunbaár)
Dunbar [dʌn'bɑr] (dunbaár)
Dunbartonshire [dʌn'bɑrtənʃaɪər] (dunbaártŏn-shīr)
Dunblane [dʌn'bleɪn] (dunbláyn)
Duncalfe, f.n. [dʌn'kɑf] (dun-kaáf)
Duncan, f.n. and C.n. ['dʌŋkən] (dúnkăn)
Duncannon, Viscount [dʌn'kænən] (dun-kánnŏn)
Dunchideock ['dʌntʃɪdək] (dúntchiddŏk)
Duncombe, f.n. ['dʌŋkəm] (dúnkŏm)
Dundarave [ˌdʌndə'reɪv] (dundáráyv)
Dundas, f.n. [dʌn'dæs] (dundáss)
Dundee [dʌn'di] (dundeé) *Appropriate also for the Earl of ~.*
Dundela, Belfast [dʌn'dilə] (dundeélá) *But the football team is pronounced* [dʌn-'delə] (dundéllá).
Dundonald [dʌn'dɒnld] (dundónnld)
Dundonian, native of Dundee [dʌn'dovnɪən] (dundŏ́niăn)
Dundrod [dʌn'drɒd] (dundród)
Dundrum [dʌn'drʌm] (dundrúm)
Dundry ['dʌndrɪ] (dúndri)
Dunedin, Viscountcy of [dʌn'idɪn] (dunneédin)
Dunfermline [dʌn'fɑrmlɪn] (dunférmlin) |
Dungannon [dʌn'gænən] (dun-gánnŏn)
Dungarvan, Viscount [dʌn'gɑrvən] (dun-gaárvăn)
Dungate, f.n. ['dʌngeɪt] (dún-gayt)
Dungavel [dʌn'geɪvl] (dun-gáyvl)
Dungeness [ˌdʌndʒɪ'nes] (dunjĕ́ness)
Dungiven [dʌn'gɪvən] (dun-gívvĕn)
Dunglass, Barony of [dʌn'glɑs] (dun-glaáss)
Dunheved [dʌn'hevɪd] (dun-hévvĕd)

Dunhill, f.n. ['dʌnhɪl] (dún-hil)
Dunholme ['dʌnəm] (dúnnŏm)
Dunino [dʌn'inov] (duneénō)
Dunipace ['dʌnɪpeɪs] (dúnnipayss)
Dunira [dʌn'ɪərə] (duneérá)
Dunkeld [dʌn'keld] (dun-kéld)
Dunkerley, f.n. ['dʌŋkərlɪ] (dúnkĕrli)
Dunkeswell ['dʌŋkɪzwel] (dúnkĕzwel)
Dunkley, f.n. ['dʌŋklɪ] (dúnkli)
Dunlop, f.n. ['dʌnlɒp] (dunlop)
Dunlop [dʌn'lɒp] (dunlóp)
Dunloy [dʌn'lɔɪ] (dunlóy)
Dunluce [dʌn'lus] (dunlooss) *Appropriate also for Viscount ~.*
Dunmore [dʌn'mɔr] (dun-mór) *Appropriate also for the Earl of ~.*
Dunmow ['dʌnmov] (dún-mō)
Dunmurry [dʌn'mʌrɪ] (dun-múrri)
Dunnet ['dʌnɪt] (dúnnĕt)
Dunnett, f.n. ['dʌnɪt] (dúnnĕt)
Dunnichen [dʌn'ɪxən] (duníchĕn)
Dunnico, f.n. [dʌnɪkov] (dúnnikō)
Dunnottar Castle [dʌn'ɒtər] (dunóttăr)
Dunoon [dʌn'un] (dunoón)
Dunphail [dʌn'feɪl] (dunfáyl)
Dunphie, f.n. ['dʌnfɪ] (dúnfi)
Dunrossil of Vallaquie, Viscount [dʌn-'rɒsɪl əv 'væləkwɪ] (dunróssil ŏv válákwi)
Duns [dʌnz] (dunz)
Dunsany, Baron of [dʌn'seɪnɪ] (dunsáyni)
Dunseverick [dʌn'severɪk] (dun-sévvĕrik)
Dunsheath, f.n. [dʌn'ʃiθ] (dun-sheéth); [dʌnz'hiθ] (dunz-heéth)
Dunsinane Hill [dʌn'sɪnən] (dun-sínnăn) *The pronunciation called for in Shakespeare's 'Macbeth' is* [ˌdʌnsɪ'neɪn] (dunsináyn) *or* ['dʌnsɪneɪn] (dúnssinayn).
Dunstaffnage Castle [dʌn'stæfnɪdʒ] (dunstáffnij)
Dunstan, f.n. ['dʌnstən] (dúnstăn)
Dunstanburgh ['dʌnstənbərə] (dúnstănbŭră)
Duntelchaig, Loch [ˌdʌntl'xeɪg] (duntl-cháyg)
Duntisbourne Rouse ['dʌntɪsbɔrn 'ravs] (dúntissborn rówss)
Duntocher [dʌn'tɒxər] (duntócher)
Duntze, f.n. [dʌnts] (dunts)
Dunure [dʌn'jʊər] (dun-yŏŏr)
Dunvant ['dʌnvənt] (dúnvănt)
Dunvegan [dʌn'vegən] (dunvéggăn); [dʌn'veɪgən] (dunváygăn)
Dunwear [dʌn'wɛər] (dunwaír); [dʌn-'wɪər] (dunweér)
Dunwich ['dʌnɪtʃ] (dúnnitch)
Dunwood ['dʌnwʊd] (dúnwŏŏd)
Dunwoody, f.n. [dʌn'wʊdɪ] (dunwŏ́ŏdi)
Dupont, f.n. [dju'pɒnt] (dewpónt); ['djupɒnt] (déwpont)
Dupplin Castle ['dʌplɪn] (dúpplin)
Dupré, f.n. [du'preɪ] (doopráy)

The form [dʌn] (dun) *used to indicate the unstressed prefix* Dun- *in Celtic names is that used in careful speech. Its occurrence as* [dən] (dŭn) *is equally frequent and acceptable.*

Duprée, *f.n.* [du'preɪ] (doopráy); [dju-'pri] (dewpreé)

Duprez, *f.n.* [du'preɪ] (doopráy); [dju-'preɪ] (dewpráy); [dju'pri] (dewpreé)

Duquemin, *f.n.* ['djukmɪn] (déwkmin)

Duquenoy, *f.n.* [djʊ'kenwɑ] (dyoōkén-waa)

Durance, *f.n.* [dju'rɑns] (dewraánss); [dju'ræns] (dewránss)

Durand, *f.n.* [djʊə'rænd] (dyoōránd); [dju'rænd] (dewránd)

Durant, *f.n.* [djuə'rænt] (dyoōránt)

Durbin, *f.n.* ['dɜrbɪn] (dúrbin)

Durden, *f.n.* ['dɜrdən] (dúrdĕn)

Durell, *f.n.* [djʊə'rel] (dyoōréll)

Duret, *f.n.* ['djʊəreɪ] (dyoōray)

Durgnat, *f.n.* ['dɜrgnæt] (dúrg-nat)

Durham ['dʌrəm] (dúrrăm) *Appropriate also for the Earldom of ~.*

Durie, *f.n.* ['djʊərɪ] (dyoōri)

Durisdeer ['dʌrɪzdɪər] (dúrrizdeer)

Durkar ['dɜrkər] (dúrkăr)

Durlacher, *f.n.* ['dɜrlækər] (dúrlacker)

Durness ['dɜrnɪs] (dúrnĕss)

Duror ['dʊərər] (dóōrŏr)

Durrad, *f.n.* ['dʌrəd] (dúrrăd)

Durrant, *f.n.* ['dʌrənt] (dúrránt)

Durrell, *f.n.* ['dʌrəl] (dúrrĕl) *Appropriate for Lawrence ~, author and poet, and for Gerald ~, author and zoologist.*

Dursley ['dɜrzlɪ] (dúrzli)

Durweston ['dʌrɪstən] (dúrrĕston)

Duthie, *f.n.* ['dʌθɪ] (dúthi)

Duthil ['dʌθɪl] (dúthil)

Duthoit, *f.n.* [du'θɔɪt] (doo-thóyt)

Dutoit, *f.n.* [dju'twɑ] (dewtwaá)

Dutot, *f.n.* [dy'toʊ] (dütő)

Duval, *f.n.* [dju'væl] (dewvál)

Dwan, *f.n.* [dwɒn] (dwon)

Dwight, *f.n.* [dwaɪt] (dwīt)

Dwygyfylchi [ˌdʊɪgə'vʌlxɪ] (dŏō-i-gắvúl-chi)

Dwynwen, *Welsh C.n.* ['dʊɪnwen] (dŏō-in-wen)

Dwyran ['dʊɪræn] (dŏō-i-ran)

Dwyryd, *f.n.* ['dʊɪrɪd] (dŏō-i-rid)

Dwyryd, River ['dʊɪrɪd] (dŏō-i-rid)

Dyas, *f.n.* ['daɪəs] (dí-áss)

Dyball, *f.n.* ['daɪbɒl] (díbawl)

Dyche, *f.n.* [daɪtʃ] (dítch)

Dyde, *f.n.* [daɪd] (dīd)

Dyer, *f.n.* ['daɪər] (dí-er)

Dyfatty [dʌ'vætɪ] (duvvátti)

Dyffryn ['dʌfrɪn] (dúffrin)

Dyffryn Ardudwy ['dʌfrɪn ɑr'dɪdʊɪ] (dúffrin aardeédŏō-i)

Dyffryn Maelor ['dʌfrɪn 'maɪlɒr] (dúffrin mflor)

Dyfi, River ['dʌvɪ] (dúvvi) *Another spelling is Dovey.*

Dyfnallt, *Welsh Bardic or C.n.* ['dʌvnæɪt] (dúvnahlt)

Dykes, *f.n.* [daɪks] (dīks)

Dylan, *C.n.* ['dʌlən] (dúllăn); ['dɪlən] (díllăn) *See Dylan Thomas under his surname.*

Dyment, *f.n.* ['daɪmənt] (dímĕnt)

Dymock, *f.n.* ['dɪmək] (dímmŏk)

Dymock ['dɪmək] (dímmŏk)

Dymoke, *f.n.* ['dɪmək] (dímmŏk)

Dymond, *f.n.* ['daɪmənd] (dímŏnd)

Dyneley, *f.n.* ['daɪnlɪ] (dínli)

Dynevor, *f.n.* ['dɪnɪvər] (dínnĕvŏr) *Appropriate also for Baron ~.*

Dynevor Castle ['dɪnɪvər] (dínnĕvŏr) *This is the English form and pronunciation used outside and, to some extent, inside Wales. ~ Grammar School in Swansea, however, is pronounced* [dɪ'nevər] (dinévvŏr). *The Welsh language spelling is Dinefwr, q.v.*

Dyrham ['dɪrəm] (dírrăm)

Dysart, Countess of ['daɪsərt] (díssárt)

Dysart ['daɪzərt] (dízărt)

Dyserth ['dɪsərθ] (dissĕrth)

Dyson, *f.n.* ['daɪsən] (díssŏn)

Dysyny, River [də'sʌnɪ] (dŭssúnni)

Dytham, *f.n.* ['daɪθəm] (díthăm)

E

Eaborn, *f.n.* ['ibɔrn] (eéborn)

Eadie, *f.n.* ['idɪ] (eédi)

Eadon, *f.n.* ['idən] (eédŏn)

Eady, *f.n.* ['idɪ] (eédi)

Eager, *f.n.* ['igər] (eéger)

Eagger, *f.n.* ['igər] (eéger)

Eaglescarnie [ˌiglz'kɛərnɪ] (eeglzkaírni)

Eaglesham ['iglʃəm] (eégl-shăm)

Eakring ['ekrɪŋ] (éckring); ['eɪkrɪŋ] (áykring)

Eales, *f.n.* [ilz] (eelz)

Eames, *f.n.* [imz] (eemz); [eɪmz] (aymz)

Eamonn, *C.n.* ['eɪmən] (áymŏn)

Eamont ['imənt] (eémŏnt); ['jæmənt] (yámmŏnt)

Earby ['ɪərbɪ] (eérbi)

Eardisland ['ɜrdzlənd] (érdzlănd)

Eardisley ['ɜrdzlɪ] (érdzli)

Eardly, *f.n.* ['ɜrdlɪ] (érdli)

Earengey, *f.n.* ['ɛərɪndʒeɪ] (aírĕnjay)

Earith ['ɪərɪθ] (eérith)

Earley, *f.n.* ['ɜrlɪ] (érli)

Earley ['ɜrlɪ] (érli)

Earls Colne ['ɜrlz 'koʊn] (érlz kŏn)

Earl Stonham ['ɜrl 'stɒnəm] (érl stónnăm)

Earlstoun ['ɜrlztən] (érlztŏn)

Earn, Loch *and* River [ɜrn] (ern)

Earp, *f.n.* [ɜrp] (erp)

Earsdon ['ɜrzdən] (érzdŏn)

Earsham ['ɜrʃəm] (ér-shăm)

Earsman, *f.n.* ['ɪərzmən] (eérzmăn)
Earwaker, *f.n.* ['ɑːrəkər] (ér-ăker); ['erə-kər] (érráker); ['ɪərweɪkər] (eérwayker)
Earwicker, *f.n.* ['erɪkər] (érricker)
Eashing ['iʃɪŋ] (eéshing)
Easington ['izɪŋtən] (eézingtŏn)
Eason, *f.n.* ['isən] (eéssŏn)
Eassie ['isɪ] (eéssi)
East Bergholt ['ist ˌ'bɜrghoʊlt] (eést bérg-hŏlt)
East Bierley ['ist 'baɪərlɪ] (eést bírli)
East Challow ['ist 'tʃæloʊ] (eést chálŏ)
East Donyland ['ist 'dɒnɪlənd] (eést dónniland)
East Freugh ['ist 'frux] (eést fro͞och)
East Hartlepool ['ist 'hɑrtlɪpul] (eést haártlipool)
East Heslerton ['ist 'heslərtən] (eést hésslěrtŏn)
East Hoathly ['ist hoʊθ'laɪ] (eést hŏth-lí)
East Horsley ['ist 'hɔrzlɪ] (eést hórzli)
East Kirby ['ist 'kɜrbɪ] (eést kírbi)
East Lothian ['ist 'loʊðɪən] (eést lóthiăn)
East Yelland ['ist 'jelənd] (eést yélländ)
Eastaugh, *f.n.* ['istɔ] (eéstaw)
Eastbourne ['istbɔrn] (eéstborn)
Eastcote ['istkoʊt] (eéstkŏt)
Easterbrook, *f.n.* ['istərbrʊk] (eéstěr-bro͞ok)
Eastham ['istəm] (eéstăm)
Easthampstead ['ist'hæmpstɪd] (eést-hámpstěd); ['istəmsted] (eéstămsted)
Eastleigh ['ist'li] (eést-leé)
Easton Mauduit ['istən 'mɔdɪt] (eéstŏn máwdit)
Eastry ['istrɪ] (eéstri)
Eastwood, *f.n.* ['istwʊd] (eéstwŏŏd)
Eaton, *f.n.* ['itən] (eétŏn)
Eaton Socon ['itən 'soʊkən] (eétŏn sŏkŏn)
Eaudyke ['oʊdaɪk] (ŏdík)
Eayrs, *f.n.* [eərz] (airz)
Ebbisham, *Baron* ['ebɪʃəm] (ébbi-shăm)
Ebbutt, *f.n.* ['ebət] (ébbŭt)
Ebbw Vale ['ebu 'veɪl] (ébboo váyl)
Eberle, *f.n.* ['ebərlɪ] (ébběrli)
Ebernoe House, *Sussex* ['ebərnoʊ] (ébběrnŏ)
Ebor, *Archbishop of York's signature* ['ibɔr] (eébor)
Ebor Handicap, *horse-race* ['ibɔr] (eébor)
Eboracum, *Roman name for York* [i'bɒrəkəm] (eebórrăkŭm)
Ebrington ['ebrɪŋtən] (ébbringtŏn); ['jʌbərtən] (yúbběrtŏn) *The first is appropriate for Viscount ~. The other, strictly local and used largely by older residents, is a legacy of an earlier form of the name.*
Ebury, *Baron* ['ibərɪ] (eébŭri)
Ecchinswell ['etʃɪnzwel] (étchinzwel)
Ecclefechan [ekl'fexən] (eckl-féchăn)
Ecclesall ['eklzɔl] (écklzawl)
Eccleshall ['eklʃəl] (éckl-shăl); ['eklʃɔl] (éckl-shawl)

Ecclesmachan [eklz'mæxən] (ecklz-máchăn)
Echlin, *f.n.* ['exlɪn] (échlin); ['eklɪn] (écklin)
Eckersall, *f.n.* ['ekərsl] (éckěrssl)
Eckersley, *f.n.* ['ekərzlɪ] (éckěrzli)
Edale ['ideɪl] (eédayl)
Eday ['ideɪ] (eéday)
Eddrachillis [ˌedrə'kɪlɪs] (edrăkílliss)
Ede, *f.n.* [id] (eed)
Edeirnion, Vale of, *also spelt* **Edeyrnion** [ə'daɪərnjɒn] (ědírn-yon)
Edelman, *f.n.* ['edlmən] (éddlmăn); ['eɪdlmən] (áydlmăn)
Edelsten, *f.n.* ['edlstən] (éddlstěn)
Eden, *f.n.* ['idən] (eéděn)
Edenbridge ['idənbrɪdʒ] (eéděn-brij)
Edenderry [ˌidən'derɪ] (eeděndérri)
Edenfield ['idənfɪld] (eéděnfeeld)
Edensor ['enzər] (énzŏr); ['ensər] (énssŏr)
Edern, *also spelt* **Edeyrn** ['eɪdɛərn] (áydairn)
Ederney ['edərnɪ] (édděrni)
Edeyrn *see* Edern.
Edeyrnion *see* Edeirnion.
Edgbaston ['edʒbəstən] (éj-băstŏn)
Edgcumbe, *Baron* ['edʒkəm] (éjkŭm)
Edgebolton [edʒ'boʊltən] (ej-bŏltŏn)
Edgecombe, *f.n.* ['edʒkəm] (éj-kŏm)
Edgell, *f.n.* ['edʒəl] (éjjěl)
Edgoose, *f.n.* [ed'gus] (ed-go͞oss)
Edholm, *f.n.* ['edhoʊm] (éd-hŏm)
Edial ['edɪəl] (éddiăl)
Edinburgh ['edɪnbərə] (éddinbŭră); ['ednbərə] (éddnbŭră)
Edinger, *f.n.* ['edɪndʒər] (éddinjer)
Edington ['idɪŋtən] (eédingtŏn)
Edisbury, *f.n.* ['edɪsbərɪ] (éddissbŭri)
Edlingham ['edlɪŋʒəm] (éddlinjăm)
Edmond, *f.n.* ['edmənd] (édmŏnd)
Edmondstone, *f.n.* ['edmənstoʊn] (éd-mŏnstŏn)
Edney, *f.n.* ['ednɪ] (édni)
Edolls, *f.n.* ['edəlz] (éddŏlz)
Edradour *Distillery* [ˌedrə'daʊər] (edrădówr)
Edradynate [ˌedrə'daɪnɪt] (edrădínit)
Edrich, *f.n.* ['edrɪtʃ] (édritch)
Edridge, *f.n.* ['edrɪdʒ] (édrij)
Edwalton [ed'wɔltən] (edwáwltŏn)
Edward, *C.n.* ['edwərd] (édwărd)
Edwardian, *pertaining to the era of King Edward VII* [ed'wɔrdɪən] (edwáwrdiăn); [ed'wɑrdɪən] (edwaárdiăn)
Edzell ['edzl] (edzl)
Eele, *f.n.* [il] (eel)
Efail Isaf ['evaɪl 'ɪsæv] (évvīl íssav)
Egan, *f.n.* ['iɡən] (eégăn)
Egerton, *f.n.* ['edʒərtən] (éjjěrtŏn)
Egerton ['edʒərtən] (éjjěrtŏn)
Eggesford ['egzfərd] (éggzfŏrd); ['egɪzfərd] (éggizfŏrd)
Eggington ['egɪŋtən] (éggingtŏn)
Egginton, *f.n.* ['egɪntən] (éggintŏn)
Egginton ['egɪntən] (éggintŏn)

Eglingham ['eglɪndʒəm] (égglinjăm)
Eglinton and Winton, Earl of ['eglɪntən ənd 'wɪntən] (égglintŏn ănd wíntŏn)
Eglish ['eglɪʃ] (égglish)
Egloshayle [ˌegləs'heɪl] (eglŏss-háyl)
Egloskerry [ˌegləs'kerɪ] (eglŏsskérri)
Egluiseg [e'gluɪseg] (egloó-isseg)
Eglwysfach [ˌeglʊɪs'vɑx] (eglŏóissvaá_ch_)
Eglwyswrw [ˌeglʊɪs'ʊəru] (eglŏóissŏóroo)
Egmanton ['egməntən] (éggmăntŏn)
Egmere ['egmɪər] (éggmeer)
Egremont, Cheshire, Cumberland ['egrɪmənt] éggrĕmŏnt)
Ehen, River ['iən] (eé-ĕn)
Eidda ['aɪðə] (f_thá_)
Eiddwen, Welsh C.n. ['aɪðwɪn] (f_thwĕn)
Eifion, Welsh C.n. ['aɪvɪɒn] (ívi-on)
Eigg [eg] (egg)
Eighton Banks ['eɪtən 'bæŋks] (áytŏn bánks); ['aɪtən 'bæŋks] (ítŏn bánks)
Eigra, Welsh C.n. ['aɪgrə] (ígrá)
Eil, Loch [il] (eel)
Eildon Hills ['ildən] (eéldŏn)
Eilean More ['elən 'mɔr] (éllăn mór)
Eilian, Welsh Bardic and C.n. ['aɪlɪən] (ílián)
Eiloart, f.n. ['aɪlovɑrt] (ílŏ-aart)
Einion, Welsh C.n. ['aɪnɪɒn] (íni-on)
Eira, Welsh C.n. ['aɪrə] (írá)
Eirene, C.n. [aɪ'rinɪ] (ireéni)
Eite, f.n. [aɪt] (ít)
Elan Valley Reservoir ['ilən] (eélăn)
Elboz, f.n. ['elbɒz] (élbozz)
Elburton ['elbərtən] (élbŭrtŏn)
Elchies ['elxɪz] (él_chiz_)
Elcho, Lord ['elkov] (élkŏ)
Elderslie, Ayr. ['eldərzlɪ] (éldĕrzli)
Elderslie, Renfrew. [ˌeldərz'li] (eldĕrzleé); ['eldərzlɪ] (éldĕrzli)
Eldred, f.n. ['eldrɪd] (éldrĕd); ['eldred] (éldred)
Eldridge, f.n. ['eldrɪdʒ] (éldrij)
Element, f.n. ['elɪmənt] (éllĕmĕnt)
Elerch ['eɪlərx] (áylĕr_ch_)
Eley, f.n. ['ilɪ] (eéli)
Elfed, Welsh C.n. ['elved] (élved)
Elford, f.n. ['elfərd] (élfŏrd)
Elgar, Sir Edward, composer ['elgɑr] (élgaar) Although this is the pronunciation by which the composer is usually known, there is a suggestion that he may have called himself ['elgər] (élgăr).
Elger, f.n. ['elgər] (élger)
Elgin ['elgɪn] (élgin) Appropriate also for the Earl of ~ and Kincardine, q.v., and for the ~ Marbles.
Elgin and Kincardine, Earl of ['elgɪn ənd kɪn'kɑrdɪn] (élgin ănd kinkaárdin)
Elgoll ['elgɒl] (élgol)
Elham ['iləm] (eélăm)
Elia, pen-name of Charles Lamb ['ilɪə] (eéliá)
Elias, f.n. [ɪ'laɪəs] (ĕlí-áss)
Elibank, Baron ['elɪbæŋk] (éllibank)

Elidyr-Fawr [e'lɪdər 'vauər] (elídder vówr)
Elie ['ilɪ] (eéli)
Eling ['ilɪŋ] (eéling)
Eliot, f.n. ['elɪət] (éllĭŏt)
Eliott, f.n. ['elɪət] (éllĭŏt)
Elkan, f.n. ['elkən] (élkăn); ['elkɑn] (élkaan) The second is appropriate for Benno ~, sculptor.
Elkesley ['elkslɪ] (élksli)
Elkind, f.n. ['elkaɪnd] (élkínd)
Elkins, f.n. ['elkɪnz] (élkinz)
Ell, f.n. [el] (ell)
Ellerman, f.n. ['elərmən] (éllĕrmăn)
Elles, f.n. ['elɪs] (élléss)
Ellesborough ['elzbərə] (élzbŭră)
Ellesmere, Earl of ['elzmɪər] (élzmeer)
Ellesmere Port ['elzmɪər 'pɔrt] (élzmeer pórt)
Ellinger, f.n. ['elɪndʒər] (éllinjer)
Ellingham ['elɪndʒəm] (éllinjăm)
Elliot, f.n. ['elɪət] (éllĭŏt)
Elliott, f.n. ['elɪət] (éllĭŏt)
Ellis, f.n. ['elɪs] (élliss)
Ellough ['elov] (éllŏ)
Elmham, North and South ['elməm] (élmăm)
Elmsall ['emsl] (emssl)
Elphick, f.n. ['elfɪk] (élfick)
Elphinstone, f.n. ['elfɪnstən] (élfinstŏn); ['elfɪnstovn] (élfinstŏn) The first is appropriate for Baron ~.
Elrig ['elrɪg] (élrig)
Else, f.n. [els] (elss)
Elsecar [ˌelsɪ'kɑr] (elssĕkaár)
Elsham ['elʃəm] (él-shám)
Elsing ['elzɪŋ] (élzing)
Elslack [el'slæk] (elssláck)
Elsom, f.n. ['elsəm] (élssŏm)
Elstow ['elstov] (élsstŏ)
Elswick ['elsɪk] (élssick)
Elswood, f.n. ['elzwvd] (élzwŏŏd)
Elt, f.n. [elt] (elt)
Eltham ['eltəm] (éltăm)
Eltisley ['eltɪzlɪ] (éltizli)
Eltringham ['eltrɪndʒəm] (éltrinjăm)
Eluned, Welsh C.n. [e'linɪd] (eleénĕd)
Elveden ['elvdən] (élvdĕn); ['eldən] (éldĕn) The second is appropriate for Viscount ~.
Elwell, f.n. ['elwəl] (élwĕl)
Elwes, f.n. ['elwɪz] (élwĕz)
Elwick, Durham ['elwɪk] (élwick)
Elwick, Northumberland ['elɪk] (éllick)
Elwy, River ['elvɪ] (éllŏŏ-i)
Ely, f.n. ['ilɪ] (eéli)
Ely ['ilɪ] (eéli)
Ely, River ['ilɪ] (eéli)
Elyhaugh ['ilɪhɑf] (eéli-haaf)
Embery, f.n. ['embərɪ] (émbĕri)
Emeleus, f.n. [ˌemɪ'liəs] (emmĕleé-ŭss)
Emeney, f.n. ['emɪnɪ] (émmĕni)
Emeny, f.n. ['emɪnɪ] (émmĕni)
Emere, f.n. [e'mɪər] (emmeér)
Emlyn, f.n. ['emlɪn] (émlin)

Emmet, *f.n.* ['emɪt] (émmĕt) *Appropriate also for Baroness* ~.

Emptage, *f.n.* ['emptɪdʒ] (émptij)

Emrys, *Welsh C.n.* ['emrɪs] (émriss)

Emyr, *Welsh C.n.* ['emɪər] (émmeer)

Endellion [ən'delɪən] (ĕndélliŏn)

Energlyn ['enərglɪn] (énnĕrglin)

Engelbach, *f.n.* ['eŋglbæk] (éng-gl-back)

Enham Alamein ['enəm 'æləmeɪn] (énnăm álămayn)

Ennals, *f.n.* ['enlz] (ennlz)

Ennisdale, *Barony of* ['enɪsdeɪl] (énniss-dayl)

Enniskillen [,enɪs'kɪlən] (enniskíllĕn) *Appropriate also for the Earl of* ~.

Enochdhu ['ɪnəx'du] (eėnŏch-doŏ)

Enraght, *f.n.* ['enrɪt] (énrit)

Enright, *f.n.* ['enraɪt] (énrīt)

Ensor, *f.n.* ['ensɔr] (énssor)

Enterkin ['entərkɪn] (éntĕrkin)

Enterkinfoot [,entərkɪn'fʊt] (entĕrkin-foŏt)

Enthoven, *f.n.* ['enθoʊvən] (ént-hōvĕn); [en'toʊvən] (entóvĕn)

Enticknap, *f.n.* ['entɪknæp] (éntick-nap); [,entɪk'næp] (enticknáp)

Entract, *f.n.* ['ɒntrækt] (óntrackt)

Entwistle, *f.n.* ['entwɪsl] (éntwissl)

Enys, *f.n.* ['enɪz] (énniz)

Enzie ['enɪ] (éng-i)

Eochar ['ɪəxər] (eė-ŏchăr) *The Gaelic spelling is* Iochdor, *q.v.*

Eport, *Loch* ['ɪpɔrt] (eėport)

Eppstein, *f.n.* ['epstaɪn] (épstīn)

Eppynt ['epɪnt] (éppint)

Epsom ['epsəm] (épssŏm)

Epstein, Sir Jacob, *sculptor* ['epstaɪn] (épstīn)

Ercall ['ɑrkl] (aarkl)

Erchless Castle ['ɛərklɪs] (áirklĕss)

Eresby ['ɪərzbɪ] (eėrzbi)

Erewash, *River* ['erɪwɒʃ] (érri-wosh)

Eriboll, *Loch* ['erɪbɒl] (érribol)

Ericht, *Loch and River* ['erɪxt] (érricht)

Ericsson, *f.n.* ['erɪksən] (érriksŏn)

Eridge Castle ['erɪdʒ] (érrij)

Eridge Green ['erɪdʒ 'grin] (érrij greén)

Eriska ['erɪskə] (érriskă)

Eriskay ['erɪskeɪ] (érriskay); ['erɪskɪ] (érriski)

Eriswell ['erɪswəl] (érrisswĕl)

Erith ['ɪərɪθ] (eėrith)

Erlanger, *f.n.* [ɛər'læŋər] (airláng-er)

Erlbeck, *f.n.* ['ɜrlbek] (érlbeck)

Erlestoke ['ɜrlstoʊk] (érl-stōk)

Erlich, *f.n.* ['ɛərlɪx] (áirlich)

Erne, *Earl of* [ɜrn] (ern)

Ernle, *Barony of* ['ɜrnlɪ] (érnli)

Errigal, *Co. Tyrone* ['erɪgəl] (érrigăl) *In the title of Viscount Alexander of Tunis and of* ~, *derived from* ~ *in Co. Donegal in the Republic of Ireland, the pronunciation is* ['erɪgɔl] (érrigawl).

Errochty Water ['erəxtɪ 'wɔtər] (érrŏchti wáwter)

Erroll, *Countess of* ['erəl] (érrŏl)

Erskine, *f.n.* ['ɜrskɪn] (érsskin)

Erskine ['ɜrskɪn] (érsskin)

Ervine, *f.n.* ['ɜrvɪn] (érvin)

Ervine, St. John, *author and dramatist* ['sɪndʒən 'ɜrvɪn] (sínjŏn érvin)

Erw ['eru] (érroo)

Erwood ['erʊd] (érrŏŏd)

Esclusham [es'klʊʃəm] (eskloóshăm)

Escoffey, *f.n.* [ɪs'kɒfɪ] (ĕskóffi)

Esdaile, *f.n.* ['ezdeɪl] (ézdayl)

Esgairgeiliog [,esgaɪər'gaɪljɒg] (essgīrgíl-yog)

Esh [eʃ] (esh)

Esha Ness ['eʃə nes] (éshă ness)

Esher ['iʃər] (eėsher) *Appropriate also for Viscount* ~.

Esholt ['eʃɒlt] (ésholt)

Eskdalemuir ['eskdeɪl'mjʊər] (éskdayl-myoŏr)

Esk Hause ['esk 'hɔz] (ésk háwz)

Eskmeals ['eskmɪlz] (éskmeelz)

Esler, *f.n.* ['eslər] (éssler)

Esmond, *f.n. and C.n.* ['ezmənd] (ézmŏnd)

Esmonde, *f.n.* ['ezmənd] (ézmŏnd)

Espinasse, *f.n.* ['espɪnæs] (éspinass)

Essame, *f.n.* ['eseɪm] (éssaym)

Essendine ['esəndaɪn] (éssĕndīn)

Essenhigh, *f.n.* ['esənhaɪ] (éssĕn-hī)

Essex ['esɪks] (éssĕks)

Esslemont, *f.n.* ['eslmənt] (ésslmŏnt)

Esthwaite Water ['esθweɪt 'wɔtər] (éss-thwayt wáwter)

Etal ['ɪtəl] (eétăl)

Etches, *f.n.* ['etʃɪz] (étchĕz)

Etchingham [,etʃɪŋ'hæm] (etching-hám)

Etheredge, *f.n.* ['eθərɪdʒ] (éthĕrij)

Etherege, *f.n.* ['eθərɪdʒ] (éthĕrėj)

Etheridge, *f.n.* ['eθərɪdʒ] (éthĕrij)

Etherton, *f.n.* ['eðərtən] (éthĕrtŏn)

Etive, *Loch and River* ['etɪv] (éttiv)

Etonian, *one educated at Eton College* [i'toʊnɪən] (eetóniăn)

Ettershank, *f.n.* ['etərʃæŋk] (éttĕr-shank)

Ettlinger, *f.n.* ['etlɪŋər] (étling-er)

Ettrick ['etrɪk] (étrick)

Etty, *f.n.* ['etɪ] (étti)

Etwall ['etwɒl] (étwawl)

Euler, *f.n.* ['julər] (yoóler); ['ɔɪlər] (óyler)

Eunson, *f.n.* ['junsən] (yoónssŏn)

Eurich, *f.n.* ['jʊərɪk] (yoŏrick)

Euston ['justən] (yoóstŏn)

Euxton ['ekstən] (éckstŏn)

Evand, *f.n.* ['evənd] (évvănd)

Evans, Beriah Gwyndaf, *Welsh divine* [bə'raɪə 'gwɪndæv 'evənz] (bĕriá gwíndav évvănz)

Evedon ['ivdən] (eévdŏn)

Eveleigh, *f.n.* ['ivlɪ] (eévli)

Eveleigh-de-Moleyns, *f.n.* ['ivlɪ 'deməlɪnz] (eévli démmŏleenz) *Family name of Baron Ventry.*

Eveline, *C.n.* ['ivlɪn] (eévlin)

Eveling, *f.n.* ['ivlɪŋ] (eévling)

Evely, f.n. ['ivlɪ] (eèvlĭ)
Evelyn, C.n. ['ivlɪn] (eèvlĭn); ['evlɪn] (évlĭn)
Evenjobb [,evən'dʒɒb] (evvĕnjób)
Evenley ['ivənlɪ] (eèvĕnli)
Evennett, f.n. ['evɪnet] (évvĕnet)
Everest, f.n. ['evərɪst] (évvĕrĕst)
Everett, f.n. ['evərɪt] (évvĕrĕt)
Everill, f.n. ['evərɪl] (évvĕrĭl)
Everingham, f.n. ['evərɪŋəm] (évvĕring-ăm)
Evers, f.n. ['evərz] (évvĕrz)
Evershed, f.n. ['evərʃed] (évvĕr-shed)
Eversholt ['evərʃɒlt] (évvĕr-sholt)
Every, f.n. ['evrɪ] (évvri); ['evərɪ] (évvĕri)
Evetts, f.n. ['evɪts] (évvĕts)
Evie ['ivɪ] (eèvi)
Evill, f.n. ['evɪl] (évvil)
Evington ['ivɪŋtən] (eèvingtŏn)
Ewart, f.n. ['juərt] (yoò-ărt)
Ewart ['juərt] (yoò-ărt)
Ewe, Loch [ju] (yoo)
Ewell ['juəl] (yoò-ĕl)
Ewelme ['juelm] (yoò-elm)
Ewen, f.n. ['juɪn] (yoò-ĕn)
Ewenny [ɪ'wenɪ] (ĕ-wénni)
Ewing, f.n. ['juɪŋ] (yoò-ing)
Ewloe ['julou] (yoòlō)
Ewood Bridge ['iwʊd 'brɪdʒ] (eè-woòd brij)
Exceat ['eksɪt] (éckseet)
Excell, f.n. [ek'sel] (eckséll)
Exe, River [eks] (ecks)
Exeter ['eksɪtər] (écksĕter) *Appropriate also for the Marquess of ~.*
Exford ['eksfɔrd] (écksford)
Exmouth ['eksmauθ] (écksmowth)
Exstance, f.n. ['ekstəns] (éckstănss)
Exwick ['ekswɪk] (éckswick)
Ey, River [eɪ] (ay)
Eyam, f.n. [im] (eem)
Eyam [im] (eem)
Eyck, f.n. [aɪk] (īk)
Eyden, f.n. ['eɪdən] (áydĕn)
Eydon ['idən] (eèdŏn)
Eye, *Hereford., Northants., Suffolk* [aɪ] (ī)
Eyemouth ['aɪmauθ] (ímowth)
Eyers, f.n. [εərz] (airz)
Eyet, f.n. ['aɪət] (í-ĕt)
Eyke [aɪk] (īk)
Eyles, f.n. [aɪlz] (īlz)
Eynesbury ['eɪnzbərɪ] (áynzbŭrĭ)
Eynon, Welsh C.n. ['aɪnən] (ínŏn)
Eynsford ['eɪnsfərd] (áynssfŏrd)
Eynsham ['enʃəm] (én-shăm); ['eɪnʃəm] (áyn-shăm)
Eype [ip] (eep)
Eyre, f.n. [εər] (air)
Eyre and Spottiswoode, publishers ['εər ənd 'spɒtɪswʊd] (aír ănd spóttis-woòd)
Eyres, f.n. [εərz] (airz)
Eysenck, f.n. ['aɪzeŋk] (ízenk)
Eyston, f.n. ['istən] (eèstŏn)
Eythorne ['eɪθərn] (áy-thorn)

Eyton, f.n. ['aɪtən] (ítŏn); ['itən] (eètŏn)
Eyton ['eɪtən] (áytŏn)
Eyton-on-the-Weald Moors ['aɪtən ɒn ðə 'wild 'muərz] (ítŏn on thē weéld moòrz)

F

Faber, f.n. ['feɪbər] (fáyber)
Fabian, f.n. ['feɪbɪən] (fáybi-ăn)
Fâche, f.n. [faʃ] (faash)
Facit ['feɪsɪt] (fáyssit)
Fada, Loch ['fædə] (fáddă)
Faed, f.n. [feɪd] (fayd)
Fage, f.n. [feɪdʒ] (fayj)
Fageant, f.n. ['feɪdʒənt] (fáyjănt)
Fagence, f.n. ['feɪdʒəns] (fáyjĕnss)
Fahie, f.n. ['feɪɪ] (fáy-i); ['faɪ] (faà-i)
Faichney, f.n. ['feɪxnɪ] (fáychni)
Faifley ['feɪflɪ] (fáyfli)
Fairbank, f.n. ['fεərbæŋk] (faírbank)
Fairbanks, f.n. ['fεərbæŋks] (faírbanks)
Fairclough, f.n. ['fεərklʌf] (faírkluff); ['fεərklou] (faírklō)
Fairfoull, f.n. ['fεərfaul] (faírfowl)
Fairley, f.n. ['fεərlɪ] (faírli)
Fairmaner, f.n. ['fεərmænər] (faír-manner); [fεər'mænər] (fairmánner)
Fairminer, f.n. ['fεərmɪnər] (faírminner)
Fairwarp ['fεərwɔrp] (faírwawrp)
Fakenham ['feɪkənəm] (fáykĕnăm)
Fala ['fælə] (fálă)
Falcon, f.n. ['fɔkən] (fáwkŏn)
Falconbridge, f.n. ['fɔkənbrɪdʒ] (fáwkŏn-brij)
Falconer, f.n. ['fɔlkənər] (fáwlkŏner); ['fɔknər] (fáwkner); ['fɒlkənər] (fól-kŏner)
Faldingworth ['fɔldɪŋwɜrθ] (fáwlding-wurth)
Falfield ['fælfɪld] (fálfeeld)
Falk, f.n. [fɒlk] (fawlk); [fɔk] (fawk)
Falkiner, f.n. ['fɔknər] (fáwkner)
Falkirk ['fɔlkərk] (fáwlkirk)
Falkland, Viscount ['fɔklənd] (fáwklănd)
Falkland ['fɒlklənd] (fáwlklănd)
Falkus, f.n. ['fɔlkəs] (fáwlkŭss)
Falla, f.n. ['fælə] (fálă)
Fallapit ['fæləpɪt] (fálăpit)
Falle, f.n. [fɒl] (fawl)
Faller, f.n. ['fælər] (fáler)
Fallin [fə'lɪn] (fălín)
Fallodon ['fælədən] (fálŏdŏn)
Falmouth ['fælməθ] (fálmŭth) *Appropriate also for Viscount ~.*
Falstone ['fælstoun] (fálstōn)
Fannich, Mountains, River, *and* Loch ['fænɪx] (fánnich)
Fantham, f.n. ['fænθəm] (fán-thăm)

Fanum House, *London* ['fernəm] (fáy-nŭm)
Faragher, *f.n.* ['færəgər] (fárrăger)
Farcet ['farsɪt] (faarssĕt)
Far Cotton ['far 'kɒtən] (faar kóttŏn)
Farey, *f.n.* ['fɛərɪ] (faíri)
Fargie, *f.n.* ['farɡɪ] (faárgi)
Faris, *f.n.* ['færɪs] (fárriss)
Farmbrough, *f.n.* ['farmbrə] (faármbră)
Farncombe, *f.n.* ['farnkəm] (faárnkŏm)
Farnell ['farnəl] (faárnĕl)
Farquhar, *f.n.* ['farkər] (faárkăr); ['fark-wər] (faárkwăr) *Both are used for George* ~, *the 17th-c. Irish dramatist.*
Farquharson, *f.n.* ['farkərsən] (faár-kărssŏn); ['farkwərsən] (faárkwărssŏn)
Farragon ['færəɡən] (fárrăgŏn)
Farrar, *f.n.* ['færər] (fárrăr)
Farrington Gurney ['færɪŋtən 'ɡɜrnɪ] (fárringtŏn gúrni)
Farvis, *f.n.* ['farvɪs] (faárviss)
Faskally, *Loch* ['faskəlɪ] (faáskăli); ['fasklɪ] (faáskli)
Faslane *Bay* [fæz'leɪn] fazláyn); [fə'sleɪn] (făssláyn)
Fasnakyle [ˌfæsnə'kaɪl] (fassnăkíl)
Faucett, *f.n.* ['fɔsɪt] (fáwssĕt)
Faucitt, *f.n.* ['fɒsɪt] (fáwssit)
Faugh [fæf] (faff); [fɑf] (faaf)
Faughan, *River* ['fɒxən] (fóchăn)
Fauldhouse ['fɒldhaʊs] (fáwld-howss)
Faulds, *f.n.* [fouldz] (földz); [fɔldz] (fawldz)
Faulkbourne ['fɒbɜrn] (fáwburn); ['fɒbɔrn] (fáwborn)
Faulkes, *f.n.* [fɔlks] (fawlks)
Faulkner, *f.n.* ['fɒknər] (fáwkner)
Faulks, *f.n.* [foʊks] (föks)
Faupel, *f.n.* [fou'pel] (föpéll)
Faure, *f.n.* [fɔr] (for)
Fausset, *f.n.* ['fɒsɪt] (fáwssĕt); ['fɒsɪt] (fóssĕt)
Fauvel, *f.n.* [fou'vel] (fövéll)
Faux, *f.n.* [fɒks] (fawks); [fou] (fö)
Favarger, *f.n.* [fə'varʒər] (făvaárzher)
Favell, *f.n.* ['fervl] (fayvl)
Faversham ['fævərʃəm] (fávvĕr-shăm)
Faville, *f.n.* ['fævɪl] (fávvil); ['fervɪl] (fáyvil)
Favor Royal ['fervər 'rɔɪəl] (fáyvŏr róyăl)
Fawcett, *f.n.* ['fɒsɪt] (fáwssĕt); ['fɒsɪt] (fóssĕt)
Fawdry, *f.n.* ['fɒdrɪ] (fáwdri)
Fawssett, *f.n.* ['fɒsɪt] (fáwssĕt)
Fayer, *f.n.* [fɛər] (fair); ['feɪər] (fáy-er)
Fayers, *f.n.* [fɛərz] (fairz); ['feɪərz] (fáy-ĕrz)
Fayrer, *f.n.* ['fɛərər] (faírer)
Fazackerley, *f.n.* [fə'zækərlɪ] (făzáckĕrli)
Fazakerley, *f.n.* [fə'zækərlɪ] (făzáckĕrli)
Fazakerley [fə'zækərlɪ] (făzáckĕrli)
Fazan, *f.n.* [fə'zæn] (făzánn)
Fazekas, *f.n.* [fə'zeɪkəs] (făzáykăss)
Fazeley ['feɪzlɪ] (fáyzli)

Fearenside, *f.n.* ['fɜrnsaɪd] (férn-síd)
Fearn, *f.n.* [fɜrn] (fern); [fɛərn] (fairn)
Fearn [fɜrn] (fern)
Fearnan ['fɜrnən] (férnăn)
Fearne, *f.n.* [fɜrn] (fern); [fɛərn] (fairn)
Fearon, *f.n.* ['fɪərən] (feérŏn)
Featherstonehaugh, *f.n.*, *also spelt* **Featherstonhaugh, Fetherstonhaugh** ['feðərstənhə] (féthĕrstŏn-haw); ['fænʃə] (fán-shaw); ['festənhɒ] (féstŏn-haw); ['fɪsənheɪ] (feéssŏn-hay); ['fɪərstənhə] (feérstŏn-haw)
Feavearyear, *f.n.* ['fevjər] (fév-yer)
Feaver, *f.n.* ['fivər] (feéver)
Fechlie, *f.n.* ['fexlɪ] (féchli)
Feeny ['finɪ] (feéni)
Feighan, *f.n.* ['fiən] (fee-än)
Feilden, *f.n.* ['fildən] (feéldĕn)
Feilding, *f.n.* ['fildɪŋ] (feélding)
Feiling, *f.n.* ['faɪlɪŋ] (fíling)
Feist, *f.n.* [fist] (feest)
Felindre, *Radnor* [ve'lɪndreɪ] (velíndray) *cf.* Velindre.
Felin-foel [ˌvelɪn'vɔɪl] (vellinvóyl)
Felin-hen [ˌvelɪn'heɪən] (vellin-háy-ĕn)
Fellowes, *f.n.* ['telouz] (féllöz)
Felmersham ['felmərʃəm] (félmĕr-shăm)
Felpham ['felphəm] (félp-hăm); ['felpəm] (félpăm); ['felfəm] (félfăm)
Feltham ['feltəm] (féltăm)
Feltwell ['feltwel] (féltwel)
Fenay Bridge ['fenɪ 'brɪdʒ] (fénni bríj)
Feniscowles ['fenɪskoulz] (fénnisskölz)
Fennell, *f.n.* ['fenl] (fennl)
Fennelly, *f.n.* ['fenəlɪ] (fénnĕli)
Fentiman, *f.n.* ['fentɪmən] (féntimăn)
Fenwick, *f.n.* ['fenɪk] (fénnick); ['fenwɪk] (fén-wick)
Fenwick ['fenɪk] (fénnick)
Feock ['fiɒk] (fee-ŏk)
Feoffees Town Hall, The, *Colyton* ['fifɪz] (feéfeez)
Ferbrache, *f.n.* ['fɜrbræʃ] (férbrash)
Fereday, *f.n.* ['ferɪdeɪ] (férrĕday)
Ferens, *f.n.* ['ferənz] (férrĕnz)
Ferguslie [ˌfɜrɡəs'li] (fergüssleé)
Ferguson, *f.n.* ['fɜrɡəsən] (férgüssŏn)
Fergusson, *f.n.* ['fɜrɡəsən] (férgüssŏn)
Ferintosh [fɜrn'tɒʃ] (ferntósh)
Fermanagh [fər'mænə] (férmánnă) *Appropriate also for Baron* ~.
Fernald, *f.n.* ['fɜrnəld] (férnăld)
Fernau, *f.n.* ['fɜrnou] (férnö)
Fernie, *f.n.* ['fɜrnɪ] (férni)
Fernihough, *f.n.* ['fɜrnɪhou] (férni-hö)
Fernyhalgh ['fɜrnɪhʌf] (férni-huff); ['fɜrnɪhælʃ] (férni-halsh)
Fernyhough, *f.n.* ['fɜrnɪhou] (férni-hö)
Ferrier, *f.n.* ['ferɪər] (férri-er)
Ferriggi, *f.n.* [fə'rɪdʒɪ] (fĕreéji)
Ferryside [ˌferɪ'saɪd] (ferri-síd)
Fertel, *f.n.* ['fɜrtəl] (fértĕl)
Feshie, *River* ['feʃɪ] (féshi)
Feshie Bridge ['feʃɪ 'brɪdʒ] (féshi bríj)
Festiniog [fes'tɪnjɒɡ] (festín-yog)

Fethaland Point ['feðəlænd] (féthăland)
Fetherstonhaugh, *f.n. see Featherstone-
haugh.*
Fetlar ['fetlər] (féttlår)
Fettes, *f.n.* ['fetɪz] (féttĕz); ['fetɪs] (féttĕss)
Fettes College ['fetɪs] (féttĕss)
Fettesian, *one educated at Fettes College*
[fə'tizɪən] (fĕtéeziăn)
Feversham, *Baron* ['fevərʃəm] (févvĕr-
shăm)
Fewtrell, *f.n.* ['fjutrəl] (féwtrĕl)
Ffair-fach [ˌfaɪər'vax] (ffīrváa__ch__)
Ffaldau ['fældaɪ] (fáldī)
Ffion, *Welsh C.n.* ['fɪɒn] (fee-on)
Ffolkes, *f.n.* [fouks] (fōks)
Fforest-fach [ˌfɒrɪst'vax] (forrĕst-vaa__ch__)
Fforest Fawr [ˌfɒrɪst 'vauər] (forrĕst
vówr)
Ffoulkes, *f.n.* [fouks] (fōks); [fuks] (fooks)
Ffrangcon, *f.n.* ['fræŋkən] (fránkŏn)
Ffrangcon-Davies,Gwen, *actress* ['gwen
'fræŋkən 'deɪvɪs] (gwén fránkŏn dáyviss)
Ffrwd-wyllt, *River* [frud'wɪłt] (frŏŏd-
wíhlt)
Ffynnongroyw [ˌfʌnən'groɪu] (funnŏn-
gróy-oo)
Fiddes ['fɪdɪs] (fíddĕss)
Fidler, *f.n.* ['fɪdlər] (fídler); ['fɪdlər]
(féedler)
Fidra ['fɪdrə] (fídră) *Appropriate for ~
Island lighthouse.*
Field Dalling ['fɪld 'dolɪŋ] (féeld dáwling)
Fielding, *f.n.* ['fɪldɪŋ] (féelding)
Appropriate for Henry ~, 18th-c. author.
Fienburgh, *f.n.* ['fɪnbərə] (féenbŭră)
Fiennes, *f.n.* [faɪnz] (fīnz)
Fife [faɪf] (fīf)
Figgis, *f.n.* ['fɪgɪs] (fíggiss)
Figgures, *f.n.* ['fɪgərz] (fíggŭrz)
Figheldean ['faɪldɪn] (fíldeen)
Figures, *f.n.* ['fɪgərz] (fíggŭrz)
Filby, *f.n.* ['fɪlbɪ] (fílbi)
Fildes, *f.n.* [faɪldz] (fīldz)
Filey ['faɪlɪ] (fíli)
Filleigh ['fɪlɪ] (fílli)
Fillongley ['fɪlɒŋlɪ] (fíllong-li)
Filmer, *f.n.* ['fɪlmər] (fílmer)
Finaghy ['fɪnəxɪ] (fínná__ch__i)
Finborough Parva ['fɪnbərə 'parvə]
(fínbŭră paárvă)
Fincastle [fɪn'kɑsl] (fin-káassl) *Appro-
priate also for Viscount ~.*
Finchale ['fɪŋkl] (fínkl) *Appropriate also
for ~ Abbey.*
Fincham, *f.n.* ['fɪntʃəm] (fíntchăm)
Finchampstead ['fɪnʃəmsted] (fínshăm-
sted)
Finchingfield ['fɪnʃɪŋfɪld] (fínshing-
feeld)
Findern ['fɪndərn] (fíndĕrn)
Findhorn ['fɪndhɔrn] (fínd-horn)
Findlater, *f.n.* ['fɪnlətər] (fínláter);
['fɪndlətər] (fíndláter)
Findlater ['fɪndlətər] (fíndláter)
Findlay, *f.n.* ['fɪnlɪ] (fínli); ['fɪndlɪ] (fíndli)

Findley, *f.n.* ['fɪndlɪ] (fíndli)
Findochty ['fɪndɒxtɪ] (fín-do__ch__ti); [fɪ-
'nextɪ] (finé__ch__ti)
Finedon ['faɪndən] (fíndŏn)
Finer, *f.n.* ['faɪnər] (fíner)
Fingal, *Norse hero* ['fɪŋgəl] (fíng-găl)
Fingal's Cave ['fɪŋgəlz 'keɪv] (fíng-gălz
káyv)
Fingalian, *pertaining to Fingal* [fɪŋ'geɪ-
lɪən] (fíng-gáyliăn)
Fingall, *Earl of* [fɪŋ'gɔl] (fíng-gáwl)
Fingest ['fɪndʒɪst] (fínjĕst)
Fingland, *f.n.* ['fɪŋlənd] (fíng-lánd)
Fingringhoe ['fɪŋrɪŋhou] (fíng-ring-hō)
Finlay, *f.n.* ['fɪnlɪ] (fínli)
Finlayson, *f.n.* ['fɪnlɪsən] (fínlissŏn)
Finnart ['fɪnərt] (fínnărt)
Finney, *f.n.* ['fɪnɪ] (fínni)
Finnie, *f.n.* ['fɪnɪ] (fínni)
Finnieston ['fɪnɪstən] (fínnistŏn)
Finnucane, *f.n.* [fɪ'nukən] (finoókăn);
[fɪ'njukən] (finéwkăn)
Finsbury Park ['fɪnzbərɪ 'park] (fínzbŭri
paárk)
Finstown ['fɪnstən] (fínsstŏn)
Fintona ['fɪntənə] (fíntŏnă)
Finucane, *f.n.* [fɪ'nukən] (finoókăn);
[fɪ'njukən] (finéwkăn)
Finvoy [fɪn'vɔɪ] (finvóy)
Finzean ['fɪŋən] (fíng-ăn)
Finzi, Gerald, *composer* ['fɪnzɪ] (fínzi)
Fionda, *f.n.* [fɪ'ɒndə] (fi-óndă)
Fior, *f.n.* ['fɪɔr] (fee-or)
Firle [fɜrl] (firl)
Firmager, *f.n.* ['fɜrmədʒər] (fírmăjer)
Firminger, *f.n.* ['fɜrmɪndʒər] (fírminjer)
Firth, *f.n.* [fɜrθ] (firth)
Fisherie ['fɪʃərɪ] (físhĕri)
Fishguard ['fɪʃgɑrd] (físhgaard)
Fishwick, *f.n.* ['fɪʃwɪk] (físh-wick)
Fison, *f.n.* ['faɪsən] (físsŏn)
Fitzailwyn, *f.n.* ['fɪts'eɪlwɪn] (fits-áylwin)
Fitzgerald, *f.n.* [fɪts'dʒerəld] (fits-jérrăld)
Fitzgibbon, *f.n.* [fɪts'gɪbən] (fits-gíbbŏn)
Fitzhardinge, *f.n.* [fɪts'hardɪŋ] (fits-
haárding)
Fitzpatrick, *f.n.* [fɪts'pætrɪk] (fits-
pátrick)
Fitzrandolph, *f.n.* [fɪts'rændɒlf] (fits-
rándolf)
Fitzroy, *f.n.* ['fɪtsrɔɪ] (fítsroy)
Fitzsimons, *f.n.* [fɪts'saɪmənz] (fits-
símŏnz)
Flackes, *f.n.* [flæks] (flacks)
Flaherty, *f.n.* ['flahərtɪ] (flaáhĕrti);
['flaərtɪ] (flaá-ĕrti)
Flannan Islands ['flænən] (flánnăn)
Flavell, *f.n.* ['fleɪvl] (flayvl); [flə'vel]
(flăvéll)
Flavin, *f.n.* ['fleɪvɪn] (fláyvin)
Flawith ['flɔ-ɪθ] (fláw-ith); [flɔɪθ] (floyth)
Flax Bourton ['flæks 'bɔrtən] (flácks
bórtŏn)
Fleggburgh ['flegbərə] (flégbŭră)
Fleischman, *f.n.* ['flaɪʃmən] (flíshmăn)

Fleming, f.n. ['flemɪŋ] (flémming) *Appropriate also for Sir Alexander ~, bacteriologist.*

Flessati, f.n. [flə'satɪ] (flĕssaáti)

Fletchamstead ['fletʃəmsted] (flétchámsted)

Fletcher, f.n. ['fletʃər] (flétcher)

Fleur de Lis [‚flɜr də 'li] (flur dĕ leé)

Fleure, f.n. [flɜr] (flur)

Flewin, f.n. ['flʌɪn] (floó-in)

Flint [flɪnt] (flint)

Flitwick ['flɪtɪk] (flíttick)

Floate, f.n. [flout] (flōt)

Floore see Flore.

Flore, also spelt **Floore** [flor] (flor)

Florey, f.n. ['florɪ] (fláwri) *Appropriate also for Barony of ~.*

Floris, f.n. ['florɪs] (flórriss)

Floud, f.n. [flʌd] (fludd)

Flury, f.n. ['flʊərɪ] (floóri)

Flux, f.n. [flʌks] (flucks)

Fochabers ['fɒxəbərz] (fóchăbĕrz)

Fochriw ['vɒxrɪu] (vóchri-oo)

Fogarty, f.n. ['fougərtɪ] (fōgắrti)

Fogerty, f.n. ['fougərtɪ] (fōgĕrti)

Fogou Caves ['fugu] (foógoo)

Folan, f.n. ['foulən] (fōlăn)

Foljambe, f.n. ['fuldʒəm] (fŏóljăm) *Family name of the Earl of Liverpool.*

Folkard, f.n. ['foukərd] (fōkárd); ['foulkard] (fōl-kaard); ['fɒlkard] (fól-kaard)

Folke [fouk] (fōk)

Folkes, f.n. [fouks] (fōks)

Folkestone ['foukstən] (fōkstŏn) *Appropriate also for Viscount ~.*

Folkingham ['fɒkɪŋəm] (fócking-ăm)

Folkington ['fouɪŋtən] (fó-ingtŏn)

Folwell, f.n. ['fɒlwəl] (fól-wĕl)

Fomison, f.n. ['fɒmɪsən] (fómmissŏn)

Fontaine, f.n. ['fɒnteɪn] (fóntayn)

Fonteyn, Dame Margot, ballerina ['margou 'fɒnteɪn] (maárgō fóntayn); [fɒn'teɪn] (fóntáyn) *Dame Margot herself finds that the stress varies according to the context.*

Foord, f.n. [ford] (ford)

Foort, f.n. [fort] (fort)

Footdee [fʊt'di] (fŏot-deé); ['fɪtɪ] (fítti)

Footler, f.n. ['fʊtlər] (fŏotler)

Forbes, f.n. ['fɒrbɪs] (fórbĕss); [fɔrbz] (forbz) *The first, which is appropriate for Baron ~ and for the Master of ~, is more usual in Aberdeenshire, the home county of the Clan Forbes.*

Forbes-Sempill, f.n. ['fɔrbɪs 'sempl] (fórbĕss sémpl) *Family name of the Barons of Sempill.*

Ford, Ford Madox, author ['ford 'mædəks 'fɔrd] (fórd máddŏcks fórd) *Formerly Ford Madox Hueffer, q.v.*

Forde, f.n. [ford] (ford)

Fordell [fɔr'del] (fordéll)

Fordoun [fɔr'dun] (fordoón)

Fordred, f.n. ['fordrɪd] (fórdrĕd)

Fordwich ['fordwɪtʃ] (fórdwitch); ['forditʃ] (fórditch)

Fordyce, f.n. [fɔr'daɪs] (fordíss)

Fordyce [fɔr'daɪs] (fordíss)

Foren, f.n. ['fɒrən] (fáwrĕn)

Forestier, f.n. ['fɒrɪstjər] (fórrĕst-yer)

Forfar ['fɔrfər] (fórfăr)

Forgan, f.n. ['fɔrgən] (fórgăn)

Forgandenny [‚fɔrgən'denɪ] (forgăn-dénni)

Forncett St. Mary ['fɔrnsɪt snt 'meərɪ] (fórnsĕt sĭnt maíri)

Forncett St. Peter ['fɔrnsɪt snt 'pitər] (fórnsĕt sĭnt peéter)

Fornsete, John of, 13th-c. composer ['fɔrnset] (fórnsett)

Forrabury ['fɒrəbərɪ] (fórrăbŭri)

Forres ['fɒrɪs] (fórrĕss) *Appropriate also for Baron ~.*

Forster, f.n. ['fɔrstər] (fórster); ['fɒstər] (fósster) *The first is appropriate for E. M. ~, author.*

Forster of Harraby, Baron ['fɒstər əv 'hærəbɪ] (fósster ŏv hárrăbi)

Forsyth, f.n. [fɔr'saɪθ] (forssíth)

Forsythe, f.n. [fɔr'saɪθ] (forssíth)

Fortbreda [fɔrt'brɪdə] (fortbreédă)

Forte, f.n. ['fɔrtɪ] (fórti)

Forter Castle ['fɔrtər] (fórter)

Fortescue, Earl ['fɔrtɪskju] (fórtĕskew)

Forteviot [fɔr'tɪvɪət] (forteéviŏt) *Appropriate also for Baron ~.*

Fortingall ['fɔrtɪŋgəl] (fórting-găl)

Fortrose ['fɒrtrouz] (fórtrōz)

Fortuin, f.n. ['fɔrtjuɪn] (fórt-yŏóin); [fɔr'taɪn] (fortín)

Foryd ['vɒrɪd] (vórrid)

Fosdyke ['fɒzdaɪk] (fózdík); ['fɒsdaɪk] (fóssdík)

Foster, f.n. ['fɒstər] (fósster)

Fotheringhay ['fɒðərɪŋheɪ] (fóthĕringhay); ['fɒðərɪŋgeɪ] (fóthĕring-gay) *The first is the village pronunciation today. The other is more usual for historic ~ Castle.*

Foudland ['faudlənd] (fówdländ)

Foula ['fulə] (foólă)

Foulden ['fuldən] (foóldĕn)

Foulds, f.n. ['fouldz] (fōldz) *Appropriate also for John ~, composer.*

Foulger, f.n. ['fuldʒər] (foóljer); ['fuldʒər] (fŏóljer); ['fouldʒər] (fóljer); ['fɒldʒər] (fóljer); ['fulgər] (foólger)

Foulis, f.n. [faulz] (fowlz)

Foulis [faulz] (fowlz) *Appropriate also for ~ Castle.*

Foulis Ferry ['faulz 'ferɪ] (fówlz férri)

Foulkes, f.n. [fouks] (fōks); [fauks] (fowks)

Foulness ['faul'nes] (fówl-néss)

Foulridge ['foulrɪdʒ] (fōlrij)

Foulsham, f.n. ['fulʃəm] (fŏol-shăm)

Foulsham ['foulʃəm] (fōl-shăm); ['fulʃəm] (fŏol-shăm); ['foulsəm] (fōlssăm)

Foulshiels ['faul'ʃilz] (fówl-sheélz)

Foux, *f.n.* [fuks] (fooks)
Fovant ['fɒvənt] (fóvvănt)
Foweraker, *f.n.* ['faʊəreɪkər] (fówĕr-ayker)
Fowey [fɔɪ] (foy)
Fowke, *f.n.* [foʊk] (fōk); [faʊk] (fowk)
Fowkes, *f.n.* [foʊks] (fōks); [faʊks] (fowks)
Fowlis Easter ['faʊlz 'istər] (fówlz eéster)
Fowlis Wester ['faʊlz 'westər] (fówlz wéster)
Fownhope ['faʊnhoʊp] (fówn-hōp)
Fox, Uffa, *yacht designer* ['ʌfə 'fɒks] (úffă fócks)
Foxell, *f.n.* ['fɒksl] (focksl)
Foxen, *f.n.* ['fɒksən] (fócksĕn)
Foxhole ['fɒkshoʊl] (fócks-hōl)
Foy, *f.n.* [fɔɪ] (foy)
Foyle, *f.n.* [fɔɪl] (foyl)
Fradin, *f.n.* ['freɪdɪn] (fráydin)
Fraenkel, *f.n.* ['freŋkl] (frankl)
Framingham ['freɪmɪŋəm] (frámming-ăm)
Francillon, *f.n.* [fræn'sɪlən] (fran-síllŏn)
Francke, *f.n.* ['fræŋkɪ] (fránki)
Franey, *f.n.* ['freɪnɪ] (fráyni)
Frankau, *f.n.* ['fræŋkoʊ] (fránkō); ['fræŋkaʊ] (fránkow) *The first is appropriate for Gilbert ~, author, and for Pamela ~, author.*
Frankel, *f.n.* ['fræŋkl] (frankl)
Frankell, *f.n.* ['fræŋkl] (frankl)
Franklin, *f.n.* ['fræŋklɪn] (fránklin)
Frant [frænt] (frant)
Fraser, *f.n.* ['freɪzər] (fráyzer)
Fraserburgh ['freɪzərbərə] (fráyzĕrbŭră)
Frater, *f.n.* ['freɪtər] (fráyter)
Frating ['freɪtɪŋ] (fráyting)
Frazer, *f.n.* ['freɪzər] (fráyzer)
Freake, *f.n.* [frik] (freek)
Freakes, *f.n.* [friks] (freeks)
Frears, *f.n.* [frɛərz] (frairz)
Fredman, *f.n.* ['fredmən] (frédmăn)
Freeson, *f.n.* ['frisən] (freésson)
Freethy, *f.n.* ['friθɪ] (freéthi)
Freke, *f.n.* [frik] (freek)
Fremantle, *f.n.* ['frimæntl] (freémantl); [fri'mæntl] (freemántl)
Fremington ['fremɪŋtən] (frémmingtŏn)
French, *f.n.* [frenʃ] (frensh)
Frenchay ['frenʃeɪ] (frén-shay)
Frere, *f.n.* [frɪər] (freer); [frɛər] (frair)
Fressanges, *f.n.* ['fresɑːʒ] (fréssaa*ng*zh)
Freswick ['frezwɪk] (frézwick); ['frezɪk] (frézzick)
Freuchie ['fruxɪ] (froóchi)
Freugh, East *and* **West** [frux] (frooch)
Freyberg, *Baron* ['fraɪbərg] (fríberg)
Freyer, *f.n.* ['friər] (freé-er); ['fraɪər] (frí-er)
Fricker, *f.n.* ['frɪkər] (fricker)
Frideswide, *8th-c. abbess* ['frɪdɪswɪdə] (fríddĕssweedĕ)
Frieght, *f.n.* [freɪt] (frayt); [fraɪt] (frīt)

Friel, *f.n.* [fril] (freel)
Friend, *f.n.* [frend] (frend)
Friern Barnet ['fraɪərn 'bɑːrnɪt] (frí-ĕrn baárnĕt)
Friesden *see* Frithsden.
Friese-Greene, William, *motion picture pioneer* ['friz 'grin] (freéz green)
Frieth [friθ] (freeth)
Frindsbury ['frɪndzbərɪ] (fríndzbŭri)
Friockheim ['frɪkɪm] (freéckim)
Frise, *f.n.* [friz] (freez)
Friskney ['frɪsknɪ] (frískni)
Friters, *f.n.* ['frɪtərz] (freétĕrz)
Frithelstock ['frɪθlstɒk] (fríthl-stock); ['frɪstɒk] (frístock)
Frithsden, *also spelt* **Friesden** ['frɪzdən] (freézdĕn); ['frɪzdən] (frízdĕn)
Frizelle, *f.n.* [frɪ'zel] (frizéll)
Frizinghall ['fraɪzɪŋhɔl] (frízing-hawl)
Frizington ['frɪzɪŋtən] (frízzingtŏn); ['fraɪzɪŋtən] (frízingtŏn)
Frocester ['frɒstər] (frósster)
Frodingham ['frɒdɪŋəm] (fródding-ăm)
Frodsham ['frɒdʃəm] (fród-shăm)
Froest, *f.n.* ['froʊɪst] (frō-ĕst)
Fromanteel, *f.n.* ['froʊməntil] (frōmăn-teel)
Frome [frum] (froom)
Frome, River, *Dorset, Somerset* [frum] (froom)
Frome Vauchurch ['frum 'voʊtʃərtʃ] (froóm vŏchurtch)
Fron [vrɒn] (vron)
Fronallt ['vrɒnəɬt] (vrónnăhlt)
Froncysyllte, *also spelt* **Froncysylltau, Vroncysyllte** [ˌvrɒnkə'sʌɬteɪ] (vron-kăssúhltay)
Frongoch [vrɒn'goʊx] (vron-gó*ch*)
Frood, *f.n.* [frud] (frood)
Frossard, *f.n.* ['frɒsɑrd] (fróssaard)
Frostenden ['frɒsəndən] (fróssĕndĕn)
Froswick ['frɒsɪk] (fróssick)
Froud, *f.n.* [fraʊd] (frowd)
Froude, *f.n.* [frud] (frood) *Appropriate also for James Anthony ~, 19th-c. historian.*
Frow, *f.n.* [fraʊ] (frow)
Frowde, *f.n.* [fraʊd] (frowd)
Fryirs, *f.n.* ['fraɪərz] (frí-ĕrz)
Fryston ['fraɪstən] (frísstŏn)
Fuchs, *f.n.* [fuks] (fooks); [fuks] (fooks) *The first is appropriate for Sir Vivian ~, geologist and explorer.*
Fugaccia, *f.n.* [fu'gætʃɪə] (fŏŏgátchiă)
Fuge, *f.n.* [fjudʒ] (fewj)
Fuinary, *f.n.* ['fjunərɪ] (féwnări)
Fujino, *f.n.* ['fjudʒɪnoʊ] (féwjinō)
Fulbourn ['fʊlbərn] (foólborn)
Fulham ['fʊləm] (foólăm)
Fulke, *f.n. and C.n.* [fʊlk] (foólk)
Fulker, *f.n.* ['fʊlkər] (foólker)
Fulking ['fʊlkɪŋ] (foólking)
Fullom, *f.n.* ['fʊləm] (foólŏm)
Fulmodestone ['fʊlmɪstən] (foólmĕstŏn)
Fulstow ['fʊlstoʊ] (foólsstō)

Fulwell ['fʊlwel] (fŏŏl-wel)
Fundenhall ['fʌndənhɔl] (fúndĕn-hawl)
Furlonge, *f.n.* ['fɜrlɒŋ] (fúrlong)
Furnace ['fɜrnɪs] (fúrniss)
Furnas, *f.n.* ['fɜrnəs] (fúrnăss)
Furneaux, *Viscount* ['fɜrnoʊ] (fúrnō)
Furnell, *f.n.* [fɜr'nel] (furnéll)
Furness, *f.n.* ['fɜrnɪs] (fúrnĕss); [fɜr'nes] (furnéss) *The first is appropriate for Viscount ～.*
Furness ['fɜrnɪs] (fúrnĕss)
Furneux Pelham ['fɜrnɪks 'peləm] (fúrnicks péllăm); ['fɜrnoʊ 'peləm] (fúrnō péllăm)
Furnivall, *Baroness* ['fɜrnɪvəl] (fúrnivăl)
Furth, *f.n.* [fɜrθ] (furth)
Fuseli, *Henry, 18-19th-c. painter* [fju-'zelɪ] (fewzélli) *Perhaps the most commonly accepted of a variety of pronunciations. He was originally Johann Heinrich Füssli, a Swiss subject.*
Fushiebridge ['fʊʃɪbrɪdʒ] (fŏŏshibrij)
Fussell, *f.n.* ['fʌsl] (fussl)
Fussey, *f.n.* ['fʌsɪ] (fússi)
Futrille, *f.n.* ['fjutrɪl] (féwtril)
Fyfield, *f.n.* ['faɪfɪld] (fífeeld)
Fyfield ['faɪfɪld] (fífeeld)
Fylde [faɪld] (fild)
Fyleman, *f.n.* ['faɪlmən] (fílmăn)
Fylingdales ['faɪlɪŋdeɪlz] (fíling-daylz)
Fysh, *f.n.* [faɪʃ] (fish)
Fyvel, *f.n.* ['faɪvl] (fívl)
Fyvie ['faɪvɪ] (fívi)

G

Gabain, *f.n.* [gə'beɪn] (găbáyn)
Gabalfa [gə'bælvə] (găbálvă)
Gabbitas, *f.n.* ['gæbɪtæs] (gábbitass)
Gaber, *f.n.* ['geɪbər] (gáyber)
Gabor, *f.n.* ['gabor] (gaábor)
Gabriel, *f.n. and C.n.* ['geɪbrɪəl] (gáybri-ĕl)
Gaddarn, *f.n.* [gə'darn] (gădaárn)
Gaddesby ['gædzbɪ] (gádzbi)
Gaddesden ['gædzdən] (gádzdĕn)
Gadfan, *Welsh C.n.* ['gædvən] (gádvăn)
Gadie Burn ['gadɪ 'bɜrn] (gaádi búrn)
Gadlys ['gædlɪs] (gádliss)
Gaenor, *Welsh C.n.* ['geɪnər] (gáynŏr)
Gaenor, *f.n.* ['geɪnər] (gáynŏr)
Gaerwen ['gaɪərwən] gírwĕn)
Gaetjens, *f.n.* ['geɪtjənz] (gáyt-yĕnz)
Gage, *f.n.* [geɪdʒ] (gayj)
Gahan, *f.n.* ['geɪən] (gáy-ăn); [gɑn] (gaan)
Gaick Forest ['gaɪk] (gaá-ick); [gaɪk] (gĭk)

Gaillard, *f.n.* ['geɪlard] (gáylaard); ['gaɪɑrd] (gí-aard)
Gainsborough ['geɪnzbərə] (gáynzbŭră) *Appropriate also for the Earl of ～.*
Gair, *f.n.* [gɛər] (gair)
Gairdner, *f.n.* ['gardnər] (gaárdner); ['gɛərdnər] (gaírdner)
Gaire, *f.n.* [gɛər] (gair)
Gairloch ['gɛərlɒx] (gaírloch)
Gaisgill ['geɪzgɪl] (gáyzgil)
Gaitens, *f.n.* ['geɪtənz] (gáytĕnz)
Gaitskell, *f.n.* ['geɪtskəl] (gáytskĕl) *Appropriate also for Baroness ～.*
Galashiels [ˌgælə'ʃilz] (gală-sheélz)
Galbally [gæl'bælɪ] (galbáli)
Galbraith, *f.n.* [gæl'breɪθ] (galbráyth)
Galby ['gɔlbɪ] (gáwlbi)
Galgate ['golgeɪt] (gáwlgayt)
Galgorm [gæl'gɔrm] (galgórm)
Gall, *f.n.* [gɔl] (gawl)
Gallacher, *f.n.* ['gæləxər] (gáláɥher)
Gallagher, *f.n.* ['gæləxər] (gálaɥher)
Gallannaugh, *f.n.* ['gæləno] (gálănaw)
Gallati, *f.n.* [gə'lætɪ] (gălátti)
Gallovidian, *native of Galloway* [ˌgæloʊ-'vɪdɪən] (galōvíddián)
Galloway ['gæləweɪ] (gálŏ-way)
Galmpton ['gæmptən] (gámptŏn)
Galpern, *f.n.* ['gælpərn] (gálpĕrn)
Galpin, *f.n.* ['gælpɪn] (gálpin)
Galston ['golstən] (gáwlsstŏn)
Galsworthy, *f.n.* ['golzwɜrðɪ] (gáwlzwurthi);['gælzwɜrðɪ] (gálzwurthi)*Although the first was the pronunciation of John ～, author, some members of the family prefer to use the second.*
Galwally [gæl'wælɪ] (galwáli)
Galway, *Viscount* ['gɔlweɪ] (gáwlway)
Gaman, *f.n.* ['geɪmən] (gáymăn)
Gamjee, *f.n.* ['gæmdʒɪ] (gámjee)
Gamlingay ['gæmlɪŋgeɪ] (gámling-gay)
Gammans, *f.n.* ['gæmənz] (gámmänz)
Gammell, *f.n.* ['gæml] (gamml)
Gamon, *f.n.* ['geɪmən] (gáymŏn)
Gampell, *f.n.* ['gæmpl] (gampl)
Gandar, *f.n.* ['gændər] (gándăr)
Gandee, *f.n.* ['gændɪ] (gándi)
Gangel, *f.n.* ['gæŋgl] (gáng-gl)
Gannaway ['gænəweɪ] (gánnă-way)
Gaping Gill ['geɪpɪŋ 'gɪl] (gáyping gíll)
Garard, *f.n.* ['gɛrərd] (gárraard)
Garboldisham['garblʃəm](gaárbl-shăm)
Garcia, *f.n.* ['garsɪə] (gaárssiá); ['garʃɪə] (gaárshiă)
Garcke, *f.n.* ['garkɪ] (gaárki)
Gardyne, *f.n.* [gar'daɪn] (gaardín)
Gare Loch, *The* ['gɛər lɒx] (gaír loch)
Garendon ['gærəndən] (gárrĕndŏn)
Garigue, *f.n.* ['gærɪgju] (gárrigew)
Garin, *f.n.* ['gærɪn] (gárrin)
Garioch, *f.n.* ['gɛrɪox] (gárriŏch)
Garioch ['gɪərɪ] (geéri)
Garlieston ['garlɪstən] (gaárlistŏn)
Garlinge Green ['garlɪndʒ 'grin] (gaárlinj greén)

Garmonsway, f.n. ['gɑrmənzweɪ] (gáar-mŏnzway)
Garmoyle, f.n. [gɑr'mɔɪl] (gaarmóyl)
Garnant ['gɑrnænt] (gaárnant)
Garndiffaith [gɑrn'dɪfaɪθ] (gaarndíffīth)
Garnedd-wen, *Flint., Merioneth* [ˌgɑr-nəð'wen] (gaarnĕth-wén)
Garneddwen, *Merioneth* [gɑr'neðwən] (gaarnéth-wĕn)
Garnet, f.n. ['gɑrnɪt] (gaárnĕt)
Garnethill [ˌgɑrnɪt'hɪl] (gaarnĕt-híll)
Garnett, f.n. ['gɑrnɪt] (gaárnĕt)
Garn-fach [gɑrn'vɑx] (gaarnvaách)
Garnsworthy, f.n. ['gɑrnzwɜrðɪ] (gaárnz-wurthi) *Appropriate also for Baron* ∼.
Garrard, f.n. ['gærɑrd] (gárraard)
Garrett, f.n. ['gærɪt] (gárrĕt)
Garry, River ['gærɪ] (gárri)
Garryduff [ˌgærɪ'dʌf] (garridúff)
Garsven ['gɑrʃven] (gaársh-ven)
Gartcosh [gɑrt'kɒʃ] (gaart-kósh)
Garten, Loch ['gɑrtən] (gaártĕn)
Garthbeibio [gɑrθ'baɪbjou] (gaarth-bíb-yō)
Garthbrengy [gɑrθ'breŋgɪ] (gaarth-bréng-gi)
Gartheli [gɑrθ'elɪ] (gaarthélli)
Gartocharn [ˌgɑrtə'xɑrn] (gaartŏchaárn)
Gartsherrie [gɑrt'ʃerɪ] (gaart-shérri)
Garvagh, f.n. ['gɑrvə] (gaárvă)
Garvagh ['gɑrvə] (gaárvă) *Appropriate also for Baron* ∼.
Garvald, *Dumfries., East Lothian* ['gɑr-vəld] (gaárvăld)
Garvellach Isles, *also spelt* **Garvelloch** [gɑr'veləx] (gaarvéllách)
Garvestone ['gɑrvɪstən] (gaárvĕstŏn)
Garvice, f.n. ['gɑrvɪs] (gaárviss)
Garw ['gæru] (gárroo)
Garwell, f.n. ['gɑrwel] (gaárwel)
Gary, f.n. ['gɛərɪ] (gaíri)
Gascoigne, f.n. ['gæskɔɪn] (gásskoyn)
Gascoin, f.n. ['gæskɔɪn] (gásskoyn)
Gascoine, f.n. ['gæskɔɪn] (gásskoyn)
Gascoyne, f.n. ['gæskɔɪn] (gásskoyn)
Gaselee, f.n. ['geɪzlɪ] (gáyzli)
Gassiot, f.n. ['gæsɪət] (gássiŏt)
Gatacre, f.n. ['gætəkər] (gáttăker)
Gateacre ['gætəkər] (gáttăker)
Gatehouse of Fleet ['geɪthaʊs əv 'flit] (gáyt-howss ŏv fleét)
Gater, f.n. ['geɪtər] (gáyter)
Gateshead ['geɪtshed] (gáyts-hed)
Gathorne, f.n. ['geɪθɔrn] (gáy-thorn)
Gathurst ['gæθərst] (gáthŭrst)
Gatward, f.n. ['gætwɔrd] (gátwawrd)
Gatwick Airport ['gætwɪk] (gátwick)
Gaubert, f.n. ['goʊbɛər] (gốbair)
Gaudin, f.n. ['gɔdɪn] (gáwdin)
Gauld, f.n. [gɔld] (gawld)
Gault, f.n. [gɔlt] (gawlt); [gɒlt] (golt)
Gauna, f.n. ['gɔnə] (gáwnă)
Gaussen, f.n. ['goʊsən] (gốssĕn)
Gavall, f.n. [gə'væl] (găvál)
Gaved, f.n. ['gævɪd] (gávvĕd)

Gavegan, f.n. ['gævɪgən] (gávvĕgăn); [gə'vegən] (găvéggăn)
Gavey, f.n. ['geɪvɪ] (gáyvi)
Gavin, C.n. ['gævɪn] (gávvin)
Gavith, f.n. ['gaʊɪθ] (gów-ith); ['geɪwɪθ] (gáy-with)
Gaymer, f.n. ['geɪmər] (gáymer)
Gayton ['geɪtən] (gáytŏn)
Geake, f.n. [gik] (geek)
Geard, f.n. [gɪərd] (geerd)
Geary, f.n. ['gɪərɪ] (geéri)
Geaussent, f.n. ['ʒoʊsɒŋ] (zhốssong)
Gebbie, f.n. ['gebɪ] (gébbi)
Gebhard, f.n. ['gebhɑrd] (géb-haard)
Geddes, f.n. ['gedɪs] (géddĕss) *Appropriate also for Baron* ∼.
Geddinge ['gedɪndʒ] (géddinj)
Geddington ['gedɪŋtən] (géddingtŏn)
Geduld, f.n. ['gedəld] (géddŭld)
Gedye, f.n. ['gedɪ] (géddi)
Gee, f.n. [dʒi] (jee)
Geevor ['givər] (geévŏr)
Geffen, f.n. ['gefən] (géffĕn)
Geffrye Museum, *London* ['dʒefrɪ] (jéffri)
Gegan, f.n. ['gigən] (geégăn)
Gegg, f.n. [geg] (geg)
Geiger, f.n. ['gaɪgər] (gíger)
Geikie, f.n. ['gaɪkɪ] (geéki)
Geldeston ['geldstən] (géldstŏn); ['geldə-stən] (géldestŏn); ['gelstən] (gélstŏn)
Geliot, f.n. ['dʒelɪət] (jélliŏt)
Gell, f.n. [gel] (gell); [dʒel] (jell)
Gellan, f.n. ['gelən] (géllăn)
Gellatly, f.n. ['gelətlɪ] (géllátli); [gə'lætlɪ] (gĕlátli)
Gellender, f.n. ['geləndər] (géllĕnder)
Geller, f.n. ['gelər] (géller)
Gelli ['geɪɪ] (géhli)
Gelliceidrim [ˌgeɪɪ'kaɪdrɪm] (gehli-kídrim)
Gelli-gaer [ˌgeɪɪ'gaɪər] (gehli-gír)
Gellilydan [ˌgeɪɪ'lɑdən] (gehli-lúddăn)
Gelli Uchaf [ˌgeɪɪ 'ɪxæv] (gehli íchavv); [ˌgeɪɪ 'ɪxɑv] (gehli eéchaav)
Gemmell, f.n. ['geml] (gemml)
Gemmill, f.n. ['geml] (gemml)
Gendros ['gendrɒs] (géndross)
Genese, f.n. [dʒɪ'nis] (jĕneéss)
Genn, f.n. [gen] (gen)
Gent, f.n. [dʒent] (jent)
Gentry, f.n. ['dʒentrɪ] (jéntri)
Geoghegan, f.n. ['geɪgən] (gáygăn)
Georgeham ['dʒɔrdʒhæm] (jórj-ham)
Georgiadis, f.n. [ˌdʒɔrdʒɪ'ɑdɪs] (jorji-aádiss)
Geraghty, f.n. ['gerətɪ] (gérrăti)
Geraint, Welsh C.n. ['geraɪnt] (gérrīnt)
Gerald, f.n. and C.n. ['dʒerəld] (jérráld)
Gerber, f.n. ['dʒɜrbər] (jérber)
Gerdes, f.n. [gɜr'diz] (gerdeéz)
Gerhardie, William, author [dʒər'hɑrdɪ] (jĕr-haárdi)
Gerhold, f.n. ['gɜrhoʊld] (gér-hōld)
Gerin, f.n. [ʒə'ræ] (zhĕráng)

Germain, f.n. ['dʒɜːmeɪn] (jérmayn)
Germoe ['gɜːmoʊ] (gérmō)
Gerngross, f.n. ['gɜːrngrɒs] (gérn-gross)
Gerrans ['gerənz] (gérränz)
Gershon, f.n. ['gɜːrʃən] (gér-shŏn)
Gervis, f.n. ['dʒɑːrvɪs] (jaárviss)
Getgood, f.n. ['getgʊd] (gét-gŏŏd)
Gethin, f.n. ['geθɪn] (géth-in)
Gething, f.n. ['geθɪŋ] (géth-ing)
Ghey, f.n. [dʒaɪ] (jī)
Gibberd, f.n. ['gɪbərd] (gíbbĕrd)
Gibbes, f.n. [gɪbz] (gibz)
Gibbon, f.n. ['gɪbən] (gíbbŏn)
Gibbons, f.n. ['gɪbənz] (gíbbŏnz)
Gibbons, Grinling, *17-18th-c. wood-carver and sculptor* ['grɪnlɪŋ 'gɪbənz] (grínling gíbbŏnz)
Gibbs, f.n. [gɪbz] (gibz)
Gicht Castle, *Aberdeen.* [gɪxt] (gi<u>ch</u>t)
Gick, f.n. [dʒɪk] (jick)
Giddens, f.n. ['gɪdənz] (gíddĕnz)
Gidding ['gɪdɪŋ] (gídding)
Gielgud, Sir John, *actor* ['gilgʊd] (geél-gŏŏd)
Gieve, f.n. [giv] (geev)
Giffard, f.n. ['dʒɪfərd] (jíffárd) ; ['gɪfɑːrd] (giffaard)
Giffnock ['gɪfnək] (gíffnŏk)
Gifford, f.n. ['dʒɪfərd] (jíffŏrd) ; ['gɪfərd] (giffŏrd); *The first is appropriate for Baron ~, the second for the ~ Lectureships at the University of St. Andrews.*
Gigha ['giə] (geé-ä)
Gilberdyke, *also spelt* **Gilberdike** ['gɪlbərdaɪk] (gílbĕrdīk)
Gilbert, f.n. and C.n. ['gɪlbərt] (gílbĕrt)
Gilbey, f.n. ['gɪlbɪ] (gílbi)
Gilbreath, f.n. [gɪl'breɪθ] (gilbráyth)
Gilcomston ['gɪlkəmstən] (gílkŏmstŏn)
Gilcrux ['gɪlkruz] (gílkrooz)
Gildea, f.n. ['gɪldeɪ] (gíldayʹ); [gɪl'deɪ] (gildáy)
Gilder, f.n. ['gɪldər] (gílder)
Gilderoy, f.n. ['gɪldərɔɪ] (gíldĕroy)
Gildersome ['gɪldərsəm] (gíldĕrssŏm)
Giles, f.n. [dʒaɪlz] (jīlz)
Gileston ['dʒaɪlztən] (jílztŏn)
Gilfach Fargoed ['gɪlvax 'vargoɪd] (gílvaa<u>ch</u> vaárgoyd)
Gilfach Goch ['gɪlvax 'goux] (gílvaa<u>ch</u> gó<u>ch</u>)
Gilford ['gɪlfərd] (gílfŏrd)
Gilham, f.n. ['gɪləm] (gílläm)
Gilhooley, f.n. [gɪl'hulɪ] (gil-hoóli)
Gilkes, f.n. [dʒɪlks] (jĭlks)
Gilks, f.n. [dʒɪlks] (jĭlks)
Gill, f.n. [gɪl] (gill)
Gillam, f.n. ['gɪləm] (gílläm)
Gillan Creek ['gɪlən 'krik] (gíllän kreék)
Gillard, f.n. ['gɪlɑːrd] (gíllaard) ; [gɪ'lɑːrd] (gilaárd) ; ['gɪlɑːrd] (gíllárd)
Gilles, f.n. ['gɪlɪs] (gíllĕss)
Gillespie, f.n. [gɪ'lespɪ] (gilésspi)
Gillett, f.n. ['gɪlɪt] (gíllĕt) ; [dʒɪ'let] (jilétt)

Gilletts Crossing ['dʒɪlets 'krɒsɪŋ] (jíllets króssing)
Gilley, f.n. ['gɪlɪ] (gílli)
Gilliam, f.n. ['gɪləm] (gílliäm)
Gilliat, f.n. ['gɪlɪət] (gílliát)
Gillick, f.n. ['gɪlɪk] (gíllick)
Gillie, f.n. ['gɪlɪ] (gílli)
Gillies, f.n. ['gɪlɪs] (gílliss)
Gilling, f.n. ['gɪlɪŋ] (gílling)
Gilling ['gɪlɪŋ] (gílling)
Gillingham, f.n. ['gɪlɪŋəm] (gílling-äm); ['dʒɪlɪŋəm] (jílling-äm)
Gillingham, *Dorset, Norfolk* ['gɪlɪŋəm] (gílling-äm)
Gillingham, *Kent* ['dʒɪlɪŋəm] (jílling-äm)
Gillingwater, f.n. ['gɪlɪŋwɔtər] (gíllingwawter)
Gillis, f.n. ['gɪlɪs] (gílliss)
Gillott, f.n. ['dʒɪlət] (jíllŏt) ; ['gɪlət] (gíllŏt)
Gilman, f.n. ['gɪlmən] (gílmän)
Gilmorehill ['gɪlmərˈhɪl] (gílmŏr-híll)
Gilmour, f.n. ['gɪlmər] (gílmūr); ['gɪlmɔːr] (gilmor)
Gilnahirk [ˌgɪlnəˈhɜːrk] (gilnähírk)
Gilpin, f.n. ['gɪlpɪn] (gílpin)
Gilroy, f.n. ['gɪlrɔɪ] (gílroy)
Gilsland ['gɪlzlənd] (gílzländ)
Gilwell Park, *Essex* ['gɪlwəl 'pɑːrk] (gílwĕl paárk)
Gilwern ['gɪlwərn] (gílwĕrn)
Gilwhite, f.n. ['gɪlʍaɪt] (gil-whīt)
Gilzean, f.n. [gɪˈlin] (gileén); [gɪlˈzin] (gilzeén)
Gimbert, f.n. ['gɪmbərt] (gímbĕrt)
Gimingham ['gɪmɪŋəm] (gímming-äm)
Gimson, f.n. ['gɪmsən] (gímssŏn); ['dʒɪmsən] (jímssŏn)
Ginclough ['dʒɪmklʌf] (jín-klúff)
Ginever, f.n. ['dʒɪnɪvər] (jínnĕver)
Gingell, f.n. ['gɪndʒəl] (ginjĕl); ['dʒɪndʒel] (jínjel)
Ginley, f.n. ['gɪnlɪ] (gínli)
Ginn, f.n. [gɪn] (gin)
Ginner, f.n. ['dʒɪnər] (jínner)
Ginsburg, f.n. ['gɪnzbərg] (gínzburg)
Ginsbury, f.n. ['gɪnzbərɪ] (gínzbŭri)
Giovene, f.n. [dʒɪˈouvənɪ] (ji-óvĕni)
Gipping, *River* ['gɪpɪŋ] (gípping)
Gipps, f.n. [gɪps] (gips)
Gipson, f.n. ['gɪpsən] (gípssŏn)
Girthon ['gɜːrθən] (gírthŏn)
Girvan ['gɜːrvən] (gírvän)
Girvin, f.n. ['gɜːrvɪn] (gírvin)
Gisborough, Baron ['gɪzbərə] (gízbŭrä)
Gisburn ['gɪsbərn] (gíssburn)
Gisleham ['gɪzləm] (gízläm); ['gɪsləm] (gíssläm)
Gislingham ['gɪzlɪŋəm] (gizling-äm)
Gissane, f.n. [gɪˈseɪn] (gissáyn)
Gissing ['gɪsɪŋ] (gíssing)
Gitsham, f.n. ['gɪtʃəm] (gít-shäm)
Gittins, f.n. ['gɪtɪnz] (gíttinz)
Gittisham ['gɪtɪsəm] (gíttissäm); ['gɪtɪʃəm] (gitti-shäm); ['gɪtsəm] (gítssäm)
Gittoes, f.n. ['gɪtoʊz] (gíttōz)

Givons Grove, *Surrey* ['dʒɪvənz 'grouv] (jívvŏnz grốv)

Gladestry ['gleɪdstrɪ] (gláyd-stri)

Gladstone, f.n. ['glædstən] (gládstŏn)

Gladstone of Hawarden, Barony of ['glædstən əv 'hardən] (gládstŏn ŏv haárdĕn)

Gladwell, f.n. ['glædwəl] (gládwĕl)

Glais [glaɪs] (gliss)

Glaisdale ['gleɪzdeɪl] (gláyzdayl)

Glaisher, f.n. ['gleɪʃər] (gláysher)

Glaister, f.n. ['gleɪstər] (gláysster)

Glamis [glɑmz] (glaamz) *Appropriate also for Baron* ~.

Glamorgan [glə'mɔrgən] (glămórgăn)

Glancy, f.n. ['glænsɪ] (glánssi)

Glanely, Barony of [glæn'ilɪ] (glaneéli)

Glanffrwd, Welsh C.n. ['glænfrud] (glánfrood)

Glangwili [glæn'gwɪlɪ] (glan-gwílli)

Glan Llugwy [glæn 'ɬɪgʊɪ] (glan ḫlígŏŏ-i)

Glan-rhyd [glæn'hrid] (glanreéd)

Glanville, f.n. ['glænvɪl] (glánvil)

Glanwydden [glæn'wɪðən] (glanwíthĕn)

Glanyllin [ˌglænə'ɬɪn] (glannă-ḫlín)

Glanyrafon [ˌglænər'ævən] (glannĕrávvŏn)

Glaramara ['glærəmɑrə] (glárrămaará)

Glarryford ['glærɪfərd] (glárriford)

Glas Island [glas] (glaass)

Glasbury ['gleɪzbərɪ] (gláyzbŭri)

Glasby, f.n. ['glæzbɪ] (glázbi)

Glascodine, f.n. ['glæskoudaɪn] (glásskōdĭn)

Glascoed, *Denbigh., Monmouth.* ['glæskɔɪd] (glásskoyd)

Glascwm, *Montgomery., Radnor* ['glæskum] (glásskŏŏm)

Glasfryn ['glæsvrɪn] (glássvrin)

Glasgow ['glɑsgou] (gláassgŏ); ['glɑskou] (gláasskŏ); ['glɑzgou] (gláazgŏ)

Glasgow Celtic *football club* ['séltɪk] (séltick)

Glaslyn ['glæslɪn] (glásslin)

Glassalt Shiel Lodge, *Aberdeen.* ['glæsəlt 'ʃil] (glássălt sheel)

Glassary ['glæsərɪ] (glássări) *Appropriate also for Baron* ~.

Glasscock, f.n. ['glɑskɒk] (gláasskock); ['glɑskou] (gláasskŏ)

Glasser, f.n. ['glæsər] (glásser)

Glass Houghton ['glɑs 'haʊtən] (gláass hówtŏn)

Glaston ['gleɪstən] (gláysstŏn)

Glastonbury ['glɑstənbərɪ] (gláasstŏnbŭri)

Glaswegian, native of Glasgow [glɑs-'widʒən] (glaass-weéján)

Glazebury ['gleɪzbərɪ] (gláyzbŭri)

Glazer, f.n. ['gleɪzər] (gláyzer)

Glazier, f.n. ['gleɪzɪər] (gláyzi-er)

Gleadless ['glidlɪs] (gleédlĕss)

Gleadow, f.n. ['gledou] (gléddŏ)

Gleadowe, f.n. ['gledou] (gléddŏ)

Gleadthorpe Grange ['glidθɔrp 'greɪndʒ] (gleéd-thorp gráynj)

Gleichen, f.n. ['glaɪxən] (glíchĕn)

Glen Chas [glen 'tʃæs] (glen cháss)

Glen Dochart [glen 'dɒxərt] (glen dóchărt)

Glen Errochty [glen 'erəxtɪ] (glen érrŏchti)

Glen Fernait [glen 'fɜrnɪt] (glen férnit)

Glen Finglass [glen 'fɪŋləs] (glen fíngláss); [glen 'fɪŋgləs] (glen fíng-gláss)

Glen Ogle [glen 'ougl] (glen ógl)

Glen Shira [glen 'ʃɪərə] (glen sheéră)

Glenalmond [glen'amənd] (glenaámŏnd)

Glenanne [glen'æn] (glenán)

Glenapp, Viscount [glen'æp] (glenáp)

Glenariff [glen'ærɪf] (glenárrif)

Glenarm [glen'ɑrm] (glenaárm)

Glenartney [glen'ɑrtnɪ] (glenaártni)

Glenavy [glen'eɪvɪ] (glenáyvi)

Glenbervie [glen'bɜrvɪ] (glenbérvi)

Glenboig [glen'bouɪg] (glenbő-ig)

Glenbruar [glen'bruər] (glenbroó-ăr)

Glenbuchat [glen'bʌkət] (glenbúckăt)

Glencaple [glen'keɪpl] (glen-káypl)

Glencarse [glen'kɑrs] (glen-kaárss)

Glencoe [glen'kou] (glen-kố)

Glenconner, f.n. [glen'kɒnər] (glenkónner) *Appropriate also for Baron* ~.

Glencross, f.n. [glen'krɒs] (glen-króss)

Glenday, f.n. ['glendeɪ] (glénday)

Glendevon [glen'devən] (glendévvŏn)

Glendower, Owen, 14-15th-c. Welsh chieftain ['ouɪn glen'dauər] (ố-ĕn glendówr) *The Welsh form is Owain Glyndwr, q.v.*

Glendyne, Baron [glen'daɪn] (glendín)

Gleneagles [glen'iglz] (gleneéglz)

Glenegedale Airport [glen'egɪdeɪl] (glenéggĕdayl)

Glenelg [glen'elg] (glenélg)

Glenfarg [glen'fɑrg] (glenfaárg)

Glenfernate [glen'fɜrnɪt] (glenférnit)

Glenfeshie [glen'feʃɪ] (glenféshi)

Glenfiddich Distillery [glen'fɪdɪx] (glenfíddich)

Glenfinnan [glen'fɪnən] (glenfínnăn)

Glengormley [glen'gɔrmlɪ] (glen-górmli)

Glenisla [glen'aɪlə] (glenílă)

Glenkinchie Distillery [glen'kɪnʃɪ] (glen-kínshi)

Glenlee [glen'li] (glen-leé)

Glenlivet [glen'lɪvɪt] (glen-lívvĕt)

Glenlochar [glen'lɒxər] (glen-lóchăr)

Glenmanus [glen'mænəs] (glenmánnŭss)

Glenmorangie Distillery [ˌglenmə-'rændʒɪ] (glen-mŏránji)

Glenorchy [glen'ɔrxɪ] (glenórchi) *Appropriate also for Lord* ~.

Glenrinnes [glen'rɪnɪs] (glenrínnĕss)

Glenrothes, *Fife* [glen'rɒθɪs] (glen-róthĕss)

Glenshane Pass [glen'ʃeɪn] (glen-sháyn)

Glenshee [glen'ʃi] (glen-sheé)
Glenshesk, River [glen'ʃesk] (glen-shésk)
Glentanar, Baron [glen'tænər] (glentánnǎr)
Glentham ['glenθəm] (glén-thǎm)
Glentoran, Baron [glen'tɔrən] (glentáwrǎn)
Glenview ['glenvju] (glénvew)
Glenwherry [glen'hwerɪ] (glen-whérri)
Glerawly, Viscount [glə'rɔlɪ] (glěráwli)
Glevum, Roman name for Gloucester ['gli:vəm] (gleévŭm)
Gliksten, f.n. ['glɪkstən] (glíckstěn)
Glimps Holm ['glɪmps houm] (glímps hōm)
Gloag, f.n. [gloug] (glōg)
Gloddaeth ['glɒðaɪθ] (glóthīth)
Glomach, Falls of ['glouməx] (glómǎch)
Glossop, f.n. ['glɒsəp] (glóssŏp)
Gloucester ['glɒstər] (glósster) Appropriate also for H.R.H. the Duke of ~.
Glover, f.n. ['glʌvər] (glúvver)
Glubb, f.n. [glʌb] (glub)
Gluckman, f.n. ['glʌkmən] (glúckmǎn)
Gluckstein, f.n. ['glʌkstin] (glúcksteen)
Glyder Fach ['glɪdər 'vax] (glídder vaách)
Glyder Fawr ['glɪdər 'vauər] (glídder vówr)
Glyders, The ['glɪdərz] (glídděrz)
Glyme, River [glaɪm] (glīm)
Glympton ['glɪmptən] (glímptŏn)
Glyn, f.n. [glɪn] (glin)
Glyncorrwg [glɪn'kɒrug] (glin-kórrŏog)
Glynde [glaɪnd] (glīnd)
Glyndebourne ['glaɪndbɔːn] (glíndborn) Home of the ~ Opera.
Glyndwr, Owain, 14-15th-c. Welsh chieftain ['ouaɪn glɪn'duər] (ó-īn glin-doŏr); ['ouɪn glɪn'duər] (ó-ĕn glindoŏr) The English form is Owen Glendower, q.v.
Glyndyfrdwy [glɪn'dʌvərdui] (glin-dúvvěrdoŏ-i)
Glynn, f.n. [glɪn] (glin)
Glynn [glɪn] (glin)
Glynne, f.n. [glɪn] (glin)
Glynogwr [glɪn'ouguər] (glinógŏŏr)
Glyntawe [glɪn'tauei] (glintów-ay)
Glyn Traian [glɪn 'traɪən] (glin trī-ǎn)
Glyn-y-Groes [ˌglɪnə'grɔɪs] (glin-ǎgróyss)
Gnosall ['nousl] (nōssl)
Goacher, f.n. ['gouʃər] (gósher)
Goatcher, f.n. ['goutʃər] (gótcher)
Goathland ['gouθlənd] (góthlǎnd)
Goathurst ['gouθərst] (gó-thurst)
Gobernuisgach Lodge, Sutherland [ˌgoubər'nɪsgəx] (góběrniss-gǎch)
Gobey, f.n. ['goubɪ] (góbi)
Gobowen [gɒb'ouɪn] (gobbó-ĕn)
Godalming ['gɒdlmɪŋ] (góddl-ming)
Godber, f.n. ['gɒdbər] (gódber)
Godbold, f.n. ['gɒdbould] (gódbōld)

Goddard, f.n. ['gɒdərd] (góddǎrd); ['gɒdɑːd] (góddaard) The first is appropriate for Baron ~.
Godde, f.n. [goud] (gōd)
Godden, f.n. ['gɒdən] (góddĕn)
Godefroy, f.n. ['gɒdɪfrɔɪ] (góddĕfroy)
Godin, f.n. ['goudɪn] (gódin)
Godiva, Lady, Saxon heroine [gə'daɪvə] (gŏdīvǎ)
Godmanchester ['gɒdmən'tʃestər] (gódmǎn-chéster)
Godmersham ['gɒdmərʃəm] (gódměrshǎm)
Godolphin [gə'dɒlfɪn] (gŏdólfin) Appropriate also for the Barony of ~.
Godreaman [ˌgɒdrɪ'æmən] (goddriámmǎn)
Godre'r-graig [ˌgɒdrər'graɪg] (godrěrgríg)
Godrevy [gə'drivɪ] (gŏdreévi)
Godshill ['gɒdzhɪl] (gódz-hil)
Goehr, f.n. [gɜr] (gur) Appropriate for Alexander ~, composer, and Walter ~, conductor.
Gogay, f.n. [gə'geɪ] (gŏgáy)
Gogerddan [gou'geərðən] (gōgaírthǎn)
Golant [gou'lænt] (gōlánt)
Golborne ['goulbɔrn] (gólborn)
Golcar ['goukər] (gókǎr)
Goldesgeyne, f.n. ['gouldɪzgeɪm] (góldězgaym)
Golding, f.n. ['gouldɪŋ] (gólding)
Goldington ['gouldɪŋtən] (góldingtŏn)
Goldrei, f.n. ['gouldrɪ] (góldri)
Goldsithney ['gould'sɪθnɪ] (góld-síthni)
Goldsmid, f.n. ['gouldsmɪd] (góld-smid)
Goldstone, f.n. ['gouldstoun] (góld-stōn)
Goldsworthy, f.n. ['gouldzwɜrðɪ] (góldzwurthi)
Golfa ['gɒlvə] (gólvǎ)
Golightly, f.n. [gə'laɪtlɪ] (gŏlítli)
Gollancz, Sir Victor, author and publisher [gə'lænts] (gŏlánts)
Golspie ['gɒlspɪ] (gólsspi)
Gomeldon ['gɒmɪldən] (gómmĕldŏn)
Gomersal ['gɒmərsl] (gómměrssl)
Gomme, f.n. [gɒm] (gomm)
Gomperts, f.n. ['gɒmpərts] (gómpěrts)
Gompertz, f.n. ['gɒmpərts] (gómpěrts)
Gomshall ['gɒmʃəl] (góm-shǎl); ['gʌmʃəl] (gúm-shǎl)
Gonvena ['gɒnvɪnə] (gónveenǎ)
Gonville and Caius College, University of Cambridge ['gɒnvɪl ənd 'kiz] (gónvil ǎnd keéz)
Gooch, f.n. [gutʃ] (gootch)
Goodale, f.n. ['gudeɪl] (goŏdayl)
Goodameavy [ˌgudə'mivɪ] (goŏdámeévi)
Goodden, f.n. ['gudən] (goŏděn)
Goode, f.n. [gud] (goŏd)
Goodenough, f.n. ['gudɪnʌf] (goŏděnuff)
Gooding, f.n. ['gudɪŋ] (goŏding)
Goodnestone ['gudnestən] (goŏdnesstŏn); ['gʌnstən] (gúnsstŏn)
Goodrick, f.n. ['gudrɪk] (goŏdrick)

Goodwick ['gʊdɪk] (gŏŏdick)
Goodyear, f.n. ['gʊdjər] (gŏŏd-yer)
Goonbell [gun'bel] (goonbéll)
Goonhavern [gə'næværn] (gŏnávvĕrn);
[gun'hævərn] (goon-hávvĕrn)
Goonhilly [gʊn'hɪlɪ] (gŏŏn-hílli)
Goonvrea [gun'vreɪ] (goonvráy)
Goosnargh ['gusnər] (gŏŏssnär)
Goossens, Sir Eugene, composer and
conductor [ju'ʒeɪn 'gusənz] (yoozháyn
gŏŏssĕnz)
Goossens, Léon, oboist ['leɪɒn 'gusənz]
(láy-on gŏŏssĕnz)
Goossens, Sidonie, harpist [sɪ'doʊnɪ
'gusənz] (sidóni gŏŏssĕnz)
Goraghwood ['gɔrəwʊd] (gáwră-wŏŏd)
Goran Haven see Gorran Haven.
Gordon, f.n. and C.n. ['gɔrdən] (górdŏn)
Gordonstoun School ['gɔrdənztən] (gór-
dŏnztŏn)
Gore, f.n. [gɔr] (gor)
Gorell, f.n. ['gʊrəl] (górrĕl) Appropriate
also for Baron ~.
Goren, f.n. ['gɔrən] (górən)
Gorhambury ['gʊrəmbərɪ] (górrămbŭri)
Goring, f.n. ['gɔrɪŋ] (gáwring)
Goring ['gɔrɪŋ] (gáwring)
Gorleston ['gɔrlstən] (górlsstŏn)
Gorman, f.n. ['gɔrmən] (górmăn)
Gormanston, Viscount ['gɔrmənstən]
(górmănstŏn)
Gorran Haven ['gʊrən 'heɪvən] (górrăn
háyvĕn)
Gorsedd ['gɔrseð] (górsseth)
Gorseinon [gɔrs'aɪnən] (gorssínŏn)
Gors-las [gɔrs'laɑs] (gorsslaáss)
Gortin ['gɔrtjɪn] (górt-yin)
Gosberton Clough ['gɒzbərtən 'klaʊ]
(gózbĕrtŏn klów)
Goschen, Viscount ['goʊʃən] (gŏ-shĕn)
Goscote ['gɒskoʊt] (gósskŏt)
Goss, f.n. [gɒs] (goss)
Gossage, f.n. ['gɒsɪdʒ] (góssij)
Goswick ['gɒzɪk] (gózzick)
Gotham ['goʊtəm] (gŏtăm)
Gotla, f.n. ['gɒtlə] (góttlá)
Gotobed, f.n. ['gɒtəbed] (góttŏbed);
['goʊtəbed] (gŏtŏbed)
Gottwaltz, f.n. ['gɒtwolts] (gótwawlts)
Goudge, f.n. [gudʒ] (gooj) Appropriate for
Elizabeth ~, author.
Goudhurst ['gaʊdhɜrst] (gówd-hurst)
Goudie, f.n. ['gaʊdɪ] (gówdi)
Goudy, f.n. ['gaʊdɪ] (gówdi)
Gouge, f.n. [gaʊdʒ] (gowj)
Gough, f.n. [gɒf] (goff) Appropriate also
for Viscount ~.
Goulburn, f.n. ['gulbɜrn] (gŏŏlburn)
Goulceby ['goʊlsbɪ] (gŏlssbi)
Gould, f.n. [guld] (goold); [goʊld] (gŏld)
Gouldbourn, f.n. ['goʊldbɔrn] (gŏld-
born)
Goulden, f.n. ['guldən] (gŏŏldĕn); ['goʊl-
dən] (gŏldĕn)
Goulding, f.n. ['guldɪŋ] (gŏŏlding)

Gouldsmith, f.n. ['goʊldsmɪθ] (gŏld-
smith)
Goullart, f.n. ['gulɑrt] (gŏŏlaart)
Goullet, f.n. [gu'let] (goolétt)
Gourgey, f.n. ['gʊərdʒɪ] (gŏŏrji)
Gourlay, f.n. ['gʊərlɪ] (gŏŏrli)
Gourley, f.n. ['gʊərlɪ] (gŏŏrli)
Gourlie, f.n. ['gʊərlɪ] (gŏŏrli)
Gourock ['gʊərək] (gŏŏrŏk)
Goutthrappel [gaʊt'θræpl] (gowt-
thráppl)
Govan, f.n. ['gʌvən] (gúvvăn)
Govan ['gʌvən] (gúvvăn)
Gove, f.n. [goʊv] (gŏv)
Gover, f.n. ['goʊvər] (gŏver)
Goveton ['gʌvɪtən] (gúvvĕtŏn)
Govett, f.n. ['gʌvɪt] (gúvvĕt)
Gower, f.n. ['gaʊər] (gówer); [gɔr] (gor)
see also Leveson-Gower.
Gowerton ['gaʊərtən] (gówĕrtŏn)
Gowing, f.n. ['gaʊɪŋ] (gówing)
Gowling, f.n. ['gaʊlɪŋ] (gówling)
Gowrie ['gaʊərɪ] (gówri) Appropriate also
for the Earl of ~.
Grace Dieu ['greɪs 'dju] (gráyss déw)
Gracie, f.n. ['greɪsɪ] (gráyssi)
Gradon, f.n. ['greɪdən] (gráydŏn)
Gradwell, f.n. ['grædwel] (grádwel)
Graeme, f.n. [greɪm] (graym)
Graffham ['græfəm] (gráffăm)
Grafftey, f.n. ['grɑftɪ] (graáfti)
Grafham, Hunts. ['grɑfəm] (graáfăm)
Grafham, Surrey ['græfəm] (gráffăm)
Graham, f.n. ['greɪəm] (gráy-ăm)
Graham of Claverhouse, John, Scot-
tish soldier ['greɪəm əv 'kleɪvərhaʊs]
(gráy-ăm ŏv kláyvĕr-howss)
Grahamston ['greɪəmstən] (gráy-ăm-
stŏn)
Graig [graɪg] (grīg)
Graig Wen [graɪg 'wen] (grīg wén)
Grainger, f.n. ['greɪndʒər] (gráynjer)
Grampians, The ['græmpɪənz] (grám-
piănz)
Grampound ['græmpaʊnd] (grámpownd)
Grandison, f.n. ['græmpaʊnd] (grándissŏn)
Grandtully['grantlɪ](graántli);['græntlɪ]
(grántli)
Gransha ['grænʃə] (grán-shă)
Grant, f.n. [grant] (graant); [grænt]
(grant)
Grantchester ['grantʃɪstər] (graán-
chĕster); ['græntʃɪstər] (gránchĕster)
The first is appropriate for Baron ~.
Grantham, f.n. ['grænθəm] (grán-thăm)
Grantham ['grænθəm] (grán-thăm)
Granthier, f.n. ['grænθɪər] (gránthi-er)
Granton ['græntən] (grántŏn)
Grantown-on-Spey ['græntaʊn ɒn
'speɪ] (grántown on spáy); ['græntən ɒn
'speɪ] (grántŏn on spáy)
Grantshouse ['grantshaʊs] (graánts-
howss)
Granville, f.n. ['grænvɪl] (gránvil)
Grassington ['grasɪŋtən] (graássingtŏn)

Grasso, *f.n.* ['grɑsoʊ] (graássō)
Grateley ['greɪtlɪ] (gráytli)
Gratiaen, *f.n.* ['greɪʃən] (gráy-shĕn)
Grattan, *f.n.* ['grætən] (gráttăn)
Graveley, *f.n.* ['greɪvlɪ] (gráyv-li)
Graveley ['greɪvlɪ] (gráyv-li)
Gravelly Hill ['græv|ɪ 'hɪl] (grávvl-i hĭll)
Graveson, *f.n.* ['greɪvsən] (gráyvssŏn)
Gravett, *f.n.* ['grævɪt] (grávvĕt)
Gravina, *f.n.* [grə'vinə] (grăvéenă)
Gray, *f.n.* [greɪ] (gray)
Greasby ['grizbɪ] (greézbi)
Great Alne ['greɪt 'ɒn] (gráyt áwn); ['greɪt 'ɒln] (gráyt áwln)
Great Bromley ['greɪt 'brɒmlɪ] (gráyt brómli)
Great Creaton ['greɪt 'kritən] (gráyt kreétŏn)
Great Cumbrae ['greɪt 'kʌmbreɪ] (gráyt kúmbray)
Great Harrowden ['greɪt 'hærəʊdən] (gráyt hárrŏdĕn)
Great Hautbois ['greɪt 'hɒbɪs] (gráyt hóbbiss)
Great Houghton, *Northants.* ['greɪt 'hoʊtən] (gráyt hótŏn)
Great Houghton, *Yorks.* ['greɪt 'hɒtən] (gráyt háwtŏn)
Great Staughton ['greɪt 'stɒtən] (gráyt stáwtŏn)
Great Totham ['greɪt 'tɒtəm] (gráyt tóttăm)
Great Waltham ['greɪt 'wɒltəm] (gráyt wáwltăm)
Great Wyrley ['greɪt 'wɜrlɪ] (gráyt wúrli)
Great Yarmouth ['greɪt 'jɑrməθ] (gráyt yaármŭth)
Greatham, *Co. Durham* ['gritəm] (greétăm)
Greatham, *Hants.*, *Sussex* ['gretəm] (gréttăm)
Greathead, *f.n.* ['greɪthed] (gráyt-hed)
Greatorex, *f.n.* ['greɪtəreks] (gráytŏrecks)
Greaves, *f.n.* [greɪvz] (grayvz); [grivz] (greevz) *The first is appropriate for the Countess of Dysart's family name.*
Greenaway, *f.n.* ['grinəweɪ] (greénă-way)
Greenbaum, *Kyla*, *pianist* ['kaɪlə 'grinbaʊm] (kílă greénbowm)
Greene, *f.n.* [grin] (green)
Greengross, *f.n.* ['gringrɒs] (greén-gross)
Greenhalgh,*f.n.*['grinhælʃ](green-halsh); ['grinhɒlʃ] (green-holsh); ['grinhældʒ] (green-haldj); ['grinhɒl] (green-hawl)
Greenhalgh ['grinhælʃ] (green-halsh); ['grinhɒlʃ] (green-hawlsh)
Greenhough, *f.n.* ['grinɒf] (greénoff); ['grinhɒf] (green-hoff); ['grinhoʊ] (green-hō); ['grinhaʊ] (green-how); ['grinhʌf] (green-huff) ['grinʌf] (greénuff)
Greenhow, *f.n.* ['grinoʊ] (greénō); ['grinhaʊ] (green-how)
Greenisland [grin'aɪlənd] (greenflánd)

Greenlaw ['grinlo] (greén-law)
Greenock ['grinək] (greénŏk)
Greenough, *f.n.* ['grinoʊ] (greénō)
Greensilhaugh ['grinsɪlhɑf] (greénssil-haaf)
Greenslade,*f.n.* ['grinsleɪd] (green-slayd)
Greenwich ['grɪnɪdʒ] (grínnij); ['grɪnɪtʃ] (grínnitch); ['grenɪtʃ] (grénnitch)
Greenwood of Holbourne, *Viscount* ['grinwʊd əv 'hɒlbʊərn] (greénwŏod ŏv hólbŏorn)
Gregg, *f.n.* [greg] (greg)
Gregoire, *f.n.* ['gregwɑr] (grégwaar)
Gregorowski, *f.n.* [ˌgregə'rɒskɪ] (greggŏrósski)
Gregynog [grɪ'gʌnɒg] (grĕgúnnog)
Greig, *f.n.* [greg] (greg)
Greim, *f.n.* [grim] (greem)
Grein, *f.n.* [graɪn] (grīn)
Grenfell, *f.n.* ['grenfəl] (grénfĕl)
Grenofen ['grenəfən] (grénnŏfĕn)
Grenoside ['grenoʊsaɪd] (grénnŏssíd)
Gresham, *f.n.* ['greʃəm] (gréshăm); ['gresəm] (gréssăm)
Gresham ['greʃəm] (gréshăm)
Gresley, *f.n.* ['grezlɪ] (grézli)
Gressingham ['gresɪŋəm] (gréssing-ăm)
Gretabridge ['gritəbrɪdʒ] (greétăbrij)
Greta Hall, *Cumberland* ['gritə 'hɒl] (greétă háwl)
Greville, *Baron* ['grevɪl] (grévvil)
Grey de Ruthyn, *Barony of* ['greɪ də 'ruθɪn] (gráy dĕ roóthin)
Greysouthen ['greɪsun] (gráyssoon)
Greystoke ['greɪstɒk] (gráy-stock)
Greywell ['greɪ'wel] (gráy-wéll); ['gruəl] (groó-ĕl)
Grianan ['grinən] (greénăn)
Gribbin Head ['grɪbɪn 'hed] (gríbbin héd)
Grice, *f.n.* [graɪs] (gríss)
Gridley, *f.n.* ['grɪdlɪ] (grídli)
Grier, *f.n.* [grɪər] (greer)
Grierson, *f.n.* ['grɪərsən] (greérssŏn)
Grieve, *f.n.* [griv] (greev)
Griew, *f.n.* [gru] (groo)
Grimethorpe ['graɪmθɔrp] (grím-thorp)
Grimond, *f.n.* ['grɪmənd] (grímmŏnd)
Grimscar ['graɪmzkɑr] (grímzkaar)
Grimsetter ['grɪmstər] (grímster)
Grimshaw, *f.n.* ['grɪmʃɔ] (grím-shaw)
Grindale ['grɪndl] (grindl)
Grinke, *f.n.* ['grɪŋkɪ] (grínki)
Grisdale, *f.n.* ['grɪzdeɪl] (grízdayl)
Grisdale ['graɪzdeɪl] (grízdayl)
Grisewood, *f.n.* ['graɪzwʊd] (grízwŏod)
Groby ['grʊbɪ] (groóbi)
Grocyn, *William*, *15-16th-c. priest and scholar* ['groʊsɪn] (gróssin)
Groeslon ['grɔɪslɒn] (gróysslon)
Grogan, *f.n.* ['groʊgən] (grógăn)
Grogarry ['grɒgərɪ] (gróggări)
Gronau, *Rees Howell*, *19th-c. Welsh author* ['ris 'haʊəl 'grɒnoʊ] (reéss hówĕl grónnō)

Groombridge ['grum'brɪdʒ] (groóm-bríj)
Groomsport ['grumzpɔrt] (groómzport)
Grose, *f.n.* [groʊs] (grōss)
Groser, *f.n.* ['groʊsər] (grṓsser)
Grosmont, *Monmouth.* ['grɒsmənt] (gróssmŏnt)
Grosmont, *Yorks.* ['groʊmənt] (grṓmŏnt); ['groʊsmənt] (grṓssmŏnt)
Gross, *f.n.* [grɒs] (gross); [groʊs] (grōss)
Grosseteste, *Robert, 13th-c. Bishop of Lincoln, also spelt* **Grossetete**, **Grossetête** ['groʊsteɪt] (grṓsstayt); ['groʊstest] (grṓsstest) *The first pronunciation is appropriate for all three spellings.*
Grosvenor, *f.n.* ['groʊvnər] (grṓv-nōr); ['groʊvənər] (grṓvĕnŏr) *The first is appropriate for the family name of the Duke of Westminster.*
Grote, *f.n.* [groʊt] (grōt)
Groton ['grotən] (gráwtŏn); ['groʊtən] (grṓtŏn)
Grouse, *f.n.* [graʊs] (growss)
Grout, *f.n.* [graʊt] (growt)
Gruenberg, *f.n.* ['grunbərg] (groónberg)
Gruffydd, *f.n.* ['grɪfɪð] (gríffith)
Gruinard Bay, Island *and* River ['grɪnjərd] (grín-yârd)
Grundisburgh ['grʌndzbərə] (grúndz-bŭrá)
Grunert, *f.n.* ['grunərt] (grṓōnĕrt)
Grupe, *f.n.* [grup] (groop)
Grygar, *f.n.* ['graɪɡɑr] (grígaar)
Guare, *f.n.* [gweər] (gwair)
Guay [gaɪ] (gī)
Gudgin, *f.n.* ['gʌdʒɪn] (gújjin)
Guedalla, *f.n.* [gwɪ'dælə] (gwĕdálá)
Gueroult, *f.n.* ['geroʊ] (gérrō)
Guerrier, *f.n.* ['gerɪər] (gérri-er)
Guest, *f.n.* [gest] (gest)
Guggisberg, *f.n.* ['gʌgɪsbərg] (gúggiss-berg)
Guignard, *f.n.* ['ginjɑr] (geén-yaar)
Guihard, *f.n.* ['gihɑrd] (geéhaard)
Guildford ['gɪlfərd] (gílfŏrd)
Guilding, *f.n.* ['gɪldɪŋ] (gílding)
Guilford, *f.n.* ['gɪlfərd] (gílfŏrd)
Guillamore, *Viscountcy of* ['gɪləmɔr] (gíllămor)
Guillaume, *f.n.* ['gioʊm] (geé-ōm)
Guillebaud, *f.n.* ['gilboʊ] (geélbō); ['gɪlboʊ] (gíllibō) *The first is appropriate for Claude ∼, economist.*
Guillemard, *f.n.* ['gɪlmɑr] (gílmaar)
Guillermin, *f.n.* ['gɪlərmɪn] (gíllĕrmin)
Guillery, *f.n.* ['gɪlərɪ] (gíllĕri)
Guilmant, *f.n.* ['gɪlmɒnt] (gílmont)
Guilsfield ['gɪlzfild] (gílzfeeld)
Guinan, *f.n.* [gɪ'næn] (ginán)
Guinane, *f.n.* [gɪ'næn] (ginán)
Guinee, *f.n.* ['gɪnɪ] (gínni)
Guinnane, *f.n.* [gɪ'næn] (ginán)
Guinness, *f.n.* ['gɪnɪs] (gínnĕss)
Guisborough ['gɪzbərə] (gízbŭrá)
Guise, *f.n.* [gaɪz] (giz)

Guiseley ['gaɪzlɪ] (gízli)
Guist [gaɪst] (gīsst)
Guiting Power ['gaɪtɪŋ 'paʊər] (gíting pówer)
Guiver, *f.n.* ['gaɪvər] (gíver)
Gulbenkian Foundation [gʊl'benkɪən] (gŏŏlbénkiän)
Guldeford ['gɪlfərd] (gílfŏrd)
Gullane ['gɪlən] (gíllăn)
Gulleford, *f.n.* ['gʌlɪfərd] (gúllifŏrd)
Gulvain ['gʊlvɪn] (goólvin)
Gulval ['gʌlvəl] (gúlvăl)
Gummery, *f.n.* ['gʌmərɪ] (gúmmĕri)
Gunderson, *f.n.* ['gʌndərsən] (gúndĕrssŏn)
Gunnell, *f.n.* ['gʌnl] (gunnl)
Gunnislake ['gʌnɪzleɪk] (gúnnizlayk)
Gunter, *f.n.* ['gʌntər] (gúnter)
Gunwalloe [gʌn'wɒloʊ] (gun-wóllō)
Gunwalloe Towans [gʌn'wɒloʊ 'taʊənz] (gun-wóllō tówänz)
Gunyon, *f.n.* ['gʌnjən] (gún-yŏn)
Gurnards Head ['gɜrnərdz 'hed] (gúrn- árdz héd)
Gurnos ['gɜrnɒs] (gúrnoss)
Gurteen, *f.n.* ['gɜrtin] (gúrteen)
Gustard, *f.n.* ['gʌstərd] (gústărd)
Gutch, *f.n.* [gʌtʃ] (gutch)
Guthrie, Sir Tyrone, *theatrical producer* [tɪ'roʊn 'gʌθrɪ] (tirrṓn gúthri)
Gutteridge, *f.n.* ['gʌtərɪdʒ] (gúttĕrij)
Guyer, *f.n.* ['gaɪər] (gí-er)
Guyatt, *f.n.* ['gaɪət] (gí-ăt)
Guyler, *f.n.* ['gaɪlər] (gíler)
Guyon, *f.n.* ['gaɪən] (gí-ŏn)
Guyot, *f.n.* ['gaɪət] (gí-ŏt)
Guyott, *f.n.* ['gaɪət] (gí-ŏt)
Gwaelod-y-Garth ['gwaɪlɒd ə 'gɑrθ] (gwílod ă gaárth)
Gwaen-cae-Gurwen *see* Gwaun-cae-Gurwen.
Gwaenysgor *see* Gwaunysgor.
Gwalchmai ['gwælxmaɪ] (gwálchmī)
Gwastaden [gwəs'tædən] (gwástáddĕn)
Gwatkin, *f.n.* ['gwɒtkɪn] (gwótkin)
Gwaun-cae-Gurwen, *also spelt* Gwaen-cae-Gurwen ['gwaɪn kə 'gɜrwən] (gwín kă gúrwĕn)
Gwaunysgor, *also spelt* Gwaenysgor [gwaɪn'ʌsgər] (gwínússgor)
Gwbert ['gʊbərt] (gŏŏbĕrt)
Gweek [gwik] (gweek)
Gwenddwr ['gwendʊər] (gwéndŏŏr)
Gwendraeth Fach ['gwendraɪθ 'vax] (gwéndrīth vaách)
Gwendraeth Fawr ['gwendraɪθ 'vaʊər] (gwéndrīth vówr)
Gwennap ['gwenəp] (gwénnăp)
Gwersyllt ['gwɜrsɪłt] (gwaírssihlt)
Gwespyr ['gwespər] (gwéssper)
Gwinear ['gwɪnɪər] (gwínneer)
Gwineas Rock, *also called* Gwinges Rock, *q.v.* ['gwɪnɪəs] (gwínniáss)
Gwinges Rock, *also called* Gwineas Rock, *q.v.* ['gwɪndʒɪz] (gwínjēz)

Gwion, Welsh C.n. ['gwiɒn] (gweé-on)
Gwithian ['gwɪðɪən] (gwíthiǎn)
Gwnnws ['gunus] (gŏŏnŏŏss)
Gwrych [gwrix](gwreech) ; [grix](greech)
In order to pronounce the first of these as one syllable, Welsh speakers treat the 'w' as a rounding of the lips to accompany the 'r'.
Gwy, River ['guɪ] (gŏŏ-i) *This is the Welsh name of the* Wye, *q.v.*
Gwyddelwern [gwɪð'elwɜrn] (gwithél-wern)
Gwydion, Welsh C.n. ['gwɪdɪən] (gwíddi-ŏn)
Gwynant, Lake ['gwɪnænt] (gwínnant)
Gwyndâf, Welsh Bardic name ['gwɪndæv] (gwíndav)
Gwynedd, Viscount ['gwɪnəð] (gwínnĕth)
Gwynedd, Hywel ab Owain, 12th-c. Welsh prince ['hauəl æb 'ouɪn 'gwɪnəð] (hówĕl ab ŏ-ĕn gwínnĕth)
Gwynfe ['gwɪnvə] (gwínvǎ)
Gwynfil ['gwɪnvɪl] (gwínvil)
Gwynfor, Welsh C.n. ['gwɪnvɔr] (gwínvor)
Gwynn, f.n. [gwɪn] (gwin)
Gwyther, f.n. ['gwaɪðər] (gwíther) ; ['gwɪðər] (gwíther)
Gwytherin [gwɪð'erɪn] (gwithérrin)
Gyde, f.n. [gaɪd] (gīd)
Gye, f.n. [dʒaɪ] (jī)
Gyffylliog [gə'fʌɪjɒg] (gǔfúhl-yog)
Gyle, f.n. [gaɪl] (gīl)
Gymer, f.n. ['gaɪmər] (gímer)
Gyngell, f.n. ['gɪndʒl] (ginjl)
Gyppeswyke Plate, sheep-farming trophy ['gɪpswɪk] (gíps-wick)

H

Haacke, f.n. ['hækɪ] (hácki)
Habermehl, f.n. ['habərmeɪl] (haábĕr-mayl)
Haceby ['heɪsbɪ] (háyssbi)
Hackett, f.n. ['hækɪt] (háckĕt)
Hackshaw, f.n. ['hækʃɔ] (háck-shaw)
Hacquoil, f.n. ['hækwɔɪl] (háckwoyl)
Hadath, Gunby, author ['gʌnbɪ 'hædəθ] (gúnbi háddǎth)
Haddow, f.n. ['hædou] (háddŏ)
Haddrill, f.n. ['hædrɪl] (hádril)
Haden, f.n. ['heɪdən] (háydĕn)
Hadnall ['hædnəl] (hád-nǎl)
Hadow, f.n. ['hædou] (háddŏ)
Hadrian's Wall ['heɪdrɪənz 'wɔl] (háydriǎnz wáwl)
Hadzor ['hædzər] (hádzŏr)
Hafner, f.n. ['hæfnər] (háffner)

Hafod ['hævɒd] (hávvod)
Hafodyrynys ['hævɒdər'ʌnɪs] (hávvod-ǎrúnniss)
Hagan, f.n. ['heɪgən] (háygǎn)
Hagen, f.n. ['heɪgən] (háygĕn)
Haggar, f.n. ['hægər] (hággaar) ; ['hægər] (hággǎr)
Hague, f.n. [heɪg] (hayg)
Hahessy, f.n. ['heɪɪsɪ] (háy-ĕssi)
Haig, f.n. [heɪg] (hayg) *Appropriate also for Earl ~.*
Haigh, f.n. [heɪg] (hayg)
Haigh, Lancs. [heɪ] (hay)
Haigh, Yorks. [heɪg] (hayg)
Haight, f.n. [haɪt] (hīt)
Haighton ['haɪtən] (hítŏn)
Hailes, Baron [heɪlz] (haylz)
Hailes Castle, *East Lothian* [heɪlz] (haylz)
Haileyburian, one educated at Haileybury College [ˌheɪlɪ'bjuərɪən] (haylibyŏŏriǎn)
Hailsham ['heɪlʃəm] (háyl-shǎm) *Appropriate also for the Viscountcy of ~.*
Hainault ['heɪnɔt] (háynawt)
Haire, f.n. [hɛər] (hair) *Appropriate also for the Barony of ~.*
Hairmyres [hɛər'maɪərz] (hairmírz)
Hakin ['heɪkɪn] (háykin)
Hakluyt, Richard, 16th-c. historian and geographer ['hæklut] (háckloot) ; ['hæklwɪt] (háckl-wit) *The former is much the more usual traditional pronunciation.*
Halahan, f.n. ['hæləhən] (hálǎhǎn)
Halas, f.n. ['hæləs] (hálǎss)
Halcrow, f.n. ['hælkrou] (hálkrŏ)
Haldane, f.n. ['hɒldən] (háwldǎn) ; ['hɒldern] (háwldayn)
Haldon ['hɒldən] (háwldŏn) *Appropriate also for the Barony of ~.*
Halebarns [heɪl'bɑrnz] (haylbaárnz)
Haler, f.n. ['heɪlər] (háyler)
Halesowen [heɪlz'ouɪn] (haylzŏ-ĕn)
Halewood [heɪl'wʊd] (haylwŏŏd)
Haley, f.n. ['heɪlɪ] (háyli)
Halford, f.n. ['hælfərd] (hálfŏrd) ; ['hɒlfərd] (háwlford)
Halford, Salop ['hɒlfərd] (háwlfŏrd)
Halford, Warwick. ['hælfərd] (hálfŏrd) ; ['hɒfərd] (haáfŏrd)
Halfpenny, f.n. ['hɑfpənɪ] (haáfpĕni)
Halket, f.n. ['hælkɪt] (hálkĕt)
Halkett, f.n. ['hælkɪt] (hálkĕt) ; ['hɒlkɪt] (háwlkĕt) ; ['hækɪt] (háckĕt)
Halkirk ['hɒlkɜrk] (háwlkirk)
Halkyn ['hælkɪn] (hálkin)
Hallam, f.n. ['hæləm] (hálǎm)
Hallam, *parliamentary division* ['hæləm] (hálǎm)
Halland ['hælənd] (hálǎnd)
Hallas, f.n. ['hæləs] (hálǎss)
Hallaton ['hælətən] (hálǎtŏn)
Hallé, f.n. ['hæleɪ] (hálay) *Appropriate also for the ~ Orchestra.*
Hallen ['hælən] (hálĕn)
Hallett, f.n. ['hælɪt] (hálĕt)

*Halley, Edmond, astronomer and mathe-
matician* ['hælɪ] (háli)
Halliday, f.n. ['hælɪdeɪ] (háliday)
Hallin ['hælɪn] (hálin)
Hallinan, f.n. ['hælɪnən] (hálinǎn)
Halling ['hɔlɪŋ] (háwling)
Hallingbury ['hɔlɪŋbərɪ] (hóllingbŭri);
['hɔlɪŋbərɪ] (háwlingbŭri)
Hallisey, f.n. ['hælɪsɪ] (hálissi)
Hall i' th' Wood ['hɔlɪt 'wʊd] (háwlit
wŏŏd)
Halliwell, f.n. ['hælɪwel] (háli-wel)
Halmore ['hælmɔr] (hálmor)
Halnaker ['hænəkər] (hánnáker)
Halpern, f.n. ['hælpərn] (hálpĕrn)
Halpin, f.n. ['hælpɪn] (hálpin)
Halsall, f.n. ['hælsl] (halssl)
Halsall ['hɔlsl] (hawlssl)
Halsbury, Earl of ['hɔlzbərɪ] (háwlzbŭri)
Halse, f.n. [hæls] (halss); [hɔls] (hawlss)
Halse [hæls] (halss); [hɔs] (hawss)
Halsetown ['hɔlztaʊn] (háwlztown)
Halsey, f.n. ['hælsɪ] (hálssi); ['hɔlzɪ]
(háwlzi); ['hɔlsɪ] (háwlssi)
Halstan, f.n. ['hɔlstən] (háwlstǎn)
Halstead, Essex, Kent ['hælsted] (hál-
sted)
Halstock ['hɔlstɒk] (háwlstock)
Halstow, Lower ['lovər 'hælstoʊ] (lŏ-er
hálstŏ)
Halswell, f.n. ['hælzwel] (hálzwel)
Haltemprice ['hɔltəmpraɪs] (háwltĕm-
prĭss)
Halton Holgate, also spelt Halton Hole-
gate ['hɔltən 'hoʊlgeɪt] (háwltŏn hŏl-
gayt); ['hɔltən 'hɒlgeɪt] (háwltŏn hóllĕ-
gayt)
Halward, f.n. ['hælwərd] (hálwǎrd)
Halwell ['hælwel] (hálwel); ['hɒlwel]
(háwlwel)
Halwill ['hælwɪl] (hálwil); ['hɒlwɪl]
(háwlwil)
Hambloch, f.n. ['hæmblɒk] (hámblock)
Hambourg, f.n. ['hæmbɜrg] (hámburg)
Hambro, f.n. ['hæmbroʊ] (hámbrŏ);
['hæmbrə] (hámbrǎ)
Hamburger, f.n. ['hæmbɜrgər] (hám-
burger)
Hamer, f.n. ['heɪmər] (háymer)
Hameringham ['hæmərɪŋəm] (hammĕr-
ing-ǎm)
Hamey, f.n. ['heɪmɪ] (háymi)
Hamfallow [hæm'fæloʊ] (hamfálŏ)
Hamilton, f.n. ['hæmltən] (hámmltŏn)
Hamilton of Dalzell, Baron ['hæmltən
əv di'el] (hámmltŏn ŏv dee-éll)
Hamilton ['hæmltən] (hámmltŏn)
Hamiltonsbawn [ˌhæmltənz'bɒn]
(hammltŏnzbáwn)
Hamish, C.n. ['heɪmɪʃ] (háymish)
Hammant, f.n. ['hæmənt] (hámmǎnt)
Hammill, f.n. ['hæmɪl] (hámmil)
Hamnett, f.n. ['hæmnɪt] (hám-nĕt)
Hamoaze ['hæmoʊz] (hámmŏz)
Hamond, f.n. ['hæmənd] (hámmŏnd)

Hampden, Viscountcy of ['hæmdən]
(hámdĕn)
Hampden Park, Eastbourne, Glasgow
['hæmdən 'park] (hámdĕn paárk)
Hampshire ['hæmpʃər] (hámp-sher)
Hampson, f.n. ['hæmsən] (hámssŏn)
Hampstead ['hæmpstɪd] (hámpstĕd);
['hæmpsted] (hámpsted)
Hamsey ['hæmzɪ] (hámzi)
Hanbury, f.n. ['hænbərɪ] (hánbŭri)
Hanchant, f.n. ['hænʃənt] (hán-shánt)
Hancock, f.n. ['hænkɒk] (hán-kock);
['hæŋkɒk] (háng-kock)
Handcock, f.n. ['hændkɒk] (hándkock)
Handel, George Frederick, composer
['hændl] (handl) The original German was
Händel, pronounced ['hendl] (hendl).
Handelian, pertaining to Handel [hæn-
'dilɪən] (handeeliǎn)
Hankin, f.n. ['hæŋkɪn] (hánkin)
Hannahstown ['hænəztaʊn] (hánnǎz-
town)
Hanrahan, f.n. ['hænrəhən] (hánrǎhǎn)
Hanratty, f.n. [hæn'rætɪ] (hanrátti)
Hanslope ['hænsloʊp] (hánsslŏp)
Happisburgh ['heɪzbərə] (háyzbŭrǎ)
Harberton ['harbərtən] (haárbĕrtŏn)
Appropriate also for Viscount ∼.
Harbertonford ['harbərtənford] (haár-
bĕrtŏnford)
Harcourt, f.n. ['harkɔrt] (haárkort);
['harkɜrt] (haárkŭrt) The second is appro-
priate for Viscount ∼.
Hardaker, f.n. ['hardeɪkər] (haárdayker)
Harden, f.n. ['hardən] (haárděn)
Hardenhuish ['harnɪʃ] (haárnish)
Hardhaugh ['hardhaf] (haárd-haaf)
Harding, f.n. ['hardɪŋ] (haárding)
Hardinge, f.n. ['hardɪŋ] (haárding);
['hardɪndʒ] (haárdinj) The first is appro-
priate for Viscount ∼.
Hardres, f.n. [hardz] (haardz)
Hardres [hardz] (haardz)
Hardress, f.n. ['hardres] (haárdress)
Hardwicke, Sir Cedric, actor ['sidrɪk
'hardwɪk] (seédrick haárdwick)
Hardwick Woods ['hardwɪk 'wʊdz]
(haárdwick wŏŏdz); ['hardɪk 'wʊdz]
(haárdick wŏŏdz)
Hardy, f.n. ['hardɪ] (haárdi)
Harefield ['hɛərfɪld] (háirfeeld)
Harehaugh ['hɛərhaf] (háir-haaf)
Harenc, f.n. ['hɛərɒŋ] (hárrong)
Haresceugh ['hɛərskjuf] (háirskewf)
Harewood, f.n. ['hɛərwʊd] (háirwŏŏd)
Harewood ['harwʊd] (haárwŏŏd); ['hɛər-
wʊd] (háirwŏŏd) The first is appropriate
for the Earl of ∼ and for ∼ House in
Yorkshire. The second is usual in the
village.
Harford, f.n. ['harfərd] (haárfŏrd)
Harger, f.n. ['hardʒər] (haárjer)
Hargham ['harfəm] (haárfǎm)

Hargreaves, *f.n.* ['hɑrgrivz] (haár-greevz) ; ['hɑrgreɪvz] (haárgrayvz) *In its native North of England, the first is appropriate. The second was that of Mrs. Alice ~, the original Alice in Wonderland.*

Haringey ['hærɪŋgeɪ] (hárring-gay)

Harington, *f.n.* ['hærɪŋtən] (hárringtŏn)

Harkness, *f.n.* ['hɑrknɪs] (haárknĕss)

Harlaxton ['hɑrləkstən] (haárlăkstŏn)

Harle, *f.n.* [hɑrl] (haarl)

Harlech ['hɑrləx] (haárlĕch) *Appropriate also for Baron ~.*

Harlesden ['hɑrlzdən] (haárlzdĕn)

Harleston ['hɑrlstən] (haárlstŏn)

Harlestone ['hɑrlstən] (haárlstŏn)

Harlow ['hɑrloʊ] (haárlō)

Harmondsworth ['hɑrməndzwɜrθ] (haármŏndzwurth)

Haroldswick ['hærəldzwɪk] (hárröldz-wick)

Harpham, *f.n.* ['hɑrpəm] (haárpăm)

Harpwood, *f.n.* ['hɑrpwʊd] (haárpwŏŏd)

Harraby ['hærəbɪ] (hárrăbi)

Harragin, *f.n.* ['hærəgɪn] (hárrăgin)

Harrap, *f.n.* ['hærəp] (hárrăp)

Harray ['hærɪ] (hárri)

Harries, *f.n.* ['hærɪs] (hárriss)

Harrietsham ['hærɪətʃəm] (hárrĭĕt-shăm) ; ['hærɪʃəm] (hárrishăm)

Harris, *f.n.* ['hærɪs] (hárriss)

Harriseahead ['hærɪsɪ'hed] (hárrissee-héd)

Harrod, *f.n.* ['hærəd] (hárrŏd)

Harrop, *f.n.* ['hærəp] (hárrŏp)

Harrovian, *one educated at Harrow School* [hə'roʊvɪən] (hărōviăn)

Harrow, *f.n.* ['hæroʊ] (hárrō)

Harrow ['hæroʊ] (hárrō)

Harrowden, Great *and* **Little** ['hæroʊdən] (hárrōdĕn)

Harrup, *f.n.* ['hærəp] (hárrŭp)

Hart, *f.n.* [hɑrt] (haart)

Hartcup, *f.n.* ['hɑrtkʌp] (haárt-kup)

Hartham ['hɑrtəm] (haártăm)

Hartismere ['hɑrtɪsmɪər] (haártiss-meer)

Hartlebury ['hɑrtlbərɪ] (haártlbŭri)

Hartlepool ['hɑrtlɪpuːl] (haártlipool)

Hartley Wespall ['hɑrtlɪ 'wespəl] (haártli wéspawl)

Hartopp, *f.n.* ['hɑrtɒp] (haártop)

Hartshorn, *f.n.* ['hɑrtshɔrn] (haárts-horn)

Hartshorne, *f.n.* ['hɑrtshɔrn] (haárts-horn)

Hartsilver, *f.n.* ['hɑrtsɪlvər] (haártsilver)

Harvey of Tasburgh, *Baron* ['hɑrvɪ əv 'teɪzbərə] (haárvi ŏv táyzbŭră)

Harwich ['hærɪdʒ] (hárrij) ; ['hærɪtʃ] (hárritch)

Harwood, *f.n.* ['hɑrwʊd] (haárwŏŏd)

Haselbech, *f.n.* ['heɪzlbɪtʃ] (háyzlbeetch)

Haseldine, *f.n.* ['hæzldaɪn] (házzldīn)

Haseler, *f.n.* ['heɪzlər] (háyzler)

Haseley ['heɪzlɪ] (háyzli)

Haselor ['heɪzlɔr] (háyzlor)

Hashagen, *f.n.* ['hæʃəgən] (háshăgĕn)

Hasketon ['hæskɪtən] (hásskĕtŏn)

Haslam, *f.n.* ['hæzləm] (házlăm)

Haslemere ['heɪzlmɪər] (háyzlmeer)

Hasler, *f.n.* ['hæzlər] (házler)

Haslett, *f.n.* ['heɪzlɪt] (háyzlĕt) ; ['hæzlɪt] (házlĕt)

Haslingden ['hæzlɪŋdən] (házlingdĕn)

Haslingfield ['heɪzlɪŋfɪld] (háyzlingfeeld)

Hassall, *f.n.* ['hæsl] (hassl)

Hassard, *f.n.* ['hæsɑrd] (hássaard)

Hastie, *f.n.* ['heɪstɪ] (háyssti)

Hastings, *f.n.* ['heɪstɪŋz] (háyysstingz)

Hastings ['heɪstɪŋz] (háyysstingz)

Haswell, *f.n.* ['hæzwel] (házwel)

Hatch Beauchamp ['hætʃ 'bitʃəm] (hátch béetchăm)

Hatfield Peverel ['hætfɪld 'pevərəl] (hát-feeld pévvĕrĕl)

Hathaway, *f.n.* ['hæθəweɪ] (háthă-way)

Hathern ['hæðərn] (háthĕrn)

Hathersage ['hæðərseɪdʒ] (háthĕr-sayj)

Hathorn, *f.n.* ['hɔθɔrn] (háwthorn); ['heɪθɔrn] (háythorn); ['hæθɔrn] (háethorn)

Hattersley, *f.n.* ['hætərzlɪ] (háttĕrzli)

Hauger, *f.n.* ['hɔgər] (háwger)

Haugh, *Lincs.* [hɔ] (haw)

Haugh, Nether *and* **Upper**, *Yorks.* [hɒf] (hawf)

Haugh of Urr ['hɒx əv 'ɜr] (haách ŏv úr)

Haugham, *Kent* ['hʌfəm] (húffăm)

Haugham, *Lincs.* ['hæfəm] (háffăm)

Haughley ['hɒlɪ] (háwli)

Haughmond Hill ['hɒmənd 'hɪl] (háw-mŏnd híll); ['hɜrmənd 'hɪl] (háymŏnd híll)

Haughney, *f.n.* ['hɒxnɪ] (hóchni)

Haughton, *f.n.* ['hɒtən] (háwtŏn)

Haughton-le-Skerne ['hɒtən lə 'skɜrn] (háwtŏn lĕ skérn)

Haulbowline Rock [hɒl'boʊlɪn] (hawlbŏlin)

Haulgh [hɒf] (hoff)

Hauser, *f.n.* ['hozər] (háwzer)

Hautbois, Great *and* **Little** ['hɒbɪs] (hóbbiss)

Hauxwell ['hɒkswel] (háwkswell)

Havant ['hævənt] (hávvănt)

Havard, *f.n.* ['hævərd] (hávvărd)

Havell, *f.n.* ['hævl] (havvl) *Appropriate also for E. B. ~, Indian art historian.*

Havenhand, *f.n.* ['heɪvənhænd] (háyvĕn-hand)

Haverah Park ['hævərə 'pɑrk] (hávvĕră paárk)

Haverfordwest [,hævərfərd'west] (havvĕrfórd-wést); [,hɑrfərd'west] (haar-fórd-wést)

Havergate Island ['hævərgeɪt] (hávvĕr-gayt)

Haverhill ['heɪvrɪl] (háyvril)

Haverigg ['hævərɪg] (hávvĕrig)

Havering-atte-Bower ['heɪvərɪŋ ætɪ 'baʊər](háyvěring atti bówer)
Haveringland ['heɪvərɪŋlənd] (háyvěring-lånd)
Havers, f.n. ['heɪvərz] (háyvěrz)
Haverton Hill ['hævərtən 'hɪl](hávvěrtŏn hill)
Haviland, f.n. ['hævɪlənd] (hávvilånd)
Haward, f.n. ['heɪwərd] (háywård); ['hɔərd] (háw-ård); [hɑrd] (haard); [hɔrd] (hord)
Hawarden, f.n. ['hɑrdən] (haárděn)
Hawarden ['hɑrdən] (haárděn) *Appropriate also for the Barony of Gladstone of* ~.
Haweis, f.n. ['hɔ-ɪs] (háw-iss)
Hawick ['hɔ-ɪk] (háw-ick)
Hawkes, f.n. [hɔks] (hawks)
Hawkinge ['hɔkɪndʒ] (háwkinj)
Haworth, f.n. ['haʊərθ] (hów-ŭrth)
Haworth ['haʊərθ] (hów-ŭrth); ['hɔərθ] (háw-ŭrth)
Hawridge ['hærɪdʒ] (hárrij)
Hawtrey, f.n. ['hɔtrɪ] (háwtri)
Haxell, f.n. ['hæksl] (hacksl)
Haxey ['hæksɪ] (hácksi)
Haycock, f.n. ['heɪkɒk] (háykock)
Hayden, f.n. ['heɪdən] (háyděn)
Haydn, C.n. ['heɪdn] (haydn)
Haydock ['heɪdɒk] (háydock)
Haydon, f.n. ['heɪdən] (háydŏn) *Appropriate for Benjamin* ~, *19th-c. historical painter.*
Hayes, f.n. [heɪz] (hayz)
Hayhow, f.n. ['heɪhoʊ] (háy-hō)
Hayhurst, f.n. ['heɪhərst] (háy-hŭrst)
Hayland, f.n. ['heɪlənd] (háylånd)
Hayle [heɪl] (hayl)
Hays, f.n. [heɪz] (hayz)
Haysom, f.n. ['heɪsəm] (háyssŏm)
Hayter, f.n. ['heɪtər] (háyter)
Haytor ['heɪ'tər] (háy-tór)
Hayward, f.n. ['heɪwərd] (háywård)
Hazell, f.n. ['heɪzl] (hayzl)
Hazlerigg, f.n. ['heɪzlrɪg] (háyzlrig)
Hazlitt, f.n. ['heɪzlɪt] (háyzlĕt); ['hæzlɪt] (házlĕt) *Although the second is now usual, the first was that of William* ~, *essayist and critic, and is still used by his descendants.*
Hazlitt Gallery, *London* ['hæzlɪt] (házlit)
Heacham ['hetʃəm] (hétchăm); ['hɪtʃəm] (heétchăm)
Headfort, Marquess of ['hedfərt] (hédfŏrt)
Headingley ['hedɪŋlɪ] (hédding-li)
Headlam, f.n. ['hedləm] (hédlăm)
Heaf, f.n. [hif] (heef)
Heage [hidʒ] (heej)
Heaks, f.n. [hiks] (heeks)
Heal, f.n. [hil] (heel)
Healaugh ['hilə] (heélă)
Heald, f.n. [hild] (heeld)
Healy, f.n. ['hilɪ] (heéli)
Heamoor ['heɪmɔr] (háymor)
Heanen, f.n. ['hinən] (heéněn)

Heanor ['hinər] (heénŏr); ['heɪnər] (háynŏr)
Heanton Punchardon ['hentən 'pʌnʃərdən](héntŏn pún-shárdŏn); ['hetən 'pʌnʃərdən] (háyntŏn pún-shárdŏn)
Heape, f.n. [hip] (heep)
Heaslip, f.n. ['heɪslɪp] (háysslip)
Heathcoat, f.n. ['heθkət] (héthkŏt)
Heathcoat Amory, f.n. ['heθkət 'eɪmərɪ] (héthkŏt áymŏri)
Heathcock, f.n. ['hiθkɒk] (heéthkock)
Heathcote, f.n. ['heθkət] (héthkŏt); ['hiθkaʊt] (heéthkŏt)
Heather ['hiðər] (heéther)
Heathery Cleugh ['heðərɪ 'klʌf] (héthěri klúff)
Heathfield ['hiθfild] (heéthfeeld)
Heathpool ['heθpul] (héthpool)
Heathrow ['hiθroʊ] (heéth-rô)
Heatlie, f.n. ['hitlɪ] (heétli)
Heaviside, f.n. ['hevɪsaɪd] (hévvissíd)
Heawood ['heɪwʊd] (háywŏŏd)
Heaword, f.n. ['heɪwərd] (háywŭrd)
Hebburn ['hebɜrn] (hébburn)
Heber, f.n. ['hibər] (heéber)
Hebert, f.n. ['hibərt] (heébĕrt)
Heckmondwike ['hekməndwaɪk] (héckmöndwík)
Hedgecock, f.n. ['hedʒkɒk] (héjkock)
Hedgehope ['hedʒəp] (héjjŏp)
Hednesford ['hensfərd] (hénssförd); ['hedʒfərd] (héjförd)
Hedon ['hedən] (héddŏn)
Heelas, f.n. ['hiləs] (heéláss)
Heffernan, f.n. ['hefərnən] (héffĕrnăn)
Hegarty, f.n. ['hegərtɪ] (héggärti)
Heggie, f.n. ['hegɪ] (héggi)
Heigham ['heɪəm] (háy-ăm)
Heighington, *Co. Durham* ['heɪŋtən] (háy-ingtŏn); ['haɪŋtən] (hí-ingtŏn); ['haɪntən] (híntŏn)
Heighington, *Lincs.* ['heɪˈɪŋtən] (hay-ingtŏn)
Heighton, f.n. ['heɪtən] (háytŏn)
Heighway, f.n. ['heɪweɪ] (háy-way)
Heilbron, f.n. ['haɪlbrɒn] (hílbron)
Heilgers, f.n. ['haɪlgərz] (hílgĕrz)
Heilpern, f.n. ['haɪlpərn] (hílpĕrn)
Heinekey, f.n. ['haɪnɪkɪ] (hínĕki)
Heisker ['haɪskər] (híssker)
Hele, f.n. [hil] (heel); ['hɪlɪ] (heéli)
Hele Stone ['hil stoʊn] (heél stŏn)
Helhoughton ['hel'haʊtən] (hel-hótŏn); [hel'haʊtən] (hel-hówtŏn)
Helland ['helənd] (héllånd)
Hellicar, f.n. ['helɪkɑr] (héllikaar)
Hellingly [ˌhelɪŋ'laɪ] (helling-lí)
Helliwell, f.n. ['helɪwel] (hélliwel)
Hellyar, f.n. ['heljər] (hél-yár)
Helme, f.n. [helm] (helm)
Helmingham ['helmɪŋəm] (hélming-ăm)
Helmore, f.n. ['helmɔr] (hélmor)
Helmsley ['helmzlɪ] (hélmzli); ['hemzlɪ] (hémzli)
Helston ['helstən] (hélsstŏn)

Helvellyn [hel'velɪn] (helvéllin)
Helwick Shoals *and* **lightship** ['helɪk] (héllick)
Hely, *f.n.* ['hilɪ] (héeli)
Helyer, *f.n.* ['helɪər] (hélli-er)
Heman, *f.n.* ['himən] (heémän)
Heming, *f.n.* ['hemɪŋ] (hémming)
Hemingbrough ['hemɪŋbrʌf] (hémming-bruff)
Hemmerde, *f.n.* ['hemərdɪ] (hémměrdi)
Hemswell ['hemzwel] (hémzwel)
Hemy, *f.n.* ['hemɪ] (hémmi)
Hemyock ['hemjɒk] (hém-yock); ['hemɪɒk] (hémmi-ock)
Hendreforgan [,hendrɪ'vɔrgən] (hendrivórgăn)
Hene, *f.n.* ['hinɪ] (heéni)
Hene ['hinɪ] (heéni)
Heneage, *f.n.* ['henɪdʒ] (hénnij) *Appropriate also for the Barony of ~.*
Henebery ['henɪbərɪ] (hénněběri)
Heneghan, *f.n.* ['henɪgən] (hénněgăn)
Heneglwys [hen'eglʊɪs] (henéglŏo-iss)
Heneker, *f.n.* ['henɪkər] (hénněker)
Hengoed ['heŋgɔɪd] (héng-goyd)
Heniarth ['henjɑrθ] (hén-yaarth); ['henɪɑrθ] (hénni-aarth)
Henig, *f.n.* ['henɪg] (hénnig)
Henlere, *f.n.* ['henlɪər] (hénleer)
Henllan ['henɬæn] (hén-ḫlan)
Henllan Fallteg ['henɬæn 'vælteg] (hénḫlan váḫlteg)
Hennessey, *f.n.* ['henɪsɪ] (hénněssi)
Hennessy, *f.n.* ['henɪsɪ] (hénněssi)
Henniker, *Baron* ['henɪkər] (hénniker)
Henocq, *f.n.* ['henɒk] (hénnock)
Henriques, *f.n.* [hen'rikɪz] (henreékěz)
Henschel, *Sir George, composer* ['henʃl] (henshl)
Hensher, *f.n.* ['henʃər] (hén-sher)
Henstead ['henstɪd] (hénstěd)
Henwick ['henwɪk] (hénwick)
Heolgerrig [,heɪɒl'gerɪg] (hay-ŏl-gérrig)
Heol-y-cyw [,heɪɒl ə 'kju] (hay-ŏl ă kéw)
Hepburn, *f.n.* ['heb3rn] (hébburn); ['hebərn] (hébbŭrn)
Hepburn ['heb3rn] (hébburn)
Heppell, *f.n.* ['hepl] (heppl)
Heppenstall, *f.n.* ['hepənstɔl] (héppěnstawl)
Hepplewhite, *f.n.* ['heplʍaɪt] (hépplwhīt)
Hepworth, *f.n.* ['hepw3rθ] (hépwurth)
Herapath, *f.n.* ['herəpɑθ] (hérrăpaath)
Herbison, *f.n.* ['h3rbɪsən] (hérbissŏn)
Hereford ['herɪfərd] (hérrěfŏrd) *Appropriate also for Viscount ~.*
Hergest Ridge ['hargɪst] (haargěst)
Herincx, Raimund, *opera singer* ['reɪmənd 'herɪŋks] (ráymŭnd hérrinks)
Heriot ['herɪət] (hérriŏt)
Herklots, *f.n.* ['h3rklɒts] (hérklots)
Herkness, *f.n.* ['hɑrknɪs] (haárkněss)
Herkomer, *f.n.* ['h3rkəmər] (hérkŏmer)
Herlihy, *f.n.* ['h3rlɪhɪ] (hérlihi)

Hermaness ['h3rmənes] (hérmăness)
Hermes, *f.n.* ['h3rmiz] (hérmeez)
Hermges, *f.n.* ['h3rmdʒiz] (hérmjeez)
Herner, *f.n.* ['h3rnər] (hérner)
Herriard ['herɪərd] (hérriărd)
Herries, *Baron* ['herɪs] (hérriss)
Herringshaw, *f.n.* ['herɪŋʃɒ] (hérringshaw)
Herriot, *f.n.* ['herɪət] (hérriŏt)
Herschell, *f.n.* ['h3rʃl] (hershl)
Herstmonceux, *also spelt* **Hurstmonceux, Hurstmonceaux** [,h3rstmən'sju] (herstmŏn-séw); [,h3rstmən'su] (herstmŏn-soŏ)
Hertford ['harfərd] (haárfŏrd) *Appropriate also for the Marquess of ~.*
Hertingfordbury ['hartɪŋfərdberɪ] (haártingfŏrdberri)
Hervey, *f.n.* ['harvɪ] (haárvi)
Herwald, *f.n.* ['h3rwəld] (hérwăld)
Heseltine, *f.n.* ['hesltaɪn] (héssltīn) *Also the pronunciation of Peter Warlock, composer, for his nom-de-plume of Philip ~.*
Heselton, *f.n.* ['hesltən] (héssltŏn)
Heshel, *f.n.* ['heʃl] (heshl)
Hesilrige, *f.n.* ['hezɪlrɪdʒ] (hézzilrij)
Hesleden ['hesldən] (héssldĕn)
Heslerton, East *and* **West** ['heslərtən] (hésslĕrtŏn)
Hesmondhalgh, *f.n.* ['hezməndhælʃ] (hézmŏnd-halsh); ['hezməndhɒ] (hézmŏnd-haw)
Hespe, *f.n.* [hesp] (hessp)
Hessary Tor ['hesərɪ 'tɒr] (héssări tór)
Hessé, *f.n.* ['hesɪ] (héssi)
Hessenford ['hesənfərd] (héssěnfŏrd)
Hessett ['hesɪt] (héssĕt)
Hession, *f.n.* ['hesɪən] (héssiŏn)
Hessle ['hezl] (hezzl)
Heston ['hestən] (hésstŏn)
Heswall ['hezwəl] (hézwăl)
Hethel ['hiθl] (heethl); ['heθl] (hethl)
Hetley, *f.n.* ['hetlɪ] (hétli)
Heugh, *f.n.* [hju] (hew)
Heugh, *Northumberland* [hjuf] (hewf)
Heulwen, *Welsh C.n.* ['haɪlwen] (hílwen)
Heuston, *f.n.* ['hjustən] (héwstŏn)
Hever ['hivər] (heéver)
Hewardine, *f.n.* ['hjuərdin] (héw-ärdeen)
Hewaswater ['hjuəswɒtər] (héw-ásswawter)
Hewett, *f.n.* ['hjuɪt] (héw-ĕt)
Hewitson, *f.n.* ['hjuɪtsən] (héw-itsŏn)
Hewitt, *f.n.* ['hjuɪt] (héw-it)
Hewlett, *f.n.* ['hjulɪt] (héwlĕt)
Heycock, *f.n.* ['heɪkɒk] (háykock)
Heydon ['heɪdən] (háydŏn)
Heyes, *f.n.* [heɪz] (hayz)
Heyford, Lower *and* **Upper,** *Northants., Oxon.* ['heɪfərd] (háyfŏrd)
Heyford, Nether ['neðər 'heɪfərd] (néther háyfŏrd)
Heyford at Bridge, *also called* Lower Heyford ['heɪfərd ət 'brɪdʒ] (háyfŏrd ăt bríj)

Heyford Warren, *also called* Upper Heyford **'heɪfərd** ['wɒrən] (háyförd wórrĕn)

Heygate, *f.n.* ['heɪgeɪt] (háygayt); ['heɪgɪt] (háygit)

Heygen, *f.n.* ['heɪgən] (háygĕn)

Heyner, *f.n.* ['heɪnər] (háyner)

Heyop ['heɪəp] (háy-ŏp)

Heyrod ['herəd] (hérrŏd)

Heys, *f.n.* [heɪz] (hayz)

Heysham ['hiʃəm] (heé-shăm)

Heyshott ['heɪʃɒt] (háy-shot)

Heytesbury, *Baron* ['hetsbərɪ] (hétsbŭri)

Heytesbury ['heɪtsbərɪ] (háytsbŭri)

Heythrop ['hiθrəp] (heéthrŏp) *Appropriate also for the ~ Hunt.*

Heyting, *f.n.* ['heɪtɪŋ] (háyting)

Heywood ['heɪwʊd] (háywŏŏd)

Hibaldstow ['hɪblstoʊ] (híbblstō)

Hibberd, *f.n.* ['hɪbərd] (híbbĕrd)

Hibbert, *f.n.* ['hɪbərt] (híbbĕrt)

Hibbitt, *f.n.* ['hɪbɪt] (híbbit)

Hickin, *f.n.* ['hɪkɪn] (híckin)

Hickinbotham, *f.n.* ['hɪkɪnbɒθəm] (híckinbothăm)

Hickling ['hɪklɪŋ] (híckling)

High Coniscliffe ['haɪ 'kɒnɪsklɪf] (hí kónniss-kliff)

High Halden ['haɪ 'hɔldən] (hí háwldĕn)

High Legh ['haɪ 'li] (hí leé)

High Wych ['haɪ 'waɪtʃ] (hí wítch)

High Wycombe ['haɪ 'wɪkəm] (hí wíckŏm)

Higham, *f.n.* ['haɪəm] (hí-ăm)

Higham, *East Suffolk, West Suffolk* ['haɪəm] (hí-ăm); ['hɪgəm] (híggăm)

Higham, *Kent* ['haɪəm] (hí-ăm)

Higham, *Yorks.* ['haɪəm] (hí-ăm); ['hɪkəm] (híckăm)

Higham Ferrers ['haɪəm 'ferərz] (hí-ăm férrĕrz)

Higham Gobion ['haɪəm 'goʊbɪən] (hí-ăm gṓbiŏn)

Higham's Park ['haɪəmz 'pɑrk] (hí-ămz paárk)

Highbury ['haɪbərɪ] (híbŭri)

Highgate, *f.n.* ['haɪgeɪt] (hígayt)

Highgate ['haɪgɪt] (hígit); ['haɪgeɪt] (hígayt)

Hiley, *f.n.* ['haɪlɪ] (híli)

Hilgay ['hɪlgeɪ] (hílgay)

Hill of Luton, *Baron* ['hɪl əv 'lutən] (hill ŏv lootŏn)

Hillcoat, *f.n.* ['hɪlkoʊt] (hílkōt)

Hilleary, *f.n.* ['hɪlərɪ] (híllĕri)

Hiller, *f.n.* ['hɪlər] (híller)

Hillery, *f.n.* ['hɪlərɪ] (híllĕri)

Hillhead ['hɪl'hed] (hill-héd)

Hillsborough ['hɪlzbərə] (hílzbŭră)

Hillswick ['hɪlzwɪk] (hílzwick)

Hincheliffe, *f.n.* ['hɪnʃklɪf] (hínsh-kliff)

Hinchingbrooke, *Viscountcy of* ['hɪnʃɪŋbrʊk] (hínshing-brŏŏk)

Hind, *f.n.* [haɪnd] (hínd); [hɪnd] (hind)

Hindell, *f.n.* ['hɪndl] (hindl)

Hinderclay ['hɪndərkleɪ] (híndĕrklay)

Hinderwell ['hɪndərwel] (híndĕrwel)

Hindle, *f.n.* ['hɪndl] (hindl)

Hindley, *f.n.* ['hɪndlɪ] (híndli); ['haɪndlɪ] (híndli)

Hindley ['hɪndlɪ] (híndli)

Hindlip ['hɪndlɪp] (híndlip) *Appropriate also for Baron ~.*

Hindmarsh, *f.n.* ['haɪndmɑrʃ] (híndmaarsh)

Hindolveston, *also spelt* **Hindolvestone** ['hɪndl'vestən] (híndlvéstŏn); ['hɪlvɪstən] (hílvĕstŏn)

Hindsley, *f.n.* ['haɪndzlɪ] (híndzli)

Hindson, *f.n.* ['haɪndsən] (híndssŏn)

Hints [hɪnts] (hints)

Hinwick ['hɪnɪk] (hínnick)

Hiorns, *f.n.* ['haɪərnz] (hí-örnz)

Hipkin, *f.n.* ['hɪpkɪn] (hípkin)

Hippisley, *f.n.* ['hɪpslɪ] (hípsli)

Hirnant ['hɜrnænt] (hírnant)

Hiron, *f.n.* ['haɪərɒn] (híron)

Hirons, *f.n.* ['haɪərɒnz] (híronz)

Hirwaun, *also spelt* **Hirwain** ['hɪərwaɪn] (heérwīn); ['hɜrwɪn] (hírwin)

Hitchcock, *f.n.* ['hɪtʃkɒk] (hítch-kock)

Hitchens, *f.n.* ['hɪtʃənz] (hítchĕnz)

Hoar, *f.n.* [hɔr] (hor)

Hoare, *f.n.* [hɔr] (hor)

Hoathly, East *and* **West** [hoʊθ'laɪ] (hōth-lí)

Hoban, *f.n.* ['hoʊbən] (hṓbăn)

Hobbins, *f.n.* ['hɒbɪnz] (hóbbinz)

Hobday, *f.n.* ['hɒbdeɪ] (hóbday)

Hobley, *f.n.* ['hoʊblɪ] (hóbli)

Hobourn, *f.n.* ['hoʊbɜrn] (hṓburn)

Hobsbaum, *f.n.* ['hɒbzbaʊm] (hóbzbowm)

Hobsbawm, *f.n.* ['hɒbzbɒm] (hóbzbawm)

Hoby, *f.n.* ['hoʊbɪ] (hṓbi)

Hodder & Stoughton, *publishers* ['hɒdər ənd 'staʊtən] (hódder ánd stówtŏn)

Hoddesdon ['hɒdzdən] (hódzdŏn)

Hoddinott, *f.n.* ['hɒdɪnɒt] (hóddinot)

Hodgart, *f.n.* ['hɒdʒərt] (hójjárt)

Hodgens, *f.n.* ['hɒdʒənz] (hójjĕnz)

Hodghton, *f.n.* ['hɒdʒtən] (hójtŏn)

Hodgson, *f.n.* ['hɒdʒsən] (hójssŏn)

Hodsoll, *f.n.* ['hɒdsl] (hodssl)

Hoenes, *f.n.* ['hoʊnes] (hóness)

Hoey, *f.n.* ['hoʊɪ] (hṓ-i); [hɔɪ] (hoy)

Hoffe, *f.n.* [hɒf] (hoff)

Hogan, *f.n.* ['hoʊgən] (hṓgăn)

Hogarth, *f.n.* ['hoʊgɑrθ] (hṓgaarth); ['hɒgərt] (hóggárt) *The first is traditional for William ~, painter and engraver. The second is usual in Cumberland and Westmorland.*

Hoggan, *f.n.* ['hɒgən] (hóggăn)

Hoggard, *f.n.* ['hɒgɑrd] (hóggaard)

Hoggarth, *f.n.* ['hɒgərt] (hóggárt)

Hogh, *f.n.* [hoʊ] (hō)

Hoghton, *f.n.* ['hɒtən] (háwtŏn)

Hoghton ['hɒtən] (háwtŏn)

Hoghton Towers ['hotən 'tauərz] (háwtŏn tówěrz); ['houtən 'tauərz] (hótŏn tówěrz)

Hogsflesh, *f.n.* ['houfleɪ] (hóflay); ['hɒgzfleʃ] (hógzflesh)

Holbeach ['hɒlbitʃ] (hólbeetch)

Holbech, *f.n.* ['hɒlbitʃ] (hólbeetch)

Holbeton ['houlbɪtən] (hólbětŏn)

Holborn, *f.n.* ['hɒlbərn] (hólbŭrn)

Holborn, *Caithness* [houl'bərn] (hōlbórn)

Holborn, *district of London* ['houbərn] (hóbŭrn); ['houlbərn] (hólbŭrn)

Holborne, *f.n.* ['houbərn] (hóbŭrn)

Holbourne *see Greenwood of ~, Viscount.*

Holbrook ['houlbruk] (hólbrŏŏk)

Holbrooke, *Joseph, composer, also spelt Josef* ['houlbruk] (hólbrŏŏk)

Holburn, *district of Aberdeen* ['houbərn] (hóburn)

Holcombe, *f.n.* ['houlkəm] (hólkŏm)

Holcombe ['hɒlkəm] (hólkŏm)

Holcombe Burnell ['houkəm 'bərnel] (hókŏm búrnel)

Holcombe Rogus ['houkəm 'rougəs] (hókŏm rógŭss)

Holden, *Barony of* ['houldən] (hóldĕn)

Holderness, *f.n.* ['houldərnɪs] (hóldĕrnĕss)

Holderness ['houldərnes] (hóldĕrness)

Holdsworth, *f.n.* ['houldzwərθ] (hóldzwürth)

Holdtum, *f.n.* ['houltəm] (hóltŭm)

Holford, *Baron* ['hɒlfərd] (hólfŏrd)

Holgate, *f.n.* ['houlgeɪt] (hólgayt)

Holinshed, Raphael, *16th-c. chronicler* ['hɒlɪnʃed] (hóllin-shed) *Traditional pronunciation.*

Holker ['hukər] (hŏŏker)

Holkham ['hɒlkəm] (hól-kăm)

Holland, *f.n.* ['hɒlənd] (hólländ)

Hollesley ['houzlɪ] (hózli)

Hollies ['hɒlɪz] (hólliz)

Hollingshead ['hɒlɪŋzhed] (hóllingz-hed)

Hollingsworth, *f.n.* ['hɒlɪŋzwərθ] (hóllingzwurth)

Hollingworth, *f.n.* ['hɒlɪŋwərθ] (hóllingwurth)

Hollinshead ['hɒlɪnzhed] (hóllinz-hed)

Holm of Skaw ['hɒlm əv 'skɔ] (hólm ŏv skáw)

Holm Patrick, *Baron* ['houm 'pætrɪk] (hóm pátrick)

Holman, *f.n.* ['houlmən] (hólmăn)

Holmbury St. Mary ['houmbərɪ snt 'mɛərɪ] (hómbŭri sĭnt máiri)

Holme, *f.n.* ['houm] (hōm)

Holme, *Norfolk* ['houm] (hōm)

Holme Moss ['houm 'mɒs] (hóm móss)

Holmer Green ['houmər 'grin] (hómer greén)

Holmes, *f.n.* ['houmz] (hōmz)

Holmes à Court, *f.n.* ['houmz ə 'kɔrt] (hómz ă kórt) *Family name of Baron Heytesbury.*

Holmesdale, *f.n.* ['houmzdeɪl] (hómzdayl)

Holmfirth ['houm'fərθ] (hóm-fírth)

Holmpton ['houmtən] (hómtŏn)

Holmstrom, *f.n.* ['houmstrɒm] (hómstrom)

Holne [houn] (hōn)

Holness, *f.n.* ['houlnɪs] (hólnĕss)

Holnest ['hɒlnest] (hólnest)

Holnicote ['hʌnɪkət] (húnnikŏt)

Holroyd, *f.n.* ['hɒlrɔɪd] (hólroyd)

Holst, Gustav, *composer* ['gustav 'houlst] (gŏŏstaav hólst)

Holsworthy ['houlzwərðɪ] (hólzwurthi)

Holtby, *f.n.* ['houltbɪ] (hóltbi)

Holter, *f.n.* ['houltər] (hólter)

Holtham, *f.n.* ['houlθəm] (hól-thăm); ['houθəm] (hó-thăm); ['hɒlθəm] (hólthăm)

Holton ['hɒltən] (hóltŏn); ['houltən] (hóltŏn)

Holton Heath ['hɒltən 'hiθ] (hóltŏn heéth)

Holton-cum-Beckering ['houltən kʌm 'bekərɪŋ] (hóltŏn kum béckĕring)

Holtum, *f.n.* ['houltəm] (hóltŭm)

Holtye [houl'taɪ] (hóltî)

Holverston ['hɒlvərstən] (hólvĕrstŏn)

Holwell ['hɒlwəl] (hólwĕl)

Holwill, *f.n.* ['hɒlwɪl] (hólwil)

Holybourne ['hɒlɪbɔrn] (hólliborn)

Holyhead ['hɒlɪ'hed] (hólli-héd); ['hɒlɪhed] (hólli-hed)

Holyport ['hɒlɪpɔrt] (hólliport)

Holyroodhouse, *Palace of* ['hɒlɪrud'haus] (hóllirood-hówss)

Holystone ['hɒlɪstoun] (hólistŏn)

Holytown ['hɒlɪtaun] (hóllitown)

Holywell, *Flint., Oxon., Somerset* ['hɒlɪwel] (hólliwel)

Holywell Row ['hɒlɪwel 'rou] (hólliwel ró)

Holywood ['hɒlɪwud] (hólliwŏŏd)

Homa, *f.n.* ['houmə] (hómă)

Homan, *f.n.* ['houmən] (hómăn)

Homard, *f.n.* ['houmard] (hómaard)

Home, *f.n.* [hjum] (hewm); [houm] (hōm) *The first is appropriate for the Earldom of ~.*

Homer Green ['houmər 'grin] (hómer greén)

Homersfield ['hɒmərzfɪld] (hómmĕrzfeeld); ['hʌmərzfɪld] (húmmĕrzfeeld)

Homfray, *f.n.* ['hɒmfrɪ] (hómfri)

Honddu, *River* ['hɒnðɪ] (hónthi)

Hone, *f.n.* [houn] (hōn)

Honess, *f.n.* ['hounes] (hóness)

Honey, *f.n.* ['hʌnɪ] (húnni)

Honicknowle ['hɒnɪknoul] (hónnick-nōl)

Honiley ['hɒnɪlɪ] (hónnili)

Honing ['hounɪŋ] (hóning)

Honingham ['hʌnɪŋəm] (húnning-ăm)

Honington, *Suffolk* ['hɒnɪŋtən] (hónningtŏn); ['hʌnɪŋtən] (húnningtŏn)

Honiton ['hʌnɪtən] (húnnitŏn); ['hɒnɪtən] (hónnitŏn)

Honley ['hɒnlɪ] (hónlï)
Honney, *f.n.* ['hʌnɪ] (húnni)
Honywood, *f.n.* ['hʌnɪwʊd] (húnniwood)
Hooe [hu] (hoo)
Hooke, *f.n.* [hʊk] (hook)
Hoo St. Werburgh ['hu snt 'wɜrbɜrg] (hóo sïnt wérburg)
Hooson, *f.n.* ['husən] (hoóossŏn)
Hooton Pagnell ['hutən 'pægnəl] (hoótŏn págnĕl) ; ['hʌtən 'pænl] (húttŏn pánl)
Hopetoun ['hoʊptən] (hóptŏn) *Appropriate also for the Earl of ~.*
Hopkins, *f.n.* ['hɒpkɪnz] (hópkinz)
Hoptrough, *f.n.* ['hɒptroʊ] (hóptrō)
Hopwas ['hɒpwəs] (hópwăss) ; ['hɒpəs] (hóppáss)
Horabin, *f.n.* ['hɒrəbɪn] (hórrăbin)
Horam, *f.n.* ['hɒrəm] (háwrăm)
Horan, *f.n.* ['hɒrən] (háwrăn)
Hore-Belisha, *Barony of* ['hɔr bə'liʃə] (hór bĕleeshă)
Hore-Ruthven, *f.n.* ['hɔr 'rɪvən] (hór rívvĕn)
Horham ['hɒrəm] (hórrăm)
Horlick, *f.n.* ['hɔrlɪk] (hórlick)
Horninglow ['hɔrnɪŋloʊ] (hórning-lō)
Hornsea ['hɔrnsi] (hórnssee)
Hornsey ['hɔrnzɪ] (hórnzi)
Horrigan, *f.n.* ['hɒrɪgən] (hórrigăn)
Horringer ['hɒrɪndʒər] (hórrinjer)
Horsbrugh, *f.n.* ['hɔrsbrə] (hórssbră)
Horsell ['hɔrsl] (horssl)
Horsey ['hɔrsɪ] (hórssi)
Horseye [hɔr'saɪ] (horssí)
Horsfall, *f.n.* ['hɔrsfɒl] (hórssfawl)
Horsfield, *f.n.* ['hɔrsfild] (hórssfeeld)
Horsham ['hɔrʃəm] (hór-shăm)
Horsham-St.-Faith ['hɔrʃəm snt 'feɪθ] (hór-shăm sïnt fáyth)
Horsley, East *and* West ['hɔrzlɪ] (hórzli)
Horsmonden [ˌhɔrsmən'den] (horssmŏndén)
Horsted Keynes ['hɔrstɪd 'keɪnz] (hórsstĕd káynz)
Horwich ['hɒrɪtʃ] (hórritch)
Hoseason, *f.n.* [hoʊ'sizən] (hōsseézŏn) ; [ˌhoʊsɪ'eɪsən] (hōssi-áyssŏn) ; [ˌhoʊsɪ'æsən] (hōssi-ássŏn)
Hosford, *f.n.* ['hɒsfərd] (hóssfŏrd)
Hosier, *f.n.* ['hoʊzɪər] (hŏzi-er)
Hoste [hoʊst] (hōst)
Hotham, *f.n.* ['hʌðəm] (húthăm) *Appropriate also for Baron ~.*
Hotham ['hʌðəm] (húthăm)
Hothfield ['hɒθfild] (hóthfeeld) *Appropriate also for Baron ~.*
Hotine, *f.n.* ['hoʊtin] (hŏteen)
Hoton ['hoʊtən] (hŏtŏn)
Hotwells ['hɒtwelz] (hótwelz)
Houblon, *f.n.* ['hublõ] (hoóoblŏng)
Houchen, *f.n.* ['haʊtʃɪn] (hówtchĕn)
Houchin, *f.n.* ['haʊtʃɪn] (hówtchin)
Hough, *f.n.* [hʌf] (huff) ; [hɒf] (hoff) ; [haʊ] (how)
Hough [hʌf] (huff)

Hough Green ['hʌf 'grin] (húff gréen)
Hough-on-the-Hill ['hʌf ɒn ðə 'hɪl] (húff on thē hill) ; ['hɒf ɒn ðə 'hɪl] (hóff on thē hill)
Houghall ['hɒfl] (hoffl)
Hougham, *f.n.* ['hʌfəm] (húffăm)
Hougham ['hʌfəm] (húffăm)
Houghton, *f.n.* ['hotən] (háwtŏn) ; ['haʊtən] (hówtŏn) ; ['hoʊtən] (hŏtŏn) *The second is appropriate for Douglas ~, politician and broadcaster.*
Houghton, *Hants.* ['hoʊtən] (hŏtŏn) ; ['haʊtən] (hówtŏn)
Houghton, *Hunts.* ['hoʊtən] (hŏtŏn)
Houghton, *Lancs.* ['hotən] (háwtŏn) ; ['haʊtən] (hówtŏn)
Houghton, *Norfolk* ['haʊtən] (hówtŏn) ; ['hoʊtən] (hŏtŏn)
Houghton, Glass ['glɑs 'haʊtən] (glaáss hówtŏn)
Houghton, Great *and* Little, *Northants.* ['hoʊtən] (hŏtŏn)
Houghton, Great *and* Little, *Yorks.* ['hotən] (háwtŏn)
Houghton Bridge ['hoʊtən 'brɪdʒ] (hŏtŏn bríj) ; ['haʊtən 'brɪdʒ] (hówtŏn bríj)
Houghton Conquest ['haʊtən 'kɒŋkwest] (hówtŏn kónkwest)
Houghton Regis ['haʊtən 'ridʒɪs] (hówtŏn reéjiss)
Houghton-le-Side ['haʊtən lə 'saɪd] (hówtŏn lĕ síd) ; ['haʊtən lɪ 'saɪd] (hówtŏnli síd)
Houghton-le-Spring ['hoʊtən lə 'sprɪŋ] (hŏtŏn lĕ spríng) ; ['hoʊtən lɪ 'sprɪŋ] (hŏtŏnli spríng)
Houghton-on-the-Hill ['hoʊtən ɒn ðə 'hɪl] (hŏtŏn on thē hill)
Houlden, *f.n.* ['hoʊldən] (hŏldĕn) ; ['huldən] (hoóoldĕn)
Houldsworth, *f.n.* ['hoʊldzwɜrθ] (hŏldzwurth)
Houlgate, *f.n.* ['hoʊlgeɪt] (hŏlgayt)
Houlton, *f.n.* ['hoʊltən] (hŏltŏn)
Hourd, *f.n.* [hʊərd] (hoŏrd)
Hourigan, *f.n.* ['hʊərɪgən] (hoŏrigăn)
Hourn, Loch [hʊərn] (hoŏrn)
Housden, *f.n.* ['haʊzdən] (hówzdĕn)
House of Gight ['haʊs əv 'gɪxt] (hówss ŏv gícht)
Housley, *f.n.* ['haʊzlɪ] (hówzli)
Housman, *f.n.* ['haʊsmən] (hówssmăn) *This is appropriate for A. E. ~, poet, and for his brother Laurence, artist and playwright. The latter particularly confirmed that they pronounced it with -s, not -z.*
Houston *f.n.* ['hustən] (hoóostŏn) ; ['hjustən] (héwsstŏn) ; ['haʊstən] (hówsstŏn)
Houston, *Renfrew., West Lothian* ['hustən] (hoóostŏn)
Houstoun, *f.n.* ['hustən] (hoóostŏn)
Houthuesen, *f.n.* ['haʊtʃɪsən] (hówchĕssĕn)
Hove [hoʊv] (hōv)

Hovell, f.n. ['hɒvl] (hovvl); ['houvl] (hôvl)
Hoveringham ['hɒvərɪŋəm] (hóvvĕring-ăm)
Hovers ['houvərz] (hóvĕrz)
Hoveton ['hɒftən] (hófftŏn); ['hʌftən] (húfftŏn); ['hɒvɪtən] (hóvvĕtŏn)
Hovey ['houvɪ] (hóvi)
Hovingham ['hɒvɪŋəm] (hóvving-ăm)
Howard, f.n. ['hauərd] (hówărd)
Howard de Walden, *Baron* ['hauərd də 'wɔldən] (hówărd dĕ wáwldĕn)
Howard of Glossop, *Baron* ['hauərd əv 'glɒsəp] (hówărd ŏv glóssŏp)
Howard of Penrith, *Baron* ['hauərd əv 'penrɪθ] (hówărd ŏv pénrith)
Howarth, f.n. ['hauərθ] (hówărth)
Howden, f.n. ['haudən] (hówdĕn)
Howden ['haudən] (hówdĕn)
Howdon-on-Tyne ['haudən ɒn 'taɪn] (hówdŏn on tín)
Howells, f.n. ['hauəlz] (hówĕlz)
Howgill, f.n. ['haugɪl] (hówgil)
Howick ['houɪk] (hó-ick)
Howick of Glendale, *Baron* ['houɪk əv glen'deɪl] (hó-ick ŏv glendáyl)
Howie, f.n. ['hauɪ] (hówi)
Howitt, f.n. ['hauɪt] (hów-it)
Howlett, f.n. ['haulɪt] (hówlĕt)
Howley ['houlɪ] (hóli)
Howorth, f.n. ['hauərθ] (hówŭrth)
Howsham ['hauʃəm] (hów-shăm); ['hauzəm] (hówzhăm); ['hauzəm] (hówzăm)
Howson, f.n. ['hausən] (hówssŏn)
Hoxne ['hɒksən] (hócksĕn)
Hoy Island [hɔɪ] (hoy)
Hoyer, f.n. ['hɔɪər] (hóyer)
Hozier, f.n. ['houzɪər] (hózi-er)
Huband, f.n. ['hjubænd] (héwband)
Hubbard, f.n. ['hʌbərd] (húbbărd)
Hubbart, f.n. ['hʌbərt] (húbbărt)
Huby ['hjubɪ] (héwbi)
Huccaby ['hʌkəbɪ] (húckăbi)
Hucclecote ['hʌklkout] (húcklkōt)
Hudis, f.n. ['hjudɪs] (héwdiss)
Hudspith, f.n. ['hʌdspɪθ] (húdsspith)
Hueffer, Ford Madox, *author* ['fɔrd 'mædəks 'hwefər] (fórd máddŏcks whéffer) *Original name of Ford Madox Ford, q.v.*
Huelin ['hjulɪn] (héwlin)
Hugessen, f.n. ['hjugɪsən] (héwgĕssĕn)
Huggate ['hʌgɪt] (húggit)
Hughes, f.n. ['hjuz] (hewz)
Hugill, f.n. ['hjugɪl] (héwgil)
Hugill ['hjugɪl] (héwgil)
Huish, f.n. ['hjuɪʃ] (héw-ish)
Huish ['hjuɪʃ] (héw-ish)
Hulbert, f.n. ['hʌlbərt] (húlbĕrt)
Hulke, f.n. ['hʌlk] (hulk)
Hullah, f.n. ['hʌlə] (húllă)
Hullavington [hʌl'ævɪŋtən] (hullávvington); ['hʌlɪŋtən] (húllingtŏn)
Hulme, f.n. ['hjum] (hewm)
Hulme, *Lancs.* [hjum] (hewm)

Hulme, *Staffs.* [hjum] (hewm); [hum] (hoom)
Hummel, f.n. ['hʌml] (humml)
Hummerston, f.n. ['hʌmərstən] (húmmĕrstŏn)
Humpherston, f.n. ['hʌmfərstən] (húmfĕrstŏn)
Humphrey, f.n. and C.n. ['hʌmfrɪ] (húmfri)
Humphreys, f.n. ['hʌmfrɪz] (húmfriz)
Humshaugh ['hʌmzhɒf] (húmz-haaf)
Huna ['hunə] (hoónă)
Huncote ['hʌnkout] (húnkŏt)
Hungarton, *Barony of* ['hʌŋgərtən] (húng-gărtŏn)
Hungarton, *also spelt* **Hungerton** ['hʌŋgərtən] (húng-gărtŏn)
Hungerford Newtown ['hʌŋgərfərd 'njutaun] (húng-gĕrfŏrd néwtown)
Hungerton *see* Hungarton.
Hunmanby ['hʌnmənbɪ] (húnmänbi)
Hunslet ['hʌnslɪt] (húnsslĕt)
Hunstanton ['hʌnstən] (húnsstŏn); [hʌn-'stæntən] (hunsstántŏn)
Hunter, f.n. ['hʌntər] (húnter)
Hunterian, *pertaining to John Hunter, 18th-c. Scottish surgeon* [hʌn'tɪərɪən] (hunteĕriăn)
Huntingdon ['hʌntɪŋdən] (húntingdŏn) *Appropriate also for the Earl of ~.*
Huntshaw ['hʌnʃɔ] (hún-shaw)
Huntspill ['hʌntspɪl] (húntspil)
Hunwick, *Baron* ['hʌnwɪk] (húnwick)
Hurcomb, Baron ['hɜrkəm] (húrkŏm)
Hurren, f.n. ['hʌrən] (húrrĕn)
Hurstmonceaux *see* Herstmonceux.
Hurstmonceux *see* Herstmonceux.
Hurstpierpoint ['hɜrstpɪər'pɔɪnt] (húrstpeerpóynt)
Hussey, f.n. ['hʌsɪ] (hússi)
Hutber, f.n. ['hʌtbər] (hútber)
Hutchens, f.n. ['hʌtʃənz] (hútchĕnz)
Hutcheson, f.n. ['hʌtʃɪsən] (hútchĕssŏn)
Hutchings, f.n. ['hʌtʃɪŋz] (hútchingz)
Hutchinson, f.n. ['hʌtʃɪnsən] (hútchinssŏn)
Huth, f.n. [huθ] (hooth)
Huthwaite ['hʌθweɪt] (húthwayt); ['hjuθweɪt] (héwthwayt)
Hutton Buscel, *also spelt* **Hutton Bushel** ['hʌtən 'buʃl] (húttŏn bŏoshl)
Hutton-le-Hole ['hʌtənlɪ'houl] (húttŏn-li-hŏl)
Huw, Welsh C.n. [hju] (hew)
Huxley, Aldous, *author* ['ɔldəs 'hʌkslɪ] (áwldŭss húcksli)
Huyton ['haɪtən] (híftŏn)
Huyton with Roby ['haɪtən wɪð 'roubɪ] (híftŏn with róbi)
Huzzard, f.n. ['hʌzərd] (húzzaard)
Hyde, f.n. [haɪd] (hīd)
Hydleman, f.n. ['haɪdlmən] (hídlmän)
Hykeham, North *and* **South** ['haɪkəm] (híkăm)
Hylton, f.n. ['hɪltən] (híltŏn)

Hymans, f.n. ['haɪmənz] (hímănz)
Hynd, f.n. [haɪnd] (hínd)
Hyndhope ['haɪndhoʊp] (hínd-hōp)
Hyndley, Viscountcy of ['haɪndlɪ] (híndli)
Hyndman, f.n. ['haɪndmən] (híndmăn)
Hytch, f.n. [haɪtʃ] (hítch)
Hywel, Welsh C.n. ['haʊəl] (hówĕl)

I

Iain, C.n., also spelt Ian ['iən] (eé-ăn)
I'Anson, f.n. [aɪ'ænsən] (ī-ánssŏn)
Ianthe, C.n. [aɪ'ænθɪ] (ī-ánthi)
Ibbs, f.n. [ɪbz] (ibbz)
Ibrox Park, Glasgow ['aɪbrɒks 'pɑrk] (íbrocks paárk)
Iceni, ancient British tribe [aɪ'sinaɪ] (īsseéni)
Iceton, f.n. ['aɪstən] (ísstŏn)
Icke, f.n. [aɪk] (īk) ; [ɪk] (ick)
Ickes, f.n. ['ɪkɪs] (íckĕss)
Icklesham ['ɪklʃəm] (íckl-shăm)
Icomb ['ɪkəm] (íckŏm)
Iddesleigh ['ɪdzlɪ] (ídzli) *Appropriate also for the Earl of ~.*
Ide [id] (eed)
Ideford ['ɪdfərd] (ídfŏrd)
Iden, f.n. ['aɪdən] (ídĕn)
Iden ['aɪdən] (ídĕn)
Idiens, f.n. ['ɪdɪənz] (íddiĕnz)
Idle ['aɪdl] (ídl)
Idless ['ɪdlɪs] (eédlĕss)
Idloes, Welsh C.n. ['ɪdlɔɪs] (ídloyss)
Idridgehay ['aɪdrɪdʒheɪ] (ídrij-hay) ; ['ɪdɪseɪ] (íthĕssay)
Idris, f.n. ['ɪdrɪs] (ídriss)
Idwal, Welsh C.n. ['ɪdwəl] (ídwăl)
Iestyn, Welsh C.n. ['jestɪn] (yéstin)
Ieuan, Welsh C.n. ['jarjən] (yí-yăn)
Ievers, f.n. ['aɪvərz] (ívĕrz)
Ife, f.n. [aɪf] (īf)
Ifor, Welsh C.n. ['ivor] (eévor) ; ['aɪvər] (fvŏr)
Ightham, f.n. ['aɪtəm] (ítăm)
Ikin, f.n. ['aɪkɪn] (íkin)
Ilam ['aɪləm] (fflăm)
Ilbert, f.n. ['ɪlbərt] (ílbĕrt)
Ilchester ['ɪltʃɪstər] (íltchĕster) *Appropriate also for the Earl of ~.*
Ilett, f.n. ['aɪlɪt] (flĕt)
Ilford ['ɪlfərd] (ílfŏrd)
Iline, f.n. ['aɪlaɪn] (flīn)
Ilkeston ['ɪlkɪstən] (ílkĕstŏn) *Appropriate also for the Barony of ~.*
Ilketshall ['ɪlkɪʃɒl] (ílkĕ-shawl)
Illingworth, f.n. ['ɪlɪŋwɜrθ] (ílling-wurth)
Illogan [ɪ'lʌgən] (illúggăn)
Illtud, Welsh C.n. ['ɪɬtɪd] (ihltid)

Ilott, f.n. ['aɪlɒt] (flot)
Imeson, f.n. ['aɪmɪsən] (fmĕssŏn) ; ['aɪmsən] (fmssŏn)
Imhof, f.n. ['ɪmhoʊf] (ím-hōf)
Imison, f.n. ['aɪmɪsən] (fmissŏn)
Imisson, f.n. ['ɪmɪsən] (ímmissŏn)
Imlach, f.n. ['ɪmləx] (ímláḫ)
Immingham ['ɪmɪŋhəm] (ímming-hăm)
Ince, f.n. [ɪns] (inss)
Inchcape, Earl of [ɪnʃ'keɪp] (insh-káyp)
Inchcruin [ɪnʃ'kruɪn] (insh-kroóin)
Inchinnan [ɪnʃ'ɪnən] (insh-ínnăn)
Inchiquin, Baron of ['ɪntʃɪkwɪn] (íntchikwin)
Inchnadamph [ˌɪnʃnə'dæmf] (inshnădámf)
Inchrye Abbey [ɪnʃ'raɪ] (insh-rí)
Inchture [ɪnʃ'tjʊər] (insh-tyőŏr)
Inchtuthil [ɪnʃ'tjuθɪl] (insh-téwthil)
Inchyra [ɪnʃ'aɪərə] (inshíră) *Appropriate also for Baron ~.*
Ind Coope, brewers ['ɪnd 'kup] (índ koóp)
Ingatestone ['ɪŋɡeɪtstoʊn] (íng-gaytstōn)
Inge, f.n. [ɪŋ] (ing)
Ingelow, f.n. ['ɪndʒɪloʊ] (ínjĕlō)
Ingestre, Viscount ['ɪŋɡɪstrɪ] (íng-gĕstri)
Ingham, f.n. ['ɪŋəm] (íng-ăm)
Inglis, f.n. ['ɪŋɡlz] (íng-glz) ; ['ɪŋɡlɪs] (íng-gliss) *The first is Scottish, the second Northern Irish and Southern English.*
Ingliston ['ɪŋɡlztən] (ing-glz-tŏn)
Ingold, f.n. ['ɪŋɡoʊld] (íng-gōld)
Ingpen, f.n. ['ɪŋpen] (íng-pen)
Ingram, f.n. ['ɪŋɡrəm] (íng-grăm)
Ingrebourne ['ɪŋɡrɪbɔrn] (íng-grĕborn)
Ingress, f.n. ['ɪŋɡrɪs] (íng-grĕss)
Ingwersen, f.n. ['ɪŋwɜrsən] (ing-wĕrssĕn)
Inishanier [ˌɪnɪʃ'æniər] (innish-ánni-er)
Inishargie [ˌɪnɪʃ'ɑrɡɪ] (innish-aárgi)
Inisharoan [ˌɪnɪʃ'erən] (innish-érrăn)
Innellan [ɪn'elən] (inéllăn)
Innerleithen [ˌɪnər'liðən] (innĕrleéthĕn)
Innerwick, East Lothian, Perth. [ˌɪnər'wɪk] (innĕrwíck)
Innes, f.n. ['ɪnɪs] (innĕss) ; ['ɪnɪz] (ínnĕz)
Innes of Edingight, f.n. ['ɪnɪs əv 'ɪdɪŋɡɪxt] (innĕss ŏv éedin-gĭcht)
Innes of Learney, Sir Thomas, Lord Lyon King of Arms ['ɪnɪs əv 'lɜrnɪ] (innĕss ŏv laírni)
Innes-Ker, f.n. ['ɪnɪs 'kɑr] (innĕss kaár) ; ['ɪnɪs 'kɛər] (innĕss kaír) *The first is appropriate for the Duke of Roxburghe's family name.*
Inns, f.n. [ɪnz] (innz)
Instone, f.n. ['ɪnstoʊn] (ínstōn)
Instow ['ɪnstoʊ] (ínstō)
Inver ['ɪnvər] (ínver)
Inverallochy [ˌɪnvər'æləxɪ] (invĕrálŏchi)
Inveraray [ˌɪnvər'ɛərɪ] (invĕráiri) ; [ˌɪnvər'ɛərə] (invĕráiră)
Inverarity [ˌɪnvər'ærɪtɪ] (invĕrárriti)
Inveravon [ˌɪnvər'an] (invĕraán)

Inverbervie [ˌɪnvər'bɜrvɪ] (invĕrbérvi)
Invereighty [ˌɪnvər'aɪtɪ] (invĕríti)
Inverey [ˌɪnvər'eɪ] (invĕráy)
Inverkeilor [ˌɪnvər'kilər] (invĕrkeélŏr)
Inverkeithing [ˌɪnvər'kiðɪŋ] (invĕrkeé-thing)
Inverlochy [ˌɪnvər'lɒxɪ] (invĕrlóchi)
Invermoriston [ˌɪnvər'mɒrɪstən] (invĕr-mórristŏn)
Inverness [ˌɪnvər'nes] (invĕrnéss)
Invernessian, native of Inverness [ˌɪn-vər'nizɪən] (invĕrneéziăn)
Inverquharity [ˌɪnvər'hwɒrɪtɪ] (invĕr-wháwriti); [ˌɪnvər'hwarɪtɪ] (invĕr-whaáriti)
Inversnaid [ˌɪnvər'sneɪd] (invĕr-snáyd)
Inveruglas [ˌɪnvər'uɡləs] (invĕroóglàss)
Inverurie [ˌɪnvər'ʊərɪ] (invĕróŏri)
Ioan, Welsh C.n. ['jouən] (yŏ-ăn)
Iochdor ['iəxkər] (eé-ŏchkăr) see also Eochar.
Iolo, Welsh C.n. ['joʊloʊ] (yŏlŏ)
Iona [aɪ'oʊnə] (I-ŏnă)
Ionides, f.n. [aɪ'ɒnɪdiz] (ī-ónnideez)
Iorns, f.n. ['aɪərnz] (í-ürnz)
Iorwerth, Welsh C.n. ['jɔrwɛərθ] (yór-wairth)
Iredell, f.n. ['aɪərdel] (írdel)
Iremonger, f.n. ['aɪərmʌŋɡər] (írmung-ger)
Ireson, f.n. ['aɪərsən] (írssŏn)
Irfonwy, Welsh C.n. [ɜr'vɒnuɪ] (irvónŏŏ-i)
Irongray ['aɪərəŋɡreɪ] (írŏn-gray)
Irthlingborough ['ɜrθlɪŋbərə] (írthling-bŭră)
Irvine, f.n. ['ɜrvɪn] (írvin)
Irvine ['ɜrvɪn] (írvin)
Irvinestown ['ɜrvɪnztaʊn] (írvinztown)
Irving, f.n. ['ɜrvɪŋ] (írving)
Irwell, River ['ɜrwel] (írwel)
Isacke, f.n. ['aɪzək] (ízák)
Isard, f.n. ['ɪzard] (ízzaard)
Isbister, f.n. ['aɪzbɪstər] (ízbister)
Isfield ['ɪsfɪld] (íssfeeld)
Isham, f.n. ['aɪʃəm] (í-shăm)
Isherwood, f.n. ['ɪʃərwʊd] (íshĕrwŏŏd)
Isington ['ɪzɪŋtən] (ízzingtŏn)
Isla, River and Glen ['aɪlə] (ílă)
Islandmagee [ˌaɪləndmə'ɡi] (ílăndmăgeé)
Islay ['aɪlə] (ílă); ['aɪleɪ] (ílay)
Isle of Wight ['aɪl əv 'waɪt] (íl ŏv wít)
Isleworth ['aɪzlwɜrθ] (ízl-wurth)
Islington ['ɪzlɪŋtən] (ízzlingtŏn)
Islip, f.n. ['ɪzlɪp] (ízlip) Appropriate also for the ~ Chapel in Westminster Abbey.
Islip ['ɪzlɪp] (ízlip)
Islwyn, Welsh C.n. ['ɪslʊɪn] (ísslŏŏ-in)
Ismay, f.n. ['ɪzmeɪ] (ízmay) Appropriate also for the Barony of ~.
Istance, f.n. ['aɪstəns] (ístănss)
Itchenor ['ɪtʃɪnər] (ítchĕnor)
Ithell, f.n. ['aɪθl] (íthl)
Ithon, River ['aɪθən] (íthŏn)
Iveagh, Earl of ['aɪvə] (ívă)
Iveagh ['aɪveɪ] (ívay)

Ivelaw, f.n. ['aɪvɪlɒ] (fvĕlaw)
Ives, f.n. [aɪvz] (ívz)
Iveson, f.n. ['aɪvsən] (fv-sŏn)
Ivimey, f.n. ['aɪvɪmɪ] (fvimi)
Ivin, f.n. ['aɪvɪn] (fvin)
Iwan, Welsh C.n. ['juən] (yoó-ăn)
Iwerne Courtney ['juɜrn 'kɔrtnɪ] (yoó-ern kórtni)
Ixer, f.n. ['ɪksər] (íckser)
Izard, f.n. ['aɪzard] (ízaard); ['aɪzərd] (ízărd); ['ɪzərd] (ízzărd)
Izatt, f.n. ['aɪzət] (ízăt)
Izen, f.n. ['aɪzən] (ízĕn)
Izod, f.n. ['ɪzəd] (ízzŏd)
Izzard, f.n. ['ɪzard] (ízzaard); ['ɪzərd] (ízzărd)
Izzett, f.n. ['aɪzɪt] (ízĕt)

J

Jackett, f.n. ['dʒækɪt] (jáckĕt)
Jacobs, f.n. ['dʒeɪkəbz] (jáykŏbz)
Jacobstow ['dʒeɪkəbstoʊ] (jáykŏb-stŏ)
Jacoby, f.n. [dʒə'koʊbɪ] (jăkóbi); ['dʒæ-kəbɪ] (jáckŏbi)
Jacot, f.n. ['dʒækoʊ] (jáckŏ)
Jacottet, f.n. ['dʒækəteɪ] (jáckŏtay)
Jacques, f.n. [dʒeɪks] (jayks); [dʒæks] (jacks)
Jaeger, f.n. ['jeɪɡər] (yáyger)
Jaffe, f.n. ['dʒæfɪ] (jáffi)
Jaffray, f.n. ['dʒæfrɪ] (jáffri)
Jago, f.n. ['dʒeɪɡoʊ] (jáygŏ)
Jagoe, f.n. ['dʒeɪɡoʊ] (jáygŏ)
Jakins, f.n. ['dʒeɪkɪnz] (jáykinz)
Jakobi, f.n. ['dʒækəbɪ] (jáckŏbi)
Jalland, f.n. ['dʒælənd] (jáländ)
Jamblin, f.n. ['dʒæmblɪn] (jámblin)
Jameson, f.n. ['dʒemɪsən] (jémmissŏn); ['dʒɪmɪsən] (jímmissŏn); ['dʒeɪmsən] (jáymssŏn); ['dʒæmɪsən] (jámmissŏn)
Jamieson, f.n. ['dʒɪmɪsən] (jímmissŏn); ['dʒemɪsən] (jémmissŏn); ['dʒeɪmɪsən] (jáymissŏn); ['dʒæmɪsən] (jámmissŏn)
Janis, f.n. ['dʒænɪs] (jánniss)
Janisch, f.n. ['jeɪnɪʃ] (yáynish)
Janson, f.n. ['dʒænsən] (jánssŏn)
Japhet, f.n. ['dʒæfɪt] (jáffĕt)
Jaque, f.n. [dʒeɪk] (jayk)
Jaques, f.n. [dʒeɪks] (jayks); [dʒæks] (jacks)
Jaquest, f.n. ['dʒeɪkwɪst] (jáykwĕst)
Jaray, f.n. ['dʒæreɪ] (járray)
Jarché, f.n. ['dʒarʃeɪ] (jaár-shay)
Jardine, f.n. ['dʒardin] (jaárdeen)
Jarlshof ['jarlzhɒf] (yaárlz-hoff)
Jarman, f.n. ['dʒarmən] (jaármăn)
Jarred, f.n. ['dʒærəd] (járrĕd)

Jarrett, f.n. ['dʒærɪt] (járrĕt)
Jarvis, f.n. ['dʒɑrvɪs] (jaárviss)
Jast, f.n. [dʒæst] (jasst)
Jaywick ['dʒeɪwɪk] (jáy-wick)
Jeacock, f.n. ['dʒiːkɒk] (jéekock)
Jeacocke, f.n. ['dʒeɪkoʊ] (jáykō)
Jeaffreson, f.n. ['dʒefərsən] (jéffĕrssŏn); ['dʒefrɪsən] (jéfrĕssŏn)
Jeans, f.n. [dʒiːnz] (jeenz)
Jeater, f.n. ['dʒiːtər] (jéeter)
Jeavons, f.n. ['dʒevənz] (jévvŏnz)
Jeayes, f.n. [dʒeɪz] (jayz)
Jedburgh ['dʒedbərə] (jédbŭrǎ) *Appropriate also for Baron ~.*
Jeffares, f.n. ['dʒefərz] (jéffǎrz)
Jeffcock, f.n. ['dʒefkɒk] (jéfkock)
Jefferies, f.n. ['dʒefrɪz] (jéffriz)
Jefferis, f.n. ['dʒefərɪs] (jéffĕriss)
Jeffress, f.n. ['dʒefrɪs] (jéffrĕss)
Jeffries, f.n. ['dʒefrɪz] (jéffriz)
Jeger, f.n. ['dʒeɪgər] (jáyger)
Jekyll, f.n. ['dʒiːkɪl] (jéekil); ['dʒekɪl] (jéckil); ['dʒɪkl] (jeekl)
Jellicoe, Earl ['dʒelɪkoʊ] (jéllikō)
Jenks, f.n. [dʒeŋks] (jenks)
Jenner, f.n. ['dʒenər] (jénner)
Jennings, f.n. ['dʒenɪŋz] (jénningz)
Jenyns, f.n. ['dʒenɪnz] (jénninz)
Jephcott, f.n. ['dʒefkɒt] (jéffkot)
Jerdein, f.n. [dʒər'diːn] (jĕrdéen)
Jerrom, f.n. ['dʒerəm] (jérrŏm)
Jersey, Earl of ['dʒɜrzɪ] (jérzi)
Jervaulx, f.n. ['dʒɜrvɪs] (jérviss)
Jervaulx ['dʒɜrvoʊ] (jérvō) *Appropriate also for ~ Abbey. It appears that an old pronunciation,* ['dʒɑrvɪs] (jaárviss), *is still used by some local speakers.*
Jervis, f.n. ['dʒɜrvɪs] (jérviss); ['dʒɑrvɪs] (jaárviss) *The first is appropriate for the family name of the 18th-c. admiral, the Earl of St. Vincent.*
Jervois, f.n. ['dʒɑrvɪs] (jaárviss)
Jervoise, f.n. ['dʒɜrvɪs] (jérviss)
Jesse, f.n. ['dʒesɪ] (jéssi)
Jessel, f.n. ['dʒesl] (jessl)
Jeudwine, f.n. ['dʒuːdwaɪn] (joódwÍn); ['dʒuːdwɪn] (joódwin)
Jeune, f.n. [ʒɜn] (zhön); [ʒuːn] (zhoon)
Jeyes, f.n. [dʒeɪz] (jayz)
Joad, f.n. [dʒoʊd] (jōd)
Job, f.n. [dʒoʊb] (jōb)
Jocelyn, C.n. ['dʒɒslɪn] (jósslin)
Jocelyn, Viscount ['dʒɒslɪn] (jósslin)
Jodrell, f.n. ['dʒɒdrəl] (jódrĕl) *Appropriate also for the ~ Chair of Zoology and Comparative Anatomy in the University of London.*
Jodrell Bank experimental station ['dʒɒdrəl 'bæŋk] (jódrĕl bánk)
Joekes, f.n. ['juːks] (yoókĕss)
Johnes, f.n. [dʒoʊnz] (jōnz)
Johnian Society, St. John's College, Cambridge ['dʒoʊnɪən] (jōnián)
Johnston, f.n. ['dʒɒnstən] (jónstŏn); ['dʒɒnsən] (jónssŏn)

Johnstone ['dʒɒnstən] (jónsstŏn)
Johnstown ['dʒɒnztaʊn] (jónztown)
Joldwynds ['dʒoʊldwɪndz] (jóldwindz)
Joll, f.n. [dʒɒl] (joll)
Jolliff, f.n. ['dʒɒlɪf] (jóllif)
Jolliffe, f.n. ['dʒɒlɪf] (jóllif)
Jonasson, f.n. ['dʒɒnəsən] (jónnǎssŏn)
Jones, f.n. [dʒoʊnz] (jōnz)
Jonesborough ['dʒoʊnzbərə] (jónzbŭrǎ)
Jordanhill ['dʒɔrdən'hɪl] (jórdǎn-híll)
Jory, f.n. ['dʒɔrɪ] (jáwri)
Joubert de la Ferté, f.n. ['ʒuːbɛər də la 'fɛərteɪ] (zhoóbair dĕ laa faírtay)
Joughin, f.n. ['dʒoʊɪn] (jō-in)
Joule, f.n. [dʒuːl] (jool); [dʒoʊl] (jōl); [dʒaʊl] (jowl) *Information obtained for the BBC in 1933 by the late Professor Arthur Lloyd James and evidence submitted by scientists to 'Nature' in September-November 1943 show that the first of these is correct for James Prescott ~, the 19th-c. scientist, after whom the unit of energy was named.*
Joules, f.n. [dʒuːlz] (joolz)
Jourdain, f.n. [ʒʊər'deɪn] (zhoŏrdáyn)
Journeaux, f.n. ['ʒʊərnoʊ] (zhoŏrnō)
Jousiffe, f.n. ['ʒuːzɪf] (zhŏzif)
Jowers, f.n. ['dʒaʊərz] (jówĕrz)
Jowett, f.n. ['dʒaʊɪt] (jów-ĕt); ['dʒoʊɪt] (jō-ĕt)
Jowitt, f.n. ['dʒaʊɪt] (jów-it); ['dʒoʊɪt] (jō-it) *The second is appropriate for the Earldom of ~.*
Jowle, f.n. [dʒaʊl] (jowl); [dʒuːl] (jool); [dʒoʊl] (jōl)
Joynson, f.n. ['dʒɔɪnsən] (jóynssŏn)
Jubb, f.n. [dʒʌb] (jubb)
Juckes, f.n. [dʒuːks] (jooks)
Juett, f.n. ['dʒuːɪt] (joó-ĕt)
Juler, f.n. ['dʒuːlər] (joóler)
Julnes, f.n. [dʒʊlnz] (jŏolnz)
Julyan, f.n. ['dʒuːljən] (joól-yǎn)
Junor, f.n. ['dʒuːnər] (joónŏr)
Jura ['dʒʊərə] (joórǎ)
Jurby ['dʒɜrbɪ] (júrbi)
Justicz, f.n. ['dʒʌstɪs] (jústiss)
Juta, f.n. ['dʒuːtə] (joótǎ)

K

Kaberry, f.n. ['keɪbərɪ] (káybĕri)
Kadisch, f.n. ['kɑdɪʃ] (kaádish)
Kadleigh, f.n. ['kædlɪ] (kádli)
Kahan, f.n. [kə'hɑn] (kǎ-haán)
Kahn, f.n. [kɑn] (kaan)
Kalindjian, f.n. [kə'lɪndʒən] (kǎlínjǎn)
Kanareck, f.n. ['kænərek] (kánnǎreck)
Kanocz, f.n. ['kɒnɒts] (kónnawts)

Karpeles, f.n. ['kɑrpɪliz] (káarpĕleez)
Kassell, f.n. ['kæsl] (kassl)
Katin, f.n. ['keɪtɪn] (káytin)
Katrine, Loch ['kætrɪn] (kátrin)
Kaufman, f.n. ['kɔfmən] (káwfmăn)
Kavanagh, f.n. ['kævənə] (kávvănă);
['kə'vænə] (kăvánnă)
Kay, f.n. [keɪ] (kay)
Kazantzis, f.n. [kə'zæntsɪs] (kăzántsiss)
Kea [ki] (kee)
Keadby ['kɪdbɪ] (keédbi)
Keady ['kɪdɪ] (keédi)
Kealey, f.n. ['kɪlɪ] (keéli)
Keane, f.n. [kin] (keen); [keɪn] (kayn)
Kearey, f.n. ['kɪərɪ] (keéri)
Kearley, f.n. ['kɪərlɪ] (keérli)
Kearney, f.n. ['kɜrnɪ] (kérni); ['kɑrnɪ]
(káarni)
Kearney ['kɜrnɪ] (kérni)
Kearsey, f.n. ['kɜrzɪ] (kérzi)
Kearsley ['kɜrzlɪ] (kérzli)
Kearsney ['kɜrznɪ] (kérzni)
Kearton, f.n. ['kɪərtən] (keértŏn)
Keating, f.n. ['kitɪŋ] (keéting)
Keatinge, f.n. ['kitɪŋ] (keéting)
Keatley, f.n. ['kitlɪ] (keétli)
Keats, f.n. [kits] (keets)
Keay, f.n. [keɪ] (kay)
Keble, f.n. ['kibl] (keebl) *Appropriate also
for John ~, 19th-c. divine and poet.*
Kedington, also spelt Ketton ['kedɪŋtən]
(kéddingtŏn); ['ketən] (kéttŏn) *Older
residents use only the second pronuncia-
tion.*
Kedleston ['kedlstən] (kédlstŏn)
Keeble, f.n. ['kibl] (keebl)
Keele [kil] (keel)
Keeling, f.n. ['kilɪŋ] (keéling)
Keene, f.n. [kin] (keen)
Kegie, f.n. ['kigɪ] (keégi)
Kehelland [kɪ'helənd] (kĕhéllănd)
Kehoe, f.n. [kjoʊ] (kyō)
Keig, f.n. [kig] (keeg)
Keig [kig] (keeg)
Keighley, f.n. ['kiθlɪ] (keéthli); ['kilɪ]
(keéli)
Keighley ['kiθlɪ] (keéthli)
Keightley, f.n. ['kitlɪ] (keétli)
Keigwin, f.n. ['kegwɪn] (kégwin)
Keill, f.n. [kil] (keel)
Keiller, f.n. ['kilər] (keéler)
Keinton Mandeville ['kentən 'mændɪvɪl]
(kéntŏn mándĕvil)
Keir, f.n. [kɪər] (keer)
Keir [kɪər] (keer)
Keisby ['keɪzbɪ] (káyzbi); ['keɪsbɪ] (káyss-
bi)
Keiss [kis] (keess)
Keith, f.n. [kiθ] (keeth)
Keith [kiθ] (keeth)
Kekewich, f.n. ['kekɪwɪtʃ] (kéckĕwitch);
['kekwɪtʃ] (kéckwitch); ['kekwɪdʒ] (kéck-
wij)
Kelburn, Viscount of ['kelbərn] (kélbŭrn)
Kelcey, f.n. ['kelsɪ] (kélssi)

Kelk, f.n. [kelk] (kelk)
Kelland, f.n. ['kelənd] (kéllănd)
Kelleher, f.n. ['kelɪhər] (kéllĕher)
Kellett, f.n. ['kelɪt] (kéllĕt)
Kelley, f.n. ['kelɪ] (kélli)
Kellock, f.n. ['kelɒk] (kéllock)
Kelmscot ['kemskət] (kémskŏt)
Kelsall, f.n. ['kelsl] (kelssl)
Kelsey, f.n. ['kelsɪ] (kélssi); ['kelzɪ] (kélzi)
Kelso ['kelsoʊ] (kélssō)
Kelvedon ['kelvɪdən] (kélvĕdŏn)
Kelvinhaugh ['kelvɪnhɔ] (kélvin-haw);
['kelvɪnhɒx] (kélvin-hoch)
Kelynack [ke'laɪnək] (kelínăk); ['klaɪnək]
(klínăk)
Kemeys-Tynte, f.n. ['kemɪs 'tɪnt]
(kémmiss tínt) *Family name of Baron
Wharton*
Kempsey ['kemsɪ] (kémssi); ['kemzɪ]
(kémzi)
Kempshall, f.n. ['kempʃəl] (kémp-shăl)
Kemptown ['kemptaʊn] (kémptown)
Kemsley, Viscount ['kemzlɪ] (kémzli)
Kendall, f.n. ['kendl] (kendl)
Kendoon [ken'dun] (kén-doón)
Kendrick, f.n. ['kendrɪk] (kéndrick)
Kenfig Hill ['kenfɪg 'hɪl] (kénfig híll)
Kenidjack [kɪ'nɪdʒæk] (kĕníjack)
Kenlis, Baron [ken'lɪs] (kenlíss)
Kenmare, Earldom of [ken'mɛər] (ken-
maír)
Kenmore ['kenmɔr] (kénmor)
Kennair, f.n. [ke'nɛər] (kenaír)
Kennaird, f.n. [ke'nɛərd] (kenaírd)
Kennard, f.n. ['kenɑrd] (kénaard);
[ke'nɑrd] (kenaárd)
Kennardington [ken'ɑrdɪŋtən] (ken-
aárdingtŏn)
Kennethmont [ken'eθmənt] (kenéth-
mŏnt)
Kennett, f.n. ['kenɪt] (kénnĕt)
Kennoway, f.n. ['kenəweɪ] (kénnŏ-way)
Kennoway ['kenəweɪ] (kénnŏ-way)
Kenshole, f.n. ['kenzhoʊl] (kénz-hōl);
['kenʃoʊl] (kén-shōl)
Kent, f.n. [kent] (kent)
Kent [kent] (kent)
Kenward, f.n. ['kenwərd] (kénwărd)
Kenwick ['kenɪk] (kénnick)
Kenwyn ['kenwɪn] (kénwin)
Kenyon, f.n. ['kenjən] (kén-yŏn)
Keogh, f.n. ['kioʊ] (keé-ō); [kjoʊ] (kyō)
Keohane, f.n. [ki'oʊn] (kee-ŏn); [ki'eɪn]
(kee-áyn); [ki'æn] (kee-án)
Keough, f.n. ['kioʊ] (keé-ō); [kjoʊ] (kyō)
Keown, f.n. [kjoʊn] (kyŏn); [ki'oʊn] (kee-
ŏn); ['kioʊn] (keé-ōn)
Kepier ['kipjər] (keép-yer)
Keppel, f.n. ['kepl] (keppl)
Keppochhill ['kepəx'hɪl] (képpŏch-híll)
Ker, f.n. [kɜr] (ker); [kɛər] (kair); [kɑr]
(kaar)
Kerby, f.n. ['kɜrbɪ] (kérbi)
Keren, Viscountcy of ['kerən] (kérrĕn)
Keresley ['kɑrzlɪ] (káarzli)

Kerfoot, *f.n.* ['kɜrfʊt] (kérfŏŏt)
Kermode, *f.n.* [kər'moʊd] (kĕrmôd)
Kernaghan, *f.n.* ['kɜrnəhən] (kérnăhăn)
Kernahan, *f.n.* ['kɜrnəhən] (kérnăhăn)
Kernoghan, *f.n.* ['kɜrnəhən] (kérnŏhăn)
Kernohan, *f.n.* ['kɜrnəhən] (kérnŏhăn)
Kerr, *f.n.* [kɜr] (ker); [kɛər] (kair); [kɑr] (kaar)
Kerrera ['kerərə] (kérrĕră)
Kerrigan, *f.n.* ['kerɪgən] (kérrigăn)
Kerruish, *f.n.* [kə'ruːʃ] (kĕroŏsh)
Kersal ['kɜrzl] (kerzl)
Kershaw, *f.n.* ['kɜrʃɔ] (kér-shaw)
Kershope ['kɜrsəp] (kérssŏp)
Kerslake, *f.n.* ['kɑrzleɪk] (kaárzlayk)
Kersner, *f.n.* ['kɜrznər] (kérzner)
Kesgrave ['kezɡreɪv] (kézgrayv)
Kesteven ['kestɪvən] (késstĕvĕn) *Appropriate also for the Barony of* ~.
Keswick, *f.n.* ['kezɪk] (kézzick) ; ['kezwɪk] (kéz-wick)
Keswick, *Cumberland, Norfolk* ['kezɪk] (kézzick)
Ketelbey, Alfred, *composer* [kɪ'telbɪ] (kĕtélbi)
Kettering ['ketərɪŋ] (kéttĕring)
Ketton, *f.n.* ['ketən] (kéttŏn)
Ketton, *Suffolk see* Kedington.
Kettyle, *f.n.* ['ketl] (kettl)
Kevill, *f.n.* ['kevɪl] (kévvil)
Keville, *f.n.* ['kevɪl] (kévvil)
Key, *f.n.* [ki] (kee)
Keyes, *Baron* [kiz] (keez)
Keyingham ['keɪɪŋhəm] (káy-ing-hăm); ['kenɪnhəm] (kénnin-hăm); ['kenɪŋhəm] (kénning-hăm)
Keymer, *f.n.* ['kiːmər] (keémer)
Keymer ['kiːmər] (keémer); ['kaɪmər] (kímer)
Keynes, *Barony of* [keɪnz] (kaynz)
Keynsham ['keɪnʃəm] (káyn-shăm)
Keyser, *f.n.* ['kizər] (keézer); ['kaɪzər] (kízer)
Keysoe ['kisoʊ] (keéssō)
Keyte, *f.n.* [kaɪt] (kīt); [kɪt] (keet)
Kidwelly [kɪd'welɪ] (kidwélli)
Kielder ['kildər] (keélder)
Kielty, *f.n.* ['kɪltɪ] (keélti)
Kiely, *f.n.* ['kɪlɪ] (keéli)
Kiessimal Castle *see* Kishmul Castle.
Kiggell, *f.n.* ['kɪgl] (kiggl)
Kighley, *f.n.* ['kɪlɪ] (keéli)
Kilbarchan [kɪl'bɑrxən] (kilbaárchăn)
Kilbowie [kɪl'baʊɪ] (kilbów-i)
Kilbride [kɪl'braɪd] (kilbríd)
Kilbroney [kɪl'broʊnɪ] (kilbrŏ́ni)
Kilbucho [kɪl'bʌxoʊ] (kilbŏ́ŏchō)
Kilburn, *f.n.* ['kɪlbɜrn] (kílburn)
Kilburn, *Derby.* ['kɪlbərn] (kílburn)
Kilburn, *London* ['kɪlbərn] (kílbŭrn); ['kɪlbɜrn] (kílburn)
Kilcalmonell [kɪl'kælmə'nel] (kilkálmŏnéll)
Kilchattan, *Argyll* [kɪl'xætən] (kilcháttăn)

Kilchattan Bay [kɪl'kætən 'beɪ] (kilkáttăn báy)
Kilchoan [kɪl'xoʊən] (kilchŏ́-ăn); [ˌkɪlə'xoʊən] (killáchŏ́-ăn)
Kilchrenan [kɪl'krenən] (kilkrénnăn)
Kilchrist ['kɪlkrɪst] (kílkrist)
Kilchurn, *f.n.* [kɪl'xɜrn] (kilchúrn)
Kilchurn Castle [kɪl'tʃɜrn] (kiltchúrn)
Kilclief [kɪl'klif] (kil-kleéf)
Kilcoan [kɪl'koʊn] (kilkŏn)
Kilconquhar [kɪl'kɒŋkər] (kilkónkăr); [kɪ'nʌxər] (kinúchăr)
Kilcoursie, *Viscount* [kɪl'kɔrsɪ] (kilkórssi)
Kilcreggan [kɪl'kregən] (kil-kréggăn)
Kildare, *Marquess of* [kɪl'dɛər] (kildaír)
Kildonan [kɪl'dɒnən] (kildónnăn)
Kildwick ['kɪldwɪk] (kíldwick)
Kilfedder, *f.n.* [kɪl'fedər] (kilfédder)
Kilgetty [kɪl'getɪ] (kilgétti)
Kilgour, *f.n.* [kɪl'gaʊər] (kilgówr)
Kilgraston [kɪl'græstən] (kilgrásstŏn)
Kilham, *f.n.* ['kɪləm] (kíllăm)
Kilian, *f.n.* ['kɪliən] (kílli-ăn)
Kilkeel [kɪl'kil] (kilkeél)
Kilkhampton [kɪlk'hæmptən] (kilkhámptŏn)
Killadeas [ˌkɪlə'dis] (killádeéss)
Killagan [kɪ'lægən] (kilággăn)
Killamarsh ['kɪləmɑrʃ] (killámarsh)
Killanin, *Baron* [kɪ'lænɪn] (kilánnin)
Killay [kɪ'leɪ] (kiláy)
Killea [kɪ'leɪ] (kiláy)
Killead [kɪ'leɪd] (kiláyd)
Killearn, *Baron* [kɪ'lɜrn] (kilérn)
Killelagh [kɪ'leɪlɪ] (kiláyli)
Killermont, *district of Glasgow* ['kɪlərmənt] (kíllĕrmŏnt) *The pronunciation of* ~ *Golf Course is* [kɪ'lɜərmənt] (kiláïrmŏnt).
Killichronan [ˌkɪlɪx'roʊnən] (killichrŏ́năn)
Killick, *f.n.* ['kɪlɪk] (kíllick)
Killiechangie [ˌkɪlɪ'hæŋɪ] (killi-háng-i)
Killiechassie [ˌkɪlɪ'hæsɪ] (killi-hássi)
Killiecrankie [ˌkɪlɪ'kræŋkɪ] (killikránki)
Killin [kɪ'lɪn] (kilín)
Killinchy [kɪ'lɪnʃɪ] (kilínshi)
Killingholme ['kɪlɪŋhoʊm] (kílling-hōm)
Killisport ['kɪlɪsport] (kíllisport)
Killough [kɪ'lɒx] (kilóch)
Killowen [kɪ'loʊən] (kilŏ́-ĕn)
Killwick, *f.n.* ['kɪlwɪk] (kílwick)
Killylea [ˌkɪlɪ'leɪ] (killiláy)
Killyleagh [ˌkɪlɪ'leɪ] (killiláy)
Killywhan [ˌkɪlɪ'hwɒn] (killi-whón)
Kilmacolm [ˌkɪlmə'koʊm] (kilmăkŏ́m)
Kilmarnock [kɪl'mɑrnək] (kilmaárnŏk) *Appropriate also for Baron* ~.
Kilmaronock [ˌkɪlmə'rɒnək] (kilmărónnŏk)
Kilmorack [kɪl'mɒrək] (kilmáwrăk)
Kilmorey, *Earl of* [kɪl'mʌrɪ] (kilmúrri)
Kilmuir, *Earldom of* [kɪl'mjʊər] (kilmyŏ́ŏr)
Kilmun [kɪl'mʌn] (kilmún)

Kilndown ['kɪlndaʊn] (kílndown)
Kilninver [kɪl'nɪnvər] (kilnínver)
Kilpheder [kɪl'fedər] (kilfédder)
Kilraughts [kɪl'ræts] (kilráts)
Kilrea [kɪl'reɪ] (kilráy)
Kilroot [kɪl'rut] (kilroót)
Kilry ['kɪlrɪ] (kílri)
Kilsyth [kɪl'saɪθ] (kil-síth)
Kilve [kɪlv] (kílv)
Kilwaughter [kɪl'wotər] (kilwáwter)
Kilwinning [kɪl'wɪnɪŋ] (kilwínning)
Kimball, f.n. ['kɪmbl] (kímbl)
Kimberley, f.n. ['kɪmbərlɪ] (kímbĕrli)
Kimbolton [kɪm'boʊltən] (kimbóltŏn)
Kimche, f.n. ['kɪmtʃɪ] (kímtchi)
Kimmance ['kɪməns] (kímmănss)
Kinahan, f.n. ['kɪnəhən] (kínnăhăn)
Kinally, f.n. [kɪ'nælɪ] (kináli)
Kinbane ['kɪn'bon] (kinbáwn)
Kincaid, f.n. [kɪn'keɪd] (kin-káyd)
Kincairney, f.n. [kɪn'kɛərnɪ] (kin-káĭrni)
Kincardine, *Fife, Inverness., Perth.* [kɪn'kardɪn] (kin-ka̐ardin)
Kincardine O'Neil [kɪn'kardɪn oʊ'nil] (kin-ka̐ardin ŏneĕl)
Kinclaven [kɪn'kleɪvən] (kin-kláyvĕn)
Kincraig [kɪn'kreɪg] (kin-kráyg)
Kinder Scout ['kɪndər skaʊt] (kínnder skowt)
Kindregan, f.n. [kɪn'drigən] (kindreégăn)
Kine, f.n. [kaɪn] (kīn)
Kineton ['kaɪntən] (kíntŏn)
Kingdon, f.n. ['kɪŋdən] (kíngdŏn)
Kingennie [kɪn'genɪ] (kin-génni)
Kingham, f.n. ['kɪŋəm] (kíng-ăm)
Kinglake, f.n. ['kɪŋleɪk] (kíng-layk)
Kinglassie [kɪn'glæsɪ] (kin-glássi); [kɪn-'glæsɪ] (king-glássi)
Kingoldrum [kɪn'goʊldrəm] (kin-góldrŭm)
King's Caple ['kɪŋz 'keɪpl] (kíngz káypl)
King's Somborne ['kɪŋz 'sɒmbərn] (kíngz sómborn)
Kings Tamerton ['kɪŋz 'tæmərtən] (kíngz támmĕrtŏn)
Kingsale, Baron [kɪn'seɪl] (kin-sáyl)
Kingsbury, f.n. ['kɪŋzbərɪ] (kíngzbŭri)
Kingscavil [kɪŋz'keɪvɪl] (kingz-káyvil)
Kingscote, f.n. ['kɪŋzkət] (kíngzkŏt)
Kingscott, f.n. ['kɪŋzkɒt] (kíngzkot)
Kingsford, f.n. ['kɪŋzfərd] (kíngzfŏrd)
Kingskerswell [kɪŋz'kɜrzwəl] (kingz-kérzwĕl)
Kingsley, f.n. ['kɪŋzlɪ] (kíngzli)
Kingsnympton ['kɪŋz'nɪmtən] (kíngz-nímtŏn)
Kingsteignton ['kɪŋz'teɪntən] (kíngz-táyntŏn)
Kingsterndale [kɪŋ'stɜrndeɪl] (king-stérndayl)
Kingston Bagpuize, *also spelt* **Bagpuize** ['kɪŋstən 'bægpjuz] (kíngstŏn bágpewz)
Kingston Blount ['kɪŋstən 'blʌnt] (kíngstŏn blúnt)

Kingston Buci ['kɪŋstən 'bjusɪ] (kíngstŏn béwssi)
Kingston Matravers ['kɪŋstən mə'trævərz] (kíngstŏn mătrávvĕrz)
Kingston-upon-Hull ['kɪŋstən əpən 'hʌl] (kíngstŏn ŭpŏn húll)
Kingswear ['kɪŋzwɪər] (kíngzweer)
Kingswinford [kɪŋ'swɪnfərd] (king-swínfŏrd)
Kingussie [kɪŋ'jusɪ] (king-yoóssi)
Kininmonth, f.n. [kɪ'nɪnmənθ] (kinnínmŏnth); ['kɪnɪnmənθ] (kínninmŏnth)
Kininmonth [kɪ'nɪnmənθ] (kinnínmŏnth)
Kinloch, f.n. [kɪn'lɒx] (kinlóch)
Kinlocheil ['kɪnlɒx'il] (kínlocheél)
Kinlochewe ['kɪnlɒx'ju] (kínloch-yoó)
Kinlochleven ['kɪnlɒx'livən] (kínloch-leévĕn)
Kinlochmoidart ['kɪnlɒx'mɔɪdərt] (kínlochmóydárt)
Kinlochourn ['kɪnlɒx'huərn] (kínlochhoôrn)
Kinloch Rannoch ['kɪnlɒx 'rænəx] (kínloch ránnŏch)
Kinloss [kɪn'lɒs] (kinlóss) *Appropriate also for Baroness* ~.
Kinmel Park ['kɪmməl 'park] (kínmĕl paárk)
Kinmond, f.n. ['kɪnmənd] (kínmŏnd)
Kinnaber Junction [kɪ'neɪbər] (kináyber)
Kinnaird [kɪ'nɛərd] (kina̐ird) *Appropriate also for Baron* ~.
Kinne, f.n. ['kɪnɪ] (kínni)
Kinnear, f.n. [kɪ'nɪər] (kineér); [kɪ'nɛər] (kina̐ir)
Kinnegar ['kɪnɪgər] (kínnĕgăr)
Kinneil [kɪ'nil] (kineél)
Kinnesswood [kɪ'neswʊd] (kinéss-wŏŏd)
Kinnimonth, f.n. [kɪ'nɪmmənt] (kinnínmŏnt); [kɪ'nɪnmənθ] (kinnínmŏnth)
Kinnoull [kɪ'nul] (kinoól) *Appropriate also for the Earl of* ~.
Kinoulton [kɪ'naʊltən] (kinówltŏn)
Kinrade, f.n. ['kɪnreɪd] (kínrayd)
Kinross [kɪn'rɒs] (kinróss) *Appropriate also for Baron* ~.
Kinsella, f.n. ['kɪnsələ] (kínssĕlă); [kɪn'selə] (kinsséllă)
Kinsey, f.n. ['kɪnzɪ] (kínzi)
Kintore [kɪn'tor] (kintór) *Appropriate also for the Countess of* ~.
Kintyre [kɪn'taɪər] (kintír)
Kintyre and Lorne, Marquess of [kɪn'taɪər ənd 'lorn] (kintír ănd lórn)
Kinvig, f.n. [kɪn'vɪg] (kinvíg)
Kinwarton ['kɪnərtən] (kínnártŏn); ['kɪnwərtən] (kínwártŏn)
Kipling, Rudyard, author ['rʌdjərd 'kɪplɪŋ] (rúd-yárd kípling)
Kipling Cotes ['kɪplɪŋ 'koʊts] (kípling kŏts)
Kirby ['kɜrbɪ] (kírbi)
Kirby Bedon ['kɜrbɪ 'bidən] (kírbi beédŏn)

Kirbye, f.n. ['kɜrbɪ] (kírbi)
Kirkbean [kɜrk'biːn] (kirkbeen)
Kirkbride, f.n. [kɜrk'braɪd] (kirkbríd)
Kirkbride [kɜrk'braɪd] (kirkbríd)
Kirkburton [kɜrk'bɜrtən] (kirkbúrtŏn)
Kirkby ['kɜrbɪ] (kírbi)
Kirkby Lonsdale ['kɜrbɪ 'lɒnzdeɪl] (kírbi lónzdayl)
Kirkby Malham ['kɜrbɪ 'mæləm] (kírbi málăm)
Kirkby Mallory ['kɜrkbɪ 'mælərɪ] (kírkbi málŏri)
Kirkby Malzeard ['kɜrbɪ 'mælzərd] (kírbi málzărd)
Kirkby Moorside ['kɜrbɪ 'mʊərsaɪd] (kírbi mŏor-síd)
Kirkby Stephen ['kɜrbɪ 'stivən] (kírbi steévĕn)
Kirkby Thore ['kɜrbɪ 'θɔr] (kírbi thór)
Kirkby-in-Ashfield ['kɜrkbɪ ɪn 'æʃfɪld] (kírkbi in áshfeeld)
Kirkby - in - Malhamdale ['kɜrbɪ ɪn 'mæləmdeɪl] (kírbi in málămdayl) *see also* Kirkby Malham.
Kirkcaldy [kər'kɒdɪ] (kirkóddi); [kər-'kɒdɪ] (kirkáwdi)
Kirkcubbin [kɜr'kʌbɪn] (kirkúbbin)
Kirkcudbright [kər'kubrɪ] (kirkoóbri)
Kirk Deighton [kɜrk 'diːtən] (kirk deétŏn)
Kirkden [kɜrk'den] (kirkdén)
Kirkgunzeon [kɜr'gʌnjən] (kirgún-yŏn)
Kirkhaugh ['kɜrkhɑf] (kírkhaaf); ['kɜrkhɔ] (kírkhaw)
Kirkheaton [kɜrk'hiːtən] (kirk-heétŏn)
Kirkhill ['kɜrk'hɪl] (kírk-híll)
Kirkhope ['kɜrkhoʊp] (kírkhŏp)
Kirkliston [kɜrk'lɪstən] (kirklístŏn)
Kirkmichael, *Ayr., I.o.M.* [kɜrk'maɪkl] (kirkmíkl)
Kirkmichael, *Perth.* [kɜrk'maɪkl] (kirkmíkl); [kɜrk'maɪxl] (kirkmíchl)
Kirkoswald [kɜrk'ɒzwɒld] (kirk-ózwäld)
Kirkpatrick, f.n. [kɜrk'pætrɪk] (kirkpátrick)
Kirkstall Abbey ['kɜrkstɒl] (kírkstawl)
Kirkstone Pass ['kɜrkstən] (kírkstŏn)
Kirkup, f.n. ['kɜrkəp] (kírkŭp)
Kirkwall ['kɜrkwɒl] (kírkwawl) *Appropriate also for Viscount ~.*
Kirriemarian, native of Kirriemuir [ˌkɪrɪ'mɛərɪən] (kirrimaíriăn)
Kirriemuir [ˌkɪrɪ'mjʊər] (kirri-myŏor)
Kirtomy [kɜr'tɒmɪ] (kirtómmi)
Kirwan, f.n. ['kɜrwən] (kírwăn)
Kishmul Castle, *also spelt* Kismull, Kiessimal ['kɪʃməl] (kíshmŭl)
Kismeldon Bridge, *Cornwall* [kɪz-'meldən] (kizméldŏn)
Kismull Castle *see* Kishmul Castle.
Kitcat, f.n. ['kɪtkæt] (kítkat)
Kitchell, f.n. ['kɪtʃl] (kitchl)
Kitchen, f.n. ['kɪtʃɪn] (kítchĕn)
Kitchener, f.n. ['kɪtʃɪnər] (kítchĕner)
Kitchin, f.n. ['kɪtʃɪn] (kítchin)

Kitshowe Bridge, *Westmorland* ['kɪtshaʊ] (kíts-how)
Kitson, f.n. ['kɪtsən] (kítsŏn)
Kiveton ['kɪvɪtən] (kívvĕtŏn)
Kleinvort, f.n. ['klaɪnwɔrt] (klín-wawrt)
Klimcke, f.n. ['klɪmkɪ] (klímki)
Klugg, f.n. [klʌg] (klug)
Klugh, f.n. [klu] (kloo)
Kluth, f.n. [kluːθ] (kluth)
Knaith [neɪð] (nayth); [neɪθ] (nayth)
Knaresborough ['nɛərzbərə] (naírzbŭră)
Knatchbull, f.n. ['nætʃbʊl] (nátchbŏol)
Knave-Go-By ['neɪvgoʊbaɪ] (náyvgŏbī)
Knavesmire Race Course, *York* 'neɪvzmaɪər] (náyvz-mīr)
Kneen, f.n. [nin] (neen)
Knevett, f.n. ['nevɪt] (névvĕt)
Knighton, f.n. ['naɪtən] (nítŏn)
Knighton, *Hants.* [kɪ'naɪtən] (kinítŏn)
Knighton, *Radnor* ['naɪtən] (nítŏn)
Knights Enham ['naɪts 'enəm] (níts énnăm)
Kniveton ['naɪvtən] (nívtŏn); ['nɪftən] (níftŏn)
Knock [nɒk] (nock)
Knockagh ['nɒkə] (nóckă)
Knockando [nɒk'ændoʊ] (nockándŏ)
Knockbracken [nɒk'brækən] (nock-bráckĕn)
Knockbreda [nɒk'breɪdə] (nockbráydă)
Knockdow, f.n. [nɒk'du] (nockdoó)
Knockholt ['nɒkhoʊlt] (nóck-hŏlt)
Knocklayd [nɒk'leɪd] (nockláyd)
Knocknacarry [ˌnɒknə'kærɪ] (nocknă-kárri)
Knocknagoney [ˌnɒknə'gɒnɪ] (nocknă-gónni); [ˌnɒknə'goʊnɪ] (nocknăgŏni)
Knockshinnoch [nɒk'ʃɪnəx] (nock-shínnŏch)
Knodishall ['nɒdɪʃəl] (nóddi-shăl)
Knokin *see* Baroness Strange.
Knole [noʊl] (nŏl)
Knollys, Viscount [noʊlz] (nŏlz)
Knott, f.n. [nɒt] (nott)
Knowesgate ['naʊzgeɪt] (nówzgayt)
Knowle [noʊl] (nŏl)
Knowler, f.n. ['noʊlər] (nŏler)
Knowles, f.n. [noʊlz] (nŏlz)
Knowsley ['noʊzlɪ] (nŏzli)
Knoydart ['nɔɪdərt] (nóydărt)
Knucklas ['nʌkləs] (núcklăss)
Knussen, f.n. ['nʌsən] (nússĕn)
Knuston ['nʌstən] (nússtŏn)
Knutsford, f.n. ['nʌtsfərd] (nútsfŏrd)
Knypersley ['naɪpərzlɪ] (nípĕrzli)
Knyvett, f.n. ['nɪvɪt] (nívvĕt)
Kortright, f.n. ['kɔrtraɪt] (kórtrīt)
Kough, f.n. [kjoʊ] (kyŏ)
Kraay, f.n. [kreɪ] (kray)
Krumb, f.n. [krʌm] (krum)
Kruse, f.n. [kruz] (krooz)
Kuggar ['kagər] (kúggăr); ['kɪgər] (kíggăr)
Kuipers, f.n. ['kaɪpərz] (kípĕrz)
Kumm, f.n. [kʊm] (kŏom)

Kyffin, *f.n.* [ˈkʌfɪn] (kúffin); [ˈkɪfɪn] (kíffin)
Kyleakin [kaɪlˈækɪn] (kīláckin)
Kyle of Lochalsh [ˈkaɪl əv lɒˈxælʃ] (kīl ŏv lochálsh)
Kyle Rhea [ˈkaɪl ˈreɪ] (kīl ráy)
Kyle Sku [ˈkaɪl ˈskjuː] (kīl skéw)
Kyles of Bute [ˈkaɪlz əv ˈbjuːt] (kīlz ŏv béwt)
Kyles Morar [ˈkaɪlz ˈmɔrər] (kīlz máwrăr)
Kyllachy, *f.n.* [ˈkaɪləxɪ] (kíláchi)
Kylsant, *Barony of* [kɪlˈsænt] (kilssánt)
Kynance [ˈkaɪnəns] (kínănss)
Kynaston, *f.n.* [ˈkɪnəstən] (kínnăstŏn)
Kynsey, *f.n.* [ˈkɪnzɪ] (kínzi)
Kynynmound, *f.n.* [kɪˈnɪnmənd] (kinnínmŭnd)

L

La Belle Sauvage Yard, *London* [la ˈbel souˈvaʒ] (laa béll sōvaázh)
La Brooy, *f.n.* [la ˈbruːɪ] (laa brŏo-i)
La Fontaine, *f.n.* [lə ˈfɒnteɪn] (lă fóntayn)
La Nauze, *f.n.* [lə ˈnɒz] (lă náwz)
La Roche, *f.n.* [la ˈrɒʃ] (laa rósh)
La Terriere, *f.n.* [la ˈterɪɛər] (laa térriair)
La Touche, *f.n.* [la ˈtuʃ] (laa tóosh)
Labbett, *f.n.* [ˈlæbɪt] (lábbĕt)
Labone, *f.n.* [ləˈboun] (lăbón)
Labouchere, *f.n.* [ˌlæbuˈʃɛər] (laboosháïr); [ˈlæbuʃɛər] (lábooshair)
Lacaille, *f.n.* [ləˈkeɪ] (lăkáy)
Lacey, *f.n.* [ˈleɪsɪ] (láyssi)
Lachmann, *f.n.* [ˈlakmən] (laákmăn)
Lackenby [ˈlækənbɪ] (láckĕnbi)
Lacock [ˈleɪkɒk] (láykock) *Appropriate also for ~ Abbey.*
Lacon, *f.n.* [ˈleɪkən] (láykŏn)
Ladbroke, *f.n.* [ˈlædbrʊk] (ládbrŏŏk)
Ladbrook, *f.n.* [ˈlædbrʊk] (ládbrŏŏk)
Laddow Rocks [ˈlædou] (láddō)
Ladefoged, *f.n.* [ˈlædɪfougɪd] (láddĕfōgĕd)
Ladell, *f.n.* [læˈdel] (ladéll)
Ladhope [ˈlædoup] (láddōp)
Ladock [ˈlædək] (láddŏck)
Lafcadio, *f.n.* [læfˈkadɪou] (lafkaádiō)
Laffan, *f.n.* [ləˈfæn] (lăfán)
Laffeaty, *f.n.* [ˈlæfɪtɪ] (láffĕti)
Lafontaine, *f.n.* [ləˈfɒnteɪn] (lăfóntayn)
Lagan, *River* [ˈlægən] (lággăn)
Laggan, *Loch* [ˈlægən] (lággăn)
Lahee, *f.n.* [ləˈhiː] (lăheé)
Laid [leɪd] (layd)
Laighwood [ˈleɪxwʊd] (láychwŏŏd)

Laindon [ˈleɪndən] (láyndŏn)
Laindon Hills, *also called* **Langdon Hills**, *q.v.* [ˈleɪndən ˈhɪlz] (láyndŏn híllz)
Laing, *f.n.* [leɪŋ] (layng); [læŋ] (lang)
Laira [ˈlɛərə] (laïră)
Laird, *f.n.* [lɛərd] (laird)
Lairig Ghru [ˌlærɪˈgruː] (larrigroó)
Lakenham [ˈleɪkənəm] (láykĕnăm)
Lakenheath [ˈleɪkənhiθ] (láykĕn-heeth)
Lamancha [ləˈmæŋkə] (lămánkă)
Lamarsh [laˈmarʃ] (laamaársh); [ˈlæmərʃ] (lámmărsh)
Lamas, *also spelt* **Lammas** [ˈlæməs] (lámmăss)
Lamb, *f.n.* [læm] (lam)
Lambeg [læmˈbeg] (lambég)
Lambelet, *f.n.* [ˈlæmbəlɪt] (lámbĕlĕt)
Lambert, *f.n.* [ˈlæmbərt] (lámbĕrt)
Lambeth [ˈlæmbəθ] (lámbĕth)
Lambethan, *pertaining to Lambeth* [læmˈbiθən] (lambeéthăn)
Lambhill [ˈlæmˈhɪl] (lám-híll)
Lamb Holm [ˈlæm houm] (lám hōm)
Lambie, *f.n.* [ˈlæmbɪ] (lám-bi)
Lambley, *f.n.* [ˈlæmlɪ] (lámli)
Lamerton [ˈlæmərtən] (lámmĕrtŏn)
Lamesley [ˈleɪmzlɪ] (láymzli)
Lamington [ˈlæmɪŋtən] (lámmingtŏn) *Appropriate also for the Barony of ~.*
Lamlash [ləmˈlæʃ] (lăm-lásh); [læmˈlæʃ] (lam-lásh)
Lammas *see* Lamas.
Lamond, *f.n.* [ˈlæmənd] (lámmŏnd)
Lamont, *f.n.* [ˈlæmənt] (lámmŏnt); [ləˈmɒnt] (lămónt) *The first is the usual Scottish pronunciation, the second the Northern Irish.*
Lamorbey [ˈlæmərbɪ] (lámmŏrbi)
Lamorna [læˈmɔrnə] (lammórnă)
Lamorran [læˈmɒrən] (lammórrăn)
Lamotte, *f.n.* [ləˈmɒt] (lămótt)
Lampe, *f.n.* [læmp] (lamp); [ˈlæmpɪ] (lámpi)
Lampeter [ˈlæmpɪtər] (lámpĕter)
Lamphey [ˈlæmfɪ] (lámfi)
Lamplugh, *f.n.* [ˈlæmplu] (lám-ploo)
Lamplugh [ˈlæmplu] (lám-ploo); [ˈlæmplə] (lám-plă)
Lanark [ˈlænərk] (lánnărk)
Lancashire [ˈlæŋkəʃər] (lánkăsher)
Lancaster, *f.n.* [ˈlæŋkəstər] (lánkáster)
Lancaster [ˈlæŋkəstər] (lánkáster)
Lancaut [læŋˈkout] (lang-kŏt)
Lance, *f.n. and C.n.* [lɑns] (laanss)
Lancefield, *f.n.* [ˈlɑnsfɪld] (laánssfeeld)
Lancelot, *C.n.* [ˈlɑnslɒt] (laánssĕlot); [ˈlɑnslɒt] (laánsslot)
Lancing [ˈlɑnsɪŋ] (laánssing)
Landau, *f.n.* [ˈlændou] (lándō)
Lander, *f.n.* [ˈlændər] (lánder)
Landewednack [ˌlændɪˈwednək] (landiwédnăk)
Landoger Trow, The, *historic Bristol inn* [ˈlændʊgər ˈtrou] (lándogger trów)
Landone, *f.n.* [ˈlændən] (lándŏn)

Landore [læn'dɔr] (landór)
Landrake [læn'dreɪk] (landráyk)
Landulph [læn'dʌlf] (landúlf)
Lanercost ['lænərkɒst] (lánnĕrkost)
Lanfine House, *Ayrshire* [læn'fin] (lanfeèn)
Langar ['læŋgər] (láng-găr)
Langbaurgh ['læŋbɑrf] (lángbaarf)
Langdon Hills, *also called* Laindon Hills, *q.v.* ['læŋdən 'hɪlz] (lángdŏn híllz)
Lange, f.n. [lændʒ] (lanj)
Langenhoe ['læŋgənhou] (láng-gĕn-hŏ)
Langer, f.n. ['læŋər] (láng-er)
Langford, f.n. ['læŋfərd] (lángfŏrd)
Langham, f.n. ['læŋəm] (láng-ăm)
Langho ['læŋou] (láng-ō)
Langholm ['læŋəm] (láng-ŏm)
Langley, f.n. ['læŋlɪ] (láng-li)
Langloan ['læŋ'loun] (láng-lŏn)
Langold ['læŋgould] (láng-gōld)
Langridge, f.n. ['læŋgrɪdʒ] (láng-grij)
Langstaff, f.n. ['læŋstɑf] (lángstaaf)
Langstone, *parliamentary division oj Portsmouth* ['læŋstən] (lángstŏn)
Langton Matravers ['læŋtən mə-'trævərz] (lángtŏn mătrávvĕrz)
Lanherne [læn'hɜrn] (lan-hérn)
Lanhydrock [læn'haɪdrək] (lan-hídrŏk)
Lanier, f.n. ['lænjər] (lán-yer)
Lanivet [læn'ɪvɪt] (lanívvĕt)
Lanjeth [læn'dʒeθ] (lanjéth)
Lankester, f.n. ['læŋkɪstər] (lánkĕster)
Lanlivery [læn'lɪvərɪ] (lan-lívvĕri)
Lanreath [læn'reθ] (lanréth)
Lansdown, f.n. ['lænzdaun] (lánzdown)
Lanteglos [læn'teglɒs] (lantégloss) ; [læn-'teɪglɒs] (lantáygloss)
Lanyon Cromlech ['lænjən 'krɒmlek] (lán-yŏn krómleck)
Lapage, f.n. [lə'peɪdʒ] (lăpáyj)
Laphroaig Distillery [lə'frɔɪg] (lăfróyg)
Lappage, f.n. [lɑ'peɪdʒ] (laapáyj)
Larkby, f.n. ['lɑrkbɪ] (laárkbi)
Larkins, f.n. ['lɑrkɪnz] (laárkinz)
Larmor, f.n. ['lɑrmɔr] (laármŏr)
Larmour, f.n. ['lɑrmər] (laármŭr)
Lascelles, Viscount ['læslz] (lasslz)
Lasdun, f.n. ['læzdən] (lázdŭn)
Lasham ['læsəm] (lássăm) ; ['læʃəm] (láshăm) *The first is the traditional village pronunciation. The second is familiar to those using the Gliding Centre.*
Lashmar, f.n. ['læʃmɑr] (láshmaar)
Laslett, f.n. ['læzlɪt] (lázlĕt)
Lassodie [læ'soudɪ] (lassódi)
Lasswade [læs'weɪd] (lasswáyd)
Latey, f.n. ['leɪtɪ] (láyti)
Latham, f.n. ['leɪθəm] (láythăm) ; ['leɪ-ðəm] (láythăm) *The first pronunciation is appropriate for Baron ∼.*
Lathan, f.n. ['leɪθən] (láythăn)
Lathbury, f.n. ['læθbərɪ] (láthbŭri)
Latheron ['læðərən] (láthĕrŏn)
Lathey, f.n. ['leɪθɪ] (láythi)

Lathom, f.n. ['leɪθəm] (láythŏm) ; ['leɪ-ðəm] (láythŏm)
Lathom ['leɪðəm] (láythŏm)
Latimer, f.n. ['lætɪmər] (láttimer)
Latreille, f.n. [lə'treɪl] (lătráyl) ; [lə'trɪl] (lătreèl) ; [lɑ'treɪ] (laatráy)
Latymer, Baron ['lætɪmər] (láttimer)
Lauder, f.n. ['lɔdər] (láwder)
Lauder ['lɔdər] (láwder)
Lauderdale ['lɔdərdeɪl] (láwdĕrdayl)
Laugharne [lɑrn] (laarn)
Laugherne House, *Worcs.* [lɔrn] (lorn)
Laughlan, f.n. ['lɒxlən] (lóchlăn)
Laughland, f.n. ['lɒxlənd] (lóchlănd)
Laughton, f.n. ['lɔtən] (láwtŏn)
Laughton, *Leics., Lincs., Sussex, Yorks.* ['lɔtən] (láwtŏn)
Launcells ['lɑnslz] (laansslz) ; ['lænslz] (lansslz)
Launceston ['lɑnsən] (laánssŏn) ; ['lɑn-stən] (laánstŏn) ; ['lɒnsən] (láwnssŏn)
Laurie, f.n. ['lɒrɪ] (lórri)
Laurier, f.n. ['lɒrɪər] (lórri-er)
Lauriston, f.n. ['lɒrɪstən] (lórristŏn)
Lauwerys, f.n. ['laʊərɪs] (lówĕríss)
Lavant ['lævənt] (lávvănt)
Lavarack, f.n. ['lævəræk] (lávvărack)
Lavecock, f.n. ['lævɪkɒk] (lávvĕkock)
Lavell, f.n. ['lævl] (lavvl) ; [lə'vel] (lăvéll)
Lavendon ['lævəndən] (lávvĕndŏn)
Lavenham ['lævənəm] (lávvĕnăm)
Laver, f.n. ['leɪvər] (láyver)
Laver, River ['lavər] (laáver)
Laverick, f.n. ['lævərɪk] (lávvĕrick)
Lavers, f.n. ['leɪvərz] (láyvĕrz)
Laverstock ['lævərstɒk] (lávvĕrstock)
Laverstoke ['lævərstoʊk] (lávvĕrstŏk)
Laville, f.n. [lə'vɪl] (lăvíll)
Lavin, f.n. ['lævɪn] (lávvin)
Lavington, West ['lævɪŋtən] (lávving-tŏn)
Lawhitton [lɒ'hwɪtən] (law-whíttŏn); [lɑ'hwɪtən] (laa-whíttŏn)
Lawler, f.n. ['lɔlər] (láwler)
Lawrence, f.n. ['lɒrəns] (lórrĕnss)
Lawrie, f.n. ['lɒrɪ] (lórri)
Lawshall ['lɔʃl] (lawshl)
Lawson, f.n. ['lɔsən] (láwssŏn)
Lawther, f.n. ['lɔðər] (láwthĕr)
Laxey ['læksɪ] (lácksi)
Layard, f.n. ['leɪɑrd] (láy-aard) ; ['leɪərd] (láy-ărd)
Layer Breton ['leɪər 'bretən] (láy-er bréttŏn)
Layer de la Haye ['leɪər də lɑ 'heɪ] (láy-er dĕ laa háy)
Layham ['leɪəm] (láy-ăm)
Layton, f.n. ['leɪtən] (láytŏn)
Lazar, f.n. [lə'zɑr] (lăzáar)
Lazard, f.n. ['læzɑrd] (lázzaard)
Lazell, f.n. [lə'zel] (lăzéll)
Lazonby, f.n. ['leɪzɒnbɪ] (láyzŏnbi)
Lazonby ['leɪzɒnbɪ] (láyzŏnbi)
Le Bars, f.n. [lə 'bɑrz] (lĕ baárz)
Le Court ['li 'kɔrt] (leè kórt)

Le Cren, *f.n.* [lə 'kren] (lĕ krén)
Le Despencer, *Baron* [lə dɪ'spensər] (lĕ dĕspénsser)
Le Fanu, *f.n.* ['lefənu] (léffánoo) ; ['lefən-ju] (léffănew)
Le Feuvre, *f.n.* [lə 'fɪvər] (lĕ feéver)
Le Fevre, *f.n.* [lə 'feɪvr] (lĕ fáyvr)
Le Fleming, *f.n.* [lə 'flemɪŋ] (lĕ flémming)
Le Gallienne, *f.n.* [lə 'gæljen] (lĕ gál-yen)
Le Grice, *f.n.* [lə 'graɪs] (lĕ gríss)
Le Gros, *f.n.* [lə 'grou] (lĕ grṓ)
Le Huray, *f.n.* [lə 'hjuəreɪ] (lĕ hyóoray)
Le Lacheur, *f.n.* [lə 'læʃər] (lĕ lásher)
Le Maitre, *f.n.* [lə 'meɪtr] (lĕ máytr)
Le Marchant, *f.n.* [lə 'martʃənt] (lĕ maártchănt) ; [lə 'marʃənt] (lĕ maár-shănt)
Le Masurier, *f.n.* [lə mə'zjuəriər] (lĕ mă-zyŏóri-er)
Le Mauviel, *f.n.* [lə 'mouvjəl] (lĕ mṓv-yĕl)
Le Mesurier, *f.n.* [lə 'meʒərər] (lĕ mézhĕrer)
Le Neve, *f.n.* [lə 'niv] (lĕ neév)
Le Patourel, *f.n.* [lə 'pætuərel] (lĕ pátŏórel)
Le Poer, *f.n.* [lə 'puər] (lĕ pŏór)
Le Quesne, *f.n.* [lə 'keɪn] (lĕ káyn)
Le Queux, *f.n.* [lə 'kju] (lĕ kéw)
Le Rougetel, *f.n.* [lə 'ruʒtel] (lĕ rŏózhtel)
Le Sage, *f.n.* [lə 'saʒ] (lĕ saázh)
Le Sueur, *f.n.* [lə 'swɜr] (lĕ swúr)
Le Surf, *f.n.* [lə 'sɜrf] (lĕ súrf)
Leach, *f.n.* [litʃ] (leetch)
Leacock, *f.n.* ['likɒk] (leécock) ; ['leɪkɒk] (láycock)
Leadbeater, *f.n.* ['ledbitər] (lédbeeter) ; ['ledbɪtər] (lédbitter) ; ['lidbitər] (leéd-beeter) ; ['lebɪtər] (lébbiter)
Leadbetter, *f.n.* ['ledbetər] (lédbetter) ; [led'betər] (ledbétter)
Leadbitter, *f.n.* ['ledbitər] (lédbitter)
Leadenhall Street, *London* ['ledənhɒl] (léddĕnhawl)
Leadenham ['ledənəm] (léddĕnăm)
Leadgate ['ledgit] (léd-git)
Leahy, *f.n.* ['lihɪ] (leéhi)
Leakey, *f.n.* ['likɪ] (leéki)
Leal, *f.n.* [lil] (leel)
Leamington ['lemɪŋtən] (lémmingtŏn)
Lean, *f.n.* [lin] (leen)
Leaning, *f.n.* ['linɪŋ] (leéning)
Leaphard, *f.n.* ['lepərd] (léppărd)
Learmonth, *f.n.* ['lɜrmənθ] (lérmŏnth) ; ['lɜərmənθ] (laírmŏnth) ; ['lɪərmənθ] (leér-mŏnth) ; ['lɜrmənt] (lérmŏnt)
Learney ['lɜərnɪ] (laírni)
Learoyd, *f.n.* ['lɪərɔɪd] (leér-oyd)
Learthart, *f.n.* ['lɪərθart] (leér-thaart)
Leasingthorne ['lizɪŋθɔrn] (leézing-thorn)
Leask, *f.n.* [lisk] (leesk)
Leasowe ['lisou] (leéssō)
Leaston ['leɪstən] (láysstŏn)

Leatham, *f.n.* ['liθəm] (leéthăm) ; ['liðəm] (leéthăm)
Leathart, *f.n.* ['liθart] (leé-thaart)
Leather, *f.n.* ['leðər] (léther)
Leathers, *Viscount* ['leðərz] (léthĕrz)
Leathes, *f.n.* [liðz] (leethz)
Leavening ['livnɪŋ] (leév-ning)
Leavesden ['livzdən] (leévzdĕn)
Leavey, *f.n.* ['livɪ] (leévi)
Leavins, *f.n.* ['levɪnz] (lévvinz)
Leavis, *f.n.* ['livɪs] (leéviss)
Leay, *f.n.* [leɪ] (lay)
Lebon, *f.n.* ['libɒn] (leébon)
Lebor, *f.n.* [lə'bɔr] (lĕbór)
Leburn, *f.n.* ['libɜrn] (leéburn)
Lebus, *f.n.* ['libəs] (leébŭss)
Leche, *f.n.* [leʃ] (lesh)
Lechlade ['letʃleɪd] (létch-layd)
Lechmere, *f.n.* ['letʃmɪər] (létchmeer) ; ['leʃmɪər] (léshmeer)
Leconfield ['lekənfild] (léckŏnfeeld)
Lecropt ['lekrɒpt] (léckropt)
Lecumpher [lə'kamfər] (lĕkúmfer)
Ledeboer, *f.n.* ['ledibuər] (léddĕbŏór)
Ledgard, *f.n.* ['ledʒard] (léjjaard)
Ledoux, *f.n.* [lə'du] (lĕdoó)
Leech, *f.n.* [litʃ] (leetch)
Leedell, *f.n.* [li'del] (leedéll)
Leeds [lidz] (leedz)
Leedstown ['lidztaun] (leédztown)
Leese, *f.n.* [lis] (leess)
Lefanu, *f.n.* ['lefənju] (léffănew) ; [lə-'fanu] (lĕfaánoo)
Lefeaux, *f.n.* [lə'fou] (lĕfṓ)
Lefebure, *f.n.* ['lefəbjuər] (léffĕbyŏór)
Lefebvre, *f.n.* [lə'fivər] (lĕfeéver)
Lefeuvre, *f.n.* [lə'fɜvr] (lĕfốvr)
Lefevre Galleries, *London* [lə'fɜːvr] (lĕfévvr)
Lefroy, *f.n.* [lə'frɔɪ] (lĕfróy)
Legacurry, *f.n.* [ˌlegə'karɪ] (leggăkúrri)
Legacy ['legəsɪ] (léggăssi)
Legard, *f.n.* ['ledʒərd] (léjjărd)
Legat, *f.n.* [lə'gæt] (lĕgát)
Leger Galleries, *London* ['ledʒər] (léjjer)
Legerton, *f.n.* ['ledʒərtən] (léjjĕrtŏn)
Legerwood ['ledʒərwud] (léjjĕrwŏŏd)
Leggate, *f.n.* ['legeɪt] (léggayt)
Leggatt, *f.n.* ['legət] (léggăt)
Legge, *f.n.* [leg] (leg)
Leggett, *f.n.* ['legɪt] (léggĕt)
Legh, *f.n.* [li] (lee)
Lehane, *f.n.* [lə'han] (lĕ-haán)
Leicester ['lestər] (lésster) *Appropriate also for the Earl of ~.*
Leigh, *f.n.* [li] (lee) *Appropriate also for Baron ~.*
Leigh, *Dorset, Kent, Surrey* [laɪ] (li)
Leigh, *Lancs., Staffs.* [li] (lee)
Leigh Court ['laɪ 'kɔrt] (lí kórt)
Leigh Delamere ['li 'deləmɪər] (leé déllămeer)
Leigh Green ['li 'grin] (leé greén)
Leigh Sinton ['laɪ 'sɪntən] (lí síntŏn)

Leigh-on-Mendip ['laɪ ɒn 'mendɪp] (lī on méndip); ['li ɒn 'mendɪp] (leė on méndip)

Leigh-on-Sea ['li ɒn 'si] (leė on seė)

Leighton, *f.n.* ['leɪtən] (láytŏn)

Leighton ['leɪtən] (láytŏn); ['letən] (léttŏn)

Leintwardine ['lentwərdaɪn] (léntwárdīn); ['lentwərdin] (léntwárdeen); ['læntərdin] (lántěrdeen)

Leire [lɪər] (leer); [lɛər] (lair)

Leishman, *f.n.* ['liʃmən] (leėshmǎn); ['lɪʃmən] (líshmǎn)

Leisten, *f.n.* ['listən] (leėsstěn)

Leister, *f.n.* ['lestər] (lésster)

Leiston ['leɪstən] (láysstŏn)

Leitch, *f.n.* [liːtʃ] (leetch)

Leith, *f.n.* [liθ] (leeth)

Leith [liθ] (leeth)

Leither, *f.n.* ['litər] (leėter)

Leitholm ['litəm] (leėtŏm)

Leitrim ['litrɪm] (leėtrim) *Appropriate also for the Earldom of ~*.

Leland, *f.n.* ['lilənd] (leėlánd)

Lelant [le'lænt] (lellánt)

Lelean, *f.n.* [lə'lin] (lěleén)

Leleu, *f.n.* [lə'lu] (lěloo)

Lely, Sir Peter, *17th-c. painter* ['lili] (leėli)

Leman, *f.n.* ['lemən] (lémmǎn); ['limən] (leėmǎn)

Lemare, *f.n.* [lə'mɛər] (lěmáir)

Lemoine, *f.n.* [lə'mɔɪn] (lěmóyn)

Lemon, *f.n.* ['lemən] (lémmŏn)

Lempfert, *f.n.* ['lempfərt] (lémpfěrt)

Lempriere, *f.n.* ['lemprɪəər] (lémpri-air)

Lenaderg [,lenə'dɜrg] (lennáděrg)

Lenanton, *f.n.* [lə'næntən] (lěnántŏn)

Leney, *f.n.* ['lini] (leėni)

Lentaigne, *f.n.* [len'teɪn] (lentáyn)

Lenthall, *f.n.* ['lentɒl] (léntawl); ['lentl] (lentl)

Lenton, *f.n.* ['lentən] (léntŏn)

Lenzie, *f.n.* ['lenzi] (lénzi)

Leochel-Cushnie ['lɒxl 'kʌʃni] (lóchl kúshni)

Leode [led] (led)

Leofric, *Saxon lord of Coventry* ['leɪəfrɪk] (láy-ŏ-frick)

Leominster ['lemstər] (lémsster)

Leon, *f.n.* ['liən] (leė-ŏn)

Leonard, *f.n.* ['lenərd] (lénnǎrd)

Leonowens, *f.n.* ['liənoʊənz] (leėŏn-ŏěnz)

Lephard, *f.n.* ['lepɑrd] (léppaard)

Lepine, *f.n.* [lə'pin] (lěpeén)

Leppard, *f.n.* ['lepɑrd] (lépaard)

Lerwegian, *native of Lerwick* [lɜr-'widʒən] (lerweéján)

Lerwick ['lɜrwɪk] (lérwick)

Lescudjack [ləs'kʌdʒæk] (lěskújjack)

Lesmahagow [,lesmə'heɪgoʊ] (lessmáhaygŏ)

Lesnewth [lez'njuθ] (lez-néwth)

Lesser, *f.n.* ['lesər] (lésser)

Lessness ['lesnɪs] (léssněss)

Lessore, *f.n.* [lə'sɔr] (lěssór)

Lestocq, *f.n.* ['lestɒk] (lésstock)

L'Estrange, *f.n.* [lə'streɪndʒ] (lěstráynj)

Leswalt [les'wɒlt] (lesswáwlt)

Letham ['leθəm] (léthǎm)

Lethbridge, *f.n.* ['leθbrɪdʒ] (léthbrij)

Lethem, *f.n.* ['leθəm] (léthěm)

Lethendy ['leθəndɪ] (léthěndi)

Lethnot ['leθnət] (léthnŏt)

Letterkenny [,letər'keni] (lettěrkénni)

Leuchars ['luxərz] (lòochárz)

Levander, *f.n.* [lɪ'vændər] (lěvánder)

Levant [le'vænt] (levvánt)

Levarne, *f.n.* [lɪ'vɑrn] (lěva'arn)

Leven, *f.n.* ['livən] (leėvěn); ['levən] (lévvěn)

Leven ['livən] (leėvěn)

Leven, *Loch, Argyll-Inverness., Kinross* ['livən] (leėvěn)

Leven, *River, Argyll-Inverness., Dunbarton., Kinross-Fife* ['livən] (leėvěn)

Leven and Melville, *Earl of* ['livən ənd 'melvɪl] (leėvěn ǎnd mélvil)

Levens, *f.n.* ['levənz] (lévvěnz)

Levens ['levənz] (lévvěnz)

Levenshulme ['levənzhjum] (lévvěnz-hewm)

Leventon, *f.n.* ['levəntən] (lévvěntŏn)

Lever, *f.n.* ['livər] (leėver)

Leverhulme, *Viscount* ['livərhjum] (leėvěr-hewm)

Leverstock Green ['levərstɒk 'grin] (lévvěrstock greén)

Leverton, *f.n.* ['levərtən] (lévvěrtŏn)

Leverton, North *and* **South** ['levərtən] (lévvěrtŏn)

Leveson-Gower, *f.n.* ['lusən 'gɔr] (lòossŏn gór) *Family name of Earl Granville*

Levey, *f.n.* ['livɪ] (leėvi); ['levɪ] (lévvi)

Levi, *f.n.* ['levɪ] (lévvi)

Levic, *f.n.* ['levɪk] (lévvick)

Levien, *f.n.* [lə'vin] (lěveén)

Levin, *f.n.* ['levɪn] (lévvin)

Levinge, *f.n.* ['levɪŋ] (lévving)

Levita, *f.n.* [lə'vitə] (lěveétá)

Levy, *f.n.* ['livɪ] (leėvi); ['levɪ] (lévvi)

Lewannick [lə'wɒnɪk] (lě-wónnick)

Lewarne, *f.n.* [lə'wɔrn] (lě-wórn)

Lewarne [lə'wɔrn] (lě-wórn)

Lewdown, *also spelt* **Lew Down** ['lu-'daʊn] (lòo-dówn)

Lewell, *f.n.* ['luəl] (lòo-ěl)

Lewenstein, *f.n.* ['luənstin] (lòo-ěnssteen)

Lewes ['luɪs] (lòo-ěss)

Lewey, *f.n.* ['luɪ] (lòo-i)

Lewin, *f.n.* ['luɪn] (lòo-in)

Lewitter, *f.n.* [lə'wɪtər] (lě-wítter)

Lewknor, *f.n.* ['luknɔr] (lòoknor)

Lews Castle [luz] (looz)

Lewsey, *f.n.* ['ljusɪ] (léwssi)

Lewthwaite, *f.n.* ['luθweɪt] (lòothwayt)

Lewtrenchard, *also spelt* **Lew Trenchard** ['lu'trenʃərd] (lòo-trén-shárd)

Ley, *f.n.* [leɪ] (lay); [li] (lee)

Leybourne ['leɪbɔːn] (láyborn)

Leyburn ['leɪbɜːn] (láyburn)

Leycester, f.n. ['lestər] (lésster)

Leycett ['liset] (leésset); ['laɪset] (lísset)

Leyhill, *Bucks.* ['leɪhɪl] (láy-hil)

Leyhill, *Derby.* ['lihɪl] (leé-hil)

Leyland, f.n. ['leɪlənd] (láylănd)

Leyland ['leɪlənd] (láylănd)

Leys, f.n. [liz] (leez)

Leysdown ['leɪzdaʊn] (láyzdown)

Leyshon, f.n. ['laɪʃən] (lí-shŏn); ['leɪʃən] (láy-shŏn) *The first is usual in Wales.*

Leyton ['leɪtən] (láytŏn)

Leytonstone ['leɪtənstoʊn] (láytŏn-stōn)

Lezant [le'zænt] (lezzánt)

Leziate ['lezɪət] (lézziăt); ['ledʒɪt] (léjjĕt)

Liardet, f.n. [liːˈɑːdet] (lee-aárdet)

Lias, f.n. ['laɪəs] (lí-ăss)

Libanus ['lɪbənəs] (líbbănŭss)

Liberton ['lɪbərtən] (líbbĕrtŏn)

Lickess, f.n. ['lɪkɪs] (líckĕss)

Lickis, f.n. ['lɪkɪs] (líckiss)

Lickiss, f.n. ['lɪkɪs] (líckiss)

Licswm *see* Lixwm.

Liddell, f.n. ['lɪdl] (liddl); [lɪ'del] (lidéll) *The first, which is still much the more usual for this spelling, is appropriate for Henry George ~, joint editor of Liddell and Scott's Greek-English lexicon, and for his daughter Alice ~, the heroine of 'Alice in Wonderland'.*

Liddle, f.n. ['lɪdl] (liddl)

Lidell, f.n. ['lɪdl] (liddl); [lɪ'del] (lidéll)

Lidgate ['lɪdgeɪt] (líd-gayt)

Lidgett, f.n. ['lɪdʒɪt] (líjjĕt)

Lidstone, f.n. ['lɪdstən] (lídstŏn)

Liebert, f.n. ['libərt] (leébĕrt)

Lienhardt, f.n. ['liənhɑːt] (leé-ĕn-haart)

Liesching, f.n. ['liʃɪŋ] (leéshing)

Lightbown, f.n. ['laɪtbaʊn] (lítbown)

Lightoller, f.n. ['laɪtɒlər] (líttoller)

Ligoniel [ˌlɪgəˈnil] (liggŏneél)

Likeman, f.n. ['laɪkmən] (lík măn)

Lilburn, f.n. ['lɪlbɜːn] (lílburn)

Lilleshall ['lɪlɪʃəl] (lílli-shál)

Lilley, f.n. ['lɪlɪ] (lílli)

Lillistone, f.n. ['lɪlɪstən] (líllistŏn)

Lillywhite, f.n. ['lɪlɪhwaɪt] (lílli-whīt)

Limavady [ˌlɪməˈvædɪ] (límmăváddi)

Limpenhoe ['lɪmpənhoʊ] (límpĕn-hō)

Limpkin, f.n. ['lɪmpkɪn] (límpkin)

Linacre, f.n. ['lɪnəkər] (línnăker)

Lincoln, f.n. ['lɪŋkən] (línkŏn)

Lincoln ['lɪŋkən] (línkŏn)

Lind, f.n. [lɪnd] (lind)

Lindgren, Baron ['lɪngrən] (lín-grĕn)

Lindholme ['lɪndhoʊm] (línd-hōm)

Lindisfarne ['lɪndɪsfɑːn] (líndiss-faarn)

Lindley, *Leics., Yorks.* ['lɪmdlɪ] (líndli)

Lindridge, f.n. ['lɪndrɪdʒ] (líndrij)

Lindsay, Earl of ['lɪndzɪ] (líndzi)

Lindsay, f.n. ['lɪndzɪ] (líndzi)

Lindsell, f.n. ['lɪndzl] (lindzl)

Linehan, f.n. ['lɪnəhən] (línnăhăn)

Lingay, f.n. ['lɪŋgɪ] (líng-gi)

Lingen, f.n. ['lɪŋən] (líng-ĕn)

Lingstrom, f.n. ['lɪŋstrəm] (líng-strŏm)

Linhope ['lɪnəp] (línnŏp)

Linkinhorne ['lɪŋkɪnhɔːn] (línkin-horn)

Linklater, Eric, author ['lɪŋklətər] (línklăter) *The author has confirmed this as his family pronunciation, although others frequently call him* ['lɪŋkleɪtər] (línklayter),

Linlathen [lɪn'læθən] (linláthĕn)

Linley, Viscount ['lɪnlɪ] (línli)

Linlithgow [lɪn'lɪθgoʊ] (linlíthgō) *Appropriate also for the Marquess of ~.*

Linnell, f.n. ['lɪnl] (línnl)

Linnhe, *Loch* ['lɪnɪ] (línni)

Linslade ['lɪnzleɪd] (línz-layd)

Linstead, *f.n.* ['lɪnsted] (línsted)

Lintott, f.n. ['lɪntɒt] (líntot)

Lintrathen [lɪn'treɪðən] (lintráythĕn)

Linzell, f.n. [lɪn'zel] (línzéll)

Lippiatt, f.n. ['lɪpɪət] (líppi-ăt)

Lippiett, f.n. ['lɪpɪət] (líppi-ĕt)

Lipscomb, f.n. ['lɪpskəm] (lípskŏm)

Lipyeat, f.n. ['lɪpɪət] (líppi-ăt)

Lisahally [ˌlɪsəˈhælɪ] (lissăháli)

Lisam, f.n. ['laɪsəm] (líssăm)

Lisbane [lɪs'bæn] (lissbán)

Lisbellaw [ˌlɪsbɪˈlɔ] (lissbĕláw)

Lisbuoy [lɪs'bɔɪ] (lissbóy)

Lisburn ['lɪsbɜːn] (líssburn)

Lisdoonan [lɪs'dunən] (lissdoónăn)

Liskeard [lɪs'kɑːd] (lisskaárd)

Lisle, f.n. [laɪl] (līl)

Lismoyne [lɪs'mɔɪn] (lissmóyn)

Lisnacrea [ˌlɪsnəˈkri] (lissnăkreé)

Lisnalinchy [ˌlɪsnəˈlɪnʃɪ] (lissnálínshi)

Lisnamallard [ˌlɪsnəˈmælərd] (lissnámálărd)

Lisnaskea [ˌlɪsnəˈski] (lissnă-skeé)

Lisney, f.n. ['lɪznɪ] (lízni)

Lissan ['lɪsən] (líssăn)

Lister, f.n. ['lɪstər] (lísster) *Appropriate for Joseph Jackson ~, microscopist, and for his son Joseph, later Baron ~, surgeon.*

Listooder [lɪs'tudər] (lisstoóder)

Listowel, Earl of [lɪs'toʊəl] (lisstṓ-ĕl)

Lisvane [lɪz'veɪn] (lizváyn) *The Welsh name is* Llys-faen, *q.v.*

Litheby, f.n. ['lɪðɪbɪ] (líthĕbi)

Lithgow, f.n. ['lɪθgoʊ] (líthgō)

Littell, f.n. [lɪ'tel] (litéll)

Little Alne ['lɪtl 'ɒn] (líttl áwn); ['lɪtl 'ɒln] (líttl áwln)

Little Creaton ['lɪtl 'kriːtən] (líttl kreétŏn)

Little Cumbrae ['lɪtl 'kʌmbreɪ] (líttl kúmbray)

Little Frome ['lɪtl 'frum] (líttl froóm)

Little Harrowden ['lɪtl 'hærəʊdən] (líttl hárrŏdĕn)

Little Hautbois ['lɪtl 'hɒbɪs] (líttl hóbbiss)

Little Houghton, *Northants.* ['lɪtl 'hoʊtən] (líttl hŏtŏn)

Little Houghton, *Yorks.* ['lɪtl 'hotən] (líttl háwtŏn)
Little Ponton ['lɪtl 'pɒntən] (líttl póntŏn)
Little Staughton ['lɪtl 'stɔtən] (líttl stáwtŏn)
Little Stonham ['lɪtl 'stɒnəm] (líttl stónnăm)
Little Totham ['lɪtl 'tɒtəm] (líttl tóttăm)
Little Wakering ['lɪtl 'weɪkərɪŋ] (líttl wáykĕring)
Little Waltham ['lɪtl 'wɒltəm] (líttl wáwltăm)
Littlebrough ['lɪtlbrə] (líttlbră)
Littlestone-on-Sea ['lɪtlstən ɒn 'si] (líttlstŏn on seé)
Litton Cheney ['lɪtən 'tʃeɪnɪ] (líttŏn cháyni)
Lium, *f.n.* ['liəm] (leé-ŭm)
Liveing, *f.n.* ['lɪvɪŋ] (lívving)
Livens, *f.n.* ['lɪvənz] (lívvĕnz)
Liver Building, *Liverpool* ['laɪvər] (líver)
Liverpool ['lɪvərpul] (lívvĕrpool)
Liverpudlian, *native of Liverpool* [ˌlɪvər'pʌdliən] (livvĕrpúdlián)
Livesey, *f.n.* ['lɪvsɪ] (lívssi); ['lɪvzɪ] (lívzi)
Livingstone, *f.n.* ['lɪvɪŋstən] (lívvingstŏn); ['lɪvɪŋstoʊn] (lívving-stŏn)
Lixwm, *also spelt* Licswm ['lɪksʊm] (lícksoŏm)
Lizard ['lɪzərd] (lízzărd)
Llai, *also spelt* Llay [ɬaɪ] (hl̄í)
Llain-goch [ɬaɪn'goʊx] (hl̄ín-góch)
Llanaelhaiarn [ˌɬænaɪl'haɪərn] (hl̄anīlhí-ärn)
Llanafan [ɬæn'ævən] (hl̄anávvăn)
Llanafan Fawr [ɬæn'ævən 'vaʊər] (hl̄anávvăn vówr)
Llanallgo [ɬæn'æɬgoʊ] (hl̄anáhl̄gŏ)
Llanarmon, *Caernarvon., Denbigh.* [ɬæn'ɑrmɒn] (hl̄anaármon)
Llanarmon Dyffryn Ceiriog [ɬæn'ɑrmɒn 'dʌfrɪn 'kaɪərjɒg] (hl̄anaármon dúffrin kír-yog)
Llanarth ['ɬænɑrθ] (hl̄ánaarth)
Llan-arth Fawr [ɬæn'ɑrθ 'vaʊər] (hl̄an-aárth vówr)
Llanarthney [ɬæn'ɑrθnɪ] (hl̄anaárthni)
Llanasa [ɬæn'æsə] (hl̄anássă)
Llanbadarn Fawr [ɬæn'bædərn 'vaʊər] (hl̄anbáddărn vówr)
Llanbadarn-y-Creuddyn [ɬæn'bædərn ə 'kraɪðɪn] (hl̄anbáddărn ă krf̄thin)
Llanbadoc [ɬæn'bædɒk] (hl̄anbáddock)
Llanbadrig [ɬæn'bædrɪg] (hl̄anbádrig)
Llanbedr, *Brecon., Merioneth* ['ɬænbedər] (hl̄ánbedder)
Llan-bedr, *Monmouth.* [ɬæn'bedər] (hl̄anbédder)
Llanbedr-goch ['ɬænbedər'goʊx] (hl̄ánbedder-góch)
Llanbedrog [ɬæn'bedrɒg] (hl̄anbédrog)
Llanbedrycennin ['ɬænbedərə'kenɪn] (hl̄ánbeddĕr-ă-kénnin)
Llanberis [ɬæn'berɪs] (hl̄anbérriss)

Llanbister [ɬæn'bɪstər] (hl̄anbísster)
Llanblethian [ɬæn'bleðɪən] (hl̄an-bléthi-ăn)
Llanboidy [ɬæn'bɔɪdɪ] (hl̄anbóydi)
Llanbradach [ɬæn'brædəx] (hl̄anbráddách)
Llanbrynmair [ˌɬænbrɪn'maɪər] (hl̄anbrin-mír)
Llancaiach, *also spelt* Llancaeach [ɬæn'kaɪəx] (hl̄an-kí-ách)
Llancynfelin [ˌɬænkɪn'velɪn] (hl̄an-kin-véllin)
Llandaff ['ɬændəf] (lándăff); ['ɬændæf] (hl̄ándaff) *Although the first is widespread local usage, the second is preferred by the clergy of* ~ *Cathedral and by the BBC in Cardiff. The Welsh language form is* Llandaf, *pronounced* [ɬæn'dav] (hl̄andáav).
Llandarcy [ɬæn'dɑrsɪ] (hl̄andaárssi)
Llanddaniel [ɬæn'ðænjəl] (hl̄anthán-yĕl)
Llanddarog [ɬæn'ðærɒg] (hl̄anthárrog)
Llanddeiniol [ɬæn'ðaɪnjɒl] (hl̄anthín-yol)
Llanddeiniolen [ˌɬænðaɪn'jɒlən] (hl̄an-thín-yóllĕn)
Llandderfel [ɬæn'ðɛərvel] (hl̄anthaírvel)
Llanddetty [ɬæn'ðetɪ] (hl̄anthétti)
Llanddeusant, *Anglesey, Carmarthen.* [ɬæn'ðaɪsænt] (hl̄anthíssant)
Llanddew ['ɬændoʊ] (lándŏ); [ɬæn'ðju] (hl̄an-théw)
Llanddewi Aberarth [ɬæn'ðewɪ ˌæbər'arθ] (hl̄anthé-wi abbĕraárth); [ɬæn'ðjuɪ ˌæbər'arθ] (hl̄anthéw-i abbĕraárth)
Llanddewi Brefi [ɬæn'ðewɪ 'breɪvɪ] (hl̄anthé-wi bráyvi); [ɬæn'ðjuɪ 'breɪvɪ] (hl̄anthéw-i bráyvi)
Llanddewi Velfrey [ɬæn'ðewɪ 'velfreɪ] (hl̄anthé-wi vélfray)
Llanddewi'r Cwm [ɬæn'ðewɪər 'kʊm] (hl̄anthé-weer kŏŏm); [ɬæn'ðjuər 'kʊm] (hl̄anthéw-er kŏŏm)
Llanddona [ɬæn'ðɒnə] (hl̄anthónnă)
Llanddowror [ɬæn'ðaʊrɒr] (hl̄anthówror)
Llanddulas [ɬæn'ðɪləs] (hl̄anthílláss)
Llanddyfnan [ɬæn'ðʌvnən] (hl̄anthúvnăn)
Llandebie [ˌɬændə'bier] (hl̄andĕbeé-ay)
Llandecwyn [ɬæn'dekwɪn] (hl̄andéckwin)
Llandefaïlog [ˌɬændə'vaɪlɒg] (hl̄andĕvflog)
Llandefaïlog-fach [ˌɬændə'vaɪlɒg 'vax] (hl̄andĕvflog vaách)
Llandefalle [ˌɬændə'væɬeɪ] (hl̄andĕváhl̄ay)
Llandefeilog [ˌɬændə'vaɪlɒg](hl̄andĕvflog)
Llandegai [ˌɬændə'gaɪ] (hl̄andĕgí)
Llandegfan [ˌɬæn'degvæn] (hl̄andégvan)
Llandegla [ɬæn'deglə] (hl̄andĕglá)
Llandegley [ɬæn'degleɪ] (hl̄andéglay)
Llandeilo *also spelt* Llandilo [ɬæn'daɪloʊ] (hl̄andflŏ)
Llandeilo Graban [ɬæn'daɪloʊ 'græbən] (hl̄andflŏ grábbăn)
Llandeilo'r-fân [ɬæn'daɪlɒr'van] (hl̄andflor-vaán)
Llandeloy [ˌɬændə'lɔɪ] (hl̄andĕlóy)
Llandenny [ɬæn'denɪ] (hl̄andénni)

Llandewi Ystradenny [ɬænˈdewɪ ˌʌstrədˈenɪ] (hlandé-wi usstrádénni); [ɬænˈdjuɪ ˌʌstrədˈenɪ] (ḥlandéw-i ussträdénni)

Llandilo *see* Llandeilo.

Llandinam [ɬænˈdinæm] (ḥlandeénam)
Llandinorwig [ˌɬændɪnˈɔrwɪg] (ḥlandinórwig)
Llandogo [ɬænˈdougou] (ḥlandógŏ)
Llandough [lænˈdɒk] (landóck)
Llandovery [ɬænˈdʌvrɪ] (ḥlandúvvri)
Llandow [lænˈdau] (landów)
Llandre [ˈɬændreɪ] (ḥlándray)
Llandrillo [ɬænˈdrɪɬou] (ḥlandríḥlŏ)
Llandrindod Wells [ɬænˈdrɪndɒd ˈwelz] (ḥlandríndod wéllz)
Llandrinio [ɬænˈdrɪnjou] (ḥlandrín-yŏ)
Llandrygar [ɬænˈdrʌɡɑr] (ḥlandrúggaar)
Llandudno [ɬænˈdɪdnou] (ḥlandídnŏ)
Llandulas [lænˈdɪləs] (ḥlandíllàss)
Llandwrog [ɬænˈdurɒɡ] (ḥlandóˈbrog)
Llandyfodwg [ˌɬændəˈvoudug] (ḥlandăvódŏg)
Llandyfriog [ˌɬændəˈvrɪɒg] (ḥlandăvreé-og)
Llandyfrydog [ˌɬændəˈvrʌdɒg] (ḥlandăvrúddog)
Llandygai [ˌɬændəˈgaɪ] (ḥlandägí)
Llandygwydd [ɬænˈdʌgwɪð] (ḥlandúg-with)
Llandyrnog [ɬænˈdɜrnɒg] (ḥlandúrnog)
Llandysilio [ˌɬændəˈsɪljou](ḥlandǘssíl-yŏ)
Llandysiliogogo [ˌɬændəˈsɪljouˈgougou] (ḥlandǘssíl-yŏ-gógŏ)
Llandysul, *Cardigan., Montgomery.* [ɬænˈdɪsɪl] (ḥlandíssíl); [ɬænˈdʌsɪl] (ḥlandússíl)
Llanedwen [ɬænˈedwɪn] (ḥlanédwĕn)
Llanedy [ɬænˈerdɪ] (ḥlanáydi)
Llanegryn [ɬænˈegrɪn] (ḥlanégrin)
Llanegwad [ɬænˈegwəd] (ḥlanégwàd)
Llaneilian [ɬænˈaɪljən] (ḥlanfí-yăn)
Llanelian [ɬænˈeljən] (ḥlanél-yăn)
Llanelidan [ˌɬænɪˈlidən] (ḥlannĕleédăn)
Llanelieu [ɬænˈɪlju] (ḥlaneélew); [lænˈɪlju] (laneélew)
Llanellen [ɬænˈelɪn] (ḥlanélĕn)
Llanelli, *Brecon., Carmarthen.* [ɬænˈeɬi] (ḥlanéɬi).
Llanelltyd [ɬænˈeɬtɪd] (ḥlanéɬltid)
Llanelly *see* Llanelli.
Llanelwedd [ɬænˈelwɪð] (ḥlanélwĕth)
Llanenddwyn [ɬænˈenðuɪn] (ḥlanénthŏŏ-in)
Llanengan [ɬænˈenən] (ḥlanéng-ăn)
Llanerchymedd [ˌɬænɛərxəˈmeɪð] (ḥlanairchámáyth)
Llanerfyl [ɬænˈɛərvɪl] (ḥlanáírvil)
Llaneugrad [ɬænˈaɪgræd] (ḥlanfgrad)

Llanfabon [ɬænˈvæbən] (ḥlanvábbŏn)
Llanfachreth, *Anglesey, Merioneth* [ɬænˈvæxrəθ] (ḥlanvácḥrĕth)
Llanfaelog [ɬænˈvaɪlɒg] (ḥlanvílog)
Llan-faes [ɬænˈvaɪs] (ḥlanvíss)
Llanfaethlu [ɬænˈvaɪθlɪ] (ḥlanvíthli)
Llanfair [ˈɬænvaɪər] (ḥlánvīr)
Llanfair-ar-y-bryn [ˈɬænvaɪər ær ə ˈbrɪn] (ḥlánvir-arrä-brín)
Llanfair Caereinion [ˈɬænvaɪər kɑrˈaɪnjɒn] (ḥlánvīr kaarín-yon)
Llanfair Clydogau [ˈɬænvaɪər klɪˈdougaɪ] (ḥlánvīr klidŏgí)
Llanfairfechan [ˌɬænvaɪərˈvexən] (ḥlanvīr-véchăn)
Llanfair-is-gaer [ˈɬænvaɪər ɪs ˈgaɪər] (ḥlánvīr-eess-gír)
Llanfair Kilgeddin [ˈɬænvaɪər kɪlˈgedɪn] (ḥlánvīr kilgéddin)
Llanfair Mathafarn Eithaf [ˈɬænvaɪər məθˈæfarn ˈaɪθæv] (ḥlánvīr mätháffaarn íthav)
Llanfair Nant-y-gof [ˈɬænvaɪər ˌnæntəˈgouv] (ḥlánvīr nant-ä-góv)
Llanfair Pwllgwyngyll[1] [ˈɬænvaɪər puɬˈgwɪŋgɪɬ] (ḥlánvīr pooɬl-gwin-giɬl) *The accepted abbreviation is* Llanfair P.G. *At the other end of the scale, however, it is traditionally the longest Welsh place name, and, as such, it appears at the bottom of this page.*
Llanfair Talhaiarn [ˈɬænvaɪər tælˈhaɪərn] (ḥlánvīr tal-hf-ärn)
Llanfairynghornwy [ˌɬænvaɪərəŋˈhornuɪ] (ḥlánvīr-íng-hórnŏŏ-i)
Llanfallteg [ɬænˈvæɬteg] (ḥlanváɬlteg)
Llan-fawr [ɬænˈvauər] (ḥlanvówr)
Llanfechain [ɬænˈvexaɪn] (ḥlanvéchīn)
Llanfechan [ɬænˈvexən] (ḥlanvéchăn)
Llanfechell [ɬænˈvexeɬ] (ḥlanvéchehl)
Llanferres [ɬænˈveres] (ḥlanvérress)
Llan-ffwyst, *also known as* Llanfoist, *q.v.* [ɬænˈfuɪst] (ḥlanfŏŏ-ist)
Llanfigael [ɬænˈvigaɪl] (ḥlanveégīl)
Llanfihangel [ˌɬænvɪˈhæŋəl] (ḥlanvi-háng-ĕl)
Llanfihangel Abercywyn [ˌɬænvɪˈhæŋəl ˌæbərˈkauɪn](ḥlanvi-háng-ĕl abbĕrkówin)
Llanfihangel-ar-arth [ˌɬænvɪˈhæŋəl ɑrˈarθ] (ḥlanviháng-ĕl-aar-aárth)
Llanfihangel Cwm Du [ˌɬænvɪˈhæŋəl kum ˈdi] (ḥlanviháng-ĕl kŏŏm deé)
Llanfihangel Esceifiog [ˌɬænvɪˈhæŋəl esˈkaɪvjɒg] (ḥlanviháng-ĕl eskív-yog)
Llanfihangel Fechan [ˌɬænvɪˈhæŋəl ˈvexən] (ḥlanviháng-ĕl véchăn)
Llanfihangel Glyn Myfyr [ˌɬænvɪˈhæŋəl glɪn ˈmʌvər] (ḥlanviháng-ĕl glin múvver)

---

[1] Llanfair-pwllgwyngyll-gogerychwyrndrobwll-llandysilio-gogogoch [ˈɬænvaɪərpuɬˈgwɪŋgɪɬgouˈgerəˈxwɜrnˈdroubuɬɬændəˈsɪrougougouˈgoux] (ḥlánvīr-pooɬl-gwín-giɬl-gŏgérrä-chwírn-drŏbooɬl-ḥlandǘssílli-ŏ-gŏgŏgóch) *See* Llanfair Pwllgwyngyll *above.*

Llanfihangel Nant Brân [ˌɬænvɪˈhæŋəl nænt ˈbrɑn] (ɬlanvihángg-ĕl nant brâan)

Llanfihangel Rhyd-y-Clafdy [ˌɬænvɪˈhæŋəl hrɪd ə ˈklævdɪ] (ɬlanvihángg-ĕl reed-ă-klávdi)

Llanfihangel Tal-y-llyn [ˌɬænvɪˈhæŋəl ˌtæləˈɬɪn] (ɬlanvihángg-ĕl tal-ă-ɬlín)

Llanfihangel Ystrad [ˌɬænvɪˈhæŋəl ˈʌstræd] (ɬlanvihángg-ĕl ússtrad)

Llanfilo [ɬænˈvɪlou] (ɬlanvíllō)

Llanfoist, *also known as* **Llan-ffwyst**, *q.v.* [ɬænˈvɔɪst] (ɬlanvóysst)

Llanfrechfa [ɬænˈvrexvə] (ɬlanvréchvă)

Llanfrothen [ɬænˈvrɒθən] (ɬlanvróthĕn)

Llanfrynach [ɬænˈvrʌnəx] (ɬlanvrúnnăch)

Llanfwrog [ɬænˈvurɒg] (ɬlanvóŏrog)

Llanfyllin [ɬænˈvʌɬɪn] (ɬlanvúɬlin)

Llanfynydd, *Carmarthen.*, *Flint.* [ɬænˈvʌnɪð] (ɬlanvúnnith)

Llanfyrnach [ɬænˈvɜrnəx] (ɬlanvúrnăch)

Llangadfan [ɬænˈgædvən] (ɬlan-gádván)

Llangadog [ɬænˈgædɒg] (ɬlan-gáddog)

Llangadwaladr, *Anglesey*, *Denbigh.* [ˌɬænɡædˈwælədər] (ɬlan-gadwáládĕr)

Llangaffo [ɬænˈgæfou] (ɬlan-gáffō)

Llangammarch [ɬænˈgæmɑrx] (ɬlan-gámmaarch)

Llanganten [ɬænˈgæntən] (ɬlan-gántĕn)

Llangar [ˈɬæŋgɑr] (ɬláng-gár)

Llangathen [ɬænˈgæθən] (ɬlan-gáthĕn)

Llangattock, *Barony of* [læŋˈgætək] (lang-gáttŏk)

Llangattock [ɬænˈgætɒk] (ɬlan-gáttock)

Llangedwyn [ɬænˈgedwɪn] (ɬlan-gédwin)

Llangefni [ɬænˈgevnɪ] (ɬlan-gévni)

Llangeinor [ɬænˈgaɪnɒr] (ɬlan-gínor)

Llangeinwen [ɬænˈgaɪnwen] (ɬlan-gínwen)

Llangeitho [ɬænˈgaɪθou] (ɬlan-gíthō)

Llangeler [ɬænˈgelər] (ɬlan-géller)

Llangelynin, *Caernarvon.*, *Merioneth* [ˌɬænɡɪˈlʌnɪn] (ɬlan-gĕlúnnin)

Llangendeirne [ˌɬænɡɪnˈdaɪərn] (ɬlan-gĕndírn)

Llangennech [ɬænˈgenəx] (ɬlan-génnĕch)

Llangenny [ɬænˈgenɪ] (ɬlan-génni)

Llangernyw [ɬænˈgeərnju] (ɬlan-gaírnew)

Llangian [ɬænˈgiən] (ɬlan-geé-ăn)

Llangibby [ɬænˈgɪbɪ] (ɬlan-gíbbi)

Llanginning, *now* **Llangynin**, *q.v.* [ɬænˈgɪnɪŋ] (ɬlan-gínning)

Llangiwg [ɬænˈgjuk] (ɬlan-géwk)

Llanglydwen [ɬænˈglɪdwen] (ɬlan-glídwen)

Llangoed [ˈɬæŋgɔɪd] (ɬláng-goyd)

Llangoedmor [ɬænˈgɔɪdmɒr] (ɬlan-góydmor)

Llangollen [ɬænˈgɒlən] (ɬlan-góɬlĕn)

Llangorse [ɬænˈgɔrs] (ɬlan-górss)

Llangower, *also spelt* **Llangywer**, **Llangywair** [ɬænˈgauər] (ɬlan-gówer)

Llangranog [ɬænˈgrænɒg] (ɬlan-gránnog)

Llangristiolus [ˌɬænɡrɪstɪˈɒlɪs] (ɬlan-gristi-ólliss)

Llangrwyney, *also spelt* **Llangrwyn** [ɬænˈgruɪneɪ] (ɬlan-groŏ-inay)

Llangua [ɬænˈgiə] (ɬlan-geé-ă)

Llangunllo [ɬænˈgʌnɬou] (ɬlan-gún-ɬlō)

Llangunnock [ɬænˈgʌnɒk] (ɬlan-gúnnock)

Llangunnor [ɬænˈgʌnɒr] (ɬlan-gúnnor)

Llangurig [ɬænˈgɪrɪg] (ɬlan-gírrig)

Llangwm, *Denbigh.*, *Pembroke.* [ˈɬæŋgʊm] (ɬláng-gŏŏm)

Llan-gwm, *Monmouth.* [ɬænˈgʊm] (ɬlan-gŏŏm)

Llangwnnadl [ɬænˈgʊnædl] (ɬlan-gŏŏn-addl)

Llangwstenin [ˌɬænɡʊstˈenɪn] (ɬlan-gŏŏsténnin)

Llangwyfan [ɬænˈguɪvən] (ɬlan-goŏ-ivăn)

Llangwyllog [ɬænˈgwɪɬɒg] (ɬlan-gwíɬlog)

Llangwyryfon [ˌɬænɡwɪərˈʌvən] (ɬlan-gweerúvvŏn)

Llangybi, *Caernarvon.*, *Cardigan.* [ɬænˈgʌbɪ] (ɬlan-gúbbi)

Llangyfelach [ˌɬænɡəˈveləx] (ɬlan-gŭvéllăch)

Llangynhafal [ˌɬænɡʌnˈhævəl] (ɬlan-gun-hávvăl)

Llangynidr [ɬænˈgʌnɪdər] (ɬlan-gúnnider)

Llangyniew [ɬænˈgʌnju] (ɬlan-gúnnew)

Llangynin, *formerly* **Llanginning**, *q.v.* [ɬænˈgʌnɪn] (ɬlan-gúnnin)

Llangynog, *Brecon.*, *Carmarthen.*, *Montgomery.* [ɬænˈgʌnɒg] (ɬlan-gúnnog)

Llangynwyd [ɬænˈgʌnuɪd] (ɬlan-gúnnoŏ-id)

Llangywair *see* Llangower.

Llangywer *see* Llangower.

Llanhamlach [ɬænˈhæmlæx] (ɬlan-hámlach)

Llanharan [ɬænˈhærən] (ɬlan-hárrăn)

Llanhilleth [ɬænˈhɪləθ] (ɬlan-híllĕth)

Llanhowell [ɬænˈhauəl] (ɬlan-hówĕl)

Llanidan [ɬænˈidən] (ɬlaneédăn)

Llanidloes [ɬænˈɪdlɔɪs] (ɬlanídloyss)

Llaniestyn [ɬænˈjestɪn] (ɬlan-yésstin)

Llanigon [ɬænˈaɪgən] (ɬlanígŏn)

Llanilar [ɬænˈilɑr] (ɬlaneélaar)

Llanishen, *Glamorgan.*, *Monmouth.* [ɬænˈɪʃən] (ɬlaníshĕn)

Llanllawddog [ɬænˈɬauðɒg] (ɬlan-ɬlówthog)

Llanllechid [ɬænˈɬexɪd] (ɬlan-ɬléchid)

Llanlleonfel [ˌɬænɬeɪˈɒnvel] (ɬlan-ɬlayónvel)

Llanllowel [ɬænˈɬauəl] (ɬlan-ɬlówĕl)

Llanllugan [ɬænˈɬigən] (ɬlan-ɬlíggăn)

Llanllwchaiarn, *Cardigan.*, *Montgomery.* [ˌɬænɬuxˈhaɪərn] (ɬlan-ɬlooch-hí-árn)

Llanllwni [ɬænˈɬunɪ] (ɬlan-ɬlŏŏni)

Llanllyfni [ɬænˈɬʌvnɪ] (ɬlan-ɬlúvni)

Llanmorlais [ɬænˈmɔrlaɪs] (ɬlan-mórlíss)

Llannefydd [ɬænˈevið] (ɬlanévvith)

Llan-non [ɬænˈɒn] (ɬlanón)

Llannor [ˈɬænɒr] (ɬlánnor)

Llanon [ɬænˈɒn] (ɬlanón)

Llanpumsaint, *formerly spelt* Llanpump-saint [ˌɫæn'pɪmsaɪnt] (ɫlan-pímssïnt)

Llanrhaeadr ym Mochnant [ɫæn-'hraɪədər ʌm 'mʊxnənt] (ɫlanrf-áder um móchnänt)

Llanrhaiadr yn Cinmerch [ɫæn'hraɪədər ʌn 'kɪnmɜrx] (ɫlanrf-áder un kínmerch)

Llanrhidian [ɫæn'hrɪdjən] (ɫlan-ríd-yän)

Llanrhychwyn [ɫæn'hrʌxwɪn] (ɫlanrúch-win)

Llanrhyddlad [ɫæn'hrɪðlæd] (ɫlanríthlad)

Llanrhystyd [ɫæn'hrʌstɪd] (ɫlanrússtid)

Llanrug [ɫæn'rɪg] (ɫlanreég)

Llanrwst [ɫæn'rʊst] (ɫlanroóst)

Llansadwrn, *Anglesey, Carmarthen.* [ɫæn'sæduərn] (ɫlan-sáddǒörn)

Llansaint ['ɫæn'saɪnt] (ɫlán-sïnt)

Llansamlet [ɫæn'sæmlɪt] (ɫlan-sámlĕt)

Llansantffraid, *Cardigan., Montgomery.* [ˌɫænsænt'fraɪd] (ɫlan-santfríd)

Llansawel [ɫæn'sauəl] (ɫlan-sówĕl)

Llansilin [ɫæn'sɪlɪn] (ɫlan-síllin)

Llanspyddid [ɫæn'spʌðɪd] (ɫlan-spúthid)

Llanstadwell [ɫæn'stædwel] (ɫlan-stádwel)

Llanstephan [ɫæn'stefən] (ɫlan-stéffän)

Llantarnam [ɫæn'tɑrnəm] (ɫlantaárnám)

Llanthony [ɫæn'tounɪ] (ɫlantǒni)

Llantilio [ɫæn'tɪljou] (ɫlantíl-yō)

Llantilio Crossenny [ɫæn'tɪljou krʊ-'senɪ] (ɫlantíl-yō krossénni)

Llantood ['læntud] (lántood)

Llantrisaint [ɫæn'trɪsaɪnt] (ɫlantríssïnt)

Llantrisaint Fawr, *also spelt* Llantris-sent Fawr [ɫæn'trɪsənt 'vauər] (ɫlan-tríssänt vówr)

Llantrisant [ɫæn'trɪsənt] (ɫlantríssänt)

Llantrissent Fawr *see* Llantrisaint Fawr.

Llantrithyd [ɫæn'trɪθɪd] (ɫlantríthid)

Llantwit Fardre ['ɫæntwɪt 'vɑrdreɪ] (ɫlántwit vaárdray)

Llantwit Major ['læntwɪt 'meɪdʒər] (lántwit máyjŏr)

Llantysilio [ˌɫæntə'sɪljou] (ɫlantüssíl-yō)

Llanuwchllyn [ɫæn'juxlɪn] (ɫlannéwch-lin)

Llanvaches [ɫæn'væxɪs] (ɫlanváchĕss)

Llanvair Discoed ['ɫænvaɪər 'dɪskoɪd] (ɫlánvïr dísskoyd)

Llanvetherine [ɫæn'veθrɪn] (ɫlanvéthrin) *The Welsh form is* Llanwytherin, *q.v.*

Llanwarne [ɫæn'worn] (ɫlan-wórn)

Llanwddyn [ɫæn'ʊðɪn] (ɫlanǒŏthin)

Llanwenarth [ɫæn'wenɑrθ] (ɫlan-wénaarth)

Llanwenllwyfo [ˌɫænwɪn'ɫuɪvou] (ɫlan-wĕn-ɫǒŏ-ivŏ)

Llanwenog [ɫæn'wenɒg] (ɫlan-wénnog)

Llanwern [ɫæn'wɜrn] (ɫlan-waírn)

Llanwinio [ɫæn'wɪnjou] (ɫlan-wín-yō)

Llanwnda, *Caernarvon., Pembroke.* [ɫæn'ʊndə] (ɫlanǒŏndä)

Llanwnen [ɫæn'ʊnən] (ɫlanǒŏnĕn)

Llanwnog [ɫæn'ʊnɒg] (ɫlanǒŏnog)

Llanwonno [ɫæn'wʌnou] (ɫlan-wúnnŏ)

Llanwrda [ɫæn'ʊərdə] (ɫlanǒŏrdä)

Llanwrin [ɫæn'ʊrɪn] (ɫlanǒŏrin)

Llanwrthwl [ɫæn'ʊərθʊl] (ɫlanǒŏrthǒŏl)

Llanwrtyd [ɫæn'ʊərtɪd] (ɫlanǒŏrtid)

Llanwyddelan [ˌɫænwɪ'ðelən] (ɫlanwi-théllän)

Llanwytherin [ˌɫænwɪ'θerɪn] (ɫlanwi-thérrin) *The English form is* Llan-vetherine, *q.v.*

Llanyblodwell [ˌɫænə'blɒdwəl] (ɫlanä-blódwĕl)

Llanybyther [ˌɫænə'bʌðər] (ɫlanäbúther)

Llan-y-cefn [ˌɫænə'kevn] (ɫlanäkévvn)

Llanychâr [ˌɫænə'xɑr] (ɫlanáchaár)

Llanychllwydog [ˌɫænəx'ɫuɪdɒg] (ɫlan-äch-ɫǒŏ-idog)

Llanycil [ɫæn'ʌkɪl] (ɫlanúckil)

Llan-y-crwys [ˌɫænə'kruɪs] (ɫlanäkrǒŏ-iss)

Llanymawddwy [ˌɫænə'mauðuɪ] (ɫlanä-mówthǒŏ-i)

Llanymynech [ˌɫænə'mʌnəx] (ɫlanä-múnnĕch)

Llanynghenedl [ˌɫænəŋ'henɪdl] (ɫlanüng-hénnĕdl)

Llanynis [ɫæn'ʌnɪs] (ɫlanúnniss)

Llanynys ,Rhewl [ɫæn'ʌnɪs hrɪ'ul] (ɫlan-únniss ri-oól)

Llanyrafon [ˌɫænər'ævən] (ɫlanárávvŏn)

Llanyre [ɫæn'ɪər] (ɫlaneér)

Llanystumdwy [ˌɫænə'stɪmduɪ] (ɫlanä-stímdŏŏ-i)

Llawhaden [ɫau'hædən] (ɫlow-háddĕn)

Llay *see* Llai.

Llechryd ['ɫexrɪd] (ɫléchrid)

Llech-y-Fedach [ˌɫeɪxə'vedəx] (ɫlaych-ä-véddäch)

Llechylched [ɫeɪx'ʌlxɪd] (ɫlaychúlchĕd)

Lletty Brongu ['ɫetɪ 'brɒŋgɪ] (ɫlétti bróng-gi)

Llewellin, Barony of [lə'welɪn] (lĕ-wéllin)

Llewellyn, f.n. [ɫə'welɪn] (ɫlĕ-wéllin) ; [lə'welɪn] (lĕ-wéllin)

Llewelyn, f.n. [[ɫə'welɪn] (ɫlĕ-wéllin) ; [lə'welɪn] (lĕ-wéllin) ; [lu'elɪn] (loo-éllin)

Lleyn Peninsula [ɫin] (ɫleen)

Llidiart-y-Waun ['ɫɪdjɑrtə'waɪn] (ɫlíd-yaart-ä-wín)

Lligwy *see* Llugwy.

Llinos, Welsh C.n. ['ɫɪnɒs] (ɫleénoss)

Llithfaen ['ɫɪθvaɪn] (ɫlíth-vīn)

Lliwedd ['ɫiweð] (ɫleé-weth)

Llongborth ['ɫɒŋbɔrθ] (ɫlóng-borth)

Llowes ['ɫouɪs] (ɫlǒ-ĕss)

Lloyd, f.n. [lɔɪd] (loyd) *Appropriate also for Baron* ~.

Lloyd George of Dwyfor, Earl ['lɔɪd 'dʒɔrdʒ əv 'duɪvər] (lóyd jórj ŏv dǒŏ-i-vor)

Llugwy, *also spelt* Lligwy ['ɫiguɪ] (ɫleégŏŏ-i)

Llwchwr ['ɫuxuər] (ɫloóchǒŏr)

Llwydcoed ['ɫuɪdkɒd] (ɫlǒŏ-idkod)

Llwydiarth ['ɬʊɪdjarθ] (ɬlṓо-id-yaarth)
Llwyn Madoc [ˌɬʊɪn 'mædɒk] (ɬlṓо-in máddock)
Llwyn-on Reservoir ['ɬʊɪn'ɒn] (ɬlṓо-in-ón)
Llwyncelyn, *Cardigan., Pembroke.* [ˌɬʊɪn'kelɪn] (ɬlṓо-in-kéllin)
Llwyngwril [ˌɬʊɪn'ɡʊərɪl] (ɬlṓо-in-gṓоril)
Llwynhendy [ˌɬʊɪn'hendɪ] (ɬlṓо-in-héndi)
Llwynypia [ˌɬʊɪnə'pɪə] (ɬlṓо-in-ápeè-ă)
Llyn Cau [ɬɪn 'kaɪ] (ɬlin kí)
Llyn Mymbyr [ɬɪn 'mʌmbər] (ɬlin múmber)
Llyn Ogwen [ɬɪn 'ɒgwen] (ɬlin ógwen)
Llyn Padarn [ɬɪn 'pædərn] (ɬlin páddărn)
Llyn Safaddan [ˌɬɪn sə'væðən] (ɬlin săváthăn)
Llynclys ['ɬʌŋklɪs] (ɬúnkliss); ['ɬʌŋklɪs] (ɬlúnkliss)
Llysfaen, *Denbigh.* ['ɬɪsvaɪn] (ɬleèssvín)
Llys-faen, *Glamorgan* [ɬɪs'vaɪn] (ɬleèssvín) *The English name is* Lisvane, *q.v.*
Llys-wen [ɬɪs'wen] (ɬleèsswén)
Llysworney [ɬɪz'wɜrnɪ] (lizwúrni)
Llys-y-frân [ˌɬɪsə'vran] (ɬleèssăvraán)
Llywelyn, *f.n.* [ɬə'welɪn] (ɬlĕ-wéllin)
Loanhead ['loʊn'hed] (lṓn-héd)
Lobjoit, *f.n.* ['lɒbdʒɔɪt] (lóbjoyt)
Lobscombe Corner ['lɒbzkəm 'kɔrnər] (lóbzkŏm kórner)
Loch, Baron [lɒx] (loch)
Loch an Athain ['lɒx ən 'an] (lóch ăn aán)
Loch na Creitheach ['lɒx nə 'krihəx] (lóch nă kreè-hăch)
Loch an Eilean ['lɒx ən 'ilən] (lóch ăn eèlăn)
Loch of Lintrathen ['lɒx əv lin'treɪðən] (lóch ŏv lintráythĕn)
Loch of the Lowes ['lɒx əv ðə 'laʊz] (lóch ŏv thĕ lówz)
Loch nan Uamh ['lɒx nən 'uəv] (lóch năn oó-ăv)
Lochaber [lɒ'xabər] (lochaáber)
Lochailort [lɒ'xaɪlərt] (lochflórt)
Lochaline [lɒ'xælɪn] (lochálin)
Lochalsh [lɒ'xælʃ] (lochálsh)
Lochboisdale [lɒx'bɔɪzdeɪl] (lochbóyzdayl)
Lochearnhead [lɒ'xɜrn'hed] (lochérnhéd)
Lochee [lɒ'xi] (locheè)
Locheilside [lɒ'xil'saɪd] (locheèl-síd)
Locheport [lɒ'xɪpɔrt] (locheèport)
Lochgelly [lɒx'gelɪ] (lochgélli)
Lochgilphead [lɒx'gɪlphed] (lochgílphed)
Lochiel, *f.n.* [lɒ'xil] (locheèl)
Lochinvar [ˌlɒxɪn'var] (lochinvaár)
Lochinver [lɒ'xɪnvər] (lochínver)
Lochlea ['lɒxlɪ] (lóchli)
Lochlee [lɒx'li] (lochleè)
Lochluichart [lɒx'luɪxərt] (lochloó-ichărt); [lɒx'luxərt] (lochloóchărt)

Lochmaben [lɒx'meɪbən] (lochmáybĕn)
Lochmaddy [lɒx'mædɪ] (lochmáddi)
Lochrane, *f.n.* ('lɒxrən] (lóchrăn); ['lɒxrən] (lókrăn)
Lochranza [lɒx'rænzə] (loch-ránză)
Lochtreighead [lɒx'trighed] (lochtreèghed)
Lockerbie ['lɒkərbɪ] (lóckĕrbi)
Lockhart, *f.n.* ['lɒkərt] (lóckărt); ['lɒkhart] (lóck-haart) *The first is appropriate for the family name,* Bruce ~.
Lockie, *f.n.* ['lɒkɪ] (lócki)
Lockinge, East and **West** ['lɒkɪndʒ] (lóckinj)
Lockspeiser, *f.n.* ['lɒkspaɪzər] (lóckspizer)
Lockyer, *f.n.* ['lɒkjər] (lóck-yer)
Locock, *f.n.* ['loʊkɒk] (lókock)
Loddiswell ['lɒdɪzwel] (lóddizwel)
Loddon, River ['lɒdən] (lóddŏn)
Loder, *f.n.* ['loʊdər] (lóder)
Loelia, *C.n.* ['lilɪə] (leèliă)
Loewe, *f.n.* [loʊ] (lō); ['loʊɪ] (lō-i)
Loewen, *f.n.* ['loʊɪn] (lō-ĕn)
Lofthouse, *f.n.* ['lɒfthaʊs] (lóft-howss)
Logan, *f.n.* ['loʊgən] (lógăn)
Logie, *f.n.* ['loʊgɪ] (lógi)
Logie, *Fife, Moray.* ['loʊgɪ] (lógi)
Logiealmond [ˌloʊgɪ'amənd] (lōgi-aámŏnd)
Logie Coldstone [ˌloʊgɪ 'koʊlstən] (lōgi kólsstŏn)
Logierait [ˌloʊgə'reɪt] (lōgĕráyt); [ˌloʊgɪ'reɪt] (lōgiráyt)
Logue, *f.n.* ['loʊg] (lōg)
Lois, *C.n.* ['loʊɪs] (lṓ-iss)
Loman, *f.n.* ['loʊmən] (lṓmăn)
Lomas, *f.n.* ['loʊməs] (lṓmăss)
Lombe, *f.n.* ['loʊm] (lōm)
Lomond, Loch ['loʊmənd] (lṓmŏnd)
Londesborough, Baron ['lɒndzbərə] (lóndzbŭră)
London ['lʌndən] (lúndŏn)
London Colney ['lʌndən 'koʊnɪ] (lúndŏn kóni)
Londonderry [ˌlʌndən'derɪ] (lundŏndérri); ['lʌndəndərɪ] (lúndŏndĕri) *The second is appropriate for the Marquess of ~.*
Long Mynd ['lɒŋ mɪnd] (lóng minnd)
Long Stow ['lɒŋ stoʊ] (lóng stō)
Longannet Point [lɒŋ'ænɪt] (long-ánnĕt)
Longforgan [lɒŋ'forgən] (longfórgăn)
Longformacus [ˌlɒŋfər'meɪkəs] (longförmáykŭss)
Longham ['lɒŋ'hæm] (lóng-hám)
Longhorsley ['lɒŋ'hɔrslɪ] (lóng-hórssli)
Longhoughton ['lɒŋ'haʊtən] (lóng-hówtŏn); ['lɒŋ'hoʊtən] (lóng-hótŏn)
Longleat ['lɒŋlit] (lóng-leet)
Longlevens ['lɒŋ'levənz] (lóng-lévvĕnz)
Longney ['lɒŋnɪ] (lóng-ni)
Longnor ['lɒŋnər] (lóng-nŏr)
Longsleddale [lɒŋ'slɪdl] (long-slíddl)

Longsowerby [lɒŋ'sauərbɪ] (long-sówĕrbi)
Longuet, *f.n.* ['lɒŋgɪt] (lóng-gĕt)
Lonie, *f.n.* ['louni] (lóni)
Lonmay [lɒn'meɪ] (lonmáy)
Lon-y-Glyder ['loun ə 'glɪdər] (lón ă glídder)
Looe [lu] (loo)
Loose [luz] (looz)
Loosley Row ['luzlɪ 'rou] (loózli rṓ)
Lorenz, *f.n.* ['lɒrənz] (lórrĕnz)
Loretto School [lə'retou] (lŏréttō)
Lorettonian, *one educated at Loretto School* [ˌlɒrɪ'tounɪən] (lorrĕtṓniăn)
Lorie, *f.n.* ['lɒrɪ] (lórri)
Lorimer, *f.n.* ['lɒrɪmər] (lórrimer)
Lorne, *f.n. and C.n.* [lɔrn] (lorn)
Lorne [lɔrn] (lorn) *Appropriate also for the Marquess of ~ and for the Firth of ~.*
Lorrimer, *f.n.* ['lɒrɪmər] (lórrimer)
Loseley Park, *Surrey* ['louzlɪ 'park] (lṓzli paárk)
Loshak, *f.n.* ['loufæk] (lṓ-shack)
Lossiemouth [ˌlɒsɪ'mauθ] (lossimówth)
Lostock Hall ['lɒstɒk 'hɔl] (lósstock háwl)
Lostwithiel [lɒst'wɪθɪəl] (losstwíthi-ĕl)
Lothbury, *City of London* ['louθbərɪ] (lṓthbŭri); ['lɒθbərɪ] (lóthbŭri)
Lothian, *Marquess of* ['louðɪən] (lṓthi-ăn)
Lothians, The ['louðɪənz] (lṓthiănz)
Lotterby, *f.n.* ['lɒtərbɪ] (lóttĕrbi)
Louarch, *f.n.* ['louərk] (lṓ-ärk)
Loudan, *f.n.* ['laudən] (lówdăn)
Loudon, *f.n.* ['laudən] (lówdŏn)
Loudoun, *f.n.* ['laudən] (lówdŏn)
Loudoun ['laudən] (lówdŏn) *Appropriate also for the Countess of ~.*
Lough, *f.n.* [lʌf] (luff); [lou] (lṓ); [lɒx] (loch)
Loughans, *f.n.* ['lʌfənz] (lúffănz)
Loughborough ['lʌfbərə] (lúffbŭră)
Loughbrickland [lɒx'brɪklənd] (loch-brícklănd)
Loughgall [lɒx'gɔl] (lochgáwl)
Loughgiel [lɒx'giːl] (lochgeél)
Loughlin, *f.n.* ['lɒxlɪn] (lóchlin); ['lɒklɪn] (lócklin)
Loughmuck [lɒx'mʌk] (lochmúck)
Loughor ['lʌxər] (lúchŏr)
Loughran, *f.n.* ['lɒxrən] (lóchrăn)
Loughrigg ['lʌfrɪg] (lúffrig)
Loughton, *Bucks., Essex* ['lautən] (lówtŏn)
Loukes, *f.n.* [lauks] (lowks)
Lourie, *f.n.* ['lauərɪ] (lówri)
Lousada, *f.n.* [lu'sadə] (loossaádă); [lu'zadə] (loozaádă)
Lousley, *f.n.* ['lauzlɪ] (lówzli)
Louth, *Baron* [lauθ] (lowth)
Louth [lauθ] (lowth)
Loutit, *f.n.* ['lutɪt] (loótit)
Louttit, *f.n.* ['lutɪt] (loótit)
Lovat, *Baron* ['lʌvət] (lúvvăt)
Lovejoy, *f.n.* ['lʌvdʒɔɪ] (lúvjoy)

Lovell, *f.n.* ['lʌvl] (lúvvl)
Loveridge, *f.n.* ['lʌvrɪdʒ] (lúvrij)
Lovett, *f.n.* ['lʌvɪt] (lúvvĕt)
Loveys, *f.n.* ['lʌvɪz] (lúvviz)
Lovibond, *f.n.* ['lʌvɪbɒnd] (lúvvibond)
Lovill, *f.n.* ['lʌvɪl] (lúvvil)
Low, *f.n.* [lou] (lṓ)
Lowater, *f.n.* ['louətər] (lṓ-ăter)
Lowbury, *f.n.* ['loubərɪ] (lṓbŭri)
Lowca ['laukə] (lówkă)
Low Coniscliffe ['lou 'kɒnɪsklɪf] (lṓ kónniss-kliff)
Lowder, *f.n.* ['laudər] (lówder)
Lowdham ['laudəm] (lówdăm)
Lowe, *f.n.* [lou] (lṓ)
Lowenthal, *f.n.* ['louɪntæl] (lṓ-ĕntal)
Lower Halstow ['louər 'hælstou] (lṓ-er hálstō)
Lower Heyford, *Northants.* ['louər 'heɪfərd] (lṓ-er háyfŏrd)
Lower Heyford, *Oxon., also sometimes called Heyford at Bridge* ['louər 'heɪfərd] (lṓ-er háyfŏrd)
Lowes, *f.n.* [louz] (lōz)
Lowesby ['louzbɪ] (lṓzbi)
Lowestoft ['loustɒft] (lṓsstoft); ['loustəft] (lṓsstŏft); ['loustəf] (lṓsstŏf)
Loweswater ['louzwɒtər] (lṓzwawter)
Lowick, *Lancs., Northants.* ['louɪk] (lṓ-ick)
Lowick, *Northumberland* ['louɪk] (lṓ-ick); ['lauɪk] (lówick)
Lowis, *f.n.* ['louɪs] (lṓ-iss); ['lauɪs] (lówiss)
Lowke, *f.n.* [louk] (lōk)
Lowles, *f.n.* [loulz] (lōlz); [laulz] (lowlz)
Lown, *f.n.* [laun] (lown)
Lownie, *f.n.* ['launɪ] (lówni)
Lowry, *f.n.* ['lauərɪ] (lówri)
Lowson, *f.n.* ['lousən] (lṓssŏn)
Lowther, *f.n.* ['lauðər] (lówther); ['louðər] (lṓther)
Lowther ['lauðər] (lówther)
Lowthers, The ['lauðərz] (lówthĕrz)
Lowthian, *f.n.* ['louðɪən] (lṓthiăn)
Lowton ['loutən] (lṓtŏn)
Loydall, *f.n.* ['lɔɪdl] (loydl)
Lozells [lou'zelz] (lōzéllz)
Luard, *f.n.* ['luard] (loó-aard)
Lubbock, *f.n.* ['lʌbək] (lúbbŏk)
Lubenham ['lʌbənəm] (lúbbĕnăm)
Lubnaig, *Loch* ['lubneɪg] (loób-nayg); ['lubnɪg] (loób-nig)
Lucan, *Earl of* ['lukən] (loó-kăn)
Lucas, *f.n.* ['lukəs] (loókăss)
Lucasian, *pertaining to Lucas* [lu'keɪzɪən] (lookáyziăn)
Luccombe ['lʌkəm] (lúckŏm)
Luchford, *f.n.* ['lʌtʃfərd] (lútchfŏrd)
Lucock, *f.n.* ['lʌkɒk] (lúckock)
Lucraft, *f.n.* ['lukraft] (loó-kraaft)
Luddesdown ['lʌdzdaun] (lúdzdown)
Ludgershall ['lʌdgərʃəl] (lúd-gĕr-shăl); ['lʌgərʃəl] (lúggĕr-shăl)
Ludgvan ['lʌdʒən] (lújjăn)
Ludlow ['lʌdlou] (lúdlō)

Luffness [lʌf'nes] (luff-néss)
Lugar ['lugər] (loo͞gǎr)
Lugard, *Barony of* [lu'gard] (loogáard)
Lugg, *f.n.* [lʌg] (lug)
Lugwardine ['lʌgwərdin] (lúgwǎrdeen)
Luib ['luɪb] (loo͞-ib)
Luing [lɪŋ] (ling)
Luker, *f.n.* ['lukər] (loo͞-ker)
Lulsgate ['lʌlzgeɪt] (lúllzgayt)
Lumley, *f.n.* ['lʌmlɪ] (lúmli)
Lummis, *f.n.* ['lʌmɪs] (lúmmiss)
Lumphanan [ləm'fænən] (lŭmfánnăn)
Lumsden, *f.n.* ['lʌmzdən] (lúmzdĕn)
Lunan, *f.n.* ['lunən] (loo͞nǎn)
Lunan ['lunən] (loo͞nǎn)
Luncarty ['lʌŋkərtɪ] (lúnkǎrti)
Lund, *f.n.* [lʌnd] (lund)
Lundie, *f.n.* ['lʌndɪ] (lúndi)
Lune, *f.n.* [lun] (loon)
Lune, *River* [lun] (loon)
Lunghi, *f.n.* ['lʌŋgɪ] (lúng-gi)
Lunnes, *f.n.* ['lʌnɪs] (lúnnĕss)
Lunt, *f.n.* [lʌnt] (lunt)
Lupino, *f.n.* [lu'pinoʊ] (loo͞peénō)
Lupton, *f.n.* ['lʌptən] (lúptŏn)
Lurgan ['lɜrgən] (lúrgǎn) *Appropriate also for Baron* ~.
Lurgashall ['lɜrgəʃəl] (lúrgǎ-shǎl)
Lurigethan [ˌlʌrɪ'giən] (lurrigeé-ǎn)
Luscombe, *f.n.* ['lʌskəm] (lússkŏm)
Lush, *f.n.* [lʌʃ] (lush)
Luss [lʌs] (luss)
Lussa ['lʌsə] (lússǎ)
Lustgarten, *f.n.* ['lʌstgartən] (lústgaartĕn)
Lustleigh ['lʌstlɪ] (lústlee)
Lutener, *f.n.* ['lutənər] (loo͞tĕner)
Luton ['lutən] (loo͞tŏn)
Luttrell, *f.n.* ['lʌtrəl] (lúttrĕl)
Lutwyche, *f.n.* ['lʌtwɪtʃ] (lútwitch)
Lutyens, *f.n.* ['lʌtjənz] (lút-yĕnz) *Appropriate for Sir Edward* ~, *architect, and Elizabeth* ~, *composer.*
Luxulyan [lʌk'sɪljən] (luckssíl-yǎn); [lʌk'sʌljən] (luckssúl-yǎn)
Luya, *f.n.* ['lujə] (loo͞-yǎ)
Luyt, *f.n.* [leɪt] (layt)
Lyall, *f.n.* ['laɪəl] (lí-ǎl); [laɪl] (lil)
Lybster ['laɪbstər] (líbster)
Lyburn, *f.n.* ['laɪbɜrn] (líburn)
Lycett, *f.n.* ['laɪsɪt] (líssĕt)
Lydd [lɪd] (lid)
Lydden ['lɪdən] (líddĕn)
Lydekker, *f.n.* [lɪ'dekər] (liddécker); [laɪ'dekər](lídécker); ['laɪdekər](lídecker)
Lyden, *f.n.* ['laɪdən] (lídĕn)
Lydford, *f.n.* ['lɪdfərd] (lídfŏrd)
Lydgate ['lɪdgɪt] (líd-git); ['lɪgɪt] (líggit)
Lydiard Park, *Wilts.* ['lɪdɪərd 'park] (líddiǎrd paáark)
Lydiate ['lɪdɪət] (líddiǎt)
Lydney ['lɪdnɪ] (líd-ni)
Lydway ['laɪdweɪ] (lídway)
Lyell, *f.n.* ['laɪəl] (lí-ĕl)
Lyford, *f.n.* ['laɪfərd] (lífŏrd)

Lygoe, *f.n.* ['laɪgoʊ] (lígō)
Lygon, *f.n.* ['lɪgən] (líggŏn)
Lyle, *f.n.* [laɪl] (lil)
Lyly, *f.n.* ['lɪlɪ] (lílli) *Usually associated also with John* ~, *16th-c. dramatist and novelist.*
Lymbery, *f.n.* ['lɪmbərɪ] (límbĕri)
Lyme Regis ['laɪm 'ridʒɪs] (lím reéjiss)
Lyminge ['lɪmɪndʒ] (límminj); ['laɪmɪndʒ] (lífminj)
Lymington ['lɪmɪŋtən] (límmingtŏn) *Appropriate also for Viscount* ~.
Lyminster ['lɪmɪnstər] (límminster)
Lymm [lɪm] (lim)
Lympany, Moura, *pianist* ['muərə 'lɪmpənɪ] (mo͞orǎ límpǎni)
Lympne [lɪm] (lim)
Lympstone ['lɪmpstən] (límpstŏn)
Lynas, *f.n.* ['laɪnəs] (línǎss)
Lynch, *f.n.* [lɪnʃ] (linsh)
Lyndon, *f.n.* ['lɪndən] (líndŏn)
Lyne, *f.n.* [laɪn] (lín)
Lynedoch ['lɪndʊx] (líndoch)
Lyneham ['laɪnəm] (línǎm)
Lynemouth ['laɪnmaʊθ] (lín-mowth)
Lynher, *River* ['laɪnər] (líner)
Lynmouth ['lɪnməθ] (lín-mŭth)
Lynturk [lɪn'tɜrk] (lintúrk)
Lyons, *f.n.* ['laɪənz] (lí-ŏnz)
Lysaght, *f.n.* ['laɪsət] (líssǎt); ['laɪsat] (líssaat) *The first is appropriate for Baron Lisle's family name.*
Lysons, *f.n.* ['laɪsənz] (líssŏnz)
Lyster, *f.n.* ['lɪstər] (líster)
Lytchett Matravers ['lɪtʃɪt mə'trævərz] (lítchĕt mǎtrávvĕrz)
Lyte, *f.n.* [laɪt] (lít)
Lyth, *f.n.* [laɪθ] (líth)
Lyth [laɪθ] (líth)
Lythall, *f.n.* ['laɪθl] (líth-l)
Lytham St. Annes ['lɪðəm snt 'ænz] (líthǎm sĭnt ánz)
Lyttle, *f.n.* ['lɪtl] (líttl)
Lyttleton, *f.n.* ['lɪtltən] (líttltŏn)
Lytton, *Earl of* ['lɪtən] (líttŏn)
Lyulph, *C.n.* ['laɪəlf] (lí-ŭlf)
Lyveden ['lɪvdən] (lívdĕn) *Appropriate also for Baron* ~.
Lywood, *f.n.* ['laɪwʊd] (lí-wo͞od)

M

McAdam, *f.n.* [mə'kædəm] (mǎkáddǎm)
Macadie, *f.n.* [mə'kædɪ] (mǎkáddi)
Macafee, *f.n.* ['mækəfi] (máckǎfee)
McAleese, *f.n.* [ˌmækə'lis] (mackǎleéss)
McAlery, *f.n.* [ˌmækə'lɪərɪ] (mackǎleéri)

McAlister, *f.n.* [məˈkælɪstər] (măkálister)
McAllister, *f.n.* [məˈkælɪstər] (măkálister)
McAloon, *f.n.* [ˌmækəˈluːn] (mackáloŏn)
Macalpine, *f.n.* [məˈkælpɪn] (măkálpin); [məˈkælpaɪn] (măkálpīn)
McAlpine, *f.n.* [məˈkælpɪn] (măkálpin); [məˈkælpaɪn] (măkálpīn)
Macan, *f.n.* [məˈkæn] (măkán)
McAnally, *f.n.* [ˌmækəˈnælɪ] (mackănáli)
Macara, *f.n.* [məˈkɑrə] (măkaárá); [məˈkærə] (măkárrá))
McArdle, *f.n.* [məˈkɑrdl] (măkaárdl)
MacArthur, *f.n.* [məˈkɑrθər] (măkaárthŭr)
McAslin, *f.n.* [məˈkɒzlɪn] (măkáwzlin)
McAteer, *f.n.* [ˈmækətɪər] (máckăteer)
McAvoy, *f.n.* [ˈmækəvɔɪ] (máckăvoy)
MacBain, *f.n.* [məkˈbeɪn] (măkbáyn)
McBean, *f.n.* [məkˈbeɪn] (măkbáyn); [məkˈbiːn] (măkbeén)
MacBeath, *f.n.* [məkˈbeθ] (măkbéth)
MacBeth, *f.n.* [məkˈbeθ] (măkbéth)
McBirney, *f.n.* [məkˈbɜrnɪ] (măkbírni)
McBrain, *f.n.* [məkˈbreɪn] (măkbráyn)
MacBrayne, *f.n.* [məkˈbreɪn] (măkbráyn)
McBrien, *f.n.* [məkˈbraɪən] (măkbrí-ĕn)
McBrinn, *f.n.* [məkˈbrɪn] (măkbrín)
McCahearty, *f.n.* [ˌmækəˈhɑrtɪ] (mackăhaárti)
McCaig, *f.n.* [məˈkeɪg] (măkáyg)
McCall, *f.n.* [məˈkɒl] (măkáwl)
McCallin, *f.n.* [məˈkælɪn] (măkálin)
MacCallum, *f.n.* [məˈkæləm] (măkálŭm)
McCalmont, *f.n.* [məˈkælmənt] (măkálmŏnt)
McCammon, *f.n.* [məˈkæmən] (măkámmŏn)
McCance, *f.n.* [məˈkæns] (măkánss)
McCann, *f.n.* [məˈkæn] (măkán)
McCarthy, *f.n.* [məˈkɑrθɪ] (măkaárthi)
McCartney, *f.n.* [məˈkɑrtnɪ] (măkaártni)
McCaughan, *f.n.* [məˈkæxən] (măkáchăn); [məˈkɒn] (măkáwn)
McCaughey, *f.n.* [məˈkæxɪ] (măkáchi); [məˈkɛhɪ] (măká-hi); [məˈkɒfɪ] (măkóffi)
McCheane, *f.n.* [məkˈtʃiːn] (măk-tcheén); [məkˈtʃeɪn] (măk-tcháyn)
MacCheyne, *f.n.* [məkˈʃeɪn] (măk-sháyn)
McChlery, *f.n.* [məˈklɪərɪ] (măkleéri)
McClatchie, *f.n.* [məˈklætʃɪ] (măklátchi)
McClenaghan, *f.n.* [məˈklenəxən] (măklénăchăn)
McClenahan, *f.n.* [məˈklenəhən] (măklénăhăn)
McClenaughan, *f.n.* [məˈklenəxən] (măklénăchăn)
McCloughin, *f.n.* [məˈkluɪn] (măkloŏ-in)
McCloughry, *f.n.* [məˈklɒrɪ] (măklórri)
McCloy, *f.n.* [məˈklɔɪ] (măklóy)
MacColl, *f.n.* [məˈkɒl] (măkól)
McComb, *f.n.* [məˈkoʊm] (măkṓm)
McCombe, *f.n.* [məˈkoʊm] (măkṓm)
MacConachie, *f.n.* [məˈkɒnəxɪ] (măkónnăchi)

McConachy, *f.n.* [məˈkɒnəxɪ] (măkónnăchi)
McConaghy, *f.n.* [məˈkɒnəxɪ] (măkónnăchi)
McConalogue, *f.n.* [məˈkoʊnəloʊg] (măkōnălōg)
McConnach, *f.n.* [məˈkɒnəx] (măkónnăch)
McCormack, *f.n.* [məˈkɔrmək] (măkórmăk)
McCorquodale, *f.n.* [məˈkɔrkədeɪl] (măkórkŏdayl)
McCracken, *f.n.* [məˈkrækən] (măkráckĕn)
McCrae, *f.n.* [məˈkreɪ] (măkráy)
McCraw, *f.n.* [məˈkrɔ] (măkráw)
McCrea, *f.n.* [məˈkreɪ] (măkráy)
McCreadie, *f.n.* [məˈkrɪdɪ] (măkreédi); [məˈkredɪ] (măkréddi)
McCready, *f.n.* [məˈkrɪdɪ] (măkreédi); [məˈkredɪ] (măkréddi)
McCreechan, *f.n.* [məˈkrɪxən] (măkreéchăn)
McCrindle, *f.n.* [məˈkrɪndl] (măkríndl)
McCrirrick, *f.n.* [məˈkrɪrɪk] (măkrírrik)
McCrudden, *f.n.* [məˈkrʌdən] (măkrúddĕn)
MacCue, *f.n.* [məˈkjuː] (măkéw)
McCue, *f.n.* [məˈkjuː] (măkéw)
McCullagh, *f.n.* [məˈkʌlə] (măkúllă)
McCulloch, *f.n.* [məˈkʌləx] (măkúllŏch); [məˈkʌlək] (măkúllŏk)
McCullough, *f.n.* [məˈkʌləx] (măkúllŏch)
McCutcheon, *f.n.* [məˈkʌtʃən] (măkútchĕn)
McDermid, *f.n.* [məkˈdɜrmɪd] (măkdérmid)
MacDermot, *f.n.* [məkˈdɜrmət] (măkdérmŏt)
McDiarmid, *f.n.* [məkˈdɜrmɪd] (măkdérmid)
McDona, *f.n.* [məkˈdʌnə] (măkdúnnă); [məkˈdɒnə] (măkdónnă)
McDonagh, *f.n.* [məkˈdʌnə] (măkdúnnă); [məkˈdɒnə] (măkdónnă)
Macdonald, *f.n.* [məkˈdɒnld] (măkdónnld)
Macdonald of Gwaenysgor, Baron [məkˈdɒnld əv gwaɪnˈʌsgər] (măkdónnld ŏv gwīnússgor)
Macdonell, *f.n.* [məkˈdɒnl] (măkdónnl); [ˌmækdəˈnel] (mackdŏnéll) *The second is appropriate for the author, A. G.* ~.
McDonell, *f.n.* [məkˈdɒnl] (măkdónnl); [ˌmækdəˈnel] (mackdŏnéll)
McDonnell, *f.n.* [məkˈdɒnl] (măkdónnl); [ˌmækdəˈnel] (mackdŏnéll)
McDonogh, *f.n.* [məkˈdʌnə] (măkdúnnă); [məkˈdɒnə] (măkdónnă)
McDonough, *f.n.* [məkˈdʌnə] (măkdúnnă); [məkˈdɒnə] (măkdónnă)
McDouall, *f.n.* [məkˈduəl] (măkdoŏ-ăl)
McDougall, *f.n.* [məkˈdugl] (măkdoŏgl)
McDowall, *f.n.* [məkˈdaʊəl] (măkdówăl)

McDowell, *f.n.* [mək'dauəl] (măkdów-ĕl) [mək'douəl] (măkdṓ-ĕl)

MacDuff, *f.n.* [mək'dʌf] (măkdúff)

McEacharn, *f.n.* [mə'kexərn] (mă-kéchárn); [mə'kexrən] (măkéchrăn); [mə'kekrən] (măkéckrăn)

McEachern, *f.n.* [mə'kexərn] (mă-kéchěrn); [mə'kexrən] (măkéchrĕn); [mə'kekrən] (măkéckrĕn)

McEachran, *f.n.* [mə'kexrən] (mă-kéchrăn)

McEchern, *f.n.* [mə'kexərn] (mă-kéchěrn); [mə'kexrən] (măkéchrĕn)

MacElderry, *f.n.* ['mækldərɪ] (máckl-derrɪ)

McEldowney, *f.n.* [ˌmækl'daunɪ] (mackl-dównɪ); ['mækldaunɪ] (máckldownɪ)

McElhone, *f.n.* ['mæklhoun] (máckl-hōn)

McElligott, *f.n.* [mə'kelɪgət] (măkélligŏt)

McElroy, *f.n.* ['mæklrɔɪ] (mácklroy)

McEneaney, *f.n.* [ˌmækə'ninɪ] (mackĕ-neéni)

McEnroe, *f.n.* ['mækənrou] (máckěnrō)

MacEntagart, *f.n.* [ˌmækən'tægərt] (mackĕntággărt)

McEntee, *f.n.* [ˌmækən'ti] (mackĕnteé); [mə'kentɪ] (măkénti)

MacEntegart, *f.n.* [ˌmækən'tegərt] (mackĕntéggărt); [mə'kentɪgɑrt] (mă-kéntĕgaart)

MacEnteggart, *f.n.* [ˌmækən'tegərt] (mackĕntéggărt)

McEvoy, *f.n.* ['mækɪvɔɪ] (máckĕvoy)

McEwen, *f.n.* [mə'kjuɪn] (măkéwĕn)

McFadyean, *f.n.* [mək'fædjən] (măk-fád-yĕn)

Macfadyen, *f.n.* [mək'fædjən] (măk-fád-yĕn)

McFadzean, *f.n.* [mək'fædjən] (măkfád-yĕn) *Appropriate also for Baron ~.*

MacFarlane, *f.n.* [mək'fɑrlən] (măk-faárlăn)

MacFarquhar, *f.n.* [mək'fɑrkər] (măk-faárkăr)

McFie, *f.n.* [mək'fi] (măkfeé)

McFinn, *f.n.* [mək'fɪn] (măkfín)

McGahern, *f.n.* [mə'gæxərn] (măgáchĕrn)

McGaughey, *f.n.* [mə'gɔɪ] (măgóy)

MacGeach, *f.n.* [mə'geɪ] (măgáy)

McGeagh, *f.n.* [mə'geɪ] (măgáy)

MacGee, *f.n.* [mə'gi] (măgeé)

McGee, *f.n.* [mə'gi] (măgeé)

McGeoch, *f.n.* [mə'giəx] (măgeé-ŏch)

McGeough, *f.n.* [mə'gou] (măgṓ)

McGeown, *f.n.* [mə'gjoun] (măg-yōn)

MacGhee, *f.n.* [mə'gi] (măgeé)

McGhee, *f.n.* [mə'gi] (măgeé)

McGhie, *f.n.* [mə'gi] (măgeé)

MacGill, *f.n.* [mə'gɪl] (măgíll)

McGillewie, *f.n.* [mə'gɪləwɪ] (măgíllĕ-wi)

McGillicuddy, *f.n.* ['mæglɪkʌdɪ] (mágli-kuddi)

McGilligan, *f.n.* [mə'gɪlɪgən] (măgílligăn)

McGillivray, *f.n.* [mə'gɪlɪvrɪ] (măgílliv-ri); [mə'gɪlvrɪ] (măgílvri); [mə'gɪlɪvreɪ] (măgíllivray)

McGimpsey, *f.n.* [mə'dʒɪmpsɪ] (mă-jímpsi)

MacGladdery, *f.n.* [mə'glædərɪ] (mă-gláddĕri)

McGladdery, *f.n.* [mə'glædərɪ] (mă-gláddĕri)

MacGladery, *f.n.* [mə'glædərɪ] (mă-gláddĕri)

McGladery, *f.n.* [mə'glædərɪ] (mă-gláddĕri)

McGlone, *f.n.* [mə'gloun] (măglṓn)

McGoffen, *f.n.* [mə'gɒfən] (măgóffĕn)

McGonagall, *f.n.* [mə'gɒnəgl] (mă-gónnăgl) *Appropriate for William ~, Scottish doggerel poet.*

McGonagle, *f.n.* [mə'gɒnəgl] (mă-gónnăgl)

MacGonnigle, *f.n.* [mə'gɒnɪgl] (mă-gónnigl)

MacGoohan, *f.n.* [mə'guən] (măgoó-ăn)

McGoohan, *f.n.* [mə'guən] (măgoó-ăn)

McGougan, *f.n.* [mə'gugən] (măgoógăn)

McGovern, *f.n.* [mə'gʌvərn] (măgúvvĕrn)

McGowan, *f.n.* [mə'gauən] (măgówăn)

McGrath, *f.n.* [mə'grɑ] (măgraá); [mə'græθ] (măgráth)

McGredy, *f.n.* [mə'gridɪ] (măgreédi)

Macgregor, *f.n.* [mə'gregər] (măgréggŏr)

MacGregor, *f.n.* [mə'gregər] (măgréggŏr)

McGregor, *f.n.* [mə'gregər] (măgréggŏr)

M'Gregor, *f.n.* [mə'gregər] (măgréggŏr)

McGrigor, *f.n.* [mə'gregər] (măgréggŏr); [mə'grɪgər] (măgríggŏr) *The first is appropriate for the late Admiral Sir Rhoderick ~.*

McGroarty, *f.n.* [mə'grɔrtɪ] (măgrórti)

McGrogan, *f.n.* [mə'grougən] (măgrṓgăn)

McGuigan, *f.n.* [mə'gwigən] (măgweé-găn); [mə'gwɪgən] (măgwíggăn)

McGuinness, *f.n.* [mə'gɪnɪs] (măgínnĕss)

McGuire, *f.n.* [mə'gwaɪər] (măgwír)

McHale, *f.n.* [mək'heɪl] (măk-háyl)

McIldowie, *f.n.* [ˌmækɪl'dui] (mackil-doó-i); [ˌmækɪl'dauɪ] (mackildów-i)

MacIlhatton, *f.n.* [ˌmækɪl'hætən] (mackil-háttŏn)

McIlroy, *f.n.* ['mækɪlrɔɪ] (máckilroy); [ˌmækɪl'rɔɪ] (mackilróy)

MacIlvenna, *f.n.* [ˌmækɪl'venə] (mackil-vénnă)

McIlwraith, *f.n.* ['mækɪlreɪθ] (máckil-rayth)

McInally, *f.n.* [ˌmækɪ'nælɪ] (mackináli)

MacInerney, *f.n.* [ˌmækɪ'nɜrnɪ] (macki-nérni)

McInerny, *f.n.* [ˌmækɪ'nɜrnɪ] (macki-nérni)

MacInnes, *f.n.* [mə'kɪnɪs] (măkínnĕss)

McInroy, *f.n.* ['mækɪnrɔɪ] (máckinroy)

McIntosh, *f.n.* ['mækɪntɒʃ] (máckintosh)

Macintyre, *f.n.* ['mækɪntaɪər] (máckin-tīr)

MacIntyre, *f.n.* ['mækɪntaɪər] (máckintĭr)

McIntyre, *f.n.* ['mækɪntaɪər] (máckintĭr)

McIver, *f.n.* [mə'kaɪvər] (mákíver); [mə'kɪvər] (mákeéver)

McIvor, *f.n.* [mə'kaɪvər] (mákívŏr); [mə'kɪvər] (mákeévŏr)

Mackarness, *f.n.* ['mækərnes] (máckărness)

McKarness, *f.n.* ['mækərnes] (máckărness)

Mackay, *f.n.* [mə'kaɪ] (mákí)

McKay, *f.n.* [mə'kaɪ] (mákí)

McKeag, *f.n.* [mə'kig] (mákeég)

McKean, *f.n.* [mə'kin] (mákeén)

McKeand, *f.n.* [mə'kind] (mákeénd); [mə'kiənd] (mákeé-ánd)

McKee, *f.n.* [mə'ki] (mákeé)

McKellar, *f.n.* [mə'kelər] (mákéllár)

Mackendrick, *f.n.* [mə'kendrɪk] (mákéndrick)

MacKendrick, *f.n.* [mə'kendrɪk] (mákéndrick)

McKenna, *f.n.* [mə'kenə] (mákénnă)

Mackenzie, *f.n.* [mə'kenzɪ] (mákénzi)

McKenzie, *f.n.* [mə'kenzɪ] (mákénzi)

Mackeown, *f.n.* [mə'kjoun] (mákyŏn)

McKeown, *f.n.* [mə'kjoun] (mákyŏn); [mə'kjuɪn] (mákéwŏn)

Mackereth, *f.n.* [mə'kerəθ] (mákérrĕth)

McKernan, *f.n.* [mə'kɜrnən] (mákérnăn)

McKey, *f.n.* [mə'kaɪ] (mákí)

McKibbin, *f.n.* [mə'kɪbɪn] (mákíbbin)

MacKie, *f.n.* [mə'ki] (mákeé)

McKie, *f.n.* [mə'ki] (mákeé); [mə'kaɪ] (mákí) *The second is appropriate for Sir William* ~, *organist and one time Master of the Choristers at Westminster Abbey.*

McKinlay, *f.n.* [mə'kɪnlɪ] (mákínli)

McKinnon, *f.n.* [mə'kɪnən] (mákínnŏn)

McKnight, *f.n.* [mək'naɪt] (máknít)

Mackrill, *f.n.* [mə'krɪl] (mákríll)

McLachlan, *f.n.* [mə'klɒxlən] (máklóchlăn); [mə'klɒklən] (máklócklăn)

McLafferty, *f.n.* [mə'klæfərtɪ] (máklåfferti)

McLagan, *f.n.* [mə'klægən] (máklággăn)

McLaine, *f.n.* [mə'kleɪn] (mákláyn)

Maclaren, *f.n.* [mə'klærən] (máklárrĕn) '

MacLaren, *f.n.* [mə'klærən] (máklárrĕn)

McLauchlan, *f.n.* [mə'klɒxlən] (máklóchlăn); [mə'klɒklən] (máklócklăn)

McLauchlin, *f.n.* [mə'klɒxlɪn] (máklóchlin); [mə'klɒklɪn] (máklócklin)

McLaughlin, *f.n.* [mə'klɒxlɪn] (máklóchlin); [mə'glɒxlɪn] (mágLóchlin); [mə-'klɒklɪn] (máklócklin)

McLaurin, *f.n.* [mə'klɒrɪn] (mákláwrin); [mə'klɒrɪn] (máklórrin)

Maclay, *f.n.* [mə'kleɪ] (mákláy) *Appropriate also for Baron* ~.

McLay, *f.n.* [mə'kleɪ] (mákláy)

McLea, *f.n.* [mə'kleɪ] (mákláy)

Maclean, *f.n.* [mə'kleɪn] (mákláyn)

McLean, *f.n.* [mə'kleɪn] (mákláyn)

McLear, *f.n.* [mə'klɪər] (mákleér)

McLeavy, *f.n.* [mə'klɪvɪ] (mákleévi)

McLeay, *f.n.* [mə'kleɪ] (mákláy)

McLeish, *f.n.* [mə'klɪʃ] (mákleésh)

McLeiland, *f.n.* [mə'klelənd] (mákléllănd)

Maclennan, *f.n.* [mə'klenən] (máklénnăn)

Macleod, *f.n.* [mə'klaud] (máklówd)

MacLeod, *f.n.* [mə'klaud] (máklówd) *Appropriate for Dame Flora* ~ *of* ~.

McLeod, *f.n.* [mə'klaud] (máklówd)

Maclise, *f.n.* [mə'klis] (mákleéss)

McLoughlin, *f.n.* [mə'klɒxlɪn] (máklóchlin)

MacLurg, *f.n.* [mə'klɜrg] (máklúrg)

McMahon, *f.n.* [mək'man] (mákmaán)

Macmanaway, *f.n.* [mək'mænəweɪ] (mákmánnáway)

McManus, *f.n.* [mək'mænəs] (mákmánnŭss); [mək'manəs] (mákmaánŭss); [mək'meɪnəs] (mákmáynŭss)

MacMath, *f.n.* [mək'maθ] (mákmaáth)

McMenemey, *f.n.* [mək'menɪmɪ] (mákménnĕmi)

McMenemy, *f.n.* [mək'menɪmɪ] (mákménnĕmi)

MacMillan, *f.n.* [mək'mɪlən] (mákmíllăn)

McMullen, *f.n.* [mək'mʌlən] (mákmúllĕn)

MacMurdie, *f.n.* [mək'mɜrdɪ] (mákmúrdi)

McMynn, *f.n.* [mək'mɪn] (mákmín)

MacNab, *f.n.* [mək'næb] (máknáb)

McNaghton, *f.n.* [mək'notən] (máknáwtŏn)

Macnalty [mək'noltɪ] (máknáwlti)

Macnamara, *f.n.* [ˌmæknə'marə] (mácknámaárá)

McNamee, *f.n.* [ˌmæknə'mi] (mácknámeé)

McNaught, *f.n.* [mək'not] (máknáwt)

McNaughton, *f.n.* [mək'notən] (máknáwtŏn)

MacNeice, *f.n.* [mək'nis] (mákneéss)

McNeil, *f.n.* [mək'nil] (mákneél)

MacNeilage, *f.n.* [mək'nilɪdʒ] (mákneélij)

McNeill, *f.n.* [mək'nil] (mákneél)

McNichol, *f.n.* [mək'nɪkl] (máknickl)

MacNiven, *f.n.* [mək'nɪvən] (máknívvĕn)

Maconachie, *f.n.* [mə'kɒnəxɪ] (mákónnáchi); [mə'kɒnəkɪ] (mákónnáki)

Maconochie, *f.n.* [mə'kɒnəxɪ] (mákónnŏchi); [mə'kɒnəkɪ] (mákónnŏki)

McOstrich, *f.n.* [mə'kɒstrɪtʃ] (mákóstritch)

MacOwan, *f.n.* [mə'kouən] (mákŏ-án)

McPhail, *f.n.* [mək'feɪl] (mákfáyl)

MacPhee, *f.n.* [mək'fi] (mákfeé)

McPherson, *f.n.* [mək'fɜrsən] (mákférssŏn)

McQuade, *f.n.* [mə'kweɪd] (mákwáyd)

McQuarrie, *f.n.* [mə'kwɒrɪ] (mákwórri)

McQuisten, *f.n.* [məˈkwɪstən] (măkwíss-těn)
McQuoid, *f.n.* [məˈkwɔɪd] (măkwóyd)
McQuown, *f.n.* [məˈkjuɪn] (măkéwĕn)
Macready, *f.n.* [məˈkriːdɪ] (măkreédi) *Appropriate also for William Charles* ∼, *19th-c. actor-manager.*
McReady, *f.n.* [məˈkriːdɪ] (măkreédi); [məˈkredɪ] (măkréddi)
McReay, *f.n.* [məˈkreɪ] (măkráy)
McRorie, *f.n.* [məˈkrɔːrɪ] (măkráwri)
McRory, *f.n.* [məˈkrɔːrɪ] (măkráwri)
McShane, *f.n.* [məkˈʃeɪn] (măk-sháyn)
McSwiney, *f.n.* [məkˈswɪnɪ] (măk-sweéni); [məkˈswɪnɪ] (măkswínni)
McTaggart, *f.n.* [məkˈtægərt] (măk-tággărt)
McVay, *f.n.* [məkˈveɪ] (măkváy)
McVean, *f.n.* [məkˈveɪn] (măkváyn); [məkˈvɪn] (măkveén)
McVey, *f.n.* [məkˈveɪ] (măkváy)
McVittie, *f.n.* [məkˈvɪtɪ] (măkvítti)
McWatters, *f.n.* [məkˈwɒtərz] (măk-wáwtĕrz)
McWhirter, *f.n.* [məkˈhwɜːrtər] (măk-whírter)
MacWilliam, *f.n.* [məkˈwɪljəm] (măk-wíl-yăm)
Maas, *f.n.* [mɑz] (maaz)
Mabane, *Barony of* [məˈbeɪn] (măbáyn)
Mabayn, *f.n.* [məˈbeɪn] (măbáyn)
Mabe [meɪb] (mayb)
Maberly, *f.n.* [ˈmæbərlɪ] (mábbĕrli)
Mably, *f.n.* [ˈmæblɪ] (mábli)
Mabon, *f.n.* [ˈmæbɒn] (mábbon); [ˈmeɪbən] (máybŏn) *The first is the Welsh pronunciation, the second the Scottish.*
Macclesfield [ˈmæklzfɪld] (mácklz-feeld)
Maccoby, *f.n.* [ˈmækəbɪ] (máckŏbi)
Macedo, *f.n.* [məˈsidoʊ] (másseédō)
Macfin [mækˈfɪn] (mackfín)
Machell, *f.n.* [ˈmeɪtʃl] (maytchl)
Machen, *f.n.* [ˈmeɪtʃɪn] (máytchĕn); [ˈmækɪn] (máckĕn); [ˈmæxən] (máchĕn) *The third is the Welsh pronunciation.*
Machen [ˈmæxən] (máchĕn)
Machent, *f.n.* [ˈmeɪtʃənt] (máytchĕnt)
Machin, *f.n.* [ˈmeɪtʃɪn] (máytchin)
Machlis, *f.n.* [ˈmæklɪs] (máckliss)
Machpelah [mækˈpiːlə] (mackpeélă)
Machray, *f.n.* [məˈkreɪ] (măkráy)
Machrihanish [ˌmæxrɪˈhænɪʃ] (măchri-hánnish)
Machynlleth [məˈxʌnɬəθ] (măchún- hlĕth)
Mackeson, *f.n.* [ˈmækɪsən] (máckĕssŏn)
Mackesy, *f.n.* [ˈmækɪsɪ] (máckĕssi)
Mackey, *f.n.* [ˈmækɪ] (mácki)
Mackie, *f.n.* [ˈmækɪ] (mácki)
Mackworth [ˈmækwɜːθ] (máckwurth)
Maclehose, *f.n.* [ˈmæklɪhoʊz] (mácklĕ-hŏz); [ˈmæklhoʊz] (mácklhŏz)
Maconchy, Elizabeth, *composer* [məˈkɒŋkɪ] (măkónki)
Macosquin [məˈkɒskɪn] (măkósskin)

Madan, *f.n.* [ˈmædən] (máddăn)
Madden, *f.n.* [ˈmædən] (máddĕn)
Madderty [ˈmædərtɪ] (máddĕrti)
Madel, *f.n.* [məˈdel] (mădéll)
Madeley [ˈmeɪdlɪ] (máydli)
Maden, *f.n.* [ˈmædən] (máddĕn)
Madian, *f.n.* [ˈmeɪdɪən] (máydi-ăn)
Madin, *f.n.* [ˈmeɪdɪn] (máydin)
Madresfield [ˈmædərzfɪld] (máddĕrz-feeld)
Madron [ˈmædrən] (mádrŏn)
Maegraith, *f.n.* [məˈɡreɪθ] (măgráyth)
Maenan [ˈmaɪnən] (mínăn) *Appropriate also for the Barony of* ∼.
Maenclochog [maɪnˈklɒxɒɡ] (mīn-klóchog)
Maendy [ˈmaɪndɪ] (míndi)
Maentwrog [maɪnˈtʊrɒɡ] (mīntóŏrog)
Maer [mɛər] (mair)
Maer Rocks [mɛər] (mair)
Maerdy [ˈmɑrdɪ] (maárdi)
Maes-car [maɪsˈkɑr] (mīsskaár)
Maes-du [maɪsˈdiː] (mīssdeé)
Maesgeirchen [maɪsˈɡaɪərxən] (mīss-gírchĕn); [maɪsˈɡɛərxæn] (mīssgaírchan)
Maes-glas, *Flint., Monmouth.* [maɪs-ˈɡlɑs] (mīssglaáss)
Maesglasau [maɪsˈɡlæsaɪ] (mīssglássī)
Maes-llwch Castle [maɪsˈɬux] (mīss-hlóŏch)
Maesmynis [maɪsˈmʌnɪs] (mīssmúnniss)
Maesteg [maɪsˈteɪɡ] (mīsstáyg)
Maes-y-coed, *Flint., Glamorgan* [ˌmaɪsə-ˈkɔɪd] (mīss-ă-kóyd)
Maesycrugiau [ˌmaɪsəˈkrɪɡjaɪ] (mīssă-kríg-yī)
Maesycwmmer [ˌmaɪsəˈkumər] (mīssă-kŏŏmer)
Maes - y - dderwen [ˌmaɪsəˈðɛərwen] (mīss-ă-tháirwen)
Maes-y-dre [ˌmaɪsəˈdreɪ] (mīss-ă-dráy)
Magarshack, *f.n.* [ˈmæɡərʃæk] (mággăr-shack)
Magdalen [ˈmæɡdəlɪn] (mágdălĕn)
Magdalen College, *University of Oxford* [ˈmɔdlɪn] (máwdlĕn)
Magdalene College, *University of Cambridge* [ˈmɔdlɪn] (máwdlĕn)
Magee, *f.n.* [məˈɡiː] (măgeé)
Magennis, *f.n.* [məˈɡenɪs] (măgénniss)
Mager, *f.n.* [ˈmeɪdʒər] (máyjer); [ˈmeɪɡər] (máyger)
Maggs, *f.n.* [mæɡz] (maggz)
Maghaberry [məˈɡæbərɪ] (măgábbĕri)
Maghera [ˌmæxəˈrɑ] (machĕraá)
Magherafelt [ˈmɑrəfelt] (maárăfelt); [ˈmæxərəfelt] (máchĕrăfelt)
Magheragall [ˌmærəˈɡɒl] (marrăgáwl)
Magherahoghill [ˌmæxrəˈhɒxɪl] (machră-hóchil)
Magheralin [ˌmærəˈlɪn] (marrălín)
Magheramorne, *Barony of* [ˌmɑrəˈmɔrn] (maarămórn)
Magheramorne [ˌmæxrəˈmɔrn] (machră-mórn)

Magheraveely [ˌmæxrəˈvilɪ] (ma<u>ch</u>rǎ-veéli)
Maghery [ˈmæxərɪ] (má<u>ch</u>ĕri)
Maghull [məˈgʌl] (mǎgúll)
Magill, *f.n.* [məˈgɪl] (mǎgíll)
Magilligan [məˈgɪlɪgən] (mǎgílligǎn)
Appropriate also for ~ *Strand.*
Maginess, *f.n.* [məˈgɪnɪs] (mǎgínnĕss)
Maginnis, *f.n.* [məˈgɪnɪs] (mǎgínniss)
Magnac, *f.n.* [ˈmænjæk] (mán-yack)
Magnay, *f.n.* [ˈmægneɪ] (mágnay); [ˈmægnɪ] (mágni); [mægˈneɪ] (magnáy)
Magniac, *f.n.* [ˈmænjæk] (mán-yack)
Magnus, *C.n.* [ˈmægnəs] (mágnŭss)
Magnusson, *f.n.* [ˈmægnəsən] (mágnŭssŏn)
Magonet, *f.n.* [ˈmægənet] (mággŏnet)
Magor [ˈmeɪgər] (máygŏr)
Magrath, *f.n.* [məˈgrɑ] (mǎgraá)
Maguire, *f.n.* [məˈgwaɪər] (mǎgwír)
Maguiresbridge [məˈgwaɪərzˈbrɪdʒ] (mǎgwírzbríj)
Mahaddie, *f.n.* [məˈhædɪ] (mǎháddi)
Mahan, *f.n.* [mɑn] (maan)
Mahany, *f.n.* [ˈmɑnɪ] (maáni)
Mahee [məˈhi] (mǎheé)
Maher, *f.n.* [mɑr] (maar)
Mahir, *f.n.* [ˈmeɪhər] (máy-her)
Mahon, *f.n.* [mɑn] (maan)
Mahoney, *f.n.* [ˈmɑənɪ] (maá-ŏni); [məˈhoʊnɪ] (mǎhŏni)
Mahony, *f.n.* [ˈmɑnɪ] (maáni)
Mahy, *f.n.* [ˈmaɪ] (maá-i)
Maia, *f.n.* [ˈmaɪə] (mí-ǎ)
Maidstone [ˈmeɪdstoʊn] (máydstŏn)
Mailer, *f.n.* [ˈmeɪlər] (máyler)
Maillard, *f.n.* [ˈmeɪlɑrd] (máylaard)
Maindee [ˈmeɪndɪ] (máyndi)
Maindy [ˈmeɪndɪ] (máyndi); [ˈmaɪndɪ] (míndi)
Maingot, *f.n.* [ˈmæŋgoʊ] (máng-gŏ)
Mainland Island [ˈmeɪnlænd] (máynland)
Mainwaring, *f.n.* [ˈmænərɪŋ] (mánnǎring); [ˈmeɪnwərɪŋ] (máynwáring)
Mair, *f.n.* [mɛər] (mair)
Mairants, *f.n.* [ˈmɛərənts] (maírǎnts)
Maire, *f.n.* [mɛər] (mair)
Mairet, *f.n.* [ˈmɛərɪ] (maíri)
Mairhi, *C.n.* [ˈmɑrɪ] (maári)
Mais, *f.n.* [meɪz] (mayz)
Maisemore [ˈmeɪzmɔr] (máyzmor)
Maison, *f.n.* [ˈmeɪsən] (máyssŏn)
Maison Dieu Hall, *Dover* [ˈmeɪz ˈdju] (máyzŏng déw); [ˈmeɪzən ˈdju] (máyzŏn déw)
Maitland, *f.n.* [ˈmeɪtlənd] (máytlǎnd)
Majdalany, *f.n.* [ˌmædʒdəˈleɪnɪ] (majdǎláyni)
Majendie, *f.n.* [ˈmædʒəndɪ] (májjĕndi)
Major, *f.n.* [ˈmeɪdʒər] (máyjŏr)
Makerstoun [ˈmækərstən] (máckĕrstŏn)
Makgill, *f.n.* [məˈgɪl] (mǎgíll)
Makins, *f.n.* [ˈmeɪkɪnz] (máykinz)
Makower, *f.n.* [məˈkaʊər] (mǎkówer)

Malan, *f.n.* [ˈmælən] (málǎn); [məˈlɑn] (mǎlaán); [məˈlæn] (mǎlán)
Malbon, *f.n.* [ˈmælbən] (málbŏn)
Malborough [ˈmɒlbərə] (máwlbŭrǎ)
Malcolm, *f.n.* [ˈmælkəm] (málkŏm); [ˈmɒlkəm] (máwlkŏm)
Malden, *f.n.* [ˈmɒldən] (máwldĕn)
Malden [ˈmɒldən] (máwldĕn)
Maldon [ˈmɒldən] (máwldŏn)
Maldwyn, *C.n.* [ˈmældwɪn] (máldwin); [ˈmɒldwɪn] (máwldwin) *The first is the Welsh pronunciation.*
Malempre, *f.n.* [məˈlempreɪ] (mǎlémpray)
Malet, *f.n.* [ˈmælɪt] (málĕt)
Maley, *f.n.* [ˈmeɪlɪ] (máyli)
Malim, *f.n.* [ˈmeɪlɪm] (máylim)
Malindine, *f.n.* [ˈmælɪndaɪn] (málindīn)
Malkin, *f.n.* [ˈmælkɪn] (málkin)
Mall, The [ðə ˈmæl] (th̯e mál)
Mallabar, *f.n.* [ˈmæləbɑr] (málǎbaar)
Mallaby, *f.n.* [ˈmæləbɪ] (málǎbi)
Mallaig [ˈmæleɪg] (málayg)
Mallalieu, *f.n.* [ˈmæləlju] (málǎlew); [ˈmæləljɜ] (málál-yö)
Malldraeth Bay [ˈmæɬdraɪθ] (má<u>hl</u>drīth)
Mallet, *f.n.* [ˈmælɪt] (málĕt)
Malletsheugh [ˈmælɪtʃux] (málĕt-shoo<u>ch</u>)
Malling, East *and* **West** [ˈmɒlɪŋ] (máwling)
Malloch, *f.n.* [ˈmæləx] (málŏ<u>ch</u>)
Mallone, *f.n.* [məˈloʊnɪ] (mǎlŏni)
Mallowan, *f.n.* [ˈmæloʊən] (málŏ-ǎn)
Mallow Ghyll [ˈmæloʊ ˈgɪl] (málŏ gíll)
Mallusk [məˈlʌsk] (mǎlúsk)
Mallwyd [ˈmæɬʊɪd] (má<u>hl</u>oᴐ-id)
Malmesbury [ˈmɑmzbərɪ] (maámzbŭri) *Appropriate also for the Earl of* ~.
Malone, *f.n.* [məˈloʊn] (mǎlŏn)
Malpas, *f.n.* [ˈmælpəs] (málpǎss)
Malpas, *Cheshire* [ˈmɒlpəs] (máwlpǎss); [ˈmælpəs] (málpǎss); [ˈmɒpəs] (máwpǎss)
Malpas, *Cornwall* [ˈmoʊpəs] (mŏpǎss)
Malpass, *f.n.* [ˈmælpæs] (málpass)
Maltby, *f.n.* [ˈmɒltbɪ] (máwltbi)
Malthus, Thomas, *19th-c. economist* [ˈmælθəs] (mál-thŭss)
Malthusian, *pertaining to Malthus* [mælˈθjuzɪən] (mal-théwziǎn)
Malton [ˈmɒltən] (máwltŏn)
Malvern [ˈmɒlvərn] (máwlvĕrn); [ˈmɒvərn] (máwvĕrn)
Malycha, *f.n.* [ˈmælɪkɪ] (máliki)
Malyon, *f.n.* [ˈmæljən] (mál-yŏn)
Mamhilad [mæmˈhaɪləd] (mam-hílǎd)
Mamore deer forest [məˈmɔr] (mǎmór)
Manaccan [məˈnækən] (mǎnáckǎn)
Manadon [ˈmænədən] (mánnǎdŏn)
Manafon [mænˈævən] (manávvŏn)
Manaton [ˈmænətən] (mánnǎtŏn)
Manbré, *f.n.* [ˈmænbreɪ] (mánbray)
Mance, *f.n.* [mæns] (manss)
Manchée, *f.n.* [mænˈʃi] (man-sheé); [mɒnˈʃeɪ] (mon-sháy)

Manchester ['mæntʃɪstər] (mántchĕs-ter); ['mæntʃester] (mántchester)
Manchip, f.n. ['mænʃɪp] (mán-ship)
Mancunian, native of Manchester [mæn-'kjunɪən] (mankéwniăn)
Mandel, f.n. [mæn'del] (mandéll)
Mandelstam, f.n. ['mændlstəm] (mándlstăm)
Mander, f.n. ['mændər] (mánder); ['mɑndər] (maánder) The first is usual in Staffordshire.
Manders, f.n. ['mændərz] (mándĕrz)
Manderson, f.n. ['mændərsən] (mándĕrssŏn)
Manea ['meɪnɪ] (máyni)
Maney, f.n. ['meɪnɪ] (máyni)
Mangin, f.n. ['mæŋɡɪn] (máng-gin)
Mangold, f.n. ['mæŋɡoʊld] (máng-gōld)
Mangotsfield ['mæŋɡətsfɪld] (mánggŏtsfeeld)
Manhood, f.n. ['mænhʊd] (mán-hŏŏd)
Manktelow, f.n. ['mæŋktɪloʊ] (mánktĕlō)
Manley, f.n. ['mænlɪ] (mánli)
Mann, f.n. [mæn] (man)
Manners, f.n. ['mænərz] (mánnĕrz)
Manning, f.n. ['mænɪŋ] (mánning)
Manningham, f.n. ['mænɪŋəm] (mánning-ăm)
Manod ['mænɒd] (mánnod)
Manorbier [ˌmænər'bɪər] (mannŏrbeér)
Manordeifi [ˌmænər'daɪvɪ] (mannŏrdívi)
Manordilo [ˌmænər'daɪloʊ] (mannŏrdílō)
Manordougherty [ˌmænər'dɒxərtɪ] (mannŏrdóchĕrti)
Manor Powis ['mænər 'paʊɪs] (mánnŏr pówiss)
Mansel, f.n. ['mænsl] (manssl)
Mansell, f.n. ['mænsl] (manssl)
Mansergh, f.n. ['mænzər] (mánzer); 'mænsər] (mánsser); ['mænsɜrdʒ] (mánsserj)
Mansergh ['mænzər] (mánzer)
Mansey, f.n. ['mænsɪ] (mánssi)
Mansfield, f.n. ['mænsfɪld] (mánssfeeld)
Manson, f.n. ['mænsən] (mánssŏn)
Manton, f.n. ['mæntən] (mántŏn)
Mantovani, f.n. [ˌmæntə'vɑnɪ] (mantŏvaáni)
Manuden ['mænjʊdən] (mán-yŏŏdĕn)
Manuel, f.n. ['mænjʊəl] (mán-yŏŏ-ĕl)
Manus, f.n. ['meɪnəs] (máynŭss)
Manwaring, f.n. ['mænərɪŋ] (mánnăring)
Manx, pertaining to the Isle of Man [mæŋks] (manks)
Manzoni, f.n. [mæn'zoʊnɪ] (manzŏni)
Maple, f.n. ['meɪpl] (maypl)
Mapledurwell [ˌmeɪpl'dɜrwel] (maypldúrwel)
Mapleton ['meɪpltən] (máypltŏn); ['mæpltən] (máppltŏn)
Maplin Sands ['mæplɪn 'sændz] (máplin sándz)
Maquarie, f.n. [mə'kwɒrɪ] (măkwórri)
Maralin [ˌmærə'lɪn] (marrálín)

Marazion [ˌmærə'zaɪən] (marrăzí-ŏn)
March [mɑrtʃ] (maartch)
Marchesi, f.n. [mɑr'kɪsɪ] (maarkeéssi)
Marchwiel [mɑrx'wɪəl] (maarchweé-ĕl)
Marcousé, f.n. [mɑr'kuzeɪ] (maarkoózay)
Marden ['mɑrdən] (maárdĕn)
Maree, Loch [mə'ri] (măreé)
Mareham ['mɛərəm] (maírăm)
Marett, f.n. ['mærɪt] (márrĕt)
Margach, f.n. ['mɑrɡə] (maárgă)
Margam ['mɑrɡəm] (maárgăm)
Margaretting [ˌmɑrɡə'retɪŋ] (maargárétting)
Margary, f.n. ['mɑrɡərɪ] (maárgări)
Margate ['mɑrɡeɪt] (maárgayt)
Margerison, f.n. [mɑr'dʒerɪsən] (maarjérrissŏn); ['mɑrdʒərɪsən] (maárjérissŏn)
Margesson, f.n. ['mɑrdʒɪsən] (maárjĕssŏn) Appropriate also for Viscount ~.
Margetson, f.n. ['mɑrɡɪtsən] (maárgĕtsŏn)
Margetts, f.n. ['mɑrɡɪts] (maárgĕts)
Margochis, f.n. [mɑr'ɡoʊʃɪ] (maargŏshi)
Margolin, f.n. [mɑr'ɡoʊlɪn] (maargŏlin)
Margoliouth, f.n. [mɑr'ɡoʊlɪəθ] (maargŏli-ŭth) Appropriate for D. S.~, classical scholar and orientalist.
Margolyes, f.n. ['mɑrɡəlɪz] (maárgŏleez)
Margulies, f.n. ['mɑrɡulɪs] (maárgooliss); ['mɑrɡʊlɪs] (maárgŏŏleess); [mɑr'ɡulɪz] (maargoóliz)
Marham ['mærəm] (márrăm); ['mɑrəm] (maárăm) The first is the traditional local pronunciation. The second is used for the Royal Air Force station by R.A.F. personnel.
Marhamchurch ['mærəmtʃɜrtʃ] (márrăm-churtch)
Marholm ['mærəm] (márrŏm)
Marian-glas [ˌmærɪən'ɡlɑs] (marriăn-glaáss)
Marillier, f.n. [mə'rɪljər] (măríl-yer)
Marindin, f.n. [mə'rɪndɪn] (măríndin)
Marino [mə'rinoʊ] (măreénō)
Marischal, f.n. ['mɑrʃl] (maarshl)
Marischal College, University of Aberdeen ['mɑrʃl] (maarshl)
Marjoribanks, f.n. ['mɑrtʃbæŋks] (maártch-banks)
Market Bosworth ['mɑrkɪt 'bɒzwərθ] (maárkĕt bózwŭrth)
Market Rasen ['mɑrkɪt 'reɪzən] (maárkĕt ráyzĕn)
Market Weighton ['mɑrkɪt 'wɪtən] (maárkĕt weétŏn)
Markham, f.n. ['mɑrkəm] (maárkăm)
Markillie, f.n. [mɑr'kɪlɪ] (maarkílli)
Markinch ['mɑrkɪnʃ] (maárk-ínsh)
Marklew, f.n. ['mɑrklu] (maárkloo)
Marklye [mɑrk'laɪ] (maarklí)
Markova, Alicia, ballerina [ə'lɪsɪə mɑr'kouvə] (áleéssiă maarkŏvă)
Marks of Broughton, Baron ['mɑrks əv 'brɒtən] (maárks ŏv bráwtŏn)

Marks Tey ['mɑrks 'teɪ] (maárks táy)

Markshall ['mɑrkshəl] (maárks-hawl); ['mɑrksl] (maarkssl)

Markwick, f.n. ['mɑrkwɪk] (maárkwick)

Markyate Street ['mɑrkjeɪt strit] (maárk-yayt street)

Marlborough, Duke of ['mɔlbrə] (máwlbrǎ)

Marlborough ['mɔlbrə] (máwlbrǎ); ['mɔlbərə] (máwlbŭrǎ)

Marlborough House, *London* ['mɔlbrə] (máwlbrǎ); ['mɔlbərə] (máwlbŭrǎ)

Marlburian, one educated at Marlborough College [mɔl'bjʊərɪən] (mawlbyǒorián)

Marler, f.n. ['mɑrlər] (maárler)

Marloes ['mɑrloʊz] (maárlōz)

Marlow ['mɑrloʊ] (maárlō)

Marlowe, f.n. ['mɑrloʊ] (maárlō)

Marnham, f.n. ['mɑrnəm] (maárnǎm)

Marnhull ['mɑrnəl] (maárnŭl)

Marochan, f.n. ['mærəkən] (márrōkǎn)

Marown [mə'raʊn] (márówn)

Marquand, f.n. ['mɑrkwɒnd] (maárkwond); ['mɑrkwənd] (maárkwŏnd)

Marques, f.n. [mɑrks] (maarks)

Marquis, f.n. ['mɑrkwɪs] (maárkwiss)

Marreco, f.n. [mə'rekoʊ] (máréckō)

Marriott, f.n. ['mærɪət] (márriŏt)

Marris, f.n. ['mærɪs] (márriss)

Marsden, f.n. ['mɑrzdən] (maárzdĕn)

Marshall, f.n. ['mɑrʃl] (maarshl)

Marsham, *Norfolk* ['mɑrʃəm] (maárshăm)

Marsh Baldon ['mɑrʃ 'bɔldən] (maársh báwldŏn)

Marsingall, f.n. ['mɑrsɪŋgl] (maárssinggl)

Marson, f.n. ['mɑrsən] (maárssŏn)

Martel, f.n. [mɑr'tel] (maartéll)

Martell, f.n. [mɑr'tel] (maartéll)

Martens, f.n. ['mɑrtənz] (maártĕnz); [mɑr'tenz] (maarténz)

Martham ['mɑrθəm] (maár-thǎm)

Martin, f.n. and C.n. ['mɑrtɪn] (maártin)

Martineau, f.n. ['mɑrtɪnoʊ] (maártinō)

Martlesham ['mɑrtlʃəm] (maártl-shǎm)

Martletwy [ˌmɑrtl'twaɪ] (maartl-twî)

Martyr, f.n. ['mɑrtər] (maárter)

Martyr Worthy ['mɑrtər 'wɜrðɪ] (maárter wúrthi)

Marvell, f.n. ['mɑrvl] (maarvl) *Appropriate for Andrew ~, 17th-c. poet and satirist.*

Marvin, f.n. ['mɑrvɪn] (maárvin)

Marwick, f.n. ['mɑrwɪk] (maárwick)

Maryculter [ˌmɛərɪ'kutər] (mairi-koóter)

Maryhill ['mɛərɪ'hɪl] (maíri-híll)

Marylebone ['mærələbən] (márrĕlĕbŏn); ['mærɪbən] (márribŏn); ['mɑrlɪbən] (maárlibŏn)

Mary Tavy ['mɛərɪ 'teɪvɪ] (maíri táyvi)

Masbrough ['mæzbərə] (mázbŭrǎ)

Mascherpa, f.n. [mə'ʃɑrpə] (mǎshérpǎ)

Mase, f.n. [meɪs] (mayss)

Masham, f.n. ['mæsəm] (mássăm); ['mæʃəm] (máshăm)

Masham ['mæsəm] (mássăm) *Appropriate also for Baron ~.*

Masham, *breed of sheep* ['mæsəm] (mássăm); ['mæʃəm] (máshăm) *Those acquainted with the place generally use the first pronunciation.*

Maskell, f.n. ['mæskl] (masskl)

Maskelyne, f.n. ['mæskɪlɪn] (másskĕlin)

Maskrey, f.n. ['mæskrɪ] (másskri)

Maslen, f.n. ['mæzlən] (mázlĕn)

Mason, f.n. ['meɪsən] (máyssŏn)

Massee, f.n. ['mæsi] (mássee)

Massereene ['mæsərɪn] (mássĕreen)

Massereene and Ferrard, *Viscount* ['mæsərɪn ənd 'ferɑrd] (mássĕreen ănd férraard)

Massey, f.n. ['mæsɪ] (mássi)

Massie, f.n. ['mæsɪ] (mássi)

Massinger, f.n. ['mæsɪndʒər] (mássinjer) *Considered appropriate also for Philip ~, 16-17th-c. dramatist.*

Masson, f.n. ['mæsən] (mássŏn)

Masters, f.n. ['mɑstərz] (maásstĕrz)

Masterton, f.n. ['mɑstərtən] (maásstĕrtŏn)

Matalon, f.n. ['mætələn] (máttălon)

Mateer, f.n. [mə'tɪər] (mátéer)

Mather, f.n. ['mæðər] (máther); ['meɪðər] (máyther)

Matherne ['mæðərn] (máthĕrn)

Mathers, f.n. ['meɪðərz] (máythĕrz) *Appropriate also for the Barony of ~.*

Mathers, E. Powys, *author and scholar* ['poʊɪs 'meɪðərz] (pō-iss máythĕrz)

Matheson, f.n. ['mæθɪsən] (máthĕssŏn)

Mathias, f.n. [mə'θaɪəs] (máthî-áss)

Mathie, f.n. ['mæθɪ] (máthi)

Mathrafal, *also spelt* **Mathraval** [mæθ'rævəl] (mathrávvǎl)

Mathry ['mæθrɪ] (máthri)

Matier, f.n. [mə'tɪər] (mátéer)

Matlaske ['mætlæsk] (mátlassk)

Maton, f.n. ['meɪtən] (máytŏn)

Matravers [mə'trævərz] (mătrávvĕrz)

Mattacks, f.n. ['mætəks] (máttáks)

Mattersey ['mætərsɪ] (máttĕrssi)

Matthay, f.n. ['mæteɪ] (máttay)

Matthes, f.n. ['mæθɪz] (máthĕz)

Matthias, f.n. [mə'θaɪəs] (máthî-áss)

Maturin, f.n. ['mætjʊərɪn] (mát-yǒorin)

Mauchline ['mʊxlɪn] (móchlin)

Maude, f.n. [mɔd] (mawd)

Mauduit, f.n. ['moʊdwi] (mṓdwee)

Maufe, Sir Edward, architect [mɔf] (mawf)

Mauger, f.n. ['meɪdʒər] (máyjer)

Maugersbury ['mozbərɪ] (máwzbŭri)

Maugham, f.n. [mɔm] (mawm); ['mɒfəm] (móffǎm) *The first is appropriate for Viscount ~.*

Maugham, Somerset, *author* ['sʌmərsɪt 'mɔm] (súmmĕrssĕt máwm)

Maughan, f.n. [mɒn] (mawn)

Maughenby ['mæfənbɪ] (máffĕnbi)
Maughold, *I.o.M.* ['mækəld] (máckŏld)
Maule, *f.n.* [mol] (mawl)
Mauleverer, *f.n.* [mɔ'levərər] (mŏ-lévvĕrer); [mɔ'levərər] (mawlévvĕrer)
Maumbury Rings ['mombərɪ] (máwmbŭri)
Maund, *f.n.* [mɔnd] (mawnd)
Maunder, *f.n.* ['mɔndər] (máwnder)
Maunsell, *f.n.* ['mænsl] (manssl)
Maurice, *f.n.* ['mɒrɪs] (mórriss); [mə'ris] (mŏreéss)
Mautby ['mɔbɪ] (máwbi)
Mavius, *f.n.* ['meɪvɪəs] (máyviŭss)
Mavor, *f.n.* ['meɪvər] (máyvŏr) *Appropriate for Dr. O. H.* ~, *whose pen name was James Bridie, q.v.*
Mavrogordato, *f.n.* [ˌmævroʊɡɔr'dɑtoʊ] (mavrōgordaátō)
Mawddach, River ['mauðəx] (mówthǎch)
Mawdesley, *f.n.* ['mɔdzlɪ] (máwdzli)
Mawnan ['mɔnən] (máwnǎn)
Maxen, *f.n.* ['mæksən] (mácksĕn)
Maxim, *f.n.* ['mæksɪm] (mácksim)
Maxse, *f.n.* ['mæksɪ] (mácksi)
Maxwell, *f.n.* ['mækswəl] (máckswĕl)
Maxwelltown ['mækswəltaʊn] (máckswĕltown); ['mækswəltən] (máckswĕltŏn)
Maxwelton['mækswəltən](máckswĕltŏn)
May, *f.n.* [meɪ] (may)
Mayall, *f.n.* ['meɪəl] (máy-ăl)
Mayb [meɪb] (mayb)
Maybole [meɪ'boʊl] (maybṓl)
Maydon, *f.n.* ['meɪdən] (máydŏn)
Mayer, *f.n.* ['meɪər] (máy-er)
Mayger, *f.n.* ['meɪdʒər] (máyjer)
Mayhew, *f.n.* ['meɪhju] (máy-hew)
Maynard, *f.n.* ['meɪnərd] (máynărd); ['meɪnɑrd] (máynaard)
Mayne, *f.n.* [meɪn] (mayn)
Mayneard, *f.n.* ['meɪnɪɑrd] (máyni-aard)
Mayo, *Earl of* ['meɪoʊ] (máy-ō)
Mayobridge [ˌmeɪoʊ'brɪdʒ] (may-ō-bríj)
Mayon, *also spelt* Mean [meɪn] (mayn)
Meacher, *f.n.* ['mitʃər] (meétcher)
Meade, *f.n.* [mid] (meed)
Meaden, *f.n.* ['midən] (meédĕn)
Meaford ['mefərd] (méffŏrd)
Meagher, *f.n.* [mɑr] (maar)
Meaker, *f.n.* ['mikər] (meéker)
Meakin, *f.n.* ['mikɪn] (meékin)
Mean *see* Mayon.
Mearles, *f.n.* [mɜrlz] (merlz)
Mearns, The [ðə 'mɛərnz] (thĕ maírnz)
Mears, *f.n.* [mɪərz] (meerz)
Measach, Falls of ['mesəx] (méssăch)
Meath, *Earl of* [miθ] (meéth)
Meathop ['miθəp] (meé-thŏp)
Meaux [mjus] (mewss)
Meavy ['mivɪ] (meévi)
Meazey, *f.n.* ['meɪzɪ] (máyzi)
Medawar, *f.n.* ['medəwər] (médăwăr)
Medcraft, *f.n.* ['medkrɑft] (médkraaft)
Meddings, *f.n.* ['medɪŋz] (méddingz)
Medhurst, *f.n.* ['medhɜrst] (méd-hurst)

Medlicott, *f.n.* ['medlɪkɒt] (médlikot)
Medmenham ['mednəm] (méd-nǎm)
Medomsley ['medəmzlɪ] (méddŏmzli)
Medus, *f.n.* ['midəs] (meédŭss)
Meehan, *f.n.* ['miən] (meé-ǎn)
Meekums, *f.n.* ['mikəmz] (meékŭmz)
Meert, *f.n.* [mɪərt] (meert)
Meeth [miθ] (meeth)
Megan, *Welsh C.n.* ['meɡən] (méggǎn)
Megaw, *f.n.* [mɪ'ɡɔ] (mĕgáw)
Meggison, *f.n.* ['meɡɪsən] (méggissŏn)
Mehan, *f.n.* ['miən] (meé-ǎn)
Meharg, *f.n.* [mɪ'hɑrɡ] (mĕhaárg)
Mehew, *f.n.* ['mihju] (meéhew); ['miu] (meé-oo)
Meifod ['maɪvɒd] (mífvod)
Meigh, *f.n.* [mi] (mee); [meɪ] (may)
Meigle ['miɡl] (meegl)
Meikle, *f.n.* ['mikl] (meekl)
Meiklejohn, *f.n.* ['mɪkldʒɒn] (míckljon); ['mikldʒɒn] (meékljon)
Meikleour [mɪ'kluər] (mĕklṓŏr)
Meilen, *f.n.* ['maɪlən] (mílĕn)
Mein, *f.n.* [min] (meen)
Meinciau ['maɪŋkjaɪ] (mínk-yī)
Meinertzhagen, *f.n.* ['maɪnərtshaɡən] (mínĕrts-haagĕn)
Meir [mɪər] (meer)
Mekie, *f.n.* ['mikɪ] (meéki)
Melachrino, *f.n.* [ˌmelə'krinoʊ] (mellákreénō)
Melbury Abbas ['melbərɪ 'æbəs] (mélbŭri ábbǎss)
Melchett, *Baron* ['meltʃɪt] (méltchĕt)
Melcio, *f.n.* ['melsɪoʊ] (mélssi-ō)
Meldrum, *f.n.* ['meldrəm] (méldrŭm)
Melgund, *Viscount* ['melɡʌnd] (mélgund)
Melhuish, *f.n.* ['melhjuɪʃ] (mél-hewish); [mel'hjuɪʃ] (mel-héwish); [mel'juɪʃ] (melléwish); ['melɪʃ] (méllish)
Melia, *f.n.* ['milɪə] (meéliǎ)
Meliden ['melɪdən] (méllidĕn)
Melincryddan [ˌmelɪn'krʌðən] (mellinkrúthǎn)
Melindwr [me'lɪndʊər] (mellíndṓŏr)
Melin Ifan Ddu ['melɪn 'ɪvən 'ði] (méllin ívvǎn theé)
Melksham ['melkʃəm] (mélk-shǎm)
Mellaart, *f.n.* ['melɑrt] (méllaart)
Mellinger, *f.n.* ['melɪndʒər] (méllinjer)
Mellingey [me'lɪndʒɪ] (mellínji)
Mellis ['melɪs] (mélliss)
Mellor, *f.n.* ['melɔr] (méllor)
Mellors, *f.n.* ['melɔrz] (méllŏrz)
Melmerby ['melmərbɪ] (mélmĕrbi); ['melərbɪ] (méllĕrbi)
Meloy, *f.n.* [mɪ'lɔɪ] (mĕlóy)
Melrose ['melroʊz] (mélrōz)
Meltham ['meləm] (mél-thǎm)
Melton Constable ['meltən 'kʌnstəbl] (méltŏn kúnstǎbl)
Melton Mowbray ['meltən 'moʊbreɪ] (méltŏn mṓbray)
Melvich ['melvɪx] (mélvich)
Melville, *f.n.* ['melvɪl] (mélvil)

Memus ['miməs] (meémŭss)

Menabilly [ˌmenə'bılı] (mennăbílli)

Menage, f.n. [mı'naʒ] (mĕnaáz̲h̲)

Menai Bridge ['menaı 'brıdʒ] (ménnı bríj)

Menai Strait ['menaı] (ménnı̄)

Menary, f.n. ['menərı] (ménnări)

Menaul, f.n. [me'nɔl] (menáwl)

Mendel, f.n. ['mendl] (mendl)

Meneely, f.n. [mı'nilı] (mĕneéli)

Meneer, f.n. [mı'nıər] (mĕneér)

Menell, f.n. ['menl] (mennl)

Menevia, *Welsh bishopric* [mı'nivıə] (mĕneéviă)

Menges, f.n. ['meŋgız] (méng-giz); ['menıs] (méng-ĕss) *The first is appropriate for Herbert ~, conductor and composer.*

Menheniot [mən'henıət] (mĕn-hénniŏt)

Mennell, f.n. [mı'nel] (mĕnéll)

Mennich, f.n. ['menıʃ] (ménnish)

Menpes, f.n. ['menpes] (ménpess); ['menpız] (ménpiz)

Menstrie ['menstrı] (ménsstri)

Menteith, Lake of [mən'tiθ] (mĕnteéth)

Menteth, f.n. [mən'tiθ] (mĕnteéth)

Menuhin, Yehudi, violinist [jə'hudı 'menjuın] (yĕ-hoŏdi mén-yoŏ-in) *Mr. Menuhin himself accepts the above popular English pronunciation. The Russian and Hebrew version is* [mə'nuxın] (mĕnoŏc̲h̲in).

Menzies, f.n. ['mıŋıs] (míng-iss); ['menız] méng-iz); ['menzız] (ménziz) *The first two are indigenous Scottish pronunciations.*

Meo, f.n. ['meıoʊ] (máy-ō)

Meole Brace ['mil 'breıs] (meél bráyss)

Meols, *Cheshire* [mels] (melss)

Meols, *Lancs.* [milz] (meelz)

Meon, River ['mıən] (meé-ŏn)

Meon, East *and* **West** ['mıən] (meé-ŏn)

Meopham ['mepəm] (méppăm)

Mepal ['mipl] (meepl)

Meppershall ['mepərʃəl] (méppĕr-shăl)

Merbecke, John, 16th-c. musician and composer ['marbek] (maárbeck)

Merchant, f.n. ['martʃənt] (mértchănt)

Merchiston ['mɜrkıstən] (mérkistŏn)

Merchistoun Hall, *Hants.* ['mɜrtʃıstən] (mértchistŏn)

Mercy, f.n. ['mɜrsı] (mérssi)

Meredith, f.n. and C.n. [mə'redıθ] (mĕréddith); ['merədıθ] (mérrĕdith) *The first is the Welsh pronunciation.*

Meredydd, Welsh f.n. and C.n. [mə'rediδ] (mĕréddit̲h̲); [mə'rediθ] (mĕréddith)

Merevale ['merıveıl] (mérrĕvayl)

Mereweather, f.n. ['merıweðər] (mérriwet̲h̲er)

Merewether, f.n. ['merıweðər] (mérriwet̲h̲er)

Mereworth, Baron ['merıwərθ] (mérrĕwürth)

Mereworth ['merıwɜrθ] (mérrĕwurth)

Merfyn, Welsh C.n. ['mɜrvın] (mérvin)

Meriden ['merıdən] (mérridĕn)

Merioneth [ˌmerı'ɒnəθ] (merri-ónnĕth) *Appropriate also for the Earl of ~.*

Mermagen, f.n. ['mɜrməgən] (mérmăgĕn)

Merrell, f.n. ['merəl] (mérrĕl)

Merrion, f.n. ['merıən] (mérriŏn)

Merryweather, f.n. ['merıweðər] (mérriwet̲h̲er)

Merse [mɜrs] (merss)

Mersea, East *and* **West** ['mɜrzı] (mérzi)

Merstham ['mɜrstəm] (mérstăm)

Merthyr ['mɜrθər] (mérther) *Appropriate also for Baron ~.*

Merthyr Tydfil ['mɜrθər 'tıdvıl] (mérther tídvil)

Meryweather, f.n. ['merıweðər] (mérriwet̲h̲er)

Mescall, f.n. ['meskl] (messkl)

Meshaw ['meʃə] (mésh-aw)

Messel, f.n. ['mesl] (messl)

Messenger, f.n. ['mesındʒər] (méssĕnjer)

Messent, f.n. ['mesənt] (méssĕnt)

Messer, f.n. ['mesər] (mésser)

Messervy, f.n. [mı'sɜrvı] (mĕssérvi)

Messina, f.n. [mı'sinə] (mĕsseénă)

Mestel, f.n. [mes'tel] (mestéll)

Metcalfe, f.n. ['metkaf] (métkaaf); ['metkəf] (métkăf)

Meteyard, f.n. ['metjard] (mét-yaard)

Metherall, f.n. ['meðərol] (mét̲h̲ĕrawl)

Methil ['meθıl] (méth-il)

Methley ['meθlı] (méthli)

Methold [f.n.] ['meθoʊld] (méth-ōld)

Methuen, Baron ['meθʊın] (méthoŏ-ĕn)

Methven, f.n. ['meθvən] (méthvĕn)

Methven ['meθvən] (méthvĕn)

Meurant, f.n. [mjuə'rænt] (myoŏránt)

Meurig, Welsh C.n. ['maırıg] (mí-rig)

Meux, f.n. [mjuks] (mewks); [mjuz] (mewz); [mju] (mew) *The first is appropriate for the firm of brewers.*

Mevagissey [ˌmevə'gısı] (mevvăgíssi); [ˌmevə'gızı] (mevvăgízzi)

Mewes, f.n. ['mevıs] (mévvĕss) *This is appropriate for the architectural firm of ~ and Davis, builders of the London Ritz Hotel.*

Mewett, f.n. ['mjuıt] (méw-ĕt)

Mey [meı] (may) *Appropriate also for the Castle of ~.*

Meyer, f.n. ['maıər] (mí-er); [mɛər] (mair); ['meıər] (máy-er); [mıər] (meer)

Meyerstein, f.n. ['maıərstaın] (mí-ĕrsstīn)

Meyjes, f.n. ['meız] (mayz)

Meyllteyrn [meɬ'taıərn] (meḷ̲ltírn)

Meynell, f.n. ['menl] (mennl)

Meyrick, f.n. ['merık] (mérrick)

Meysey, f.n. ['meızı] (máyzi)

Mhachair, Loch ['væxər] (vác̲h̲ăr)

Miall, f.n. ['maıəl] (mí-ăl)

Michael, f.n. and C.n. ['maıkl] (mīkl)

Michaelis, f.n. [mı'keılıs] (mickáyliss); [mı'kaılıs] (mickíliss)

Michaelston - y - fedw ['maɪklstən ə 'vedu] (mǐklsstǒn ǎ véddoo)
Michaelstow ['maɪklstoʊ] (mǐklsstǒ)
Micheldever['mɪtʃldevər](mǐtchldevver)
Michelham, *Baron* ['mɪtʃələm] (mǐtchělǎm)
Michell, *f.n.* [mɪ'ʃel] (mǐshéll)
Michelli, *f.n.* [mɪ'kelɪ] (mǐkélli)
Michelmore, *f.n.* ['mɪtʃlmɔr] (mǐtchlmor)
Michelson, *f.n.* ['mɪtʃlsən] (mǐtchlssǒn)
Michie, *f.n.* ['mɪxɪ] (mǐchi); ['mɪxɪ] (meéchi); ['mɪkɪ] (mǐcki)
Mickel, *f.n.* ['mɪkl] (mǐckl)
Micklebring ['mɪklbrɪŋ] (mǐcklbring)
Midanbury ['mɪdənbərɪ] (mǐddǎnbüri)
Middle Stoughton ['mɪdl 'stɔtən] (mǐddl stáwtǒn)
Middle Wallop ['mɪdl 'wɒləp] (mǐddl wóllǒp)
Middlemiss, *f.n.* ['mɪdlmɪs] (mǐddlmiss)
Middlesbrough ['mɪdlzbrə] (mǐddlzbrǎ)
Middleton, *f.n.* ['mɪdltən] (mǐddltǒn)
Middleton Tyas ['mɪdltən 'taɪəs] (mǐddltǒn tí-ǎss)
Middletown ['mɪdltaʊn] (mǐddltown)
Middleweek, *f.n.* ['mɪdlwik] (mǐddlweek)
Middlewich ['mɪdlwɪtʃ] (mǐddlwitch) ¡
Midgley, *f.n.* ['mɪdʒlɪ] (mǐjjli)
Midleton, *Earl of* ['mɪdltən] (mǐddltǒn)
Midlothian [mɪd'loʊðɪən] (midlǒthián) *Appropriate also for the Earl of ~.*
Midsomer Norton ['mɪdsʌmər 'nɔrtən] (mídsummer nórtǒn)
Miesch, *f.n.* [miʃ] (meesh)
Miéville, *f.n.* ['mjeɪvɪl] (myáyvil)
Mighall, *f.n.* ['maɪəl] (mí-ǎl)
Mighell, *f.n.* ['maɪəl] (mí-ěl)
Mikardo, *f.n.* [mɪ'kɑrdoʊ] (mikaárdǒ)
Mikellatos, *f.n.* [ˌmɪkɪ'lɑtɒs] (mickělaátoss)
Mikes, George, *author* ['mikeʃ] (meékesh)
Milbourne, *f.n.* ['mɪlbɔrn] (mílborn)
Milburn, *f.n.* ['mɪlbɜrn] (mílburn)
Milburne, *f.n.* ['mɪlbɜrn] (mílburn)
Mildenhall, *Suffolk* ['mɪldənhɔl] (mílděnhawl)
Mildenhall, *Wilts.* ['mɪldənhɔl] (mílděnhawl) *Sometimes spelt* **Minal** *and pronounced* ['maɪnɔl] (mínawl).
Mildmay, *f.n.* ['maɪldmeɪ] (mǐldmay)
Mildmay of Flete, *Barony of* ['maɪldmeɪ əv 'flit] (mǐldmay ǒv fleét)
Mildwater, *f.n.* ['maɪldwɔtər] (mǐldwawter)
Miles, *f.n.* [maɪlz] (mílz)
Milkina, Nina, *pianist* ['ninə 'mɪlkinə] (neénǎ mílkeenǎ)
Millais, Sir John, *painter* ['mɪleɪ] (míllay)
Millar, *f.n.* ['mɪlər] (míllǎr)
Millard, *f.n.* ['mɪlɑrd] (míllaard)
Millbay [mɪl'beɪ] (milbáy)
Miller, *f.n.* ['mɪlər] (míller)
Milles, *f.n.* [mɪlz] (millz)

Milliband, *f.n.* ['mɪlɪbænd] (mílliband)
Millichap, *f.n.* ['mɪlɪtʃæp] (míllitchap)
Milligan, *f.n.* ['mɪlɪgən] (mílligǎn)
Milliken, *f.n.* ['mɪlɪkɪn] (mílliken)
Millings, *f.n.* ['mɪlɪŋz] (míllingz)
Millington, *f.n.* ['mɪlɪŋtən] (míllingtǒn)
Millisle [mɪl'aɪl] (millíl)
Millwall ['mɪl'wɔl] (míll-wáwl); ['mɪlwəl] (mílwǎl)
Millward, *f.n.* ['mɪlwɔrd] (mílwawrd)
Milmo, *f.n.* ['mɪlmoʊ] (mílmǒ)
Milnathort [ˌmɪlnə'θɔrt] (milnǎ-thórt)
Milne, *f.n.* [mɪln] (miln); [mɪl] (mill)
Milner, *f.n.* ['mɪlnər] (mílner)
Milnes, *f.n.* [mɪlnz] (milnz); [mɪlz] (millz)
Milngavie [mɪl'gaɪ] (milgí); [mʌl'gaɪ] (mulgí)
Miltimber [mɪl'tɪmbər] (miltímber)
Milton, *f.n.* ['mɪltən] (míltǒn)
Milward, *f.n.* ['mɪlwərd] (mílwǎrd)
Mimran, *River* ['mɪmræn] (mímran)
Minack ['mɪnək] (mínnǎk)
Minal *see* Mildenhall, *Wilts.*
Minay, *f.n.* ['maɪneɪ] (mínay)
Minchinton, *f.n.* ['mɪntʃɪntən] (mínchintǒn)
Minell, *f.n.* [mɪ'nel] (minéll)
Minera [mɪ'nerə] (minérrǎ)
Mines, *f.n.* [maɪnz] (mínz)
Mineter, *f.n.* ['mɪnɪtər] (mínněter)
Minety ['maɪntɪ] (mínti)
Minffordd ['mɪnfɔrð] (mínforth)
Mingary, Loch ['mɪŋgərɪ] (míng-gǎri)
Mingulay ['mɪŋgʊleɪ] (míng-gǒolay)
Miningsby ['mɪnɪŋzbɪ] (mínningzbi)
Minns, *f.n.* [mɪnz] (minnz)
Minoprio, *f.n.* [mɪ'noʊprɪoʊ] (minǒpriǒ)
Minshull, *f.n.* ['mɪnʃl] (minshl)
Minshull Vernon ['mɪnʃl 'vɜrnən] (mínshl vérnǒn)
Minsmere ['mɪnzmɪər] (mínzmeer)
Minster Lovell ['mɪnstər 'lʌvl] (mínsster lúvvl)
Minter, *f.n.* ['mɪntər] (mínter)
Mintlaw ['mɪnt'lɔ] (mínt-láw)
Minto ['mɪntoʊ] (míntǒ) *Appropriate also for the Earl of ~.*
Mirfin, *f.n.* ['mɜrvɪn] (mírvin)
Miscampbell, *f.n.* [mɪs'kæmbl] (miskámbl)
Miserden ['mɪzərdən] (mízzěrděn)
Mishcon, *f.n.* ['mɪʃkɒn] (míshkon)
Mishnish ['mɪʃnɪʃ] (míshnish)
Miskin ['mɪskɪn] (mísskin)
Mitcham ['mɪtʃəm] (mítchǎm)
Mitchamian, *native of Mitcham* [mɪ'tʃeɪmɪən] (mitcháymián)
Mitchell, *f.n.* ['mɪtʃl] (mitchl)
Mitchenere, *f.n.* [ˌmɪtʃɪ'nɛər] (mitchěnaír)
Mitford, *f.n.* ['mɪtfərd] (mítfǒrd)
Mithian ['mɪðɪən] (míthián)
Mivart, *f.n.* ['maɪvərt] (mívǎrt)
Mizen, *f.n.* ['maɪzən] (mízěn)

Mizler, f.n. ['mɪzlər] (mízzler)
Mizzi, f.n. ['mɪtsɪ] (mítsi)
Moate, f.n. [moʊt] (mōt)
Moberly, f.n. ['moʊbərlɪ] (mṓbĕrli)
Mobsby, f.n. ['mɒbzbɪ] (móbzbi)
Mocatta, f.n. [moʊ'kætə] (mōkáttă)
Mochan, f.n. ['mɒkən] (móckăn)
Mochdre, *Denbigh., Montgomery.* ['mɒxdreɪ] (móchdray)
Mochrum ['mɒxrəm] (móchrŭm)
Moelfre ['mɔɪlvreɪ] (móylvray)
Moelwyn, Welsh C.n. ['mɔɪlwɪn] (móylwin)
Moelyci [mɔɪ'lʌkɪ] (moylúcki)
Moeran, f.n. ['mɔərən] (máwrăn)
Moffat, f.n. ['mɒfət] (móffăt)
Moffat ['mɒfət] (móffăt)
Moger, f.n. ['moʊdʒər] (mṓjer)
Mogey, f.n. ['moʊgɪ] (mṓgi)
Moidart ['mɔɪdərt] (móydărt)
Moilliet, f.n. ['mɔɪlɪet] (móyli-et)
Moir, f.n. ['mɔɪər] (moyr)
Moira ['mɔɪərə] (móyră)
Moiseiwitsch, Benno, pianist ['benoʊ mɔɪ'zeɪɪvɪtʃ] (bénnō moyzáy-ivitch)
Moiser, f.n. ['mɔɪzər] (móyzer)
Molash ['moʊlæʃ] (mṓlash)
Mold [moʊld] (mōld)
Molesey, East *and* **West** ['moʊlzɪ] (mṓlzi)
Moline, f.n. [moʊ'lin] (mōleén)
Molineux football stadium, *Wolverhampton* ['mɒlɪnjuː] (móllinew)
Mollard, f.n. ['mɒlɑrd] (móllaard)
Molloy, f.n. [mə'lɔɪ] (mōlóy)
Molony, f.n. [mə'loʊnɪ] (mōlṓni)
Molson, f.n. ['moʊlsən] (mṓlssŏn) *Appropriate also for Baron ~.*
Molteno, f.n. [mɒl'tinoʊ] (molteénō)
Molyneux, f.n. ['mʌlɪnjuks] (múllinewks); ['mɒlɪnjuks] (móllinewks); ['mʌlɪnjuː] (múllinew); ['mɒlɪnjuː] (móllinew)
Momerie, f.n. ['mʌmərɪ] (múmmĕri)
Monadhliadh Mountains ['moʊnəˈliə] (mṓnăleé-ă)
Monaghan, f.n. ['mɒnəhən] (mónnăhăn)
Monahan, f.n. ['mɒnəhən] (mónnăhăn)
Monair, Loch [mɒ'nɛər] (monnáir)
Monar, Loch ['moʊnər] (mṓnăr)
Moncaster, f.n. ['mʌŋkəstər] (múnkăster)
Monck, f.n. [mʌŋk] (munk) *Appropriate also for Viscount ~.*
Monckton, f.n. ['mʌŋktən] (múnktŏn)
Moncreiff, f.n. [mən'krɪf] (mŏn-kreéf) *Appropriate also for Baron ~.*
Moncreiffe, f.n. [mən'krɪf] (mŏn-kreéf) *Appropriate also for Sir Iain ~ of that Ilk.*
Moncrieff, f.n. [mən'krɪf] (mŏn-kreéf)
Moncrieffe, f.n. [mən'krɪf] (mŏn-kreéf)
Moncur, f.n. [mɒn'kɜr] (mon-kúr)
Mondynes [mɒn'daɪnz] (mondínz)
Monea [mʌ'neɪ] (munnáy)
Money, f.n. ['mʌnɪ] (múnni)
Moneydie [mɒ'nɪdɪ] (monneédi); [mɒ'naɪdɪ] (monnídi)

Moneyglass [ˌmʌnɪ'glɑs] (munniglaáss)
Moneymore [ˌmʌnɪ'mɔr] (munnimór)
Moneypenny, f.n. ['mʌnɪpenɪ] (múnnipenni); ['mɒnɪpenɪ] (mónnipenni)
Moneyreagh [ˌmʌnɪ'reɪ] (munniráy)
Mongeham ['mʌndʒəm] (múnjăm)
Monger, f.n. ['mʌŋgər] (múng-ger)
Mongewell ['mʌndʒwel] (múnjwel)
Moniaive [ˌmɒnɪ'aɪv] (monni-ív)
Monifieth [ˌmʌnɪ'fiθ] (munnifeéth)
Monikie [mə'nɪkɪ] (mōneéki)
Monkhouse, f.n. ['mʌŋkhaʊs] (múnkhowss)
Monkman, f.n. ['mʌŋkmən] (múnkmăn)
Monks Eleigh [mʌŋks 'ilɪ] (munks eéli)
Monkton ['mʌŋktən] (múnktŏn)
Monkwearmouth [mʌŋk'wɪərmaʊθ] (munk-weérmowth)
Monlough ['mɒnlɒx] (mónloch)
Monmouth ['mʌnməθ] (múnmŭth); ['mɒnməθ] (mónmŭth)
Monnow, River ['mʌnoʊ] (múnnō); ['mɒnoʊ] (mónnō)
Monquhitter [mɒn'hwɪtər] (mon-whítter)
Monro, f.n. [mən'roʊ] (mŏnrṓ); [mʌn'roʊ] (munrṓ)
Monsarrat, f.n. ['mɒnsəræt] (mónssărat); [ˌmɒnsə'ræt] (monssărát)
Monsell, f.n. ['mʌnsl] (munssl) *Appropriate also for Viscount ~.*
Monsey, f.n. ['mʌnsɪ] (mónssi)
Monslow, f.n. ['mɒnzloʊ] (mónzlō)
Monson, f.n. ['mʌnsən] (múnssŏn); ['mɒnsən] (mónssŏn) *The first is appropriate for Baron ~.*
Montacute ['mɒntəkjut] (móntăkewt)
Montagnon, f.n. [mɒn'tænjō] (montányōng); [mō'tænjō] (mōng-tán-yōng)
Montagu of Beaulieu, Baron ['mɒntəgju əv 'bjulɪ] (móntăgew ŏv béwli)
Monteagle, Baron [mən'tigl] (mōnteégl)
Montefiore, f.n. [ˌmɒntɪ'fjɔrɪ] (montĕfyáwri)
Monteith, f.n. [mɒn'tiθ] (monteéth)
Montgomerie, f.n. [mənt'gʌmərɪ] (mŏntgúmmĕri); [mən'gʌmərɪ] (mŏn-gúmmĕri); [mənt'gɒmərɪ] (mŏntgómmĕri)
Montgomery, f.n. [mənt'gʌmərɪ] (mŏntgúmmĕri); [mən'gʌmərɪ] (mŏn-gúmmĕri); [mənt'gɒmərɪ] (mŏntgómmĕri)
Montgomery [mənt'gʌmrɪ] (mŏntgúmri); [mənt'gɒmərɪ] (mŏntgómmĕri)
Montgomery of Alamein, Viscount [mənt'gʌmərɪ əv 'æləmeɪn] (mŏntgúmmĕri ŏv álămayn)
Montresor, f.n. ['mɒntrezər] (móntrezzŏr)
Montrose [mɒn'troʊz] (montrṓz); [mən'troʊz] (mŏntrṓz) *The first is appropriate for the Duke of ~.*
Monyash ['mʌnɪæʃ] (múnni-ash)
Monymusk [ˌmɒnɪ'mʌsk] (monnimúsk)
Monzie [mɒ'ni] (monneé); [mə'ni] (mōneé)
Monzievaird [ˌmɒnɪ'vɛərd] (monniváird)

Moonie, f.n. ['muːnɪ] (moóni)
Moonzie ['muːnzɪ] (moónzi)
Moorat, f.n. ['mʊəræt] (mŏŏrat)
Moore, f.n. [mʊər] (mŏŏr)
Moorfoot, f.n. ['mʊərfʊt] (mŏŏrfŏŏt)
Moorhead, f.n. ['mʊərhed] (mŏŏr-hed)
Moos, f.n. [mus] (mooss)
Moran, f.n. ['mɒrən] (máwrăn); ['mɒrən] (mórrăn); [məˈræn] (mŏrán) *The first is appropriate for Baron ~.*
Morant, f.n. [məˈrænt] (mŏránt)
Morar ['mɒrər] (máwrăr)
Moray ['mʌrɪ] (múrri) *Appropriate also for the Earl of ~ and the ~ Firth.*
Morcom, f.n. ['mɔːkəm] (mórkŏm)
Mordaunt, f.n. ['mɔːdənt] (mórdănt); ['mɔːdɒnt] (mórdawnt)
Mordiford ['mɔːdɪfərd] (mórdifŏrd)
Mordue, f.n. ['mɔːdjʊ] (mórdew)
More, f.n. [mɔːr] (mor)
Morebath ['mɔːbɑːθ] (mórbaath)
Morehen, f.n. ['mɔːhen] (mór-hen)
Moreing, f.n. ['mɔːrɪŋ] (máwring)
Morel, f.n. [mɒˈrel] (mawréll); [məˈrel] (mŏréll)
Moreland, f.n. ['mɔːlənd] (mórlănd)
Moreleigh ['mɔːlɪ] (mórli)
Morell, f.n. [mɒˈrel] (morréll)
Morena, f.n. [mɒˈriːnə] (morreénă)
Moresby, f.n. ['mɔːzbɪ] (mórzbi)
Moresby ['mɒrɪsbɪ] (mórrĕssbi)
Moreton Morrell ['mɔːtən 'mɒrəl] (mórtŏn mórrĕl)
Morey, f.n. ['mɔːrɪ] (máwri)
Morfudd, Welsh C.n. [ˈmɔːrvɪð] (mórvith)
Morgan, f.n. ['mɔːgən] (mórgăn)
Morgenstern, f.n. ['mɔːgənstɜːn] (mórgĕnsstern)
Moriarty, f.n. [ˌmɒrɪˈɑːtɪ] (morri-aárti)
Morice, f.n. ['mɒrɪs] (mórriss)
Morin, f.n. ['mɔːrɪn] (máwrin)
Morison, f.n. ['mɒrɪsən] (mórrissŏn)
Morissy, f.n. ['mɒrɪsɪ] (mórrissi)
Morland, f.n. ['mɔːlənd] (mórlănd)
Morley, f.n. ['mɔːlɪ] (mórli)
Moro, f.n. ['mɒrou] (mórrō)
Morpeth ['mɔːpəθ] (mórpĕth)
Morpurgo, f.n. [mɔːˈpɜːgou] (morpúrgō)
Morrah, f.n. ['mɒrə] (mórră)
Morrell, f.n. [məˈrel] (mŏréll); [mɒˈrel] (morréll); ['mʌrəl] (múrrĕl)
Morrick, f.n. ['mɒrɪk] (mórrick)
Morris, f.n. ['mɒrɪs] (mórriss)
Morrison, f.n. ['mɒrɪsən] (mórrissŏn)
Morrissey, f.n. ['mɒrɪsɪ] (mórrissi)
Morrow, f.n. ['mɒrou] (mórrō)
Morse, f.n. [mɔːs] (morss)
Morshead, f.n. ['mɔːzhed] (mórz-hed)
Mortehoe ['mɔːthou] (mórt-hō)
Morteshed, f.n. ['mɔːtʃed] (mórtĕ-shed)
Mortimer, f.n. ['mɔːtɪmər] (mórtimer)
Mortlach ['mɔːtləx] (mórtlăch)
Mortlake ['mɔːtleɪk] (mórt-layk)
Morton, f.n. ['mɔːtən] (mórtŏn)

Morton of Henryton, *Baron* ['mɔːtən əv 'henrɪtən] (mórtŏn ŏv hénritŏn)
Morvah ['mɔːvə] (mórvă)
Morvena, Welsh C.n. [mɔːˈwenə] (morwénnă)
Morwenstow ['mɔːwɪnstou] (mórwĕnsstō)
Moseley, f.n. ['mouzlɪ] (mōzli)
Mosley, f.n. ['mouzlɪ] (mōzli); ['mɒzlɪ] (mózzli)
Mosley Common ['mɒzlɪ 'kɒmən] (móssli kómmŏn)
Mosside [mɒsˈsaɪd] (moss-síd)
Mossley ['mɒslɪ] (móssli)
Mostyn ['mɒstɪn] (mósstin) *Appropriate also for Baron ~.*
Mothecombe ['mʌðɪkəm] (múthĕkŭm)
Motley, f.n. ['mɒtlɪ] (móttli)
Mottershead, f.n. ['mɒtərzhed] (móttĕrzhed)
Motteux, Peter Anthony, 17-18th-c. translator and dramatist ['mɒts] (móttō)
Mottistone, Baron ['mɒtɪstən] (móttistŏn)
Motyer, f.n. [məˈtɪər] (mŏteér)
Mouat, f.n. ['mouət] (mō-ăt)
Moubray, f.n. ['moubreɪ] (mōbray)
Moughtin, f.n. ['moutɪn] (máwtin)
Moughton, f.n. ['moutən] (mōtŏn)
Mouland, f.n. ['mulənd] (moólănd); [muˈlænd] (moolánd)
Moule, f.n. [moul] (mōl)
Moulin ['mulɪn] (moólin)
Moulinearn [ˌmulɪnˈɑːn] (moolinaárn)
Moulsecoomb ['moulskum] (mōlsskoom)
Moulsford ['moulzfərd] (mōlzfŏrd)
Moulsham ['moulʃəm] (mōl-shăm)
Moulsoe ['moulsou] (mōlssō)
Moulson, f.n. ['moulsən] (mōlssŏn)
Moulton, Barony of ['moultən] (mōltŏn)
Moulton, *Cheshire, Lincs.* ['moultən] (mōltŏn)
Moulton Eaugate ['moultən 'igeɪt] (mōltŏn eégayt)
Moultrie, f.n. ['mutrɪ] (moótri)
Mouncer, f.n. ['maunsər] (mównsser)
Mount Edgcumbe, Earl of [maunt 'edʒkəm] (mownt éjkŭm)
Mount Edgcumbe and Valletort, Viscount [maunt 'edʒkəm ənd 'vælɪtɔrt] (mownt éjkŭm ănd válitort)
Mount Kedar [maunt 'kidər] (mownt keédăr)
Mountain Ash ['mauntɪn 'æʃ] (mówntin ásh)
Mountbatten of Burma, Earl [maunt-'bætən əv 'bɜːmə] (mowntbáttĕn ŏv búrmă)
Mountfort, f.n. ['mauntfort] (mówntfort); [maunt'fort] (mowntfórt)
Mountjoy, f.n. [maunt'dʒɔɪ] (mownt-jóy); ['mauntdʒɔɪ] (mównt-joy)
Mountpottinger [maunt'pɒtɪndʒər] (mownt-póttinjer)

Mountsorrel [maunt'sɒrəl] (mownt-sórrĕl)

Mourne Mountains [mɔrn] (morn)

Mousa ['muzə] (moóză)

Mousehold ['maushould] (mówss-hōld) *Appropriate also for* ~ Heath.

Mousehole ['mauzl] (mowzl)

Mouswald ['musl] (moossl)

Moutell, *f.n.* [mou'tel] (mōtéll)

Movers Lane ['muvərz 'leɪn] (moóvĕrz láyn)

Movilla [mou'vɪlə] (mōvíllă)

Mowat, *f.n.* ['mouət] (mŏ-ăt); ['mauət] (mów-ăt)

Mowbray, Segrave and Stourton, Baron ['moubrɪ 'sɪɡreɪv ənd 'stɜrtən] (mŏbri seégrayv ănd stúrtŏn)

Mow Cop ['mau 'kɒp] (mów kóp)

Mower, *f.n.* ['mouər] (mŏ-er)

Mowlem, *f.n.* ['mouləm] (mŏlĕm)

Mowling, *f.n.* ['moulɪŋ] (mŏling)

Mowll, *f.n.* [moul] (mōl)

Mowsley ['mauzlɪ] (mówzli); ['mouzlɪ] (mózli)

Moya, *f.n.* ['mɔɪə] (móy-ă)

Moyallon [mɔɪ'ælən] (moy-álŏn)

Moyarget [mɔɪ'arɡɪt] (moy-aárgĕt)

Moyers, *f.n.* ['mɔɪərz] (móyĕrz)

Moyes, *f.n.* [mɔɪz] (moyz)

Moygashel [mɔɪ'ɡæʃl] (moygáshl)

Moylena [mɔɪ'linə] (moyleénă)

Moynihan, Baron ['mɔɪnɪən] (móyni-ăn)

Moyola [mɔɪ'oulə] (moy-ōlă)

Moys, *f.n.* [mɔɪz] (moyz)

Moyse, *f.n.* [mɔɪz] (moyz)

Muchalls ['mʌxlz] (múchlz)

Muchelney ['mʌtʃəlnɪ] (mútchĕlni)

Muck [mʌk] (muck)

Muckamore ['mʌkəmɔr] (múckămor)

Muckle Flugga ['mʌkl 'flʌɡə] (múckl flúggă)

Mudeford ['mʌdɪfərd] (múddĕfŏrd)

Mudell, *f.n.* [mə'del] (mŭdéll)

Mudie, *f.n.* ['mjudɪ] (méwdi)

Muggerhanger ['mʊərhæŋər] (moŏr-hang-er)

Muggeridge, *f.n.* ['mʌɡərɪdʒ] (múggĕrij)

Mugginton ['mʌɡɪntən] (múggintŏn)

Muggoch, *f.n.* ['mʌɡəx] (múggŏch)

Mugiemoss ['mʌɡɪmɒs] (múggimoss)

Mugliston, *f.n.* ['mʌɡlɪstən] (múgglistŏn)

Mugridge, *f.n.* ['mʌɡrɪdʒ] (múgrij)

Muick, Loch and River [mɪk] (mick)

Muil, *f.n.* [mjul] (mewl)

Muill, *f.n.* [mjul] (mewl)

Muille, *f.n.* [mjul] (mewl)

Muir, *f.n.* [mjuər] (myoŏr)

Muirden, *f.n.* [mjuər'den] (myoŏrdén)

Muirhead, *f.n.* ['mjuərhed] (myoŏr-hed)

Muirhouses ['mʌrɪz] (múrriz)

Muir of Ord ['mjuər əv 'ɔrd] (myoŏr ŏv órd)

Mukle, *f.n.* ['mjuklɪ] (méwkli)

Mulben [mʌl'ben] (mulbén)

Mulcaghey, *f.n.* [mʌl'kæxɪ] (mulká̱chi)

Mulcahy, *f.n.* [mʌl'kæhɪ] (mulká-hi)

Mulchrone, *f.n.* [mʌl'kroun] (mulkrŏ̄n)

Mulcock, *f.n.* ['mʌlkɒk] (múlkock)

Mulder, *f:n.* ['mʌldər] (múlder)

Mule, *f.n.* [mjul] (mewl)

Mulhall, *f.n.* [məl'hɒl] (mŭl-háwl)

Mulholland, *f.n.* [mʌl'hɒlənd] (mul-hóllănd)

Mull [mʌl] (mull) *Appropriate also for the Sound of* ~.

Mull of Kintyre ['mʌl əv kɪn'taɪər] (múll ŏv kintír)

Mull of Oa ['mʌl əv 'ou] (múll ŏv ŏ̄)

Mullaghboy [ˌmʌlə'bɔɪ] (mulláboy)

Mullaghglass [ˌmʌlə'ɡlɑs] (mulláglaáss)

Mullagh Ouyre, *I.o.M.* ['mulək 'auər] (moŏlăck ówr)

Mullally, *f.n.* [mʌ'lælɪ] (mulláli)

Mullaly, *f.n.* [mʌ'leɪlɪ] (mulláyli)

Mullan, *f.n.* ['mʌlən] (múllăn)

Mullans, *f.n.* ['mʌlənz] (múllănz)

Mullardoch, Loch [mʌ'lardɒx] (mulláardo̱ch)

Mullen, *f.n.* ['mʌlən] (múllĕn)

Muller, *f.n.* ['mʌlər] (múller)

Mulley, *f.n.* ['mʌlɪ] (múlli)

Mulligan, *f.n.* ['mʌlɪɡən] (múlligăn)

Mullinar, *f.n.* ['mʌlɪnar] (múllinär)

Mulliner, *f:n.* ['mʌlɪnər] (múlliner)

Mullineux, *f.n.* ['mʌlɪnə] (múllinä)

Mullins, *f.n.* ['mʌlɪnz] (múllinz)

Mullion ['mʌlɪən] (múlliŏn)

Mullo, *f.n.* ['mʌlou] (múllō)

Mullyard [ˌmʌlɪ'ard] (mulli-aárd)

Mulot, *f.n.* ['mjulou] (méwlō)

Muncaster, *f:n.* ['mʌŋkəstər] (múnkäster)

Munday, *f.n.* ['mʌndeɪ] (múnday)

Mundesley ['mʌnzlɪ] (múnzli)

Mundford ['mʌndfərd] (múndfŏrd)

Mungo, *C.n.* ['mʌŋɡou] (múng-gō)

Mungrisdale [mʌŋ'ɡraɪzdeɪl] (mung-grízdayl)

Munnelly, *f.n.* ['mʌnəlɪ] (múnnĕli)

Munns, *f:n.* [mʌnz] (munnz)

Munro, *f.n.* [mən'rou] (mŭnrŏ̄)

Munthe, *f.n.* ['mʌntɪ] (múnti)

Muraille, *f.n.* [mjuə'reɪl] (myoŏráyl)

Murdoch, *f.n.* ['mɜrdəx] (múrdŏ̱ch); ['mɜrdɒk] (múrdock)

Mure, *f.n.* [mjuər] (myoŏr)

Murgett, *f.n.* ['mɜrɡɪt] (múrgĕt)

Murie, *f.n.* ['mjuərɪ] (myoŏri)

Murlough ['mɜrlɒx] (múrlo̱ch)

Murnaghan, *f.n.* ['mɜrnəhən] (múrnähăn)

Murphy, *f.n.* ['mɜrfɪ] (múrfi)

Murrant, *f.n.* ['mʌrənt] (múrrănt)

Murray, *f.n.* ['mʌrɪ] (múrri)

Murrell, *f.n.* ['mʌrəl] (múrrĕl); [mʌ'rel] (murréll)

Murroes ['mʌrouz] (múrrōz)

Murtagh, *f.n.* ['mɜrtə] (múrtă)

Murthly ['mɜrθlɪ] (múrthli)

Murtle ['mɜrtl] (murtl)

Muschamp, *f.n.* ['mʌskəm] (músskăm)

Musgrave, *f.n.* ['mʌzɡreɪv] (múzzgrayv)

Musselburgh ['mʌslbərə] (músslbŭră)
Muston ['mʌstən] (músstŏn); ['mʌsən] (mússŏn)
Muthill ['mjuθɪl] (méw-thǐl)
Mutley ['mʌtlɪ] (múttli)
Mutter, f.n. ['mʌtər] (mútter)
Muybridge, f.n. ['maɪbrɪdʒ] (mībrij)
Myatt, f.n. ['maɪət] (mí-ăt)
Mycock, f.n. ['maɪkɒk] (mīkock); ['maɪkou] (mīkō)
Myddfai ['mʌðvaɪ] (múthvī)
Myddleton, f.n. ['mɪdltən] (míddltŏn)
Mydrim ['maɪdrɪm] (mídrim)
Myers, f.n. ['maɪərz] (mí-ĕrz)
Myerscough, f.n. ['maɪərskou] (mí-ĕrsskō); ['maɪərskɒf] (mí-ĕrsskoff)
Myfanwy, Welsh C.n. [mə'vænwɪ] (mŭvánwi)
Myles, f.n. [maɪlz] (mīlz)
Mylne, f.n. [mɪln] (miln)
Mylod, f.n. ['maɪlɒd] (mīlod)
Mylor ['maɪlər] (mīlŏr)
Mylrea, f.n. [mɪl'reɪ] (milráy)
Mynachdy, Cardiff [mə'nækdɪ](mŭnákdi)
Mynett, f.n. ['maɪnɪt] (mínĕt)
Mynors, f.n. ['maɪnərz] (mínŏrz)
Mynott, f.n. ['maɪnət] (mínŏt)
Mynyddcerrig [ˌmʌnɪð'kerɪg] (munnith-kérrig)
Mynyddislwyn[ˌmʌnɪð'ɪsluɪn](munnith-isslōō-in)
Myrddin-Evans, Sir Guildhaume, international labour expert ['gɪldoum 'mɜrðɪn 'evənz] (gíldŏm múrthin évvänz)
Myroe [maɪə'rou] (mīrō)
Mytchett ['mɪtʃɪt] (mítchĕt)
Mytholm ['maɪðəm] (míthŏm)
Mytholmroyd [ˌmaɪðəm'rɔɪd] (mīthŏm-róyd)
Mythop ['mɪθɒp] (míth-op)
Mytton, f.n. ['mɪtən] (míttŏn)

N

Naar, f.n. [nɑr] (naar)
Naas, Baron [neɪs] (nayss)
Nabarro, f.n. [nə'bɑrou] (năbaárō)
Naden, f.n. ['neɪdən] (náydĕn)
Naesmith, f.n. ['neɪsmɪθ] (náyssmith)
Nagel, f.n. ['neɪgl] (naygl); ['nɑgl] (naagl)
Nagele, f.n. [nə'gelɪ] (năgélli)
Nairn [nɛərn] (nairn)
Nairne, Baroness [nɛərn] (nairn)
Naish, f.n. [neɪʃ] (naysh)
Nalder, f.n. ['nɒldər] (náwlder)
Nall, f.n. [nɒl] (nawl)
Nally, f.n. ['nælɪ] (náli)
Nalty, f.n. ['næltɪ] (nálti)

Namier, f.n. ['neɪ-mɪər] (náy-meer)
Nancegollan [ˌnænsɪ'gɒlən] (nanssĕ-góllán)
Nancekivell, f.n. [næns'kɪvl] (nanss-kívvl); ['nænskɪvl] (nánsskivvl); [ˌnæns-kɪ'vel] (nansskivéll)
Nancekuke [næns'kjuk] (nansskéwk)
Nancledra [næn'kledrə] (nan-klédră)
Nanjizal Bay [næn'dʒɪzl] (nanjízzl)
Nankeville, f.n. ['nænkɪvɪl] (nánkĕvil)
Nanmor ['nænmɔr] (nán-mor)
Nannerch ['nænɛərx] (nánairch)
Nantbwlch-yr-Haiarn [nænt'bʊlx ər 'haɪərn] (nantbŏŏlch ŭr hī-ărn)
Nantclwyd [nænt'kluɪd] (nantklŏŏ-id)
Nantcwnlle [nænt'kunɫeɪ] (nantkŏŏn-hlay)
Nanteos [nænt'eɪɒs] (nantáy-oss)
Nantffrancon [nænt'fræŋkən] (nant-fránkŏn)
Nantgaredig [ˌnæntgər'edɪg] (nant-gáréddig)
Nantgarw [nænt'gæru] (nantgárroo)
Nantgwynant [nænt'gwɪnənt] (nant-gwínnănt)
Nantlle ['næntɫeɪ] (nánt-hlay)
Nantmel ['næntmel] (nántmel)
Nant Peris [nænt 'perɪs] (nant pérriss)
Nantwich ['næntwɪtʃ] (nántwitch); ['næntwaɪtʃ] (nántwītch)
Nant-y-bwch [ˌnæntə'bux](nantăbŏŏch)
Nant - y - caws [ˌnæntə'kaus] (nantă-kówss)
Nantyffyllon [ˌnæntə'fʌɫɒn] (nantă-fúhlon)
Nant-y-glo [ˌnæntə'glou] (nantăglŏ)
Nant-y-groes [ˌnæntə'grɔɪs] (nantă-gróyss)
Nant-y-moel [ˌnæntə'mɔɪl] (nantămóyl)
Nantyronen [ˌnæntər'ounən] (nantă-rŏ̆nĕn)
Napier, f.n. ['neɪpjər] (náyp-yer); [nə'pɪər] (năpéer) The first is appropriate for John ~, inventor of logarithms.
Napier and Ettrick, Baron ['neɪpjər ənd 'etrɪk] (náyp-yer ănd éttrick)
Napier of Magdala, Baron ['neɪpjər əv 'mægdələ] (náyp-yer ŏv mágdălă)
Napley, f.n. ['næplɪ] (nápli)
Narberth ['nɑrbərθ] (naárbĕrth)
Nares, f.n. [nɛərz] (nairz)
Nasmith, f.n. ['neɪsmɪθ] (náyssmith)
Nason, f.n. ['neɪsən] (náyssŏn)
Nasse, f.n. ['næsɪ] (nássi)
Nathan, Baron ['neɪθən] (náythăn)
Natt, f.n. [næt] (nat)
Naulls, f.n. [nɒlz] (nawlz)
Navan ['nævən] (návván)
Navar ['neɪvər] (náyvár)
Navenby ['neɪvənbɪ] (náyvĕnbi)
Navin, f.n. ['nævɪn] (návvin)
Naworth ['navʊərθ] (nów-ŭrth); ['nawərθ] (naá-wŭrth)
Naylor, f.n. ['neɪlər] (náylŏr)
Nazeing ['neɪzɪŋ] (náyzing)

Neagh, Lough [lɒx 'neɪ] (lo<u>ch</u> náy)
Neal, f.n. [niːl] (neel)
Neale, f.n. [niːl] (neel)
Neaman, Yfrah, violinist ['ifrə 'nimən] (eéfrá neémán)
Nears, f.n. [nɪərz] (neerz)
Neath [niːθ] (neeth)
Neath, River [niːθ] (neeth)
Neatishead ['niːtstɪd] (neétstĕd); ['niːtɪs-hed] (neétiss-hed) *The first is the traditional village pronunciation. The second is used by Service personnel for the local R.A.F. Station.*
Neave, f.n. [niːv] (neev)
Neaverson, f.n. ['nevərsən] (névvĕr-ssŏn); ['nivərsən] (neévĕrssŏn)
Nebo ['nebəʊ] (nébbō)
Nechells ['nitʃlz] (neétchlz)
Neden, f.n. ['nidən] (neédĕn)
Needle, f.n. ['niːdl] (needl)
Neidpath Castle ['nidpɑːθ] (neédpaath)
Neild, f.n. [niːld] (neeld)
Neill, f.n. [niːl] (neel)
Neilson, f.n. ['nilsən] (neélssŏn)
Nelmes, f.n. [nelmz] (nelmz)
Nelson ['nelsən] (nélssŏn)
Nene, River [nen] (nen); [niːn] (neen)
Nepean, f.n. [nɪ'pin] (nĕpeén)
Nercwys, *also spelt* **Nerquis** ['neərkwɪs] (naírkwiss); ['nɜrkwɪs] (nérkwiss)
Nerquis *see* Nercwys.
Nesbitt, f.n. ['nezbɪt] (nézbit)
Ness, Loch *and* River [nes] (ness)
Nessler, f.n. ['neslər] (néssler)
Nethan, River ['neθən] (néthăn)
Nether Alderley ['neðər 'ɔldərlɪ] (né<u>ther</u> áwldĕrli)
Nether Broughton ['neðər 'brɔtən] (né<u>ther</u> bráwtŏn)
Nether Haugh ['neðər 'hɔf] (né<u>ther</u> háwf)
Nether Heyford ['neðər 'heɪfərd] (né<u>ther</u> háyfŏrd)
Nether Wallop ['neðər 'wɒləp] (né<u>ther</u> wóllŏp)
Netheravon ['neðəreɪvən] (né<u>th</u>ĕrayvŏn)
Nethercote ['neðərkət] (né<u>th</u>ĕrkŏt)
Netherne ['neðərn] (né<u>th</u>ĕrn)
Nethy Bridge ['neθɪ 'brɪdʒ] (néthi bríj)
Nettel, f.n. [nɪ'tel] (nĕtéll)
Netteswell ['netswel] (nétswel)
Nettleingham, f.n. ['netlɪŋhəm] (néttling-hăm)
Neubert, f.n. ['njubərt] (néwbĕrt)
Neven, f.n. ['nevən] (névvĕn)
Nevendon ['nevəndən] (névvĕndŏn)
Nevern, f.n. ['nevərn] (névvĕrn)
Nevin ['nevɪn] (névvin)
Nevis, Loch ['nevɪs] (névviss)
Nevisburgh ['nevɪsbərə] (névvissbŭrá)
New Byth ['nju 'baɪθ] (néw bíth)
New Clipstone ['nju 'klɪpstoʊn] (néw klípstŏn)
New Galloway [nju 'gæləweɪ] (new gálŏ-way)
New Kyo ['nju 'kaɪoʊ] (néw kí-ō)

New Quay ['nju 'ki] (néw keé)
New Romney ['nju 'rɒmnɪ] (néw rómni); ['nju 'rʌmnɪ] (néw rúmni)
Newark ['njuərk] (néwărk)
Neway, f.n. ['njuweɪ] (néw-way)
Newbegin, f.n. ['njubɪgɪn] (néwbiggin)
Newberry, f.n. ['njubərɪ] (néwbĕri)
Newbert ['njubərt] (néwbĕrt)
Newbery, f.n. ['njubərɪ] (néwbĕri)
Newbigging, f.n. ['njubɪgɪn] (néwbigging); [nju'bɪgɪn] (newbigging)
Newbigin, f.n. ['njubɪgɪn] (néwbiggin)
Newbold, f.n. ['njuboʊld] (néwbōld)
Newborough, *Anglesey, Northants., Staffs.* ['njubərə] (néwbŭrá)
Newbould, f.n. ['njuboʊld] (néwbōld)
Newboult, f.n. ['njuboʊlt] (néwbōlt)
Newbrough ['njubrʌf] (néwbruff)
Newburgh, *Aberdeen., Fife* ['njubərə] (néwbŭrá)
Newbury, f.n. ['njubərɪ] (néwbŭri)
Newby, f.n. ['njubɪ] (néwbi)
Newcastle, *Co. Down* ['njukasl] (néwkaassl)
Newcastle Emlyn ['njukasl 'emlɪn] (néwkaassl émlin)
Newcastle-under-Lyme ['njukasl ʌndər 'laɪm] (néwkaassl undĕr lím)
Newcastle upon Tyne ['njukasl əpən 'taɪn] (néwkaassl ŭpŏn tín); [nju'kæsl əpən 'taɪn] (newkássl ŭpŏn tín) *The second, being the local pronunciation, should normally take precedence over the other. Here, however, is a case where the first is firmly established national usage.*
Newcraighall ['njukreɪg'hɔl] (néwkrayg-háwl)
Newdigate, Sir Roger, *18th-c. antiquary* ['njudɪgeɪt] (néwdigayt); ['njudɪgɪt] (néwdigit) *Appropriate also for the ~ prize for English verse.*
Newell, f.n. ['njuəl] (néwĕl)
Newens, f.n. ['njuənz] (néwĕnz)
Newfound ['njufaʊnd] (néwfownd)
Newham, *Essex* ['njuəm] (néw-ăm); ['njuhəm] (néw-hăm)
Newham, *Northumberland* ['njuəm] (néw-ăm)
Newhaven ['njuheɪvən] (néw-hayvĕn)
Newington, f.n. ['njuɪŋtən] (néwingtŏn)
Newland ['njulænd] (néwland)
Newlove, f.n. ['njulʌv] (néwluv)
Newlyn ['njulɪn] (néwlin)
Newman, f.n. ['njumən] (néwmăn)
Newmark, f.n. ['njumark] (néwmaark)
Newmarket ['njumarkɪt] (néwmaarkĕt)
Newmills, *Fife* [nju'mɪlz] (newmíllz)
Newmilns [nju'mɪlz] (newmíllz)
Newnes, f.n. [njunz] (newnz)
Newport Pagnell ['njuport 'pægnəl] (néwport págnĕl)
Newquay ['nju-ki] (néw-kee)
Newrick, f.n. ['njurɪk] (néw-rick)
Newry ['njʊərɪ] (nyṓri)
Newsome, f.n. ['njusəm] (néwssŏm)

Newsome ['nju:zəm] (néwzŏm)
Newson, f.n. ['nju:sən] (néwssŏn)
Newstone, f.n. ['nju:stən] (néwsstŏn)
Newth, f.n. [nju:θ] (newth)
Newtimber ['nju:tɪmbər] (néwtimber)
Newton, f.n. ['nju:tən] (néwtŏn)
Newton Flotman ['nju:tən 'flɒtmən] (néwtŏn flóttmǎn)
Newton Kyme ['nju:tən 'kaɪm] (néwtŏn kim)
Newton Mearns ['nju:tən 'mɛərnz] (néwtŏn maírnz)
Newton Morrell ['nju:tən 'mɒrəl] (néwtŏn mórrĕl)
Newton Purcell ['nju:tən 'pərsl] (néwtŏn púrssl)
Newton Reigny ['nju:tən 'reɪnɪ] (néwtŏn ráyni)
Newton St. Boswells ['nju:tən snt 'bɒzwəlz] (néwtŏn sĭnt bózwĕlz)
Newton St. Cyres ['nju:tən snt 'saɪərz] (néwtŏn sĭnt sírz)
Newton St. Loe ['nju:tən snt 'loʊ] (néwtŏn sĭnt lŏ); ['nju:tən snt 'lu:] (néwtŏn sĭnt lŏó)
Newtonmore ['nju:tən'mɔːr] (néwtŏnmór)
Newtown, Montgomery ['nju:taʊn] (néwtown)
Newtown Crommelin ['nju:tən 'krʌmlɪn] (néwtŏn krúmlĭn)
Newtownards ['nju:tən'ɑːdz] (néwtŏn-aárdz)
Newtownbreda ['nju:tən'briːdə] (néwtŏn-breèdá); ['nju:tən'breɪdə] (néwtŏnbráydá)
Newtownbutler ['nju:tən'bʌtlər] (néwtŏnbúttler)
Newtownhamilton ['nju:tən'hæmɪltən] (néwtŏn-hámmiltŏn)
Newtownstewart ['nju:tən'stjʊərt] (néwtŏn-styŏó-árt)
Neyland ['neɪlənd] (náylǎnd)
Neyroud, f.n. ['neɪrud] (náy-rood)
Niall, f.n. and C.n. [nil] (neel); ['naɪəl] (ní-ál)
Nian, f.n. ['niən] (neè-ǎn)
Nias, f.n. ['naɪəs] (ní-ǎss)
Nice, f.n. [nis] (neess)
Nicholls, f.n. ['nɪklz] (nicklz)
Nicholson, f.n. ['nɪklsən] (nícklssŏn)
Nickalls, f.n. ['nɪklz] (nicklz)
Nickels, f.n. ['nɪklz] (nicklz)
Nicklin, f.n. ['nɪklɪn] (nick-lin)
Nickolls, f.n. ['nɪklz] (nicklz)
Nicoll, f.n. ['nɪkl] (nickl)
Nicolson, f.n. ['nɪklsən] (nícklssŏn)
Niddrie ['nɪdrɪ] (níddri)
Niddry ['nɪdrɪ] (níddri)
Nidon ['naɪdən] (nídŏn)
Nieman, Alfred, composer ['naɪmən] (nímǎn)
Niemeyer, f.n. ['nimaɪər] (neèmí-er)
Nigel, f.n. and C.n. ['naɪdʒl] (níjl)
Nihill, f.n. ['naɪhɪl] (níhil)
Nilsson, f.n. ['nɪlsən] (nílssŏn)
Nimmie, f.n. ['nɪmɪ] (nímmi)
Nimmo, f.n. ['nɪmoʊ] (nímmŏ)

Nimmy, f.n. ['nɪmɪ] (nímmi)
Nind, f.n. [nɪnd] (ninnd)
Nineham, f.n. ['naɪnəm] (nínǎm)
Nisbet, f.n. ['nɪzbɪt] (nízbĕt)
Nisbett, f.n. ['nɪzbɪt] (nízbĕt)
Niton ['naɪtən] (nítŏn)
Niven, f.n. ['nɪvən] (nívvĕn)
Nixon, f.n. ['nɪksən] (níckssŏn)
Noakes, f.n. [noʊks] (nōks)
Noblet, f.n. ['nɒblɪt] (nóbblĕt)
Nolan, f.n. ['noʊlən] (nólǎn)
Nonely ['nʌnəlɪ] (núnnĕli)
Nonsuch Palace ['nʌnsʌtʃ] (nún-sutch); ['nɒnsʌtʃ] (nón-sutch) The first of these is usual among scholars. Locally, however, at Nonsuch Park, where the site of the original Tudor palace is to be found, the second is current today.
Nonsuch Park ['nɒnsʌtʃ] (nón-sutch)
Nont Sarah's ['nɒnt 'sɛərəz] (nónt saírǎz)
Nonweiller, f.n. ['nɒnwilər] (nónweeler)
Norbury, f.n. ['nɔːbərɪ] (nórbūri)
Norfolk ['nɔːfək] (nórfŏk)
Norham ['nɒrəm] (nórrǎm)
Norie, f.n. ['nɒrɪ] (nórri)
Norledge, f.n. ['nɔːlɪdʒ] (nórlĕj)
Normanbrook, Barony of ['nɔːmənbrʊk] (nórmǎnbrŏŏk)
Normansell, f.n. ['nɔːmənsl] (nórmǎnssl)
Normanton, f.n. ['nɔːməntən] (nórmǎntŏn)
Normanton ['nɔːməntən] (nórmǎntŏn) Appropriate also for the Earl of ~.
Norquoy, f.n. ['nɔːkɪ] (nórki)
Norreys, Baron ['nɒrɪs] (nórriss)
Norris, f.n. ['nɒrɪs] (nórriss)
North Baddesley ['nɔːθ 'bædzlɪ] (nórth bádzli)
North Elmham ['nɔːθ 'elmǝm] (nórth élmǎm)
North Hykeham ['nɔːθ 'haɪkəm] (nórth híkǎm)
North Leigh ['nɔːθ 'li] (nórth leè)
North Leverton ['nɔːθ 'levərtən] (nórth lévvĕrtŏn)
North Ronaldsay ['nɔːθ 'rɒnldseɪ] (nórth rónnld-say); ['rɒnldfeɪ] (rónnld-shay)
North Tawton ['nɔːθ 'tɔːtən] (nórth táwtŏn)
North Walsham ['nɔːθ 'wɒlʃəm] (nórth wáwl-shǎm)
Northall, f.n. ['nɔːθɔl] (nórthawl)
Northam, f.n. ['nɔːðəm] (nórᴛ̱ǎm)
Northam ['nɔːðəm] (nórᴛ̱ǎm)
Northampton [nɔːˈθæmptən] (northámptŏn); [nɔːθˈhæmptən] (north-hámptŏn) The first is appropriate for the Marquess of ~.
Northbourne, Baron ['nɔːθbərn] (nórthbŭrn)
Northcliffe, f.n. ['nɔːθklɪf] (nórthkliff)
Northcote, f.n. ['nɔːθkət] (nórthkŏt)
Northenden ['nɔːðəndən] (nórᴛ̱ĕndĕn)
Northiam ['nɔːðɪəm] (nórᴛ̱iǎm)

Northleigh, *nr. Colyton, Devon* ['nɔrθli] (nórthlee)

Northleigh, *nr. Goodleigh, Devon* ['nɔrθli] (nórthlee); ['nɔrli] (nórlee)

Northmaven [nɔrθ'meɪvən] (northmáy-věn)

Northolme ['nɔrθoʊm] (nór-thōm)

Northowram [nər'θaʊərəm] (nŏr-thówrăm)

Northrepps ['nɔrθreps] (nórthreps)

Northsceugh ['nɔrθskjuf] (nórth-skewf)

Northumberland [nɔr'θʌmbərlənd] (northúmběrlănd)

Northumbrian, pertaining to Northumberland [nɔr'θʌmbrɪən] (northúmbriăn)

Northwich ['nɔrθwɪtʃ] (nórth-witch)

Norton Hawkfield ['nɔrtən 'hɔkfild] (nórtŏn háwkfeeld)

Norwich ['nɒrɪdʒ] (nórrij); ['nɒrɪtʃ] (nórritch)

Norwick ['nɔrwɪk] (nórwick)

Norwood, f.n. ['nɔrwʊd] (nórwŏŏd)

Nosworthy, f.n. ['nɒzwɜrðɪ] (nózwurthi)

Nothe Promontory, The [noʊð] (nōth)

Notley, f.n. ['nɒtlɪ] (nóttli)

Nott, f.n. [nɒt] (nott)

Nottingham ['nɒtɪŋəm] (nótting-ăm)

Novar [noʊ'vɑr] (nōvaár)

Novar Toll [noʊ'vɑr 'toʊl] (nōvaár tōl)

Novocastrian, native of Newcastle upon Tyne [ˌnoʊvoʊ'kæstrɪən] (nōvōkásstriăn)

Nowell, f.n. ['noʊəl] (nō-ĕl)

Nowlin, f.n. ['noʊlɪn] (nōlin)

Nowton ['noʊtən] (nótŏn)

Nudd, f.n. [nʌd] (nudd)

Nugent, f.n. ['njudʒənt] (néwjĕnt)

Nunburnholme, Baron [nʌn'bɜrnəm] (nunbúrnŏm)

Nuneaton [nʌn'itən] (nuneétŏn)

Nuneham Courtenay ['njunəm 'kɔrtnɪ] (néwnăm kórtni)

Nunns, f.n. [nʌnz] (nunnz)

Nunwick ['nʌnɪk] (núnnick)

Nupen, f.n. ['njupən] (néwpĕn)

Nuthall, f.n. ['nʌtɔl] (núttawl)

Nuthall ['nʌtl] (nuttl)

Nuttall, f.n. ['nʌtɔl] (núttawl)

Nuttgens, f.n. ['nʌtdʒənz] (nútjĕnz)

Nygaard, f.n. ['naɪgɑrd] (nígaard)

Nyholm, f.n. ['naɪhoʊm] (ní-hōm)

Nymans ['naɪmənz] (nímănz)

Nymet Rowland ['nɪmɪt 'roʊlənd] (nímmĕt rōlănd)

Nymet Tracey ['nɪmɪt 'treɪsɪ] (nímmĕt tráyssi)

O

O'Brien, f.n. [oʊ'braɪən] (ōbrí-ĕn)

O'Callaghan, f.n. [oʊ'kæləhən] (ōkáláhăn); [oʊ'kæləgən] (ōkálágăn)

O'Clarey, f.n. [oʊ'klɛərɪ] (ōkláiri)

O'Clee, f.n. [oʊ'kli] (ōkleé)

O'Connor, f.n. [oʊ'kɒnər] (ōkónnŏr)

O'Dea, f.n. [oʊ'di] (ōdeé); [oʊ'deɪ] (ōdáy)

O'Doherty, f.n. [oʊ'dɒxərtɪ] (ōdóchĕrti)

O'Donell, f.n. [oʊ'dɒnl] (ōdónnl)

O'Donovan, f.n. [oʊ'dʌnəvən] (ōdúnnŏvăn)

O'Ferrall, f.n. [oʊ'færəl] (ōfárrĕl)

O'Flaherty, f.n. [oʊ'flahərtɪ] (ōfláahĕrti); [oʊ'flɑərtɪ] (ōflaá-ĕrti)

O'Gara, f.n. [oʊ'gɑrə] (ōgaárá)

O'Grady, f.n. [oʊ'greɪdɪ] (ōgráydi)

O'Hagan, f.n. [oʊ'heɪgən] (ō-háygăn)

O'Halloran, f.n. [oʊ'hælərən] (ō-hálŏrăn)

O'Hana, f.n. [oʊ'hænə] (ō-hánná)

O'Hear, f.n. [oʊ'hɛər] (ō-haír)

O'Keefe, f.n. [oʊ'kif] (ōkeéf)

O'Keeffe, f.n. [oʊ'kif] (ōkeéf)

O'Leary, f.n. [oʊ'lɪərɪ] (ōleéri)

O'Loghlen, f.n. [oʊ'lɒxlən] (ōlóchlĕn)

O'Loughlin, f.n. [oʊ'lɒxlɪn] (ōlóchlin)

O'Malley, f.n. [oʊ'mælɪ] (ōmáli); [oʊ'meɪlɪ] (ōmáyli)

O'Mara, f.n. [oʊ'mɑrə] (ōmaárá)

O'Meara, f.n. [oʊ'mɑrə] (ōmaárá); [oʊ'mɛərə] (ōmaírá)

O'Neill, f.n. [oʊ'nil] (ōneél)

O'Reilly, f.n. [oʊ'raɪlɪ] (ō-rílí)

O'Rorke, f.n. [oʊ'rɔrk] (ō-rórk)

O'Rourke, f.n. [oʊ'rɔrk] (ō-rórk)

O'Shagar, f.n. [oʊ'ʃagər] (ō-shaagár)

O'Shaughnessy, f.n. [oʊ'ʃɒnɪsɪ] (ō-sháwnĕssi)

O'Shea, f.n. [oʊ'ʃeɪ] (ō-sháy); [oʊ'ʃi] (ō-sheé)

Oa [oʊ] (ō)

Oadby ['oʊdbɪ] (ŏdbi)

Oakenclough ['oʊkənklju] (ŏkĕn-klew); ['oʊkənklaʊ] (ŏkĕn-klow); ['oʊkənklʌf] (ŏkĕn-kluff)

Oaksey, Baron ['oʊksɪ] (ŏksi)

Oaten, f.n. ['oʊtən] (ŏtĕn)

Oates, f.n. [oʊts] (ōts)

Oath [oʊð] (ōth)

Oaze Deep ['oʊz 'dip] (ōz deép)

Oban ['oʊbən] (ŏbăn)

Obbard, f.n. ['oʊbard] (ŏbaard)

Oby ['oʊbɪ] (ŏbi)

Ochil Hills ['oʊxl] (ōchl)

Ochiltree, *Ayr.* ['ɒxɪltrɪ] (óchiltree); ['ʊxltrɪ] (óchiltree) *Appropriate also for* ~ *Castle.*

Ochs, f.n. [ɒks] (ocks)

Ochterlony, f.n. [ˌɒxtər'loʊnɪ] (ochtĕr-lŏni)

Ochtertyre [ˌɒxtər'taɪər] (ochtĕrtír)

Ocklynge ['ɒklɪndʒ] (ócklinj)

Ocle Pychard ['oʊkl 'pɪtʃərd] (ŏkl pítchărd)

Odam, f.n. ['oʊdəm] (ŏdăm)

Odey, f.n. ['oʊdɪ] (ŏdi)

Odiham ['oʊdɪəm] (ŏdi-ăm)

Odlum, f.n. ['ɒdləm] (óddlŭm)

Odom, *f.n.* ['oʊdʊm] (ódom)
Odsal ['ɒdzl] (óddzl)
Oertling, *f.n.* ['ɜːtlɪŋ] (úrtling)
Oettle, *f.n.* ['ɒʊtl] (ótl)
Oetzmann, *f.n.* ['oʊtsmən] (ótsmăn)
Offaly, *Earl of* ['ɒfəlɪ] (óffáli)
Offham ['ɒʊfəm] (ófăm); ['ɒfəm] (óffăm)
Oghill ['ɒxɪl] (óchil)
Ogilvie, *f.n.* ['oʊglvɪ] (óglvi)
Ogilvy, *f.n.* ['oʊglvɪ] (óglvi)
Ogley, *f.n.* ['ɒglɪ] (óggli)
Ogmore ['ɒgmər] (ógmor)
Ogof Ffynnonddu ['oʊgɒv ˌfʌnən'ðiː] (ógov funnŏn-thée)
Ogwell ['oʊgwel] (ógwel)
Ogwen ['ɒgwən] (ógwĕn)
Ogwen, *Lake* ['ɒgwən] (ógwĕn)
Okehampton [oʊk'hæmptən] (ōk-hámptŏn)
Okell, *f.n.* ['oʊkl] (ōkl)
Olantigh Towers, *Kent* ['ɒləntɪ 'taʊərz] (óllănti tówĕrz)
Old Meldrum ['oʊld 'meldrəm] (óld méldrŭm)
Old Romney ['oʊld 'rɒmnɪ] (óld rómni); ['oʊld 'rʌmnɪ] (óld rúmni)
Oldbury - on - Severn ['oʊldbərɪ ɒn 'severn] (óldbŭri on sévvĕrn)
Olderfleet ['oʊldərflɪt] (óldĕrfleet)
Oldhamstocks [oʊld'hæmstɒks] (óldhámstocks)
Olding, *f.n.* ['oʊldɪŋ] (ólding)
Oldpark ['oʊldpɑrk] (óldpaark)
Olender, *f.n.* [ə'lendər] (ŏlénder)
Olerenshaw, *f.n.* [ˌɒlɪ'renʃə] (ollĕrén-shaw)
Olivere, *f.n.* [ˌɒlɪ'vɪər] (ollivéer)
Olivier, *f.n.* [ə'lɪvɪeɪ] (ŏlívvi-ay); [ɒ'lɪvɪər] (ollívvi-er) *The first is appropriate for Sir Laurence ~, actor.*
Ollerenshaw, *f.n.* [ˌɒlɪ'renʃə] (ollĕrén-shaw); ['ɒlərɪnʃə] (óllĕrĕn-shaw)
Olliffe, *f.n.* ['ɒlɪf] (óllif)
Ollivant, *f.n.* ['ɒlɪvənt] (óllivănt)
Olliver Duchet watch tower ['ɒlɪvər 'dʌkɪt] (ólliver dúckĕt)
Olney ['oʊlnɪ] (ólni); ['oʊnɪ] (óni)
Olrig ['ɒlrɪg] (ólrig)
Olsen, *f.n.* ['oʊlsən] (ólssĕn)
Olsson, *f.n.* ['oʊlsən] (ólssŏn)
Olton ['oʊltən] (óltŏn)
Olver, *f.n.* ['ɒlvər] (ólver)
Olveston ['oʊlvɪstən] (ólvĕsstŏn); ['oʊlstən] (ólsstŏn)
Omagh ['oʊmə] (ómă)
Oman, *f.n.* ['oʊmən] (ómăn)
Omand, *f.n.* ['oʊmənd] (ómănd)
Ombersley ['ɒmbərzlɪ] (ómbĕrzli)
Ommanney, *f.n.* ['ɒmənɪ] (ómmăni)
Omoa [oʊ'moʊə] (ōmŏ-ă)
Onchan, *I.o.M.* ['ɒŋkən] (ónkăn)
Onecote ['ɒnkət] (ón-kŏt)
Ongar ['ɒŋgɑr] (óng-gaar)
Onibury ['ɒnɪbərɪ] (ónnibŭri)
Onich ['oʊnɪx] (ónich)

Onions, *f.n.* ['ʌnjənz] (únn-yŏnz); [oʊ'naɪənz] (ōnf-ŏnz) [ə'naɪənz] (ŏnf-ŏnz) *The first is appropriate for C. T. ~, philologist, grammarian and an editor of the Oxford English Dictionary; also for Oliver ~, author.*
Onllwyn ['ɒnɬʊɪn] (ónhlŏŏ-in)
Onny, *River* ['ɒnɪ] (ónni)
Onslow, *f.n.* ['ɒnzloʊ] (ónzlŏ) *Appropriate also for the Earl of ~.*
Openshaw, *f.n.* ['oʊpənʃə] (ópĕn-shaw)
Openshaw ['oʊpənʃə] (ópĕn-shaw)
Opie, *f.n.* ['oʊpɪ] (ópi)
Oppenheim, *f.n.* ['ɒpənhaɪm] (óppĕn-hīm)
Oram, *f.n.* ['ɒrəm] (áwrăm)
Oranmore and Browne, *Baron* ['ɒrənmor ənd 'braʊn] (órránmor ănd brówn)
Orbach, *f.n.* ['ɒrbæk] (órback)
Orcadian, *native of the Orkney Islands* [ɒr'keɪdɪən] (orkáydiăn)
Orchy *see* Bridge of Orchy.
Orczy, *Baroness, author* ['ɒrtsɪ] (órtsi)
Orda, *f.n.* ['ɒrdə] (órdă)
Orde-Powlett, *f.n.* ['ɒrd 'pɒlɪt] (órd páwlĕt) *Family name of Baron Bolton.*
Ordiquhill [ˌɒrdɪ'hwɪl] (ordi-whíll)
Orfordness ['ɒrfərd'nes] (órförd-néss)
Orgel, *f.n.* ['ɒrgl] (orgl)
Orgelist, *f.n.* ['ɒrdʒɪlɪst] (órjĕlist)
Oriel, *f.n.* ['ɒrɪəl] (áwri-ĕl)
Oritor ['ɒrɪtər] (órritŏr)
Orkney ['ɒrknɪ] (órkni)
Orlebar, *f.n.* ['ɒrlɪbɑr] (órlĕbaar)
Orlestone ['ɒrlstən] (órlsstŏn)
Orleton ['ɒrltən] (órltŏn)
Orlock ['ɒrlɒk] (órlock)
Ormeau [ɒr'moʊ] (ormó)
Ormelie, *f.n.* ['ɒrmɪlɪ] (órmĕli)
Ormerod, *f.n.* ['ɒrmrɒd] (órmrod); ['ɒrmərɒd] (órmĕrod)
Ormiston ['ɒrmɪstən] (órmisstŏn)
Ormiston ['ɒrmɪstən] (órmisstŏn)
Ormonde, *f.n.* ['ɒrmənd] (órmŏnd)
Ormonde, *Marquess of* ['ɒrmənd] (órmŏnd)
Ormrod, *f.n.* ['ɒrmrɒd] (órmrod)
Ornadel, *f.n.* ['ɒrnədel] (órnădel)
Oronsay ['ɒrənzeɪ] (órrŏnzay)
Orpin, *f.n.* ['ɒrpɪn] (órpin)
Orr, *f.n.* [ɒr] (or)
Orrell ['ɒrəl] (órrĕl)
Orridge, *f.n.* ['ɒrɪdʒ] (órrij)
Orton Longueville ['ɒrtən 'lɒŋvɪl] (órtŏn lóng-vil)
Ortzen, *f.n.* ['ɒrtsən] (órtsĕn)
Osbaldeston [ˌɒzbəl'destən] (ozbáldéss-tŏn)
Osbaston ['ɒzbəstən] (ózbásstŏn)
Osborn, *f.n.* ['ɒzbɔrn] (ózborn); ['ɒzbərn] (ózbŭrn)
Osborne, *f.n.* ['ɒzbɔrn] (ózborn); ['ɒzbərn] (ózbŭrn)
Osbourne, *f.n.* ['ɒzbɔrn] (ózborn); ['ɒzbərn] (ózbŭrn)

Osea Island ['ouzɪ] (ŏzi); ['ousɪ] (ŏssi)

Osers, f.n. ['ouzərz] (ŏzĕrz)

Osland, f.n. ['ɒzlənd] (ŏzzlánd)

Osler, f.n. ['ouslər] (ŏssler); ['ɒslər] (ŏssler); ['ɒzlər] (ŏzler)

Osmaston ['ɒzməstən] (ŏzmásstŏn)

Osney ['ouznɪ] (ŏzni)

Ospringe ['ɒsprɪndʒ] (ŏssprinj)

Ossett ['ɒsɪt] (ŏssĕt)

Ostler, f.n. ['oustlər] (ŏstler)

Oswestry ['ɒzwəstrɪ] (ŏzwĕstri); ['ɒzɪstrɪ] (ŏzzĕstri)

Otham ['ɒtəm] (óttăm)

Othery ['ouðərɪ] (ŏthĕri)

Othick, f.n. ['ɒθɪk] (óthick)

Otley, f.n. ['ɒtlɪ] (óttli)

Otley Chevin ['ɒtlɪ 'ʃevɪn] (óttli shévvin); ['ɒtlɪ 'ʃɪvɪn] (óttli shívvin)

Otterham ['ɒtərəm] (óttĕrăm)

Ottery St. Mary ['ɒtərɪ snt 'mɛərɪ] (óttĕri sĭnt maíri)

Ottinge ['ɒtɪndʒ] (óttinj)

Ottolangui, f.n. [,ɒtou'læŋgwɪ] (ottŏláng-gwi)

Ottoway, f.n. ['ɒtəweɪ] (óttŏ-way)

Ough, f.n. [ou] (ŏ)

Ougham, f.n. ['ɔəm] (áw-ăm)

Oughtershaw ['autərʃə] (ówtĕr-shaw)

Oughterside ['autərsaɪd] (ówtĕrssīd)

Oughtibridge ['utɪbrɪdʒ] (oótibrij); ['autɪbrɪdʒ] (ówtibrij); ['ɒtɪbrɪdʒ] (óttibrij); (áwtibrij); ['outɪbrɪdʒ] (ótibrij)

Oughton, f.n. ['autən] (ówtŏn); ['ɒtən] (áwtŏn)

Oughtrington ['utrɪŋtən] (oótringtŏn)

Ouin, f.n. ['ouɪn] (ŏ-in)

Ould, f.n. [ould] (ŏld); [uld] (oold)

Ouless, f.n. ['ulɪs] (oólĕss)

Oulton, f.n. ['oultən] (ŏltŏn)

Oulton, Staffs., Suffolk, Yorks. ['oultən] (ŏltŏn)

Oulton Broad ['oultən 'brɔd] (ŏltŏn bráwd)

Oulton Park ['oultən 'park] (ŏltŏn paárk)

Oundle ['aundl] (owndl)

Oury, f.n. ['urɪ] (oó-ri); ['uərɪ] (oŏri)

Ousby ['uzbɪ] (oózbi)

Ousdale ['auzdeɪl] (ówzdayl)

Ousden, also spelt **Owsden** ['auzdən] (ówzdĕn)

Ouseley, f.n. ['uzlɪ] (oózli)

Ousey, f.n. ['uzɪ] (oózi)

Ousley, f.n. ['uzlɪ] (oózli)

Ousman, f.n. ['uzmən] (oózmăn)

Ouston, f.n. ['austən] (ówsstŏn)

Ouston ['austən] (ówsstŏn)

Outen, f.n. ['autən] (ówtĕn)

Outhwaite, f.n. ['auθweɪt] (ówthwayt); ['ouθweɪt] (ŏthwayt); ['uθweɪt] (oóthwayt)

Outlane ['autleɪn] (ówtlayn)

Outram, f.n. ['utrəm] (oótrăm); ['autrəm] (ówtrăm) The first is appropriate for George ~ & Co., newspaper publishers.

Outred, f.n. ['utred] (oótred); ['autred] (ówtred)

Outstack, The ['autstæk] (ówt-stack)

Ouvry, f.n. ['uvrɪ] (oóvri)

Oved, f.n. [ou'ved] (ŏvéd)

Ovenden, f.n. ['ouvəndən] (ŏvĕndĕn)

Ovenden ['ɒvəndən] (óvvĕndĕn)

Ovens, f.n. ['ʌvənz] (úvvĕnz)

Over, Cheshire ['ouvər] (ŏver)

Over, Glos. ['uvər] (oóver)

Over Alderley ['ouvər 'ɒldərlɪ] (ŏver áwldĕrli)

Over Wallop ['ouvər 'wɒləp] (ŏver wóllŏp)

Over Whitacre ['ouvər 'hwɪtəkər] (ŏver whíttăker)

Overcombe ['ouvərkum] (ŏvĕrkoom)

Overend, f.n. ['ouvərend] (ŏvĕrend)

Overton, f.n. ['ouvərtən] (ŏvĕrtŏn)

Overton ['ouvərtən] (ŏvĕrtŏn); ['ɒvərtən] (óvvĕrtŏn)

Oving, Bucks., Sussex ['ouvɪŋ] (ŏving)

Ovingham ['ɒvɪndʒəm] (óvvinjăm)

Ovington, Norfolk ['ouvɪŋtən] (ŏvingtŏn)

Ovington, Yorks. ['ɒvɪŋtən] (óvvingtŏn)

Owen, f.n. and C.n. ['ouɪn] (ŏ-ĕn)

Ower, f.n. ['auər] (ów-er)

Owermoigne ['ouərmɔɪn] (ŏ-ĕrmoyn)

Owers, f.n. ['ouərz] (ŏ-ĕrz); ['auərz] (ów-ĕrz)

Owers light-vessel ['auərz] (ów-ĕrz)

Owersby ['auərzbɪ] (ów-ĕrzbi)

Owler Bar ['oulər 'bar] (ŏler baár)

Owlerton ['oulərtən] (ŏlĕrtŏn)

Owles, f.n. [oulz] (ŏlz); [aulz] (owlz); [ulz] (oolz)

Owmby ['oumbɪ] (ŏmbi)

Owsden see Ousden.

Owslebury ['ʌslbərɪ] (ússlbŭri); ['ʌzlbərɪ] (úzzlbŭri)

Owst, f.n. [oust] (ŏsst)

Owtram, f.n. ['autrəm] (ówtrăm)

Oxford ['ɒksfərd] (ócksfŏrd)

Oxford and Asquith, Earl of ['ɒksfərd ənd 'æskwɪθ] (ócksfŏrd ănd ásskwith)

Oxley, f.n. ['ɒkslɪ] (ócksli)

Oxnard, f.n. ['ɒksnərd] (ócksnărd)

Oxonian, member of Oxford University [ɒk'souniən] (ocksŏniăn)

Ozell, f.n. [ou'zel] (ŏzéll)

Ozengell Grange, Kent ['ouzəngel 'greɪndʒ] (ŏzĕn-gel gráynj)

P

Pabo ['pæbou] (pábbŏ)

Packer, f.n. ['pækər] (pácker)

Packham, f.n. ['pækəm] (páckăm)

Padarn, Lake ['pædərn] (páddărn)

Paddock, *f.n.* ['pædək] (páddŏk)
Padel, *f.n.* ['padəl] (paádĕl)
Padell, *f.n.* [pa'del] (paadéll)
Padiham ['pædɪəm] (páddi-ăm)
Padmore, *f.n.* ['pædmɔr] (pádmor)
Padog ['pædɒg] (páddog)
Padstow ['pædstoʊ] (pádsstō)
Paget, *f.n.* ['pædʒɪt] (pájjĕt)
Paget of Beaudesert, *Baron* ['pædʒɪt əv 'boʊdɪzɛər] (pájjĕt ŏv bṓdĕzair)
Pagham ['pægəm] (pággăm)
Pagin, *f.n.* ['peɪgɪn] (páygin)
Paignton ['peɪntən] (páyntŏn)
Pain, *f.n.* [peɪn] (payn)
Painswick ['peɪnzwɪk] (páynzwick)
Paish, *f.n.* [peɪʃ] (paysh)
Paisley ['peɪzlɪ] (páyzli)
Pakenham, *f.n.* ['pækənəm] (páckĕnăm) *Appropriate for the Earl of Longford's family name and for Baron ~.*
Pakenham ['pækənəm] (páckĕnăm)
Pakington, *f.n.* ['pækɪŋtən] (páckingtŏn)
Palairet, *f.n.* ['pæləret] (pálăret)
Paley, *f.n.* ['peɪlɪ] (páyli)
Palfery, *f.n.* ['pɒlfrɪ] (páwlfri)
Palfrey, *f.n.* ['pɒlfrɪ] (páwlfri)
Palfry, *f.n.* ['pɒlfrɪ] (páwlfri)
Palgrave, *f.n.* ['pælgreɪv] (pálgrayv); ['pɒlgreɪv] (páwlgrayv) *The first is correct for Sir Francis ~, 19th-c. Professor of Poetry at the University of Oxford and compiler of The Golden Treasury.*
Palgrave ['pælgreɪv] (pálgrayv)
Palin, *f.n.* ['peɪlɪn] (páylin)
Paling, *f.n.* ['peɪlɪŋ] (páyling)
Palk, *f.n.* [pɔk] (pawk); [pɒlk] (pawlk)
Pallant, *f.n.* ['pælənt] (pálănt)
Palles, *f.n.* ['pælɪs] (páless)
Palling ['pɒlɪŋ] (páwling)
Pallion ['pælɪən] (páli-ŏn)
Palliser, *f.n.* ['pælɪsər] (pálisser)
Pall Mall ['pæl 'mæl] (pál mál); ['pel 'mel] (péll méll)
Pallot, *f.n.* ['pæloʊ] (pálō)
Palm, *f.n.* [pɑm] (paam)
Palmer, *f.n.* ['pɑmər] (paámer)
Palmes, *f.n.* [pɑmz] (paamz)
Palnackie [pæl'nækɪ] (palnácki)
Palsgrave, *f.n.* ['pælzgreɪv] (pálzgrayv)
Pampisford ['pæmpɪsfərd] (pámpissfŏrd)
Panchen, *f.n.* ['pæntʃɪn] (pántchĕn)
Paneth, *f.n.* ['pænəθ] (pánnĕth)
Pankhurst, *f.n.* ['pæŋkhɜrst] (pánkhurst)
Panmure [pæn'mjʊər] (pan-myṓr)
Pannal ['pænl] (pannl)
Pannell, *f.n.* ['pænl] (pannl)
Panteg [pæn'teɪg] (pantáyg)
Pant-glas, *Caernarvon., Monmouth.* [pænt'glas] (pant-gláass)
Pantlin, *f.n.* ['pæntlɪn] (pántlin)
Pantycelyn [ˌpæntə'kelɪn] (pantăkéllin)
Pant-y-dŵr [ˌpæntə'dʊər] (pantădṓŏr)
Pantyffynnon [ˌpæntə'fʌnən] (pantăfúnnŏn)

Pantygasseg [ˌpæntə'gæseg] (pantăgásseg)
Pantygraig - wen [ˌpæntəgraɪg'wen] (pantăgrĭg-wén)
Pant-y-mwyn [ˌpæntə'mʊɪn] (pantămṓb-in)
Pantyscallog [ˌpæntə'skælɒg] (pantăskáhlog)
Pant-y-waun [ˌpæntə'waɪn] (pantă-wín)
Papa Stour ['papə 'stʊər] (paápá stṓŏr)
Papa Westray ['papə 'westreɪ] (paápá wéstray)
Papillon, *f.n.* [pə'pɪlən] (păpíllŏn)
Papworth, *f.n.* ['pæpwɜrθ] (pápwurth)
Paravicini, *f.n.* [ˌpærəvɪ'tʃɪnɪ] (parrăvitcheéni)
Parcell, *f.n.* [par'sel] (paarsséll)
Pardoe, *f.n.* ['pardoʊ] (paárdō)
Pardovan [par'dʌvən] (paardúvvăn)
Pares, *f.n.* [pɛərz] (pairz)
Pargiter, *f.n.* ['pardʒɪtər] (paárjitter)
Parham, *f.n.* ['pærəm] (párrăm)
Parham, *Suffolk, Sussex* ['pærəm] (párrăm)
Parham Park, *Sussex* ['pærəm 'park] (párrăm paárk)
Paris, *f.n.* ['pærɪs] (párriss)
Parish, *f.n.* ['pærɪʃ] (párrish)
Parker, *f.n.* ['parkər] (paárker)
Parkeston ['parkstən] (paárkstŏn)
Parkeston Quay ['parkstən 'ki] (paárkstŏn keé)
Parkgate ['parkgeɪt] (paárk-gayt)
Parkin, *f.n.* ['parkɪn] (paárkin)
Parkinson, *f.n.* ['parkɪnsən] (paárkinssŏn)
Parkmore [park'mɔr] (paarkmór)
Parkstone ['parkstən] (paárkstŏn)
Parlane, *f.n.* [par'leɪn] (paarláyn)
Parlour, *f.n.* ['parlər] (paárlŭr)
Parmenter, *f.n.* ['parmentər] (paármĕnter)
Parminter, *f.n.* ['parmɪntər] (paárminter)
Parmiter, *f.n.* ['parmɪtər] (paármitter)
Parnell, *f.n.* [par'nel] (paarnéll); ['parnəl] (paárnĕl)
Parnwell, *f.n.* ['parnwəl] (paárnwĕl)
Parotte, *f.n.* [pə'rɒt] (părótt)
Parracombe ['pærəkum] (párrăkoom)
Parry, *f.n.* ['pærɪ] (párri)
Parsley, *f.n.* ['parzlɪ] (paárzli)
Parslow, *f.n.* ['parzloʊ] (paárzlō)
Partick ['partɪk] (paártick)
Partickhill ['partɪk'hɪl] (paártick-hĭll)
Partridge, *f.n.* ['partrɪdʒ] (paártrij)
Pasco, *f.n.* ['pæskoʊ] (pásskō)
Pashley, *f.n.* ['pæʃlɪ] (páshli)
Pask, *f.n.* [pæsk] (passk)
Pasley, *f.n.* ['peɪzlɪ] (páyzli)
Passant, *f.n.* ['pæsənt] (pássănt)
Paston, *f.n.* ['pæstən] (pásstŏn)
Patchett, *f.n.* ['pætʃɪt] (pátchĕt)
Patel, *f.n.* [pə'tel] (pătéll)
Paterson, *f.n.* ['pætərsən] (páttĕrssŏn)

Patey, f.n. ['peɪtɪ] (páyti)
Path of Condie ['paθ əv 'kɒndɪ] (paáth ŏv kóndi)
Paton, f.n. ['peɪtən] (páytŏn)
Patrick, f.n. and C.n. ['pætrɪk] (pátrick)
Patrington ['pætrɪŋtən] (pátringtŏn)
Patriss, f.n. ['pætrɪs] (pátriss)
Patrixbourne ['pætrɪksbɔrn] (pátricksborn)
Patterson, f.n. ['pætərsən] (páttĕrssŏn)
Pattie, f.n. ['pætɪ] (pátti)
Pattishall ['pætɪʃl] (páttishl)
Pattison, f.n. ['pætɪsən] (páttissŏn)
Pattreiouex, f.n. ['pætrɪoʊ] (pátri-ō)
Pauer, f.n. ['paʊər] (pówer)
Paulerspury ['pɔlərzpərɪ] (páwlĕrzpŭri)
Paulina, one educated at St. Paul's Girls' School [pɔ'laɪnə] (pawlínă)
Pauline, one educated at St. Paul's School ['pɔlaɪn] (páwlīn)
Paulton, f.n. ['poʊltən] (pṓltŏn)
Pauncefort, f.n. ['pɒnsfərt] (páwnssfŏrt)
Pauncefote, f.n. ['pɒnsfət] (páwnssfŏt)
Appropriate also for the Barony of ~.
Pauperhaugh ['pɔpərhɒf] (páwpĕr-haaf)
Pavely, f.n. ['peɪvlɪ] (páyvli)
Pavenham ['peɪvənəm] (páyvĕnăm)
Paver, f.n. ['peɪvər] (páyver)
Pavey, f.n. ['peɪvɪ] (páyvi)
Paviere, f.n. ['pævjɪər] (páv-yair)
Paviour, f.n. ['peɪvjər] (páyv-yŭr)
Pavitt, f.n. ['pævɪt] (pávvit)
Pavlow, f.n. ['pævloʊ] (pávlō)
Pavy, f.n. ['peɪvɪ] (páyvi)
Pawley, f.n. ['pɔlɪ] (páwli)
Pawsey, f.n. ['pɔzɪ] (páwzi)
Paxton, f.n. ['pækstən] (páckstŏn)
Paynter, f.n. ['peɪntər] (páynter)
Paynting, f.n. ['peɪntɪŋ] (páynting)
Peabody, f.n. ['pibədɪ] (peébŏdi); ['pibɒdɪ] (peéboddi); ['peɪbɒdɪ] (páyboddi)
Peacey, f.n. ['pisɪ] (peéssi)
Peachell, f.n. ['pitʃl] (peetchl)
Peachey, f.n. ['pitʃɪ] (peétchi)
Peacock, f.n. ['pikɒk] (peékock)
Peaker, f.n. ['pikər] (peéker)
Pear, f.n. [pɪər] (peer)
Pearce, f.n. [pɪərs] (peerss)
Pearmain, f.n. ['pɛərmeɪn] (páirmayn)
Pearn, f.n. [pɜrn] (pern)
Pears, f.n. [pɪərz] (peerz); [pɛərz] (pairz) *The first is appropriate for Peter ~, singer.*
Pearson, f.n. ['pɪərsən] (peérssŏn)
Peart, f.n. [pɪərt] (peert)
Pease, f.n. [piz] (peez)
Peasgood, f.n. ['pizgʊd] (peézgŏod)
Peaston ['peɪstən] (páysstŏn)
Peate, f.n. [pit] (peet)
Peay, f.n. ['pieɪ] (peé-ay)
Pebardy, f.n. ['pebərdɪ] (pébbărdi)
Peberdy, f.n. ['pebərdɪ] (pébbĕrdi)
Pechell, f.n. ['pitʃl] (peetchl)
Peckham ['pekəm] (péckăm)

Pecorini, f.n. [ˌpekə'rinɪ] (peckŏreéni)
Pedair Ffordd ['pedaɪər 'fɔrð] (péddir fórth)
Peden, f.n. ['pidən] (peédĕn)
Peden ['pidən] (peédĕn)
Pedlow, f.n. ['pedloʊ] (pédlō)
Pedraza, f.n. [pɪ'drazə] (pĕdraáză)
Peebles ['piblz] (peeblz)
Pegna, f.n. ['penjə] (pén-yă)
Pegnall, f.n. ['pegnəl] (pégnăl)
Pegram, f.n. ['pigrəm] (peégrăm)
Peierls, f.n. ['paɪərlz] (pí-ĕrlz)
Peile, f.n. [pil] (peel)
Peill, f.n. [pil] (peel)
Peirce, f.n. [pɪərs] (peerss)
Peirse, f.n. [pɪərz] (peerz)
Peirson, f.n. ['pɪərsən] (peérssŏn)
Peiser, f.n. ['paɪzər] (pízer)
Peisley, f.n. ['pizlɪ] (peézli)
Pelaw ['pilə] (peélă) ; ['pilɒ] (peélaw)
Pelham, f.n. ['peləm] (péllăm)
Pelletier, f.n. ['peltɪeɪ] (pélti-ay)
Pelloe, f.n. ['peloʊ] (péllō)
Pellsyeat ['pelzjit] (péllz-yeet)
Pelynt [pə'lɪnt] (pĕlínt); [plɪnt] (plint)
Pembrey [pem'breɪ] (pembráy)
Pembroke, f.n. ['pembrʊk] (pémbrŏŏk)
Pembroke, *Wales* ['pembrʊk] (pémbrŏŏk) ; ['pembrɒk] (pémbrŏk)
Pembroke College, *University of Cambridge and University of Oxford* ['pembrʊk] (pémbrŏŏk)
Pen-allt [pen'ælt] (penáhlt)
Penally [pen'ælɪ] (penáli)
Penally Point [pen'ælɪ] (penáli)
Penarth [pə'narθ] (pĕnaárth)
Penberth [pen'bɜrθ] (penbérth)
Penberthy, f.n. [pen'bɜrðɪ] (penbérthi); ['penbərðɪ] (pénbĕrthi); [pen'bɜrθɪ] (penbérthi); ['penbərθɪ] (pénbĕrthi)
Penboyr [pen'bɔɪər] (penbóyr)
Penbuallt [pen'biælt] (penbeé-ahlt)
Pencader [pen'kædər] (pen-kádder)
Pencaitland [pen'keɪtlənd] (pen-káytländ)
Pencalenick [ˌpenkə'lenɪk] (pen-kălénnik)
Pencarnisiog [ˌpenkɑr'nɪsjɒg] (pen-kaarníss-yog); [ˌpenkɑr'nɪʃɒg] (pen-kaarníshog)
Pencarreg [pen'kæreg] (pen-kárreg)
Pencerig [pen'kerɪg] (pen-kérrig)
Pen-clawdd [pen'klaʊð] (pen-klówth)
Pencoed [pen'kɔɪd] (pen-kóyd)
Pencoys [pen'kɔɪz] (pen-kóyz)
Pencraig, *Hereford.* ['pen'kreɪg] (pén-kráyg)
Pencraig, *Radnor* ['penkraɪg] (pén-krīg)
Pendarves [pen'dɑrvɪs] (pendaárvĕss)
Pendeen [pen'din] (pendeén)
Pendell Court, *Surrey* ['pendl 'kɔrt] (péndl kórt)
Pendennis [pen'denɪs] (pendénniss)
Penderyn [pen'derɪn] (pendérrin)
Pendine [pen'daɪn] (pendín)

Pendlebury, f.n. ['pendlbərɪ] (péndlbŭri)
Pendomer [pen'doʊmər] (pendṓmer)
Pendrea [pen'dreɪ] (pendráy)
Pendrous, f.n. ['pendrəs] (péndrŭss)
Pendse, f.n. ['pendzɪ] (péndzi)
Pendyrys [pen'dʌrɪs] (pendúrriss)
Penegoes [pen'egɔɪs] (penéggoyss)
Penfold, f.n. ['penfoʊld] (pénfōld)
Penfound House, *Cornwall* [pən'faʊnd 'haʊs] (pĕnfównd hówss)
Pengam ['peŋgəm] (péng-găm)
Pengegon [pen'gegən] (pen-géggŏn)
Pengelly, f.n. [peŋ'gelɪ] (peng-gélli)
Pengersick [pen'gɜrsɪk] (pen-gérssick)
Pengwern, *Caernarvon., Flint., Merioneth* ['pengwɜrn] (pén-gwern)
Pen-hydd [pen'hɪð] (pen-heéth)
Penicuik ['penɪkʊk] (pénnikŏok)
Peniel ['penjəl] (pén-yĕl)
Penifiler [ˌpenɪ'fɪlər] (pennifeéler)
Penistone ['penɪstən] (pénnistŏn)
Pen-lan [pen'læn] (penlán)
Penlee [pen'li] (penleé)
Penlle'r-gaer [ˌpenłər'gɑr] (penhlĕr-gaár)
Pen-llin [pen'łin] (pen-hleén) *But see also* Penllyne.
Penlline *see* Penllyne.
Penllwyn-fawr [pen'łʊɪn 'vaʊər] (pen-hlŏo-in vówr)
Penllwyn-gwent [pen'łʊɪn 'gwent] (pen-hlŏo-in gwént)
Penllyn [pen'łɪn] (pén-hlin)
Penllyne, *also spelt* **Penlline** [pen'łaɪn] (pen-hlín) *These are locally accepted semi-anglicized forms. The Welsh language form is* Pen-llin, *q.v.*
Penmachno [pen'mæxnoʊ] (penmáchnō)
Penmaen - mawr [ˌpenmaɪn'maʊər] (penmĭn-mówr)
Penmon ['penmɒn] (pénmon)
Penmynydd [pen'mʌnɪð] (penmúnnith)
Pennal ['penl] (pennl)
Pennan ['penən] (pénnăn)
Pennant ['penənt] (pénnant)
Pennefather, f.n. ['penɪfeðər] (pénnifether); ['penɪfaðər] (pénnifaather)
Pennell, f.n. ['penl] (penl)
Pennells, f.n. ['penlz] (pennlz)
Pennethorne, f.n. ['penɪθɔrn] (pénnithorn)
Pennines, The ['penaɪnz] (pénnīnz)
Penninghame ['penɪŋhəm] (pénninghăm)
Pennington, f.n. ['penɪŋtən] (pénningtŏn)
Pennycuick, f.n. ['penɪkʊk] (pénnikŏok); ['penɪkwɪk] (pénni-kwick); ['penɪkjuk] (pénnikewk)
Pennyfather, f.n. ['penɪfeðər] (pénnifether); ['penɪfaðər] (pénnifaather)
Pennyman, f.n. ['penɪmən] (pénnimăn)
Penpergwm [pen'pɛərgʊm] (penpaírgŏom)
Penponds [pen'pɒndz] (penpóndz)

Penrhiw-ceiber [ˌpenʌrɪʊ'kaɪbər] (penri-oo-kíber)
Penrhiwlas [ˌpenʌrɪ'uləs] (penri-oóláss)
Penrhiwtyn [ˌpenʌrɪ'utɪn] (penri-oótin)
Pen-rhos, *Brecon., Monmouth., Montgomery.* [pen'hroʊs] (penrṓss)
Penrhos, *Caernarvon.* ['penʌrɒs] (pénross); ['penʌroʊs] (pénrōss)
Penrhos Lligwy [pen'hroʊs 'łɪgʊɪ] (penrṓss hliggŏo-i)
Penrhyn-coch [ˌpenʌrɪn'koʊx] (penrinkŏch)
Penrhyndeudraeth [ˌpenʌrɪn'daɪdraɪθ] (penrin-dídrīth)
Penrice [pen'raɪs] (penríss) *Appropriate also for ~ Castle.*
Penrith ['penrɪθ] (pénrith)
Penrose, f.n. ['penroʊz] (pénrōz); [pen'roʊz] (penrṓz)
Penryn [pen'rɪn] (penrín)
Pen-sarn [pen'sɑrn] (penssaárn)
Penselwood [pen'selwʊd] (penssélwŏod)
Penshaw ['penʃə] (pén-shá); ['penʃə] (pén-shaw)
Pentewan [pen'tjuən] (pentéw-ăn)
Pentir [pen'tɪər] (penteér)
Pentire Head [pen'taɪər] (pentír)
Pentland Firth ['pentlənd] (péntlănd)
Pentland Hills ['pentlənd] (péntlănd)
Penton, *Cumberland* [pen'tɒn] (pentón)
Pentonville ['pentənvɪl] (péntŏnvil)
Pentraeth [pen'traɪθ] (pentríth)
Pentre ['pentrə] (péntră)
Pentreath, f.n. [pen'triθ] (pentreéth)
Pentre-bach, *Brecon., Carmarthen., Flint., Glamorgan* [ˌpentrə'bax] (pentră-baách)
Pentre Celyn [ˌpentrə 'kelɪn] (pentră kéllin)
Pentrefelin [ˌpentrə'velɪn] (pentrăvéllin)
Pentrefoelas [ˌpentrə'vɔɪləs] (pentră-vóyláss)
Pentre - llyn - cymmer [ˌpentrəłɪn'kʌmər] (pentrăhlin-kúmmer)
Pentre-poeth, *Carmarthen., Glamorgan* [ˌpentrə'pɔɪθ] (pentrăpóyth)
Pentre Uchaf [ˌpentrə 'ɪxæv] (pentră íchav)
Pentrich ['pentrɪtʃ] (péntritch)
Pen-twyn, *Glamorgan, Monmouth.* [pen'tʊɪn] (pentŏo-in)
Pentwyn-mawr [penˌtʊɪn'maʊər] (pen-tŏo-in-mówr)
Pentyla [pen'tʌlə] (pentúllă); [pen'tɪlə] (pentíllă)
Pentyrch, *Glamorgan* [pen'tɜrk] (pentírk)
Pentyrch, *Montgomery.* ['pentɜrx] (péntirch)
Penwarden, f.n. [pen'wɔrdən] (penwáwrden)
Penwartha [pen'wɔrθə] (penwáwrthă)
Pen-waun [pen'waɪn] (penwĭn)
Penwill, f.n. ['penwɪl] (pénwil)
Penwith [pen'wɪθ] (penwíth)

Penwortham [ˈpenwərðəm] (pénwŭr-thăm)
Pen-y-bank [ˌpenəˈbæŋk] (pennăbánk)
Penyberth [peˈnʌbɜrθ] (penúbberth)
Pen-y-cae [ˌpenəˈkaɪ] (pennăkí)
Penydarren [ˌpenəˈdærən] (pennădárrĕn)
Pen-y-fai [ˌpenəˈvaɪ] (pennăví)
Pen-y-fan [ˌpenəˈvæn] (pennăván)
Pen-y-ffordd [ˌpenəˈfɔrð] (pennăfórth)
Penygelli [ˌpenəˈgelɪ] (pennăgéhli)
Penygenffordd [ˌpenəˈgenfɔrð] (pennă-génforth)
Penyghent [ˈpenɪgent] (pénnigent)
Pen-y-gors [ˌpenəˈgɔrs] (pennăgórss)
Pen-y-graig [ˌpenəˈgraɪg] (pennăgríg)
Pen-y-groes [ˌpenəˈgrɔɪs] (pennăgróyss)
Penygwryd [ˌpenəˈgʊərɪd] (pennăgŏórid)
Pen-y-lan [ˌpenəˈlæn] (pennălán)
Penyrheolgerrig [ˌpenrɪʊlˈgerɪg] (penri-ool-gérrig)
Pen-y-waun [ˌpenəˈwaɪn] (pennă-wín)
Penzance [penˈzæns] (penzánss)
Peock, f.n. [ˈpiək] (peé-ŏk)
Peover [ˈpivər] (peéver)
Peowrie, f.n. [ˈpaʊərɪ] (pówri)
Peper Harow [ˈpepər ˈhæroʊ] (pépper hárrō)
Peppiatt, f.n. [ˈpepɪət] (péppi-ăt)
Pepys, f.n. [ˈpepɪs] (péppiss); [pips] (peeps); [peps] (pepps) The first is appropriate for the family name of the Earl of Cottenham. The second was apparently that of the diarist, Samuel ~, and this is the pronunciation used today by the ~ Cockerell family, lineal descendants of the diarist's sister Paulina.
Pepys Cockerell, f.n. [ˈpips ˈkɒkərəl] (peéps kóckĕrĕl)
Percy, f.n. and C.n. [ˈpɜrsɪ] (pérssi)
Perdiswell Park, Worcs. [ˈpɜrdɪswəl] (pérdisswĕl)
Perebourne, f.n. [ˈperɪbɔrn] (pérrĕborn)
Perelman, f.n. [ˈperəlmən] (pérrĕlmăn)
Peress, f.n. [ˈperes] (pérress)
Perham, f.n. [ˈperəm] (pérrăm)
Perkins, f.n. [ˈpɜrkɪnz] (pérkinz)
Perks, f.n. [pɜrks] (perks)
Pernel, f.n. [pɜrˈnel] (pernéll)
Perott, f.n. [ˈperət] (pérrŏt)
Perowne, f.n. [pəˈroʊn] (pĕrṓn)
Perranarworthal [ˌperənərˈwɜrðl] (perrănărwúrthl)
Perranporth [ˌperənˈpɔrθ] (perrănpórth)
Perranuthnoe [ˌperənˈjuθnoʊ] (perrănéwthnō); [ˌperənˈʌθnoʊ] (perrănúthnō) Although the second is used extensively in the West Country, the first is the local pronunciation.
Perranwell [ˌperənˈwel] (perrănwéll)
Perranzabuloe [ˌperənˈzæbjʊloʊ] (perrănzáb-yŏŏlō)
Perret, f.n. [ˈpereɪ] (pérray)
Perrett, f.n. [ˈperɪt] (pérrĕt)
Perrin, f.n. [ˈperɪn] (pérrin)

Perring, f.n. [ˈperɪŋ] (pérring)
Perrins, f.n. [ˈperɪnz] (pérrinz)
Perris, f.n. [ˈperɪs] (pérriss)
Pershouse, f.n. [ˈpɜrshaʊs] (pérss-howss)
Persse, f.n. [pɜrs] (perss)
Perth [pɜrθ] (perth)
Pertwee, f.n. [ˈpɜrtwi] (pértwee)
Perutz, f.n. [pəˈruts] (pĕroóts)
Pery, f.n. [ˈpɪərɪ] (paíri); [ˈpɪərɪ] (peéri); [ˈperɪ] (pérri) The first is appropriate for the Earl of Limerick's family name.
Peschek, f.n. [ˈpeʃek] (pésheck)
Pestel, f.n. [ˈpestl] (pesstl)
Pestell, f.n. [pesˈtel] (pesstéll)
Pestridge, f.n. [ˈpestrɪdʒ] (pésstrij)
Peterborough [ˈpitərbərə] (peétĕrbŭră)
Peterculter [ˌpitərˈkutər] (peétĕrkoóter)
Peterhead [ˌpitərˈhed] (peetĕr-héd)
Peterkin, f.n. [ˈpitərkɪn] (peétĕrkin)
Peterlee [ˈpitərˈli] (peétĕr-leé)
Peters, f.n. [ˈpitərz] (peétĕrz)
Petersen, f.n. [ˈpitərsən] (peétĕrssĕn)
Petersham [ˈpitərʃəm] (peétĕr-shám)
Peterstone [ˈpitərstən] (peétĕrsstŏn)
Peter Tavy [ˈpitər ˈteɪvɪ] (peéter táyvi)
Petham [ˈpetəm] (péttăm)
Pethen, f.n. [ˈpeθən] (péthĕn)
Petherick, f.n. [ˈpeθərɪk] (péthĕrick)
Pethick-Lawrence, Barony of [ˈpeθɪk ˈlɒrəns] (péthick lórrĕnss)
Peto, f.n. [ˈpitoʊ] (peétō)
Petre, f.n. [ˈpitər] (peéter) Appropriate also for Baron ~.
Petrides, f.n. [pɪˈtridɪz] (pĕtreédĕz)
Petrie, f.n. [ˈpitrɪ] (peétri)
Petrockstow [ˈpetrɒkstoʊ] (pétrocksstō)
Pettener, f.n. [ˈpetnər] (péttĕnĕr)
Pettican, f.n. [ˈpetɪkən] (péttikán)
Pettifer, f.n. [ˈpetɪfər] (péttifer)
Pettigo [ˈpetɪgoʊ] (péttigō)
Pettigrew, f.n. [ˈpetɪgru] (péttigroo)
Pettingell, f.n. [ˈpetɪŋgl] (pétting-gl)
Pettistree [ˈpetɪstri] (péttisstree)
Pettit, f.n. [ˈpetɪt] (péttit)
Pevensey [ˈpevənzɪ] (pévvĕnzi)
Pevsner, Nikolaus, art historian [ˈnɪkələs ˈpevznər] (níckŏlăss pévzner)
Pewitt Island [ˈpjuɪt] (péw-it)
Pewsey [ˈpjuzɪ] (péwzi)
Pewsham [ˈpjuʃəm] (péw-shăm)
Peyre, f.n. [peər] (pair)
Peyton, f.n. [ˈpeɪtən] (páytŏn)
Pfammatter, f.n. [ˈfæmətər] (fámmăter)
Phaidon Press, publishers [ˈfeɪdən] (fáydŏn)
Phairkettle, f.n. [ˈfɛərketl] (faírkettl)
Phayre, f.n. [fɛər] (fair)
Phelops, f.n. [ˈfelɒps] (féllops)
Phelps, f.n. [felps] (felps)
Phemister, f.n. [ˈfemɪstər] (fémmisster)
Philie, f.n. [ˈfɪlɪ] (fílli)
Philiphaugh [ˈfɪlɪpˈhɒx] (fillip-hóch)
Philipson, f.n. [ˈfɪlɪpsən] (fíllipsŏn)
Phillack [ˈfɪlək] (fillák)

Philleigh ['fɪlɪ] (fílli)
Philorth [fɪ'lɔrθ] (filórth)
Phipps, f.n. [fɪps] (fipps)
Phizacklea, f.n. [fɪ'zæklɪə] (fizzácklia)
Picard, f.n. ['pɪkɑrd] (píckaard)
Picarda, f.n. [pɪ'kɑrdə] (pikaárdă)
Piccadilly [ˌpɪkə'dɪlɪ] (pickădílli)
Pickard, f.n. ['pɪkɑrd] (píckaard)
Pickavance, f.n. ['pɪkəvæns] (píckăvanss)
Pickaver, f.n. [pɪ'keɪvər] (pikáyver)
Pickering, f.n. ['pɪkərɪŋ] (píckĕring)
Pickett, f.n. ['pɪkɪt] (píckĕt)
Pickford, f.n. ['pɪkfərd] (píckfŏrd)
Pickles, f.n. ['pɪklz] (picklz)
Pickstock, f.n. ['pɪkstɒk] (píckstock)
Pickthorne, f.n. ['pɪkθɔrn] (píck-thorn)
Pickvance, f.n. ['pɪkvæns] (píckvanss)
Pidding, f.n. ['pɪdɪŋ] (pídding)
Piddinghoe [ˌpɪdɪŋ'huː] (pidding-hoŏ)
Piddletrenthide [ˌpɪdl'trentaɪd] (piddl-tréntíd)
Pidsley, f.n. ['pɪdzlɪ] (pídzli)
Piears, f.n. [pɪərz] (peerz)
Piegza, f.n. [pɪ'egzə] (pi-égză)
Pielou, f.n. [pi'luː] (peeloŏ)
Pierce, f.n. [pɪərs] (peerss)
Piercebridge ['pɪərs'brɪdʒ] (peérss-brĭj)
Piercy, f.n. ['pɪərsɪ] (peérssi) Appropriate also for Baron ~.
Pierpont, f.n. ['pɪərpənt] (peérpŏnt)
Pierrepont, f.n. ['pɪərpənt] ˌ(peérpŏnt)
Piers, C.n. [pɪərz] (peerz)
Pierssené, f.n. ['pɪərsneɪ] (peérssnay)
Pignon, f.n. ['pɪnjɒ̃] (peén-yŏng)
Pigot, f.n. ['pɪgət] (píggŏt)
Pigou, f.n. ['pɪguː] (píggoo)
Pike, f.n. [paɪk] (pík)
Pilbeam, f.n. ['pɪlbiːm] (pílbeem)
Pilbrow, f.n. ['pɪlbroʊ] (pílbrō)
Pilch, f.n. [pɪltʃ] (piltch)
Pilcher, f.n. ['pɪltʃər] (píltcher)
Pillaton ['pɪlətən] (píllătŏn)
Pilley, f.n. ['pɪlɪ] (pílli)
Pillgwenlly [pɪɬ'gwenɬɪ] (pihl-gwénhḷi)
Pillow, f.n. ['pɪloʊ] (píllō)
Pimperne ['pɪmpərn] (pímpĕrn)
Pinchbeck, f.n. ['pɪntʃbek] (pínsh-beck); ['pɪntʃbek] (píntch-beck)
Pinchen, f.n. ['pɪntʃən] (pínshĕn)
Pinches, f.n. ['pɪntʃɪz] (pínshĕz)
Pincus, f.n. ['pɪŋkəs] (pínkŭss)
Pinero, f.n. [pɪ'nɪəroʊ] (pineéro); [pɪ'nɛəroʊ] (pináíro) The first is appropriate for Sir Arthur Wing ~, playwright.
Pinfield, f.n. ['pɪnfɪld] (pínfeeld)
Pinged ['pɪŋged] (píng-ged)
Pinhoe [pɪn'hoʊ] (pin-hṓ)
Pinnegar, f.n. ['pɪnɪgər] (pínnĕgăr)
Pinnell, f.n. [pɪ'nel] (pinéll)
Pinter, f.n. ['pɪntər] (pín-ter) Appropriate for Harold ~, playwright.
Pinyoun, f.n. [pɪn'jaʊn] (pin-yówn); [pɪn'joʊn] (pin-yŏ́n)

Piper, f.n. ['paɪpər] (píper)
Pipewell ['pɪpwel] (pípwel)
Pipon, f.n. ['pɪpɒn] (peépon)
Pirant, f.n. ['pɪrənt] (pírrănt)
Piratin, f.n. [pɪ'rætɪn] (piráttin)
Pirbright ['pɜrbraɪt] (pírbrīt)
Pirie, f.n. ['pɪrɪ] (pírri)
Pirnie, f.n. ['pɜrnɪ] (pírni)
Pisciottani, f.n. [ˌpɪskɪə'tɑnɪ] (pisskiōtaáni)
Pistyll ['pɪstɪɬ] (písstihḷ)
Pitblado, f.n. [pɪt'bleɪdoʊ] (pitbláydō)
Pitcairn, f.n. [pɪt'kɛərn] (pitkaírn)
Pitcalzean House, Ross. [pɪt'kæljən] (pitkál-yĕn)
Pitfichie Castle, Aberdeen. [pɪt'fɪxɪ] (pitfíchi)
Pitfodels [pɪt'fɒdlz] (pitfóddlz)
Pitgaveny [pɪt'geɪvənɪ] (pitgáyvĕni)
Pitlochry [pɪt'lɒxrɪ] (pitlóchri)
Pitreavie [pɪt'riːvɪ] (pitreévi)
Pitscottie [pɪt'skɒtɪ] (pitskótti)
Pitsea ['pɪtsɪ] (pítsee)
Pitsligo [pɪt'slaɪgoʊ] (pitslígō)
Pittenweem [ˌpɪtən'wiːm] (pittĕnweém)
Pittodrie [pɪ'tɒdrɪ] (pitóddri)
Pittondrigh, f.n. ['pɪtəndraɪ] (píttŏndrī)
Pizey, f.n. ['paɪzɪ] (pízi)
Pizzey, f.n. ['pɪzɪ] (pízzi); ['pɪtsɪ] (pítsi)
Pladdies ['plædɪz] (pláddiz)
Plaid Cymru, Welsh National Party ['plaɪd 'kʌmrɪ] (plíd kúmri)
Plainmoor ['pleɪnmʊər] (pláynmŏŏr)
Plaisted, f.n. ['pleɪstɪd] (pláysstĕd)
Plaistow, f.n. ['pleɪstoʊ] (pláysstō)
Plaistow, Derby., Hereford. ['pleɪstoʊ] (pláysstō)
Plaistow, Essex ['plastoʊ] (pláasstō); ['plæstoʊ] (plásstō) Appropriate for the ~ Parliamentary Division.
Plaistow, Kent ['plastoʊ] (pláasstō); ['pleɪstoʊ] (pláysstō)
Plaistow, Sussex ['plæstoʊ] (plásstō)
Plaitford ['pleɪtfərd] (pláytfŏrd)
Plamenatz, f.n. ['plæmɪnæts] (plámmĕnats)
Planterose, f.n. ['plantərouz] (pláantĕrōz)
Plaskow, f.n. ['plæskoʊ] (plásskō)
Plasnewydd, Cardiff, [plæs'njuɪð] (plassnéw-ith)
Plastow, f.n. ['plæstoʊ] (plásstō)
Plater, f.n. ['pleɪtər] (pláyter)
Plath, f.n. [plæθ] (plath)
Platt, f.n. [plæt] (platt)
Platting ['plætɪŋ] (plátting)
Platts, f.n. [plæts] (platts)
Playle, f.n. [pleɪl] (playl)
Pleasance, f.n. ['plezəns] (plézzănss)
Pleasington ['plezɪŋtən] (plézzingtŏn)
Pleasley ['plezlɪ] (plézzli)
Pleass, f.n. [plis] (pleess); [ples] (pless)
Pleshey ['pleʃɪ] (pléshi)
Pleydell, f.n. ['pledl] (pleddl); [pleɪ'del] (playdéll)

Pleydell-Bouverie, f.n. ['pledl 'buvərɪ] (pléddl boóvĕri) *Family name of the Earl of Radnor.*

Pliatzky, f.n. [plɪ'ætskɪ] (pli-átski)

Plimmer, f.n. ['plɪmər] (plímmer)

Plinlimmon, *also spelt* **Plynlimon** [plɪn'lɪmən] (plinlímmŏn) *The Welsh form of the name is* Pumlumon, *q.v.*

Plomer, f.n. ['pluːmər] (plooʹmer) *Appropriate for William ~, author.*

Plomley, f.n. ['plʌmlɪ] (plúmli)

Plouviez, f.n. ['pluvɪeɪ] (ploóvi-ay)

Plowden, f.n. ['plaʊdən] (plówdĕn) *Appropriate also for Baron ~.*

Plugge, f.n. [plʌg] (plug)

Plumbe, f.n. [plʌm] (plum)

Plumbridge [plʌm'brɪdʒ] (plum-bríj)

Plume, f.n. [pluːm] (ploom)

Plumer Barracks, *Plymouth* ['pluːmər] (ploómer)

Plummer, f.n. ['plʌmər] (plúmmer)

Plumptre, f.n. ['plʌmtrɪ] (plúmtree)

Plumtre, f.n. ['plʌmtrɪ] (plúmtree)

Plungar ['plʌŋɡɑr] (plúng-gaar)

Plunkett, f.n. ['plʌŋkɪt] (plúnkĕt)

Pluscarden ['plʌskərdən] (plússkárdĕn)

Plymen, f.n. ['plaɪmən] (plíʹmĕn)

Plymouth ['plɪməθ] (plímmŭth)

Plymtree ['plɪmtrɪ] (plímtree)

Plynlimon *see* Plinlimmon.

Pochin, f.n. ['poʊtʃɪn] (pŏtchin); ['pʌtʃɪn] (pútchin)

Pocock, f.n. ['poʊkɒk] (pŏkock)

Podds, f.n. [pɒdz] (podz)

Podevin, f.n. ['poʊdəvɪn] (pŏdĕvin)

Podington ['pɒdɪŋtən] (póddingtŏn)

Poel, f.n. ['poʊel] (pŏ-el)

Poett, f.n. ['poʊɪt] (pŏ-ĕt)

Pointon, f.n. ['poɪntən] (póyntŏn)

Poirier, f.n. ['pɒrɪər] (pórri-er)

Polak, f.n. ['poʊlæk] (pŏlák); ['poʊlæk] (pŏlack)

Polapit ['pɒləpɪt] (póllăpit)

Polbathic [pɒl'bæθɪk] (polbáthick)

Polden Hill ['poʊldən 'hɪl] (pŏldĕn híll)

Poldhu [pɒl'dju] (poldéw)

Pole, f.n. [poʊl] (pŏl); [pul] (pool)

Polegate ['poʊlɡeɪt] (pŏlgayt)

Polgigga *see* Poljigga.

Pol Hill ['pɒl 'hɪl] (pól híll)

Poling ['poʊlɪŋ] (pŏling)

Poljigga, *also spelt* **Polgigga** [pɒl'dʒɪɡə] (poljíggă)

Polkemmet [pɒl'kemɪt] (polkémmĕt)

Polkerris [pɒl'kerɪs] (polkérriss)

Pollak, f.n. ['pɒlək] (póllăk)

Pollard, f.n. ['pɒlɑrd] (póllaard)

Pollock, f.n. ['pɒlək] (póllŏk)

Polmadie [ˌpɒlmə'diː] (polmădeé)

Polmont ['poʊlmənt] (pŏlmŏnt)

Polperro [pɒl'peroʊ] (polpérrŏ)

Polruan [pɒl'ruən] (polroó-ăn)

Polson, f.n. ['poʊlsən] (pŏlssŏn)

Polstead ['poʊlsted] (pŏlssted)

Poltalloch [pɒl'tæləx] (poltálŏ<u>ch</u>)

Poltimore ['poʊltɪmər] (pŏltimor) *Appropriate also for Baron ~.*

Polwarth, f.n. ['pɒlwərθ] (pólwärth) *Appropriate also for Baron ~.*

Polwarth ['poʊlwərθ] (pŏlwärth)

Polwhele, f.n. [pɒl'wiːl] (polweél)

Polwhele [pɒl'wiːl] (polweél)

Polzeath [pɒl'zeθ] (polzéth)

Pomeroy, f.n. ['poʊmrɔɪ] (pŏmroy); ['pɒmərɔɪ] (pómmĕroy) *The first is appropriate for the family name of Viscount Harberton.*

Pomfret, f.n. ['pʌmfrɪt] (púmfrĕt)

Pompey, *popular name for Portsmouth* ['pɒmpɪ] (pómpi)

Ponfeigh [pɒn'feɪ] (ponfáy)

Ponsanooth [pɒnz'nuθ] (ponz-noóth)

Ponsonby ['pʌnsənbɪ] (púnssŏnbi); ['pɒnsənbɪ] (pónssŏnbi)

Ponsonby, f.n. ['pʌnsənbɪ] (púnssŏnbi); ['pɒnsənbɪ] (pónssŏnbi)

Ponsonby of Shulbrede, Baron ['pʌnsənbɪ əv 'ʃulbrɪd] (púnssŏnbi ŏv shoólbreed)

Ponsonby of Sysonby, Baron ['pʌnsənbɪ əv 'saɪzənbɪ] (púnssŏnbi ŏv síʹzŏnbi)

Pontardawe [ˌpɒntər'daʊeɪ] (pontárdów-ay)

Pontardulais [ˌpɒntər'dɪləs] (pontárdíllăss); [ˌpɒntər'dɪlaɪs] (pontárdíllíss); [ˌpɒntər'dʌləs] (pontárdúllăss)

Pontcysyllte [ˌpɒntkə'sʌɪteɪ] (pontküssúh̲ltay)

Pont-dôl-goch [ˌpɒntdoʊl'goʊx] (pontdŏlgŏ<u>ch</u>)

Pontefract ['pɒntɪfrækt] (póntĕfrackt) *An old local form, which survives in the name of the liquorice sweets known as* 'Pomfret cakes', *is pronounced* ['pʌmfrɪt] (púmfrĕt) *or* ['pɒmfrɪt] (pómfrĕt).

Ponteland [pɒnt'ɪlənd] (ponteéländ)

Ponterwyd [pɒnt'eərwɪd] (pontáirwid)

Pontesbury ['pɒntɪzbərɪ] (póntĕzbüri)

Pontet, f.n. ['pɒntɪt] (póntĕt); ['pɒnteɪ] (póntay)

Pont-faen [pɒnt'vaɪn] (pontvín)

Pontfenny [pɒnt'venɪ] (pontvénni)

Ponthenry [pɒnt'henrɪ] (pont-hénri)

Pontlase, Pontlasse *see* Pontlassau.

Pontlassau, *also spelt* **Pontlase, Pontlasse** [pɒnt'læseɪ] (pontlássay)

Pontllan-fraith [ˌpɒntɬæn'vraɪθ] (pont-h̲lanvríth)

Pont-lliw [pɒnt'ɬju] (pont-h̲léw)

Pontllyfni [pɒnt'ɬʌvnɪ] (pont-h̲lúvni)

Pontlottyn [pɒnt'lɒtɪn] (pontlóttin)

Pontneathvaughan [ˌpɒntniθ'vɒn] (pontneethváwn) *The Welsh form is* Pontneddfechan, *q.v.*

Pontneddfechan [ˌpɒntneð'vexən] (pontneth̲véchăn) *The English form is* Pontneathvaughan, *q.v.*

Pontnewydd [pɒnt'newɪð] (pontné-wi<u>th</u>)

Pontnewynydd [ˌpɒntnə'wʌnɪð] (pontnĕ-wúnnith)

Ponton, Great *and* Little ['pɒntən] (póntŏn)

Pontop ['pɒntɒp] (póntop)

Pontop Pike ['pɒntɒp 'paɪk] (póntop pik)

Pontrhydfendigaid [ˌpɒntʰridven'digaɪd] (pontreed-vendeégid)

Pont-rhyd-y-fen [ˌpɒntʰridə'ven] (pontreedávén); [ˌpɒntʰridə'ven] (pontridávén)

Pontrilas [pɒnt'raɪləs] (pontrílăss)

Pont Sadog [pɒnt 'sædɒg] (pont sáddog)

Pontsticill [pɒnt'stɪkɪɫ] (pontstíckihl)

Pontyates [pɒnt'jeɪts] (pont-yáyts)

Pontyberem [ˌpɒntə'berəm] (pontăbérrĕm)

Pontybodkin [ˌpɒntə'bɒdkɪn] (pontăbódkin)

Pont-y-clun [ˌpɒntə'klin] (pontăkleén)

Pontycymmer [ˌpɒntə'kʌmər] (pontăkúmmer)

Pont-y-gwaith [ˌpɒntə'gwaɪθ] (pontăgwíth)

Pontymister [ˌpɒntə'mɪstər] (pontămísster)

Pontymoile [ˌpɒntə'mɔɪl] (pontămóyl)

Pontypool [ˌpɒntə'pul] (pontăpoól)

Pontypridd [ˌpɒntə'prɪð] (pontăpreéth)

Pontyrhyl [ˌpɒntə'rɪl] (pontáríll)

Poock, f.n. [puk] (pook)

Pook, f.n. [puk] (pook)

Poole, f.n. [pul] (pool)

Poolewe [pul'ju] (poŏléw)

Popham, f.n. ['pɒpəm] (póppăm)

Popkin, f.n. ['pɒpkɪn] (pópkin)

Pople, f.n. ['pɒupl] (pōpl)

Poples Bow ['pɒuplz 'bɒu] (pŏplz bŏ)

Poplett, f.n. ['pɒplɪt] (póplĕt)

Porchester, Baron ['pɔrtʃɪstər] (pórchĕsster)

Porges, f.n. ['pɔrdʒɪz] (pórjĕz)

Poringland ['pɔrɪŋlænd] (páwring-land); ['pɔrlænd] (pórland)

Porkellis [pɔr'kelɪs] (porkélliss)

Port Bannatyne [pɔrt 'bænətaɪn] (port bánnătin)

Port Eynon [pɔrt 'aɪnən] (port ínŏn)

Port Seton [pɔrt 'siːtən] (port seétŏn)

Port Talbot [pɔrt 'tɔlbət] (port táwlbŏt); [pɔrt 'tælbət] (port tálbŏt)

Portadown [ˌpɔrtə'daun] (portădówn)

Portaferry [ˌpɔrtə'ferɪ] (portăférri),

Portal, f.n. ['pɔrtl] (portl)

Portal of Hungerford, Viscount ['pɔrtl əv 'hʌŋgərfərd] (pórtl ŏv húng-gĕrfŏrd)

Portarlington, Earl of [pɔrt'arlɪŋtən] (portaárlingtŏn)

Portaskaig [pɔrt'æskeɪg] (portásskayg)

Portavo [ˌpɔrtə'vɒu] (portăvŏ)

Portavogie [ˌpɔrtə'vɒugɪ] (portăvŏgi)

Portballintrae [pɔrtˌbælɪn'treɪ] (portbalintráy)

Portbraddon [pɔrt'brædən] (portbráddŏn)

Porteous, f.n. ['pɔrtjəs] (pórt-yŭss); [ˌpɔrtɪəs] (pórti-ŭss)

Portesham ['pɔrtɪʃəm] (pórtĕ-shăm)

Portglenone [ˌpɔrtglə'nɒun] (portglĕnŏn)

Porthallow [pɔrθ'ælɒu] (porth-álŏ)

Porthcawl [pɔrθ'kɔl] (porthkáwl)

Porthcurno [pɔrθ'kɜrnɒu] (porthkúrnŏ)

Porth Dinllaen [ˌpɔrθ dɪn'ɬaɪn] (porth din-hlín) *Another form is* Portin-llaen, *q.v.*

Porthgwarra [pɔrθ'gwɒrə] (porthgwórră)

Porthleven [pɔrθ'levən] (porthlévvĕn)

Porthminster [pɔrθ'mɪnstər] (porthmínster)

Porthoustock [pɔrθ'austɒk] (porthówsstock); ['praustɒk] (prówsstock)

Porthpean [pɔrθ'pɪən] (porthpeé-ăn)

Porthtowan [pɔrθ'tauən] (porthtów-ăn)

Porth-y-rhyd [ˌpɔrθə'ʰrid] (porth-ăr
eéd)

Portincaple ['pɔrtɪnkæpl] (pórtin-kappl)

Portin-llaen [ˌpɔrtɪn'ɬaɪn] (portin-hlín) *see other form,* Porth Dinllaen.

Portishead ['pɔrtɪshed] (pórtiss-hed)

Portlethen [pɔrt'leθən] (portléthĕn)

Portloe [pɔrt'lɒu] (portlŏ)

Portmadoc [pɔrt'mædək] (portmáddŏk)

Portmahomack [ˌpɔrtmə'hɒmək] (portmăhómmăk)

Portnahaven [ˌpɔrtnə'hævən] (portnăhávvĕn)

Portnoid, f.n. ['pɔrtnɔɪd] (pórt-noyd)

Portobello [ˌpɔrtə'belɒu] (portŏbéllŏ)

Portquin [pɔrt'kwɪn] (portkwín)

Portreath [pɔr'triθ] (portreéth)

Portree [pɔr'tri] (portreé)

Portrush [pɔrt'rʌʃ] (portrúsh)

Portscatho [pɔrt'skæθɒu] (portskáthŏ)

Portskewett [pɔrt'skjurt] (portskéw-ĕt)

Portsmouth ['pɔrtsməθ] (pórtsmŭth)

Portsoy [pɔrt'sɔɪ] (port-sóy)

Portstewart [pɔrt'stjuərt] (port-styŏ̆árt)

Postcombe ['poustkəm] (pŏstkŏm)

Poster, f.n. ['pɒstər] (pósster)

Postgate, f.n. ['pousɡeɪt] (pŏst-gayt)

Postgate ['pousgeɪt] (pŏst-gayt)

Postling ['poustlɪŋ] (pŏstling)

Poston, f.n. ['pɒstən] (pósstŏn)

Postwick ['pɒzɪk] (pózzick)

Poton, f.n. ['pɒtən] (póttŏn)

Potter Heigham ['pɒtər 'heɪəm] (pótter háy-ăm); ['pɒtər 'haɪəm] (pótter hí-ăm); ['pɒtər 'hæm] (pótter hám)

Potterspury ['pɒtərzpərɪ] (póttĕrzpŭri)

Pottinger, f.n. ['pɒtɪndʒər] (póttinjer)

Pougher, f.n. ['pauər] (pówer); ['pʌfər] (púffer)

Poughill, *Cornwall* ['pɒfɪl] (póffil); ['pʌfɪl] (púffil)

Poughill, *Devon* ['pauɪl] (pów-il)

Poulett, Earl ['pɔlɪt] (páwlĕt)

Poulner ['paunər] (pówner); ['paulnər] (pówlner)

Poulshot ['poʊlʃɒt] (pṓl-shot)

Poulson, f.n. ['poʊlsən] (pṓlssŏn)

Poulter, f.n. ['poʊltər] (pṓlter)

Poultney ['poʊltnɪ] (pṓltni)

Poulton, f.n. ['poʊltən] (pṓltŏn)

Poulton-le-Fylde ['pʊltən lə 'faɪld] (pṓoltŏn lĕ ffīld)

Pounder, f.n. ['paʊndər] (pównder)

Poundstock ['paʊndstɒk] (pównd-stock)

Pounteney, f.n. ['paʊntnɪ] (pówntni)

Pountney, f.n. ['paʊntnɪ] (pówntni)

Poupart, f.n. ['pʊpɑrt] (poópaart); ['poʊpɑrt] (pṓpaart)

Pouparts Junction, London ['pʊpɑrts] (poópaarts)

Povall, f.n. ['poʊvl] (pṓvl)

Pover, f.n. [poʊvər] (pṓver)

Povey's Cross ['poʊvɪz 'krɒs] (pṓviz krṓss)

Pow, f.n. [paʊ] (pow)

Powburn ['paʊbɜrn] (pówburn)

Powe, f.n. [paʊ] (pow)

Powell, f.n. ['paʊəl] (pówĕl); ['poʊəl] (pṓ-ĕl)

Powerscourt, Viscount ['pɔrzkɔrt] (pórz-kort)

Powick ['poʊɪk] (pṓ-ick)

Powis, Earl of ['poʊɪs] (pṓ-iss)

Powis, Aberdeen. ['paʊɪs] (pówiss)

Powis Castle, Montgomery. ['poʊɪs] (pṓ-iss)

Powlett, f.n. ['pɔlɪt] (páwlĕt)

Powley, f.n. ['poʊlɪ] (pṓli)

Pownall, f.n. ['paʊnl] (pownl)

Powrie, f.n. ['paʊərɪ] (pówri)

Powys, f.n. ['poʊɪs] (pṓ-iss); ['paʊɪs] (pówiss) The first is appropriate for the family name of Baron Lilford; also for A. R. ~, church architect, John Cowper ~, poet and author, Llewelyn ~, author, Theodore Francis ~, author, and E. ~ Mathers, author and scholar.

Powys ['paʊɪs] (pówiss)

Poyntzpass [pɔɪnts'pɑs] (poyntspaáss)

Praa Sands see Prah Sands.

Praah Sands see Prah Sands.

Praed, f.n. [preɪd] (prayd)

Pragnell, f.n. ['præɡnəl] (prágnĕl)

Prah Sands, also spelt Praa, Praah ['preɪ 'sændz] (práy sándz)

Prangnell, f.n. ['præŋnəl] (práng-nĕl)

Prater, f.n. ['preɪtər] (práyter)

Pratley, f.n. ['prætlɪ] (prátli)

Praze [preɪz] (prayz)

Predannack, f.n. ['predənæk] (préddănack); ['prednæk] (préd-nack)

Preece, f.n. [pris] (preess)

Preedy, f.n. ['pridɪ] (preédi)

Prehen [prɪ'hen] (prĕhén)

Preidel, f.n. ['praɪdel] (prídel)

Prendergast, f.n. ['prendərɡæst] (prén-dĕrgasst)

Prendwick ['prendɪk] (préndick)

Prentice, f.n. ['prentɪs] (préntiss)

Prentis, f.n. ['prentɪs] (préntiss)

Prentiss, f.n. ['prentɪs] (préntiss)

Prescelly Mountains, also spelt Prescely [prɪ'selɪ] (prĕssélli)

Prestatyn [pre'stætɪn] (presstáttin)

Presteigne [pre'stin] (presteén)

Prestige, f.n. [pre'stidʒ] (presstij)

Preston ['prestən] (présstŏn)

Prestonpans ['prestən'pænz] (présstŏn-pánz)

Prestwick, Ayr. ['prestwɪk] (présstwick) Appropriate also for ~ Airport.

Prestwick, Northumberland ['prestɪk] (présstick)

Pretius, f.n. ['preʃəs] (préshŭss)

Pretty, f.n. ['prɪtɪ] (prítti); ['pretɪ] (prétti)

Pretyman, f.n. ['prɪtɪmən] (príttimän)

Prevatt, f.n. ['prɪvət] (prívvăt)

Prevezer, f.n. [prɪ'vizər] (prĕveézer)

Previté, f.n. [prɪ'vitɪ] (prĕveéti); ['prevɪtɪ] (prévviti)

Prevost, f.n. [prɪ'voʊ] (prĕvṓ); ['prevəst] (prévvŏst)

Prewer, f.n. ['pruər] (proó-er)

Preye, f.n. [preɪ] (pray)

Price, f.n. [praɪs] (priss)

Prideaux, f.n. ['prɪdoʊ] (príddō)

Prideaux ['prɪdəks] (príddŭks)

Pridham, f.n. ['prɪdəm] (príddăm)

Priestley, f.n. ['prɪstlɪ] (preésstli)

Princetown ['prɪnstaʊn] (prínsstown)

Pringle, f.n. ['prɪŋɡl] (príng-gl)

Prinknash Abbey ['prɪnɪdʒ] (prínnij)

Prinsep, f.n. ['prɪnsep] (prínssep)

Prioleau, f.n. ['prɪəloʊ] (preé-ōlō)

Prior, f.n. ['praɪər] (prí-ŏr)

Priske, f.n. [prɪsk] (prissk)

Pritchard, f.n. ['prɪtʃərd] (prítchărd); ['prɪtʃɑrd] (prítchaard)

Pritlove, f.n. ['prɪtlʌv] (prítluv)

Privett ['prɪvɪt] (prívvĕt)

Probert, f.n. ['prɒbərt] (próbbĕrt); ['proʊbərt] (prṓbĕrt)

Probus ['proʊbəs] (prṓbŭss)

Probyn, f.n. ['proʊbɪn] (prṓbin)

Procter, f.n. ['prɒktər] (próckter)

Profumo, f.n. [prə'fjumoʊ] (prŏféwmō)

Progin, f.n. ['proʊdʒɪn] (prṓjin)

Prosser, f.n. ['prɒsər] (prósser)

Prothero, f.n. ['prɒðəroʊ] (próthĕrō); ['prʌðəroʊ] (prúthĕrō)

Protheroe, f.n. ['prɒðəroʊ] (próthĕrō); ['prʌðəroʊ] (prúthĕrō)

Provan, f.n. ['prɒvən] (próvvăn); ['proʊvən] prṓvăn)

Provan ['prɒvən] (próvvăn)

Provis, f.n. ['proʊvɪs] (prṓviss)

Prudhoe ['prʌdoʊ] (prúddō); ['prʌdhoʊ] (prúd-hō)

Prue, f.n. [pru] (proo)

Prusmann, f.n. ['prʌsmən] (prússmăn)

Prynne, f.n. [prɪn] (prinn)

Prys, f.n. [pris] (preess)

Prytherch, f.n. ['prʌðərx] (prúthěrch); ['prʌðərk] (prúthěrk); ['prɪðɪk] (príthick) *The first is the Welsh pronunciation.*
Puckey, f.n. ['pʌkɪ] (púcki)
Puddefoot, f.n. ['pʌdɪfʊt] (púdděfŏŏt); ['pʊdɪfʊt] (pŏŏděfŏŏt)
Puddephat, f.n. ['pʌdɪfæt] (púdděfat)
Puddephatt, f.n. ['pʌdɪfæt] (púdděfat); ['pʊdɪfæt] (pŏŏděfat)
Puddletown ['pʌdltaʊn] (púddltown)
Pudney, f.n. ['pʌdnɪ] (púdni)
Pudsey ['pʌdsɪ] (púdssi)
Puffett, f.n. ['pʌfɪt] (púffět)
Puffin Island, *also* St. Seiriol Island, *q.v.* ['pʌfɪn] (púffin)
Pugh, f.n. [pjuː] (pew)
Pughe, f.n. [pjuː] (pew)
Pugin, f.n. ['pjuːdʒɪn] (péwjin)
Pugmire, f.n. ['pʌɡmaɪər] (púgmir)
Pulay, f.n. ['puːleɪ] (poólay)
Pulfer, f.n. ['pʊlfər] (pŏŏlfer)
Pullein, f.n. ['pʊlɪn] (pŏŏlĕn)
Pullen, f.n. ['pʊlɪn] (pŏŏlĕn)
Pulling, f.n. ['pʊlɪŋ] (pŏŏling)
Pulloxhill ['pʊləkshɪl] (pŏŏlóks-hil)
Pulteney, f.n. ['pʌltnɪ] (púltni); ['pʊltnɪ] (pŏŏltni)
Pulvertaft, f.n. ['pʌlvərtæft] (púlvěrtafft)
Pumlumon [pɪm'lɪmən] (pimlímmŏn) *see also* Plinlimmon.
Pumpherston ['pʌmfərstən] (púmfěrstŏn)
Pumpsaint ['pɪmpsaɪnt] (pímpsïnt)
Puncheston ['pʌnʃɪstən] (púnshĕsstŏn)
Puncknowle ['pʌnl] (punnl)
Punshon, f.n. ['pʌnʃən] (púnshŏn)
Purbrick, f.n. ['pɜːbrɪk] (púrbrick)
Purcell, f.n. ['pɜːsl] (purssl) *Appropriate for the 17th-c. composer, Henry ~.*
Purchese, f.n. [pɜː'tʃiːz] (purtcheéz)
Purdie, f.n. ['pɜːdɪ] (púrdi)
Purdue, f.n. ['pɜːdjuː] (púrdew)
Purdy, f.n. ['pɜːdɪ] (púrdi)
Purdysburn [ˌpɜːdɪz'bɜːn] (purdizbúrn)
Purefoy, f.n. ['pjʊərfɔɪ] (pyŏŏrfoy)
Purgavie, f.n. [pɜː'ɡeɪvɪ] (purgáyvi)
Puriton ['pjʊərɪtən] (pyŏŏritŏn)
Purleigh ['pɜːlɪ] (púrli)
Purley ['pɜːlɪ] (púrli)
Purnell, f.n. [pɜː'nel] (purnéll)
Pursey, f.n. ['pɜːzɪ] (púrzi)
Pusey, f.n. ['pjuːzɪ] (péwzi)
Putnam, f.n. ['pʌtnəm] (pútt-năm)
Putney ['pʌtnɪ] (púttni)
Putt, f.n. [pʌt] (putt)
Putteridge Bury ['pʌtərɪdʒ 'berɪ] (púttěrij bérri)
Pwll [puɬ] (poohl)
Pwllcrochan [puɬ'krɒxən] (poohl-króchăn)
Pwll-gwaun [puɬ'ɡwaɪn] (poohl-gwín)
Pwllheli [puɬ'helɪ] (poohl-héli); [pu'ɬelɪ] (poohlélli)
Pwll-Meyric [puɬ 'maɪrɪk] (poohl mírick)

Pyburn, f.n. ['paɪbɜːn] (píburn)
Pybus, f.n. ['paɪbəs] (píbüss)
Pyddoke, f.n. ['pɪdoʊk] (píddōk)
Pyecombe ['paɪkuːm] (píkoom)
Pyer, f.n. ['paɪər] (pí-er)
Pyle [paɪl] (píl)
Pylle [pɪl] (pill); [paɪl] (píl)
Pym, f.n. [pɪm] (pim)
Pyper, f.n. ['paɪpər] (píper)
Pyrah, f.n. ['paɪərə] (pírǎ)
Pyrford ['pɜːfərd] (pírfŏrd)
Pytchley ['paɪtʃlɪ] (pítchli)

Q

Quaddell, f.n. [kwə'del] (kwŏdéll)
Quadring ['kweɪdrɪŋ] (kwáydring)
Quaife, f.n. [kweɪf] (kwayf)
Quant, f.n. [kwɒnt] (kwont)
Quantock Hills ['kwɒntɒk] (kwóntock)
Quantrill, f.n. ['kwɒntrɪl] (kwóntril)
Quarff [kwɑːf] (kwaarf)
Quarles, f.n. [kwɔːlz] (kworlz) *Appropriate for Francis ~, 16th-c. poet.*
Quarles [kwɔːlz] (kworlz)
Quarley ['kwɔːlɪ] (kwórli)
Quarndon ['kwɔːndən] (kwórndŏn)
Quarr Abbey [kwɔːr] (kwor)
Quarrell, f.n. ['kwɒrəl] (kwórrĕl)
Quartermaine, f.n. ['kwɔːtərmeɪn] (kwórtěrmayn)
Quartley, f.n. ['kwɔːtlɪ] (kwórtli)
Quass, f.n. [kwɒs] (kwoss)
Quastel, f.n. ['kwɒstel] (kwósstel)
Quatermain, f.n. ['kwɒtərmeɪn] (kwáwtěrmayn)
Quatermass, f.n. ['kweɪtərmæs] (kwáytěrmass)
Quatt [kwɒt] (kwott)
Quay, f.n. [kweɪ] (kway)
Quaye, f.n. [kweɪ] (kway)
Quayle, f.n. [kweɪl] (kwayl)
Quealy, f.n. ['kwɪlɪ] (kweéli)
Quedgeley ['kwedʒlɪ] (kwéjjli)
Queenborough ['kwɪnbərə] (kweénbŭră) *Appropriate also for the Barony of ~.*
Queenslie ['kwɪnz'lɪ] (kweénz-leé)
Quelch, f.n. [kwelʃ] (kwelsh)
Quemerford ['kʌmərfərd] (kúmměrfŏrd)
Queniborough ['kwenɪbərə] (kwénnibŭră)
Quenington ['kwenɪŋtən] (kwénningtŏn) *Appropriate also for Viscount ~.*
Quennell, f.n. [kwɪ'nel] (kwěnéll)
Quentin, f.n. ['kwentɪn] (kwéntin)
Querée, f.n. ['kerɪ] (kérri)
Queripel, f.n. ['kwerɪpel] (kwérripel)
Quernmore ['kwɔːmər] (kwáwrmer); ['kwɑːmər] (kwaármer)

Quertier, f.n. ['kɜrtɪeɪ] (kérti-ay) ; ['kwɜr-tɪər] (kwérti-er)

Quesnel, f.n. [kwɪ'nel] (kwĕnéll) ; ['keɪnl] (kaynl)

Quested, f.n. ['kwestɪd] (kwésstĕd)

Quethiock ['kweðɪk] (kwéthick) ; ['kweθɪk] (kwéthick) ; ['kwɪðɪk] (kwíthick)

Quibell, f.n. [kwɪ'bel] (kwibéll) ; ['kwɪbl] (kwibbl) ; ['kwaɪbl] (kwíbl) *The third is appropriate for the Barony of ~ of Scunthorpe.*

Quicke, f.n. [kwɪk] (kwick)

Quigley, f.n. ['kwɪglɪ] (kwígli)

Quiller-Couch, Sir Arthur, author ['kwɪlər 'kutʃ] (kwíller koŏtch)

Quilliam, f.n. ['kwɪljəm] (kwíl-yăm)

Quilter, f.n. ['kwɪltər] (kwílter)

Quin, f.n. [kwɪn] (kwin)

Quinain, f.n. [kwɪ'neɪn] (kwináyn)

Quinan, f.n. ['kwaɪnən] (kwínăn)

Quinault, f.n. ['kwɪnəlt] (kwínnŭlt)

Quincey, f.n. ['kwɪnsɪ] (kwínssi)

Quincy, f.n. ['kwɪnsɪ] (kwínssi)

Quinnell, f.n. [kwɪ'nel] (kwinéll)

Quintana, f.n. [kwɪn'tanə] (kwintaánă)

Quinton, f.n. ['kwɪntən] (kwíntŏn)

Quinton ['kwɪntən] (kwíntŏn)

Quirke, f.n. [kwɜrk] (kwirk)

Quitak, f.n. ['kwɪtæk] (kwíttack)

Quixall, f.n. ['kwɪksɔl] (kwícksawl)

Quoich, Loch *and* River [kɔɪx] (koych)

Quoile, River [kɔɪl] (koyl)

Quorn *Hunt* [kwɔrn] (kworn)

Quothquan ['kwɒθ'kwɒn] (kwóth-kwón)

Quy, f.n. [kwaɪ] (kwī)

Quy [kwaɪ] (kwī)

R

Raad, f.n. [rad] (raad)

Raans Manor, *Bucks.* [reɪnz] (raynz)

Raasay ['raseɪ] (raássay)

Rabbetts, f.n. [rə'bets] (răbétts)

Rabin, f.n. ['reɪbɪn] (ráybin)

Rabinowitz, f.n. [rə'bɪnəwɪts] (răbínnŏwits)

Radcliffe, f.n. ['rædklɪf] (rádkliff)

Radcliffe ['rædklɪf] (rádkliff)

Rademon [rə'demən] (rădémmŏn)

Radford, f.n. ['rædfərd] (rádfŏrd)

Radford Semele ['rædfərd 'semɪlɪ] (rádfŏrd sémmĕli)

Radice, f.n. [rə'dɪtʃɪ] (rădeétchi)

Radleian, one educated at Radley College [ræd'liən] (radleé-ăn)

Radley, f.n. ['rædlɪ] (rádli)

Radnor ['rædnər] (rádnŏr) *Appropriate also for the Earl of ~.*

Rado, f.n. ['reɪdoʊ] (ráydŏ)

Radyr ['rædər] (rádder)

Rae, f.n. [reɪ] (ray)

Rael, f.n. [reɪl] (rayl)

Raffan, f.n. ['ræfən] (ráffăn)

Raffrey ['ræfrɪ] (ráffri)

Ragg, f.n. [ræg] (rag)

Raggett, f.n. ['rægɪt] (rággĕt)

Raghan, f.n. ['reɪgən] (ráygăn)

Raglan ['ræglən] (ráglăn) *Appropriate also for Baron ~.*

Ragosin, f.n. ['rægəsɪn] (rágŏssin)

Rahere, founder of St. Bartholomew the Great and of St. Bartholomew's Hospital ['reɪhɪər] (ráyheer) ; [rə'hɪər] (răheér)

Rahilly, f.n. ['raɪlɪ] (raá-illi)

Raholp [rə'hɒlp] (răhólp)

Raikes, f.n. [reɪks] (rayks)

Rainbow, f.n. ['reɪnboʊ] (ráynbŏ)

Raine, f.n. [reɪn] (rayn)

Rainger, f.n. ['reɪndʒər] (ráynjer)

Rainier, f.n. ['reɪnɪeɪ] (ráyni-ay) ; ['reɪn-jər] (ráyn-yer)

Rainsberry, f.n. ['reɪnzbərɪ] (ráynzbĕri)

Rainsford, f.n. ['reɪnzfərd] (ráynzfŏrd)

Raisbeck, f.n. ['rɔɪzbek] (ráyzbeck)

Raishbrook, f.n. ['reɪʃbrʊk] (ráyshbrŏŏk)

Raisman, f.n. ['reɪzmən] (ráyzmăn)

Raistrick, f.n. ['reɪstrɪk] (ráysstrick)

Rakoff, f.n. ['reɪkɒf] (ráykoff)

Ralegh, f.n. ['rɔlɪ] (ráwli) ; ['ralɪ] (ráali) ; ['rælɪ] (ráli)

Raleigh, f.n. ['ralɪ] (raáli) ; ['rælɪ] (ráli) ; ['rɔlɪ] (ráwli) *The indications are that the third of these was the personal pronunciation of the 16th-c. navigator, Sir Walter ~, but today, even among scholars, his treatment seems to vary according to taste. The second is appropriate for the ~ bicycle.*

Ralling, f.n. ['rælɪŋ] (ráling)

Raloo [rə'lu] (răloó)

Ralph, C.n. [rælf] (ralf) ; [reɪf] (rayf) ; [ræf] (raff)

Ralph, f.n. [rælf] (ralf)

Ralph Gore yachting trophy ['reɪf 'gɔr] (ráyf gór)

Ralphs, f.n. [rælfs] (ralfs)

Ralston, f.n. ['rɒlstən] (ráwlsstŏn) ; ['rælstən] (rálsstŏn)

Ralston ['rɒlstən] (ráwlsstŏn)

Ramage, f.n. ['ræmɪdʒ] (rámmij)

Rambaut, f.n. ['rɒmboʊ] (rómbŏ) ; ['rʌmboʊ] (raámbŏ)

Rame [reɪm] (raym) *Appropriate also for ~ Head.*

Ramelson, f.n. ['ræmlsən] (rámlssŏn)

Ramore Head [rə'mɔr] (rămór)

Rampisham ['ræmpɪʃəm] (rámpi-shăm)

Rampton ['ræmptən] (rámptŏn)

Ramsay, f.n. ['ræmzɪ] (rámzi) *Appropriate also for Baron ~.*

Ramsbotham, f.n. ['ræmzbɒtəm] (rámzbottăm) ; ['ræmzbʌθəm] (rámzboth-ăm) *The second is appropriate for Viscount Soulbury's family name.*

Ramseyer, *f.n.* ['ræmseɪər] (rámssay-er)

Ramsgate ['ræmzgeɪt] (rámzgayt)

Ramshaw, *f.n.* ['ræmʃɔ] (rám-shaw)

Ramus, *f.n.* ['reɪməs] (ráymŭss)

Ramuz, *f.n.* ['reɪmʌz] (ráymuz)

Ranalow, *f.n.* ['rænəloʊ] (ránnálō)

Rance, *f.n.* [ræns] (ranss)

Ranchev, *f.n.* ['ræntʃev] (rántchev)

Randall, *f.n.* ['rændl] (randl)

Randalstown ['rændlztaʊn] (rándlz-town)

Randolph, *f.n. and C.n.* ['rændɒlf] (rándolf)

Ranelagh Gardens ['rænɪlə] (ránnĕlă)

Ranfurly, *Earl of* ['rænfərlɪ] (ránfúrli)

Rangag, *Loch* ['ræŋgæg] (rán-gag)

Ranger, *f.n.* ['reɪndʒər] (ráynjer)

Ranish ['rænɪʃ] (ránnish)

Rankeillour [ræŋ'kɪlər] (rankeĕlŭr) *Appropriate also for Baron ~.*

Rankin, *f.n.* ['ræŋkɪn] (ránkin)

Rankine, *f.n.* ['ræŋkɪn] (ránkin)

Rannoch ['rænəx] (ránnŏ<u>ch</u>)

Ransome, *f.n.* ['rænsəm] (ránssŏm)

Ranulph, *C.n.* ['rænʌlf] (ránnulf)

Raper, *f.n.* ['reɪpər] (ráyper)

Raphael, *f.n.* ['reɪfl] (rayfl); ['ræfeɪl] (ráffayl); ['ræfɪəl] (ráffi-ĕl)

Raphael Park, *Essex* ['reɪfl] (rayfl)

Rapoport, *f.n.* ['ræpoʊpɔrt] (ráppōport)

Rapp, *f.n.* [ræp] (rap)

Rappitt, *f.n.* ['ræpɪt] (ráppit)

Rasharkin [rə'ʃɑrkɪn] (ră-shaárkin)

Rashee [rə'ʃi] (ră-sheé)

Rashleigh, *f.n.* ['ræʃlɪ] (ráshlee)

Rasmussen, *f.n.* ['ræsmʊsən] (rássmŏ͝ossĕn)

Rassal Ashwood ['ræsl 'æʃwʊd] (rássl áshwŏͅod)

Ratcheugh ['rætʃəf] (rátchŭff)

Ratcliff, *f.n.* ['rætklɪf] (rátkliff)

Ratcliffe, *f.n.* ['rætklɪf] (rátkliff)

Ratendone, ‖*Viscount* ['rætəndʌn] (ráttĕndun)

Rathbone, *f.n.* ['ræθboʊn] (ráthbōn); ['ræθbən] (ráthbŏn)

Rathcavan, *Baron* [ræθ'kævən] (rathkávvăn)

Rathdonnel, *f.n.* [ræθ'dɒnl] (rathdónnl)

Rathdonnell, *Baron* [ræθ'dɒnl] (rathdónnl)

Rathe, *f.n.* [reɪθ] (rayth)

Rathen ['reɪθən] (ráythĕn)

Rathfriland [ræθ'fraɪlənd] (rathfríländ)

Rathlin ['ræθlɪn] (ráthlin)

Rathmore, *f.n.* [ræθ'mɔr] (rathmór)

Ratho ['raθoʊ] (raáthō)

Rathven ['ræθvən] (ráthvĕn)

Ratigan, *f.n.* ['rætɪɡən] (ráttigăn)

Rattale, *f.n.* ['rætl] (rattl)

Rattenbury, *f.n.* ['rætənbərɪ] (ráttĕnbŭri)

Ratten Clough ['rætən 'klʌf] (ráttĕn klúff)

Rattigan, *f.n.* ['rætɪɡən] (ráttigăn)

Rattle, *f.n.* ['rætl] (rattl)

Rattray, *f.n.* ['rætrɪ] (ráttri)

Rattray ['rætrɪ] (ráttri)

Raughton Head ['rɑftən 'hed] (raáftŏn héd); ['rɒftən 'hed] (rófftŏn héd)

Raunds [rɔndz] (rawndz)

Ravelston ['rævlstən] (rávvlstŏn)

Ravendale ['reɪvəndeɪl] (ráyvĕndayl)

Ravenglass ['reɪvənglas] (ráyvĕn-glaass)

Raveningham ['rævənɪŋəm] (rávvĕningăm); ['rævɪŋəm] (rávving-ăm); ['rænɪŋəm] (ránning-ăm) *The third is particularly associated with ~ Hall.*

Ravensdale, *Baron* ['reɪvənzdeɪl] (ráyvĕnzdayl)

Ravenstruther ['reɪvənstrʌðər] (ráyvĕnstru͝ther)

Raverat, *f.n.* ['ravərə] (raávĕraa)

Ravertz, *f.n.* ['rævərts] (rávvĕrts)

Ravillious, *f.n.* [rə'vɪlɪəs] (răvílli-ŭss)

Raw, *f.n.* [rɔ] (raw)

Rawlings, *f.n.* ['rɔlɪŋz] (ráwlingz)

Rawlins, *f.n.* ['rɔlɪnz] (ráwlinz)

Raworth, *f.n.* ['reɪwərθ] (ráy-wŭrth)

Rawreth ['rɔrəθ] (ráwrĕth)

Rawtenstall ['rɒtənstɒl] (ráwtĕnstawl); ['rɒtənstɒl] (róttĕnstawl)

Rawthey, *River* ['rɒðɪ] (ráw<u>th</u>i)

Raybould, *f.n.* ['reɪboʊld] (ráybōld)

Rayel, *f.n.* ['reɪəl] (ráy-ĕl)

Rayleigh ['reɪlɪ] (ráyli) *Appropriate also for Baron ~.*

Raymont, *f.n.* ['reɪmɒnt] (ráymont)

Rayner, *f.n.* ['reɪnər] (ráyner)

Raynham, *f.n.* ['reɪnəm] (ráynăm)

Raynsford, *f.n.* ['reɪnzfərd] (ráynzfŏrd)

Razzall, *f.n.* ['ræzl] (razzl)

Rea, *f.n.* [reɪ] (ray); [ri] (ree) *The second is appropriate for Baron ~.*

Rea, *River* [reɪ] (ray)

Read, *f.n.* [rid] (reed)

Reade, *f.n.* [rid] (reed)

Reader, *f.n.* ['ridər] (reéder)

Reading ['redɪŋ] (rédding) *Appropriate also for the Marquess of ~.*

Readman, *f.n.* ['redmən] (rédmăn)

Reagh [reɪ] (ray)

Reakes, *f.n.* [riks] (reeks)

Reaney, *f.n.* ['reɪnɪ] (ráyni); ['rinɪ] (reéni) ‖ *The first is appropriate for P. H. ~, author of* A Dictionary of British Surnames.

Reavell, *f.n.* ['revl] (revvl)

Reavey, *f.n.* ['rivɪ] (reévi)

Reavgli, *f.n.* ['rivglɪ] (reévgli)

Reay, *f.n.* [reɪ] (ray)

Reay [reɪ] (ray) *Appropriate also for Baron ~.*

Rebbeck, *f.n.* ['rebek] (rébbeck)

Rebel, *f.n.* [rɪ'bel] (rĕbéll)

Recknell, *f.n.* ['reknəl] (récknĕll)

Reculver [rɪ'kʌlvər] (rĕkúlver)

Redadder, *River* ['redədər] (réddăder)

Reddick, *f.n.* ['redɪk] (réddick)

Redelinghuyes, *f.n.* ['redlɪŋhjuz] (rédling-hewz)

Redenhall ['redənhɒl] (réddĕnhawl)
Redesdale, *Baron* ['rɪdzdeɪl] (reĕdzdayl)
Redhead, *f.n.* ['redhed] (réd-hed)
Redheugh ['redhjuf] (réd-hewf); ['redjuf] (réddewf)
Redman, *f.n.* ['redmən] (rédmăn)
Redmond, *f.n.* ['redmənd] (rédmŏnd)
Redmoss ['red'mɒs] (réd-móss)
Redrup, *f.n.* ['redrup] (rédrŏŏp)
Redruth [red'ruːθ] (redroóth)
Rée, *f.n.* [reɪ] (ray)
Reed, *f.n.* [riːd] (reed)
Reekie, *f.n.* ['riːkɪ] (reéki)
Reepham, *Lincs., Norfolk* ['riːfəm] (reéfăm)
Rees, *f.n.* [riːs] (reess)
Reese, *f.n.* [riːs] (reess)
Reeves, *f.n.* [riːvz] (reevz)
Reibbit, *f.n.* ['raɪbɪt] (ríbit)
Reichel, *f.n.* ['raɪxl] (ríchl)
Reid, *f.n.* [riːd] (reed)
Reigate ['raɪgɪt] (rígit)
Reighton ['riːtn] (reétŏn)
Reilly, *f.n.* ['raɪlɪ] (ríli)
Reindorp, *f.n.* ['raɪndɔrp] (ríndorp)
Reiner, *f.n.* ['reɪnər] (ráyner); ['raɪnər] (ríner)
Reinold, *f.n.* ['raɪnould] (rínōld)
Reiss, *f.n.* [raɪs] (ríss)
Reiss [riːs] (reess)
Reiter, *f.n.* ['raɪtər] (ríter)
Reith, *f.n.* [riːθ] (reeth) *Appropriate also for Baron ~.*
Reizenstein, Franz, *pianist and composer* ['frænz 'raɪzənstaɪn] (fránz rízenstīn)
Rejerrah [rɪ'dʒerə] (rĕjérră)
Relubbas [rɪ'lʌbəs] (rĕlúbbăss)
Relugas [rɪ'luːgəs] (rĕloógăss)
Remer, *f.n.* ['riːmər] (reémer)
Renals, *f.n.* ['renlz] (rennlz)
Rendall, *f.n.* ['rendl] (rendl)
Rendell, *f.n.* ['rendl] (rendl); [ren'del] (rendéll)
Reney, *f.n.* ['reneɪ] (rénnay)
Renfrew ['renfruː] (rénfroo)
Renhold ['renld] (renld)
Renier, *f.n.* [rɪ'nɪər] (rĕneér)
Renishaw ['renɪʃɔ] (rénni-shaw) *Appropriate also for ~ Hall.*
Renish Point ['renɪʃ] (rénnish)
Rennell, *f.n.* ['renl] (rennl) *Appropriate also for Baron ~.*
Renney, *f.n.* ['renɪ] (rénni)
Rennie, *f.n.* ['renɪ] (rénni)
Renold, *f.n.* ['renld] (renld)
Renshaw, *f.n.* ['renʃɔ] (rén-shaw)
Renton, *f.n.* ['rentən] (réntŏn)
Rentoul, *f.n.* [ren'tul] (rentoól); ['rentul] (réntŏŏl)
Renwick, *f.n.* ['renɪk] (rénnick)
Renwick ['renɪk] (rénnick); ['renwɪk] (rénwick)
Rescobie [rɪ'skoubɪ] (rĕsskôbi)
Reskadinnick [ˌreskə'dɪnɪk] (resskă-dínnick)

Resolis [rɪ'soulɪs] (rĕssôliss)
Resolven [rɪ'zɒlvən] (rĕzólvĕn)
Restalrig ['reslrɪg] (réslrig)
Restieaux, *f.n.* ['restɪou] (résti-ō)
Restormel Castle [rɪ'stɔrməl] (rĕstórmĕl)
Restronguet [rɪ'strɒŋget] (rĕstróng-get)
Retallick, *f.n.* [rɪ'tælɪk] (rĕtálick)
Reuel, *f.n.* ['ruəl] (roó-ĕl)
Reuter, *f.n.* ['rɔɪtər] (róyter)
Revans, *f.n.* ['revənz] (révvănz)
Revell, *f.n.* ['revl] (revvl)
Revelstoke ['revlstouk] (révvl-stōk) *Appropriate also for Baron ~.*
Revesby ['rivzbɪ] (reévzbi)
Revie, *f.n.* ['rivɪ] (reévi)
Revill, *f.n.* ['revɪl] (révvil); ['revl] (revvl)
Revis, *f.n.* ['revɪs] (révviss)
Rew, *f.n.* [ru] (roo)
Rewe [ru] (roo)
Reydon ['reɪdən] (ráydŏn)
Reymerston ['remərstən] (rémmĕrsstŏn)
Reynard, *f.n.* ['renərd] (rénnărd); ['renard] (rénnaard); ['remard] (ráynaard)
Reynders, *f.n.* ['raɪndərz] (ríndĕrz)
Reyner, *f.n.* ['renər] (rénner); ['remər] (ráyner)
Reynolds, *f.n.* ['renldz] (renldz)
Reynoldston ['renldstən] (rénnldstŏn)
Reyrolle, *f.n.* ['rɛɪroul] (ráy-rōl)
Rhae, *f.n.* [reɪ] (ray)
Rhandir-mwyn ['hrændɪər'muɪn] (rándeer-moó-in)
Rhayader ['hraɪədər] (rí-ader) *Appropriate also for the Barony of ~.*
Rhees, *f.n.* [riːs] (reess)
Rheidol, *River* ['hraɪdɒl] (rídol)
Rhenish Tower, *Devon* ['renɪʃ] (rénnish)
Rhewl ['hreul] (ré-ōōl)
Rhian, *Welsh C.n.* ['hriən] (reé-ăn)
Rhiannon, *Welsh C.n.* [ˌhri'ænən] (ree-ánnŏn)
Rhianydd, *Welsh C.n.* [ˌhri'ænɪð] (ree-ánnith)
Rhiconich [rɪ'kounɪx] (reekônich)
Rhigos ['hrigɒs] (reégoss)
Rhind, *f.n.* [raɪnd] (rīnd); [rɪnd] (rind)
Rhinns of Galloway ['rɪnz əv 'gæləweɪ] (rínnz ŏv gálŏ-way)
Rhinns of Islay ['rɪnz əv 'aɪlə] (rínnz ŏv ílă)
Rhinns of Kells ['rɪnzˌəv 'kelz] (rínnz ŏv kéllz)
Rhinog Fach ['hrinɒg 'vax] (reénog vaách)
Rhinog Fawr ['hrinɒg 'vauər] (reénog vówr)
Rhiwbina [ru'baɪnə] (roobínă)
Rhiwderyn [ˌhriu'derɪn] (ree-oodérrin)
Rhiw-fawr [ˌhriu'vauər] (ree-oovówr)
Rhiwlas [rɪ'uləs] (ri-oólăss)
Rhodes, *f.n.* [roudz] (rōdz)
Rhondda ['hrɒnðə] (rónthă) *Appropriate also for Viscountess ~.*
Rhoose [rus] (rooss)
Rhoscolyn [hrous'kɒlɪn] (rōsskóllin)

Rhos-ddu [ʰrovs'ði] (rŏss-thée)
Rhosesmor [ʰrovs'esmər] (rŏsséssmor)
Rhosgadfan [ʰrovs'gædvən] (rŏssgád-văn)
Rhosllanerchrugog   [ʰrovs'ɫænərx-ˈrigʊg] (rŏss-hlánnĕrch-reégog)
Rhos-maen [ʰrovs'main] (rŏssmín)
Rhos-meirch [ʰrovs'mairəx] (rŏssmírch)
Rhosneigr [ʰrovs'naigər] (rŏssníger)
Rhossili [ʰrɒs'ili] (rossílli)
Rhostryfan [ʰrovs'trʌvən] (rŏsstrúvvăn)
Rhostyllen [ʰrovs'tʌɫɪn] (rŏsstúhlĕn)
Rhos-y-bol [ˌʰrovsə'bɒl] (rŏssăbóll)
Rhosymedre [ˌʰrovsə'medrei] (rŏssămédray)
Rhu [ru] (roo)
Rhuddlan [ʰriðlæn] (ríthlan)
Rhum, also spelt Rum [rʌm] (rum)
Rhyd-ddu [ʰrid'ði] (reed-thée)
Rhydderch, f.n. [ʰrʌðərx] (rúthĕrch)
Rhydding [ʰridiŋ] (ridding)
Rhydfelen [ʰrid'veilɪn] (reedváylĕn)
Rhydlafar [ʰrid'lævər] (reedlávvăr)
Rhydowen [ʰrid'ovin] (reedŏ-ĕn)
Rhydwen [ʰridwen] (reédwen)
Rhyd-y-felin [ˌʰridə'velin] (reedăvéllin)
Rhyd-y-fro [ˌʰridə'vrov] (reedăvró)
Rhyd-y-main [ˌʰridə'main] (reedămín)
Rhyd-y-mwyn [ˌʰridə'mvin] (reedămó̆o-in)
Rhyl [ʰril] (rill)
Rhymney [ʰrʌmni] (rúmni)
Rhynd [rmd] (rinnd)
Rhynie [ʰraini] (ríni)
Rhys, f.n. [ʰris] (reess); [rais] (ríss) Although the first is usual in Wales, the second is appropriate for Baron Dynevor's family name.
Riach, f.n. [ʰriəx] (reé-ăch)
Rialton Priory [ʰraiəltən] (rí-ăltŏn)
Riccarton, Ayr., Midlothian, Roxburgh. [ʰrikərtən] (ríckărtŏn)
Rice, f.n. [rais] (ríss)
Richard,   f.n.   and   C.n.   [ʰritʃərd] (rítchărd)
Richards, f.n. [ʰritʃərdz] (rítchărdz)
Richardson, Sir Ralph, actor [ʰrælf ˈritʃərdsən] (rálf rítchărdssŏn)
Riche, f.n. [ritʃ] (rich)
Richens, f.n. [ʰritʃənz] (rítchĕnz)
Richer, f.n. [ʰritʃər] (rítcher)
Richhill [ritʃ'hil] (ritch-híll)
Richmond, Surrey, Yorks. [ʰritʃmənd] (rítchmŏnd)
Rickard, f.n. [ʰrikard] (ríckaard)
Rickards, f.n. [ʰrikɑrdz] (ríckaardz)
Rickarton [ʰrikərtən] (ríckărtŏn)
Rickett, f.n. [ʰrikit] (rickĕt)
Ricketts, f.n. [ʰrikits] (rickĕts)
Rickmansworth [ʰrikmənzwɜrθ] (ríckmánzwurth)
Ricôt, f.n. [ʰrikov] (rickó); [ʰrikov] (reékŏ)
Riddell, f.n. [ʰridl] (riddl); [ri'del] (ridéll)
Riddiough, f.n. [ʰridjov] (ríd-yŏ)
Rideal, f.n. [ri'dil] (rideél)

Ridealgh, f.n. [ʰridiælʃ] (ríddi-alsh); [ʰraidældʒ] (rídalj)
Rideau, Baron [ʰridov] (reédŏ)
Ridehalgh, f.n. [ʰraidhælʃ] (rídhalsh); [ʰridihælʃ] (ríddihalsh)
Rider, f.n. [ʰraidər] (ríder)
Ridgeway, f.n. [ʰridʒwei] (ríj-way)
Ridgway, f.n. [ʰridʒwei] (ríj-way)
Riding, f.n. [ʰraidiŋ] (ríding)
Ridout, f.n. [ʰridavt] (ríddowt); [ʰraidavt] (rídowt)
Ridsdale, f.n. [ʰridzdeil] (rídzdayl)
Ridsdel, f.n. [ʰridzdəl] (rídzdĕl)
Ridz, f.n. [ridz] (riddz)
Riera, f.n. [ri'eərə] (ree-áiră)
Riesco, f.n. [ri'eskov] (ri-ésskŏ)
Rietty, f.n. [ri'eti] (ri-étti)
Rieu, f.n. [ri'u] (ri-oó); [ʰriu] (reé-oo) The first is appropriate for Dr. Emile Victor ~, Editor of the Penguin Classics.
Rievaulx, f.n. [ʰrivəz] (rívvăz)
Rievaulx   [ʰrivov]   (reévŏ);   [ʰrivəz] (rívvăz) Both appropriate for ~ Abbey.
Rigby, f.n. [ʰrigbi] (rígbi)
Rigg, f.n. [rig] (rigg)
Riggs, f.n. [rigz] (riggz)
Rigler, f.n. [ʰriglər] (ríggler)
Rimbault, f.n. [ʰrimbovlt] (rímbŏlt)
Rimell, f.n. [ʰraiml] (ríml)
Rimer, f.n. [ʰraimər] (rímer)
Rimington [ʰrimiŋtən] (rímmingtŏn)
Ringdufferin [riŋ'dʌfərin] (ringdúffĕrin)
Ringhaddy [riŋ'hædi] (ring-háddi)
Ringsend [riŋz'end] (ringz-énd)
Rinsey Head [ʰrinzi] (rínzi)
Riou, f.n. [ʰriu] (reé-oo)
Ripon [ʰripən] (ríppŏn)
Risca [ʰriskə] (rísskă)
Riseley [ʰraizli] (rízli)
Risley [ʰrizli] (rizzli)
Risman, f.n. [ʰrizmən] (rízzmăn)
Rison, f.n. [ʰraisən] (ríssŏn)
Ritchford, f.n. [ʰritʃfərd] (ritchfŏrd)
Ritchie, f.n. [ʰritʃi] (rítchi)
Rittener, f.n. [ʰritnər] (rítt-ner)
Rittermann, f.n. [ʰritərmən] (rittĕrmăn)
Ritzema, f.n. [ʰritsimə] (rítsĕmă); [ʰritˈzimə] (ridzeémă)
Rive, f.n. [raiv] (rív)
Rivelin [ʰrivəlin] (rívvĕlin)
Rivers, f.n. [ʰrivərz] (rívvĕrz)
Rivet, f.n. [ʰrivei] (reévay)
Rivett, f.n. [ri'vet] (rivétt)
Riviere, f.n. [ʰriviɛər] (rívvi-air); [riv-'jɛər] (riv-yáir); [ri'viər] (rivveér)
Rivière, f.n. [ʰriviɛər] (rívvi-air); [riv-'jɛər] (riv-yáir); [ri'viər] (rivveér)
Rivis, f.n. [ʰrivis] (rívviss)
Rivvett, f.n. [ʰrivit] (rívvĕt)
Roach, f.n. [rovtʃ] (rŏtch)
Roag, Loch [rovæg] (rŏ-ag)
Roanhead [ʰrɒnhed] (rónn-hed); [ʰrovn-hed] (rŏn-hed)
Roath [rovθ] (rŏth)
Robartes, f.n. [rə'bɑrts] (rŏbaárts)

Robarts, *f.n.* [rə'bɑrts] (rŏbaárts)
Robathan, *f.n.* ['roʊbəθən] (rṓbăthăn)
Robay, *f.n.* ['roʊbeɪ] (rṓbay)
Robbie, *f.n.* ['rɒbɪ] (róbbi)
Robbins, *f.n.* ['rɒbɪnz] (róbbinz)
Robens, *f.n.* ['roʊbənz] (rṓbĕnz) *Appropriate also for Baron ~.*
Roberts, *f.n.* ['rɒbərts] (róbĕrts)
Robertson, *f.n.* ['rɒbərtsən] (róbĕrtsŏn)
Robeston Wathen ['rɒbɪstən 'wɒðən] (róbbĕstŏn wóthĕn)
Robey, *f.n.* ['roʊbɪ] (rṓbi)
Robieson, *f.n.* ['rɒbɪsən] (róbbissŏn)
Robin, *C.n.* ['rɒbɪn] (róbbin)
Robins, *f.n.* ['rɒbɪnz] (róbbinz); ['roʊbɪnz] (rṓbinz)
Robinson, *f.n.* ['rɒbɪnsən] (róbbinssŏn)
Roborough ['roʊbərə] (rṓbŭră)
Robotham, *f.n.* [rə'boʊθəm] (rŏbṓthăm)
Robson, *f.n.* ['rɒbsən] (róbssŏn) *Appropriate for Dame Flora ~, actress.*
Roby ['roʊbɪ] (rṓbi)
Rocester ['roʊstər] (rṓsster)
Roch, *f.n.* [roʊtʃ] (rṓtch); [rɒtʃ] (rotch)
Roch [roʊtʃ] (rṓtch)
Rochdale ['rɒtʃdeɪl] (rótchdayl)
Roche, *f.n.* [roʊtʃ] (rṓtch); [roʊʃ] (rṓsh); [rɒʃ] (rosh) *The first is appropriate for the Barony of ~.*
Roche [roʊtʃ] (rṓtch)
Rochester ['rɒtʃɪstər] (rótchĕster)
Rochford ['rɒtʃfərd] (rótchfŏrd)
Rochfort, *f.n.* ['rɒtʃfərt] (rótchfŏrt)
Rockbeare ['rɒkbɪər] (róckbeer); ['rɒkbər] (róckber)
Rodbaston ['rɒdbəstən] (ródbăstŏn)
Roddis, *f.n.* ['rɒdɪs] (róddiss)
Rodel ['roʊdl] (rṓdl)
Rodger, *f.n.* ['rɒdʒər] (rójjer)
Rodgers, *f.n.* ['rɒdʒərz] (rójjĕrz)
Rodick, *f.n.* ['rɒdɪk] (róddick)
Roding ['roʊdɪŋ] (rṓding); ['ruðɪŋ] (roóthing) *The second, the historical pronunciation, has gradually given way, although not entirely succumbed, to the former. The group of villages known as The Rodings includes Abbess Roding, Aythorpe Roding, Beauchamp Roding, Berners Roding, High Roding, Leaden Roding, Margaret Roding, and White Roding or Roothing. Except in the last case, where Roothing has been retained in the name of the civil parish, it appears that Roding is now accepted as the standard spelling.*
Rodmersham ['rɒdmərʃəm] (ródmĕrshăm)
Rodnight, *f.n.* ['rɒdnaɪt] (ródnīt)
Rodon, *f.n.* ['roʊdən] (rṓdŏn)
Roe, *f.n.* [roʊ] (rṓ)
Roedean School ['roʊdin] (rṓdeen)
Roehampton [roʊ'hæmptən] (rōhámptŏn)
Roemmele, *f.n.* ['rɒmɪlɪ] (rómmĕli)
Roetter, *f.n.* ['roʊtər] (rṓter)
Rofe, *f.n.* [roʊf] (rṓf)

Roffe, *f.n.* [rɒf] (roff)
Roffey, *f.n.* ['rɒfɪ] (róffi)
Rogaly, *f.n.* [roʊ'geɪlɪ] (rōgáyli)
Rogart ['roʊgərt] (rṓgărt)
Roger, *f.n. and C.n.* ['rɒdʒər] (rójjer)
Rogers, *f.n.* ['rɒdʒərz] (rójjĕrz)
Rogerstone ['rɒdʒərstən] (rójjĕrstŏn)
Roget, *f.n.* ['roʊʒeɪ] (rṓzhay)
Rohan, *f.n.* ['roʊən] (rṓ-ăn)
Roissetter, *f.n.* ['rɒsɪtər] (róssiter)
Rokeby ['roʊkbɪ] (rṓkbi)
Rokison, *f.n.* ['roʊkɪsən] (rṓkissŏn)
Roland, *f.n. and C.n.* ['roʊlənd] (rṓlănd)
Roland Browse and **Delbanco Art Gallery,** London ['roʊlənd 'braʊz ənd del-'bæŋkoʊ] (rṓlănd brówz ánd delbánkō)
Rolfe, *f.n.* [roʊf] (rṓf) *Appropriate for John ~, 16-17th-c. colonist and husband of Pocahontas, and for Frederick ~, Baron Corvo, 19th-c. author.*
Roll, *f.n.* [roʊl] (rṓl); [rɒl] (rol)
Rollason, *f.n.* ['rɒləsən] (rólássŏn)
Rollesby ['roʊlzbɪ] (rṓlzbi)
Rolleston, *f.n.* ['roʊlstən] (rṓlsstŏn)
Rolleston, Leics., Notts., Staffs. ['roʊlstən] (rṓlstŏn)
Rollestone ['roʊlstən] (rṓlstŏn)
Rollins, *f.n.* ['rɒlɪnz] (róllinz)
Rolt, *f.n.* [roʊlt] (rṓlt)
Rolvenden ['rɒlvəndən] (rólvĕndĕn)
Romanby ['roʊmənbɪ] (rṓmănbi)
Romanes, *f.n.* [roʊ'mɑnɪz] (rōma'ánĕz [roʊ'mænɪs] (rōmánnĕss) *The first is appropriate for the ~ Lecturership, University of Oxford.*
Romanis, *f.n.* [roʊ'meɪnɪs] (rōmáyniss)
Rombaut, *f.n.* ['rɒmboʊ] (rómbō)
Romeike, *f.n.* [roʊ'mɪkɪ] (rōmeéki)
Romer, *f.n.* ['roʊmər] (rṓmer)
Romford, *f.n.* ['rʌmfərd] (rúmfŏrd); ['rɒmfərd] (rómfŏrd)
Romford, Essex, Kent ['rɒmfərd] (rómfŏrd); ['rʌmfərd] (rúmfŏrd)
Romilly, *f.n.* ['rɒmɪlɪ] (rómmili) *Appropriate also for Baron ~.*
Romney, Earl of ['rʌmnɪ] (rúmni)
Romney, *f.n.* ['rʌmnɪ] (rúmni); ['rɒmnɪ] (rómni)
Romney, New and **Old** ['rɒmnɪ] (rómni); ['rʌmnɪ] (rúmni)
Romney Marsh ['rɒmnɪ 'mɑrʃ] (rómni maársh)
Romsey ['rʌmzɪ] (rúmzi) *Appropriate also for Baron ~, a subsidiary title of Earl Mountbatten of Burma.*
Rona ['roʊnə] (rṓnă)
Ronald, *f.n. and C.n.* ['rɒnld] (ronnld)
Ronaldsay, North and **South** ['rɒnldseɪ] (rónnld-say); ['rɒnldʃeɪ] (rónnld-shay)
Ronaldshay, Earl of ['rɒnldʃeɪ] (rónnld-shay)
Ronaldsway ['rɒnldzweɪ] (rónnldzway)
Ronas Voe ['roʊnəs 'voʊ] (rṓnáss vṓ)
Ronay, *f.n.* ['rɒneɪ] (rónnay)
Ronayne, *f.n.* [roʊ'neɪn] (rōnáyn)

Roney, f.n. ['rouni] (rṓni)
Rook, f.n. [rʊk] (rŏŏk)
Room, f.n. [rum] (room)
Roome, f.n. [rum] (room)
Rooney, f.n. ['runi] (rōóni)
Roope, f.n. [rup] (roop)
Rooper, f.n. ['roupər] (rṓper)
Roos [rus] (rooss)
Roose, f.n. [rus] (rooss)
Rooss, f.n. [rus] (rooss)
Root, f.n. [rut] (root)
Rootes, f.n. [ruts] (roots)
Rootham, f.n. ['rutəm] (rōótăm)
Roper, f.n. ['roupər] (rṓper)
Ropner, f.n. ['rɒpnər] (rópner)
Roques, f.n. [rouks] (rōks)
Rosbotham,f.n. ['rɒsbɒtəm] (róssbottăm)
Roscroggan [rɒs'krɒgən] (rosskróggăn)
Rose, f.n. [rouz] (rōz)
Rosehearty [rouz'hɑrti] (rōz-haárti)
Roseingrave, f.n. ['rouzɪŋgreɪv] (rṓzingrayv) *Specifically the 17-18th-c. family of musicians.*
Rosemarkie [rouz'mɑrki] (rōzmaárki)
Rosetta [rə'zetə] (rŏzéttă)
Roseveare, f.n. ['rouzvɪər] (rṓzveer)
Roseworthy [rouz'wɜrði] (rōzwúrthi)
Rosherville ['rouʃərvɪl] (rṓshĕrvil); ['rɒzərvɪl] (rózzĕrvil)
Rosier, f.n. ['rouzɪər] (rṓzi-er)
Roskell, f.n. ['rɒskl] (rosskl)
Roskestal [rɒs'kestl] (rosskésstl)
Roslea [rɒs'leɪ] (rossláy)
Rosneath ['rouz'niθ] (rōz-neéth)
Ross, f.n. [rɒs] (ross)
Ross and Cromarty ['rɒs ənd 'krɒmərti] (róss ănd krómmárti)
Rossall School ['rɒsl] (rossl)
Rossallian, one educated at Rossall School [rɒ'seɪlɪən] (rossáylian)
Rossendale ['rɒsəndeɪl] (róssĕndayl)
Rosser, f.n. ['rɒsər] (rósser)
Rossetti, f.n. [rə'zeti] (rŏzétti); [rə'seti] (rŏssétti) *Both are accepted usage for the family of Dante Gabriel ~, 19th-c. poet and painter.*
Rossiter, f.n. ['rɒsɪtər] (róssiter)
Rost, f.n. [rɒst] (rosst)
Rostal, f.n. ['rɒstæl] (rósstal)
Rosteague [rɒs'tig] (rossteég)
Rostrevor, f.n. [rɒs'trevər] (rosstrévvŏr)
Rostrevor [rɒs'trevər] (rosstrévvŏr)
Rosyth [rə'saɪθ] (rŏssíth)
Rotblat, f.n. ['rɒtblæt] (rótblat)
Roth, f.n. [rɒθ] (roth); [rouθ] (rōth)
Rotha, f.n. ['rouθə] (rṓthă)
Rothamsted ['rɒθəmsted] (róthămsted)
Rothay, River ['rɒθeɪ] (róthay)
Rothbury ['rɒθbəri] (róthbŭri)
Rothe, f.n. [rouθ] (rōth)
Rothenstein, f.n. ['rouθənstaɪn] (rṓthĕn-stīn) *Appropriate for Sir William ~, portrait painter, Sir John ~, erstwhile Director of the Tate Gallery, and Michael ~, painter and print-maker.*

Rother, River, Yorks. ['rɒðər] (róther) *Appropriate also for the ~ Valley Parliamentary Division.*
Rothera, f.n. ['rɒðərə] (róthĕră)
Rotherfield Peppard ['rɒðərfīld 'pepard] (róthĕrfeeld péppaard)
Rotherham, f.n. ['rɒðərəm] (róthĕrăm)
Rotherham ['rɒðərəm] (róthĕrăm)
Rothermere, Viscount ['rɒðərmɪər] (róthĕrmeer)
Rotherwick, Baron ['rɒðərwɪk] (róthĕrwick)
Rothes, Fife ['rɒθɪs] (róthĕss); ['rɒθɪz] (róthĕz) *The second is appropriate for the Earl of ~.*
Rothesay ['rɒθsɪ] (róthssi)
Rothholz, f.n. ['rɒθhoults] (róth-hōlts)
Rothiemay [ˌrɒθɪ'meɪ] (rothimáy)
Rothiemurchus [ˌrɒθɪ'mɜrkəs] (rothimúrküss)
Rothienorman [ˌrɒθɪ'nɔrmən] (rothinórmăn)
Rothley ['rouθlɪ] (rṓthli)
Rothney, f.n. ['rɒθnɪ] (róthni)
Rothschild, Baron ['rɒθstʃaɪld] (róthschild)
Rothwell, f.n. ['rɒθwəl] (róthwĕl)
Rothwell, Lincs., Yorks. ['rɒθwel] (róthwell)
Rothwell, Northants. ['rɒθwel] (róthwell); ['rouəl] (rṓ-ĕl)
Rottingdean ['rɒtɪŋdin] (rótting-deen)
Roucan ['rukən] (rōōkăn)
Roud, f.n. [raʊd] (rowd)
Roudsea Wood, Lancs. ['raʊdzɪ] (rówdzi)
Rough, f.n. [rʌf] (ruff)
Rougham, Norfolk, Suffolk ['rʌfəm] (rúffăm)
Roughdown ['raʊdaʊn] (rówdown)
Roughlee ['rʌf'li] (rúff-leè)
Rought, f.n. [rɒt] (rawt); [raʊt] (rowt)
Roughton, f.n. ['raʊtən] (rówtŏn)
Roughton, Lincs. ['rutən] (rōōtŏn)
Roughton, Norfolk, Salop ['raʊtən] (rówtŏn)
Rough Tor ['raʊ 'tɔr] (rów tór)
Rouken Glen ['rukɪn 'glen] (rōōkĕn glén)
Roulston, f.n. ['roulstən] (rṓlsstŏn)
Roundhay Park, Leeds ['raʊndeɪ] (równday)
Rountree, f.n. ['raʊntri] (równtree)
Rous, f.n. [raʊs] (rowss) *Appropriate also for Baron ~.*
Rousay ['raʊzeɪ] (rówzay)
Rousdon ['ruzdən] (rōózdŏn); ['raʊzden] (rówzdŏn)
Rouse, f.n. [raʊs] (rowss)
Rousham ['raʊʃəm] (rów-shăm); ['raʊsəm] (rówssăm)
Rousky ['ruski] (rōósski)
Rous Lench ['raʊs 'lenʃ] (rówss lénsh)
Rouson, f.n. ['raʊsən] (rówssŏn)
Roussel, f.n. [ru'sel] (rōōsséll)
Rout, f.n. [raʊt] (rowt)
Routh, f.n. [raʊθ] (rowth)

Routledge, *f.n.* ['rautlɪdʒ] (rówtlĕj); ['rʌtlɪdʒ] (rútlĕj)
Routledge and Kegan Paul, *publishers* ['rautlɪdʒ ənd 'kigən 'pɔl] (rówtlĕj ănd keégán páwl)
Routley, *f.n.* ['rautlɪ] (rówtli)
Rowallan, *Baron* [rou'ælən] (rō-álăn)
Rowan, *f.n.* ['rouən] (rō-ăn); ['rauən] (rówăn) *The second is usual in Scotland.*
Rowardennan [ˌrauər'denən] (rowărdénnăn)
Rowarth ['rauərθ] (rówărth)
Rowbotham, *f.n.* ['roubɒtəm] (róbottăm)
Rowde [raud] (rowd)
Rowden, *f.n.* ['raudən] (rówdĕn)
Rowden, *Devon, Wilts.* ['raudən] (rówdĕn)
Rowdon, *f.n.* ['roudən] (ródŏn)
Rowe, *f.n.* [rou] (rō)
Rowell, *f.n.* ['rauəl] (rówĕl)
Rowena, *C.n.* [rou'inə] (rō-eénă)
Rowett Research Institute, *Bucksburn* ['rauɪt] (rówĕt)
Rowhedge ['rouhedʒ] (ró-hej); ['rauhedʒ] (rów-hej)
Rowland, *f.n.* ['roulənd] (rólănd)
Rowledge ['raulɪdʒ] (rówlĕj)
Rowlett, *f.n.* ['raulɪt] (rówlĕt)
Rowlette, *f.n.* [rou'let] (rōlétt)
Rowley, *f.n.* ['roulɪ] (róli)
Rowley Mile, *Newmarket* ['roulɪ] (róli)
Rowley Regis ['raulɪ 'ridʒɪs] (rówli reéjiss)
Rowner ['raunər] (równer)
Rowney, *f.n.* ['raunɪ] (równi); ['rounɪ] (róni)
Rowntree, *f.n.* ['rauntri] (równtree)
Rowridge ['raurɪdʒ] (rów-rij)
Rowse, *f.n.* [raus] (rowss)
Rowsell, *f.n.* ['rausl] (rowssl)
Rowsley ['rouzlɪ] (rózli)
Rowson, *f.n.* ['rausən] (rówssŏn); ['rousən] (róssŏn)
Rowston ['raustən] (rówsstŏn)
Rowton, *f.n.* ['rautən] (rówtŏn)
Rowton, *Cheshire, Salop* ['rautən] (rówtŏn) *Appropriate also for ~ Castle in Shropshire.*
Roxburgh, *f.n.* ['rɒksbərə] (rócksbŭră)
Roxburgh ['rɒksbərə] (rócksbŭră)
Roxburghe, *Duke of* ['rɒksbərə] (rócksbŭră)
Roxwell ['rɒkswel] (róckswel)
Royce, *f.n.* [rɔɪs] (royss)
Royle, *f.n.* [rɔɪl] (royl)
Royse, *f.n.* [rɔɪs] (royss)
Royston, *f.n.* ['rɔɪstən] (róysstŏn)
Royton ['rɔɪtən] (róytŏn)
Rozentals, *f.n.* [rou'zentlz] (rōzéntlz)
Ruabon [ru'æbən] (roo-ábbŏn)
Ruane, *f.n.* [ru'eɪn] (rōō-áyn)
Ruanlanihorne [ˌruən'lænɪhɔrn] (roo-ánlánnihorn)
Ruardean ['ruərdin] (róō-ărdeen)

Rubach, *f.n.* ['rubax] (roóbaach)
Rubane [ru'bæn] (roóbán)
Rubbra, *Edmund, composer* ['rʌbrə] (rúbbră)
Rubery ['rubərɪ] (roóbĕri)
Rubidge, *f.n.* ['rubɪdʒ] (roóbij)
Rubislaw ['rubslɔ] (roóbsslaw); ['rubɪslɔ] (roóbisslaw)
Ruchazie [rʌx'heɪzɪ] (ruch-háyzi)
Ruchill ['rʌxɪl] (rúchil)
Ruchlaw ['rʌxlɔ] (rúchlaw)
Rucker, *f.n.* ['rukər] (roóker)
Ruckinge ['rʌkɪndʒ] (rúckinj)
Rudd, *f.n.* [rʌd] (rudd)
Ruddell, *f.n.* ['rʌdl] (ruddl)
Rudgard, *f.n.* ['rʌdgard] (rúd-gaard)
Rudgwick ['rʌdʒwɪk] (rújwick); ['rʌdʒɪk] (rújjick)
Rudhall ['rʌdɔl] (rúddawl)
Rudham, *f.n.* ['rʌdəm] (rúddăm)
Rudkin, *f.n.* ['rʌdkɪn] (rúdkin)
Rudry ['rʌdrɪ] (rúddri)
Ruff, *f.n.* [rʌf] (ruff)
Rugbeian, *one educated at Rugby School* [rʌg'biən] (rugbeé-ăn)
Rugby ['rʌgbɪ] (rúgbi)
Rugeley ['rudʒlɪ] (roójli)
Ruggles-Brise, *f.n.* ['rʌglz 'braɪz] (rúgglz bríz)
Ruishton ['ruɪʃtən] (roó-ishtŏn)
Ruislip ['raɪslɪp] (ríssslip)
Rum *see* **Rhum.**
Rumbelow, *f.n.* ['rʌmbɪlou] (rúmbĕlō)
Rumbold, *f.n.* ['rʌmbould] (rúmbōld)
Rumens, *f.n.* ['rumɪnz] (roóměnz)
Rumney, *f.n.* ['rʌmnɪ] (rúmni)
Rumney ['rʌmnɪ] (rúmni)
Rumsam, *f.n.* ['rʌmsəm] (rúmssăm)
Runacres, *f.n.* ['rʌnəkərz] (rúnnăkĕrz)
Runciman, *Viscount* ['rʌnsɪmən] (rúnssimăn)
Runcorn of Heswall, *Barony of* ['rʌŋkorn əv 'hezwəl] (rúnkorn ŏv hézwăl)
Rundall, *f.n.* ['rʌndl] (rundl)
Runge, *f.n.* [rʌndʒ] (runj)
Runkerry [rʌn'kerɪ] (rŏon-kérri)
Runtz, *f.n.* [rʌnts] (runts)
Rupp, *f.n.* [rʌp] (rupp)
Ruse, *f.n.* [rus] (rooss)
Rushall, *Hereford., Staffs.* ['rʌʃɔl] (rúshawl)
Rushall, *Norfolk* ['rʌʃhɔl] (rúsh-hawl)
Rushall, *Wilts.* ['rʌʃəl] (rúshăl)
Rushen, *I.o.M.* ['rʌʃən] (rúshĕn)
Rusholme ['rʌʃhoum] (rúsh-hōm) *Appropriate also for Baron ~.*
Rushyford ['rʌʃɪford] (rúshi-ford)
Rusland ['rʌzlənd] (rúzzlănd)
Russell, *f.n.* ['rʌsl] (russl)
Russell of Killowen, *Barony of* ['rʌsl əv kɪ'louɪn] (rússl ŏv kiló-ĕn)
Rusthall ['rʌsthɔl] (rúst-hawl)
Ruswarp ['rʌsərp] (rússărp)
Rutherford, *f.n.* ['rʌðərfərd] (rútherford)
Rutherglen ['rʌðərglen] (rútherglen)

Ruthin ['rɪθɪn] (ríthin)
Ruthrieston ['rʌðərstən] (rúth̲ẖ̲ĕrstŏn)
Ruthven, Baroness ['rɪvən] (rívvĕn)
Ruthven, f.n. ['rɪvən] (rívvĕn); ['ruθvən] (roóthvĕn)
Ruthven, Aberdeen. ['rʌθvən] (rúthvĕn)
Ruthven, Angus ['rɪvən] (rívvĕn)
Ruthven, Loch, Inverness. ['rʌθvən] (rúthvĕn)
Ruthven of Canberra, Viscount ['rɪvən əv 'kænbərə] (rívvĕn ŏv kánbĕră)
Ruthwaite ['rʌθwert] (rúthwayt; ['rʌθət] (rúth-ăt)
Ruthwell ['rʌθwəl] (rúthwĕl); ['rʌðwəl] (rúth̲ẖ̲wĕl); ['rɪðl] (rithl)
Rutland, f.n. ['rʌtlənd] (rútlănd)
Rutland ['rʌtlənd] (rútlánd)
Ruyton-Eleven-Towns ['raɪtən ɪ'levəntaʊnz] (rítŏn-ĕlévvĕntownz)
Ryan, f.n. ['raɪən] (rí-ăn)
Ryarsh ['raɪɑrʃ] (rí-aarsh)
Rydal ['raɪdl] (rídl) *Appropriate also for ~ Water.*
Ryhope ['raɪəp] (rí-ŏp)
Rykwert, f.n. ['rɪkwərt] (ríckwĕrt)
Ryland, f.n. ['raɪlənd] (ríländ)
Ryme Intrinsica ['raɪm ɪn'trɪnsɪkə] (rīm intrínssikă)
Rynd, f.n. [rɪnd] (rinnd)
Rysanek, f.n. ['raɪsənek] (ríssăneck)
Ryton-on-Dunsmore ['raɪtən ɒn 'dʌnzmər] (rítŏn on dúnzmor)
Ryves, f.n. [raɪvz] (rīvz)

S

Sabel, f.n. ['serbl] (saybl)
Sabelli, f.n. [sə'belɪ] (săbélli)
Sabeston, f.n. ['sæbɪstən] (sábbĕstŏn)
Sabin, f.n. ['serbɪn] (sáybin); ['sæbɪn] (sábbin)
Sabine, f.n. ['sæbaɪn] (sábbīn)
Sabit, f.n. ['sæbɪt] (sábbit)
Sach, f.n. [serʧ] (saytch); [serʃ] (saysh)
Sacher, f.n. ['sækər] (sácker)
Sachs, f.n. [sæks] (sacks)
Sackley, f.n. ['sæklɪ] (sáckli)
Sackur, f.n. ['sækər] (sáckŭr)
Sacombe ['serkəm] (sáykŏm)
Sacriston Heugh ['sækrɪstən 'hjuf] (sáckristŏn héwf)
Sadberge ['sædbɜrdʒ] (sádberj)
Saffell, f.n. ['sæfl] (saffl); [sə'fel] (săféll)
Saffron Walden ['sæfrən 'wɒldən] (sáffrŏn wáwldĕn)
Sagar, f.n. ['serɡər] (sáygăr)
Sager, f.n. ['serɡər] (sáyger)
Saggar, f.n. ['sæɡar] (sággaar)

Saham Toney ['serəm 'toʊnɪ] (sáy-ăm tŏni)
Saich, f.n. [serʃ] (saysh)
Saighton ['sertən] (sáytŏn)
Sainsbury, f.n. ['seɪnzbərɪ] (sáynzbŭri) *Appropriate also for Baron ~.*
Saint, f.n. [seɪnt] (saynt)
St. Agnes [snt 'ægnɪs] (sĭnt ágnĕss)
St. Albans [snt 'ɒlbənz] (sĭnt áwlbănz) *Appropriate also for the Duke of ~.*
St. Aldate's, Oxford [snt 'ɒldɪts] (sĭnt áwldits); [snt 'oʊldz] (sĭnt ŏ́ldz)
St. Aldwyn, Earl [snt 'ɒldwɪn] (sĭnt áwldwin)
St. Aloysius [snt ˌæloʊ'ɪʃəs] (sĭnt alŏ-íshŭss)
St. Alphege [snt 'ælfɪdʒ] (sĭnt álfĕj)
St. Andrews [snt 'ændruz] (sint ándrooz) *Appropriate also for Earl of ~.*
St. Anthony in Meneage [snt 'æntənɪ ɪn mɪ'niɡ] (sĭnt ántŏni in mĕne̅e̅g); [snt 'æntənɪ ɪn mɪ'neɪɡ] (sĭnt ántŏni in mĕnáyg)
St. Asaph [snt 'æsəf] (sĭnt ássăff)
St. Athan [snt 'æθən] (sĭnt áthăn)
St. Aubyn, f.n. [snt 'ɒbɪn] (sĭnt áwbin)
St. Audries, Baron [snt 'ɒdrɪz] (sĭnt áwdriz)
St. Austell [snt 'ɒstl] (sĭnt áwsstl); [snt 'ɒsl] (sĭnt áwssl)
St. Benet's Abbey, Norfolk [snt 'benɪts] (sĭnt bénnĕts)
St. Beuno [snt 'baɪnə] (sĭnt bínaw)
St. Botolph [snt 'bɒtɒlf] (sĭnt bóttolf)
St. Breock [snt 'briək] (sĭnt bree̅-ŏk)
St. Breward [snt 'bruərd] (sĭnt broo̅-árd)
St. Briavels [snt 'brevlz] (sĭnt brévvlz)
St. Bronach [snt 'broʊnəx] (sĭnt brŏ́nách)
St. Budeaux [snt 'bjudoʊ] (sĭnt béwdŏ)
St. Buryan [snt 'bʌrɪən] (sĭnt búrri-ăn); [snt 'berɪən] (sĭnt bérri-ăn)
St. Chloe [snt 'kloʊɪ] (sĭnt klŏ́-i)
St. Chrysostom [snt 'krɪsəstəm] (sĭnt kríssŏsstŏm)
St. Clair, f.n. [snt 'kleər] (sĭnt kláïr); ['sɪŋkleər] (sínklair)
St. Clare, f.n. ['sɪŋklər] (sínklăr)
St. Clears [snt 'kleərz] (sĭnt kláïrz)
St. Clement Danes, London [snt 'klemənt 'deɪnz] (sĭnt klémmĕnt dáynz)
St. Clements [snt 'klemənts] (sĭnt klémmĕnts)
St. Clether [snt 'kleðər] (sĭnt kléther)
St. Cloud [snt 'klu] (sĭnt klŏ́o)
St. Colmanell [snt ˌkɒlmə'nel] (sĭnt kolmánéll)
St. Columb [snt 'kʌləm] (sĭnt kúllŭm); [snt 'kɒləm] (sĭnt kóllŭm)
St. Columba [ˌsnt kə'lʌmbə] (sĭnt kŏlúmbă)
St. Comgall [snt 'kɒmɡəl] (sĭnt kómgăl)
St. Cyres, Viscount [snt 'saɪərz] (sĭnt sírz)
St. Dennis [snt 'denɪs] (sĭnt dénniss)

St. **Dogmaels** [snt ˈdɒgməlz] (sĭnt dógmĕlz)

St. **Dogwells** [snt ˈdɒgwəlz] (sĭnt dógwĕlz)

St. **Dominick** [snt ˈdɒmɪnɪk] (sĭnt dómminick)

St. Donard [snt ˈdɒnərd] (sĭnt dónnărd)

St. **Donat's** [snt ˈdɒnəts] (sĭnt dónnăts) *Appropriate also for* ~ *Castle.*

St. Dunstan [snt ˈdʌnstən] (sĭnt dúnsstăn)

St. Eansvythe [snt ˈiənswɪθ] (sĭnt eeănsswith)

St. Ebbe [snt ˈeb] (sĭnt ébb)

St. **Endellion** [ˌsnt enˈdelɪən] (sĭnt endélliŏn)

St. **Enoder** [snt ˈenədər] (sĭnt énnŏder)

St. **Enodoc** [snt ˈenədɒk] (sĭnt énnŏdock)

St. **Erth** [snt ˈɜːθ] (sĭnt érth)

St. Etheldreda [snt ˈeθldrɪdə] (sĭnt éthldreedă)

St. **Eval** [snt ˈevl] (sĭnt évvl)

St. **Ewe** [snt ˈjuː] (sĭnt yoŏ)

St. **Fagan's** [snt ˈfægənz] (sĭnt fággănz)

St. **Feock** [snt ˈfiɒk] (sĭnt fee-ock)

St. **Fillan's** [snt ˈfɪlənz] (sĭnt fíllănz)

St. **Gennys** [snt ˈgenɪs] (sĭnt génniss)

St. **Germans**, *Cornwall, Norfolk* [snt ˈdʒɜːrmənz] (sĭnt jérmănz)

St. **Giles' Cathedral**, *Edinburgh* [snt ˈdʒaɪlz] (sĭnt jīlz) *Traditionally, no optional possessive -s is used in the spelling, nor* [-ɪz] *(-ĕz) in the pronunciation.*

St. **Gluvias** [snt ˈgluvɪəs] (sĭnt gloŏviăss)

St. **Gorran**, *also spelt* St. **Goran** [snt ˈgɒrən] (sĭnt górrăn)

St. **Govan's Head** [snt ˈgɒvənz] (sĭnt góvvănz); [snt ˈgʌvənz] (sĭnt gúvvănz) *The first is the Welsh pronunciation. The second tends to be heard on the English side of the Bristol Channel.*

St. Helena [snt ˈhelɪnə] (sĭnt héllĕnă)

St. Helier [snt ˈheljər] (sĭnt héll-yer)

St. **Hilary** [snt ˈhɪlərɪ] (sĭnt hĭllări)

St. Hyacinth [snt ˈhaɪəsɪnθ] (sĭnt hĭăssinth)

St. Ia [snt ˈiə] (sĭnt ee-ă)

St. Illtyd [snt ˈɪɫtɪd] (sĭnt íḥḷtid)

St. **Ippolyts** [snt ˈɪpəlɪts] (sĭnt íppŏlits)

St. **Issey** [snt ˈɪzɪ] (sĭnt izzi)

St. **Ive** [snt ˈiv] (sĭnt eev)

St. **Ives**, *Cornwall, Hunts.* [snt ˈaɪvz] (sĭnt īvz)

St. John, *f.n.* [ˈsɪndʒən] (sínjŏn); [snt ˈdʒɒn] (sĭnt jŏn) *The first is appropriate for Viscount Bolingbroke's family name.*

St. John of Bletso, *Baron* [ˈsɪndʒən əv ˈbletsoʊ] (sínjŏn ŏv blétsŏ)

St. **John's Point** [snt ˈdʒɒnz ˈpɔɪnt] (sĭnt jónz póynt)

St. **Juliot** [snt ˈdʒulɪət] (sĭnt joŏli-ŏt); [snt ˈdʒɪlt] (sĭnt jílt)

St. Just, *Baron* [snt ˈdʒʌst] (sĭnt júst)

St. **Just in Penwith** [snt ˈdʒʌst ɪn penˈwɪθ] (sĭnt júst in penwíth)

St. Kentigern [snt ˈkentɪgərn] (sĭnt kéntigĕrn)

St. **Keverne** [snt ˈkevərn] (sĭnt kévvĕrn)

St. **Keyne** [snt ˈkeɪn] (sĭnt káyn); [snt ˈkɪn] (sĭnt keén)

St. **Kilda** [snt ˈkɪldə] (sĭnt kíldă)

St. Leger, *f.n.* [snt ˈledʒər] (sĭnt léjjer); [ˈselɪndʒər] (séllinjer) *The first is appropriate for Viscount Doneraile's family name, the second for the Yorkshire branch of the family.*

St. Leodegar [ˌsnt leɪˈɒdɪgɑr] (sĭnt lay-ódděgaar)

St. **Leonards-on-Sea** [snt ˈlenərdz ɒn ˈsi] (sĭnt lénnărdz on seé)

St. **Levan** [snt ˈlevən] (sĭnt lévvăn) *Appropriate also for Baron* ~.

St. **Loyes** [snt ˈlɔɪz] (sĭnt lóyz)

St. **Lythan's** [snt ˈlɪðənz] (sĭnt líthănz)

St. **Mabyn** [snt ˈmeɪbɪn] (sĭnt máybin)

St. **Machar's Cathedral**, *Aberdeen* [snt ˈmæxərz] (sĭnt máchărz)

St. **Martin in Meneage** [snt ˈmɑrtɪn ɪn mɪˈnig] (sĭnt maártin in mĕneèg); [snt ˈmɑrtɪn ɪn mɪˈneɪg] (sĭnt maártin in mĕnáyg)

St. **Martin's le Grand** [snt ˈmɑrtɪnz lə ˈgrænd] (sĭnt maártinz lĕ gránd)

St. **Mary Axe**, *City of London* [snt ˈmɛərɪ ˈæks] (sĭnt maíri ácks); [ˈsɪmərɪ ˈæks] (símmări ácks)

St. **Mary Woolnoth**, *City of London Guild church* [snt ˈmɛərɪ ˈwʊlnɒθ] (sĭnt maíri woŏlnoth)

St. **Marylebone** [snt ˈmærələbən] (sĭnt márrĕlĕbŏn) *see* Marylebone.

St. **Mary-le-Strand** [snt ˈmɛərɪ lə ˈstrænd] (sĭnt maíri lĕ stránd)

St. Maur, *f.n.* [ˈsɪmɔr] (seémor)

St. **Mawes** [snt ˈmɔz] (sĭnt máwz)

St. **Mawgan in Meneage** [snt ˈmɔgən ɪn mɪˈnig] (sĭnt máwgăn in mĕneèg); [snt ˈmɔgən ɪn mɪˈneɪg] (sĭnt máwgăn in mĕnáyg)

St. **Mawgan-in-Pydar** [snt ˈmɔgən ɪn ˈpaɪdar] (sĭnt máwgăn in pídaar)

St. **Merryn** [snt ˈmerɪn] (sĭnt mérrin)

St. **Mewan** [snt ˈmjuən] (sĭnt méw-ăn)

St. **Michael Penkevil** [snt ˈmaɪkl penˈkɪvl] (sĭnt mǐkl penkívvl)

St. **Modans** [snt ˈmoʊdənz] (sĭnt mṓdănz)

St. **Monance** [snt ˈmoʊnəns] (sĭnt mōnănss)

St. Munda [snt ˈmʌndə] (sĭnt múndă)

St. Mungo [snt ˈmʌŋgoʊ] (sĭnt múng-gō)

St. **Neot** [snt ˈniət] (sĭnt nee-ŏt)

St. **Neots** [snt ˈniəts] (sĭnt nee-ŏts)

St. **Ninian's Cathedral**, *Perth* [snt ˈnɪnɪənz] (sĭnt nínni-ănz)

St. Olave [snt ˈɒlɪv] (sĭnt ólliv)

St. **Olaves** [snt ˈɒlɪvz] (sĭnt óllivz)

St. **Osyth** [snt ˈoʊzɪθ] (sĭnt ŏzith); [snt ˈousɪθ] (sĭnt óssith)

St. **Pancras** [snt ˈpæŋkrəs] (sĭnt pánkrăss)

St. Paul's Walden Bury [snt 'pɒlz 'wɔldən 'berɪ] (sint páwlz wáwldĕn bérri)
St. Peter-at-Gowts, *Lincoln church* [snt 'pitər ət 'gauts] (sĭnt peéter ăt gówts)
St. Petrox [snt 'petrɒks] (sĭnt péttrocks)
St. Pinnock [snt 'pɪnək] (sĭnt pínnŏk)
St. Protasus [snt prə'teɪzəs] (sĭnt prŏtáyzŭss)
St. Protus [snt 'proutəs] (sĭnt prŏtúss)
St. Rollox [snt''rɒlɒks] (sĭnt róllŏcks)
St. Romaine, f.n. [ˌsnt rə'meɪn] (sĭnt rŏmáyn)
St. Ronan [snt 'rounən] (sĭnt rŏnăn)
St. Salvator's College, *University of St. Andrews* [ˌsnt sæl'veɪtərz] (sĭnt salváytŏrz)
St. Seiriol Island, *also* Puffin Island, *q.v.* [snt 'saɪərjɒl] (sĭnt sír-yoll)
St. Swithin [snt 'swɪðɪn] (sĭnt swíthin); [snt 'swɪθɪn] (sĭnt swíthin)
St. Teath [snt 'teθ] (sĭnt téth)
St. Teilo Priory, *Cardiff* [snt 'taɪlou] (sĭnt tílŏ)
St. Tudy [snt 'tjudɪ] (sĭnt téwdi)
St. Tysilio [ˌsnt tə'sɪljou] (sĭnt tŭssíl-yŏ)
St. Vedast [snt 'vɪdæst] (sĭnt veédasst)
St. Vigeans [snt 'vɪdʒənz] (sĭnt víjjänz)
St. Weonards [snt 'wenərdz] (sĭnt wénnărdz)
St. Werburgh [snt 'wɜrbɜrg] (sĭnt wérburg)
St. Wulstan [snt 'wʊlstən] (sĭnt wŏŏlstăn)
St. Wynifred's Well [snt 'wɪnɪfrɪdz] (sĭnt wínnifrĕdz)
Saintfield ['seɪntfɪld] (sáyntfeeld)
Sainton, f.n. ['seɪntən] (sáyntŏn)
Sala, George Augustus Henry, 19th-c. journalist and author ['salə] (saálă)
Salaman, f.n. ['sæləmæn] (sáláman)
Salamé, f.n. ['sæləmeɪ] (sálámay)
Salant, f.n. ['seɪlənt] (sáylănt)
Salberg, f.n. ['sɒlbɜrg] (sáwlberg)
Salcey Forest ['sɒlsɪ] (sáwlssi)
Salcombe ['sɒlkəm] (sáwlkŏm); ['sɒlkəm] (sólkŏm)
Sale [seɪl] (sayl)
Salen ['salən] (saálĕn)
Sales, f.n. [seɪlz] (saylz)
Salew, f.n. [sə'lu] (sáloó)
Salfield ['sælfɪld] (sálfeeld)
Salford, *Beds.* ['sæfərd] (sáffŏrd)
Salford, *Lancs.* ['sɒlfərd] (sólfŏrd)
Salfords ['sælfərdz] (sálfŏrdz)
Saline ['sælɪn] (sálín)
Salisbury ['sɒlzbərɪ] (sáwlzbŭri); ['sɒlzbrɪ] (sáwlzbri) *The first is appropriate for the Marquess of ~.*
Salkeld, f.n. ['sɒlkeld] (sáwlkeld)
Salkeld ['sɒlkeld] (sáwlkeld)
Sall, *also spelt* Salle [sɒl] (sawl)
Sallagh ['sælə] (sálă)
Salle *see* Sall.
Sallis, f.n. ['sælɪs] (sáliss)

Salmesbury ['samzbərɪ] (saámzbŭri)
Salmon, f.n. ['sæmən] (sámmŏn)
Salmonby ['sæmənbɪ] (sámmŏnbi); ['sælmənbɪ] (sál-mŏnbi)
Salmond, f.n. ['sæmənd] (sámmŏnd)
Salop ['sæləp] (sálŏp)
Salopian, one educated at Shrewsbury School [sə'loupɪən] (sálŏpián)
Saloway, f.n. ['sæləweɪ] (sálŏ-way)
Salpeter, f.n. ['sælpitər] (sálpeeter)
Salsburgh ['sɒlzbərə] (sáwlzbŭră)
Salt, f.n. [sɒlt] (sawlt); [sɒlt] (sollt)
Saltaire [sɒl'tɛər] (sawltaír)
Saltash [sɒl'tæʃ] (sawltásh)
Salter, f.n. ['sɒltər] (sáwlter); ['sɒltər] (sóllter)
Saltfleetby ['sɒltflitbɪ] (sáwltfleetbi); ['sɒlɒbɪ] (sóllăbi)
Salthouse ['sɒlthaus] (sáwlt-howss)
Saltley ['sɒltlɪ] (sáwltli)
Saltoun, f.n. ['sɒltən] (sáwltŏn); ['sæltən] (sáltŏn) *The first is appropriate for the Baron ~.*
Saltoun ['sɒltən] (sáwltŏn)
Salusbury, f.n. ['sɒlzbərɪ] (sáwlzbŭri)
Salvesen, f.n. ['sælvɪsən] (sálvéssĕn)
Salveson, f.n. ['sælvɪsən] (sálvéssŏn)
Salway, f.n. ['sɒlweɪ] (sáwlway)
Salwick ['sælɪk] (sálick); ['sælwɪk] (sálwick)
Salzedo, f.n. [sæl'zeɪdou] (salzáydŏ)
Samares, f.n. ['sæməreɪ] (sámmáray)
Sambles, f.n. ['sæmblz] (samblz)
Samett, f.n. ['sæmɪt] (sámmĕt)
Samlesbury ['sæmzbərɪ] (sámzbŭri); ['samzbərɪ] (saámzbŭri)
Sammes, f.n. [sæmz] (samz)
Sampford Courtenay ['sæmpfərd 'kortnɪ]; (sámpfŏrd kórtni)
Sampford Spiney ['sæmfərd 'spaɪnɪ] (sámfŏrd spíni)
Sampson, f.n. ['sæmpsən] (sámpssŏn)
Samson Island ['sæmsən] (sámssŏn)
Samuelly, f.n. [ˌsæmju'elɪ] (sam-yŏŏ-élli)
Samuels, f.n. ['sæmjuəlz] (sám-yŏŏ-ĕlz)
Sancreed [sæŋ'krid] (sankreéd)
Sandars, f.n. ['sændərz] (sándárz)
Sanday ['sændeɪ] (sánday)
Sandbach, f.n. ['sændbætʃ] (sándbatch)
Sandbach ['sændbætʃ] (sándbatch)
Sandell, f.n. ['sændl] (sandl)
Sandelson, f.n. ['sændlsən] (sándlssŏn)
Sanders, f.n. ['sandərz] (saándĕrz); ['sændərz] (sándĕrz); ['sɒndərz] (sáwndĕrz)
Sanderson, f.n. ['sandərsən] (saándĕrsson); ['sændərsən] (sándĕrssŏn)
Sandes, f.n. [sændz] (sandz)
Sandhurst Royal Military Academy ['sændhɜrst] (sándhurst)
Sandiacre ['sændɪeɪkər] (sándi-ayker)
Sandilands, f.n. ['sændɪləndz] (sándiländz)
Sandness ['sændnɪs] (sándness)

Sandringham ['sændrɪŋəm] (sándringăm)
Sandry, f.n. ['sændrɪ] (sándri)
Sands, f.n. [sændz] (sandz)
Sandwich ['sænwɪtʃ] (sánwitch); ['sændwɪtʃ] (sándwitch)
Sandwick, Orkney, Shetland ['sændwɪk] (sándwick)
Sandy, f.n. ['sændɪ] (sándi)
Sandyknowe Crags ['sændɪ'nau] (sándinów)
Sandys, f.n. [sændz] (sandz) Appropriate also for Baron ~.
Sanford, f.n. ['sænfərd] (sánförd)
Sanger, f.n. ['sæŋər] (sáng-er)
Sangster, f.n. ['sæŋstər] (sángster)
Sanquhar ['sæŋkər] (sánkär) Appropriate also for the Earl of ~.
Sapcote ['sæpkout] (sápkōt)
Saphier, f.n. ['sæfɪər] (sáffeer)
Sapiston ['sæpɪstən] (sáppistŏn)
Sapte, f.n. [sæpt] (sapt)
Sarell, f.n. ['særəl] (sárrĕl)
Sargant, f.n. ['sɑrdʒənt] (saárjánt)
Sargeaunt, f.n. ['sɑrdʒənt] (saárjĕnt)
Sargent, f.n. ['sɑrdʒənt] (saárjĕnt)
Sargisson, f.n. ['sɑrdʒɪsən] (saárjissŏn)
Sarisbury ['sɑrzbərɪ] (saárzbüri); ['sɛərzbərɪ] (saárzbüri)
Sarnau ['sɑrnaɪ] (saárnī)
Sarratt ['særət] (sárrăt)
Sarre [sɑr] (saar)
Sarson, f.n. ['sɑrsən] (saárssŏn)
Sartoris, f.n. ['sɑrtərɪs] (saártŏriss)
Sartorius, f.n. ['sɑrtərɪs] (saártŏriss)
Sarum, Roman name for Salisbury ['sɛərəm] (saírŭm)
Sasse, f.n. [sæs] (sass)
Sassoon, f.n. [sə'sun] (sǎssoón)
Satchwell, f.n. ['sætʃwel] (sátchwel)
Satow, f.n. ['satou] (saátō)
Satterleigh ['sætərlɪ] (sátterli)
Sauchie ['sɒxɪ] (sóchi)
Sauchiehall Street, Glasgow [ˌsɒxɪ'hɒl] (sochiháwl)
Sauer, f.n. [sɔr] (sor)
Saughall, Great and Little ['sɒkl] (sawkl)
Saughton ['sɒxtən] (sóchtŏn)
Saughtree ['sɒxtrɪ] (sóchtree)
Saul [sɒl] (sawl)
Saulez, f.n. ['sɒlɪ] (sáwli); ['soulɪ] (sóli)
Saumarez, f.n. ['sɒməriz] (sómmărĕz); ['soumərɪ] (sómări)
Saundby, f.n. ['sɒndbɪ] (sáwndbi)
Saunders, f.n. ['sɒndərz] (sáwndĕrz); ['sɑndərz] (saándĕrz)
Saundersfoot ['sɒndərzfut] (sáwndĕrzfŏŏt)
Saunderson, f.n. ['sɒndərsən] (sáwndĕrssŏn); ['sɑndərsən] (saándĕrssŏn)
Sauter, f.n. ['soutər] (sóter)
Sauvage, f.n. ['sævɪdʒ] (sávvij)
Savage, f.n. ['sævɪdʒ] (sávvij)
Savernake ['sævərnæk] (sávvĕrnack) Appropriate also for Viscount ~.

Savile, f.n. ['sævɪl] (sávvil)
Savins, f.n. ['sævɪnz] (sávvinz)
Savoch ['sævəx] (sávvŏch)
Savory, f.n. ['seɪvərɪ] (sáyvŏri)
Saward, f.n. ['seɪwərd] (sáywärd)
Sawbridgeworth ['sobrɪdʒwərθ] (sáwbrijwürth); ['sæpswərθ] (sápswürth)
Saweard, f.n. ['seɪwərd] (sáywärd)
Sawel ['soəl] (sáw-ĕl)
Sawrey, f.n. ['sorɪ] (sáwri)
Sawtry ['sotrɪ] (sáwtri)
Sawyer, f.n. ['sojər] (sáw-yer)
Saxilby ['sækslbɪ] (sáckslbi)
Saxmundham [sæks'mʌndəm] (sacksmúndăm)
Saxon, f.n. ['sæksən] (sácksŏn)
Saxthorpe ['sæksθorp] (sácks-thorp)
Saxton, f.n. ['sækstən] (sáckstŏn)
Saxty, f.n. ['sækstɪ] (sácksti)
Sayce, f.n. [seɪs] (sayss)
Saye and Sele, Baron ['seɪ ənd 'sɪl] (sáy ănd seél)
Sayer, f.n. [sɛər] (sair); ['seɪər] (sáy-er)
Sayers, f.n. [sɛərz] (sairz);['seɪərz](sáy-ĕrz)
Saynor, f.n. ['seɪnər] (sáynŏr)
Sayres, f.n. [sɛərz] (sairz)
Saywell, f.n. ['seɪwel] (sáywel)
Scadding, f.n. ['skædɪŋ] (skádding)
Scadgell, f.n. ['skædʒl] (skajjl)
Scafell ['sko'fel] (skáw-féll)
Scalasaig ['skæləseɪg] (skálássayg)
Scalby ['skolbɪ] (skáwlbi); ['skobɪ] (skáwbi)
Scalford ['skolfərd] (skáwlförd); ['skofərd] (skáwförd)
Scalloway ['skæləwə] (skálŏ-wǎ)
Scalpay ['skælpeɪ] (skálpay)
Scammell, f.n. ['skæml] (skamml)
Scannell, f.n. ['skænl] (skannl)
Scapa Flow ['skapə 'flou] (skaápǎ flō)
Scarba ['skɑrbə] (skaárbǎ)
Scarbrough, Earl of ['skɑrbrə] (skaárbrǎ)
Scardifield, f.n. ['skɑrdɪfɪld] (skaárdifeeld)
Scarinish ['skærɪnɪʃ] (skárrinish)
Scarisbrick, f.n. ['skɛərzbrɪk] (skaírzbrick)
Scarisbrick ['skɛərzbrɪk] (skaírzbrick)
Scarista ['skærɪstə] (skárristǎ)
Scarlett, f.n. ['skɑrlɪt] (skaárlĕt)
Scartho, also spelt Scarthoe ['skɑrθou] (skaár-thō)
Scarva ['skɑrvə] (skaárvǎ)
Scaur, The [skɔr] (skor)
Scavaig, Loch ['skæveɪg] (skávvayg)
Scawen, f.n. ['sko-ɪn] (skáw-ĕn)
Sceales, f.n. [skilz] (skeelz)
Scears, f.n. [sɪərz] (seerz)
Sceats, f.n. [skits] (skeets)
Schaffer, f.n. ['fæfər] (sháffer)
Schapiro, f.n. [ʃə'pɪərou] (shäpeérō)
Scharrer, f.n. ['ʃɑrər] (shaárer)
Schaschke, f.n. ['ʃæskɪ] (shásski)
Schellenberg, f.n. ['ʃelɪnbɜrg] (shéllĕnberg)

Scherer, f.n. [ˈʃɛərər] (sha͞irer)
Schidlof, f.n. [ˈʃɪdlɒf] (shídloff)
Schiehallion [ʃɪˈhæljən] (shēhál-yŏn)
Schilizzi, f.n. [skɪˈlɪtsɪ] (skilítsi)
Schjelderup, f.n. [ˈʃeldrəp] (shéldrŭp)
Schlaen, f.n. [ʃleɪn] (shlayn)
Schlazinger, f.n. [ˈʃlæzɪndʒər] (shlázzinjer)
Schlesinger, f.n. [ˈʃlesɪndʒər] (shléssinjer)
Schlie, f.n. [sli] (slee)
Schofield, f.n. [ˈskoʊfild] (skṓfeeld)
Scholefield, f.n. [ˈskoʊlfild] (skṓlfeeld)
Scholes, f.n. [skoʊlz] (skōlz) *Appropriate for Percy ~, musicologist.*
Scholes [skoʊlz] (skōlz)
Scholfield, f.n. [ˈskoʊfild] (skṓfeeld); [ˈskoʊlfild] (skṓlfeeld)
Schon, f.n. [ʃɒn] (shonn)
Schonell, f.n. [ʃɒˈnel] (shonnéll)
Schonfield, f.n. [ˈskɒnfild] (skónnfeeld)
Schooling, f.n. [ˈskulɪŋ] (skoʻoling)
Schoutze, f.n. [ˈʃʊtseɪ] (shoʻotsay)
Schreiber, f.n. [ˈʃraɪbər] (shrī́ber)
Schulten, f.n. [ˈskʊltən] (skoʻoltĕn)
Schuster, f.n. [ˈʃʊstər] (shoʻoster)
Schwabe, f.n. [ˈʃwɑbə] (shwaábĕ)
Schwartz, f.n. [ʃwɔrts] (shwawrts)
Sciama, f.n. [ˈʃɑmə] (shaámă)
Sciennes, f.n. [ʃinz] (sheenz)
Scillonian, native of the Isles of Scilly [sɪˈloʊnɪən] (silṓniǎn)
Scilly, Isles of [ˈsɪlɪ] (sílli)
Scissett [sɪˈset] (sissétt)
Sclanders, f.n. [ˈsklɑndərz] (sklaándĕrz)
Sclater, f.n. [ˈsleɪtər] (sláyter)
Scobell, f.n. [skoʊˈbel] (skōbéll)
Scofield, f.n. [ˈskoʊfild] (skṓfeeld)
Scole [skoʊl] (skōl)
Scollan, f.n. [ˈskɒlən] (skóllán)
Scolt Head [skɒlt] (skollt)
Scone [skun] (skoon) *Appropriate also for Baron ~ and for the Stone of ~.*
Scoones, f.n. [skunz] (skoonz)
Scopes, f.n. [skoʊps] (skōps)
Scopwick [ˈskɒpwɪk] (skópwick)
Scorer, f.n. [ˈskɔrər] (skáwrer)
Scorgie, f.n. [ˈskɔrdʒɪ] (skórji)
Scorrier [ˈskɒrɪər] (skórri-er)
Scotby [ˈskɒtbɪ] (skótbi)
Scothern, f.n. [ˈskɒθɜrn] (skóthĕrn); [ˈskɒθərn] (skóthĕrn)
Scothern [ˈskɒθɜrn] (skóthern)
Scotstoun [ˈskɒtstən] (skótstŏn)
Scott, f.n. [skɒt] (skott)
Scottow [ˈskɒtoʊ] (skóttō)
Scougal, f.n. [ˈskugl] (skoogl)
Scougall, f.n. [ˈskugl] (skoogl)
Scoular, f.n. [ˈskulər] (skoʻolár)
Scoullar, f.n. [ˈskulər] (skoʻolár)
Scouller, f.n. [ˈskulər] (skoʻoler)
Scouloudi, f.n. [skʊˈludɪ] (skoʻoloʻodi)
Scourfield, f.n. [ˈskaʊərfild] (skówrfeeld)
Scourie [ˈskaʊərɪ] (skówri)
Scovell, f.n. [skoʊˈvel] (skōvéll)

Scowen, f.n. [ˈskoʊɪn] (skṓ-ĕn)
Scrabo [ˈskræboʊ] (skrábbō)
Scrafield [ˈskreɪfild] (skráyfeeld)
Screveton [ˈskrevɪtən] (skrévvĕtŏn); [ˈskriːtən] (skreeʹtŏn)
Scridain, Loch [ˈskridən] (skreédăn)
Scrivelsby [ˈskrɪvlzbɪ] (skrívvlzbi); [ˈskrɪlzbɪ] (skreélzbi)
Scrivener, f.n. [ˈskrɪvənər] (skrívvĕner)
Scroby [ˈskroʊbɪ] (skrṓbi)
Scroggie, f.n. [ˈskrɒgɪ] (skróggi)
Scroggs, f.n. [skrɒgz] (skroggz)
Scrope, f.n. [skrup] (skroop)
Scrubey, f.n. [ˈskrubɪ] (skroʻobi)
Scruby, f.n. [ˈskrubɪ] (skroʻobi)
Scrymgeour, f.n. [ˈskrɪmdʒər] (skrímjer)
Scudamore, f.n. [ˈskjudəmɔr] (skéwdámor)
Scull, f.n. [skʌl] (skull)
Scullion, f.n. [ˈskʌljən] (skúll-yŏn)
Sculpher, f.n. [ˈskʌlfər] (skúllfer)
Scupham, f.n. [ˈskʌfəm] (skúffăm)
Scuse, f.n. [skjus] (skewss)
Scutt, f.n. [skʌt] (skutt)
Seabright, f.n. [ˈsibraɪt] (seé-brīt)
Seacy, f.n. [ˈsisɪ] (seéssi)
Seadon [ˈsidən] (seédŏn)
Seaford [siˈfɔrd] (seefórd); [ˈsifɔrd] (seéford)
Seaforde [ˈsifɔrd] (seéford)
Seager, f.n. [ˈsigər] (seéger)
Seago, f.n. [ˈsigoʊ] (seégō)
Seagoe [ˈsigoʊ] (seégō)
Seaham [ˈsiəm] (seé-ăm)
Seahouses [ˈsihaʊzɪz] (seé-howzĕz)
Searchfield, f.n. [ˈsɜrtʃfild] (sértchfeeld)
Searcy, f.n. [ˈsɪərsɪ] (seérssi)
Searell, f.n. [ˈserəl] (sérrĕl)
Searight, f.n. [ˈsiraɪt] (seé-rīt)
Searle, f.n. [sɜrl] (serl)
Sears, f.n. [sɪərz] (seerz)
Seasalter [ˈsisɔltər] (seé-sawlter)
Seascale [ˈsiskeɪl] (seé-skayl)
Seathwaite [ˈsiθweɪt] (seé-thwayt)
Seaton, f.n. [ˈsitən] (seétŏn)
Seaton Carew [ˈsitən kəˈru] (seétŏn kăroʻo)
Seaton Delaval [ˈsitən ˈdeləvəl] (seétŏn déllávál)
Seaville [ˈsevɪl] (sévvil)
Seavington [ˈsevɪŋtən] (sévvingtŏn)
Sebergham [ˈsebərəm] (sébbĕrăm)
Secombe, f.n. [ˈsikəm] (seékŏm)
Secord, f.n. [ˈsikɔrd] (seékord)
Secretan, f.n. [ˈsekrɪtən] (séckrĕtán)
Secrett, f.n. [ˈsikrɪt] (seékrĕt)
Sedbergh [ˈsedbər] (sédber); [ˈsedbɜrg] (sédberg)
Seddon, f.n. [ˈsedən] (séddŏn)
Sedgehill [ˈsedʒhɪl] (séj-hill); [ˈsedʒl] (sejjl)
Sedgwick, f.n. [ˈsedʒwɪk] (séjwick)
Seear, f.n. [ˈsɪər] (seé-ăr)
Seend [sind] (seend)

Segal, f.n. ['sɪgl] (seegl)
Seghill ['seghɪl] (ség-hill)
Segrave, f.n. ['sɪgreɪv] (seégrayv) see also Baron Mowbray, ~ and Stourton.
Segrue, f.n. ['sɪgru] (seégroo)
Seif, f.n. [sif] (seef)
Seigal, f.n. ['sɪgl] (seegl)
Seighford ['saɪfərd] (sífórd)
Seil [sil] (seel)
Seilern, f.n. ['saɪlɜrn] (sílern)
Seilibost ['ʃeɪlɪbɒst] (sháylibosst)
Seiriol, Welsh C.n. ['saɪərjɒl] (sír-yol)
Seisdon ['sizdən] (seézdŏn)
Sekers, Sir Nicholas, patron of the arts ['sekərz] (séckĕrz) Familiarly known as Miki ~, pronounced ['mɪkɪ] (mícki).
Selham ['sɪləm] (seélăm); ['seləm] (séllăm)
Seligman, f.n. ['selɪgmən] (sélligmăn)
Seligmann, f.n. ['selɪgmən] (sélligmăn)
Selkirk ['selkɜrk] (sélkirk)
Sellack ['selək] (séllăk)
Sellars, f.n. ['selərz] (séllărz)
Sellas, f.n. ['seləs] (séllăss)
Sellers, f.n. ['selərz] (séllĕrz)
Selley, f.n. ['selɪ] (sélli)
Sellindge ['selɪndʒ] (séllinj)
Selly Oak ['selɪ 'oʊk] (sélli ók)
Selmeston ['selmztən] (sélmztŏn)
Selous, f.n. [sə'lu] (sĕloó)
Selsey ['selzɪ] (sélzi)
Selsey Bill ['selzɪ 'bɪl] (sélzi bíll); ['selsɪ 'bɪl] (sélssi bíll)
Selwick ['selwɪk] (séllwick)
Selwyn, f.n. ['selwɪn] (sélwin)
Semington ['semɪŋtən] (sémmingtŏn)
Sempill, Baroness ['sempl] (sempl)
Sendall, f.n. ['sendɒl] (séndawl)
Senghenydd [seŋ'henɪð] (seng-hénnith)
Sennen ['senən] (sénnĕn)
Sensier, f.n. ['sensɪər] (sénsseer)
Serena, C.n. [sɪ'rinə] (sĕreénă)
Sergison, f.n. ['sɑrdʒɪsən] (saárjissŏn)
Serpell, f.n. ['sɜrpl] (serpl)
Serraillier, f.n. [sɪ'reɪlɪər] (sĕráyli-er)
Serret, f.n. ['serɪt] (sérrĕt)
Servaes, f.n. [sər'veɪz] (sĕrváyz)
Seskinore [ˌseskɪ'nɔr] (sesskinór)
Seton, f.n. ['sitən] (seétŏn)
Setoun, f.n. ['sitən] (seétŏn)
Sever, f.n. ['sevər] (sévver)
Severn, River ['sevərn] (sévvĕrn)
Severs, f.n. ['sevərz] (sévvĕrz)
Sevier, f.n. ['sevjər] (sév-yer); [sɪ'vɪər] (sĕveér)
Seville, f.n. ['sevɪl] (sévvil)
Seward, f.n. ['sjuərd] (syoó-ărd)
Sewell, f.n. ['sjuəl] (séwĕl)
Sewerby ['suərbɪ] (soó-ĕrbi)
Sexton, f.n. ['sekstən] (séckstŏn)
Seyd, f.n. [saɪd] (síd)
Seyers, f.n. [sɛərz] (sairz)
Seyler, Athene, actress [ə'θinɪ 'saɪlər] (ăthéeni síler)
Seymour, f.n. ['simər] (seémŭr); ['simər] (seémor); ['seɪmər] (sáymŭr) The first is

appropriate for the family name of the Duke of Somerset and of the Marquess of Hertford.
Seys, f.n. [seɪs] (sayss); [seɪz] (sayz)
Sezincote ['sizənkət] (seézin-kŏt)
Sgiwen see Skewen.
Sgurr Alasdair ['skʊər 'ælɪstər] (skoór álistăr)
Sgurr Biorach ['skʊər 'bɪrəx] (skoór bírrăch)
Sgurr Dearg, Isle of Skye ['skʊər 'derɪg] (skoór dérrĕg)
Sgurr na Banachdich ['skʊər nə 'bænəxdɪx] (skoór nă bánnăchdich)
Sgurr nan Eag ['skʊər nən 'eɪk] (skoór nán áyk)
Sgurr nan Gillean ['skʊər nən 'gɪljən] (skoór nán geél-yán)
Shackell, f.n. ['ʃækl] (shackl)
Shackleton, f.n. ['ʃækltən] (sháckltŏn) Appropriate also for Baron ~.
Shackman, f.n. ['ʃækmən] (sháckmăn)
Shaen, f.n. [ʃeɪn] (shayn)
Shaffer, f.n. ['ʃæfər] (sháffer)
Shafir, Shulamith, pianist ['ʃuləmɪθ ʃæ'fɪər] (shoólămith shafféer)
Shaftesbury ['ʃaftsbərɪ] (shaáftsbŭri) Appropriate also for the Earl of ~.
Shairp, f.n. [ʃɑrp] (shaarp)
Shakerley, f.n. ['ʃækərlɪ] (sháckĕrli)
Shakerley ['ʃækərlɪ] (sháckĕrli)
Shakerly, f.n. ['ʃækərlɪ] (sháckĕrli)
Shakespeare, f.n. ['ʃeɪkspɪər] (sháykspeer)
Shalden ['ʃɒldən] (sháwldĕn); ['ʃɒldən] (shól-dĕn)
Shaldon ['ʃɒldən] (sháwldŏn); ['ʃɒldən] (shól-dŏn)
Shalford, Essex, Surrey ['ʃælfərd] (shálfórd)
Shallcross, f.n. ['ʃælkrɒs] (shálkross)
Shalmsford Street ['ʃælmzfərd strit] (shálmzfŏrd street)
Shanbally ['ʃænbælɪ] (shánbali)
Shankill ['ʃæŋkɪl] (shánkil)
Shanklin, f.n. ['ʃæŋklɪn] (shánklin)
Shanklin ['ʃæŋklɪn] (shánklin)
Shannagh ['ʃænə] (shánnă)
Shapinsay ['ʃæpɪnseɪ] (sháppinssay)
Shapiro, f.n. [ʃə'pɪəroʊ] (shăpeèrŏ)
Shapland, f.n. ['ʃæplənd] (shápländ)
Shapley, f.n. ['ʃæplɪ] (shápli)
Shapwick ['ʃæpɪk] (sháppick)
Sharp, f.n. [ʃɑrp] (shaarp)
Sharpe, f.n. [ʃɑrp] (shaarp)
Sharpenhoe ['ʃɑrpɪnoʊ] (shaárpĕnŏ)
Sharples, f.n. ['ʃɑrplz] (shaarplz)
Sharpley, f.n. ['ʃɑrplɪ] (shaárpli)
Sharpness ['ʃɑrpnɪs] (shaárpnĕss)
Shaughnessy, f.n. ['ʃɒnɪsɪ] (sháwnĕssi) Appropriate also for Baron ~.
Shaugh Prior ['ʃɔ 'praɪər] (sháw prí-ŏr)
Shaw, f.n. [ʃɔ] (shaw)
Shawcross, f.n. ['ʃɒkrɒs] (sháwkross) Appropriate also for Baron ~.
Shea, f.n. [ʃeɪ] (shay)

Shead, *f.n.* [ʃed] (shed)
Sheaf, River [ʃif] (sheef)
Shearer, *f.n.* [ˈʃɪərər] (sheèrer)
Shearman, *f.n.* [ˈʃɜːmən] (shérmăn); [ˈʃɪərmən] (sheèrmăn)
Shearn, *f.n.* [ʃɜːn] (shern)
Shears, *f.n.* [ʃɪərz] (sheerz)
Shearsby [ˈʃɪərzbɪ] (sheèrzbi)
Shebbear [ˈʃebɪər] (shébbeer)
Shebbeare, *f.n.* [ˈʃebɪər] (shébbeer)
Sheehy, *f.n.* [ˈʃihɪ] (sheéhi)
Sheepscombe [ˈʃepskəm] (shépskŏm)
Sheffield, *f.n.* [ˈʃefild] (shéffeeld)
Sheffield [ˈʃefild] (shéffeeld)
Sheil, Loch [ʃil] (sheel)
Sheldon, *f.n.* [ˈʃeldən] (shéldŏn)
Shelfanger [ˈʃelfæŋər] (shélfang-ger)
Shelland [ˈʃelənd] (shélländ)
Shelley, *f.n.* [ˈʃelɪ] (shélli)
Shelmerdine, *f.n.* [ˈʃelmərdɪn] (shélmĕrdeen)
Shelton, *f.n.* [ˈʃeltən] (shéltŏn)
Shelvey, *f.n.* [ˈʃelvɪ] (shélvi)
Shephalbury [ˈʃeplbərɪ] (shépplbŭri)
Shephall [ˈʃepl] (sheppl)
Shepheard, *f.n.* [ˈʃepərd] (shéppĕrd)
Shepherd, *f.n.* [ˈʃepərd] (shéppĕrd)
Shepherdine [ˈʃepərdaɪn] (shéppĕrdīn)
Sheppard, *f.n.* [ˈʃepərd] (shéppărd)
Shepreth [ˈʃeprɪθ] (shéprĕth)
Shepton Beauchamp [ˈʃeptən ˈbitʃəm] (shéptŏn beètchăm)
Shepton Mallet [ˈʃeptən ˈmælɪt] (shéptŏn málĕt)
Sheraton, *f.n.* [ˈʃerətən] (shérrătŏn) *Appropriate for Thomas ~, 18th-c. cabinet-maker and furniture designer.*
Sherborne [ˈʃɜːbərn] (shérbŭrn) *Appropriate also for Baron ~.*
Shere [ʃɪər] (sheer)
Sheret, *f.n.* [ˈʃerɪt] (shérrĕt)
Sherfield, Baron [ˈʃɜːfild] (shérfeeld)
Sherfield - on - Loddon [ˈʃɜːfild ɒn ˈlɒdən] (shérfeeld on lóddŏn)
Shergold, *f.n.* [ˈʃɜːgoʊld] (shérgōld)
Sheridan, *f.n.* [ˈʃerɪdən] (shérridăn)
Sheridan, Richard Brinsley, *18th-c. dramatist* [ˈrɪtʃərd ˈbrɪnzlɪ ˈʃerɪdən] (rítchărd brínzli shérridăn)
Sheringham [ˈʃerɪŋəm] (shérring-ăm)
Sherlock, *f.n.* [ˈʃɜːlɒk] (shérlock)
Shermanbury [ˈʃɜːmənbərɪ] (shérmănbŭri)
Sherrin, *f.n.* [ˈʃerɪn] (shérrin)
Shetland [ˈʃetlənd] (shétländ)
Shettleston [ˈʃetlstən] (shéttlstŏn)
Sheuchan [ˈʃuxən] (shoóchăn)
Sheviock [ˈʃevɪɒk] (shévvi-ŏk)
Shew, *f.n.* [ʃu] (shoo)
Shewen, *f.n.* [ˈʃuɪn] (shoó-ĕn)
Shewey, *f.n.* [ˈʃoʊɪ] (shó-i)
Shiant Isles [ˈʃɪənt] (sheè-ănt)
Shields, *f.n.* [ʃildz] (sheeldz)
Shields, North *and* **South** [ʃildz] (sheeldz)

Shillaker, *f.n.* [ˈʃɪleɪkər] (shíllayker)
Shillidy, *f.n.* [ˈʃɪlɪdɪ] (shíllidi)
Shillinglaw, *f.n.* [ˈʃɪlɪŋlɒ] (shílling-law)
Shimna, River [ˈʃɪmnə] (shímnă)
Shincliffe [ˈʃɪŋklɪf] (shínk-liff)
Shinebourne, *f.n.* [ˈʃaɪnbɔːn] (shínborn)
Shinwell, *f.n.* [ˈʃɪnwəl] (shínwĕl)
Shipbourne [ˈʃɪbɜːn] (shíbburn)
Shipdam [ˈʃɪpdəm] (shípdăm); [ˈʃɪpəm] (shíppăm)
Shiplake [ˈʃɪpleɪk] (shíplayk)
Shipley, *f.n.* [ˈʃɪplɪ] (shípli)
Shipp, *f.n.* [ʃɪp] (ship)
Shippea [ˈʃɪpɪ] (shíppi)
Shipston-on-Stour [ˈʃɪpstən ɒn ˈstaʊər] (shípstŏn on stówr)
Shipton Bellinger [ˈʃɪptən ˈbelɪndʒər] (shíptŏn béllinjer)
Shirley, *f.n. and C.n.* [ˈʃɜːlɪ] (shírli)
Shirreff, *f.n.* [ˈʃɪrɪf] (shírrĕf); [ˈʃerɪf] (shérrĕf)
Shiskine [ˈʃɪskɪn] (shísskin)
Shivas, *f.n.* [ˈʃɪvəs] (sheèváss)
Shlaen, *f.n.* [ʃleɪn] (shlayn)
Shobrook, *f.n.* [ˈʃɒbrʊk] (shóbbroŏk)
Shobrooke [ˈʃoʊbrʊk] (shóbroŏk)
Shocklach [ˈʃɒklɪtʃ] (shócklitch)
Shoeburyness [ˈʃuːbərɪˈnes] (shoŏbŭrinéss)
Shoemake, *f.n.* [ˈʃuːmeɪk] (shoŏmayk)
Sholden [ˈʃoʊldən] (shóldĕn)
Sholing [ˈʃoʊlɪŋ] (shóling)
Sholto, *f.n.* [ˈʃɒltoʊ] (shóltō)
Shone, *f.n.* [ʃoʊn] (shōn)
Shonfield, *f.n.* [ˈʃɒnfild] (shónnfeeld)
Shooter, *f.n.* [ˈʃuːtər] (shoóter)
Short, *f.n.* [ʃɔːt] (short)
Shortlanesend [ˌʃɔːtleɪnzˈend] (shortlaynzénd)
Shorto, *f.n.* [ˈʃɔːtoʊ] (shórtō)
Shorwell [ˈʃɔːwel] (shórwel)
Shotesham All Saints [ˈʃɒtsəm ɔl ˈseɪnts] (shóttsăm awl sáynts)
Shotesham St. Mary [ˈʃɒtsəm snt ˈmɛərɪ] (shóttsăm sĭnt maíri)
Shottisham [ˈʃɒtsəm] (shóttsăm)
Shotwick [ˈʃɒtwɪk] (shótwick)
Shouldham [ˈʃoʊldəm] (shóldăm)
Shouldham Thorpe [ˈʃoʊldəm ˈθɔrp] (shóldăm thórp)
Shouler, *f.n.* [ˈʃuːlər] (shoóler)
Shoults, *f.n.* [ʃoʊlts] (shōlts)
Shove, Fredegond, *poet and author* [ˈfredɪgɒnd ˈʃoʊv] (fréddĕgond shóv)
Showell, *f.n.* [ˈʃoʊəl] (shó-ĕl)
Shrawardine [ˈʃreɪwərdaɪn] (shráy-wărdin)
Shrewsbury [ˈʃroʊzbərɪ] (shrózbŭri); [ˈʃruzbərɪ] (shroózbŭri) *The first is appropriate for the Earl of ~ and for the public school, but both are used in the town.*
Shrewton [ˈʃrutən] (shroótŏn)
Shrimpton, *f.n.* [ˈʃrɪmptən] (shrímptŏn)
Shrivenham [ˈʃrɪvənəm] (shrívvĕnăm)
Shroton [ˈʃroʊtən] (shrótŏn)

Shryane, f.n. ['ʃraɪən] (shrí-ăn)
Shuard, f.n. ['ʃuɑːd] (shoō-aard)
Shube, f.n. [ʃub] (shoob)
Shuckburgh, f.n. ['ʃʌkbərə] (shúckbŭră)
Shuckburgh, Lower *and* **Upper** ['ʃʌk-bərə] (shúckbŭră)
Shulbrede Priory ['ʃulbrɪd] (shoōl-breed) *see also Baron Ponsonby of Shulbrede.*
Shuldham, f.n. ['ʃuldəm] (shoōldăm)
Shults, f.n. [ʃʌlts] (shullts)
Shurmer, f.n. ['ʃɜːmər] (shúrmer)
Shurrery ['ʃʌrərɪ] (shúrrĕri)
Shute, Baron [ʃuːt] (shoot)
Sian, Welsh C.n. [ʃɑːn] (shaan)
Sibbett, f.n. ['sɪbɪt] (síbbĕt)
Sibdon Carwood ['sɪbdən 'kɑːwʊd] (síbdŏn kaárwoōd)
Sible Hedingham ['sɪbl 'hedɪŋəm] (síbbl hédding-ăm)
Sibley, f.n. ['sɪblɪ] (síbbli)
Sibree Hall, *Coventry* ['saɪbrɪ] (síbri)
Sibun, f.n. ['saɪbən] (síbŭn)
Sich, f.n. [sɪtʃ] (sitch)
Sichell, f.n. ['sɪtʃl] (sitchl); ['sɪʃl] (sishl)
Sicklesmere ['sɪklzmɪər] (sícklzmeer)
Sidcup ['sɪdkʌp] (sídkup); ['sɪdkəp] (síd-kŭp)
Siddall, f.n. ['sɪdɔl] (síddawl)
Sidebotham, f.n. ['saɪdbɒtəm] (síd-bottăm)
Sidebottom, f.n. ['saɪdbɒtəm] (seéd-bottŏm); [ˌsɪdɪbə'tɒm] (siddibŏttŏm)
Sidestrand ['saɪdstrænd] (sídstrand); ['saɪdɪstrænd] (sídĕsstrand)
Sidey, f.n. ['saɪdɪ] (sídi)
Sidford [sɪd'fɔːd] (sidfórd); ['sɪdfɔːd] (sídford)
Sidgreaves, f.n. ['sɪdgriːvz] (sídgreevz)
Sidlesham ['sɪdlsəm] (sídlssăm)
Sidmouth ['sɪdməθ] (sídmŭth)
Sieff, f.n. [sif] (seef) *Appropriate· also for Baron ~.*
Sieman, f.n. ['siːmən] (seémăn)
Siemons, f.n. ['siːmənz] (seémŏnz)
Sier, f.n. [sɪər] (seer); ['saɪər] (sīr)
Sieve, f.n. [sɪv] (seev)
Sieveking, f.n. ['sɪvkɪŋ] (seévking)
Sievier, f.n. ['sɪvjər] (seév-yer)
Sievwright, f.n. ['sɪvraɪt] (seévrīt)
Sigal, f.n. ['sɪgl] (seegl)
Siggins, f.n. ['sɪgɪnz] (sígginz)
Sigsworth, f.n. ['sɪgzwɜːθ] (síggzwurth)
Sileby ['saɪlbɪ] (sílbi)
Silhillian, native· of· Solihull [sɪl'hɪlɪən] (silhílli-ăn)
Silkin, f.n. ['sɪlkɪn] (sílkin)
Silkstone ['sɪlkstoʊn] (sílksstŏn)
Sill, f.n. [sɪl] (sill)
Sillence, f.n. [sɪ'lens] (sillénss); ['saɪləns] (sílĕnss)
Sillita, f.n. ['sɪlɪtə] (síllită)
Sillito, f.n. ['sɪlɪtoʊ] (síllitŏ)
Sillitoe, f.n. ['sɪlɪtoʊ] (síllitŏ)
Sillitto, f.n. ['sɪlɪtoʊ] (síllitŏ)

Silloth ['sɪləθ] (síllŏth)
Sillyearn [ˌsɪlɪ'ɜːn] (silli-érn)
Silsoe ['sɪlsoʊ] (sílssŏ) *Appropriate also for Baron ~.*
Silver, f.n. ['sɪlvər] (sílver)
Silverman, f.n. ['sɪlvərmən] (sílvĕrmăn)
Silverstone, f.n. ['sɪlvərstoʊn] (sílvĕr-sstŏn)
Silvester, f.n. [sɪl'vestər] (silvésster)
Silvey, f.n. ['sɪlvɪ] (sílvi)
Simche, f.n. ['sɪmtʃɪ] (símtchi)
Simeons, f.n. ['sɪmɪənz] (símmi-ŏnz)
Simister, f.n. ['sɪmɪstər] (símmister)
Simmonds, f.n. ['sɪməndz] (símmŏndz); ['sɪmənz] (símmŏnz)
Simmons, f.n. ['sɪmənz] (símmŏnz)
Simms, f.n. [sɪmz] (simmz)
Simon, f.n. ['saɪmən] (sīmŏn) *Appropriate also for Viscount ~.*
Simon of Wythenshawe, *Baron* ['saɪmən əv 'wɪðənʃoʊ] (sīmŏn ŏv wíthĕn-shaw)
Simond, f.n. ['saɪmənd] (sīmŏnd)
Simonds, f.n. ['sɪməndz] (símmŏndz); ['saɪməndz] (sīmŏndz) *The first is appropriate for Viscount ~.*
Simonis, f.n. [sɪ'moʊnɪs] (simmóniss)
Simons, f.n. ['saɪmənz] (sīmŏnz)
Simonsbath ['sɪmənzbɑːθ] (símmŏnz-baath)
Simonstone ['sɪmənstoʊn] (símmŏn-sstŏn)
Simpson, f.n. ['sɪmpsən] (símpsŏn)
Sims, f.n. [sɪmz] (simmz)
Sinclair, f.n. ['sɪŋkleər] (sínklair); ['sɪŋklər] (sínklăr) *The first is appropriate for Baron ~. The second is usual in Scotland.*
Singer, f.n. ['sɪŋər] (síng-er)
Singleton, f.n. ['sɪŋgltən] (síng-gltŏn)
Sinnatt, f.n. ['sɪnət] (sínnăt)
Sinodun Hill ['sɪnədən] (sínnŏdŭn)
Sinstadt, f.n. ['sɪnstæt] (sínstat)
Sion Mills ['zaɪən 'mɪlz] (zī-ŏn míllz)
Sired, f.n. ['saɪərɪd] (sírĕd)
Sirett, f.n. ['sɪrɪt] (sírrĕt)
Sirhowy [sɜː'haʊɪ] (sir-hówi)
Siriol, Welsh C.n. ['sɪrɪɒl] (sírri-ol)
Sisam, f.n. ['saɪsəm] (síssăm)
Sisland ['saɪzlənd] (sízlănd)
Sisley, f.n. ['sɪzlɪ] (sízzli) *Appropriate also in English usage for the Anglo-French painter, Alfred ~.*
Sissinghurst ['sɪsɪŋhɜːst] (síssing-hurst) *Appropriate also for ~ Castle.*
Siston ['saɪstən] (sísstŏn); ['saɪsən] (síssŏn)
Sisum, f.n. ['saɪsəm] (síssŭm)
Sitch, f.n. [sɪtʃ] (sitch)
Sithney ['sɪθnɪ] (síthni)
Sitwell, Sacheverell, author [sə'ʃevərəl 'sɪtwəl] (săshévvĕrĕl sítwĕl)
Sizer, f.n. ['saɪzər] (sízer)
Sizergh ['saɪzər] (sízer)
Sizewell ['saɪzwəl] (sízwĕl)

Skamacre, f.n. ['skæmeɪkər](skámayker)
Skarra Brae ['skærə 'breɪ] (skárrǎ bráy)
Skea, f.n. [ski] (skee)
Skeabost ['skeɪbɒst] (skáybosst)
Skeaping, f.n. ['skipɪŋ] (skeeping)
Skeat, f.n. [skit] (skeet)
Skeats, f.n. [skits] (skeets)
Skegoniel [ˌskegə'nil] (skeggǒneél)
Skelhorn, f.n. ['skelhɔrn] (skélhorn)
Skell, River [skel] (skell)
Skelmersdale ['skelmərzdeɪl] (skélměrz-dayl); ['skemərzdeɪl] (skémměrzdayl) *The first is appropriate for Baron ~.*
Skelmorlie ['skelmərlɪ] (skélmŏrli)
Skelsey, f.n. ['skelsɪ] (skélssi)
Skelsmergh ['skelzmər] (skélzmer); ['skelzmɪər] (skélzmeer)
Skelton, f.n. ['skeltən] (skéltŏn)
Skelwith ['skelɪθ] (skéllith)
Skemp, f.n. [skemp] (skemp)
Skempton, f.n. ['skemptən] (skémptŏn)
Skene, f.n. [skin] (skeen)
Sker [skɛər] (skair)
Skernaghan Point ['skɜrnəxən] (skér-náchǎn)
Skerritt, f.n. ['skerɪt] (skérrit)
Sketch, f.n. [sketʃ] (sketch)
Skewen, *also spelt* **Sgiwen** ['skjuɪn] (skéw-ĕn)
Skeyton ['skaɪtən] (skítŏn)
Skidmore, f.n. ['skɪdmɔr] (skídmor)
Skilbeck, f.n. ['skɪlbek] (skílbeck)
Skinburness [ˌskɪnbɜr'nes] (skinburnéss)
Skinnard, f.n. ['skɪnɑrd] (skínnaard)
Skinner, f.n. ['skɪnər] (skínner)
Skiport, Loch ['skɪpərt] (skíppŏrt)
Skirlaugh ['skɜrlou] (skírlŏ)
Skirrow, f.n. ['skɪrou] (skírrŏ)
Skirsa ['skɜrzə] (skírzǎ)
Skokholm, *also spelt* **Skokham** ['skɒk-houm] (skóck-hōm); ['skoukəm] (skó-kǎm)
Skomer Island ['skoumər] (skómer)
Skone, f.n. [skoun] (skōn)
Skrimshire, f.n. ['skrɪmʃaɪər] (skrím-shīr)
Skrine, f.n. [skrin] (skreen); [skraɪn] (skrīn)
Skye [skaɪ] (skī)
Skyrme, f.n. [skɜrm] (skirm)
Slaap, f.n. [slɑp] (slaap)
Sladden, f.n. ['slædən] (sláddĕn)
Slade, f.n. [sleɪd] (slayd)
Slaithwaite ['slæθweɪt] (sláthwayt); ['slauɪt] (slówit)
Slamannan [slə'mænən] (slǎmánnǎn)
Slamin, f.n. ['slæmɪn] (slámmin)
Slapin, Loch ['slapɪn] (sláapin)
Slater, f.n. ['sleɪtər] (sláyter)
Slatter, f.n. ['slætər] (slátter)
Slattery, f.n. ['slætərɪ] (sláttĕri)
Slaugham ['slæfəm] (sláffǎm); ['slafəm] (slaáfǎm)
Slaughdon ['slodən] (sláwdŏn)
Slaughter, f.n. ['slotər] (sláwter)

Slaughter, Lower *and* **Upper** ['slotər] (sláwter)
Sleaford ['slifərd] (sleefŏrd)
Sleat [sleɪt] (slayt)
Sleath, f.n. [sliθ] (sleeth)
Slebech ['slebetʃ] (slébbetch)
Sledmere ['sledmɪər] (slédmeer)
Sleeman, f.n. ['slimən] (sleémǎn)
Sleigh, f.n. [sleɪ] (slay); [sli] (slee)
Sleights [slaɪts] (slīts)
Slemish ['sleɪmɪʃ] (sláymish)
Slessenger, f.n. ['slesɪndʒər] (sléssĕnjer)
Slessor, f.n. ['slesər] (sléssŏr)
Slevin, f.n. ['slevɪn] (slévvin)
Slieu Lhean, *I.o.M.* ['slju 'len] (sléw lén)
Slieve Bearnagh [sliv 'bɜrnə] (sleev baírnǎ)
Slieve Donard [sliv 'dɒnərd] (sleev dónnǎrd)
Slieve-na-Man [ˌslivnə'mæn] (sleev-námán)
Slievebane [sliv'bæn] (sleevbán)
Sligachan ['sligəxən] (sleegáchǎn)
Sligo, Marquess of ['slaɪgou] (slígŏ)
Sloan, f.n. [sloun] (slōn)
Sloane, f.n. [sloun] (slōn)
Slochd [slɒx] (sloch)
Slocombe, f.n. ['sloukəm] (slókŏm)
Slough [slau] (slow)
Slowey, f.n. ['slouɪ] (sló-i)
Sloy, Loch [slɔɪ] (sloy)
Slydell, f.n. [slaɪ'del] (slīdéll)
Smaje, f.n. [smeɪdʒ] (smayj)
Smale, f.n. [smeɪl] (smayl)
Smalley ['smolɪ] (smáwli)
Smallpeice, f.n. ['smolpis] (smáwlpeess)
Smarden ['smɑrdən] (smaárdĕn); [smɑr-'den] (smaardén)
Smart, f.n. [smɑrt] (smaart)
Smeaton, f.n. ['smitən] (smeétŏn)
Smedley, f.n. ['smedlɪ] (smédli)
Smeeth [smiθ] (smeeth)
Smeeton, f.n. ['smitən] (smeétŏn)
Smellie, f.n. ['smelɪ] (smélli)
Smethurst, f.n. ['smeθɜrst] (sméthurst)
Smethwick ['smeðɪk] (sméthick)
Smibert, f.n. ['smaɪbərt] (smíbĕrt)
Smieton, f.n. ['smitən] (smeétŏn)
Smily, f.n. ['smaɪlɪ] (smíli)
Smith, f.n. [smɪθ] (smith)
Smithaleigh ['smɪðəli] (smíthǎlee)
Smithells, f.n. ['smɪðlz] (smíthlz)
Smithers, f.n. ['smɪðərz] (smíthĕrz)
Smithfield ['smɪθfild] (smíthfeeld)
Smitton, f.n. ['smɪtən] (smíttŏn)
Smollett, f.n. ['smɒlɪt] (smóllĕt)
Smurthwaite, f.n. ['smɜrθweɪt] (smúrth-wayt)
Smyth, f.n. [smɪθ] (smith); [smaɪð] (smīth); [smaɪð] (smīth) *The second is appropriate for Dame Ethel ~, composer and conductor.*
Smythe, f.n. [smaɪð] (smīth); [smaɪθ] (smīth)
Smythson, f.n. ['smaɪðsən] (smíthssŏn)

Snabdough ['snæbdʌf] (snábduff)
Snaefell, *I.o.M.* ['sneɪ'fel] (snáy-féll)
Snagge, *f.n.* [snæg] (snag)
Snailum, *f.n.* ['sneɪləm] (snáylŭm)
Snaith, *f.n.* [sneɪθ] (snayth)
Snashall, *f.n.* ['snæʃl] (snashl)
Snead, *f.n.* [snid] (sneed)
Sneezum, *f.n.* ['snizəm] (sneézŭm)
Sneinton ['snentən] (snéntŏn)
Snettisham ['snetsəm] (snétsăm); ['snetɪsəm] (snéttissăm); ['snetʃəm] (snétchăm)
Snewin, *f.n.* ['snjuɪn] (snéw-in)
Snewing, *f.n.* ['snjuɪŋ] (snéw-ing)
Sneyd, *f.n.* [snid] (sneed)
Sneyd [snid] (sneed)
Snizort ['snaɪzərt] (snízŏrt)
Snizort, Loch ['snaɪzərt] (snízŏrt)
Snoad, *f.n.* [snoud] (snōd)
Snodgrass, *f.n.* ['snɒdgrɑs] (snódgraass)
Snodland ['snɒdlənd] (snódlănd)
Snoswell, *f.n.* ['snɒzwəl] (snózzwĕl)
Snow, *f.n.* [snou] (snō) *Appropriate also for Baron ~.*
Snowdon ['snoudən] (snódŏn) *Appropriate also for the Earl of ~.*
Snowdonia [snou'dounɪə] (snōdṓniă)
Snoxell, *f.n.* ['snɒksl] (snockssl)
Soal, *f.n.* [soul] (sōl)
Soames, *f.n.* [soumz] (sōmz)
Soane, *f.n.* [soun] (sōn)
Soar ['souar] (sṓ-aar)
Soar, River [sɔr] (sor)
Soay ['souə] (sṓ-ǎ)
Sobell, *f.n.* ['soubel] (sóbell)
Sodor and Man, *bishopric* ['soudər ənd 'mæn] (sódŏr ănd mán)
Sofaer, *f.n.* [sou'fɛər] (sōfáir)
Soham ['souəm] (sō-ăm)
Sohier, *f.n.* ['soujər] (sō-yer)
Soke of Peterborough ['souk əv 'pitərbərə] (sṓk ŏv peéterbŭră)
Solent ['soulənt] (sṓlĕnt)
Solihull [ˌsoulɪ'hʌl] (sōli-húll)
Sollars, *f.n.* ['sɒlərz] (sóllărz)
Sollas ['sɒləs] (sólláss)
Solon, *f.n.* ['soulɒn] (sṓlon); ['soulən] (sṓlŏn)
Solva ['sɒlvə] (sólvă)
Solway Firth ['sɒlweɪ] (sólway)
Somerby ['sʌmərbɪ] (súmmĕrbi)
Somercotes ['sʌmərkouts] (súmmĕrkōts)
Somerfield, *f.n.* ['sʌmərfild] (súmmĕrfeeld)
Somerhough, *f.n.* ['sʌmərhɒf] (súmmĕrhoff)
Somerleyton ['sʌmərleɪtən] (súmmĕrlaytŏn)
Somers, *f.n.* ['sʌmərz] (súmmĕrz) *Appropriate also for Baron ~.*
Somersby ['sʌmərzbɪ] (súmmĕrzbi)
Somerset, *f.n.* ['sʌmərsɪt] (súmmĕrssĕt)
Somerset ['sʌmərsɪt] (súmmĕrssĕt); ['sʌmərset] (súmmĕrsset) *The first is appropriate for the Duke of ~.*

Somersham ['sʌmərʃəm] (súmmĕr-shăm)
Somerton, *f.n.* ['sʌmərtən] (súmmĕrtŏn) *Appropriate also for Viscount ~.*
Somerton, East *and* **West** ['sʌmərtən] (súmmĕrtŏn)
Somervell, *f.n.* ['sʌmərvəl] (súmmĕrvĕl)
Somerville, *f.n.* ['sʌmərvɪl] (súmmĕrvil)
Sompting ['sʌmptɪŋ] (súmpting); ['sɒmptɪŋ] (sómpting)
Sondes, *f.n.* [sɒndz] (sondz) *Appropriate also for Earl ~.*
Sonnex, *f.n.* ['sɒneks] (sónnecks)
Sonning ['sʌnɪŋ] (súnning); ['sɒnɪŋ] (sónning)
Soper, *f.n.* ['soupər] (sṓper) *Appropriate also for Baron ~.*
Soref, *f.n.* ['sɒrɪf] (sórrĕf)
Sorensen, *f.n.* ['sɒrənsən] (sórrĕnssĕn)
Sorensen of Leyton, Baron ['sɒrənsən əv 'leɪtən] (sórrĕnssĕn ŏv láytŏn)
Sorley, *f.n.* ['sɔrlɪ] (sórli)
Sorrell, *f.n.* ['sɒrəl] (sórrĕl); [sə'rel] (sŏréll)
Soskice, *f.n.* ['sɒskɪs] (sósskiss)
Sotham, *f.n.* ['sʌðəm] (súth̃ăm)
Sotheby's, *auctioneers* ['sʌðəbɪz] (súth̃ĕbiz)
Sothers, *f.n.* ['sʌðərz] (súth̃ĕrz)
Sotterley ['sɒtərlɪ] (sóttĕrli)
Soudley ['sudlɪ] (soódli)
Souez, *f.n.* ['suɪz] (soó-ĕz)
Soul, *f.n.* [sul] (sool)
Soulbury, Viscount ['soulbərɪ] (sṓlbŭri)
Soulby, *f.n.* ['soulbɪ] (sṓlbi)
Soulby ['soulbɪ] (sṓlbi)
Souldern ['souldərn] (sṓldĕrn)
Souldrop ['souldrɒp] (sṓldrop)
Soulsby, *f.n.* ['soulzbɪ] (sṓlzbi)
Sound of Mull ['saund əv 'mʌl] (sównd ŏv múll)
Sourin ['sauərɪn] (sówrin)
Sourton ['sɔrtən] (sórtŏn)
Souster, *f.n.* ['sustər] (soóster)
Soutar, *f.n.* ['sutər] (soótăr)
Souter, *f.n.* ['sutər] (soóter)
Souter Point ['sutər 'pɒɪnt] (soóter póynt)
South Baddesley ['sauθ 'bædɪzlɪ] (sówth báddĕzli); ['sauθ 'bædzlɪ] (sówth bádzli)
South Cerney ['sauθ 'sɜrnɪ] (sówth sérni)
South Croxton ['sauθ 'krousən] (sówth krṓssŏn); ['sauθ 'kroustən] (sówth krṓsston); ['sauθ 'krouzən] (sówth krṓzŏn)
South Elmham ['sauθ 'elməm] (sówth élmăm)
South Hykeham ['sauθ 'haɪkəm] (sówth hīkăm)
South Kirkby ['sauθ 'kɜrbɪ] (sówth kírbi)
South Leverton ['sauθ 'levərtən] (sówth lévvĕrtŏn)
South Ronaldsay ['sauθ 'rɒnldseɪ] (sówth rónnld-say); ['rɒnldʃeɪ] (rónnld-shay)
South Shields ['sauθ 'ʃildz] (sówth sheéldz)

South Trekeive ['saʊθ trɪ'kiv] (sówth trĕkéev)

South Walsham ['saʊθ 'wɔlʃəm] (sówth wáwl-shăm)

Southall, f.n. ['sAðɔl] (súthawl)

Southall ['saʊθɔl] (sówth-awl)

Southam, f.n. ['saʊðəm] (sówthăm)

Southam ['saʊðəm] (sówthăm)

Southampton [saʊθ'hæmptən] (sowth-hámptŏn); [saʊ'θæmptən] (sowthámptŏn)

Southby, f.n. ['saʊθbɪ] (sówthbi)

Southcombe, f.n. ['saʊθkəm] (sówthkŏm)

Southerndown ['sAðərndaʊn] (súthĕrndown)

Southerwood, f.n. ['sAðərwʊd] (súthĕrwŏŏd)

Southery ['sAðərɪ] (súthĕri)

Southey, f.n. ['saʊðɪ] (sówthi); ['sAðɪ] (súthi) *The first is appropriate for Robert ∼, Poet Laureate.*

Southgate, f.n. ['saʊθgeɪt] (sówthgayt); ['saʊθgɪt] (sówthgit)

Southgate ['saʊθgɪt] (sówthgit)

Southleigh ['saʊθ'li] (sówth-leé); ['saʊli] (sówlee)

Southminster ['saʊθ'mɪnstər] (sówth-mínster)

Southorn, f.n. ['sAðorn] (súthorn)

Southowram [saʊθ'aʊərəm] (sowthówrăm)

Southrepps ['saʊθreps] (sówthrepps)

Southrey ['sAðrɪ] (súthri)

Southron, f.n. ['sAðrən] (súthrŏn)

Southwark, f.n. ['sAðərk] (súthărk)

Southwark ['sAðərk] (súthărk) *Appropriate also for ∼ Cathedral.*

Southwell, f.n. ['sAðl] (súthl); ['saʊθwəl] (sówthwĕl) *The first is appropriate for Viscount ∼.*

Southwell ['sAðl] (súthl)

Southwick, *Dumfries., Sussex, Wilts.* ['saʊθwɪk] (sówthwick)

Southwick, *Co. Durham* ['saʊθwɪk] (sówthwick); ['sAðɪk] (súthick)

Southwick, *Hants.* ['sAðɪk] (súthick); ['saʊθwɪk] (sówthwick)

Southwick, *Northants.* ['sAðɪk] (súthick)

Southwold ['saʊθwoʊld] (sówth-wōld)

Soutra ['sutrə] (soótră)

Souttar, f.n. ['sutər] (soótăr)

Soward, f.n. ['saʊərd] (sówărd)

Sowels, f.n. ['soʊəlz] (ső-ĕlz)

Sowerbucks, f.n. ['soʊərbʌks] (ső-ĕrbucks)

Sowerby, f.n. ['soʊərbɪ] (ső-ĕrbi); ['saʊərbɪ] (sówĕrbi)

Sowerby, *North Riding of Yorks.* ['saʊərbɪ] (sówĕrbi)

Sowerby Bridge ['soʊərbɪ 'brɪdʒ] (ső-ĕrbi bríj); ['saʊərbɪ 'brɪdʒ] (sówĕrbi bríj)

Sowerby Parliamentary Division ['soʊərbɪ] (ső-ĕrbi); ['saʊərbɪ] (sówĕrbi)

Sowle, f.n. [soʊl] (sōl)

Sowrey, f.n. ['saʊərɪ] (sówri)

Sowry, f.n. ['saʊərɪ] (sówri)

Sowton ['saʊtən] (sówtŏn)

Spadeadam [speɪd'ædəm] (spaydáddăm)

Spalding ['spɔldɪŋ] (spáwlding)

Spalford ['spɔlfərd] (spáwlförd)

Spamount ['spɑmaʊnt] (spaámownt)

Spanoghe, f.n. ['spænoʊg] (spánnōg)

Sparham, f.n. ['spɑrəm] (spaárăm)

Sparham ['spærəm] (spárrăm)

Sparks, f.n. [spɑrks] (spaarks)

Sparsholt ['spɑrʃoʊlt] (spaár-shōlt)

Speaight, f.n. [speɪt] (spayt)

Spean, River ['spiən] (speé-ăn)

Spean Bridge ['spiən 'brɪdʒ] (speé-ăn bríj)

Spearman, f.n. ['spɪərmən] (speérmăn)

Spears, f.n. [spɪərz] (speerz)

Spedan, f.n. ['spidən] (speédăn)

Speight, f.n. [speɪt] (spayt)

Speir, f.n. [spɪər] (speer)

Speirs, f.n. [spɪərz] (speerz)

Speke [spik] (speek)

Spence, f.n. [spens] (spenss)

Spenceley, f.n. ['spenslɪ] (spénssli)

Spencer, f.n. ['spensər] (spénsser)

Spens, f.n. [spenz] (spenz)

Spenser, f.n. ['spensər] (spénsser)

Sperrin Mountains ['sperɪn] (spérrin)

Spetisbury ['spetsbərɪ] (spétsbŭri)

Spey, Loch *and* River [speɪ] (spay)

Speybridge ['speɪ'brɪdʒ] (spáy-bríj)

Speyer, f.n. [speər] (spair)

Speymouth ['speɪmaʊθ] (spáymowth)

Spice, f.n. [spaɪs] (spíss)

Spicer, f.n. ['spaɪsər] (spísser)

Spiegl, f.n. ['spigl] (speegl)

Spier, f.n. [spɪər] (speer)

Spillane, f.n. [spɪ'leɪn] (spilláyn)

Spiller, f.n. ['spɪlər] (spíller)

Spilsbury, f.n. ['spɪlzbərɪ] (spíllzbŭri)

Spiridion, f.n. [spɪ'rɪdɪən] (spiríddi-ŏn)

Spital ['spɪtl] (spittl)

Spital Tongues ['spɪtl 'tʌŋz] (spíttl túngz)

Spitalfields ['spɪtlfildz] (spíttlfeeldz)

Spithead ['spɪt'hed] (spit-héd)

Spittal, f.n. ['spɪtl] (spittl)

Spittal of Glenshee ['spɪtl əv glen'ʃi] (spíttl ŏv glen-sheé)

Spivey, f.n. ['spaɪvɪ] (spívi)

Spofforth, f.n. ['spofərθ] (spóffürth)

Spon, f.n. [spon] (sponn)

Spondon ['spondən] (spóndŏn); ['spundən] (spoóndŏn)

Spooner, f.n. ['spunər] (spoóner)

Sporle [spɔrl] (sporl)

Sporle with Palgrave ['spɔrl wɪð 'pælgreɪv] (spórl with pálgrayv)

Spottiswoode, f.n. ['spotɪswʊd] (spóttiswŏŏd); ['spotswʊd] (spótswŏŏd)

Spouse, f.n. [spaʊz] (spowz)

Sprague, f.n. [spreɪg] (sprayg)

Spriggs, f.n. [sprɪgz] (spriggz)

Springall, f.n. ['sprɪŋɔl] (spríng-awl)

Springburn ['sprɪŋbɜrn] (spríngburn)
Springett, f.n. ['sprɪŋɪt] (spríng-ĕt)
Springfield ['sprɪŋfɪld] (spríngfeeld)
Sproson, f.n. ['sprousən] (sprŏssŏn)
Sproughton ['sprɔtən] (spráwtŏn)
Sproule, f.n. [sproul] (sprŏl); [sprul] (sprool)
Sprouston ['spraustən] (sprówsstŏn)
Sprowston [sproustən] (sprŏsstŏn)
Sproxton, f.n. ['sprɒkstən] (spróckstŏn)
Spungin, f.n. ['spʌŋgɪn] (spúng-gin)
Spurling, f.n. ['spɜrlɪŋ] (spúrling)
Spurrell, f.n. ['spʌrəl] (spúrrĕl)
Spurrier, f.n. ['spʌrɪər] (spúrri-er)
Squier, f.n. ['skwaɪər] (skwír)
Squire, f.n. ['skwaɪər] (skwír)
Squires, f.n. ['skwaɪərz] (skwírz)
Stacey, f.n. ['steɪsɪ] (stáyssi)
Stadlen, f.n. ['stædlən] (stádlĕn)
Staffa ['stæfə] (stáffá)
Stafford ['stæfərd] (stáffŏrd)
Stainer, f.n. ['steɪnər] (stáyner)
Staines [steɪnz] (staynz)
Staithes [steɪðz] (staythz)
Stakehill ['steɪk'hɪl] (stáyk-híll)
Stalbridge ['stɔlbrɪdʒ] (stáwlbrij) Appropriate also for the Barony of ∼.
Stalham ['stæləm] (stálăm)
Stalham Green ['stæləm 'grin] (stálăm gréen)
Stalisfield ['stælɪsfɪld] (stálissfeeld)
Stalker, f.n. ['stɔkər] (stáwker); ['stælkər] (stál-ker)
Stallard, f.n. ['stælard] (stálaard)
Stallingborough ['stɔlɪŋbərə] (stáalingbŭrá)
Stallybrass, f.n. ['stælɪbras] (stálibraass)
Stalman, f.n. ['stælmən] (stálmăn)
Stalybridge ['steɪlɪbrɪdʒ] (stáylíbrij)
Stamfordham ['stæmfərdəm] (stámfŏrdăm); ['stænərtən] (stánnĕrtŏn)
Stamp, f.n. [stæmp] (stamp)
Stancliffe, f.n. ['stænklɪf] (stán-kliff)
Standaloft, f.n. ['stændəlɒft] (stándălŏft)
Standedge ['stænedʒ] (stánnej)
Standeven, f.n. ['stændivən] (stándeevĕn)
Standing, f.n. ['stændɪŋ] (stánding)
Stanford, f.n. ['stænfərd] (stánfŏrd)
Stanford - le - Hope ['stænfərdlɪ'houp] (stánfŏrdli-hŏp)
Stangboom, f.n. ['stæŋbum] (stángboom)
Stangroom, f.n. ['stæŋrum] (stángrŏm); [stæn'grum] (stan-grŏm)
Stanhill ['stænhɪl] (stánhil)
Stanhoe ['stænou] (stánnŏ)
Stanhope, f.n. ['stænəp] (stánnŏp) Appropriate also for the Earldom of ∼.
Stanhope ['stænəp] (stánnŏp)
Stanier, f.n. ['stænɪ-ər] (stánni-er)
Staniland, f.n. ['stænɪlənd] (stánnilănd)
Stanion ['stænjən] (stán-yŏn)
Stanley, f.n. and C.n. ['stænlɪ] (stánli)
Stanley of Alderley, Baron ['stænlɪ əv 'ɔldərlɪ] (stánli ŏv áwldĕrli)

Stanley ['stænlɪ] (stánli)
Stannard, f.n. ['stænard] (stánnaard)
Stansfield, f.n. ['stænzfɪld] (stánzfeeld)
Stansgate, Viscountcy of ['stænzgeɪt] (stánzgayt)
Stansted Airport ['stænsted] (stánsted)
Stansted Mountfitchet ['stænsted maunt'fɪtʃɪt] (stánsted mowntfítchĕt)
Stanton, f.n. ['stæntən] (stántŏn); ['stantən] (staántŏn)
Stanton-by-Bridge['stæntən baɪ 'brɪdʒ] (stántŏn bī brij)
Stanwick, f.n. ['stænɪk] (stánnick)
Stanwick ['stænɪk] (stánnick)
Stanwick St. John ['stænɪk snt 'dʒɒn] (stánnick sĭnt jón)
Stanwix ['stænɪks] (stánnicks)
Stapley, f.n. ['stæplɪ] (stápli); ['steɪplɪ] (stáypli)
Stareton ['startən] (staártŏn)
Stark, f.n. [stark] (staark)
Starkey, f.n. ['starkɪ] (staárki)
Starlaw ['star'lɔ] (staár-láw)
Startin, f.n. ['startɪn] (staártin)
Statham, f.n. ['steɪθəm] (stáythăm); ['steɪðəm] (stáythăm)
Stathern ['stæθərn] (stát-hern)
Staton, f.n. ['steɪtən] (stáytŏn)
Staub, f.n. [stɒb] (stawb)
Staughton, Little ['stotən] (stáwtŏn)
Staughton Green ['stotən 'grin] (stáwtŏn gréen)
Staughton Highway ['stotən 'haɪweɪ] (stáwtŏn hí-way)
Staughton Moor ['stotən 'muər] (stáwtŏn mŏŏr)
Staunton, f.n. ['stɒntən] (stáwntŏn)
Staveacre, f.n. ['steɪveɪkər] (stáyvayker)
Staveley, Derby. ['steɪvlɪ] (stáyvli)
Staveley, Westmorland ['steɪvəlɪ] (stáyvĕli)
Staverton, Glos., Northants. ['stævərtən] (stávvĕrtŏn)
Stavordale Priory ['stævərdeɪl] (stávvŏrdayl)
Staward ['stawərd] (staáwărd)
Staxigoe ['stæksɪgjou] (stácksig-yŏ)
Staythorpe ['steɪθɔrp] (stáy-thorp)
Stead, f.n. [sted] (sted); [stid] (steed)
Steart ['stɪərt] (steé-ărt)
Stechford ['stetʃfərd] (stétchfŏrd)
Steck, f.n. [stek] (steck)
Steddall, f.n. ['stedɔl] (stéddawl)
Stedeford, f.n. ['stedɪfərd] (stéddĕford)
Stedman, f.n. ['stedmən] (stédmăn)
Steeïd, f.n. [stid] (steed)
Steegman, f.n. ['stidʒmən] (steéjmăn)
Steele, f.n. [stil] (steel)
Steen, f.n. [stin] (steen)
Stein, f.n. [staɪn] (stīn); [stin] (steen)
Steinitz, f.n. ['staɪnɪtʃ] (stínits)
Steley, f.n. ['stelɪ] (stélli)
Stelling Minnis ['stelɪŋ 'mɪnɪz] (stélling mínniz)
Stenalees [ˌstenə'liz] (stennáleéz)

Stenhousemuir ['stenhaʊs'mjʊər] (sténhowss-myóŏr)
Stenigot ['stenɪgɒt] (sténnigot)
Stenning, f.n. ['stenɪŋ] (sténning)
Stentiford, f.n. ['stentɪfərd] (sténtifŏrd)
Stepaside [ˌstepə'saɪd] (stepássíd)
Stephen, C.n. ['stivən] (steévĕn)
Stephens, f.n. ['stivənz] (steévĕnz)
Stephenson, f.n. ['stivənsən] (steévĕnssŏn)
Steptoe, f.n. ['steptoʊ] (stéptŏ)
Sterke, f.n. [stark] (staark)
Sterling, f.n. ['stɜrlɪŋ] (stérling)
Sterner, f.n. ['stɜrnər] (stérner)
Sternfeld, f.n. ['stɜrnfeld] (stérnfeld)
Steuart, f.n. ['stjuərt] (stéw-árt); ['stjuərt] (styóŏ-árt)
Stevas, f.n. ['stivæs] (steévass)
Stevens, f.n. ['stivənz] (steévĕnz)
Stevenson, f.n. ['stivənsən] (steévĕnssŏn)
Steventon ['stivəntən] (steévĕntŏn)
Stevington ['stevɪŋtən] (stévvingtŏn)
Steward, f.n. ['stjuərd] (stéw-árd)
Stewart, f.n. ['stjuərt] (stéw-árt); ['stjuərt] (styóŏ-árt)
Steyne [stin] (steen)
Steyne, The, Brighton [ðə 'stin] (thĕ steén)
Steyning ['stenɪŋ] (sténning)
Steynor, f.n. ['stinər] (steénŏr)
Stickells, f.n. ['stɪklz] (sticklz)
Stiebel, f.n. ['stibl] (steebl)
Stiffkey ['stɪfkɪ] (stíffki); ['stukɪ] (stoóki); ['stjukɪ] (stéwki) The two latter are rarely heard today.
Stillwell, f.n. ['stɪlwel] (stíllwel)
Stilton ['stɪltən] (stíltŏn)
Stiperstones ['staɪpərstoʊnz] (stípĕrstŏnz)
Stirling, f.n. ['stɜrlɪŋ] (stírling)
Stirling ['stɜrlɪŋ] (stírling)
Stirton, f.n. ['stɜrtən] (stírtŏn)
Stisted ['staɪsted] (stí-sted)
Stithians ['stɪðɪ-ænz] (stíthi-ánz)
Stivichall, also spelt Styvechale ['staɪtʃl] (stítchl); ['staɪtʃl] (stítchawl)
Stixall ['stɪksɒl] (stícksawl)
Stobart, f.n. ['stoʊbart] (stóbaart)
Stobo ['stoʊboʊ] (stóbŏ)
Stoborough ['stoʊbərə] (stóbŭrá)
Stock, f.n. [stɒk] (stock)
Stocking, f.n. ['stɒkɪŋ] (stócking)
Stockins, f.n. ['stɒkɪnz] (stóckinz)
Stockleigh Pomeroy ['stɒklɪ 'pɒmərɔɪ] (stóckli pómmĕroy)
Stockley, f.n. ['stɒklɪ] (stóckli)
Stocks, f.n. [stɒks] (stocks) Appropriate also for Baroness ~.
Stockwell, f.n. ['stɒkwel] (stóckwel); ['stɒkwəl] (stóckwĕl)
Stockwell ['stɒkwel] (stóckwĕl)
Stodart, f.n. ['stɒdərt] (stóddărt); ['stoʊdart] (stõdaart); [stoʊ'dart] (stōdaárt)
Stoddart, f.n. ['stɒdərt] (stóddărt)

Stody ['stʌdɪ] (stúddi)
Stoekoe, f.n. ['stoʊkoʊ] (stókŏ)
Stoer ['stoʊər] (stó-er)
Stoessiger, f.n. ['stesɪdʒər] (stéssijer)
Stogdon, f.n. ['stɒgdən] (stógdŏn)
Stogumber [stoʊ'gʌmbər] (stŏgúmber); ['stɒgəmbər] (stóggŭmber)
Stogursey [stoʊ'gɜrzɪ] (stŏgúrzi)
Stoic, one educated at Stowe School ['stoʊɪk] (stó-ick)
Stoke Bruern ['stoʊk 'bruərn] (stók broó-ĕrn)
Stoke d'Abernon ['stoʊk 'dæbərnən] (stók dábbĕrnŏn)
Stoke Damerel ['stoʊk 'dæmərəl] (stók dámmĕrĕl)
Stoke Mandeville ['stoʊk 'mændɪvɪl] (stók mándĕvil)
Stoke Pero ['stoʊk 'pɪəroʊ] (stók peérŏ)
Stoke-in-Teignhead ['stoʊk ɪn 'tɪnhed] (stók in tínhed)
Stokenham [ˌstoʊkən'hæm] (stōkĕn-hám); ['stoʊkənəm] (stókĕnăm)
Stokes, f.n. [stoʊks] (stóks)
Stoll, f.n. [stɒl] (stoll)
Stollery, f.n. ['stɒlərɪ] (stóllĕri)
Stolz, f.n. [stɒlts] (stollts)
Stonar ['stɒnər] (stónnăr)
Stone, f.n. [stoʊn] (stōn)
Stonea ['stoʊnɪ] (stóni)
Stoneaston [stɒn'istən] (stonneésstŏn)
Stonebridge, f.n. ['stoʊnbrɪdʒ] (stónbrij)
Stonebyres ['stoʊnbaɪərz] (stónbírz)
Stoneclough ['stoʊnklʌf] (stón-kluff)
Stonedge ['stoʊnedʒ] (stóne); ['stænedʒ] (stánnej)
Stonehaven [stoʊn'heɪvən] (stōn-háyvĕn); [steɪn'haɪ] (stayn-hí) The first is appropriate also for Viscount ~.
Stonehenge ['stoʊn'hendʒ] (stón-hénj)
Stoneleigh, Surrey ['stoʊn'li] (stón-leé)
Stoneleigh, Warwick. ['stoʊnlɪ] (stónli) Appropriate also for ~ Abbey.
Stoner, f.n. ['stoʊnər] (stónER)
Stoney, f.n. ['stoʊnɪ] (stóni)
Stonham ['stɒnəm] (stónnăm) Appropriate also for Baron ~.
Stonham Aspal ['stɒnəm 'æspɒl] (stónnăm ásspawl)
Stonier, f.n. ['stoʊnɪ-ər] (stóni-er)
Stonor, f.n. ['stoʊnɒr] (stónor); ['stoʊnər] (stónnŏr) The first is appropriate for the family name of Baron Camoys.
Stonor ['stɒnər] (stónnŏr)
Stooke, f.n. [stʊk] (stoók)
Stopham ['stɒpəm] (stóppăm)
Stopher, f.n. ['stoʊfər] (stófer)
Stoppard, f.n. ['stɒpərd] (stóppaard)
Storace, f.n. ['stɒrəs] (stórráss)
Stordy, f.n. ['stɔrdɪ] (stórdi)
Storey, f.n. ['stɔrɪ] (stáwri)
Storm, f.n. [stɔrm] (storm)
Stormont, f.n. ['stɔrmənt] (stórmŏnt)
Stormont ['stɔrmənt] (stórmŏnt) Appropriate also for Viscount ~.

Stormont Castle, *Co. Down* ['stɔrmənt] (stórmŏnt)

Stormontfield ['stɔrməntfiːld] (stórmŏntfeeld)

Stormonth, *f.n.* ['stɔrmənt] (stórmŏnt)

Stornoway ['stɔrnəweɪ] (stórnŏ-way)

Storrier, *f.n.* ['stɒrɪ-ər] (stórri-er)

Storrs, *f.n.* [stɔrz] (storz)

Stothard, *f.n.* ['stɒðard] (stóthaard); ['stɒðərd] (stóthárd)

Stothert, *f.n.* ['stɒðərt] (stóthĕrt)

Stott, *f.n.* [stɒt] (stott)

Stottesdon ['stɒtɪzdən] (stóttĕzdŏn)

Stoughton, *f.n.* ['stɔtən] (stáwtŏn); ['stautən] (stówtŏn)

Stoughton, *Leics.*, *Sussex* ['stoutən] (stótŏn)

Stoughton, *Surrey* ['stautən] (stówtŏn) *Appropriate also for* ~ *Barracks.*

Stoughton, Middle *and* **West**, *Somerset* ['stɔtən] (stáwtŏn)

Stoughton Cross ['stɔtən 'krɒs] (stáwtŏn króss)

Stoulton ['stoultən] (stóltŏn)

Stour, River, *Dorset-Hants.* ['stauər] (stowr); [stuər] (stŏŏr)

Stour, River, *Kent* [stuər] (stŏŏr); ['stauər] (stowr) *Although the first is much more usual for the name of the river, see treatment of neighbouring* Stourmouth.

Stour, River, *Oxon.-Warwick.* ['stauər] (stowr); ['stouər] (stŏ-er)

Stour, River, *Suffolk-Essex* [stuər] (stŏŏr) *This is the river associated with* Constable.

Stour, River, *Worcs.* ['stauər] (stowr); ['stouər] (stŏ-er)

Stour Provost ['stauər 'prɒvəst] (stówr próvvŏst)

Stour Row *see* Stower Row.

Stourbridge ['stauərbrɪdʒ] (stówrbrij); ['stouərbrɪdʒ] (stŏ-ĕrbrij)

Stourhead House, *Wilts.* ['stɔrhed] (stór-hed); ['stauərhed] (stówr-hed)

Stourmouth ['stauərmauθ] (stówrmowth); ['stuərmauθ] (stŏŏrmowth) *Although the first of these is more usual locally for the place name, it is interesting that the neighbouring River Stour is more often pronounced* [stuər] (stŏŏr).

Stourport-on-Severn ['stauərpɔrt ɒn 'sevərn] (stówrport ŏn sévvĕrn); ['stuərpɔrt ɒn 'sevərn] (stŏŏrport ŏn sévvĕrn)

Stourton, *f.n.* ['stɜrtən] (stúrtŏn) *see also* Baron Mowbray, Segrave *and* ~.

Stourton, *Wilts.* ['stɜrtən] (stúrtŏn); ['stɔrtən] (stórtŏn)

Stourton, *Yorks.* ['stɜrtən] (stúrtŏn)

Stourton Caundle ['stɔrtən 'kɔndl] (stórtŏn káwndl)

Stout, *f.n.* [staut] (stowt)

Stovell, *f.n.* [stə'vel] (stŏvéll); [stou'vel] (stōvéll); ['stouvl] (stŏvl)

Stoven ['stʌvən] (stúvvĕn)

Stovold, *f.n.* ['stɒvould] (stóvvŏld)

Stow [stau] (stow)

Stow Bedon [stou 'biːdən] (stŏ beédŏn)

Stow Longa ['stou 'lɒŋgə] (stŏ lóng-gă)

Stow Maries [stou 'mɑrɪz] (stŏ maáriz)

Stow-on-the-Wold ['stou ən ðə 'would] (stŏ ŏn thĕ wŏld)

Stowell, *f.n.* ['stouəl] (stŏ-ĕl)

Stowell ['stouəl] (stŏ-ĕl); [stoul] (stŏl)

Stower Row, *also spelt* **Stour Row** ['stauər 'rou] (stówer rŏ)

Stowey ['stouɪ] (stŏ-i)

Stowford ['stoufərd] (stŏfŏrd)

Stowmarket ['stoumɑrkɪt] (stŏmaarkĕt)

Stowting ['stautɪŋ] (stówting)

Strabane [strə'bæn] (străbán) *Appropriate also for Viscount* ~.

Strabolgi, *Baron* [strə'bougɪ] (străbŏgi)

Stracathro [strə'kæθrou] (străkáthrŏ)

Strachan, *f.n.* ['stræxən] (stráchăn); [strɒn] (strawn)

Strachan [strɒn] (strawn)

Strachey, *f.n.* ['streɪtʃɪ] (stráytchi); ['stræxɪ] (stráchi)

Strachie, *f.n.* ['streɪtʃɪ] (stráytchi) *Appropriate also for Baron* ~.

Strachur [strə'xɜr] (străchúr)

Stradbroke ['strædbruk] (strádbrŏŏk) *Appropriate also for the Earl of* ~.

Stradey Park rugby ground, *Llanelly* ['stræeɪ 'pɑrk] (stráddi paárk)

Stradishall ['strædɪʃɔl] (stráddi-shawl)

Stradling, *f.n.* ['strædlɪŋ] (strádling)

Stradwick, *f.n.* ['strædwɪk] (strádwick)

Strahan, *f.n.* [strɒn] (strawn)

Strakosch, *f.n.* ['strækɒʃ] (stráckosh)

Straloch [strə'lɒx] (strălóch)

Strange, *f.n.* [streɪndʒ] (straynj)

Strange of Knokin, *Hungerford and De Moleyns*, *Baroness* ['streɪndʒ əv 'nɒkɪn 'hʌŋgərfərd ənd də 'mʌlɪmz] (stráynj ŏv nóckin húng-gĕrfŏrd ănd dĕ múllinz)

Stranger, *f.n.* ['streɪndʒər] (stráynjer)

Strangeways ['streɪndʒweɪz] (stráynjwayz)

Strangford ['stræŋfərd] (strángfŏrd)

Strangways, *f.n.* ['stræŋweɪz] (stráng-wayz)

Stranmillis [stræn'mɪlɪs] (stranmílliss)

Stranocum [stræn'oukəm] (stranŏkŭm)

Stranraer, *f.n.* [stræn'rɑr] (stranraár)

Stranraer [stran'rɑr] (stránraár)

Strata Florida ['strætə 'flɒrɪdə] (stráttă flórridă)

Stratfieldsaye House, *Berks.* ['strætfɪldseɪ] (strátfeeldssay)

Stratford-atte-Bowe ['strætfərd ætɪ 'bou] (strátfŏrd atti bŏ); ['strætfərd ætɪ 'bouɪ] (strátfŏrd atti bŏ-i); ['strætfərd ætə 'bouə] (strátfŏrd attĕ bŏ-ĕ) *The first is a modern pronunciation of the historic name. The others are perhaps more familiar to students of Chaucer.*

Stratford-le-Bow ['strætfərd lə 'bou] (strátfŏrd lĕ bŏ)

Stratford-upon-Avon ['strætfərd əpɒn 'eivən] (strátfŏrd ŭpon áyvŏn)
Strath, f.n. [straθ] (straath)
Strathallan [stræθ'ælən] (strathálăn)
Appropriate also for Viscount ~.
Strathardle [stræθ'ɑrdl] (stratháardl)
Strathaven ['streivən] (stráyvěn)
Strathclyde [stræθ'klaid] (strathklíd)
Appropriate also for Baron ~ and for the University of ~.
Strathcona, Baron [stræθ'kounə](strathkŏnă)
Strathdee, f.n. [stræθ'di] (strathdeé)
Strathearn [stræθ'ɜrn] (strathérn)
Stratheden, Baron [stræθ'idən] (stratheédĕn)
Strathfillan [stræθ'filən] (strathfíllăn)
Strathkinness [stræθ'kinis] (strathkínnĕss)
Strathleven [stræθ'livən] (strathleévĕn)
Strathmiglo [stræθ'miglou] (strathmíglŏ)
Strathmore [stræθ'mɔr] (strathmór)
Strathmore and Kinghorne, Earl of [stræθ'mɔr ənd 'kɪŋhɔrn] (strathmór ănd kíng-horn)
Strathnaver [stræθ'neivər] (strathnáyver)
Strathpeffer [stræθ'pefər] (strathpéffer)
Strathspey [stræθ'spei] (strath-spáy)
Appropriate also for Baron ~.
Strathtay [stræθ'tei] (strathtáy)
Straton, f.n. ['strætən] (stráttŏn)
Stratton ['strætən] (stráttŏn)
Straughan, f.n. [strɒn] (strawn)
Strauss, f.n. ['straus] (strowss)
Strauther, f.n. ['strɒðər] (stráwther)
Streat, f.n. [strit] (street)
Streatfeild, f.n. ['stretfild] (strétfeeld)
Streatfield, f.n. ['stretfild] (strétfeeld)
Streatham ['stretəm] (stréttăm)
Streather, f.n. ['streðər] (stréther)
Streatley, Beds. ['stretli] (stréttli)
Streatley, Berks. ['stritli] (streétli)
Stredwick, f.n. ['stredwik] (strédwick)
Street, f.n. [strit] (street)
Streethay ['strithei] (streét-hay)
Strensall ['strensl] (strenssl)
Strethall ['streθɔl] (strét-hawl)
Stretham ['stretəm] (stréttăm)
Stretton Sugwas ['stretən 'sʌgəs] (stréttŏn súggăss)
Strevens, f.n. ['strevənz] (strévvěnz)
Strichen ['strixən] (stríchěn)
Stride, f.n. [straid] (strīd)
Striguil Castle, Monmouth. ['strigil] (stríggil)
Stringer, f.n. ['striŋər] (stríng-er)
Striven, Loch ['strivən] (strívvěn)
Strode, f.n. [stroud] (strŏd)
Strollamus ['strɒləməs] (stróllămŭss)
Stroma ['stroumə] (strŏmă)

Stromness ['strɒmnes] (strómness); ['strʌmnes] (strúmness)
Stronachlachar ['strɒnəx'læxər] (strónnăch-láchăr)
Strong, f.n. [strɒŋ] (strong)
Stronge, f.n. [strɒŋ] (strong)
Strongitharm, f.n. ['strɒŋiθɑrm] (stróng-ithaarm)
Stronsay ['strɒnzei] (strónzay)
Strontian [strɒn'tiən] (strontee-ăn)
Strood [strud] (strood)
Stross, f.n. [strɒs] (stross)
Strother, f.n. ['strʌðər] (strúther)
Stroud, f.n. [straud] (strowd)
Stroud, Glos., Hants. [straud] (strowd)
Stroudley, f.n. ['straudli] (strówdli)
Strowan, f.n. ['strouən] (strŏ-ăn)
Strowan ['strauən] (strów-ăn); ['struən] (stroó-ăn)
Stroxton ['strosən] (stráwssŏn); ['strousən] (strŏssŏn)
Stroyan, f.n. ['stroiən] (stróyăn)
Struan ['struən] (stroó-ăn)
Strube, cartoonist ['strubi] (stroóbi)
Strule, River [strul] (strool)
Strumpshaw ['strʌmʃə] (strúm-shă)
Struve, f.n. ['struvi] (stroóvi)
Stuart, f.n. ['stjuərt] (stéw-ărt); ['stjuərt] (styŏ́-ărt)
Stuart of Findhorn, Viscount ['stjuərt əv 'findhɔrn] (styŏ́-ărt ŏv fíndhorn)
Stubbs, f.n. [stʌbz] (stubbz)
Stuchbury, f.n. ['stʌtʃbri] (stútchbri)
Stuck, f.n. [stʌk] (stuck)
Stucke, f.n. [stjuk] (stewk)
Stucley, f.n. ['stjukli] (stéwkli)
Studd, f.n. [stʌd] (studd)
Studdal ['stʌdl] (studdl)
Studdert, f.n. ['stʌdərt] (stúddĕrt)
Studholme, f.n. ['stʌdhoum] (stúdhŏm)
Stukeley, Great and Little ['stjukli] (stéwkli)
Stunell, f.n. [stə'nel] (stŭnéll)
Stunt, f.n. [stʌnt] (stunt)
Sturdy, f.n. ['stɜrdi] (stúrdi)
Sturgate ['stɜrgeit] (stúrgayt)
Sturge, f.n. [stɜrdʒ] (sturj)
Sturley, f.n. ['stɜrli] (stúrli)
Sturmer, f.n. ['stɜrmər] (stúrmer)
Sturminster Marshall ['stɜrminstər 'mɑrʃl] (stúrminster maárshl)
Sturminster Newton ['stɜrminstər 'njutən] (stúrminster néwtŏn)
Sturry ['stʌri] (stúrri)
Sturt, f.n. [stɜrt] (sturt)
Sturtevant, f.n. ['stɜrtivənt] (stúrtěvănt)
Sturtivant, f.n. ['stɜrtivənt] (stúrtivănt)
Sturton ['stɜrtən] (stúrtŏn)
Styal ['staiəl] (stí-ăl)
Styche, f.n. [staitʃ] (stītch)
Styles, f.n. [stailz] (stīlz)
Styvechale see Stivichall.

The form [stræθ-] (strath-), used to indicate the unstressed prefix Strath-, is that used in careful speech. Its occurrence as [strəθ-] (străth-) is equally frequent and acceptable.

Sudbury, *f.n.* ['sʌdbəri] (súdbŭri)
Suddes, *f.n.* ['sʌdɪs] (súddĕss)
Sudeley, *Baron* ['sjudlɪ] (séwdli)
Sudley, *Baron* ['sʌdlɪ] (súddli)
Suenson, *f.n.* ['suɪnsən] (soó-ĕnssŏn)
Sueter, *f.n.* ['sjutər] (séwter); ['sutər] (soóter)
Suffield, *f.n.* ['sʌfɪld] (súffeeld)
Suffolk ['sʌfək] (súffŏk)
Suggate, *f.n.* ['sʌgeɪt] (súggayt)
Sugrew, *f.n.* ['sugru] (soógroo)
Sugrue, *f.n.* ['sugru] (soógroo)
Sugwas Pool ['sʌgəs 'pul] (súggăss poól)
Suilven ['sʊlvɪn] (soŏlvĕn)
Suirdale, *Viscount* ['ʃɜrdl] (shurdl)
Sulby, *I.o.M.* ['sʌlbɪ] (súllbi)
Sule Skerry ['sul 'skerɪ] (soól skérri)
Sulham ['sʌləm] (súllăm)
Sulhampstead [sʌl'hæmpstɪd] (sullhámpstĕd)
Sullivan, *f.n.* ['sʌlɪvən] (súllivăn)
Sully ['sʌlɪ] (súlli)
Sulwen, *Welsh C.n.* ['sɪlwen] (seélwen)
Sumbler, *f.n.* ['sʌmblər] (súmbler)
Sumburgh Head ['sʌmbərə] (súmbŭră)
Summerfield, *f.n.* ['sʌmərfɪld] (súmmĕrfield)
Summers, *f.n.* ['sʌmərz] (súmmĕrz)
Sumption, *f.n.* ['sʌmʃən] (súm-shŏn)
Sumsion, *f.n.* ['sʌmʃən] (súm-shŏn)
Sunart, *Loch* ['sunərt] (soónărt)
Sunderland ['sʌndərlənd] (súndĕrlănd)
Surbiton ['sɜrbɪtən] (súrbitŏn)
Surfleet, *f.n.* ['sɜrflit] (súrfleet)
Surgenor, *f.n.* ['sɜrdʒɪnor] (súrjĕnor)
Surguy, *f.n.* ['sɜrgaɪ] (súrgī)
Surplice, *f.n.* ['sɜrplɪs] (súrpliss)
Surrey ['sʌrɪ] (súrri)
Surridge, *f.n.* ['sʌrɪdʒ] (súrrij)
Survaes, *f.n.* ['sɜrveɪz] (súrvayz)
Sussams, *f.n.* ['sʌsəmz] (sússămz)
Susser, *f.n.* ['sʌsər] (sússer)
Sussex ['sʌsɪks] (sússĕks)
Susskind, Walter, *conductor* ['woltər 'suskɪnd] (wáwlter soósskinnd)
Sutcliffe, *f.n.* ['sʌtklɪf] (sútkliff)
Suter, *f.n.* ['sutər] (soóter)
Sutherland, *f.n.* ['sʌðərlənd] (súthĕrlănd)
Sutherland ['sʌðərlənd] (súthĕrlănd)
Appropriate also for the Duke of ~.
Sutlieff, *f.n.* ['sʌtlif] (súttleef)
Sutro, *f.n.* ['sutroʊ] (soótrŏ)
Sutter, *f.n.* ['sʌtər] (sútter)
Suttie, *f.n.* ['sʌtɪ] (sútti)
Suttle, *f.n.* ['sʌtl] (suttl)
Sutton, *f.n.* ['sʌtən] (súttŏn)
Sutton ['sʌtən] (súttŏn)
Sutton Coldfield ['sʌtən 'koʊldfild] (súttŏn kóldfeeld)
Sutton Courtenay ['sʌtən 'kortnɪ] (súttŏn kórtni)
Sutton Scotney ['sʌtən 'skɒtnɪ] (súttŏn skóttni)
Sutton Veny ['sʌtən 'vinɪ] (súttŏn veéni)
Suzman, *f.n.* ['suzmən] (soózmăn)

Swaby ['sweɪbɪ] (swáybi)
Swadlincote ['swɒdlɪŋkoʊt] (swódlingkōt)
Swaebe, *f.n.* ['sweɪbɪ] (swáybi)
Swaffer, Hannen, *journalist and dramatic critic* ['hænən 'swɒfər] (hánnĕn swóffer)
Swaffham ['swɒfəm] (swóffăm)
Swafield ['sweɪfild] (swáyfeeld)
Swalcliffe ['sweɪklɪf] (swáykliff)
Swales, *f.n.* ['sweɪlz] (swaylz)
Swalwell ['swɒlwel] (swólwel)
Swan, *f.n.* [swɒn] (swonn)
Swanborough, *Baroness* ['swɒnbərə] (swónnbŭră)
Swanbourne ['swɒnborn] (swónnborn)
Swann, *f.n.* [swɒn] (swonn)
Swannell, *f.n.* ['swɒnl] (swonnl)
Swansea ['swɒnzɪ] (swónzi)
Swanson, *f.n.* ['swɒnsən] (swónssŏn)
Swanton Novers ['swɒntən 'noʊvərz] (swónntŏn nōvĕrz)
Swanwick, *f.n.* ['swɒnɪk] (swónnick)
Swanwick, *Derby., Hants.* ['swɒnɪk] (swónnick)
Swanzy, *f.n.* ['swɒnzɪ] (swónzi)
Swardeston ['sworstən] (swáwrsstŏn)
Swarkeston ['sworkstən] (swáwrkstŏn)
Swatman, *f.n.* ['swɒtmən] (swótmăn)
Swaton ['sweɪtən] (swáytŏn)
Swatragh ['swɒtrə] (swótră)
Swavesey ['sweɪvzɪ] (swáyvzi)
Sweatman, *f.n.* ['swetmən] (swétmăn)
Sweet, *f.n.* [swit] (sweet)
Sweetland, *f.n.* ['switlənd] (sweétlănd)
Sweetman, *f.n.* ['switmən] (sweétmăn)
Swefling ['sweflɪŋ] (swéffling)
Swenarton, *f.n.* ['swenərtən] (swénnărtŏn)
Swenerton, *f.n.* ['swenərtən] (swénnĕrtŏn)
Swetman, *f.n.* ['swetmən] (swétmăn)
Swillies Channel ['swɪlɪz] (swílliz)
Swimer, *f.n.* ['swaɪmər] (swímer)
Swinburne, *f.n.* ['swɪnbɜrn] (swínburn)
Swindall, *f.n.* ['swɪndəl] (swíndawl)
Swindell, *f.n.* ['swɪndel] (swíndell)
Swindells, *f.n.* ['swɪn'delz] (swindéllz)
Swine [swaɪn] (swīn)
Swineshead ['swaɪnzhed] (swínz-hed)
Swiney, *f.n.* ['swaɪnɪ] (swíni); ['swɪnɪ] (swínni)
Swiney ['swɪnɪ] (sweéni)
Swingler, *f.n.* ['swɪŋglər] (swíng-gler)
Switzer, *f.n.* ['swɪtsər] (swítsser)
Sword, *f.n.* [sord] (sord)
Sworder, *f.n.* ['sordər] (sórder)
Swymbridge ['swɪmbrɪdʒ] (swímbrij)
Sycharth ['sʌxarθ] (súchaarth)
Sychnant Pass ['sʌxnænt] (súchnant)
Sydenham, *Co. Down* ['sɪdnəm] (sídnăm)
Sydenham, *London* ['sɪdənəm] (síddĕnăm)
Syderstone ['saɪdərstoʊn] (sídĕrsstŏn)

Sydie, f.n. ['saɪdɪ] (sídi)
Sydling St. Nicholas ['sɪdlɪŋ snt
'nɪkələs] (síddling sïnt níckóláss)
Syers, f.n. ['saɪərz] (sí-ĕrz)
Syerston ['saɪərstən] (sí-ĕrsstŏn)
Syfret, f.n. ['saɪfrɪt] (sífrĕt)
Sygrove, f.n. ['saɪɡrouv] (sígrŏv)
Sykes, f.n. [saɪks] (síks)
Sylvester, f.n. [sɪl'vestər] (silvésster)
Symbister ['sɪmbɪstər] (símbisster)
Syme, f.n. [saɪm] (sïm)
Symene, River [saɪ'minɪ] (sïmeéni)
Symes, f.n. [saɪmz] (sïmz)
Symington, f.n. ['saɪmɪŋtən] (símingtŏn)
Symington, *Ayr., Lanark.* ['saɪmɪŋtən]
(símingtŏn)
Symon, f.n. ['saɪmən] (sïmŏn)
Symonds, f.n. ['sɪməndz] (símmŏndz);
['saɪməndz] (sïmŏndz) *The first is appro-
priate for John Addington ~, 19th-c.
author and translator.*
Symond's Yat ['sɪməndz ˈjæt]
(símmŏndz yát)
Symondsbury ['sɪmənzbərɪ] (símmŏnz-
būri)
Symons, f.n. ['sɪmənz] (símmŏnz); ['saɪ-
mənz] (sïmŏnz) *The first is that of the
authors, A. J. A. ~ and Julian ~, and of
Arthur ~, poet and critic.*
Synge, f.n. [sɪŋ] (sing)
Syon House, *Middlesex* ['saɪən] (sí-ŏn)
Syrad, f.n. ['saɪəræd] (sírad)
Syrett, f.n. ['saɪərɪt] (sírĕt)
Sysonby, Baron ['saɪzənbɪ] (sízŏnbi)
Syston, *Leics., Lincs.* ['saɪstən] (sísstŏn)
Sytchampton ['sɪtʃhæmptən] (sítch-
hamptŏn)
Sywell ['saɪwel] (sí-wel)
Szasz, f.n. [sæz] (sazz)
Szerelmey, f.n. [sɪ'relmɪ] (sĕrélmi)

T

Taaffe, f.n. [tæf] (taff)
Tabern, f.n. ['tæbərn] (tábbĕrn)
Taberner, f.n. ['tæbərnər] (tábbĕrner);
[tə'bɜrnər] (tăbérner)
Tabori, Paul, author ['pɔl tə'bɔrɪ] (páwl
tábáwri)
Tack, f.n. [tæk] (tack)
Tacolneston ['tæklstən] (tácklstŏn)
Tadcaster ['tædkæstər] (tádkasster)
Taf, River, *Pembroke.-Carmarthen.* [tav]
(taav) *The English form is* Taff, *q.v.*
Tafarnau Bach [tə'varnaɪ 'bax] (tă-
vaárnï baach)
Taff, River, *Brecon.-Glamorgan.* [tæf]
(taff)

Taff, River, *Pembroke.-Carmarthen.* [tæf]
(taff) *The Welsh form is* Taf, *q.v.*
Taffinder, f.n. ['tæfɪndər] (táffinder)
Tagliaferro, f.n. [ˌtɑliə'ferou] (taali-
áférrō)
Tahourdin, f.n. ['tavərdɪn] (tówĕrdin)
Tailyour, f.n. ['teɪljər] (táyl-yor)
Tain [teɪn] (tayn)
Tainsh, f.n. [teɪnʃ] (taynsh)
Tainton, f.n. ['teɪntən] (táyntŏn)
Tait, f.n. [teɪt] (tayt)
Takeley ['teɪklɪ] (táykli)
Talachddu [tə'læxðɪ] (tálách-thi)
Talaton ['tælətən] (tálátŏn)
Talbot, f.n. ['tɔlbət] (táwlbŏt)
Talbot de Malahide, Baron ['tɔlbət də
'mæləhaɪd] (táwlbŏt dĕ máláhïd)
Talbut, f.n. ['tɔlbət] (táwlbŭt)
Talerddig [tæl'eərðɪɡ] (taláĕrthig)
Talfan, Welsh C.n. ['tælvæn] (tálvan)
Talfourd, f.n. ['tælfərd] (tálfŏrd)
Talfryn, f.n. ['tælvrɪn] (tálvrin)
Talgarth ['tælɡarθ] (tálgaarth)
Talisker, f.n. ['tælɪskər] (tálisker)
Talkin ['tɔkɪn] (táwkin)
Talley ['tælɪ] (táli)
Tallis, Thomas, 16th-c. composer ['tælɪs]
(táliss)
Talsarnau [tæl'sarnaɪ] (tal-saárnï)
Talwrn ['tælvərn] (táluörn)
Tal-y-bont, *Caernarvon., Cardigan.,
Merioneth* [ˌtælə'bont] (talábónt)
Tal-y-llyn [ˌtælə'ɬɪn] (talá-hlín)
Tal-y-sarn [ˌtælə'sarn] (talá-saárn)
Tamar, River ['teɪmər] (táymăr)
Tamerton Foliott ['tæmərtən 'fovhət]
(támmĕrtŏn fŏli̇t)
Tamsin, C.n. ['tæmzɪn] (támzin)
Tamsyn, C.n. ['tæmzɪn] (támzin)
Tamworth ['tæmwɜrθ] (támwurth);
['tæmərθ] (támmŭrth)
Tanat, River ['tænət] (tánnăt)
Tandragee [ˌtændrə'gi] (tandrăgeé)
Tangley, Baron ['tæŋlɪ] (táng-li)
Tangmere ['tæŋmɪər] (tángmeer)
Tangye, f.n. ['tæŋɡɪ] (táng-gi)
Tanner, f.n. ['tænər] (tánner)
Tanqueray, f.n. ['tæŋkərɪ] (tánkĕri)
Tantobie [tæn'toubɪ] (tantóbi)
Tan-y-bwlch [ˌtænə'bulx] (tannăbŏŏlch)
Tanygrisiau [ˌtænə'ɡrɪsjaɪ] (tannăgríss-
yï)
Tan-y-maes [ˌtænə'maɪs] (tannámíss)
Tan-yr-allt [ˌtænər'æɬt] (tannúráhlt)
Tappenden, f.n. ['tæpəndən] (táppĕndĕn)
Tapply, f.n. ['tæplɪ] (tápli)
Tapscott, f.n. ['tæpskɒt] (tápskott)
Tapsell, f.n. ['tæpsl] (tapssl)
Tapsfield, f.n. ['tæpsfɪld] (tápsfeeld)
Tarbat ['tarbət] (taárbăt) *Appropriate
also for Viscount ~.*
Tarbert ['tarbərt] (taárbĕrt)
Tarbet ['tarbɪt] (taárbĕt)
Tarbolton [tar'boultən] (taarbóltŏn)
Tarbrax [tar'bræks] (taarbrácks)

Tardebigge ['tɑrdəbɪg] (taárdĕbig)
Tarenig, River [tə'renɪg] (tárénnig)
Target, f.n. ['tɑrdʒɪt] (taárjĕt)
Tarner, f.n. ['tɑrnər] (taárner)
Tarporley ['tɑrpərlɪ] (taárpŏrli); ['tɑrplɪ] (taárpli)
Tarran, f.n. ['tærən] (tárrăn)
Tarrant Keynston ['tærənt 'keɪnstən] (tárrănt káynsstŏn)
Tarring ['tærɪŋ] (tárring)
Tarskavaig ['tɑrskəvɪg] (taársskăvig)
Tartaraghan [tɑr'tærəhən] (taartárrăhăn)
Tarves ['tɑrvɪs] (taárvĕss)
Tasburgh ['teɪzbərə] (táyzbŭră)
Tasker, f.n. ['tæskər] (tássker)
Tassagh ['tæsə] (tássă)
Tate, f.n. [teɪt] (tayt)
Tate Gallery [teɪt] (tayt)
Tatem, f.n. ['teɪtəm] (táytĕm)
Tatenhill ['teɪtənhɪl] (táytĕnhill)
Tatham, f.n. ['teɪtθəm] (táy-thăm); ['teɪðəm] (táytħăm)
Tatham ['teɪtəm] (táytăm)
Tatt, f.n. [tæt] (tatt)
Tattersall, f.n. ['tætərsɔl] (táttĕrssawl); ['tætərsəl] (táttĕrssăl)
Tattershall ['tætərʃəl] (táttĕr-shăl)
Tattingstone ['tætɪŋstən] (táttingstŏn)
Taubman, f.n. ['tɔbmən] (táwbmăn)
Taunton ['tɔntən] (táwntŏn); ['tɑntən] (taántŏn)
Taverham ['teɪvərəm] (táyvĕrăm)
Taverne, f.n. [tə'vɜrn] (tăvérn)
Tavy, River ['teɪvɪ] (táyvi)
Tawe, River ['taueɪ] (tów-ay)
Tawell, f.n. [tɔl] (tawl); ['tɔəl] (táw-ĕl)
Tay, Loch and River [teɪ] (tay)
Taylor, f.n. ['teɪlər] (táylŏr)
Taylour, f.n. ['teɪlər] (táylŏr)
Taynuilt [teɪ'nʊlt] (taynoŏlt)
Teaffe, f.n. [tɑf] (taaf)
Tealby ['tɪlbɪ] (teélbi)
Teallach ['tʃælʌx] (chálăch)
Tean, River [tin] (teen)
Teape, f.n. [tɪp] (teep)
Teare, f.n. [tɪər] (teer)
Tearlath, Gaelic C.n. ['tʃɛərləx] (cháírlăch)
Tearle, f.n. [tɜrl] (terl)
Teasdale, f.n. ['tizdeɪl] (teézdayl)
Teastler, f.n. ['tistlər] (teéstler)
Tebay, f.n. [tɪ'beɪ] (tĕbáy)
Tebay ['tibeɪ] (teébay)
Tebbs, f.n. [tebz] (tebbz)
Tebby, f.n. ['tebɪ] (tébbi)
Tebworth ['tebərθ] (tébbŭrth)
Tecwyn, Welsh C.n. ['tekwɪn] (téckwin)
Tedburn St. Mary ['tedbɜrn snt 'mɛərɪ] (tédburn sïnt maíri)
Tedder of Glenguin, Baron ['tedər əv glen'gwɪn] (tédder ŏv glen-gwín)
Teear, f.n. ['tɪər] (teé-ăr)
Teed, f.n. [tid] (teed)
Teetgen, f.n. ['tidʒən] (teéjĕn)

Teevan, f.n. ['tivən] (teévăn)
Teggin, f.n. ['tegɪn] (téggin)
Tehidy [tɪ'hɪdɪ] (tĕhíddi)
Tei, f.n. [teɪ] (tay)
Teichman, f.n. ['taɪʃmən] (tíshmăn)
Teifi, River, also spelt Teivy ['taɪvɪ] (tívi)
Teifion, Welsh C.n. ['taɪvɪən] (tívi-ŏn)
Teigh [tiˈ] (tee)
Teign, River [tin] (teen); [tɪn] (tin)
Teigngrace ['tɪngreɪs] (teén-grayss)
Teignmouth ['tɪnməθ] (tínmŭth); ['tɪnməθ] (teénmŭth) The first is appropriate for Baron ~.
Teise, River [tiz] (teez)
Teivy, River see Teifi.
Teleri, Welsh C.n. [tɪ'lerɪ] (tĕlérri)
Telfer, f.n. ['telfər] (télfer)
Telscombe ['telskəm] (télsskŏm)
Temair see Aberdeen and ~, Marquess of.
Temme, f.n. ['temɪ] (témmi)
Temperton, f.n. ['tempərtən] (témpĕrton)
Temple, f.n. ['templ] (templ)
Temple Guiting ['templ 'gaɪtɪŋ] (témpl gíting)
Temple Sowerby ['templ 'sauərbɪ] (témpl sówĕrbi); ['templ 'sɔrbɪ] (témpl sórbi)
Templepatrick ['templ'pætrɪk] (témpl-pátrick)
Tenandry ['tenəndrɪ] (ténnándri)
Tenby ['tenbɪ] (ténbi)
Tenniel, Sir John, cartoonist ['tenjəl] (tén-yĕl)
Tennyson, f.n. ['tenɪsən] (ténnissŏn)
Tenterden ['tentərdən] (téntĕrdĕn)
Ter, River [tɑr] (taar)
Terally [tɪ'rælɪ] (tĕráli)
Terling ['tɑrlɪŋ] (taárling); ['tɜrlɪŋ] (térling)
Terregles [tɪ'reglz] (tĕrégglz)
Terrell, f.n. ['terəl] (térrĕl)
Terrington, f.n. ['terɪŋtən] (térringtŏn)
Terrot, f.n. ['terət] (térrŏt)
Terry, f.n. ['terɪ] (térri)
Terwick ['terɪk] (térrick)
Tester, f.n. ['testər] (tésster)
Teston ['tisən] (teéssŏn)
Tettenhall ['tetənhɔl] (téttĕnhawl)
Tetzner, f.n. ['tetsnər] (tétsner)
Teulon, f.n. ['tjulən] (téwlŏn)
Teviot, Baron ['tevɪət] (tévvi-ŏt)
Teviot, River ['tivɪət] (teévi-ŏt)
Teviotdale ['tivɪətdeɪl] (teévi-ŏtdayl)
Teynham ['tenəm] (ténnăm); ['teɪnəm] (táynăm) The first is appropriate for Baron ~.
Thaarup, f.n. ['tɑrʊp] (taárŏŏp)
Thacker, f.n. ['θækər] (thácker)
Thackley ['θæklɪ] (tháckli)
Thackwray, f.n. ['θækreɪ] (tháckray)
Thain, f.n. [θeɪn] (thayn)
Thakeham ['θeɪkəm] (tháykăm)
Thalben-Ball, George, organist ['θælbən 'bɔl] (thálbĕn báwl)

Thame [teɪm] (taym)
Thames, River [temz] (temz)
Thankerton [ˈθæŋkərtən] (thánkĕrtŏn)
Thavenot, *f.n.* [ˈtævənoʊ] (távvĕnō); [ˈtævənɒt] (távvĕnot)
Theakstone, *f.n.* [ˈθiːkstoʊn] (theéksstōn)
Theale [θiːl] (theel)
Theiler, *f.n.* [ˈtaɪlər] (tíler)
Thellusson, *f.n.* [ˈteləsən] (téllŭssŏn)
Thelnetham [θelˈniːəm] (thelneéthăm)
Themerson, *f.n.* [ˈtemərsən] (témmĕrsŏn)
Theobald, *f.n.* [ˈθɪəbold] (theé-ōbawld); [ˈtɪbəld] (tíbbăld) *The second is appropriate for Lewis ~, 17-18th-c. Shakespearean critic.*
Theobalds Park [ˈθɪəboldz] (theé-ōbawldz)
Theobald's Road, *London* [ˈθɪəboldz] (theé-ōbawldz); [ˈtɪbəldz] (tíbbăldz)
Thesiger, *f.n.* [ˈθesɪdʒər] (théssijer)
Thevenard, *f.n.* [ˈtevənɑrd] (tévvĕnaard)
Thew, *f.n.* [θjuː] (thew)
Thewes, *f.n.* [θjuːz] (thewz)
Theydon Bois [ˈθeɪdən ˈbɔɪz] (tháydŏn bóyz)
Thick, *f.n.* [θɪk] (thick)
Thicke, *f.n.* [θɪk] (thick)
Thicknesse, *f.n.* [ˈθɪknɪs] (thícknĕss)
Thiebault, *f.n.* [ˈθɪəbolt] (theé-ĕbawlt)
Thiman, *f.n.* [ˈtimən] (teémăn)
Thirde, *f.n.* [θɜrd] (third)
Thirer, *f.n.* [ˈθaɪərər] (thírer)
Thirkell, *f.n.* [ˈθɜrkl] (thírkl)
Thirkettle, *f.n.* [ˈθɜrketl] (thírkettl)
Thirsk [θɜrsk] (thirsk)
Thom, *f.n.* [tɒm] (tom)
Thomas, *f.n. and C.n.* [ˈtɒməs] (tómmăss)
Thomas, Dylan, *poet* [ˈdɪlən ˈtɒməs] (díllăn tómmăss) *Although the Welsh pronunciation is more nearly* [ˈdʌlən] (dúllăn), *the poet himself recommended the anglicized pronunciation of his Christian name.*
Thomason, *f.n.* [ˈtɒməsən] (tómmăssŏn)
Thompson, *f.n.* [ˈtɒmsən] (tómssŏn); [ˈtɒmpsən] (tómpssŏn)
Thonger, *f.n.* [ˈθɒŋər] (thóng-er)
Thonock [ˈθɒnək] (thónnŏk)
Thorburn, *f.n.* [ˈθɔrbɜrn] (thórburn)
Thoresby [ˈθɔrzbɪ] (thórzbi)
Thorn, *f.n.* [θɔrn] (thorn)
Thornbury [ˈθɔrnbərɪ] (thórnbŭri)
Thorne, *f.n.* [θɔrn] (thorn)
Thorne [θɔrn] (thorn)
Thorne Gyme [ˈθɔrn ˈɡaɪm] (thórn gím)
Thorneloe, *f.n.* [ˈθɔrnɪloʊ] (thórnĕlō)
Thorness [θɔrˈnes] (thornéss)
Thornham, *Norfolk* [ˈθɔrnəm] (thórnăm)
Thornham Magna [ˈθɔrnəm ˈmægnə] (thórnăm mágnă)
Thornham Parva [ˈθɔrnəm ˈpɑrvə] (thórnăm paárvă)
Thornhaugh [ˈθɔrnhɔ] (thórn-haw)
Thornhill, *f.n.* [ˈθɔrnhɪl] (thórnhil)

Thorning, *f.n.* [ˈθɔrnɪŋ] (thórning)
Thornley, *f.n.* [ˈθɔrnlɪ] (thórnli)
Thornliebank [ˈθɔrnlɪˈbæŋk] (thórnlibánk)
Thornton, *f.n.* [ˈθɔrntən] (thórntŏn)
Thornton Heath [ˈθɔrntən ˈhiːθ] (thórntŏn heéth)
Thornton Hough [ˈθɔrntən ˈhʌf] (thórntŏn húff)
Thorold, *f.n.* [ˈθɒrəld] (thórrŏld); [ˈθʌrəld] (thúrrŏld); [ˈθɒroʊld] (thórrōld)
Thorp, *f.n.* [θɔrp] (thorp)
Thorpe Davie, Cedric, *composer* [ˈsedrɪk ˈθɔrp ˈdeɪvɪ] (sédrick thórp dáyvi)
Thorpe Morieux [ˈθɔrp məˈruː] (thórp mŏroó)
Thorpe-le-Soken [ˈθɔrp lə ˈsoʊkən] (thórp lĕ sṓkĕn)
Thorrington [ˈθɒrɪŋtən] (thórringtŏn)
Thouless, *f.n.* [ˈθaʊles] (thówless)
Thousell, *f.n.* [ˈθaʊsl] (thowssl)
Thovez, *f.n.* [ˈθoʊvɪz] (thṓvĕz)
Thow, *f.n.* [θaʊ] (thow)
Threapland [ˈθriplənd] (threépländ)
Threave Castle [θriv] (threev)
Threekingham [ˈθrekɪŋəm] (thréckingăm)
Threlfall, *f.n.* [ˈθrelfɔl] (thrélfawl)
Thripp, *f.n.* [θrɪp] (thripp)
Througham [ˈθrʌfəm] (thrúffăm)
Throwley [ˈθroʊlɪ] (thrṓli); [ˈθraʊlɪ] (thrówli)
Thrupp, *f.n.* [θrʌp] (thrupp)
Thrybergh [ˈθraɪbər] (thríber); [ˈθraɪbərə] (thríbĕră)
Thubron, *f.n.* [ˈθjubrən] (théwbrŏn)
Thuillier, *f.n.* [ˈtwɪljər] (twíll-yer)
Thurgarton, *Norfolk* [ˈθɜrgərtən] (thúrgărtŏn)
Thurgarton, *Notts.* [ˈθɜrgartən] (thúrgaartŏn)
Thurgoland [ˈθɜrgoʊlænd] (thúrgōland)
Thurgood, *f.n.* [ˈθɜrgʊd] (thúrgŏŏd)
Thurleigh [θɜrˈlaɪ] (thur-lí)
Thurley, *f.n.* [ˈθɜrlɪ] (thúrli)
Thurling, *f.n.* [ˈθɜrlɪŋ] (thúrling)
Thurloxton [θɜrˈlɒkstən] (thurlóckstŏn)
Thurmaston [ˈθɜrməstən] (thúrmásstŏn)
Thurne [θɜrn] (thurn)
Thurnham [ˈθɜrnəm] (thúrnăm)
Thurnscoe [ˈθɜrnzkoʊ] (thúrnzkō)
Thurso [ˈθɜrsoʊ] (thúrssō) *Appropriate also for Viscount ~.*
Thurston, *f.n.* [ˈθɜrstən] (thúrsstŏn)
Thurstonfield [ˈθrʌstənfɪld] (thrússtŏnfeeld)
Thynne, *f.n.* [θɪn] (thin)
Tiarks, *f.n.* [ˈtiarks] (teé-aarks)
Tibbermore [ˌtɪbərˈmɔr] (tibbĕrmór)
Tibenham [ˈtɪbənəm] (tíbbĕnăm)
Ticciati, *f.n.* [tɪˈtʃɑti] (titchaáti)
Ticehurst, *f.n.* [ˈtaɪshɜrst] (tíss-hurst)
Tichborne [ˈtɪtʃbɔrn] (títchborn)
Tichelar, *f.n.* [ˈtɪtʃɪlar] (títchĕlaar)
Tickell, *f.n.* [tɪˈkel] (tickéll)

Tickhill ['tɪkhɪl] (tíckhil)
Tickle, f.n. ['tɪkl] (tickl)
Ticknall ['tɪknəl] (tícknăl)
Ticktum, f.n. ['tɪktəm] (tícktŭm)
Tidball, f.n. ['tɪdbɒl] (tídbawl)
Tideford ['tɪdrfərd] (tíddĕförd)
Tidenham ['tɪdənəm] (tíddĕnăm)
Tideswell ['taɪdzwel] (tídzwel); ['tɪdzl] (tiddzl)
Tidmarsh, f.n. ['tɪdmɑrʃ] (tídmaarsh)
Tiernan, f.n. ['tɜrnən] (teérnăn)
Tietjen, f.n. ['titʃm] (teétchĕn)
Tievenagh ['tivmə] (teévĕnă)
Tiffin, f.n. ['tɪfɪn] (tíffin)
Tigar, f.n. ['taɪgər] (tígăr)
Tighe, f.n. [taɪ] (tí)
Tighnabruaich [,taɪnə'bruəxʃ] (tīnăbroó-ăch̲); [,tɪnə'bruəx] (tinnăbroó-ăch̲)
Tilbe, f.n. ['tɪlbɪ] (tílbi)
Tilbury, f.n. ['tɪlbərɪ] (tílbŭri)
Tilbury ['tɪlbərɪ] (tílbŭri)
Tiley, f.n. ['taɪlɪ] (tíli)
Tiller, f.n. ['tɪlər] (tíller)
Tillett, f.n. ['tɪlɪt] (tíllĕt)
Tilley, f.n. ['tɪlɪ] (tílli)
Tillicoultry [,tɪlɪ'kutrɪ] (tillikoótri)
Tilling, f.n. ['tɪlɪŋ] (tílling)
Tillysburn [,tɪlɪz'bɜrn] (tillizbúrn)
Tilmanstone ['tɪlmənstoun] (tílmănstŏn)
Tilshead [tɪlz'hed] (tillz-héd)
Timberscombe ['tɪmbərzkum] (tímbĕrzkoom)
Timewell, f.n. ['taɪmwəl] (tímwĕl)
Timmins, f.n. ['tɪmɪnz] (tímminz)
Timpson, f.n. ['tɪmpsən] (tímpssŏn)
Tinbergen, f.n. ['tɪnbɜrgən] (tínbergĕn)
Tindall, f.n. ['tɪndl] (tinndl); ['tɪndəl] (tíndawl)
Tindell, f.n. ['tɪndel] (tíndel); ['tɪndl] (tinndl)
Tingewick ['tɪndʒwɪk] (tínjwick)
Tingey, f.n. ['tɪŋgɪ] (tíng-gi)
Tingrith ['tɪŋgrɪθ] (tíng-grith)
Tingwall ['tɪŋwəl] (tíng-wăl)
Tink, f.n. [tɪŋk] (tink)
Tinne, f.n. ['tɪnɪ] (tínni)
Tintagel [tɪn'tædʒl] (tintájjl)
Tintern Abbey ['tɪntərn] (tíntĕrn)
Tinwald ['tɪnl] (tinnl)
Tippett, f.n. ['tɪpɪt] (típpĕt) *Appropriate for Michael ~, composer.*
Tipping, f.n. ['tɪpɪŋ] (típping)
Tipton St. John ['tɪptən snt 'dʒɒn] (típtŏn sīnt jón)
Tirbutt, f.n. ['tɜrbət] (tírbŭt)
Tirebuck, f.n. ['taɪərbʌk] (tírbuck)
Tiree [taɪ'ri] (tī-reé)
Tirpentwys [tər'pentuɪs] (tirpéntoö-iss)
Tir-phil [tɪər'fɪl] (teer-fíll)
Tir-y-berth [,tɪrə'beərθ] (tirrăbaírth)
Tir-y-dail [,tɪrə'daɪl] (tirrădíl)
Tisi, f.n. ['tɪzɪ] (teézi)
Titheradge, f.n. ['tɪðərɪdʒ] (títhĕrij)
Titmus, f.n. ['tɪtməs] (títmŭss)

Titshall, f.n. ['tɪtsl] (tittsl)
Tittensor ['tɪtənsər] (títtĕnssor)
Tittleshall ['tɪtlʃɒl] (títtl-shawl)
Tiumpan Head ['tjumpən] (tyoómpăn)
Tiverton ['tɪvərtən] (tívvĕrtŏn)
Tivetshall ['tɪvɪtshɒl] (tívvĕts-hawl)
Tizard, f.n. ['tɪzɑrd] (tízzaard); ['tɪzərd] (tízzărd)
Tjaden, f.n. ['tʃɑdən] (chaádĕn)
Tobermore [,tʌbər'mɔr] (tubbĕrmór)
Tobermory [,toubər'mɔrɪ] (tŏbĕrmáwri)
Tobias, f.n. [tə'baɪəs] (tŏbí-áss)
Tobin, f.n. ['toubɪn] (tŏbin)
Toch, f.n. [tɒk] (tock); [tɒʃ] (tosh)
Tocher, f.n. ['tɒxər] (tócher)
Tockholes ['tɒkhoulz] (tóckhōlz)
Tockwith ['tɒkwɪθ] (tóckwith)
Todd, f.n. [tɒd] (todd)
Todds, f.n. [tɒdz] (toddz)
Todlawmoor ['tɒdlɪ'muər] (tóddlimoŏr)
Todmorden ['tɒdmərdən] (tódmördĕn); ['tɒdmərdən] (tódmordĕn)
Toghill, f.n. ['tɒghɪl] (tóg-hil)
Tokyngton ['toukɪntən] (tŏkingtŏn)
Tolcarne [tɒl'kɑrn] (tolkaárn)
Tolgullow [tɒl'gʌlou] (tolgúllō)
Tolkien, J. R. R., author and scholar ['tɒlkin] (tólkeen)
Toll, f.n. [tɒl] (tol)
Tolladay, f.n. ['tɒlədeɪ] (tóllád_ay)
Tollady, f.n. ['tɒlədɪ] (tóllădi)
Tollemache, f.n. ['tɒlmæʃ] (tólmash); ['tɒlmɑʃ] (tólmaash) *The first is appropriate for Baron ~.*
Tollerton, f.n. ['tɒlərtən] (tóllĕrtŏn)
Tollesbury ['toulzbərɪ] (tŏlzbŭri)
Tolleshunt d'Arcy ['toulzhʌnt 'dɑrsɪ] (tŏlz-hunt daárssi)
Tolleshunt Knights ['toulzhʌnt 'naɪts] (tŏlz-hunt níts)
Tolleshunt Major ['toulzhʌnt 'meɪdʒər] (tŏlz-hunt máyjör)
Tol-Pedn-Penwith [tɒl'pednpen'wɪθ] (tolpéddn-penwith)
Tolpuddle ['tɒlpʌdl] (tólpuddl); ['tɒlpɪdl] (tólpiddl)
Tolskithy [tɒl'skɪθɪ] (tolsskíthi)
Tolt Hill [tɒt] (tawt)
Tolworth ['tɒlwərθ] (tólwürth); ['toulwərθ] (tólwürth)
Tomatin [tə'mætɪn] (tŏmáttin)
Tombs, f.n. [tumz] (toomz)
Tombstone, f.n. ['tumstoun] (toómstŏn)
Tomintoul [,tɒmɪn'taul] (tommintówl)
Tomlinson, f.n. ['tɒmlɪnsən] (tómlinssŏn)
Tomnahurich [,tɒmnə'huərɪx] (tomnáhoŏrich̲)
Tomnavoulin [,tɒmnə'vulɪn] (tomnăvoólin)
Tomney, f.n. ['tɒmnɪ] (tómni)
Tompion, Thomas, 17th-c. clock-maker ['tɒmpɪən] (tómpi-ŏn)
Toms, f.n. [tɒmz] (tommz)
Tonbridge ['tʌnbrɪdʒ] (túnbrij)
Ton-du [tɒn'di] (tondeé)

Tone, River [toun] (tōn)
Toner, f.n. ['touner] (tōner)
Tonfanau [tɒn'vænaɪ] (tonvánnï)
Tong, f.n. [tɒŋ] (tong)
Tonge, f.n. [tɒŋ] (tong); [tɒndʒ] (tonj)
Tonge, Kent, Lancs., Leics. [tɒŋ] (tong)
Tonge Fold ['tɒŋ 'fould] (tóng fóld)
Tonge-cum-Breightmet ['tɒŋ kʌm 'breɪtmet] (tóng kum bráytmet); ['tɒŋ kʌm 'braɪtmet] (tóng kum brítmet)
Tongland, also spelt Tongueland ['tʌŋlənd] (túng-lǎnd)
Tongue [tʌŋ] (tung)
Tongueland, also spelt Tongland ['tʌŋlənd] (túng-lǎnd)
Tongwynlais [tɒn'gwɪnlaɪs] (ton-gwínliss)
Tonna ['tɒnə] (tónnǎ)
Tonpentre [tɒn'pentreɪ] (tonpéntray)
Tonwell ['tʌnl] (tunnl)
Tonypandy [ˌtɒnə'pændɪ] (tonnǎpándi)
Tonyrefail [ˌtɒnər'evaɪl] (tonnǎrévvïl)
Tonysguboriau [ˌtɒnəskɪ'bɒrɪaɪ] (tonnŭskibórri-ï)
Toombs, f.n. [tumz] (toomz)
Toot Baldon ['tut 'bɒldən] (toŏt báwldŏn)
Tooth, f.n. [tuθ] (tooth)
Toothill, f.n. ['tuthɪl] (toŏt-hil)
Tooting Graveney ['tutɪŋ 'greɪvnɪ] (toŏting gráyv-ni)
Toovey, f.n. ['tuvɪ] (toŏvi)
Topliss, f.n. ['tɒplɪs] (tópliss)
Toppesfield ['tɒpɪsfiːld] (tóppěssfeeld); ['tɒpsfiːld] (tópsfeeld)
Topping, f.n. ['tɒpɪŋ] (tópping)
Topsham ['tɒpsəm] (tópssǎm)
Tor Achilty ['tɔːr 'æxɪltɪ] (tór áchïlti)
Tordoff, f.n. ['tɔːdɒf] (tórdoff)
Torell, f.n. ['tɒrəl] (tórrěl)
Torksey ['tɔːksɪ] (tórksi)
Torlesse, f.n. ['tɔːlɪs] (tórlěss)
Torley, f.n. ['tɔːlɪ] (tórli)
Torlum Hill ['tɔːr'lʌm] (tór-lúm)
Tormore [tɔː'mɔːr] (tormór)
Torpantau [tɔːr'pæntaɪ] (torpántï)
Torpenhow [trɪ'penə] (tripénnǎ); ['tɔːrpənhaʊ] (tórpěnhow)
Torphichen [tɔːr'fɪxən] (torfíchěn) Appropriate also for Baron ~.
Torphins [tɔːr'fɪnz] (torfínz)
Torpoint [tɔːr'pɔɪnt] (torpóynt)
Torquay [tɔːr'kiː] (torkée)
Torquil, C.n. ['tɔːkwɪl] (tórkwil)
Torrance, f.n. ['tɒrəns] (tórránss)
Torrens, f.n. ['tɒrənz] (tórrěnz)
Torrie, f.n. ['tɒrɪ] (tórri)
Torry ['tɒrɪ] (tórri)
Torthorwald [tə'θɒrəld] (tǒr-thórrǎld); [tər'θɒrwəld] (tǒr-thórwǎld)
Toseland, f.n. ['touzələnd] (tōzělǎnd)
Tosh, f.n. [tɒʃ] (tosh)
Tossell, f.n. ['tɒsl] (tossl)
Tosside ['tɒsaɪd] (tóssïd); ['tɒsɪd] (tóssid); ['tɒsɪt] (tóssit)

Totham, Great and Little ['tɒtəm] (tóttǎm)
Tothill, f.n. ['tɒthɪl] (tótt-hil); ['tɒtɪl] (tóttil)
Totley ['tɒtlɪ] (tóttli)
Totnes ['tɒtnɪs] (tótněss)
Toton ['toutən] (tōtŏn)
Tottenham ['tɒtənəm] (tóttěnǎm)
Totternhoe ['tɒtərnhou] (tóttěrnhō)
Tottman, f.n. ['tɒtmən] (tóttmǎn)
Totton ['tɒtən] (tóttŏn)
Touch, f.n. [tautʃ] (towtch)
Touche, f.n. [tuʃ] (toosh)
Tough, f.n. [tʌx] (tooch); [tʌf] (tuff)
Tough [tux] (tooch)
Touhey, f.n. ['tuɪ] (toŏ-i)
Toulmin, f.n. ['tulmɪn] (toŏlmin)
Toulson, f.n. ['tulsən] (toŏlssŏn)
Toulston ['toulstən] (tōlsstŏn)
Tourle, f.n. [tɜːl] (turl); [tuərl] (toŏrl)
Tourneur, Turnour or Turner, Cyril, 16-17th-c. dramatist ['tɜːnər] (túrner)
Tours, f.n. [tuərz] (toŏrz)
Tovell, f.n. ['touvl] (tōvl)
Tovey, f.n. ['touvɪ] (tōvi); ['tʌvɪ] (túvvi) The first is appropriate for Sir Donald Francis ~, pianist and composer, the second for Baron ~, Admiral of the Fleet.
Tovil ['tɒvɪl] (tóvvil); ['tɒvl] (tovvl)
Toward ['tauərd] (tów-ǎrd)
Towb, f.n. [taub] (towb)
Towcester ['toustər] (tōsster)
Towednack [tou'wednək] (tō-wédnǎk)
Towell, f.n. ['tauəl] (tówěl)
Towers, f.n. ['tauərz] (tówěrz)
Towgood, f.n. ['tougud] (tōgoŏd)
Tow Law ['tau 'lɔ] (tów láw)
Towle, f.n. [toul] (tōl)
Towler, f.n. ['taulər] (tówler)
Towndrow, f.n. ['taundrou] (tówndrō)
Townsend, f.n. ['taunzend] (tównzend)
Townshend, f.n. ['taunzend] (tównzend) Appropriate also for Marquess ~.
Townshend ['taunz'end] (tównz-énd)
Townson, f.n. ['taunsən] (tównssŏn)
Towse, f.n. [tauz] (towz)
Towy, River ['tauɪ] (tówi)
Towyn ['tauɪn] (tów-in)
Toxteth ['tɒkstəθ] (tóckstěth)
Toynbee, f.n. ['tɔɪnbɪ] (tóynbi)
Toyne, f.n. [tɔɪn] (toyn)
Tracey, f.n. ['treɪsɪ] (tráyssi)
Trafalgar, Viscount [trə'fælgər] (trǎfálgǎr) The sixth Earl Nelson advocated this pronunciation, although mentioning that previous holders of the title had preferred [ˌtræfl'gɑr] (trafflgaár).
Trafalgar House, nr. Salisbury [ˌtræfl'gɑr] (trafflgaár); [trə'fælgər] (trǎfálgǎr)
Traherne, f.n. [trə'hɜːn] (trǎhérn)
Traian-glas ['traɪən'glɑs] (trí-ǎn-glaáss)
Train, f.n. [treɪn] (trayn)
Trallong ['trælɒŋ] (tráhlong)
Tranent [trə'nent] (trǎnént)

Trant, f.n. [trænt] (trannt)
Tranter, f.n. ['træntər] (tránnter)
Traprain, Viscount [trə'preɪn] (trăpráyn)
Traquair, f.n. [trə'kwɛər] (trăkwáir)
Traquair [trə'kwɛər] (trăkwáir)
Trathen, f.n. ['treɪθən] (tráythĕn)
Travers, f.n. ['trævərz] (trávvĕrz)
Travess, f.n. [trə'ves] (trăvéss)
Travis, f.n. ['trævɪs] (trávviss)
Trawscoed ['trauskɔɪd] (trówsskoyd)
Trawsfynydd [traus'vʌnɪð] (trowss-vúnnith)
Traynor, f.n. ['treɪnər] (tráynŏr)
Treacy, f.n. ['treɪsɪ] (tráyssi)
Treadwell, f.n. ['tredwəl] (trédwĕl)
Trealaw [trɪ'ælau] (tri-álow)
Treales [treɪlz] (traylz)
Trearddur Bay [treɪ'arðɪər 'beɪ] (tray-aártheer báy)
Trease, f.n. [triz] (treez)
Trebanos [trɪ'bænɒs] (trĕbánnoss)
Trebarwith [trɪ'bɑrwɪθ] (trĕbaárwith)
Trebble, f.n. ['trebl] (trebbl)
Trebehor [trɪ'bɪər] (trĕbeér)
Trebey, f.n. ['trɪbɪ] (treébi)
Trebilcock, f.n. [trɪ'bɪlkou] (trĕbílkō); [trɪ'bɪlkɒk] (trĕbílkock)
Trebullet [trɪ'bulɪt] (trĕboŏlĕt)
Trebursye [trɪ'bɜrzɪ] (trĕbúrzi)
Trecarrel [trɪ'kærəl] (trĕkárrĕl)
Trecastle [trɪ'kæsl] (trĕkássl)
Tredegar [trɪ'dɪgər] (trĕdeégăr) *Appropriate also for the Barony of ~.*
Tredennick, f.n. [trɪ'denɪk] (trĕdénnick)
Tredree, f.n. ['tredri] (trédree)
Tree, f.n. [tri] (tree)
Trefdraeth, *also spelt* Trevdraeth ['trevdraɪθ] (trévdríth)
Trefeglwys [trɪ'vegluɪs] (trĕvéglōŏ-iss)
Trefeirig [trɪ'vaɪrɪg] (trĕvírig)
Trefgarne, Baron ['trefgɑrn] (tréffgaarn)
Trefilan [trɪ'vɪlæn] (trĕveélan)
Tre-fin *see* Trevine.
Treflys ['trevlɪs] (trévliss)
Trefnant ['trevnænt] (trévnant)
Trefonen [trɪ'vɒnɪn] (trĕvónnĕn)
Trefor, Welsh C.n. ['trevɒr] (trévvŏr)
Treforest [trɪ'fɒrɪst] (trĕfórrĕst)
Trefriw ['trevrɪu] (trévri-oo)
Trefusis, f.n. [trɪ'fjusɪs] (trĕféwssiss)
Tregadillett [ˌtregə'dɪlɪt] (treggădíllĕt)
Tregajorran [ˌtregə'dʒɒrən] (treggă-jórrăn)
Tregaminian [ˌtregə'mɪnɪən] (treggă-mínni-ăn)
Treganthe [trɪ'gænθɪ] (trĕgánthi)
Tregare [trɪ'gɛər] (trĕgáir)
Tregaron [trɪ'gærən] (trĕgárrŏn)
Tregavethan [ˌtregə'veθən] (treggă-véthăn)
Tregellas, f.n. [trɪ'geləs] (trĕgéllăss)
Tregelles, f.n. [trɪ'gelɪs] (trĕgéllĕss)
Tregenna Castle [trɪ'genə] (trĕgénnă)
Tregenza, f.n. [trɪ'genzə] (trĕgénză)

Tregeseal [ˌtregɪ'sɪəl] (treggĕsseé-ăl); [ˌtregɪ'sɪl] (treggĕsseél)
Treglown, f.n. [trɪ'gloun] (trĕglŏn); [trɪ'gloun] (treeglŏn)
Tre-goed *see* Tregoyd.
Tregolls [trɪ'gɒlz] (trĕgóllz)
Tregonetha [ˌtregə'neθə] (treggŏnéthă)
Tregoning, f.n. [trɪ'gɒnɪŋ] (trĕgónning)
Tregonissey [ˌtregə'nɪsɪ] (treggŏníssi)
Tregonning [trɪ'gɒnɪŋ] (trĕgónning)
Tregony ['tregənɪ] (tréggŏni)
Tregoyd, *also spelt* Tre-goed [trɪ'gɔɪd] (trĕgóyd)
Tregrehan [tre'greɪn] (tregráyn)
Tregurrian [trɪ'gʌrɪən] (trĕgúrri-ăn)
Tregynon [trɪ'gʌnən] (trĕgúnnŏn)
Trehafod [trɪ'hævəd] (trĕhávvŏd)
Trehane, f.n. [trɪ'heɪn] (trĕháyn)
Treharris [trɪ'hærɪs] (trĕhárriss)
Trehearne, f.n. [trɪ'hɜrn] (trĕhérn)
Treherbert [trɪ'hɜrbərt] (trĕhérbĕrt)
Treig, Loch *and* River [treɪg] (treeg)
Treitel, f.n. ['traɪtl] (trítl)
Trekeive Steps [trɪ'kiv 'steps] (trĕkeév stéps)
Trekenner [trɪ'kenər] (trĕkénner)
Trelawney, f.n. [trɪ'lɒnɪ] (trĕláwni)
Trelawny, f.n. [trɪ'lɒnɪ] (trĕláwni)
Trelawnyd [trɪ'launɪd] (trĕlównid)
Treleaven, f.n. [trɪ'levən] (trĕlévvĕn)
Tre-lech a'r Betws [trɪ'leɪx ɑr 'betus] (trĕláych aar béttŏŏss)
Treleigh [trɪ'leɪ] (trĕláy)
Trelewis [trɪ'luɪs] (trĕloŏ-iss); [trɪ'ljuɪs] (trĕléw-iss)
Treligga [trɪ'lɪgə] (trĕlíggă)
Trelleck ['trelek] (trélleck)
Treloar, f.n. [trɪ'lɔr] (trĕlór)
Treluggan [trɪ'lʌgən] (trĕlúggăn)
Trematon ['tremətən] (trémmătŏn)
Tremeirchion [trɪ'maɪərxɪɒn] (trĕ-mírchi-on)
Tremenheere, f.n. ['tremɪnhɪər] (trémmĕnheer)
Tremills, f.n. ['tremlz] (tremmlz)
Trenaman, f.n. [trɪ'nɑmən] (trĕnaámăn)
Trenance [trɪ'næns] (trĕnánss)
Trenant [trɪ'nænt] (trĕnánt)
Trenchard, Viscount ['trenʃərd] (trén-shărd)
Trencrom [tren'krɒm] (tren-krómm)
Treneglos [trɪ'neglɒs] (trĕnégloss)
Trenewydd [trɪ'newɪð] (trĕné-with)
Trengwainton [trɪn'gweɪntən] (trĕn-gwáyntŏn)
Trenowth [trɪ'nauθ] (trĕnówth)
Trent, River [trent] (trent)
Trentbridge [trent'brɪdʒ] (trént-bríj)
Trentishoe ['trentɪʃou] (tréntiss-hō)
Treorchy [trɪ'ɔrkɪ] (tri-órki)
Trepass, f.n. [trɪ'pæs] (trĕpáss)
Trerice Manor [trɪ'raɪs] (trĕríss)
Trerise, f.n. [trɪ'raɪz] (trĕríz)
Trerule Foot [trɪ'rul 'fut] (trĕroŏl foŏt)

Treryn Dinus [trə'rɪn 'daɪnəs] (trĕreén dínŭss); ['trɪn 'daɪnəs] (treén dínŭss)
Tresardern, *f.n.* ['tresərdɜrn] (tréssärdern)
Tresco ['treskoʊ] (trésskŏ)
Treshnish Isles ['treʃnɪʃ] (tréshnish)
Tresillian [trɪ'sɪlɪən] (trĕssílli-än)
Treskillard [trɪs'kɪlərd] (trĕskíllärd)
Tresman, *f.n.* ['trezmən] (trézmän)
Tresmeer [trez'mɪər] (trezmeér)
Treswithian [trɪ'swɪðɪən] (trĕ-swíthi-än)
Trethewey, *f.n.* [trɪ'θjuɪ] (trĕthéw-i)
Trethewy, *f.n.* [trɪ'θjuɪ] (trĕthéw-i)
Trethowan, *f.n.* [trɪ'θaʊən] (trĕthówăn); [trɪ'θoʊən] (trĕthŏ-än)
Treuddyn ['traɪðɪn] (trɪ́thin)
Trevan, *f.n.* [trɪ'væn] (trĕván)
Trevarrack [trɪ'værək] (trĕvárräk)
Trevaskis, *f.n.* [trɪ'væskɪs] (trĕvásskiss)
Trevdraeth *see* Trefdraeth.
Trevella [trɪ'velə] (trĕvéllä)
Trevelyan, *f.n.* [trɪ'vɪljən] (trĕvíl-yän); [trɪ'veljən] (trĕvél-yän) *The first is the usual Cornish pronunciation, the second the Northumbrian. The first is appropriate for George Macaulay ~, historian, and for Baron ~, diplomatist.*
Trevena [trɪ'vinə] (trĕveénä)
Treverbyn [trɪ'vɜrbɪn] (trĕvérbin)
Treves, *f.n.* [trivz] (treevz)
Trevethick [trɪ'veθɪk] (trĕvéthick)
Trevethin, *Baron* [trɪ'veθɪn] (trĕvéthin)
Trevett, *f.n.* ['trevɪt] (trévvĕt)
Trevine, *also spelt* **Tre-fin** [trɪ'vin] (trĕveén)
Trevivian, *f.n.* [trɪ'vɪvɪən] (trĕvívvi-än)
Trevor, *f.n.* ['trevər] (trévvŏr)
Trevose Head [trɪ'voʊz] (trĕvŏz)
Trew [tru] (troo)
Trewalchmai [trɪ'wælxmaɪ] (trĕ-wálchmI)
Trewavas, *f.n.* [trɪ'wævəs] (trĕ-wávvăss)
Treweek, *f.n.* [trɪ'wik] (trĕ-weék)
Trewellard [trɪ'welərd] (trĕ-wéllärd)
Trewhela, *f.n.* [trɪ'hwelə] (trĕ-whéllä)
Trewidland [trɪ'wɪdlənd] (trĕ-wídländ)
Trewin, *f.n.* [trɪ'wɪn] (trĕ-wín)
Trewirgie [trɪ'wɜrgɪ] (trĕ-wírgi)
Trewoon ['truən] (troó-ŏn)
Treyarnon Bay [trɪ'jɑrnən] (trĕ-yaárnŏn)
Trickett, *f.n.* ['trɪkɪt] (tríckĕt)
Trier, *f.n.* [trɪər] (treer)
Trillick ['trɪlɪk] (tríllick)
Trillo, *Welsh saint* ['trɪłoʊ] (tríhlŏ)
Trimingham ['trɪmɪŋəm] (trímming-ăm)
Trimlestown, *Baron* ['trɪmlztən] (trímmlztŏn)
Trimsaran [trɪm'særən] (trim-sárrăn)
Trinafour [ˌtrɪnə'fʊər] (trinnăfoŏr)
Trinaman, *f.n.* ['trɪnəmən] (trínnămän); [trɪ'nɑmən] (trináamän)
Trinant ['trɪnænt] (trínnant)
Tring, *f.n.* [trɪŋ] (tring)
Tring [trɪŋ] (tring)

Trinity Gask ['trɪnɪtɪ 'gæsk] (trínniti gássk)
Tripp, *f.n.* [trɪp] (trip)
Trispen ['trɪspən] (trísspĕn)
Tristram, *C.n.* ['trɪstrəm] (trísstrăm)
Tritton, *f.n.* ['trɪtən] (tríttŏn)
Trocchi, *f.n.* ['trɒkɪ] (trócki)
Troedrhiw-fuwch ['trɔɪdhrɪu'vjux] (tróydri-oo-véwch)
Troedrhiw-gwair ['trɔɪdhrɪu'gwaɪər] (tróydri-oo-gwír)
Troed-yr-aur ['trɔɪdər'aɪər] (tróydárír)
Troed-y-rhiw ['trɔɪdərɪ'u] (tróydári-oó)
Trofarth ['troʊvɑrθ] (trŏvaarth)
Trollope, *f.n.* ['trɒləp] (tróllŏp)
Trostre ['trɒstreɪ] (trósstray)
Troth, *f.n.* [trɒθ] (troth)
Trotter, *f.n.* ['trɒtər] (tróttĕr)
Trottiscliffe ['trɒtɪsklɪf] (tróttiskliff); ['trɒslɪ] (tróssli)
Troubridge, *f.n.* ['trubrɪdʒ] (troóbrij)
Troughton, *f.n.* ['traʊtən] (trówtŏn)
Troup, *f.n.* [trup] (troop)
Troway ['troʊɪ] (trŏ-i)
Trowbridge ['troʊbrɪdʒ] (trŏbrij)
Trowell, *f.n.* ['traʊəl] (trówĕl); ['troʊəl] (trŏ-ĕl)
Trowell ['traʊəl] (trówĕl); ['troʊəl] (trŏ-ĕl)
Trower, *f.n.* ['traʊər] (trówer)
Trowsdale, *f.n.* ['traʊzdeɪl] (trówzdayl)
Trowse [troʊs] (trŏss)
Troy, *f.n.* [trɔɪ] (troy)
Truckle, *f.n.* ['trʌkl] (truckl)
Trueman, *f.n.* ['trumən] (troómăn)
Trueta, *f.n.* [tru'etə] (troo-éttä)
Trufitt, *f.n.* ['trufɪt] (troófit)
Truim, *River* ['truɪm] (troó-im)
Truman, *f.n.* ['trumən] (troómän)
Trunch [trʌnʃ] (trunsh)
Truro ['truəroʊ] (troŏrŏ)
Truscott, *f.n.* ['trʌskət] (trússkŏt)
Trusham ['trʌsəm] (trússăm); ['trɪsəm] (tríssăm)
Trustan ['trʌstən] (trússtăn)
Trusthorpe ['trʌsθɔrp] (trúss-thorp)
Trusthorpe Gowt ['trʌsθɔrp 'gaʊt] (trúss-thorp gówt)
Trustram, *C.n.* ['trʌstrəm] (trússtrăm)
Truzzi, *f.n.* ['trʌzɪ] (trúzzi)
Try, *f.n.* [traɪ] (trī)
Tryfan ['trʌvən] (trúvvăn)
Tryon, *f.n.* ['traɪən] (trí-ŏn) *Appropriate also for Baron ~.*
Trysull ['trɪsl] (treessl); ['trɪzl] (treezl)
Trythall, *f.n.* ['traɪθɒl] (trí-thawl)
Tschaikov, *f.n.* ['tʃaɪkɒf] (chíkoff)
Tschiffely, *A. F.*, *author* [tʃɪ'feɪlɪ] (chifáyli)
Tschirren, *f.n.* ['tʃɪrɪn] (chírrĕn)
Tuchner, *f.n.* ['tʌknər] (túckner)
Tuck, *f.n.* [tʌk] (tuck)
Tucker, *f.n.* ['tʌkər] (túcker)
Tuckett, *f.n.* ['tʌkɪt] (túckĕt)
Tuddenham, *f.n.* ['tʌdənəm] (túddĕnăm)

Tudeley ['tjudlɪ] (téwdli); ['tudlɪ] (toŏdli)
Tudhoe ['tʌdoʊ] (túddō)
Tudhope, f.n. ['tjudəp] (téwdŏp)
Tudsbery, f.n. ['tʌdzbərɪ] (túdzbĕri)
Tudur, Welsh C.n. ['tɪdɪər] (tíddeer)
Tufano, f.n. [tu'fanoʊ] (tōŏfaänō)
Tuffin, f.n. ['tʌfɪn] (túffĭn)
Tuffnell, f.n. ['tʌfnəl] (túffnĕl)
Tugendhat, f.n. ['tugənhat] (toŏgĕn-haat)
Tugwell, f.n. ['tʌgwəl] (túgwĕl)
Tuite, f.n. [tjut] (tewt)
Tuke, f.n. [tjuk] (tewk)
Tuker, f.n. ['tjukər] (téwker)
Tulchan Lodge, Forfar ['tʌlxən] (túl-chăn)
Tulk, f.n. [tʌlk] (tulk)
Tullibardine, Marquess of [ˌtʌlɪ'bardɪn] (tullibaárdin)
Tulliemet [ˌtʌlɪ'met] (tullimét)
Tulloch ['tʌləx] (túllŏch)
Tullymore [ˌtʌlɪ'mɔr] (tullimór)
Tummel, Loch and River ['tʌml] (tumml)
Tunesi, f.n. [tju'nesɪ] (tewnéssi)
Tungate, f.n. ['tʌŋgeɪt] (túng-gayt)
Tungay, f.n. ['tʌŋgeɪ] (túng-gay)
Tunnard, f.n. ['tʌnərd] (túnnărd)
Tunnell, f.n. [tə'nel] (tŭnéll)
Tunstall, Co. Durham, Staffs., Suffolk ['tʌnstəl] (túnsstăl)
Tunstall, Norfolk ['tʌnstol] (túnsstawl)
Tunstead ['tʌnstɪd] (túnsstĕd)
Tuohey, f.n. ['tuɪ] (toŏ-i)
Tuohy, f.n. ['tuɪ] (toŏ-i)
Tupper, f.n. ['tʌpər] (túpper)
Tuppholme, f.n. ['tʌphoʊm] (túpp-hōm)
Turgis Green ['tɜrdʒɪs 'grin] (túrjiss greén)
Turl, f.n. [tɜrl] (turl)
Turnbull, f.n. ['tɜrnbʊl] (túrnbŏŏl)
Turnell, f.n. [tər'nel] (tŭrnéll)
Turner, f.n. ['tɜrnər] (túrner)
Turnhouse ['tɜrnhaʊs] (túrn-howss)
Turnill, f.n. ['tɜrnɪl] (túrnil)
Turnour, f.n. ['tɜrnər] (túrnŭr)
Turnour, Cyril, 16-17th-c. dramatist see Tourneur, Cyril.
Turquand, f.n. [tɜr'kwænd] (turkwánd); ['tɜrkwənd] (túrkwănd); [tɜr'kɒŋ] (tur-kóng)
Turrell, f.n. ['tʌrəl] (túrrĕl)
Turriff ['tʌrɪf] (túrriff)
Turweston [tər'westən] (tŭrwésstŏn)
Tusa, f.n. ['tjusə] (téwssá)
Tushielaw [ˌtʌʃɪ'lə] (tushi-láw)
Tuson, f.n. ['tjusən] (téwssŏn)
Tussaud, f.n. ['tusoʊ] (toŏssō) Although members of the family themselves use this pronunciation, they expect and accept the popular versions for Madame¹ ~'s exhibition, q.v.
Tussaud's, Madame, waxworks exhibition [tə'sɔdz] (tŭssáwdz); [tə'soʊdz] (tŭssōdz)
Tutaev, f.n. [tu'taɪef] (tootí-eff)

Tuttiett, f.n. ['tʌtjet] (tút-yet)
Tuxford ['tʌksfərd] (túcksförd)
Tuyrrell, f.n. ['tɪrəl] (tírrĕl)
Twechar ['twexər] (twéchăr)
Tweddel, f.n. ['twedl] (tweddl)
Tweed, River [twid] (tweed)
Tweeddale, Marquess of ['twiddeɪl] (tweéd-dayl)
Tweedsmuir, Baron ['twidzmjʊər] (tweédz-myōŏr)
Tweseldown ['twizldaʊn] (tweézldown)
Twidell, f.n. [twɪ'del] (twidéll); ['twɪdl] (twiddl)
Twidle, f.n. ['twaɪdl] (twidl)
Twine, f.n. [twaɪn] (twīn)
Twineham ['twaɪnəm] (twínăm)
Twinhoe ['twɪnoʊ] (twínnō)
Twisly [twɪz'laɪ] (twizz-lī)
Twistleton-Wykeham-Fiennes, f.n. ['twɪsltən 'wɪkəm 'faɪnz] (twíssltŏn wíckăm fīnz) Family name of Baron Saye and Sele.
Twitchett, f.n. ['twɪtʃɪt] (twitchĕt)
Twizell ['twaɪzl] (twīzl)
Twohy, f.n. ['tuɪ] (toŏ-i)
Twomey, f.n. ['tumɪ] (toŏmi)
Twynholm ['twaɪnəm] (twínŏm)
Twyn-yr-Odyn ['tuɪn ər 'ɒdɪn] (toŏ-in ŭr óddin)
Tyacke, f.n. ['taɪæk] (tī-ack)
Tybalds Close ['tɪbəldz 'kloʊs] (tíbb-ăldz klōss)
Tyberton ['tɪbərtən] (tíbbērtŏn)
Tyburn ['taɪbərn] (tíbŭrn)
Ty-croes, Anglesey, Carmarthen. [ti-'kroɪs] (tee-króyss)
Tydd [tɪd] (tidd)
Tydeman, f.n. ['taɪdɪmən] (tídimăn); ['taɪdmən] (tídmăn)
Tyderwen [tɪ'dɜrwɪn] (tiddérwĕn)
Tydweiliog [tɪd'waɪljɒg] (tidwíl-yog)
Tye, f.n. [taɪ] (tī)
Ty-Hyll Bridge [ti 'hɪɬ] (tee híḷl)
Tyla-gwyn [ˌtʌlə'gwɪn] (tullágwin)
Tyldesley ['tɪldzlɪ] (tíldzli); ['tɪlzlɪ] (tíllzli)
Tylecote, f.n. ['taɪlkoʊt] (tílkōt)
Tylee, f.n. ['taɪlɪ] (tílee)
Tyler, f.n. ['taɪlər] (tíler)
Tylney Hall ['tɪlnɪ] (tíllni)
Tylorstown ['taɪlərztaʊn] (tílŏrztown)
Tylwch ['tʌlʊx] (túllŏŏch)
Ty-mawr [ti'maʊər] (teemówr)
Tynan, f.n. ['taɪnən] (tínăn)
Tynan ['taɪnən] (tínăn)
Tyndale, William, translator of the New Testament ['tɪndl] (tindl)
Tyndale ['tɪndeɪl] (tíndayl)
Tyndrum [taɪn'drʌm] (tīndrúm)
Tyne, River [taɪn] (tīn)
Tynemouth ['tæmmaʊθ] (tǎmmowth); ['tɪnməθ] (tínmŭth)
Tynewydd [tɪ'njuɪð] (tinnéw-ith)
Tynte, f.n. [tɪnt] (tint)
Tyntesfield ['tɪntsfɪld] (tíntsfeeld)

Tynwald, *Manx legislative assembly* ['tınwəld] (tínwáld)
Tyn-y-berth [,tınə'bɜrθ] (tinnăbérth)
Tynyfelin [,tınə'velın] (tinnăvéllin)
Tynyrheol [,tınər'herɒl] (tinnĕr-háy-ol)
Tyrell, *f.n.* ['tırəl] (tírrĕl)
Tyrella [tı'relə] (tirréllă)
Tyrer, *f.n.* ['taıərər] (tírer)
Tyringham, *f.n.* ['tırıŋəm] (tírring-ăm)
Tyrone [tı'roʊn] (tirrŏn) *Appropriate also for the Earl of* ~.
Tyrrell, *f.n.* ['tırəl] (tírrĕl)
Tyrwhitt, *f.n.* ['tırıt] (tírrit)
Tyseley ['taızlı] (tízli)
Tysoe ['taısoʊ] (tíssŏ)
Tyssen, *f.n.* ['taısən] (tíssĕn)
Tysser, *f.n.* ['taısər] (tísser)
Tytherinton ['tıðərıntən] (títhĕrintŏn)
Tytler, *f.n.* ['taıtlər] (títler)
Tywardreath [,taıwər'dreθ] (tĭ-wărd-réth)
Tywyn ['taʊ ın] (tów-in)
Tyzack, *f.n.* ['taızæk] (tízack); ['tızæk] (tízzack)

U

Ubbelohde, *f.n.* ['ʌbıloʊd] (úbbĕlŏd)
Uber, *f.n.* ['jubər] (yoóber)
Ubley ['ʌblı] (úbbli)
Ubsdell, *f.n.* ['ʌbzdəl] (úbzdĕl)
Ubysz, *f.n.* ['jubıʃ] (yoóbish)
Udal, *f.n.* ['judəl] (yoódál)
Udale, *f.n.* ['judeıl] (yoódayl); [ju'deıl] (yoodáyl)
Udall, *f.n.* ['judəl] (yoódál); ['judɒl] (yoódawl); ['judeıl] (yoódal); [ju'dæl] (yoodál); [ju'dɒl] (yoodáwl)
Udell, *f.n.* [ju'del] (yŏodéll)
Uden, *f.n.* ['judən] (yoódĕn)
Udimore ['judımɔr] (yoódimor); ['ʌdımər] (úddimor)
Udny ['ʌdnı] (úddni)
Uffculme ['ʌfkəm] (úffkŭm)
Ugglebarnby ['ʌgl'barnbı] (úggl-baárnbi)
Ugley ['ʌglı] (úggli)
Uglow, *f.n.* ['ʌgloʊ] (úgglŏ); ['jugloʊ] (yoóglŏ) *The first is usual in Cornwall.*
Ugthorpe ['ʌgθɔrp] (úg-thorp)
Uig, *Inverness.*, *Ross.* ['uıg] (oó-ig)
Uigen ['uıgən] (oó-igĕn)
Uisgean ['ʊʃgən] (oósh-găn)
Uist ['juıst] (yoó-ist); ['uıst] (oó-ist)
Ulceby ['ʌlsbı] (úlssbi); ['usbı] (oóssbi)
Ulcombe ['ʌlkəm] (úllkŏm)
Uley ['julı] (yoóli)
Ulgham ['ʌfəm] (úffăm)
Ulick, *C.n.* ['julık] (yoólick)

Ullesthorpe ['ʌlısθɔrp] (úllĕss-thorp)
Ullock, *f.n.* ['ʌlək] (úllŏk)
Uliswater ['ʌlzwɔtər] (úllz-wawter) *Appropriate also for Viscount* ~.
Ulph, *f.n.* [ʌlf] (ulf)
Ulva ['ʌlvə] (úllvă)
Ulverstone ['ʌlvərstən] (úllvĕrsstŏn)
Umberleigh ['ʌmbərlı] (úmbĕrli)
Umfreville, *f.n.* ['ʌmfrıvıl] (úmfrĕvil)
Uncles, *f.n.* ['ʌŋklz] (unklz)
Underdown, *f.n.* ['ʌndərdaʊn] (úndĕrdown)
Underhill, *f.n.* ['ʌndərhıl] (úndĕr-híl)
Underwood, *f.n.* ['ʌndərwʊd] (úndĕrwŏod)
Undery, *f.n.* ['ʌndərı] (úndĕri)
Ungar, *f.n.* ['ʌŋgər] (úng-găr)
Ungoed, *Welsh C.n.* ['ıŋgɔıd] (íng-goyd)
Ungoed, *f.n.* ['ıŋgɔıd] (íng-goyd); ['ʌŋgɔıd] (úng-goyd)
Uniacke, *f.n.* ['junıæk] (yoóni-ack)
Unst [ʌnst] (unsst)
Unstone ['ʌnstən] (únsstŏn)
Unthank, *f.n.* ['ʌnθæŋk] (ún-thank)
Unwin, *f.n.* ['ʌnwın] (únwin) *Appropriate for George Allen and* ~, *publishers.*
Up Exe ['ʌpeks] (úppecks)
Up Ottery [ʌp 'ɒtərı] (up óttĕri)
Upavon ['ʌpeıvən] (úpayvŏn)
Uphall [ʌp'hɒl] (up-háwl)
Uplowman [ʌp'loʊmən] (uplŏmăn)
Uppark, *Sussex* ['ʌpɑrk] (úp-paark)
Upper Broughton ['ʌpər 'brɒtən] (úpper bráwtŏn)
Upper Hardres ['ʌpər 'hardz] (úpper haárdz)
Upper Haugh ['ʌpər 'hɒf] (úpper háwf)
Upper Heyford, *Oxon. also sometimes called* Heyford Warren ['ʌpər 'heıfərd] (úpper háyfŏrd)
Upper Shuckburgh ['ʌpər 'ʃʌkbərə] (úpper shúckbŭră)
Upper Slaughter ['ʌpər 'slɔtər] (úpper sláwter)
Upper Tean ['ʌpər 'tin] (úpper teén)
Upper Wyche ['ʌpər 'wıtʃ] (úpper witch)
Upperdine, *f.n.* ['ʌpərdaın] (úppĕrdín)
Upperlands ['ʌpərləndz] (úppĕrlăndz)
Uprichard, *f.n.* [ju'prıtʃard] (yooprítchaard); [ju'prıtʃərd] (yooprítchărd); [ʌp'rıtʃərd] (uprítchărd)
Upton, *f.n.* ['ʌptən] (úptŏn)
Upton Hellions ['ʌptən 'helıənz] (úptŏn hélli-ŏnz)
Upwey ['ʌpweı] (úpway)
Urban, *f.n.* ['ɜrbən] (úrbăn)
Urch, *f.n.* [ɜrtʃ] (urtch)
Urchfont ['ɜrtʃfɒnt] (úrtchfont)
Ure, *f.n.* [jʊər] (yŏor)
Ure, River [jʊər] (yŏor)
Uren, *f.n.* [jʊə'ren] (yŏorén)
Uridge, *f.n.* ['jʊərıdʒ] (yŏorij)
Urmston ['ɜrmstən] (úrmsstŏn)
Urquhart, *f.n.* ['ɜrxərt] (úrchărt); ['ɜrkərt] (úrkărt)

Urquhart, *Inverness., Moray., Ross.*
['ɜrxərt] (úrҫhắrt)
Urrard House, *Perth.* ['ʌrərd] (úrrărd)
Urray ['ʌrɪ] (úrri)
Urswick ['ɜrzwɪk] (úrzwick); ['ɜrzɪk]
(úrzick)
Urwick, f.n. ['ɜrwɪk] (úrwick)
Ury, f.n. ['jʊərɪ] (yoŏri)
Usan ['uzən] (oozán)
Usborne, f.n. ['ʌzbɔrn] (úzzborn)
Ushaw ['ʌʃə] (úsh-ă); ['ʌʃɔ] (úsh-aw)
Usher, f.n. ['ʌʃər] (úsh-er)
Usherwood, f.n. ['ʌʃərwʊd] (úshĕrwŏŏd)
Usk [ʌsk] (ussk) *Appropriate also for* ~
Priory.
Usk, River [ʌsk] (ussk)
Uskmouth ['ʌskmaʊθ] (ússkmowth)
Usselby ['ʌslbɪ] (ússlbi)
Ussher, f.n. ['ʌʃər] (úsh-er)
Ustinov, f.n. ['justɪnɒf] (yoŏstinoff)
['ustɪnɒf] (oóstinoff); *Peter* ~, *film pro-
ducer, actor, and playwright, submits to
either pronunciation.*
Uswayford ['ʌzweɪfɔrd] (úzzwayford)
Usworth ['ʌzwɜrθ] (úzzwurth)
Uthwatt, f.n. ['ʌθwɒt] (úth-wott) *Ap-
propriate also for the Barony of* ~.
Utting, f.n. ['ʌtɪŋ] (útting)
Uttoxeter [ju'tɒksɪtər] (yootócksitter);
[ʌ'tɒksɪtər] (uttócksitter); ['ʌksɪtər]
(úcksitter) *There are other less common
variants.*
Uvarov, f.n. [ju'vɑrɒf] (yoováaroff)
Uvedale, Baron ['juvdeɪl] (yoŏvdayl)
Uwchygarreg [ˌjuxə'gærɛg] (yooҫhá-
gárreg)
Uwins, f.n. ['juɪnz] (yoŏ-inz)
Uxbridge ['ʌksbrɪdʒ] (úcksbrij)
Uyeasound ['juːəsaʊnd] (yoŏ-ássownd)
Uxiell, f.n. ['juzɪel] (yoŏzi-el)
Uzmaston ['ʌzməsən] (úzzmássŏn)

V

Vache, The, *Bucks.* [ðə 'vætʃ] (thĕ vátch)
Vachell, f.n. ['veɪtʃl] (vaytchl); ['vætʃl]
(vatchl)
Vachell, Horace Annesley, author
['hɒrɪs 'ænzlɪ 'veɪtʃl] (hórriss ánzli
váytchl)
Vacher, f.n. ['væʃər] (vásher) *Appro-
priate in particular for the printers of* ~'*s
Parliamentary Companion.*
Vaesen, f.n. ['veɪzən] (váyzĕn)
Vaila ['veɪlə] (váylă)
Vaillant, f.n. ['væljənt] (vál-yănt); ['vaɪ-
jɒŋ] (ví-yong)
Valency, f.n. [və'lensɪ] (vălénssi)

Valency, River [və'lensɪ] (vălénssi)
Valentin, f.n. ['væləntɪn] (válĕntin)
Valentine, f.n. and C.n. ['væləntaɪn]
(válĕntín)
Valerio, f.n. [və'lɛərɪoʊ] (vălaïrioŏ)
Valetort, f.n. ['vælɪtɔrt] (válitort)
Vallance, f.n. ['vælənss] (válánss)
Vallancey, f.n. [væ'lænsɪ] (valánssi)
Vallans, f.n. ['vælənss] (válánss)
Valle Crucis ['vælɪ 'krusɪs] (váli
kroóssiss)
Valley ['vælɪ] (váli)
Vallier, f.n. ['væljeɪ] (vál-yay)
Vallins, f.n. ['vælɪnz] (válinz)
Van Damm, f.n. [væn 'dæm] (van dám)
Van Dyck, f.n. [væn 'daɪk] (van dík)
Van Eyssen, f.n. [væn 'aɪsən] (van íssĕn)
van Geloven, f.n. [ˌvæn gɪ'loʊvən] (van
gĕlṓvĕn)
van Greenaway, f.n. [væn 'grinəweɪ]
(van greénă-way)
Van Gijseghem, f.n. [væn 'gaɪzɪgəm]
(van gízĕgĕm)
Van Moppes, f.n. [væn 'mɒpɪz] (van
móppĕz)
Van Praagh, f.n. [væn 'prɑg] (van praág)
van Straten, f.n. [væn 'strɑtən] (van
straátĕn)
van Straubenzee, f.n. [ˌvæn strɔ'benzɪ]
(van strawbénzi)
Van Thal, f.n. [væn 'tɒl] (van táwl)
Van Wyck, f.n. [væn 'waɪk] (van wík)
Van den Bergh, f.n. ['vændənbɜrg]
(vándĕnberg)
van der Burgh, f.n. ['vændərbɜrg]
(vándĕrburg)
Van Der Gucht, f.n. ['vændərgut] (ván-
dĕrgoot)
Van der Pant, f.n. ['vændərpænt] (ván-
dĕrpant)
van der Riet, f.n. ['vændərɪt] (vándĕreet)
van der Sprenkel, f.n. [ˌvæn dər
'sprɛŋkl] (van dĕr sprénkl)
Vanbrugh, f.n. ['vænbrə] (vánbră)
Vanburgh, f.n. ['vænbrə] (vánbră)
Vance, f.n. [væns] (vanss); [vɑns] (vaanss)
Vandam, f.n. [væn'dæm] (vandám)
Vandepeer, f.n. [ˌvændɪ'pɪər] (vandĕ-
peér)
Vanderbyl, f.n. ['vændərbaɪl] (vándĕrbíl)
Vanderplank, f.n. ['vændərplæŋk] (ván-
dĕrplank)
Vandyck, f.n. [væn'daɪk] (vandík)
Vange [vændʒ] (vanj)
Vanneck, f.n. [væn'ek] (vanéck)
Vans Colina, f.n. [ˌvænz kə'linə] (vanz
kŏleénă)
Vansittart, f.n. [væn'sɪtərt] (van-síttărt)
Appropriate also for the Barony of ~.
Varah, f.n. ['vɑrə] (vaáră)
Varley, f.n. ['vɑrlɪ] (vaárli)
Varndell, f.n. [vɑrn'del] (vaarndéll)
Varnel, f.n. [vɑr'nel] (vaarnéll)
Varteg, *Glamorgan, Monmouth.* ['vɑrteg]
(vaárteg)

Vasey, *f.n.* ['veɪzɪ] (váyzi)
Vaternish *see* Waternish.
Vatersay ['vætərseɪ] (váttĕrssay)
Vaudin, *f.n.* ['voʊdɪn] (vṓdin)
Vaughan, *f.n.* [vɔn] (vawn)
Vaughan Williams, Ralph, *composer* ['reɪf 'vɔn 'wɪljəmz] (ráyf váwn wíl-yämz)
Vaus, *f.n.* [vɔs] (vawss)
Vautor, Thomas, *16-17th-c. composer* ['voʊtər] (vṓtor)
Vaux, *f.n.* [vɔks] (vawks); [voʊ] (vō); [vɒks] (vocks)
Vaux of Harrowden, *Baron* ['vɒks əv 'hærʊdən] (váwks ŏv hárrṓdĕn)
Vauxhall ['vɒksɒl] (vócksawl); ['vɒkshɒl] (vócks-hawl)
Vavasour, *f.n.* ['vævəsər] (vávvässŭr)
Vavasseur, *f.n.* [ˌvævə'sɜr] (vavvässúr)
Vayne, *f.n.* [veɪn] (vayn)
Vaynol ['vaɪnɒl] (vínoll)
Vaynor ['veɪnər] (váynor); ['vaɪnɔr] (vínor)
Vear, *f.n.* [vɪər] (veer)
Veasey, *f.n.* ['viːzɪ] (veézi)
Vedrenne, *f.n.* [vɪ'dren] (vĕdrén)
Veitch, *f.n.* [viːtʃ] (veetch)
Velindre, *Cardigan., Glamorgan, Pembroke.* [ve'lɪndreɪ] (velíndray) *cf.* Felindre.
Vellenoweth, *f.n.* ['velɪnoʊɪθ] (véllĕnṓĕth); ['velnoʊθ] (vélnōth); [ˌvelɪ'naʊɪθ] (vellĕnów-ĕth); ['velnaʊθ] (véllĕnowth); ['velnəθ] (vélnōth)
Vementry ['vemɪntrɪ] (vémmĕntri)
Venables, *f.n.* ['venəblz] (vénnäblz)
Venediger, *f.n.* [vɪ'nedɪdʒər] (vĕnéddijer)
Veness, *f.n.* [vɪ'nes] (vĕnéss)
Vennachar, *Loch* ['venəxər] (vénnăchăr)
Venner, *f.n.* ['venər] (vénner)
Venning, *f.n.* ['venɪŋ] (vénning)
Venour, *f.n.* ['venər] (vénnŭr); [vɪ'nʊər] (vĕnŏŏr)
Ver, *River* [vɜr] (ver)
Vercoe, *f.n.* ['vɜrkoʊ] (vérkō)
Vercow, *f.n.* [vɜr'koʊ] (verkṓ)
Vercowe, *f.n.* [vɜr'koʊ] (verkṓ)
Vereker, *f.n.* ['verɪkər] (vérrĕker)
Verey, *f.n.* ['vɪərɪ] (veéri)
Verinder, *f.n.* ['verɪndər] (vérrinder)
Verity, *f.n.* ['verɪtɪ] (vérriti)
Verlander, *f.n.* [vər'lændər] (vĕrlánder); ['vɜrləndər] (vérländer)
Vernède, *f.n.* [vər'neɪd] (vĕrnáyd)
Verney, *f.n.* ['vɜrnɪ] (vérni)
Vernon, *f.n.* ['vɜrnən] (vérnŏn)
Verrells, *f.n.* ['verəlz] (vérrĕlz)
Verschoyle, *f.n.* ['vɜrskɔɪl] (vérsskoyl)
Vertigan, *f.n.* ['vɜrtɪgən] (vértigän)
Verulam, *Earl of* ['verʊləm] (vérrŏŏläm)
Verulamium, *Roman site near St. Albans* [ˌverʊ'leɪmɪəm] (verrŏŏláy-miŭm)
Veryan ['verɪən] (vérri-ăn)
Vesey, *f.n.* ['viːzɪ] (veézi)

Vesian, *f.n.* ['veziən] (vézzi-ăn)
Vesselo, *f.n.* [vɪ'seloʊ] (vĕsséllō)
Vevers, *f.n.* ['vivərz] (veévĕrz)
Veysey, *f.n.* ['veɪzɪ] (váyzi)
Vezin, *f.n.* ['vizɪn] (veézin)
Via Gellia ['vaɪə 'dʒeliə] (víə-ă jélli-ă)
Vialls, *f.n.* ['vaɪəlz] (ví-älz); ['vaɪɒlz] (ví-awlz)
Viant, *f.n.* ['vaɪənt] (ví-änt)
Vibart, *f.n.* ['vaɪbərt] (víbärt)
Vidal, *f.n.* ['vaɪdl] (vídl)
Videan, *f.n.* ['vɪdɪən] (víddi-ăn)
Vidler, *f.n.* ['vɪdlər] (víddler)
Vigar, *f.n.* ['vaɪgər] (vígăr); ['vaɪgɑr] (vígaar)
Vigay ['vaɪgeɪ] (vígay)
Vigers, *f.n.* ['vaɪgərz] (vígĕrz)
Vigne, *f.n.* [vaɪn] (vīn)
Vignes, *f.n.* [vɪnz] (veenz)
Vignoles, *f.n.* ['vɪnjoʊlz] (vín-yōlz); ['vɪnjoʊlz] (veén-yōlz); ['vɪnjoʊl] (veén-yōl); [vɪn'joʊlz] (vin-yṓlz); ['vɪnjɒlz] (veén-yollz)
Vigo Inn, *Kent* ['vaɪgoʊ] (vígō)
Vigor, *f.n.* ['vaɪgɔr] (vígor)
Vigurs, *f.n.* ['vaɪgərz] (vígŭrz); ['vɪgərz] (víggŭrz)
Villiers, *f.n.* ['vɪlərz] (víllĕrz); ['vɪljərz] (víl-yĕrz) *The first is appropriate for the family name of the Earl of Clarendon and of the Earl of Jersey, for Viscount ~ and for Baron de ~.*
Vinaver, *f.n.* [vɪ'nɑvər] (vinaáver)
Vincent, *f.n. and C.n.* ['vɪnsənt] (vínssĕnt)
Viner, *f.n.* ['vaɪnər] (víner)
Vinerian, *pertaining to Viner* [vaɪ'nɪərɪən] (vīneéri-ăn) *Appropriate for the ~ common law professorship and fellowships at the University of Oxford.*
Viney Hill ['vaɪnɪ 'hɪl] (víni híll)
Vintcent, *f.n.* ['vɪnsənt] (vínssĕnt)
Vinter, *f.n.* ['vɪntər] (vínter)
Vintner, *f.n.* ['vɪntnər] (víntner)
Viollet, *f.n.* ['vaɪəlɪt] (ví-ŏlĕt)
Vipont, *f.n.* ['vaɪpɒnt] (vípont)
Virginia Water [vər'dʒɪnɪə 'wɔtər] (virjínni-ă wáwter)
Viveash, *f.n.* ['vaɪvæʃ] (vívash)
Vivian, *f.n.* ['vɪvɪən] (vívvi-ăn)
Vizard, *f.n.* ['vɪzɑrd] (vízzaard)
Vley, *f.n.* [vleɪ] (vlay)
Voelcker, *f.n.* ['voʊlkər] (vṓlker)
Vogel, *f.n.* ['voʊgl] (vṓgl)
Vogt, *f.n.* [voʊkt] (vōkt); [voʊt] (vōt); [vɒt] (vott)
Vogue Beloth ['voʊg bɪ'lɒθ] (vṓg bĕlóth)
Voigt, *f.n.* [vɔɪt] (voyt)
Voisey, *f.n.* ['vɔɪzɪ] (vóyzi)
Volante, *f.n.* [və'læntɪ] (vŏlánti)
Volckman, *f.n.* ['vɒlkmən] (vólkmăn)
Volk, *f.n.* [vɒlk] (volk); [voʊlk] (vōlk) *The first is appropriate for ~'s Railway at Brighton.*
Volze, *f.n.* [voʊlz] (vōlz)

Von der Heyde, *f.n.* ['vɒndərhaɪd] (vónděr-hīd)

Von Stranz, *f.n.* [vɒn 'strænz] (von stránz)

Vortigern, *5th-c. king of the Britons* ['vɔːtɪgɜːrn] (vórtigĕrn)

Vos, *f.n.* [vɒs] (voss)

Vosburgh, *f.n.* ['vɒsbərə] (vóssbŭrǎ)

Voss, *f.n.* [vɒs] (voss)

Voules, *f.n.* [voʊlz] (vōlz); [vaʊlz] (vowlz)

Vowden, *f.n.* ['vaʊdən] (vówdĕn)

Vowles, *f.n.* [voʊlz] (vōlz); [vaʊlz] (vowlz)

Voysey, *f.n.* ['vɔɪzɪ] (vóyzi)

Vroncysyllte *see* Froncysyllte.

Vuller, *f.n.* ['vʊlər] (vŏŏler)

Vulliamy, *f.n.* ['vʌljəmɪ] (vúl-yǎmi) *Appropriate also for Benjamin Lewis ~, 18th-c. clock-maker.*

Vyrnwy, River ['vɜːrnuɪ] (vérnŏŏ-i)

Vyse, *f.n.* [vaɪz] (vīz)

Vyvyan, *f.n.* ['vɪvɪən] (vívvi-ǎn)

W

Wacey, *f.n.* ['weɪsɪ] (wáyssi)

Wach, *f.n.* [wɒtʃ] (wotch)

Wacher, *f.n.* ['wætʃər] (wátcher)

Wacton ['wæktən] (wácktŏn)

Waddell, *f.n.* ['wɒdl] (woddl); [wə'del] (wŏdéll)

Waddesdon ['wɒdzdən] (wódzdŏn)

Waddicor, *f.n.* ['wɒdɪkɔr] (wóddikor)

Waddilove, *f.n.* ['wɒdɪlʌv] (wóddiluv)

Waddon ['wɒdən] (wóddŏn)

Wade, *f.n.* [weɪd] (wayd)

Wadebridge ['weɪdbrɪdʒ] (wáydbrij)

Wadeford ['wɒdfərd] (wódfŏrd)

Wadham College, *University of Oxford* ['wɒdəm] (wóddǎm)

Wadsley, *f.n.* ['wɒdzlɪ] (wódzli)

Wadsworth, *f.n.* ['wɒdzwərθ] (wódz-wŭrth)

Waechter, *f.n.* ['veɪktər] (váykter)

Waenavon [waɪn'ævən] (wīnávvŏn)

Waenfawr, *also spelt* Waunfawr ['waɪnvaʊər] (wínvowr)

Waghen *see* Wawne.

Wagner, *f.n.* ['wægnər] (wágner)

Wahab, *f.n.* [wɒb] (wawb)

Wainfleet ['weɪnfliːt] (wáynfleet)

Wainwright, *f.n.* ['weɪnraɪt] (wáynrīt)

Waites, *f.n.* [weɪts] (wayts)

Waithman, *f.n.* ['weɪθmən] (wáythmǎn)

Wake, *f.n.* [weɪk] (wayk)

Wakefield, *f.n.* ['weɪkfiːld] (wáykfeeld)

Wakeling, *f.n.* ['weɪklɪŋ] (wáykling)

Wakering, Great *and* Little ['weɪkərɪŋ] (wáykĕring)

Wakes Colne ['weɪks 'koʊn] (wáyks kŏn)

Wakley, *f.n.* ['wæklɪ] (wáckli); ['werklɪ] (wáykli) *The first is considered appropriate for Thomas ~, 19th-c. surgeon, founder of* The Lancet.

Walberswick ['wɔlbərzwɪk] (wáwlbĕrz-wick)

Walcot, *f.n.* ['wɒlkɒt] (wáwlkott)

Walcote ['wɒlkoʊt] (wáwlkŏt)

Waldegrave, *f.n.* ['wɒlgreɪv] (wáwl-grayv); ['wɒldɪgreɪv] (wáwldĕgrayv) *The first is appropriate for Earl ~.*

Walden, *f.n.* ['wɒldən] (wáwldĕn); ['wɒldən] (wóldĕn)

Waldo, *C.n.* ['wɒldoʊ] (wáwldŏ)

Waldron, *f.n.* ['wɒldrən] (wáwldrŏn)

Waleran, *Barony of* ['wɒlrən] (wáwlrǎn)

Walesby ['weɪlzbɪ] (wáylzbi)

Waley, *f.n.* ['weɪlɪ] (wáyli)

Walford, *f.n.* ['wɒlfərd] (wáwlfŏrd); ['wɒlfərd] (wólfŏrd)

Walhampton ['wɒl'hæmptən] (wáwl-hámptŏn)

Walkden ['wɔkdən] (wáwkdĕn)

Walker, *f.n.* ['wɔkər] (wáwker)

Walkerdine, *f.n.* ['wɔkərdin] (wáwkĕr-deen)

Walkham, River ['wɒlkəm] (wáwlkǎm)

Walkley ['wɒklɪ] (wáwkli)

Wall, *f.n.* [wɒl] (wawl)

Walla, *f.n.* ['wɒlə] (wóllǎ)

Wallace, *f.n.* ['wɒlɪs] (wólliss)

Wallach, *f.n.* ['wɒlək] (wóllǎk); ['wɒlə] (wóllǎ)

Wallage, *f.n.* ['wɒlɪdʒ] (wóllij)

Wallasey ['wɒləsɪ] (wóllǎssi)

Waller, *f.n.* ['wɒlər] (wóller); ['wɒlər] (wáwler)

Wallich, *f.n.* ['wɒlɪk] (wóllick)

Walliker, *f.n.* ['wɒlɪkər] (wólliker)

Wallinger, *f.n.* ['wɒlɪndʒər] (wóllinjer)

Wallington ['wɒlɪŋtən] (wóllingtŏn)

Wallis, *f.n.* ['wɒlɪs] (wólliss)

Wallop, *f.n.* ['wɒləp] (wóllŏp)

Wallop ['wɒləp] (wóllŏp)

Wallsend ['wɔlz'end] (wáwlzénd)

Walmer ['wɒlmər] (wáwlmer)

Walmersley ['wɒmzlɪ] (wáwmzli)

Walmesley, *f.n.* ['wɒmzlɪ] (wáwmzli)

Walmisley, *f.n.* ['wɒmzlɪ] (wáwmzli)

Walmsley, *f.n.* ['wɒmzlɪ] (wáwmzli)

Walne, *f.n.* [wɒn] (wawn)

Walrond, *f.n.* ['wɒlrənd] (wáwlrŏnd)

Walsall ['wɒlsl] (wawlssl); ['wɒlsol] (wáwlssawl); ['wɒsl] (wawssl)

Walsden ['wɒlzdən] (wáwlzdĕn)

Walsh, *f.n.* [wɒlʃ] (wawlsh); [wɒlʃ] (wolsh); [welʃ] (welsh)

Walsham, North *and* South ['wɒlʃəm] (wáwl-shǎm)

Walsingham, *Baron* ['wɒlsɪŋəm] (wáwl-ssing-ǎm)

Walsingham, Great *and* Little ['wɒlzɪŋəm] (wáwlzing-ǎm)

Walsoken ['wɒlsoʊkən] (wáwlssŏkĕn)

Walston, f.n. ['wolstən] (wáwlsstŏn)
Appropriate also for Baron ~.
Walsworth, f.n. ['wolzwərθ] (wáwlz-würth)
Walter, f.n. and C.n. ['woltər] (wáwlter)
Walters, f.n. ['woltərz] (wáwltĕrz)
Waltham, f.n. ['wolθəm] (wáwl-thăm)
Waltham, *Lincs.* ['wolθəm] (wáwl-thăm)
Waltham, Great *and* Little ['woltəm] (wáwltăm)
Waltham, North ['wolθəm] (wáwl-thăm)
Waltham Abbey ['wolθəm 'æbɪ] (wáwl-thăm ábbi)
Waltham Cross ['wolθəm 'krɒs] (wáwl-thăm króss)
Waltham St. Lawrence ['wolθəm snt 'lɒrəns] (wáwl-thăm sĭnt lórrĕnss)
Waltham-on-the-Wolds ['wolθəm ɒn ðə 'woʊldz] (wáwl-thăm on thē wŏldz)
Walthamstow ['wolθəmstoʊ] (wáwl-thămsstō)
Walthew, f.n. ['wolθju] (wáwl-thew)
Walton, f.n. ['woltən] (wáwltŏn)
Walwick ['wɒlɪk] (wóllick); ['wolwɪk] (wáwlwick)
Walwyn, f.n. ['wolwɪn] (wáwlwin)
Wamil Hall, *Suffolk* ['wɒmɪl] (wómmil)
Wamphray ['wɒmfreɪ] (wómfray)
Wand, f.n. [wɒnd] (wond)
Wands, f.n. [wɒndz] (wondz)
Wandsworth ['wɒndzwərθ] (wóndzwürth)
Wanlip ['wɒnlɪp] (wónn-lip)
Wanlockhead [ˌwɒnlɒk'hed] (wonnlock-héd)
Wann, f.n. [wɒn] (wonn)
Wannop, f.n. ['wɒnəp] (wónnŏp)
Wansbeck, River ['wɒnzbek] (wónnz-beck)
Wansbeck Parliamentary Division ['wɒnzbek] (wónnzbeck)
Wansborough, f.n. ['wɒnzbərə] (wónnz-bŭră)
Wansbrough, f.n. ['wɒnzbrə] (wónnzbră)
Wansey, f.n. ['wɒnzɪ] (wónnzi)
Wansford ['wɒnzfərd] (wónnzfŏrd)
Wanstall, f.n. ['wɒnstɒl] (wónsstawl)
Wantage, f.n. ['wɒntɪdʒ] (wónntij)
Wantage ['wɒntɪdʒ] (wónntij)
Wantisden ['wɒntsdən] (wónntsdĕn)
Wapping ['wɒpɪŋ] (wópping)
Wapping Old Stairs [ˌwɒpɪŋ 'oʊld stɛərz] (wopping ŏld stairz)
Warbeck, f.n. ['wɔrbek] (wáwrbeck)
Warbstow ['wɔrbstoʊ] (wáwrbsstō)
Warburg Institute ['wɔrbɜrg] (wáwr-burg)
Warburton, f.n. ['wɔrbərtən] (wáwr-bŭrtŏn)
Warcop ['wɔrkəp] (wáwrkŏp)
Ward, f.n. [wɔrd] (wawrd)
Wardell, f.n. [wɔr'del] (wawrdéll)
Wardhaugh, f.n. ['wɔrdhɔ] (wáwrd-haw)
Waren Burn ['wɛərən] (wáirĕn)

Waren Mills ['wɛərən 'mɪlz] (wáirĕn míllz)
Warenford ['wɛərənfɔrd] (wáirĕn-ford)
Warenton ['wɛərəntən] (wáirĕntŏn)
Warham, *William*, *15-16th-c. archbishop of Canterbury* ['wɒrəm] (wórrăm)
Waring, f.n. ['wɛərɪŋ] (wáiring)
Waring ['wɛərɪŋ] (wáiring)
Waringstown ['wɛərɪŋztaʊn] (wáiringz-town)
Wark [wɔrk] (wawrk)
Warkleigh ['wɔrklɪ] (wáwrkli)
Warkworth, f.n. ['wɔrkwərθ] (wáwrk-würth)
Warkworth ['wɔrkwərθ] (wáwrkwürth)
Appropriate also for Baron ~.
Warleggan [wɔr'legən] (wawrléggăn)
Warlock, f.n. ['wɔrlɒk] (wáwrlock)
Warman, f.n. ['wɔrmən] (wáwrmăn)
Warmsworth ['wɔrmzwɜrθ] (wáwrmz-wurth)
Warmwell ['wɔrmwel] (wáwrmwel)
Warncken, f.n. ['wɔrŋkɪn] (wáwrnkĕn)
Warner, f.n. ['wɔrnər] (wáwrner)
Warnham, f.n. ['wɔrnəm] (wáwrnăm)
Warr, f.n. [wɔr] (wawr)
Warre, f.n. [wɔr] (wawr)
Warrell, f.n. ['wɒrəl] (wórrĕl)
Warren, f.n. ['wɒrən] (wórrĕn)
Warrick, f.n. ['wɒrɪk] (wórrick)
Warrin, f.n. ['wɒrɪn] (wórrin)
Warsash ['wɔrsæʃ] (wáwrssash); ['wɔrzæʃ] (wáwrzash)
Warter, f.n. ['wɔrtər] (wáwrter)
Wartle ['wɔrtl] (wawrtl)
Wartling ['wɔrtlɪŋ] (wáwrtling)
Warton, f.n. ['wɔrtən] (wáwrtŏn)
Warwick, f.n. ['wɒrɪk] (wórrick)
Warwick ['wɒrɪk] (wórrick) *Appropriate also for the Earl of ~.*
Wasdale, *also spelt* Wastdale ['wɒsdl] (wossdl) Wastdale *is the ecclesiastical spelling.*
Wasdale Head, *also spelt* Wastdale Head ['wɒsdl 'hed] (wóssdl héd)
Wash, f.n. [wɒʃ] (wosh)
Washbourne, f.n. ['wɒʃbɔrn] (wóshborn)
Wasson, f.n. ['wɒsən] (wóssŏn)
Wastell, f.n. ['wɒstl] (wosstl)
Wastie, f.n. ['wæstɪ] (wássti)
Wastwater ['wɒstwɔtər] (wósstwawter)
Watendlath [wɒ'tendləθ] (wotténdlăth)
Water of Feugh ['wɒtər əv 'fjux] (wáwter ŏv féwch)
Waterden ['wɒtərdən] (wáwtĕrdĕn)
Waterloo [ˌwɒtər'lu] (wawtĕrlóo)
Waterman, f.n. ['wɒtərmən] (wáwtĕr-măn)
Waternish, *also spelt* Vaternish ['wɒtərnɪʃ] (wáwtĕrnish)
Waterrow ['wɒtəroʊ] (wáwtĕrō)
Waters, f.n. ['wɒtərz] (wáwtĕrz)
Watford ['wɒtfərd] (wóttfŏrd)
Wath [wɒθ] (woth)

Wath upon Dearne [ˈwɒθ əpɒn ˈdɜrn] (wóth ŭpon dérn); [ˈwæθ əpɒn ˈdɜrn] (wáth ŭpon dérn)

Wathen, *f.n.* [ˈwɒθən] (wóthĕn)

Watherston, *f.n.* [ˈwɒθərstən] (wóthĕr-stŏn)

Wathes, *f.n.* [ˈwɒθɪz] (wóthĕz)

Watkin, *f.n.* [ˈwɒtkɪn] (wóttkin)

Watkins, *f.n.* [ˈwɒtkɪnz] (wóttkinz)

Watling, *f.n.* [ˈwɒtlɪŋ] (wóttling)

Watling Street [ˈwɒtlɪŋ strit] (wóttling street)

Watmough, *f.n.* [ˈwɒtmoʊ] (wóttmō)

Watney, *f.n.* [ˈwɒtnɪ] (wóttni)

Watrous, *f.n.* [ˈwɒtrəs] (wótrŭss)

Watson, *f.n.* [ˈwɒtsən] (wótssŏn)

Watt, *f.n.* [wɒt] (wott)

Watten [ˈwɒtən] (wóttĕn); [ˈwætən] (wáttĕn)

Watters, *f.n.* [ˈwɔtərz] (wáwtĕrz); [ˈwɒtərz] (wóttĕrz)

Watthews, *f.n.* [ˈwɒθjuz] (wáw-thewz)

Wattis, *f.n.* [ˈwɒtɪs] (wóttiss)

Wattisfield [ˈwɒtɪsfɪld] (wóttisfeeld)

Wattisham [ˈwɒtɪʃəm] (wótti-shăm)

Watton [ˈwɒtən] (wóttŏn)

Watts, *f.n.* [wɒts] (wotts)

Wattstown [ˈwɒtstaʊn] (wóttstown)

Wauchope, *f.n.* [ˈwɒxəp] (wóchŏp); [ˈwokəp] (wáwkŏp)

Waugh, *f.n.* [wɔ] (waw); [wɒx] (woch); [wɒf] (woff); [wɑf] (waaf)

Waunarlwydd [waɪnˈɑrlʊɪð] (wīnaárlŏŏ-ith)

Waunfawr *see* Waenfawr.

Waun-lwydd [waɪnˈlʊɪð] (wīn-lŏŏ-ith)

Waun-pound [waɪnˈpaʊnd] (wīnpównd)

Wauthier, *f.n.* [ˈvoʊtjeɪ] (vŏt-yay)

Wavell, *f.n.* [ˈweɪvl] (wayvl) *Appropriate also for the Earldom of* ~.

Wavendon [ˈwævəndən] (wávvĕndŏn)

Waveney, River [ˈweɪvənɪ] (wáyvĕni)

Waverley [ˈweɪvərlɪ] (wáyvĕrli)

Wavertree [ˈweɪvərtri] (wáyvĕrtree)

Wawne, *also spelt* **Waghen** [wɒn] (wawn)

Weacombe [ˈwiːkəm] (weékŏm)

Weal, *f.n.* [wil] (weel)

Wealdstone [ˈwildstoʊn] (weéldsstŏn)

Wealeson, *f.n.* [ˈwilsən] (weélssŏn)

Wear, River [wɪər] (weer)

Weardale [ˈwɪərdeɪl] (weérdayl)

Wearde [weərd] (waird)

Weare Giffard [ˈwɪər ˈdʒɪfərd] (weér jíffărd)

Wearing, *f.n.* [ˈweərɪŋ] (waíring)

Wearn, *f.n.* [wɜrn] (wern)

Wearne, *f.n.* [wɜrn] (wern)

Wearne [weərn] (wairn); [wɪərn] (weern); [wɜrn] (wern)

Weasenham All Saints [ˈwizənəm ɔl ˈseɪnts] (weézĕnăm awl sáynts)

Weasenham St. Peter [ˈwizənəm snt ˈpitər] (weézĕnăm sĭnt peéter)

Weaste [wist] (weesst)

Weaverham [ˈwivərhæm] (weévĕr-ham)

Webb, *f.n.* [web] (webb)

Webber, *f.n.* [ˈwebər] (wébber)

Weber, *f.n.* [ˈwebər] (wébber); [ˈwibər] (weéber)

Webster, *f.n.* [ˈwebstər] (wébsster)

Weddell, *f.n.* [ˈwedl] (weddl); [wɪˈdel] (wĕdéll)

Wedgewood, *f.n.* [ˈwedʒwʊd] (wéjwŏŏd)

Wedgwood, *f.n.* [ˈwedʒwʊd] (wéjwŏŏd) *Appropriate for Josiah and Thomas* ~, *18th-c. potters.*

Wednesbury [ˈwenzbərɪ] (wénzbŭri); [ˈwedʒbərɪ] (wéjbŭri)

Wednesfield [ˈwensfɪld] (wénssfeeld); [ˈwedʒfɪld] (wéjfeeld)

Weeks, *f.n.* [wiks] (weeks)

Weelkes, Thomas, *16th-c. organist and composer* [wilks] (weelks)

Weem [wim] (weem)

Wegg, *f.n.* [weg] (wegg)

Weguelin, *f.n.* [ˈwegəlɪn] (wéggĕlin)

Weidenfeld and Nicolson, George, *publishers* [ˈvaɪdənfelt ənd ˈnɪklsən] (vídĕnfelt ănd nícklssŏn)

Weigal, *f.n.* [ˈwaɪgl] (wígl)

Weigall, *f.n.* [ˈwaɪgəl] (wígawl); [ˈwaɪgl] (wígl)

Weighill, *f.n.* [ˈweɪhɪl] (wáyhil)

Weight, *f.n.* [weɪt] (wayt)

Weightman, *f.n.* [ˈweɪtmən] (wáytmăn)

Weil, *f.n.* [wil] (weel); [vaɪl] (vīl)

Weiland, *f.n.* [ˈwilənd] (weéländ)

Weiner, *f.n.* [ˈwaɪnər] (wíner)

Weipers, *f.n.* [ˈwaɪpərz] (wípĕrz)

Weir, *f.n.* [wɪər] (weer)

Weis, *f.n.* [wis] (weess)

Weisdale [ˈwizdeɪl] (weézdayl)

Weisner, *f.n.* [ˈwiznər] (weézner)

Weist, *f.n.* [wist] (weesst)

Weitz, *f.n.* [wits] (weets)

Weitzman, *f.n.* [ˈwaɪtsmən] (wítsmăn)

Welbourne, *f.n.* [ˈwelbɔrn] (wélborn)

Welch, *f.n.* [weltʃ] (weltch); [welʃ] (welsh)

Weldon, *f.n.* [ˈweldən] (wéldŏn)

Wellbeloved, *f.n.* [ˈwelbɪlʌvd] (wélbĕluvd)

Weller, *f.n.* [ˈwelər] (wéller)

Wellesbourne [ˈwelzbɔrn] (wélzborn)

Wellesley, *f.n.* [ˈwelzlɪ] (wélzli) *Appropriate also for Viscount* ~.

Wellesz, Egon, *composer and musicologist* [ˈeɪgɒn ˈvelɪs] (áygon vélléss)

Wellingborough [ˈwelɪŋbərə] (wélling-bŭră)

Wellington, *f.n.* [ˈwelɪŋtən] (wéllingtŏn)

Wellington [ˈwelɪŋtən] (wéllingtŏn) *Appropriate also for the Duke of* ~.

Wellman, *f.n.* [ˈwelmən] (wélmăn)

Wells, *f.n.* [welz] (wellz)

Welnetham *see* Whelnetham.

Welsh, *f.n.* [welʃ] (welsh)

Welshpool [ˈwelʃpul] (wélshpool); [ˈwelʃpul] (wélsh-poól)

Welwick [ˈwelɪk] (wéllick)

Welwyn [ˈwelɪn] (wéllin)

Welwyn Garden City ['welɪn] (wéllin)
Wem [wem] (wemm)
Wembley ['wemblɪ] (wémbli)
Wemyss [wimz] (weemz) *Appropriate also for the Earl of ~.*
Wemyss Bay ['wimz 'beɪ] (weémz báy)
Wendon, f.n. ['wendən] (wéndŏn)
Wendron ['wendrən] (wéndrŏn)
Wenffrwd Bridge ['wenfrud] (wénfrood)
Wenger, f.n. ['weŋər] (wéng-er)
Wenninger, f.n. ['wenɪndʒər] (wénninjer)
Wensley ['wenzlɪ] (wénzli)
Wensleydale ['wenzlɪdeɪl] (wénzlidayl) *Appropriate also for ~ cheese and for the ~ breed of sheep.*
Wensum, River ['wensəm] (wénssŭm)
Wentworth, f.n. ['wentwərθ] (wéntwŭrth); ['wentwɜrθ] (wéntwurth)
Wentzel, f.n. ['wentsl] (wentssl)
Wenvoe ['wenvoʊ] (wénvō)
Weobley ['weblɪ] (wébli)
Weoley Castle, *Warwick.* ['wɪəlɪ] (weé-ŏli)
Werner, f.n. ['wɜrnər] (wérner); ['wɔrnər] (wáwrner)
Werneth ['wɜrnəθ] (wérnĕth)
Wernher, f.n. ['wɜrnər] (wérner)
Wernick, f.n. ['wɜrnɪk] (wérnick)
Wern Tarw ['wɛərn 'tæru] (waírn tárroo)
Wesham ['wesəm] (wéssăm)
Weske, f.n. [wesk] (wessk)
Wesker, f.n. ['weskər] (wéssker)
Wesley, f.n. ['weslɪ] (wéssli) *Appropriate for John ~, 18th-c. evangelist and leader of Methodism, and his brother Charles.*
Wesleyan, pertaining to John and Charles Wesley ['weslɪən] (wéssli-ăn)
Wess, f.n. [wes] (wess)
West Alvington ['west 'ɒlvɪŋtən] (wést áwlvingtŏn)
West Bromwich ['west 'brɒmɪtʃ] (wést brómmitch)
West Calder ['west 'kɔldər] (wést káwlder)
West Challow ['west 'tʃæloʊ] (wést chálō)
West Freugh ['west 'frux] (wést froóch)
West Hartlepool ['west 'hɑrtlɪpul] (wést haártlipool)
West Heslerton ['west 'heslərtən] (wést hésslĕrtŏn)
West Hoathly ['west hoʊθ'laɪ] (wést hŏth-líˈ)
West Horsley ['west 'hɔrzlɪ] (wést hórzli)
West Lavington ['west 'lævɪŋtən] (wést lávvingtŏn)
West Lockinge ['west 'lɒkɪndʒ] (wést lóckinj)
West Lothian ['west 'loʊðɪən] (wést lṓthiăn)
West Malling ['west 'mɒlɪŋ] (wést máwling)
West Meon ['west 'miən] (wést meé-ŏn)

West Mersea ['west 'mɜrzɪ] (wést mérzi)
West Molesey ['west 'moʊlzɪ] (wést mṓlzi)
West Penwith ['west pen'wɪθ] (wést penwíth)
West Somerton ['west 'sʌmərtən] (wést súmmĕrtŏn)
West Stoughton ['west 'stɔtən] (wést' stáwtŏn)
West Wycombe ['west 'wɪkəm] (wést wíckŏm)
Westaby, f.n. ['westəbɪ] (wésstăbi)
Westacott, f.n. ['westəkɒt] (wésstăkot)
Westall, f.n. ['westɔl] (wésstawl)
Westbrook, f.n. ['westbrʊk] (wésstbroŏk)
Westcott, f.n. ['westkət] (wésstkŏt); ['weskət] (wésskŏt)
Westenra, f.n. ['westənrə] (wésstĕnră)
Westerglen ['westərglen] (wésstĕrglen)
Westgate, f.n. ['westgeɪt] (wésstgayt); ['westgɪt] (wésstgit)
Westhoughton ['west'hotən] (wést-háwtŏn)
Westleton ['weslton] (wéssltŏn)
Westmeath, Earl of [west'mið] (wesst-meéth)
Westminster ['wesminstər] (wésstminster)
Westmorland ['wesmərlənd] (wésstmŏrlánd) *Appropriate also for the Earl of ~.*
Westoby, f.n. ['westəbɪ] (wésstŏbi); [wes'toʊbɪ] (wesstṓbi)
Weston, f.n. ['westən] (wésstŏn)
Weston Bampfylde ['westən 'bæmfɪld] (wésstŏn bámfeeld)
Weston Favell ['westən 'feɪvl] (wésstŏn fáyvl)
Weston Zoyland ['westən 'zɔɪlənd] (wésstŏn zóylánd)
Weston-super-Mare ['westən ˌsjupər 'mɛər] (wésstŏn sewpĕr maír); ['westən ˌsjupər 'mɛərɪ] (wésstŏn sewpĕr maíri)
Westoning ['westənɪŋ] (wésstŏning)
Westray ['westreɪ] (wésstray)
Westruther ['westrʌðər] (wésstruther)
Westward [west'wɔrd] (wesst-wáwrd)
Westwater, f.n. ['westwotər] (wésstwawter)
Westwick ['westwɪk] (wésstwick)
Westwoodside ['westwʊdsaɪd] (wésstwoŏd-sīd)
Wetton, f.n. ['wetən] (wéttŏn)
Wetwang ['wetwæŋ] (wétwang)
Wevill, f.n. ['wevɪl] (wévvil)
Weybourne ['webərn] (wébbŭrn)
Weyman, f.n. ['weɪmən] (wáymăn) *Appropriate for Stanley J. ~, author.*
Weymouth ['weɪməθ] (wáymŭth) *Appropriate also for Viscount ~.*
Whaley Bridge ['weɪlɪ 'brɪdʒ] (wáyli bríj)
Whalley, f.n. ['hwɒlɪ] (whólli); ['hwɒlɪ] (wháwli); ['weɪlɪ] (wáyli)
Whalley ['hwɒlɪ] (wháwli)

Whalley Range ['wɒlɪ 'reɪndʒ] (wólli ráynj)

Whalsay ['ʍɔlseɪ] (wháwlssay)

Whannel, *f.n.* ['ʍɒnl] (whonnl); [wɒ'nel] (wonnéll)

Whaplode ['ʍɒploʊd] (whóp-lōd)

Wharam, *f.n.* ['ʍɛərəm] (whaírăm)

Wharncliffe, *Earl of* ['wornklɪf] (wórnkliff)

Wharram ['wɒrəm] (wórrăm)

Whateley, *f.n.* ['ʍeɪtlɪ] (wháytli)

Whatley, *f.n.* ['ʍɒtlɪ] (whóttli)

Whatling, *f.n.* ['ʍɒtlɪŋ] (wóttling)

Whatmough, *f.n.* ['ʍɒtmoʊ] (whóttmō)

Whatsley, *f.n.* ['wɒtslɪ] (wóttsli)

Whatstandwell [wɒt'stændwel] (wottstándwel)

Whatton, *f.n.* ['wɒtən] (wóttŏn)

Whatton ['wɒtən] (wóttŏn)

Wheadon, *f.n.* ['wɪdən] (weédŏn)

Wheare, *f.n.* [ʍɛər] (whair)

Wheatacre ['ʍɪtəkər] (whíttăker)

Wheathampstead ['ʍwetəmsted] (whéttámssted); ['ʍwitəmsted] (wheétámssted)

Wheatley, *f.n.* ['ʍɪtlɪ] (wheétli)

Wheatstone, *f.n.* ['ʍwitstən] (wheétstŏn)

Wheeler, *f.n.* ['ʍwilər] (wheéler)

Whelan, *f.n.* ['ʍwilən] (wheélăn)

Wheldon, *f.n.* ['ʍweldən] (wéldŏn)

Whelen, *f.n.* ['ʍwilən] (wheélĕn)

Whelnetham, *also spelt* **Welnetham** [wel'niθəm] (welneéthăm); ['welnetəm] (wélnettăm)

Wherstead ['wɜrsted] (wérssted)

Wherwell ['ʍwɜrwel] (whér-wel)

Wheway, *f.n.* ['ʍwiweɪ] (wheéway)

Whewell, *f.n.* ['hjuəl] (héw-ĕl)

Whibley, *f.n.* ['ʍwiblɪ] (whíbbli)

Whichcote, *f.n.* ['ʍwɪtʃkoʊt] (whítch-kōt)

Whicher, *f.n.* ['wɪtʃər] (wítcher)

Whicker, *f.n.* ['wɪkər] (wícker)

Whiddett, *f.n.* [wɪ'det] (widétt)

Whiffen, *f.n.* ['wɪfm] (wiffĕn)

Whiffin, *f.n.* ['wɪfm] (wíffin)

Whiffing, *f.n.* ['wɪfɪŋ] (wíffing)

Whigham, *f.n.* ['ʍwɪɡəm] (whíggăm)

Whilding, *f.n.* ['ʍwaɪldɪŋ] (whílding)

Whiligh ['ʍwaɪlaɪ] (whí-lī)

Whincup, *f.n.* ['wɪŋkəp] (wínkŭp)

Whinerey, *f.n.* ['ʍwɪnərɪ] (whínnĕri); ['ʍwɪnreɪ] (whínray)

Whipsnade ['ʍwɪpsneɪd] (whíp-snayd)

Whissendine ['ʍwɪsəndaɪn] (whíssĕndin)

Whistlefield ['ʍwɪslfɪld] (whísslfeeld)

Whitaker, *f.n.* ['ʍwɪtəkər] (whíttăker) *Appropriate for* ~ *'s Almanac.*

Whitbread, *f.n.* ['ʍwɪtbred] (whíttbred)

Whitby, *f.n.* ['ʍwɪtbɪ] (whíttbi)

Whitby ['ʍwɪtbɪ] (whíttbi)

Whitcher, *f.n.* ['wɪtʃər] (wítcher)

Whitchurch Canonicorum ['ʍwɪtʃɜrtʃ kə,nɒnɪ'korəm] (whíttchurch kănonnikáwrŭm)

White, *f.n.* [ʍwaɪt] (whīt)

White Colne ['ʍwaɪt 'koʊn] (whīt kōn)

White Waltham ['ʍwaɪt 'wɒlθəm] (whīt wáwl-thăm); ['ʍwaɪt 'wɒltəm] (whīt wáwltăm)

Whiteabbey [ʍwaɪt'æbɪ] (whītábbi)

Whiteadder, River ['ʍwɪtədər] (whíttăder)

Whitear, *f.n.* ['ʍwɪtɪ-ər] (whítti-ăr)

Whitebridge ['ʍwaɪtbrɪdʒ] (whítbrij)

Whitefield, *f.n.* ['ʍwɪtfɪld] (whíttfeeld); ['ʍwaɪtfɪld] (whítfeeld) *The first is appropriate for George* ~, *18th-c. preacher and evangelist, and hence for the* ~ *Memorial Church in London.*

Whitefield, *Lancs.* ['ʍwaɪtfɪld] (whítfeeld)

Whitehall ['ʍwaɪthɒl] (whít-hawl); ['ʍwaɪt'hɒl] (whīt-háwl)

Whitehaugh [ʍwaɪt'hɒ] (whīt-háw)

Whitehaven ['ʍwaɪtheɪvən] (whíthayvĕn)

Whitehead, *f.n.* ['ʍwaɪthed] (whít-hed)

Whitehead [ʍwaɪt'hed] (whīt-héd)

Whitehorn, *f.n.* ['ʍwaɪthɔrn] (whíthorn)

Whitehouse [ʍwaɪt'haʊs] (whīt-hówss)

Whiteley, *f.n.* ['ʍwaɪtlɪ] (whítli)

Whitelock, *f.n.* ['ʍwaɪtlɒk] (whítlock)

Whitemoor ['ʍwaɪtmʊər] (whítmoŏr)

Whiten Head ['ʍwaɪtən'hed] (whítĕn héd)

Whiteside, *f.n.* ['ʍwaɪtsaɪd] (whítsīd)

Whiteslea Lodge, *Norfolk* ['ʍwaɪtslɪ] (whítslee)

Whitestone, *Devon* ['ʍwɪtstən] (whíttstŏn)

Whitestone, *Hereford.* ['ʍwaɪtstoʊn] (whítstōn)

Whitfield, *f.n.* ['ʍwɪtfɪld] (whíttfeeld)

Whitfield ['ʍwɪtfɪld] (whíttfeeld)

Whithorn ['ʍwɪthɔrn] (whítt-horn)

Whiting, *f.n.* ['ʍwaɪtɪŋ] (whíting)

Whiting Bay ['ʍwaɪtɪŋ 'beɪ] (whíting báy)

Whitla Hall, *Queen's University, Belfast* ['ʍwɪtlə] (whíttlă)

Whitley, *f.n.* ['ʍwɪtlɪ] (whíttli)

Whitlock, *f.n.* ['ʍwɪtlɒk] (whíttlock)

Whitmore, *f.n.* ['ʍwɪtmɔr] (whíttmor)

Whitney, *f.n.* ['ʍwɪtnɪ] (whíttni)

Whitred, *f.n.* ['ʍwɪtrɪd] (whíttrĕd)

Whitrow, *f.n.* ['ʍwɪtroʊ] (wíttrō)

Whittaker, *f.n.* ['ʍwɪtəkər] (whíttăker)

Whittingehame ['ʍwɪtɪndʒəm] (whíttinjăm)

Whittingham, *Lancs.* ['ʍwɪtɪnhəm] (whíttin-hăm)

Whittingham, *Northumberland* ['ʍwɪtɪndʒəm] (whíttinjăm)

Whittle, *f.n.* ['ʍwɪtl] (whíttl)

Whittle-le-Woods ['ʍwɪtl lə 'wʊdz] (whíttl lĕ woŏdz)

Whittock, *f.n.* ['ʍwɪtək] (whíttŏk)

Whitton, *f.n.* ['ʍwɪtən] (whíttŏn)

Whitty, *f.n.* ['ʍwɪtɪ] (whítti)

Whitwick ['hwɪtɪk] (whíttick)
Whitworth, f.n. ['hwɪtwɜrθ] (whítt-wurth)
Whone, f.n. [woʊn] (wōn)
Whyberd, f.n. ['waɪbɜrd] (wíberd)
Whybrow, f.n. ['hwaɪbraʊ] (whíbrow)
Whyke [wɪk] (wick)
Whyman, f.n. ['waɪmən] (wímăn)
Whymant, f.n. ['waɪmənt] (wímănt)
Whymper, f.n. ['hwɪmpər] (whímper)
Whyte, f.n. [hwaɪt] (whīt)
Whyteleafe ['hwaɪtliːf] (whítleef)
Whytham, f.n. ['hwaɪtəm] (whítăm)
Wibsey ['wɪpsɪ] (wípssi); ['wɪbzɪ] (wíbzi)
Wichelo, f.n. ['wɪtʃəloʊ] (wítchĕlō)
Wichnor ['wɪtʃnər] (wítchnor)
Wick [wɪk] (wick)
Wicken, f.n. ['wɪkɪn] (wíckĕn)
Wickhambreaux ['wɪkəmbruː] (wíckăm-broo)
Wickham Skeith ['wɪkəm 'skiːθ] (wíckăm skeéth)
Wickins, f.n. ['wɪkɪnz] (wíckinz)
Wicks, f.n. [wɪks] (wicks)
Wickwar ['wɪkwɔr] (wíckwor)
Wicor ['wɪkər] (wíckŏr)
Widecombe ['wɪdɪkəm] (wíddĕkŏm)
Widemouth Bay ['wɪdməθ 'beɪ] (wíd-mŭth·báy)
Wideopen ['waɪdoʊpən] (wídōpĕn)
Wideson, f.n. ['waɪdsən] (wídssŏn)
Widlake, f.n. ['wɪdleɪk] (wídlayk)
Widnall, f.n. ['wɪdnəl] (wídnăl)
Widnes ['wɪdnɪs] (wídnĕss)
Widnesian, native of Widnes [wɪd'niziən] (widneézi-ăn)
Wieler, f.n. ['wiːlər] (weéler)
Wien, f.n. [wiːn] (ween)
Wiesenthal, f.n. ['viːsəntɑl] (veéssĕntaal)
Wigan, f.n. ['wɪgən] (wíggăn)
Wigan ['wɪgən] (wíggăn)
Wigfull, f.n. ['wɪgfəl] (wígfŭl)
Wiggall, f.n. ['wɪgɔl] (wíggawl)
Wiggins, f.n. ['wɪgɪnz] (wíggínz)
Wigham, f.n. ['wɪgəm] (wíggăm)
Wight, Isle of [waɪt] (wīt)
Wightman, f.n. ['waɪtmən] (wítmăn)
Wighton, f.n. ['waɪtən] (wítŏn)
Wightwick, f.n. ['wɪtɪk] (wíttick)
Wightwick ['wɪtɪk] (wíttick)
Wigley, f.n. ['wɪglɪ] (wíggli)
Wigmore, f.n. ['wɪgmɔr] (wígmor)
Wigoder, f.n. ['wɪgədər] (wíggŏder)
Wigram, f.n. ['wɪgrəm] (wígrăm)
Wigtown ['wɪgtaʊn] (wígtown); ['wɪg-tən] (wígtŏn)
Wigzell, f.n. ['wɪgzl] (wigzl)
Wilbarston [wɪl'bɑrstən] (wilbaársstŏn)
Wilberforce, f.n. ['wɪlbərfɔrs] (wílbĕr-forss)
Wilbraham, f.n. ['wɪlbrəm] (wílbrăm)
Wilbraham, Great and Little ['wɪl-brəhæm] (wílbrăham); ['wɪlbrəm] (wíl-brăm)
Wilburton [wɪl'bɜrtən] (wilbúrtŏn)

Wilbye, John, 16-17th-c. madrigal composer ['wɪlbɪ] (wílbi) A contemporary reference to him as Wilbee seems to discount the view held by some that the second syllable should rhyme with 'high'.
Wilcox, f.n. ['wɪlkɒks] (wílkocks)
Wild, f.n. [waɪld] (wīld)
Wildash, f.n. ['waɪldæʃ] (wīldash)
Wilde, f.n. [waɪld] (wīld)
Wildeman, f.n. ['waɪldmən] (wīldmăn)
Wildenstein Gallery, London ['wɪldən-staɪn] (wílldĕnsstīn)
Wilderhope ['wɪldərhoʊp] (wílldĕr-hōp)
Wilderspool ['wɪldərzpuːl] (wílldĕrzpool)
Wilding, f.n. ['waɪldɪŋ] (wílding)
Wildman, f.n. ['waɪldmən] (wíldmăn)
Wilen, f.n. [vɪ'leɪn] (villáyn)
Wilenski, f.n. [wɪ'lenskɪ] (willénski)
Wiles, f.n. [waɪlz] (wīlz)
Wiliam, f.n. ['wɪljəm] (wíl-yăm)
Wilkes, f.n. [wɪlks] (wilks)
Wilkie, f.n. ['wɪlkɪ] (wílki)
Wilkinson, f.n. ['wɪlkɪnsən] (wílkinssŏn)
Willapark Point ['wɪləpɑrk] (wíllăpaark)
Willard, f.n. ['wɪlɑrd] (wíllaard)
Willcocks, f.n. ['wɪlkɒks] (wílkocks)
Willcox, f.n. ['wɪlkɒks] (wílkocks)
Willemse, f.n. ['wɪləmzɪ] (wíllĕmzi)
Willenhall ['wɪlənhɔl] (wíllĕnhawl)
Willersey, f.n. ['wɪlərzɪ] (wíllĕrzi)
Willes, f.n. [wɪlz] (willz)
Willesden ['wɪlzdən] (wíllzdĕn)
Willey, f.n. ['wɪlɪ] (wílli)
Williams, f.n. ['wɪljəmz] (wíl-yămz)
Williamscot ['wɪlskət] (wílsskŏt)
Willicomb, f.n. ['wɪlɪkəm] (wíllikŏm)
Willies, f.n. ['wɪlɪz] (wílliz)
Willingale, f.n. ['wɪlɪŋgeɪl] (willing-gayl)
Willingham, f.n. ['wɪlɪŋəm] (willing-ăm)
Willis, f.n. ['wɪlɪs] (williss)
Willison, f.n. ['wɪlɪsən] (wíllissŏn)
Willmott, f.n. ['wɪlmət] (wílmŏt); ['wɪl-mɒt] (wílmott)
Willoughby, f.n. ['wɪləbɪ] (wíllŏbi)
Willoughby de Broke, Baron ['wɪləbɪ də 'brʊk] (wíllŏbi dĕ brŏŏk)
Willoughby de Eresby, Baron ['wɪləbɪ 'dɪərzbɪ] (wíllŏbi deérzbi)
Wills, f.n. [wɪlz] (willz)
Willson, f.n. ['wɪlsən] (wílssŏn)
Willum, f.n. ['wɪləm] (wíllŭm)
Wilmcote ['wɪlmkoʊt] (wílmkōt)
Wilmot of Selmeston, Barony of ['wɪl-mət əv 'selmztən] (wílmŏt ŏv sélmztŏn)
Wilmslow ['wɪlmzloʊ] (wílmzlō); ['wɪmz-loʊ] (wímzlō)
Wilnecote ['wɪlnɪkət] (wílnĕkŏt); ['wɪŋ-kət] (wínkŏt)
Wilpshire ['wɪlpʃər] (wílp-sher)
Wilshamstead, also spelt Wilstead ['wɪlʃəmsted] (wíl-shămssted); ['wɪlsted] (wíllssted)
Wilshin, f.n. ['wɪlʃɪn] (wíl-shin)
Wilson, f.n. ['wɪlsən] (wílssŏn)

Wilstead *see* Wilshamstead.

Wiltshire, *f.n.* ['wɪltʃər] (wĭlt-sher)

Wiltshire ['wɪltʃər] (wĭlt-sher); ['wɪlʃər] (wĭl-sher)

Wimbledon ['wɪmbldən] (wĭmbldŏn)

Wimbotsham ['wɪmbətʃəm] (wĭmbŏt-shăm)

Wimhurst, *f.n.* ['wɪmhɜrst] (wĭmhurst)

Wincanton [wɪn'kæntən] (win-kántŏn)

Winch, *f.n.* [wɪntʃ] (wintch)

Winchburgh ['wɪnʃbərə] (wĭnshbŭră)

Winchcombe ['wɪnʃkəm] (wĭnshkŏm)

Winchelsea ['wɪntʃlsɪ] (wĭntchlssee)

Winchester ['wɪntʃɪstər] (wĭntchĕster)

Winchilsea, Earl of ['wɪntʃlsɪ] (wĭntchlssee)

Winchwen ['wɪnʃwen] (wĭnsh-wen)

Winckless, *f.n.* ['wɪŋkləs] (wĭnkless)

Wincott, *f.n.* ['wɪŋkət] (wĭnkŏt)

Windeatt, *f.n.* ['wɪndɪət] (wĭndi-ăt)

Windebank, *f.n.* ['wɪndəbæŋk] (wĭndĕbank)

Winder, *f.n.* ['wɪndər] (wĭnder)

Windermere ['wɪndərmɪər] (wĭndĕrmeer)

Winders, *f.n.* ['wɪndərz] (wĭndĕrz)

Windeyer, *f.n.* ['wɪndɪ-ər] (wĭndi-er)

Windle, *f.n.* ['wɪndl] (windl)

Windlesham ['wɪndlʃəm] (wĭndl-shăm) *Appropriate also for Baron ~.*

Windley, *f.n.* ['wɪndlɪ] (wĭndli)

Windram, *f.n.* ['wɪndrəm] (wĭndrăm)

Windrush, River ['wɪndrʌʃ] (wĭndrush)

Windsor, *f.n.* ['wɪnzər] (wĭnzŏr)

Windsor, *Berks., Co. Antrim* ['wɪnzər] (wĭnzŏr)

Windus, *f.n.* ['wɪndəs] (wĭndŭss)

Windygates ['wɪndɪgeɪts] (wĭndigayts)

Wine, *f.n.* [waɪn] (wīn)

Winearls, *f.n.* ['wɪnɜrlz] (wĭnnerlz)

Wineham [waɪn'hæm] (wīn-hám)

Winestead ['waɪnsted] (wĭnssted)

Winfrith Heath ['wɪnfrɪθ 'hiθ] (wĭnfrith heĕth)

Winfrith Newburgh ['wɪnfrɪθ 'njubɜrg] (wĭnfrith néwburg)

Wing, *f.n.* [wɪŋ] (wing)

Wingerworth ['wɪŋərwɜrθ] (wĭng-ĕr-wurth)

Winget, *f.n.* ['wɪŋɪt] (wĭng-ĕt)

Wingham, *f.n.* ['wɪŋəm] (wĭng-ăm)

Winkleigh ['wɪŋklɪ] (wĭnkli)

Winlaton [wɪn'leɪtən] (winláytŏn); ['wɪn-letən] (wĭnlettŏn)

Winn, *f.n.* [wɪn] (winn)

Winnall, *Hants.* ['wɪnl] (winnl)

Winsborough, *f.n.* ['wɪnzbrə] (wĭnzbră)

Winser, *f.n.* ['wɪnzər] (wĭnzer)

Winsham ['wɪnsəm] (wĭnssăm)

Winshill ['wɪnzhɪl] (wĭnz-hil)

Winslade, *f.n.* ['wɪnsleɪd] (wĭnsslayd)

Winsor, *f.n.* ['wɪnzər] (wĭnzŏr)

Winspear, *f.n.* ['wɪnspɪər] (wĭnsspeer)

Winstanley, *f.n.* ['wɪnstənlɪ] (wĭnsstán-li); [wɪn'stænlɪ] (winsstánli)

Winstanley ['wɪnstənlɪ] (wĭnsstănli); [wɪn'stænlɪ] (winsstánli)

Winstock, *f.n.* ['wɪnstɒk] (wĭnsstock)

Winter, *f.n.* ['wɪntər] (wĭnter)

Winterborne Whitchurch ['wɪntər-bɔrn 'hwɪttʃərtʃ] (wĭntĕrborn whĭtchurch)

Winterbotham, *f.n.* ['wɪntərbɒtəm] (wĭntĕrbottăm)

Winterbottom, *f.n.* ['wɪntərbɒtəm] (wĭntĕrbottŏm)

Winterflood, *f.n.* ['wɪntərflʌd] (wĭntĕr-fludd)

Winther, *f.n.* ['wɪntər] (wĭnter)

Wintle, *f.n.* ['wɪntl] (winntl)

Wintour, *f.n.* ['wɪntər] (wĭntŭr)

Wintringham, *f.n.* ['wɪntrɪŋəm] (wĭn-tring-ăm)

Winward, *f.n.* ['wɪnwərd] (wĭnwărd)

Winwick, *Hunts., Lancs.* ['wɪnɪk] (wĭnnick)

Wippell, *f.n.* ['wɪpl] (wippl)

Wirksworth ['wɜrkswɜrθ] (wĭrkswurth)

Wirral ['wɪrəl] (wĭrrăl)

Wirth, *f.n.* [wɜrθ] (wirth)

Wisbech ['wɪzbɪtʃ] (wĭzbeetch)

Wisdom, *f.n.* ['wɪzdəm] (wĭzdŏm)

Wise, *f.n.* [waɪz] (wīz)

Wiseton ['waɪstən] (wĭsstŏn)

Wishart, *f.n.* ['wɪʃərt] (wĭshărt)

Wishaw, *Lanark., Warwick.* ['wɪʃɔ] (wĭshaw)

Wisher, *f.n.* ['wɪʃər] (wĭsher)

Wisley ['wɪzlɪ] (wĭzzli)

Wissington *see* Wiston, *Suffolk.*

Wistaston ['wɪstəstən] (wĭsstăsstŏn)

Wiston, *Lanark.* ['wɪstən] (wĭsstŏn)

Wiston, *Pembroke.* ['wɪsən] (wĭssŏn)

Wiston, *Suffolk, also spelt* Wissington ['wɪstən] (wĭsstŏn)

Wiston, *Sussex* ['wɪstən] (wĭsstŏn); ['wɪsən] (wĭssŏn)

Wistrich, *f.n.* ['wɪstrɪtʃ] (wĭstritch)

Witchell, *f.n.* ['wɪtʃl] (witchl)

Witham, *f.n.* ['wɪtəm] (wĭttăm)

Witham, *Essex* ['wɪtəm] (wĭttăm)

Witham, River, *Rutland-Lincs.* ['wɪðəm] (wĭthăm)

Witham Friary ['wɪtəm 'fraɪərɪ] (wĭttăm frĭ-ări); ['wɪðəm 'fraɪərɪ] (wĭthăm frĭ-ári)

Withernsea ['wɪðərnsɪ] (wĭthĕrnssee)

Witherow, *f.n.* ['wɪðərou] (wĭthĕrō)

Withers, *f.n.* ['wɪðərz] (wĭthĕrz)

Withington ['wɪðɪŋtən] (wĭthingtŏn)

Withnall, *f.n.* ['wɪðnəl] (wĭthnăl)

Withnell [wɪθnəl] (wĭthnĕl)

Withycombe Raleigh ['wɪðɪkəm 'rɒlɪ] (wĭthĭkŏm ráwli)

Withyham [ˌwɪðɪ'hæm] (withĭ-hám); ['wɪðɪhæm] (wĭthĭ-ham)

Witt, *f.n.* [wɪt] (witt)

Wittenbach, *f.n.* ['wɪtənbak] (wĭttĕn-baak)

Wittersham ['wɪtərʃəm] (wĭttĕr-shăm)

Wittkower, *f.n.* ['wɪtkouvər] (wĭttkŏver)

Wittle, *f.n.* ['wɪtl] (wittl)
Witton Gilbert ['wɪtən 'dʒɪlbərt] (wittŏn jĭlbĕrt); ['wɪtən 'gɪlbərt] (wittŏn gĭlbĕrt)
Wiveliscombe ['wɪvəlɪskəm] (wívvĕlisskŏm); ['wɪlskəm] (wílsskŏm)
Wivelsfield ['wɪvlzfɪld] (wívvlzfeeld)
Wivenhoe ['wɪvənhoʊ] (wívvĕnhō)
Wivenhoe Cross ['wɪvənhoʊ 'krɒs] (wívvĕnhō króss)
Wiverton ['waɪvərtən] (wívĕrtŏn); ['wɜrtən] (wértŏn)
Wiveton ['wɪvtən] (wívvtŏn); ['wɪvɪtən] (wívvĕtŏn)
Woburn, *Beds.* ['wuːbɜrn] (woóburn)
Woburn, *Co. Down* ['woʊbərn] (wōbŭrn)
Woburn Abbey ['wuːbɜrn] (woóburn)
Woburn Sands ['wuːbərn 'sændz] (woóbŭrn sándz)
Wodehouse, *f.n.* ['wʊdhaʊs] (wŏŏd-howss); ['wʊdəs] (wŏŏdŭss) *The first is appropriate for P. G. ~, author.*
Wodell, *f.n.* ['wɒ'del] (woddéll)
Wofford, *f.n.* ['wɒfərd] (wóffŏrd)
Wofinden, *f.n.* ['wʊfɪndən] (wŏŏfindĕn)
Woking ['woʊkɪŋ] (wōking)
Wokingham ['woʊkɪŋəm] (wōking-ăm)
Wolborough ['wʊlbərə] (wŏŏlbŭră)
Woldingham ['woʊldɪŋəm] (wōlding-ăm)
Woledge, *f.n.* ['wʊlɪdʒ] (wŏŏlĕj)
Wolfe, *f.n.* [wʊlf] (wŏŏlf)
Wolfenden, *f.n.* ['wʊlfəndən] (wŏŏlfĕndĕn)
Wolferstan, *f.n.* ['wʊlfərstən] (wŏŏlfĕrstăn)
Wolferton ['wʊlfərtən] (wŏŏlfĕrtŏn)
Wolfgang, *f.n.* ['wʊlfgæŋ] (wŏŏlfgang)
Wolfhampcote ['wʊlfəmkoʊt] (wŏŏlfámkōt)
Wolfrunian, *native of Wolverhampton* [wʊl'fruːnɪən] (wŏŏlfroónián)
Wolfsthal, *f.n.* ['wʊlfstɑl] (wŏŏlfstaal)
Wollaston, *f.n.* ['wʊləstən] (wŏŏlásstŏn)
Wollaton ['wʊlətən] (wŏŏlátŏn)
Wolmer, *f.n.* ['wʊlmər] (wŏŏlmer)
Wolpert, *f.n.* ['wʊlpərt] (wŏŏlpĕrt)
Wolrige, *f.n.* ['wʊlrɪdʒ] (wŏŏlrij)
Wolseley, *f.n.* ['wʊlzlɪ] (wŏŏlzli)
Wolsey, *f.n.* ['wʊlzɪ] (wŏŏlzi)
Wolsingham ['wʊlzɪŋəm] (wŏŏlzing-ăm)
Wolstenbury Hill ['wʊlstənbərɪ] (wŏŏlstĕnbŭri)
Wolstencroft, *f.n.* ['wʊlstənkrɒft] (wŏŏlstĕnkroft)
Wolstenholme, *f.n.* ['wʊlstənhoʊm] (wŏŏlsstĕnhōm)
Wolsty ['wʊlstɪ] (wŏŏlssti); ['wʊstɪ] (wŏŏssti)
Wolvercote ['wʊlvərkət] (wŏŏlvĕrkŏt)
Wolverhampton ['wʊlvərhæmptən] (wŏŏlvĕr-hamptŏn)
Wolverley ['wʊlvərlɪ] (wŏŏlvĕrli)
Wolviston ['wʊlvɪstən] (wŏŏlvisstŏn)
Wombourn ['wɒmbɜrn] (wómborn)
Wombridge ['wʌmbrɪdʒ] (wúmbrij)

Wombwell, *f.n.* ['wumwəl] (woómwĕl); ['wʊmwəl] (wŏŏmwĕl); ['wɒmwəl] (wómwĕl)
Wombwell ['wʊmwel] (wŏŏmwel)
Womenswold ['wɪmɪnzwoʊld] (wímmĕnzwōld); ['wɪmzwoʊld] (weémzwōld)
Womersley, *f.n.* ['wʊmərzlɪ] (wŏŏmĕrzli); ['wɒmərzlɪ] (wómmĕrzli)
Wonersh ['wɒnərʃ] (wónnersh)
Wonnacott, *f.n.* ['wɒnəkɒt] (wónnăkott)
Wontner, *f.n.* ['wɒntnər] (wónntner)
Wood, Haydn, *composer* ['heɪdn 'wʊd] (háydn wŏŏd)
Woodall, *f.n.* ['wʊdɒl] (wŏŏdawl)
Woodbridge, *f.n.* ['wʊdbrɪdʒ] (wŏŏdbrij)
Woodbridge ['wʊdbrɪdʒ] (wŏŏdbrij)
Woodburn ['wʊdbɜrn] (wŏŏdburn)
Woodchester ['wʊtʃɪstər] (wŏŏtchĕsster)
Woodford Halse ['wʊdfərd 'hɒls] (wŏŏdfŏrd hólss)
Woodgate, *f.n.* ['wʊdgeɪt] (wŏŏd-gayt)
Woodger, *f.n.* ['wʊdʒər] (wŏŏjer)
Woodget, *f.n.* ['wʊdgɪt] (wŏŏd-gĕt)
Woodhall, *f.n.* ['wʊdhɒl] (wŏŏdhawl)
Woodhatch, *f.n.* ['wʊdhætʃ] (wŏŏdhatch)
Woodhouse, *f.n.* ['wʊdhaʊs] (wŏŏdhowss)
Woodiwiss *f.n.* ['wʊdɪwɪs] (wŏŏdiwiss)
Woodland, *f.n.* ['wʊdlənd] (wŏŏdlănd)
Woodlesford ['wʊdlzfərd] (wŏŏdlzfŏrd)
Woodley, *f.n.* ['wʊdlɪ] (wŏŏdli)
Woodliff, *f.n.* ['wʊdlɪf] (wŏŏdliff)
Woodman, *f.n.* ['wʊdmən] (wŏŏdmăn)
Woodnesborough ['wʊdnɪzbərə] (wŏŏdnĕzbŭră); ['wʊnzbərə] (wŏŏnzbŭră); ['wɪnzbərə] (wínzbŭră)
Woodnutt, *f.n.* ['wʊdnʌt] (wŏŏdnutt)
Woodrooffe, *f.n.* ['wʊdrəf] (wŏŏdrŏf)
Woods, *f.n.* [wʊdz] (wŏŏdz)
Woodstock ['wʊdstɒk] (wŏŏdsstock)
Woodvale ['wʊdveɪl] (wŏŏdvayl)
Woodville, *f.n.* ['wʊdvɪl] (wŏŏdvil)
Woodward, *f.n.* ['wʊdwərd] (wŏŏdwărd)
Woof, *f.n.* [wʊf] (wŏŏf)
Woolam, *f.n.* ['wʊləm] (wŏŏlăm)
Woolard, *f.n.* ['wʊlɑrd] (wŏŏlaard)
Woolas, *f.n.* ['wʊləs] (wŏŏlăss)
Woolaston ['wʊləstən] (wŏŏlásstŏn)
Woolavington [wʊl'ævɪŋtən] (wŏŏlávvingtŏn) *Appropriate also for the Barony of ~.*
Woolbeding ['wʊlbidɪŋ] (wŏŏlbeeding)
Woolcombe, *f.n.* ['wʊlkəm] (wŏŏlkŏm)
Wooldridge, *f.n.* ['wʊldrɪdʒ] (wŏŏldrij)
Wooler, *f.n.* ['wʊlər] (wŏŏler)
Woolf, *f.n.* [wʊlf] (wŏŏlf)
Woolfardisworthy, *nr. Bideford see* Woolsery.
Woolfardisworthy, *nr. Crediton* [wʊl'fɑrdɪswɜrðɪ] (wŏŏlfaardisswurthi)
Woolford, *f.n.* ['wʊlfərd] (wŏŏlfŏrd)
Woolhampton [wʊl'hæmptən] (wŏŏlhámptŏn)

Woolhouse, *f.n.* ['wʊlhaʊs] (woŏl-howss)

Wooll, *f.n.* [wʊl] (woŏl)

Woolland, *f.n.* ['wʊlənd] (woŏlánd)

Woollard, *f.n.* ['wʊlɑrd] (woŏlaard)

Woolley, *f.n.* ['wʊlɪ] (woŏli)

Woolnough, *f.n.* ['wʊlnoʊ] (woŏlnō)

Woolsery, *formerly spelt* **Woolfardisworthy** ['wʊlzərɪ] (woŏlzěri)

Woolsington ['wʊlzɪŋtən] (woŏlzingtŏn)

Woolsthorpe ['wʊlzθɔrp] (woŏlzthorp)

Woolwich ['wʊlɪtʃ] (woŏlitch); ['wʊlɪdʒ] (woŏlij)

Woore [wɔr] (wawr)

Woosnam, *f.n.* ['wuznəm] (woŏznăm)

Wootton of Abinger, *Baroness* ['wʊtən əv 'æbɪndʒər] (woŏtŏn ŏv ábbinjer)

Wootton Wawen ['wʊtən 'wɔən] (woŏtŏn wáw-ĕn)

Worbarrow Bay ['wɔrbæroʊ 'beɪ] (wúrbarrō báy)

Worcester, *f.n.* ['wʊstər] (woŏsster)

Worcester ['wʊstər] (woŏsster)

Wordie, *f.n.* ['wɜrdɪ] (wúrdi)

Wordingham, *f.n.* ['wɜrdɪŋəm] (wúrdingăm)

Wordsworth, *f.n.* ['wɜrdzwɜrθ] (wúrdzwurth); ['wɜrdzwərθ] (wúrdzwŭrth)

Worfield, ['wɜrfɪld] (wúrfeeld)

Worfolk, *f.n.* ['wɜrfoʊk] (wúrfōk)

Work, *f.n.* [wɜrk] (wurk)

Workman, *f.n.* ['wɜrkmən] (wúrkmăn)

Worland, *f.n.* ['wɔrlənd] (wáwrlănd)

Worle [wɜrl] (wurl)

Worledge, *f.n.* ['wɜrlɪdʒ] (wúrlĕj)

Worley, *f.n.* ['wɜrlɪ] (wúrli)

Worlington ['wɜrlɪŋtən] (wúrlingtŏn)

Worlledge, *f.n.* ['wɜrlɪdʒ] (wúrlĕj)

Worlock, *f.n.* ['wɔrlɒk] (wáwrlock)

Wormald, *f.n.* ['wɜrməld] (wúrmáld)

Wormegay ['wɜrmɪgeɪ] (wúrmĕgay)

Wormelow ['wɜrmɪloʊ] (wúrmĕlō)

Wormingford ['wɜrmɪŋfərd] (wúrmingfŏrd)

Wormington, *f.n.* ['wɔrmɪŋtən] (wáwrmingtŏn)

Wormit ['wɜrmɪt] (wúrmit)

Wormleighton ['wɜrm'leɪtən] (wúrmláytŏn)

Wormley ['wɜrmlɪ] (wúrmli)

Worn, *f.n.* [wɔrn] (worn)

Worne, *f.n.* [wɔrn] (worn)

Wornum, *f.n.* ['wɜrnəm] (wúrnŭm)

Worplesdon ['wɔrplzdən] (wórplzdŏn)

Worrall, *f.n.* ['wʌrəl] (wúrrăl)

Worsley, *f.n.* ['wɜrslɪ] (wúrssli); ['wɜrzlɪ] (wúrzli) *The first, apparently much the more usual, is appropriate for the maiden name of H.R.H. the Duchess of Kent; the second for Baron ~, subsidiary title of the Earl of Yarborough.*

Worsley ['wɜrslɪ] (wúrssli)

Worsley Mesnes ['wɜrslɪ 'meɪnz] (wúrssli máynz)

Worsnop, *f.n.* ['wɜrznəp] (wúrznŏp)

Worstead ['wʊsted] (woŏssted); ['wʊstɪd] (woŏsstĕd)

Worster, *f.n.* ['wʊstər] (woŏsster)

Worsthorne, *f.n.* ['wɜrsθɔrn] (wúrss-thorn)

Worswick, *f.n.* ['wɜrsɪk] (wúrssick)

Worth, *f.n.* [wɜrθ] (wurth)

Worth Matravers ['wɜrθ mə'trævərz] (wúrth mătrávvĕrz)

Wortham ['wɜrðəm] (wúrtháм)

Worthing ['wɜrðɪŋ] (wúrthing)

Worthington, *f.n.* ['wɜrðɪŋtən] (wúrthingtŏn)

Worthley, *f.n.* ['wɜrθlɪ] (wúrthli)

Worting ['wɔrtɪŋ] (wúrting)

Wortley, *f.n.* ['wɜrtlɪ] (wúrtli)

Wortley ['wɜrtlɪ] (wúrtli)

Worton ['wɔrtən] (wúrtŏn)

Wortwell ['wɜrtwəl] (wúrtwĕl)

Wotherspoon, *f.n.* ['wʌðərspun] (wúthĕrspoon); ['wɒðərspun] (wóthĕrspoon)

Wothespoon, *f.n.* ['wʌðɪspun] (wúthĕspoon); ['wɒðɪspun] (wóthĕspoon)

Wotton, *f.n.* ['wʊtən] (woŏtŏn)

Wotton-under-Edge ['wʊtən 'ʌndrɪdʒ] (woŏtŏn úndrĕj); ['wʊtən ʌndər 'edʒ] (woŏtŏn under éjj)

Woughton ['wʊftən] (woŏftŏn)

Wouldham ['wʊldəm] (woŏldăm)

Wrafton ['ræftən] (ráftŏn)

Wrangaton ['ræŋətən] (ráng-ătŏn)

Wrangham, *f.n.* ['ræŋəm] (ráng-ăm)

Wrantage ['rɑntɪdʒ] (raántij)

Wrath, Cape [rɔθ] (rawth); [rɑθ] (raath)

Wrathall, *f.n.* ['rɒθl] (rothl)

Wraxhall, *f.n.* ['ræksl] (racksl)

Wray, *f.n.* [reɪ] (ray)

Wraysbury *see* Wyrardisbury.

Wrea Green ['reɪ 'grɪn] (ráy gréen)

Wreake, *River* [rik] (reek)

Wreay ['riə] (reé-ă)

Wreford, *f.n.* ['rɪfərd] (reéfŏrd)

Wrekenton ['rekɪntən] (réckĕntŏn)

Wrekin, The [ðə 'rikɪn] (thĕ reékin)

Wreningham ['renɪŋəm] (rénning-ăm)

Wrentham ['renθəm] (rén-thăm)

Wretham ['retəm] (réttăm)

Wrexham ['reksəm] (réckssăm)

Wrey, *f.n.* [reɪ] (ray)

Wright, *f.n.* [raɪt] (rīt)

Wrighton, *f.n.* ['raɪtən] (rítŏn)

Wrigley, *f.n.* ['rɪglɪ] (ríggli)

Wriothesley, *f.n.* ['raɪəθslɪ] (rī-ŏthsli); ['rɒtslɪ] (róttsli); ['rɒtɪslɪ] (róttĕssli); ['rɪθlɪ] (ríthli); ['rɪzlɪ] (rízzli) *This name, now historic, was the family name of the Elizabethan Earls of Southampton. The first is the pronunciation used by at least one descendant, the thirteenth Duke of Bedford. To judge by various works of reference, the others were current, singly or severally, in the fifteenth and sixteenth centuries.*

Wrisberg, *f.n.* ['rɪsbərg] (ríssberg)

Wrixon, *f.n.* ['rɪksən] (ríckssŏn)

Wrose [roʊz] (rōz)

Wrotham ['rutəm] (roótăm)

Wrottesley, f.n. ['rɒtslɪ] (róttsli) *Appropriate also for Baron ~.*
Wrottesley ['rɒtslɪ] (róttsli)
Wroughton, f.n. ['rɔtən] (ráwtŏn)
Wroughton ['rɔtən] (ráwtŏn)
Wulfrun Hall, *Wolverhampton* ['wʊlfrən] (wŏŏlfrŭn)
Wulstan, f.n. ['wʊlstən] (wŏŏlsstăn)
Wvendth, f.n. [wentθ] (went-th)
Wyatt, f.n. ['waɪət] (wí-ăt)
Wyberg, f.n. ['waɪbər] (wíber)
Wyberton ['wɪbərtən] (wíbbĕrtŏn)
Wybrew, f.n. ['waɪbru] (wíbroo)
Wybunbury ['wɪbənbrɪ] (wíbbŭnbri)
Wych Cross ['wɪtʃ 'krɒs] (wítch króss)
Wyche, f.n. [waɪtʃ] (wích)
Wyche, Lower *and* Upper [wɪtʃ] (witch)
Wychnor Bridges ['wɪtʃnɔr 'brɪdʒɪz] (wítchnor bríjjĕz)
Wychwood Forest ['wɪtʃwʊd] (wítchwŏŏd)
Wycliffe, John, 14th-c. religious reformer, also spelt *Wyclif* ['wɪklɪf] (wícklĭff)
Wycoller ['waɪkɒlər] (wíkoller)
Wycombe *see* High Wycombe, West Wycombe.
Wyddfa, Yr [ər 'ʊɪðvə] (ŭr oŏ-íthvă)
Wye, River [waɪ] (wī) *Its Welsh name is* Gwy, *q.v.*
Wyke, *Salop, Surrey, Yorks.* [waɪk] (wīk)
Wyke Regis ['waɪk 'rɪdʒɪs] (wík reéjiss)
Wykeham, f.n. ['wɪkəm] (wíckăm)
Wykeham ['waɪkəm] (wíkăm)
Wykehamist, one educated at Winchester College ['wɪkəmɪst] (wíckămist)
Wyken ['waɪkən] (wíkĕn)
Wykes, f.n. [waɪks] (wiks)
Wykey ['waɪkɪ] (wíki)
Wylam ['waɪləm] (wílăm)
Wyld, f.n. [waɪld] (wíld)
Wylde, f.n. [waɪld] (wíld)
Wylfa ['wɪlvə] (wílvă)
Wylie, f.n. ['waɪlɪ] (wíli)
Wyllie, f.n. ['waɪlɪ] (wíli)
Wylye ['waɪlɪ] (wíli)
Wymer, f.n. ['waɪmər] (wímer)
Wymering ['wɪmərɪŋ] (wímmĕring)
Wymeswold ['waɪmzwoʊld] (wímzwōld)
Wymington ['wɪmɪŋtən] (wímmingtŏn)
Wymondham, *Leics.* ['waɪməndəm] (wímŏndăm)
Wymondham, *Norfolk* ['wɪndəm] (wínndăm)
Wymondley, Great *and* Little ['waɪməndlɪ] (wímŏndli)
Wynd, f.n. [waɪnd] (wínd)
Wyndham, f.n. ['wɪndəm] (wíndăm)
Wynford, f.n. ['wɪnfərd] (wínfŏrd)
Wynn, f.n. [wɪn] (win)
Wynne, f.n. [wɪn] (win)
Wynward, f.n. ['wɪnərd] (wínnărd)
Wynyard, f.n. ['wɪnjərd] (wín-yărd)
Wynyard ['wɪnjərd] (wín-yărd)
Wyrardisbury, *also spelt* Wraysbury ['reɪzbərɪ] (ráyzbŭri)

Wyreside ['waɪərsaɪd] (wírssíd)
Wyrley, Great *and* Little ['wɜrlɪ] (wúrli)
Wysall ['waɪsl] (wíssl)
Wythall ['waɪðɒl] (wíthawl)
Wytham ['waɪtəm] (wítăm)
Wythburn ['waɪðbɜrn] (wíthburn) ; ['waɪbɜrn] (wíburn)
Wythenshawe ['wɪðənʃɒ] (wíthĕn-shaw)
Wythop ['wɪðəp] (wíthŏp)
Wyton, f.n. ['waɪtən] (wítŏn)
Wyton ['wɪtən] (wíttŏn)
Wyvis, Ben ['wɪvɪs] (wívviss) ; ['wɪvɪs] (weéviss)

X

Xavier, f.n. ['zeɪvjər] (záyv-yer)
Xerri, f.n. ['ʃerɪ] (shérri)
Xiberras, f.n. [ˌʃɪbə'ras] (shibbĕraáss)
Xuereb, f.n. ['ʃweɪrəb] (shwáy-rĕb)

Y

Yalden, f.n. ['jɒldən] (yáwldĕn)
Yalding ['jɒldɪŋ] (yáwlding)
Yar, River [jɑr] (yaar)
Yarborough, Earl of ['jɑrbərə] (yaárbŭră)
Yarburgh ['jɑrbərə] (yaárbŭră)
Yare, River [jɛər] (yair)
Yarmouth ['jɑrməθ] (yaármŭth)
Yarmouth, Great ['jɑrməθ] (yaármŭth)
Yarrow ['jærɒʊ] (yárrō)
Yates, f.n. [jeɪts] (yayts)
Yatton Keynell ['jætən 'kenl] (yáttŏn kénnl)
Yeabsley, f.n. ['jebzlɪ] (yébzli)
Yeading ['jedɪŋ] (yédding)
Yeadon, f.n. ['jɪdən] (yeédŏn) ; ['jedən] (yéddŏn)
Yeadon ['jɪdən] (yeédŏn)
Yealand Conyers ['jelənd 'kɒnjərz] (yéllănd kón-yĕrz)
Yealm, River [jæm] (yam)
Yealmpton ['jæmtən] (yámtŏn)
Yeaman, f.n. ['jeɪmən] (yáymăn) ; ['jɪmən] (yeémăn)
Yeames, f.n. [jimz] (yeemz) ; [jeɪmz] (yaymz)
Yearby ['jɜrbɪ] (yérbi)
Yearsley, f.n. ['jɪərzlɪ] (yeérzli)
Yeates, f.n. [jeɪts] (yayts)
Yeathouse ['jethaʊs] (yét-howss)
Yeatman, f.n. ['jeɪtmən] (yáytmăn)
Yeats, f.n. [jeɪts] (yayts)

Yeavering ['jevərɪŋ] (yévvĕring)
Yeaxlee, *f.n.* ['jækslɪ] (yácksli); ['jekslɪ] (yécksli)
Yell [jel] (yell)
Yelland, *f.n.* ['jelənd] (yéllánd)
Yelland ['jelənd] (yéllánd)
Yelverton ['jelvərtən] (yélvĕrtŏn)
Yeo, *f.n.* [joʊ] (yŏ)
Yeoell, *f.n.* ['joʊəl] (yŏ-ĕl)
Yeolmbridge ['joʊmbrɪdʒ] (yŏmbrij)
Yeovil ['joʊvɪl] (yŏvil)
Yeowell, *f.n.* ['joʊəl] (yŏ-ĕl)
Yerburgh, *f.n.* ['jɑrbərə] (yaárbŭrá)
Yerbury, *f.n.* ['jɜrbərɪ] (yérbŭri)
Yerling ['jɜrlɪŋ] (yérling)
Yetholm ['jetəm] (yéttŏm)
Yevele, Henry de, *14th-c. master-mason and architect* [də 'jivəlɪ] (dĕ yeévĕli)
Yglesias, *f.n.* [ɪ'gliziəs] (igleézi-áss)
Yielden ['jildən] (yeéldĕn)
Yiend, *f.n.* [jend] (yend)
Ynys Llanddwyn ['ʌnɪs 'ɬænðʊɪn] (únniss hlánthŏŏ-in)
Ynys Môn ['ʌnɪs 'mon] (únniss máwn)
Ynys Tawe ['ʌnɪs 'taʊeɪ] (únniss tów-ay)
Ynysangharad ['ʌnɪsæŋ'hærəd] (únniss-ang-hárrád)
Ynysarwed [ˌʌnɪs'ɑrwed] (unniss-aárwed)
Ynysawdre [ˌʌnɪs'aʊdreɪ] (unniss-ówdray)
Ynys-boeth [ˌʌnɪs'bɔɪθ] (unniss-bóyth)
Ynyscedwyn [ˌʌnɪs'kedwɪn] (unniss-kédwin)
Ynys-ddu [ˌʌnɪs'ðiː] (unniss-thee)
Ynys-hir [ˌʌnɪs'hɪər] (unniss-heér)
Ynyslwyd [ˌʌnɪs'lʊɪd] (unniss-lŏŏ-id)
Ynys-wen [ˌʌnɪs'wen] (unniss-wén)
Ynysybwl [ˌʌnɪsə'bʊl] (unnissábŏŏl)
Yonge, *f.n.* [jʌŋ] (yung)
Yorath, *f.n.* ['jɔrəθ] (yáwrăth)
York, *f.n.* [jɔrk] (york)
York [jɔrk] (york)
Yorke, *f.n.* [jɔrk] (york)
Youatt, *f.n.* ['juət] (yoó-ăt)
Youde, *f.n.* [jud] (yood)
Youds, *f.n.* [jaʊdz] (yowdz)
Youel, *f.n.* ['juəl] (yoó-ĕl); ['jʊəl] (yŏŏ-ĕl); [jul] (yool)
Youell, *f.n.* ['juəl] (yoó-ĕl); ['jʊəl] (yŏŏ-ĕl); [jul] (yool)
Youens, *f.n.* ['juɪnz] (yoó-ĕnz)
Youghal, *f.n.* [jɔl] (yawl)
Youings, *f.n.* ['juɪŋz] (yoó-ingz)
Youldon, *f.n.* ['juldən] (yoóldŏn)
Youlgrave ['julɡreɪv] (yoólgrayv)
Youmans, *f.n.* ['jumənz] (yoómánz)
Young, *f.n.* [jʌŋ] (yung)
Younger, *f.n.* ['jʌŋɡər] (yúng-ger)
Younghusband, *f.n.* ['jʌŋhʌzbənd] (yúng-huzbánd)
Youngman, *f.n.* ['jʌŋmən] (yúng-mán)
Younkman, *f.n.* ['jʌŋkmən] (yúnkmăn)
Younson, *f.n.* ['junsən] (yoónssŏn)
Youseman, *f.n.* ['jusmən] (yoóssmăn)
Yow, *f.n.* [jaʊ] (yow)

Yoxall, *f.n.* ['jɒksl] (yocksl)
Ypres, *Earl of* [ipr] (eepr)
Ypres Tower, *Rye* [ipr] (eepr)
Ysceifiog [ʌs'kaɪvjɒg] (usskív-yog)
Ysclydach [ʌs'klɪdəx] (ussklíddǎch)
Yspytty [ʌ'spʌtɪ] (usspútti)
Yspytty Ystwyth [ʌ'spʌtɪ 'ʌstwɪθ] (usspútti ússtwith)
Ystalyfera [ˌʌstələ'verə] (usstǎlǎvérrǎ)
Ystrad, *Carmarthen., Denbigh.* ['ʌstrəd] (ússtrăd)
Ystrad Meurig ['ʌstrəd 'maɪrɪg] (ússtrăd mírig)
Ystrad Mynach ['ʌstrəd 'mʌnəx] (ússtrăd múnnǎch)
Ystrad Rhondda ['ʌstrəd 'rɒnðə] (ússtrăd rónthǎ)
Ystradfellte [ˌʌstrəd'veɬteɪ] (usstrǎd-véhḷtay)
Ystradgynlais [ˌʌstrəd'gʌnlaɪs] (usstrăd-gúnlíss)
Ystwyth, *River* ['ʌstwɪθ] (ússtwith)
Ythan, *River* ['aɪθən] (íthǎn)
Ythanbank ['aɪθən'bæŋk] (íthǎn-bánk)
Ythanwells ['aɪθən'welz] (íthǎn-wéllz)
Yudkin, *f.n.* ['judkɪn] (yoódkin)
Yuille, *f.n.* ['juɪl] (yoó-il)

Z

Zaehner, *f.n.* ['zeɪnər] (záyner)
Zangwill, *f.n.* ['zæŋwɪl] (záng-wil)
Zealley, *f.n.* ['zɪlɪ] (zeéli)
Zeal Monachorum ['zil ˌmɒnə'kɔrəm] (zeél monnǎkáwrŭm)
Zeeman, *f.n.* ['zimən] (zeémǎn)
Zelah ['zilə] (zeélǎ)
Zennor ['zenər] (zénnŏr)
Zetland ['zetlənd] (zétlánd) *Appropriate also for the Marquess of ~.*
Zeuner, *f.n.* ['zɔɪnər] (zóyner)
Ziegler, *f.n.* ['zɪglər] (zeégler)
Zilliacus, *f.n.* [ˌzɪlɪ'akəs] (zilliaákūss)
Ziman, *f.n.* ['zaɪmən] (zímǎn)
Zinkeisen, *f.n.* ['zɪŋkaɪzən] (zínkīzĕn) *Appropriate for Anna ~, painter.*
Zoffany, John, *18-19th-c. painter* ['zɒfənɪ] (zóffǎni)
Zoller, *f.n.* ['zɒlər] (zóller)
Zorian, *f.n.* ['zɔrɪən] (záwri-ǎn)
Zorza, *f.n.* ['zɔrzə] (zórzǎ)
Zouche, *Baron* [zuʃ] (zoosh)
Zuckerman, *f.n.* ['zʊkərmən] (zŏŏkĕrmǎn) *Appropriate for Sir Solly ~, scientist.*
Zuill, *f.n.* [jul] (yool)
Zussman, *f.n.* ['zʌsmən] (zússmǎn)
Zwar, *f.n.* [zwɑr] (zwaar)
Zwemmer Gallery, *London* ['zwemər] (zwémmer)

CHANNEL ISLANDS APPENDIX

A

A'Court, *f.n.* ['eɪkɔrt] (áykort)
Ahier, *f.n.* ['ajeɪ] (aá-yay)
Albiges, *f.n.* [ˌælbɪ'ʒeɪ] (albi<u>zh</u>áy)
Alderney ['ɔldərnɪ] (áwldĕrni)
Alexandre, *f.n.* [ˌælɪk'zɒndr] (alĕkzóndr)
Allaire, *f.n.* ['ælɛər] (álair)
Allenet, *f.n.* ['ælɪneɪ] (álinay)
Alles, *f.n.* ['ɔleɪ] (áwlay)
Allez, *f.n.* ['ɔleɪ] (áwlay)
Allo, *f.n.* ['æloʊ] (álō)
Amourette, *f.n.* [ˌæmʊ'ret] (ammŏŏrét)
Andrieux, *f.n.* ['ændrɪʒ] (ándree-ö)
Anthoine, *f.n.* [ɒn'twɒn] (awntwón)
Aubert, *f.n.* ['oʊbɛər] (ŏbair)
Aubin, *f.n.* ['oʊbɪn] (ŏbin)
Audrain, *f.n.* ['oʊdrɑ] (ŏdraa)
Averty, *f.n.* [ə'vɜrtɪ] (ávérti)
Avrill, *f.n.* ['ævrɪl] (ávril)

B

Baal, *f.n.* [beɪl] (bayl)
Babbé, *f.n.* [bæ'beɪ] (babbáy)
Bailhache, *f.n.* ['bælæʃ] (bálash)
Bailiff, *f.n.* ['beɪlɪf] (báyliff)
Balleine, *f.n.* ['bæleɪn] (bálayn)
Bannier, *f.n.* ['bænjeɪ] (bán-yay)
Barbé, *f.n.* [bar'beɪ] (baarbáy)
Bataille, *f.n.* ['bætaɪ] (báttī)
Batiste, *f.n.* ['bætɪst] (bátteest)
Baudains, *f.n.* ['boʊdæ] (bŏdang)
Baudet, *f.n.* ['boʊdeɪ] (bŏday)
Beaucamps, *f.n.* ['boʊkɒn] (bŏkon)
Beauchamp, *f.n.* ['boʊʃɒ] (bŏ-shaw)
Beaugie, *f.n.* ['boʊʒɪeɪ] (bŏzhi-ay)
Beaulieu, *f.n.* ['boʊljə] (bŏl-yö)
Beauport ['boʊpɔrt] (bŏport)
Bechelet, *f.n.* ['beʃleɪ] (béshlay)
Becquet, *f.n.* ['bekeɪ] (béckay)
Beghin, *f.n.* ['begæ] (béggang)
Benest, *f.n.* ['beneɪ] (bénnay)
Bertaille, *f.n.* ['bɜrtaɪ] (bértī)
Berteau, *f.n.* ['bɜrtoʊ] (bértō)
Berthelot, *f.n.* ['bɜrtɪloʊ] (bértĕlŏ)
Besnard, *f.n.* ['bemɑrd] (báynaard)
Besquet, *f.n.* ['biskweɪ] (béesskway)
Beuzeval, *f.n.* ['bɜzvɑl] (bözvaal)
Bichard, *f.n.* ['bɪʃɑr] (bíshaar)
Billot, *f.n.* ['bɪloʊ] (bíllō)
Binet, *f.n.* ['bɪneɪ] (bínnay)
Bisset, *f.n.* ['bɪsɪt] (bíssĕt)

Bisson, *f.n.* ['bɪsɒn] (bísson); ['bɪsə] (bíssaw) *The first is a Guernsey pro-nunciation, the second a Jersey one.*
Blampied, *f.n.* [blæm'pieɪ] (blămpeé-ay); ['blɒmpieɪ] (blómpee-ay) *The first is a Guernsey pronunciation, the second a Jersey one.*
Bliault, *f.n.* ['blioʊ] (bleé-ō)
Blondel, *f.n.* ['blɒndl] (blondl)
Bois, *f.n.* [bwɑ] (bwaa)
Bonne Nuit ['bɒn 'nwi] (bón nweé)
Bouchard, *f.n.* ['bʊʃɑrd] (bŏŏshaard)
Boudin, *f.n.* ['bʊdæ] (bŏŏdang)
Bougeard, *f.n.* ['bʊʒɑrd] (bŏŏ<u>zh</u>aard)
Bougourd, *f.n.* ['bʊgʊər] (bŏŏgŏŏr)
Bouley ['bʊlɪ] (bŏŏli)
Bourgaize, *f.n.* ['bʊərgeɪz] (bŏŏrgayz)
Brâche, *f.n.* [brɑʃ] (braash)
Brechou Island ['breku] (bréckoo)
Brecqhou, *f.n.* ['breku] (bréckoo)
Brehaut, *f.n.* [breɪ'oʊ] (bray-ŏ)
Breuilly, *f.n.* ['bruɪ] (broŏ-ee)
Brouard, *f.n.* ['bruɑrd] (broŏ-aard)
Buesnel, *f.n.* ['bjunel] (béwnel); ['bjuznəl] (béwznĕl)
Burhou [bə'ru] (bŭroŏ)

C

Cabeldu, *f.n.* ['kæbldu] (kábbl-doo)
Cabot, *f.n.* ['kæboʊ] (kábbō)
Cadin, *f.n.* ['kædæ] (káddang)
Carey, *f.n.* ['kɛərɪ] (kaíri)
Carré, *f.n.* ['kareɪ] (kaáray)
Caskets ['kæskɪts] (kásskĕts) *see also* Les Casquets.
Castel, *f.n.* ['katel] (kaátel)
Castle Cornet ['kɑsl 'kɔrnɪt] (kaássl kórnĕt)
Cauvain, *f.n.* ['koʊvæ] (kŏvang)
Chevalier, *f.n.* [ʃɪ'væljeɪ] (shĕvál-yay)
Cloche, *f.n.* [klɒʃ] (klosh)
Cohu, *f.n.* ['koʊju] (kŏ-yoo)
Colin, *f.n.* ['kɒlæ] (kóllang)
Collas, *f.n.* ['koʊləs] (kŏláss)
Collenette, *f.n.* ['kɒlɪnet] (kóllĕnet)
Corbet, *f.n.* ['kɔrbɪt] (kórbĕt)
Corbière, *Guernsey* [kɔr'bɪər] (korbeér)
Corbière Point, *Jersey* [kɔr'bjɛər] (kor-byaír)
Corbin, *f.n.* ['kɔrbɪn] (kórbin)
Cordiere, *f.n.* ['kɔrdɪɛər] (kórdi-air)
Corniere, *f.n.* ['kɔrnjɛər] (kórn-yair)
Coutanche, *f.n.* ['kutɒnʃ] (koótawnsh)

D

Dallain, *f.n.* ['dælæ̃] (dálang)
De Caen, *f.n.* [də 'kã] (dě kaáng)
De Carteret, *f.n.* [də ˌkɑrtə'ret] (dě kaartěrét)
D'Eauthreau, *f.n.* ['doʊtroʊ] (dŏtrō)
De Faye, *f.n.* [də 'feɪ] (dě fáy)
De Garis, *f.n.* [də 'gɑrɪ] (dě gaáree)
De Gruchy, *f.n.* [də 'grɪʃɪ] (dě gríshi); [də 'grʊʃɪ] (dě grŏoshi); [də 'gruʃɪ] (dě groóshi)
De La Cour, *f.n.* [ˌdelə'kɔr] (dellákór)
De La Mare, *f.n.* [ˌdə lə 'mɛər] (dě lǎ maír)
De La Perrelle, *f.n.* [ˌdelə'peərel] (dellápaírel)
De Louche, *f.n.* [də 'luʃ] (dě loósh)
De Mouilpied, *f.n.* [ˌdə mul'piel] (dě moolpeě-ay)
De Putron, *f.n.* [də 'pjutrɒn] (dě péwtron)
De Ste. Croix, *f.n.* [ˌdə sæn 'krwɑ] (dě san krwaá)
De Saumarez, *f.n.* [də 'sɒməreɪ] (dě sómmáray)
De Sausmarez, *f.n.* [də 'sɒməreɪ] (dě sómmáray)
De Veulle, *f.n.* [də 'vɜl] (dě vŏll)
Decaux, *f.n.* [də'koʊ] (děkŏ)
Derouet, *f.n.* ['dɛərʊeɪ] (daírŏo-ay)
Deslandes, *f.n.* ['deɪlɒnd] (dáylawnd)
Desperques, *f.n.* [deɪ'pɜrk] (daypérk)
Digard, *f.n.* ['dɪgɑr] (díggaar)
Ditot, *f.n.* ['dɪtoʊ] (díttō)
Dixcart ['dɪkɑr] (deékaar)
Domaille, *f.n.* ['doʊmaɪl] (dŏmíl)
Dorey, *f.n.* ['dɒrɪ] (dórri); ['dɔrɪ] (dáwri) *The first is a Guernsey pronunciation, the second a Jersey one.*
Du Feu, *f.n.* [du 'fɜ] (doo fŏ)
Du Heaume, *f.n.* [du 'hoʊm] (doo hŏm)
Du Parcq, *f.n.* [du 'pɑrk] (doo paárk)
Dubras, *f.n.* [dʊ'brɑ] (dŏobraá)
Duchemin, *f.n.* ['duʃmɪn] (doóshmin)
Dupré, *f.n.* [du'preɪ] (doopráy)
Duquemin, *f.n.* ['dukmɪn] (doókmin); ['dukmæ̃] (doókmang) *The first is a Guernsey pronunciation, the second a Jersey one.*
Durell, *f.n.* [du'rel] (doo-réll)
Dutertre, *f.n.* [du'tɜrtr̩] (dootértr)

E

Ecobichon, *f.n.* [ˌekoʊ'biʃo] (eckŏ-beěshaw)
Ecrehou Islands ['ekrɪhoʊ] (éckrěhō)
Egré, *f.n.* ['egreɪ] (égray)
Eker, *f.n.* ['ikər] (eéker)

Enevoldsen, *f.n.* [en'vɒlsən] (envólssěn)
Ereaut, *f.n.* ['ɛəroʊ] (aírō)
Esnouf, *f.n.* ['eɪnuf] (áynoof)
Etienne, *f.n.* ['etjen] (ét-yen)

F

Falla, *f.n.* ['fælə] (fálaa)
Fauvel, *f.n.* ['foʊvel] (fŏvel)
Ferbrache, *f.n.* ['fɛərbrɑʃ] (faírbrush)
Filleul, *f.n.* ['fɪljɜl] (fíl-yŏll)
Fiott, *f.n.* ['fioʊ] (feě-ō)
Fosse, *f.n.* [fɒs] (foss)
Foullain, *f.n.* ['fɒlæ̃] (fóllang)
Froome, *f.n.* [frum] (froom)
Frossard, *f.n.* ['frɒsɑr] (fróssaar)

G

Gallichan, *f.n.* ['gælɪʃo] (gálishaw)
Gallienne, *f.n.* [gæ'leɪn] (galáyn)
Garignon, *f.n.* ['gærɪnjo] (gárrin-yaw)
Gaudin, *f.n.* ['goʊdɪn] (gŏdin)
Gaudion, *f.n.* ['goʊdɪɒn] (gŏdi-on)
Gautier, *f.n.* [goʊ'tieɪ] (gŏteě-ay)
Gavet, *f.n.* ['gæveɪ] (gávvay)
Gavey, *f.n.* ['gæveɪ] (gávvay)
Gibault, *f.n.* ['ʒɪboʊ] (<u>zh</u>íbbŏ)
Girard, *f.n.* ['ʒɪrɑr] (<u>zh</u>írraar)
Godel, *f.n.* ['gɒdel] (gáwdel)
Gorey [gɒ'riː] (gawreé)
Gorin, *f.n.* ['gɒræ̃] (gáwrang)
Goubert, *f.n.* ['gubeər] (goóbair)
Gouyette, *f.n.* ['gujet] (goó-yet)
Grandes Rocques ['grænd 'rɒk] (gránd róck)
Greffier, *f.n.* ['grefjeɪ] (gréff-yay)
Greve de Lecq ['greɪv də 'lek] (gráyv dě léck)
Grouville, *f.n.* [gru'vɪl] (groovíll)
Gruchy, *f.n.* ['gruʃɪ] (groóshi) *But cf. De Gruchy.*
Guegan, *f.n.* ['gigən] (geégǎn)
Guernsey ['gɜrnzɪ] (gérnzi)
Guille, *f.n.* [gil] (geel)
Guillemette, *f.n.* ['gɪlmet] (gílmet)
Guiton, *f.n.* ['gɪto] (gíttaw)

H

Hamon, *f.n.* ['hæmã] (hámaang); ['hæmɒn] (hámmon) *The first is a Guernsey pronunciation, the second a Jersey one.*

Heaume, *f.n.* [joʊm] (yōm)
Hegerat, *f.n.* [ˈhegərɑ] (héggĕraa)
Herissier, *f.n.* [hɛəˈrɪsjeɪ] (hairíss-yay)
Herivel, *f.n.* [ˈherɪvel] (hérrivel)
Herm [hɜrm] (herm)
Hervé, *f.n.* [ˈhɜrvɪ] (hérvi)
Hervieu, *f.n.* [ˈhɛərvju] (háirvew)
Houguez, *f.n.* [ˈhugeɪ] (hoógay)
Houiellebecq, *f.n.* [ˈhʊlbek] (hoólbeck)
Hucquet, *f.n.* [ˈhukeɪ] (hoókay)
Huelin, *f.n.* [ˈhjulɪn] (héwlin)

I

Icart Point [ˈikɑr] (eékaar)
Illien, *f.n.* [ˈɪljen] (íll-yen)
Ingrouille, *f.n.* [ɪnˈgruil] (in-groó-eel)

J

Jamouneau, *f.n.* [ʒæˈmunoʊ] (<u>zh</u>amoónō)
Jehan, *f.n.* [ˈdʒiæn] (jeé-an); [ˈʒiæn] (<u>zh</u>eé-an) *The first is a Guernsey pronunciation, the second a Jersey one.*
Jerrom, *f.n.* [ˈdʒerəm] (jérrŏm)
Jersey [ˈdʒɜrzɪ] (jérzi)
Jethou [ˈdʒetu] (jéttoo)
Jeune, *f.n.* [ʒɑn] (<u>zh</u>ön)
Jory, *f.n.* [ˈdʒɔrɪ] (jáwri)
Jouan, *f.n.* [ˈʒuɔ] (<u>zh</u>oó-aw)
Jouget, *f.n.* [ˈʒugeɪ] (<u>zh</u>oógay)
Journeaux, *f.n.* [ˈʒɔrnoʊ] (<u>zh</u>órnō)
Jurat, *f.n.* [ˈdʒʊərət] (joŏrát)

K

Kergozou, *f.n.* [ˈkɛərgoʊzu] (káirgōzoo)
Kerhoat, *f.n.* [ˈkɛərhwɑ] (káir-hwaa)
Keyho, *f.n.* [ˈkeɪoʊ] (káy-ō)

L

La Corbiere [lɑ ˈkɔrbɪər] (laa kórbeer)
La Coupée, *f.n.* [lɑ ˈkupeɪ] (laa koópay)
La Maseline [lɑ ˈmæzəlɪn] (laa mázzĕleen)
La Moye [lə ˈmɔɪ] (lă móy)
La Villiaze [ˌlɑ viˈjɑz] (laa vee-yaáz)
Labey, *f.n.* [ˈlæbɪ] (lábbi)
Lainé, *f.n.* [ˈleɪneɪ] (láynay)

Lamy, *f.n.* [ˈlæmɪ] (lámmi)
Langlois, *f.n.* [ˈlɒŋleɪ] (lóng-lay); [ˈlɒŋgwɑ] (láwn-gwaa) *The first is a Guernsey pronunciation, the second a Jersey one.*
Larbalestier, *f.n.* [lɑrˈbɒlestɪeɪ] (laarbólesti-ay)
Laurens, *f.n.* [ˈlɔrɔ] (láwraw)
Le Bailly, *f.n.* [lə ˈbaɪi] (lĕ bí-ee)
Le Bas, *f.n.* [lə ˈbɑ] (lĕ baá)
Le Blancq, *f.n.* [lə ˈblɒ] (lĕ bláw)
Le Boutillier, *f.n.* [lə ˈbutɪljeɪ] (lĕ boótil-yay)
Le Breton, *f.n.* [lə ˈbretɒn] (lĕ brétton)
Le Brun, *f.n.* [lə ˈbrʌn] (lĕ brúnn)
Le Cappelain, *f.n.* [lə ˈkæplæ] (lĕ káplang)
Le Chaminant, *f.n.* [lə ˈʃemmɔ] (lĕ shémminaw)
Le Chanu, *f.n.* [lə ˈʃænu] (lĕ shánnoo)
Le Cheminant, *f.n.* [lə ˈʃemmɑ] (lĕ shémminaang)
Le Clercq, *f.n.* [lə ˈklɛər] (lĕ kláir)
Le Cocq., *f.n.* [lə ˈkoʊk] (lĕ kŏk); [lə ˈkɒk] (lĕ kóck) *The first is a Guernsey pronunciation, the second a Jersey one.*
Le Cornu, *f.n.* [lə ˈkɔrnju] (lĕ kórnew)
Le Couteur, *f.n.* [lə ˈkutər] (lĕ koóter)
Le Cras, *f.n.* [lə ˈkrɑ] (lĕ kraá)
Le Cuirot, *f.n.* [lə ˈkwɪroʊ] (lĕ kwírrō)
Le Febvre, *f.n.* [lə ˈfɛːbr] (lĕ fébbr)
Le Feuvre, *f.n.* [lə ˈfivər] (lĕ feéver)
Le Fondre, *f.n.* [lə ˈfondreɪ] (lĕ fáwndray)
Le Gallais, *f.n.* [lə ˈgæleɪ] (lĕ gálay)
Le Gallez, *f.n.* [lə ˈgæleɪ] (lĕ gálay)
Le Gresley, *f.n.* [lə ˈgreɪlɪ] (lĕ gráyli)
Le Gros, *f.n.* [lə ˈgroʊ] (lĕ grŏ)
Le Hucquet, *f.n.* [lə ˈhukeɪ] (lĕ hoókay)
Le Huray, *f.n.* [ˌlə hjuˈreɪ] (lĕ hew-ráy)
Le Lacheur, *f.n.* [lə ˈlæʃər] (lĕ lásher)
Le Lievre, *f.n.* [lə ˈlivər] (lĕ leéver)
Le Machon, *f.n.* [lə ˈmæʃɑ] (lĕ máshă)
Le Main, *f.n.* [lə ˈmæ̃] (lĕ máng)
Le Maistre, *f.n.* [lə ˈmeɪtr̩] (lĕ máytr)
Le Maître, *f.n.* [lə ˈmeɪtr̩] (lĕ máytr)
Le Marchand, *f.n.* [lə ˈmarʃɔ] (lĕ maárshaw)
Le Marquand, *f.n.* [lə ˈmarkɑ̃] (lĕ maárkaang); [lə ˈmarkə] (lĕ maárkă) *The first is a Guernsey pronunciation, the second a Jersey one.*
Le Masurier, *f.n.* [ˌlə məˈsʊərɪeɪ] (lĕ mássoŏri-ay); [lə ˈmæzʊərɪeɪ] (lĕ mázoŏri-ay) *The first is a Guernsey pronunciation, the second a Jersey one.*
Le Messurier, *f.n.* [lə ˈmeʒərər] (lĕ mé<u>zh</u>ĕrer)
Le Mesurier, *f.n.* [lə ˈmezʊərɪeɪ] (lĕ mézzoŏri-ay)
Le Moisne, *f.n.* [lə ˈmwɑn] (lĕ mwaán)
Le Monnier, *f.n.* [lə ˈmɒnjeɪ] (lĕ món-yay)
Le Montais, *f.n.* [lə ˈmɒnteɪ] (lĕ móntay)
Le Noury, *f.n.* [lə ˈnʊərɪ] (lĕ noŏri)
Le Page, *f.n.* [lə ˈpɑʒ] (lĕ paá<u>zh</u>)
Le Pelley, *f.n.* [lə ˈpeleɪ] (lĕ péllay)
Le Pennec, *f.n.* [lə ˈpenek] (lĕ pénneck)

Le Poidevin, *f.n.* [lə ˈpedvɪn] (lĕ pédvin); [lə ˈpɒdvæ̃] (lĕ pódva*ng*) *The first is a Guernsey pronunciation, the second a Jersey one.*

Le Prevost, *f.n.* [lə ˈprevou] (lĕ prévvō)

Le Quesne, *f.n.* [lə ˈkeɪn] (lĕ káyn)

Le Rendu, *f.n.* [lə ˈrondu] (lĕ ráwndoo)

Le Riche, *f.n.* [lə ˈrɪʃ] (lĕ rísh)

Le Rossignol, *f.n.* [lə ˈrɒsɪnjɒl] (lĕ róssin-yol)

Le Ruez, *f.n.* [lə ˈrueɪ] (lĕ roŏ-ay)

Le Sauteur, *f.n.* [lə ˈsoutər] (lĕ sŏtur)

Le Sauvage, *f.n.* [ˌlə sɒˈvɑʒ] (lĕ sovváa*zh*)

Le Sueur, *f.n.* [lə ˈswɜr] (lĕ swúr)

Le Tissier, *f.n.* [lə ˈtɪsjeɪ] (lĕ tíss-yay)

Le Tocq, *f.n.* [lə ˈtɒk] (lĕ tóck)

Le Vesconte, *f.n.* [lə ˈveɪkɒnt] (lĕ váykont)

Les Canichers [leɪ ˈkænɪʃərz] (lay kánnishĕrz)

Les Casquets [leɪ ˈkæskɪts] (lay kásskĕts) *see also* Caskets.

Les Hanois [leɪ ˈhænwɑ] (lay hán-waa)

Les Mielles [leɪ ˈmjel] (lay myéll)

Lenfestey [lenˈfestɪ] (lenfésti)

Lihou Island [ˈliu] (leé-oo)

Loveridge, *f.n.* [ˈlʌvərɪdʒ] (lúvvĕrij)

M

Machon, *f.n.* [ˈmæʃɒn] (máshon)

Mahy, *f.n.* [ˈmɑi] (maá-ee)

Marquand, *f.n.* [ˈmɑrkɑ̃] (maárkaa*ng*)

Marquis, *f.n.* [ˈmɑrki] (maárkee)

Martel, *f.n.* [ˈmɑrtel] (maártel)

Mauger, *f.n.* [ˈmɔɪdʒər] (máyjer)

Mesny, *f.n.* [ˈmeɪnɪ] (máyni)

Michel, *f.n.* [ˈmɪʃel] (míshel)

Miere, *f.n.* [ˈmiɛər] (meé-air)

Mignot, *f.n.* [ˈmɪnjou] (mín-yō)

Minquiers [ˈmɪŋkɪz] (míngkiz); [ˈmæ̃kjeɪ] (máng-kyay)

Mollet, *f.n.* [ˈmɒleɪ] (móllay)

Montais, *f.n.* [ˈmɒnteɪ] (móntay)

Morin, *f.n.* [ˈmɒræ̃] (máwra*ng*)

Moulin Huet [ˈmulɪn wet] (moŏlin wet)

Mourant, *f.n.* [ˈmurə] (moŏ-raw)

N

Neveu, *f.n.* [ˈnevju] (névvew)

Nicholle, *f.n.* [ˈnɪkoul] (níckōl)

Noel, *f.n.* [nɒul] (nōl)

Noyon, *f.n.* [ˈnɔɪjɒn] (nóy-yon)

O

Oeillet, *f.n.* [ˈojeɪ] (áw-yay)

Ogier, *f.n.* [ˈouʒɪər] (ō*zh*eer); [ouˈʒijeɪ] (ō*zh*eé-yay) *The first is a Guernsey pronunciation, the second a Jersey one.*

Orange, *f.n.* [ˈoronʒ] (áwrawn*zh*)

Ouaisne [ˈweɪneɪ] (wáynay)

Ozanne, *f.n.* [ouˈzæn] (ōzán)

Ozouf, *f.n.* [ˈouzuf] (ōzoof)

P

Pallot, *f.n.* [ˈpælou] (pálō)

Parmentier, *f.n.* [ˌpɑrmɒnˈtɪər] (paarmonteér)

Perchard, *f.n.* [ˈpɜrʃɑrd] (pér-shaard)

Perelle, *f.n.* [ˈpɛərel] (paírel)

Perelle Bay [ˈpɛərel] (paírel)

Perrée, *f.n.* [pɛəˈreɪ] (pairáy)

Petit, *f.n.* [ˈpetɪ] (pétti)

Petit Bot [ˈpetɪ ˈbou] (pétti bŏ)

Pettiquin, *f.n.* [ˈpetɪkæ̃] (péttika*ng*)

Picot, *f.n.* [ˈpɪkou] (píckō)

Pigeon, *f.n.* [ˈpiʒo] (peé*zh*aw)

Pinchemain, *f.n.* [ˈpɪnʃmeɪn] (pínshmayn)

Pinel, *f.n.* [ˈpɪnel] (pínnel)

Pirouet, *f.n.* [ˈpɪrveɪ] (pírrŏŏ-ay)

Pleinmont Point [ˈplaɪmɒn] (plímon)

Plémont [ˈplemə] (plémmaw)

Poingdestre, *f.n.* [ˈpoɪndestər] (póyndester)

Poree, *f.n.* [ˈporeɪ] (páwray)

Potier, *f.n.* [ˈpɒtjeɪ] (pót-yay)

Priaulx, *f.n.* [ˈpriou] (preé-ō)

Procureur, *f.n.* [ˈprɒkjuərər] (próck-yŏŏrer)

Q

Quellenec, *f.n.* [ˈkelnek] (kéllĕneck)

Quentin, *f.n.* [ˈkwentɪn] (kwéntin)

Queripel, *f.n.* [ˈkerɪpel] (kérripel)

Quesnel, *f.n.* [ˈkeɪnel] (káynel)

Quevatre, *f.n.* [kɪˈvɑtr] (kĕvaátr)

Quinain, *f.n.* [kɪˈneɪn] (kináyn)

Quinquenel, *f.n.* [ˈkæŋkɪnel] (kánkinel)

Quirot, *f.n.* [ˈkwɪrou] (kwírrō)

R

Rabet, *f.n.* ['ræbeɪ] (rábbay)
Rabey, *f.n.* ['reɪbɪ] (ráybi)
Raimbault, *f.n.* ['ræmbou] (rámbō)
Rault, *f.n.* [roʊlt] (rōlt)
Rebourg, *f.n.* [re'bʊərg] (rebbŏőrg)
Rebours, *f.n.* [re'bʊər] (rebbŏőr)
Reniér, *f.n.* ['renjeɪ] (rén-yay)
Renouard, *f.n.* ['renwɑr] (rénwaar)
Renouf, *f.n.* [re'nuf] (rennoóf); ['renɒf] (rénnoff) *The first is a Guernsey pronunciation, the second a Jersey one.*
Richard, *f.n.* ['rɪʃɑr] (ríshaar)
Ricou, *f.n.* ['rɪku] (ríckoo)
Rihoy, *f.n.* ['rɪɔɪ] (reé-oy)
Rimeur, *f.n.* ['rɪmɜr] (rímmur)
Robilliard, *f.n.* [roʊ'bɪlɪərd] (rōbílli-ărd)
Robin, *f.n.* ['roʊbɪn] (rōbin)
Roche, *f.n.* [roʊʃ] (rōsh)
Rocquaine Bay [roʊ'keɪn] (rōkáyn)
Rohais, *f.n.* ['roʊheɪz] (rō-hayz)
Romerill, *f.n.* ['rɒmrɪl] (rómrill)
Rouget, *f.n.* [ru'ʒeɪ] (roozháy)
Rousseau, *f.n.* ['rusoʊ] (roóssō)
Roussel, *f.n.* [ru'sel] (roosséll)
Routier, *f.n.* ['rutɪeɪ] (roóti-ay)
Rozel ['roʊzel] (rōzel)

S

St. Aubin [snt 'oʊbɪn] (sĭnt ŏbin); [snt 'ɔbɪn] (sĭnt áwbin)
St. Brelade [ˌsnt brɪ'lɑd] (sĭnt brĕlaáad)
St. Helier [snt 'helɪər] (sĭnt hélli-er)
St. Ouen's [snt 'wɒnz] (sĭnt wónnz)
St. Peter Port [snt 'pitər pɔrt] (sĭnt peéter port)
Salsac, *f.n.* ['sælzæk] (sálzack)
Sangan, *f.n.* ['sæŋen] (sáng-en)
Sark [sɑrk] (saark)
Sarre, *f.n.* [sɑr] (saar)
Savident, *f.n.* ['sævɪdɒn] (sávvidon)
Sebire, *f.n.* ['sebɪər] (sébbeer)
Simon, *f.n.* ['sɪmɑ̃] (símmaang); ['sɪmɔ] (símmaw) *The first is a Guernsey pronunciation, the second a Jersey one.*
Sohier, *f.n.* ['sɔjeɪ] (sáw-yay)
Surcouf, *f.n.* ['sʊərkuf] (soŏrkoof)
Syvret, *f.n.* ['sɪvreɪ] (sívray)

T

Tabel, *f.n.* ['teɪbel] (táybel)
Talibard, *f.n.* ['tælɪbɑr] (tálibaar)

Tanguy, *f.n.* ['tæŋɪ] (táng-i); ['tæŋgɪ] (táng-gi) *The first is a Guernsey pronunciation, the second a Jersey one.*
Tardif, *f.n.* ['tɑrdɪf] (taárdiff)
Tardivel, *f.n.* ['tɑrdɪvel] (taárdivel)
Thoume, *f.n.* [tʊm] (toom)
Thoumine, *f.n.* [tu'min] (toomeén)
Tirel, *f.n.* ['tɪrel] (tírrel)
Torode, *f.n.* ['tɒroʊd] (tórrōd)
Tostevin, *f.n.* ['tɒstɪvɪn] (tósstĕvin)
Tourtel, *f.n.* ['tʊərtel] (toŏrtel)
Touzeau, *f.n.* ['tuzoʊ] (toŏzō)
Touzel, *f.n.* ['tuzel] (toŏzel)
Tregear, *f.n.* [trɪ'gɜr] (trĕgaír)
Trehorel, *f.n.* ['treɪɔrel] (tráy-awrel)
Troquer, *f.n.* ['troʊkeɪ] (trōkay)
Trouteaud, *f.n.* [tru'toʊ] (trootō)
Tulié, *f.n.* [ˌtulɪ'eɪ] (tooli-áy)

U

Udle, *f.n.* ['judl] (yoodl)

V

Vaillant, *f.n.* ['veɪjə] (váy-yă)
Vallois, *f.n.* ['vælwɑ] (válwaa)
Valpied, *f.n.* ['vælpɪeɪ] (válpi-ay)
Vasselin, *f.n.* ['væslɑ̃] (vásslang)
Vaudin, *f.n.* ['voʊdɪn] (vŏdin)
Vautier, *f.n.* ['voʊtjeɪ] (vŏt-yay)
Vazon Bay ['vazɒn] (vaázon)
Vibert, *f.n.* ['vaɪbərt] (víbĕrt); ['vibɛər] (veébair)
Vidamour, *f.n.* ['vɪdəmʊər] (víddămoŏr)
Viel, *f.n.* ['viel] (veé-el)
Vining, *f.n.* ['vɪnɪŋ] (vínning)
Voisin, *f.n.* ['vɔɪzɪn] (vóyzin)

Y

Yvette, *f.n. and C.n.* [i'vet] (eevét)
Yvonne, *f.n. and C.n.* [i'vɒn] (eevón)

Z

Zabiela, *f.n.* zæ'bɪlə] (zabíllă)

PRINTED IN GREAT BRITAIN
AT THE UNIVERSITY PRESS, OXFORD
BY VIVIAN RIDLER
PRINTER TO THE UNIVERSITY